GLOBALIZATION, ART, AND EDUCATION

ABOUT NAEA

The National Art Education Association is the world's largest professional visual arts education association and a leader in educational research, policy, and practice for art education. NAEA's mission is to advance art education through professional development, service, advancement of knowledge, and leadership.

Membership includes elementary and secondary art teachers, middle school and high school students in the National Art Honor Society programs, artists, administrators, museum educators, arts council staff, university professors, and students from the United States and several foreign countries. It also includes publishers, manufacturers, and suppliers of art materials; parents; students; retired art educators; and others concerned about quality art education in our schools.

NAEA publishes *Art Education, Studies in Art Education*, and other professional papers on art education; holds an annual convention; conducts research; sponsors a teacher awards program; develops standards for student learning, school programs, and teacher preparation; and co-sponsors workshops, seminars, and institutes on art education. For further information, visit our website at www.arteducators.org.

To order a copy of this book or obtain additional information, contact National Art Education Association: www.arteducators.org or 800-299-8321.

Order No. 305
ISBN 978-1-890160-43-2

NaeA

Globalization, Art, and Education is endorsed by the United States Society for Education through Art and the International Society for Education through Art.

GLOBAL
IZATION
ART&
EDUCATION

Elizabeth Manley Delacruz

Alice Arnold

Ann Kuo

Michael Parsons

EDITORS

Contents

SECTION I
CULTURAL IDENTITIES, CULTURAL HERITAGE SITES, AND EDUCATIONAL PRACTICES

SECTION II
ART, ARTISTIC PRACTICES, AND GLOBAL VISUAL CULTURE

Foreword

Elizabeth Manley Delacruz, Alice Arnold, Ann Kuo, Michael Parsons

Globalization has been called the new world order and the demise of democracy; the next step toward world peace, stability, and prosperity; and the latest stage in the destruction of the earth and its inhabitants. In answer to our call for scholarly investigations and insights about the implications of globalization, this ambitious book brings together provocative and timely essays and case studies from 49 scholars from all over the world. *Globalization, Art, and Education* began with a conversation in a café at the Art Institute of Chicago in 2006 at the Annual Convention of the National Art Education Association. At that time, the co-editors agreed that this would be a much needed and worthwhile contribution to the theoretical, methodological, and professional/practical discourse concerning the interface of globalization, art, and education.

Early on, we sought and found support in this endeavor from The International Society for Education through Art (InSEA), and the United States Society for Education through Art (USSEA). Without their initial commitments and encouragement, this book would not have gone forward. We also found tremendous support from colleagues, scholars, artists, and educators, near and far, and ultimately from our publisher, the National Art Education Association. We owe all of these organizations and individuals, especially the National Art Education Association, our deepest gratitude in bringing this important publication forward. *Globalization, Art, and Education* comes full circle at Annual Conventions of the National Art Education Association, in authors' presentations in two Super Sessions in Minneapolis, Minnesota in 2009, and four additional sessions in Baltimore, Maryland in 2010.

In creating a focus for this book, we asked the authors to look at the impact of various forms of globalization on human creativity and at the problems and possibilities it creates for visual arts education, highlighting three principal areas of interest:

- **The changing nature of cultural production in a globalized world economy.** Our questions were: In what ways do cultural practices in different parts of the world contribute to or reflect globalization? How do artists adapt to various forms of globalization? What happens to images, designs, and arts and crafts industries as they are affected by globalization tendencies? How do new digital multi-media and mass media play into these tendencies? How are museums, educational institutions, local traditions, and heritage sites affected by globalization?

- **New ways of thinking about nations, cultures, communities, and individuals,** asking: What policies do nations design in response to globalization? What are the challenges of scholarly understandings and public policy formation when people are understood not only as members of a particular country but also in terms of (post)colonial indigenous communities, migrations, and with dual citizenship arrangements; or when private institutions expand beyond political and geographic boundaries, and undermine nation-state sovereignty?

- ***Case studies of youth culture, youth artistic expressions, and art educational practices,*** asking: How is child art impacted by globalization? What are some trends in the globalization of youth culture? How do emerging tourist industries use local arts, historical sites, and "cultural" festivals to inform arts and educational programming? What art educational programs can be identified that promote new forms of creative cultural expression, intercultural understandings, and citizen empowerment? And finally, in what ways have international research, collaboration, and teaching transformed art education theory and practices?

Planning, development, solicitations, correspondences, exchanges, revisions, and discussions ensued with intensity and focus throughout the past 3 years, and have resulted in the chapters that now comprise *Globalization, Art, and Education.* Our authors have examined complex and varied ways globalization interfaces not only with art and education, but also with local and regional cultural practices and identities, economies, political strategies and reactions, and ecological-environmental concerns of different people and places in the world. Utilizing a range of research methodologies and scholarly formats, authors share philosophical discussions, historical and critical analyses, ethnographies, case studies, and creatively written narratives, plays, conversations, and dialogues to frame their discourse about selected people, cultures, practices, phenomena, and understandings in and across specific localities in the world (including but not limited to Australia, Austria, Brazil, Canada, Cuba, China, Ecuador, Guatemala, Hong Kong, Jamaica, Kenya, Korea, Palestine/Israel, Singapore, Spain, Suriname, Taiwan, United Kingdom, and the United States of America). Befitting to the goals of this anthology, many authors developed their insights through cross-cultural and trans-national investigations, and, not surprisingly, several have focused on the Internet and the World Wide Web as their primary site for investigation.

Global systems and structures, globalization, and globalism, although interrelated, have different meanings in global studies discourse. *Global systems* are generally understood as inter-governmental and supranational geopolitical, economic, and cultural institutions and arrangements involving commerce, communication, and cultural flows across regions of the world. *Globalization* refers to dynamic processes and phenomena underlying such arrangements: interconnectivity, mobility, transformation, acceleration, intensification, and so forth. And *globalism* is a worldview or way of thinking about one's place in an increasingly interconnected world. Themes that emerged in the chapters that comprise this book include considerations central to our understandings of all three: systems, processes, and ideologies.

Many of the authors in this book take a critical stance toward globalization, reconceptualizing aspects of what may seem like the inevitability and pervasiveness of globalization and offering insights and recommendations that promote alternatives to its negative consequences. Constructs and phenomena broached by these authors include examinations of "ethnocentrism," "heterogeneity," "hegemony," and "homogenization" in a world of unequal players on the global stage. Given here are also perspectives that view individuals not as victims of overwhelming global forces but as active agents in the creation of unique "glocal" practices both at home and abroad. Permeating these chapters are discussions of "border crossing," "transculturalism," "hybridization," "creolization," "interculturalism," and "cosmopolitanism" in consideration of new meanings of old concepts like "identity," "tradition," and "citizenship." Some authors spotlight recent creative examples of cultural expression, cultural celebration, and cultural revivalism amongst individuals, groups, and nations, highlighting changing understandings in varying places about longstanding values and expectations. For others, themes of self-reflexivity, generosity, and ecological and ethical action are offered as critical elements of an emerging conceptual framework for future inquiry and action in the global arena, as authors consider their own roles as privileged researchers, cultural workers, border crossers, and citizens. Authors also provide provocative explanations and insights regarding current notions of visual literacy, visuality, visual and material culture, mass culture, media culture, cyber-culture, digital online artistic communities, netizens, distance education, and media education insofar as these have become prominent features of the age of global digital media and communication technologies. Finally, many of the chapters in this book present widely divergent philosophical considerations, penetrating discussions, and challenging new views about the changing nature and role of art in a globalized world, and what this means for visual arts education.

The chapters of this book are organized thematically into four sections: Section I: Cultural Identities, Cultural Heritage Sites, and Educational Practices; Section II: Art, Artistic Practices, and Global Visual Culture; Section III: Global and Local Youth Cultures & Sites, and Online and On-Site School Practices with Young People; and Section IV: Case Studies and Philosophical Speculations about Higher Education International Practices—College-Level Faculty & Students' Transformations. Each of the four sections is preceded by an introduction to focus readers on the contents of the particular section. Although this structure seems logical, given the focus of individual chapters, the contents and concerns of these chapters overlap considerably, and many other arrangements were possible.

From a variety of locations and disciplinary dispositions, the authors of the 41 chapters in this book offer diverse perspectives about globalization. Uniting these perspectives is an unspoken optimism in the value of scholarly investigations and publications such as this, our reliance on thoughtful inquiry about the conditions of people in the world, and a privileging of creative cultural expression as a testament to human imagination, an incomplete and complicated project, fraught with self-contradictions and inconsistencies, by anyone's estimation. Our hopes in publishing *Globalization, Art, and Education* are both to shed light on and spur further investigations of the multilayered and complicated facets of globalization and their relation to art, culture, and education. In doing so, we hope to foster commitments to the vital, albeit changing, role of art, creative cultural expression, and education in furthering progression toward global civil society.

Introduction
Globalization, Art, and Education: Mapping the Terrain

Elizabeth Manley Delacruz

"I am a citizen of the world."

—DIOGENES[1]

Globalization is one of the most hotly contested, contradictory, and critical facets of contemporary life on earth. We can't help but be awed by the marvels of human ingenuity; the vibrancy and diversity of human creativity and cultural expressiveness; advancements in computing, communication, and access to information; unprecedented opportunities for personal and professional self-actualization and lifelong learning; the proliferation of interdisciplinary inquiry, scientific discovery, and cross-cultural exchange; the rise of a worldwide entrepreneurial creative sector; inter-institutional and international collaborations aimed at solving the world's most pressing problems; the emergence of multicultural, multinational, multidisciplinary global civil society; increased recognition of the nature and value of the individual, local, and indigenous; worldwide preservation and conservation efforts; a worldwide movement toward democratization; increased efforts at defining and protecting universal human rights; and an unprecedented amount of attention to and investments in the youth of today.

At the same time, at the writing of this Introduction we are in the midst of a worldwide recession tied to the collapse of deeply intertwined global economies; evidence of coming cataclysmic climate change attributable to reckless human consumption,[2] waste,[3] and destruction of the natural environment; transmittal of diseases of tremendous harm to plants and animals, now spread worldwide by birds, rodents, frogs, mosquitoes, beetles, pigs, and humans;[4] violent regional conflicts and atrocities stemming from centuries-old hatreds and entrenched religious and ethnic rivalries; fear of looming nuclear and biological warfare;[5] increasing worldwide poverty, hunger, disease,[6] and disparities between "haves" and "have nots"; and the unchecked ascent of powerful supranational governing entities and transnational corporate conglomerates that interpenetrate virtually every aspect of human life and hold allegiance to no sovereign country, culture, religion, or value system other than to a materialist ideology of worldwide production, consumption, and wealth accumulation.

Advocates celebrate globalization as the triumph of modernization, progress, innovation, and freedom throughout the world—linking these to the achievements of capitalism, democracy, technology, and Western ideology. Opponents decry globalization's oppressive neoliberal rationality and its resulting excesses, human suffering, social fragmentation, and devastation of entire ecosystems. Regardless of how one sees the world, we understand and experience with increasing sophistication that old adage from the *whole earth*[7] era that what happens globally also impacts us locally and in the classroom.[8] It is also important to understand and appreciate that what happens in the classroom and locally can also impact what happens globally (Blandy, personal communication, January 21, 2009). It is with these thoughts in mind that I map the terrain of globalization discourse in this Introduction. As do the other authors in this anthology, I find globalization, art, and education to be inextricably linked, and I suggest broad themes and areas of inquiry with confidence that visual arts educators and others will find meaningful connections between these themes and their own praxis.

What is Globalization?

Globalization is an ambiguous and complicated

construct with multiple overlapping dimensions and competing definitions arising from different academic, commercial, political, and ideological foci. Global studies in academia are informed by scholarship in world history, political theory, economics, anthropology, cultural studies, area studies, feminist and multicultural studies, education, media studies and communications, environmental studies, and critical theory. Globalization is also studied by governmental agencies, think tanks, corporations, consulting agencies, foundations, and nongovernmental entities from virtually every sector of society, each representing diverse points of views and competing agendas. Across these sectors, globalization is understood through consideration of the modes and motivations of human activities and aspirations in the arenas of commerce, culture, and governance, as these interlinking and overlapping spheres of human conduct occur within and impact local, regional, and world affairs.

Globalization is conceptualized, varyingly, as a long-term historical process of human development and evolution (Gunder Frank & Gills, n. d.; Wallerstein, 2000), a complex social and cultural project (Kellner, 2002), a recent phenomenon resulting from the rise of the West and the now worldwide economic system of free market capitalism (Barber, 1996, 2002; Friedman, 1999; Hardt & Negri, 2000), and a new paradigm for the future (Friedman, 2007; Hardt & Negri, 2004; Rheingold, 2002). The term *globalization* is also commonly meant to refer to those fundamental global transformations of human societies brought about by transnational expansion, integration, and interdependency of human social networks and flows of resources, goods, ideas, and culture; the geopolitical, economic, legal, and cultural reorganization of human social life on a global scale; a movement away from particularistic tribal, ethnic, regional, religious, or nation-state systems; and a conscious acceptance or reconceptualization of humanity itself by people worldwide toward the idea of *globalism:* an ecological, holistic one-world/whole earth point of view. Included in the dynamics of globalization examined by scholars are the opposing forces of empire-building or global cultural hegemony vs. local, cultural diversity, heterogeneity, resistance, and rivalry. In this mix are cultural inventions, adaptations, and responses to globalization, including a dazzling array of unique and hybridized cultural practices, identities, forms of expression, and conceptualizations about oneself in relation to others in the world. In most if not all writings on globalization, the strength and acceleration of global forces and their impact on life on earth are of central interest, and theorists are converging on the position that globalization is indeed the new world system, the distinguishing trend, and the defining moment of the present era.

A Brief History of Globalization

Describing globalization as a process of human social and political development, historians, sociologists, anthropologists, political theorists, and economists have identified and analyzed cooperative and rivalrous social arrangements and impacts arising from trade, commerce, and intercultural exchanges across societies in varying parts of the world in different eras, noting important structural transitions in regions of the world as human societies shifted from tribal to feudal to capitalist economic systems, and from nomadic to agrarian to urban to national cultural-political geo-economic formations, and finally—some argue—to transnational, polymorphous, and sometimes free-floating or deterritorialized entities. Many analyses include observations about how the need for resources (land, natural materials, and human labor), the production of surplus goods, and the creation and maintenance of trade routes across territories or dominions relied on and were accompanied by a quest for domination, consumption, wealth accumulation, and military superiority. The stability or well being of societies (or at least the elites within these societies) created social/political systems capable of maintaining trade infrastructures, divisions of labor, bourgeois professional specializations, governing institutions, and international agreements and conquests that fostered their own internal sustenance and growth. Where world historians and world systems theorists differ is in their views about when globalization began, what facets of globalization are currently most in need of scrutiny and understanding, and ultimately whether or not globalization is good for humanity.[9]

Although some currently conceptualize globalization as a relatively recent late 20th-century phenomenon, social historian Immanuel Wallerstein (2000) posits that the processes of globalization have existed for some 500 years with the long ascent of a Euro-centered Western system of capitalism from 1450 to the present, and that this process is best understood as a part of a cycle of genesis, expansion, and terminal decline. Social critic and philosopher Jurgen Habermas (1974) describes some of the social transformations taking place during this era, as European nation states shifted from public (princely) ownership and control of public goods and resources to privatization (private ownership and control of property and enterprises of commerce), and finally to the present system in which what were formerly public goods and resources (land, food, energy, and information, for example) are now privately owned by corporations. Similarly, political theorist and popular writer Benjamin Barber (1996) traces the transition in England from a monarchy with its guilds and merchants through a series of constitutional reforms that lead—ultimately—to democratization, and which in turn fostered a form of entrepreneurial capitalism that spread to other countries and set the stage for the current international system.

Scholars observe that during this era European explorers, colonists, military expeditions, missionaries, traders, intellectuals, and travelers carried their worldviews, science, technologies, cultural patterns, and political systems to all parts of the globe (Boli & Lechter, 2002). The loci of power gradually shifted from Europe to the United States in the 20th century; and since 1945, the US has come to shape the new world order by dominating global and regional markets, political life, and cultural systems through a variety of political, economic, and military arrangements and interventions throughout the world (Berger, 2002; Friedman, 1999; Hardt & Negri, 2000; Wallerstein, 2000).

In Wallerstein's world system view, the current world order relies on a system of domination by core societies and of subordination of peripheral societies (or nations), of exploitation and extraction of natural and human resources of peripheral societies by dominant societies for the accumulation of surplus capital, and the creation and control of worldwide markets for the distribution of the products of core societies. Challenging Wallerstein's Eurocentric view but not his assessment of underlying processes of globalization, German economic historian and sociologist Andre Gunder Frank and global politics scholar Barry Gills posit the idea of a "continuous history and development of a single world system for at least 5,000 years" (¶ 1, n. d.). Arguing that the advent of capitalism was

neither an invention of Europe or the seismic shift that occurred in 1400s, Gunder Frank and Gills observe that there existed extensive capital producing activities throughout human history, with recurrent trade, migrations, invasions, and their accompanying cultural/technological diffusions, and that these activities have been part of a global, one-world system encompassing much of Afro-Eurasia by the 3rd millennium BC or earlier. The world economy prior to the rise of Europe already had a far-flung division of labor; and an intricate trade system built around the production and distribution of commodities; extraction, exploitation, and investments in natural resources (timber and metals), agricultural products (wool, silk, and spices), and people (technicians, merchants, and migrant and slave laborers); the building and military protection of trade route infrastructures (roads, canals, bridges, ports, and regional hubs of commerce); and social institutions (governing centers, banks, guilds, and religious and educational systems) designed to secure and foster those sectors of society involved in serving the interests of the ruling elite or nation-state. According to Gunder Frank and Gills, in the 1400s the Europeans entered into this already well-established mercantile system of trade and capital accumulation in their exploitation of global differences in resources, production and prices, in order to maximize their profits as middlemen and to cover European monarchies' own massive trade imbalances with other regional powers at the time.

Whether economists, social historians, and political theorists argue for a long (5000 years), a shorter (500 years), or a recent (10-50 years) view of globalization, there is general agreement that globalization is fueled by economic and military quests for territory, resources, and domination made possible through creation and maintenance of transportation and communication infrastructures, through investments in the acquisition of knowledge about the world and the education of those in need of such knowledge, and through technological advancements (Friedman, 2007; Ludden, n. d.; Wallerstein, 2000). In contrast to disjunctive and Eurocentric explanations attempting to describe the nature and history of globalization, Gunder Frank and Gills posit instead a continuous, cyclical, single-world, humanocentric, and holistic approach, one that takes into account not only the transitions and developments of early human social interactions across territories but also, importantly, consideration of human history in relation to geography, climate, demography, and technology. Such a framework posits a cosmopolitan view that recognizes our common history and shared future, places the study and understanding of globalization within a larger ecological framework, connects global studies to environmentalism and geo-politics, and refocuses attention on fundamental issues of today in global politics: sustainability, ecology, transparency, accountability, citizen polity, equity, and cultural- and bio-diversity.[10]

New World Order or Clash of Civilizations?

Many accounts of the current global system follow along the general explanations given thus far, with variations and disagreements over important facets concerning the role of commerce, citizen polity, the nature of cultural identity, and the future of democracy in the new world order. Scholars now consider the intricate and complicated relationships that have developed between privatization/capitalism and concomitant forms of democracy, protections of the individual within the state, the nature of cultural identities, and new meanings of citizenship. For example, globalization scholar John Tomlinson describes the "emergence of 'hybrid' cultural identities as a consequence both of the multicultural constitution of modern nation-states and of the emergence of transnational forms of popular culture" and observes that "political subjects can now experience and express, without contradiction, both attachments to the nation, multi-ethnic allegiances and cosmopolitan sensibilities" (2003, p.275). Similarly, sociologists John Boli and Frank Lechter describe what they see as an emerging world culture, explaining it as a "cultural complex of foundational assumptions, forms of knowledge, and prescriptions for action that underlie globalized flows, organizations, and institutions" (Boli & Lechter, 2002, p. 6261).

By most accounts, the US currently stands as the sole hegemonic power in the world, although some scholars also believe that the US is in decline. Acknowledging the fundamental role of the US in the development and maintenance of the current world system, American literary and political theorist Michael Hardt and Italian born political philosopher and formerly imprisoned militant activist Antoni Negri[11] currently argue that the

world has now moved beyond a period of imperialism or expansionism and into a new global geopolitical order or era of *Empire*, one that *in its totality* transcends and subsumes nation states and regional and ethnic rivalries (2004). Empire, they argue, operates through its own supranational ideology,[12] and is given legal authority conferred through international agreements that address political and economic policies and practices in localities worldwide.[13] For example, American economist, Nobel laureate, and former Senior Vice President of the World Bank, Joseph Stiglitz condemns the devastating consequences of the market fundamentalism of the new supranationals on developing countries (2002).[14]

Arguments both for and against the emergence of supranational authority or one-world governance center on issues of sovereignty, democracy, and the opposing forces of homogenization and Western hegemony vs. preserving heterogeneity or cultural plurality.[15] American political scientist Samuel Huntington (1996) describes the post-Cold War shift of power away from Western hegemony with the rise of East Asian Sinic and Islamic power, and an impending clash of civilizations stemming from cultural and religious rivalries. Wallerstein and many others conclude that the present, now U.S.-centered worldwide capitalist system has reached its inevitable critical point of crisis and decline, that we are currently entering a period of transition (one with an uncertain future).[16]

As globalization scholars point out, relationships and rivalries resulting from globalization are not between equal players on this world stage; rather they are played out by core (dominant) and peripheral (subordinate) societies or nations, whereby core societies expand and impose their ideology, ways of life, and interests on peripheral societies, and peripheral societies adapt, assimilate into, resist, or are subsumed or destroyed by core societies (Berger, 2002; Gunder Frank & Gills, n. d.; Wallerstein, 2000). At the same time, scholars, economists, governing agencies, and civil society activists now recognize *creolization, mestizzae, hybridization,* and *glocalization* as important forms of cultural adaptation and expression. Once considered to be localized and regional with both loose and tight webs of international interconnections, these global/local relationships, rivalries, and reactions, like globalization itself, now have consequences of epic proportions.

Technology

Regardless of whether scholars and theorists view globalization positively or negatively,[17] most recognize that one of the most important recent facets of globalization has been the impact of the scientific and technological revolutions in which the world is currently immersed. Understanding globalization now requires conceptualizing it as both a product of technological advancements and their impacts on the current global restructuring, in which economic, technological, political, and cultural facets are intertwined (Kellner, 2002).

Attributing the 19th- and early 20th-century era of globalization to the invention of the railroad, the steamship, and the automobile—all of which reduced transportation costs and facilitated world flows of resources, goods, and people—and seeing the end of the Cold War in 1989 as an indicator of a new era of globalization, Pulitzer Prize winner and *New York Times* foreign affairs columnist Thomas Friedman claims that globalization has brought about the integration of technology, finance, and information across national borders (1999, 2007). For Friedman, this confluence of technology, finance, and information has democratized nations and societies throughout the world, and it privileges the work ahead of the talented, entrepreneurial, connected individual in the *new global village*. In Friedman's globalist worldview,[18] the technology and information revolution is built around advancements in electronic telecommunications (microchips, satellites, fiber optics, and the Internet) that now weave the world together tightly (1999, 2007). This also means, Friedman asserts, that developing countries no longer have to harvest and exploit their raw materials in return for finished products in a marketplace of commodities exchange; rather they can now be big time producers in the worldwide information and service economy.

Although not entirely agreeing with all aspects Friedman's optimistic assessment and arguments, media and communications scholar Douglas Kellner essentially affirms this view in his assessment that "the human species is evolving into a novel, postindustrial techno society, culture, and condition in which technology, knowledge, and information are the axial or organizing principles" (Kellner, 2002, p. 287). The acceleration, proliferation, and worldwide impact of globalization due to recent technological advancements is so dramatic and profound that some theorists posit such advancements as signaling a new and qualitatively different era in human evolution to be distinguished from the "previous mode of industrial production, characterized by heavy industry, mass production and consumption, bureaucratic organization, and social conformity" (Kellner, 2002, p. 287).

Now seeing the tech-savvy people of the world as a polymorphous mass of deterritorialized, networked organizers, creators, and consumers of popular world culture (Shirkey, 2008), scholars refer to these masses as "smart mobs" (Rheingold, 2002), "multitudes" (Hardt & Negri, 2004), and, in simplest terms, *global culture* (Tomlinson, 1999). The online world of young people in particular is of great interest to both educators and market analysts, as media scholars are quick to note (Montgomery, 2007). The following two vignettes illustrate, each in their own way, how technology, international commerce, cultural identity, citizenship, and education come together in the online world that young people, aka *millennials* (Lancaster, 2003),[19] now inhabit.

Chinese Cool. China Youthology™ is a new, hip marketing firm in China, dedicated to understanding and describing contemporary Chinese youth communities, experiences, and aspirations, both online and offline, and operating in promotion of Chinese economic, social, creative, and cultural interests. The owners/creators of China Youthology™, Zafka Zhang and Lisa Li, actively seek out, participate in, and help foster China's emerging creative sector. That is, they create interactive content, research, arts and cultural news highlights, marketing information, entertainment, and products for their blog and website. They also organize real world cultural events. Included among China Youthology™ posts are descriptions, images, and videos from the 2008 Shanghai eARTS festival—organized by Zhang and Li and attended by a new generation of creative, mobile, tech-savvy, edgy Chinese youth. Also available on the site are discussions of Chinese youth today as diverse, tolerant, and globalized; commentary about contemporary designers' commercial adaptations of traditional Chinese aesthetics and symbolism; discussion of an "indie" creative flea market for young design-lovers to display and sell their own products; discussion of Chinese emerging skateboarding culture (only 1 million "sk8borders" in China as of 2008); photographs of people giving blood after the Sichuan earthquake; and a commentary about Chinese government leaders' growing fan base among youth, who search and share pictures of Chairman Hu and Premier Wen in daily life, find them handsomer than thought in old pictures, and talk about them as if talking about their uncle ... all unimaginable a generation ago and emerging as a result of China's recent economic and political transformations.

What one may also learn from this website is that the local governments of major cities throughout China have decided to build hardware and software infrastructures to boost the *creative industry*, which the Chinese national government now views as a major pillar of economic development. This in turn has brought about tremendous demand for and investments in state-of-the-art technology and creative-related entertainment; commercial and educational enterprises and educational programming throughout the country; along with increased youth participation in music festivals, art exhibitions, book stores, live shows, and Internet-based p2p creating, sharing, collaboration, consumption, and learning.[20] One also learns that Chinese youth today, as described by Li, are fast-changing and diversified, growing toward greater responsibility, diversity, and tolerance, and "enterprising spirits (seeking self-achievement via hard work), and love and care towards the country."[21] They are also aware of the impact of trends from Japan and the US, and interested in creating their own local, retro-hybridized but independent version of *Chinese Cool*.[22]

1 World Manga. Teaming up with Viz,™ a leading English-language manga publisher, in 2005 the World Bank launched a series of 6 manga-styled books, each highlighting a key "development" issue identified by the World Bank. *1 World Manga* is a story about Rei, an orphaned teenager who dreams of becoming the greatest fighter in the world, and through a series of adventures, or passages, "discovers that the only way to become a true warrior is to understand the challenges facing the poor and disadvantaged people he befriends along the way."[23] In each of the six books, aka *passages*, Rei's spirit guide takes him on a different journey. These journeys deal with the theme of each of the six books: Poverty, HIV/Aids, Global Warming, Child Soldiers, Girls' Education, and Corruption. Available for purchase on the World Bank's youth website, *Youthink!*, proceeds from sales go to charities.[24]

The World Bank's *Youthink!* is a multimedia interactive website designed to raise awareness about world issues, with extensive educational materials designed especially for young people and teachers. *Youthink!* is said by the World Bank to be one of the most popular of its websites, receiving 15,000 visitors per month.[25] In June 2006 the *Youthink!* Web design team was included among the recipients of the 10th Annual Webby Awards, conferred by the International Academy of Digital Arts and Sciences, a global organization recognizing excellence in web design, creativity, usability, and functionality. *Youthink!* was recognized by the academy for activism. Noting that almost a billion people are now online—almost one sixth of the world's population—Tiffany Schlain, who created the Webbys in 1996, observed that "The youthink. worldbank.org Webby Award nomination is a testament to the skill, ingenuity, and vision of its creators" (2006).[26] In March 2007, the World Bank adapted *1 World Manga Passage 1* into a pilot anime (Japanese-style animation) and made it available as a downloadable wmv file or a streaming video anime from both the World Bank and *Youthink!* websites. The anime was also posted to YouTube.™ Text posts in the YouTube™ Commentary section, apparently from anime-knowledgeable young people, were critical—not because of the World Bank's heavy-handed policies and actions in developing nations (*ala* Stiglitz and his followers), but based on criteria derived from their own aesthetic system:[27]

> This is really incredible—I never thought I'd see the day where anime would have a good message such as this—to help children be aware of what's going on in the world and how they can help. But I really don't like how they made this into an American Anime type thing—it should be authentic Japanese anime. (Simba92)
>
> ...this anime adaptation is TERRIBLE. The majority of the good dialogue is gone, the characters are not fleshed out, and it feels like an animated After School Special. Read the manga, but DON'T watch the anime. (vamspapi)
>
> this looks like US anime/manga clone from Cartoon Network, Fox Kids look alike, LOL (CaptCamping)

There can be no doubt that advancements in technology (electronic information, communication networks, and digital multimedia) have contributed to the phenomenon of global youth culture, that young people's cultural experiences are shaped by globalization, that all of this is tied to capitalism or commerce, and that a sort-of world mass culture is forming with, within, and/or because of new digital media. One can't but help being both awed by and drawn into new media and mass culture, or by the amazing agility that young people seem to have with new technologies (Delacruz, 2009; Lenhart & Madden, 2005; Montgomery, 2007; McPhearson, 2007). And that young people are early adopters of digital technologies is no surprise to many. Media and cultural observers are quick to point out that people of all ages are now part of the online world for all kinds of good reasons, and that the previous generations have been instrumental in building and making the new online world possible (Brand, 1995; Turner, 2006). Uncertain about the exact nature or implications of such a grandiose vision of a world culture online, cultural studies scholar David Oswell asks, "Is it possible to have a common culture—or a culture of the commons—that is at once heterogeneous, global, and collective?" (2006, p. 95). Moreover, critics are quick to note that benefits of technological advancements have not been shared by a vast majority of the world's population, and that new technologies have also provided new and better means of intrusion into local and regional cultures and environments.[28] In addition to all of the purportedly marvelous things now possible online, the Internet also facilitates global terrorism networks, hate sites, the digital divide, and ever more intrusions into our privacy and sense of security. Our fascination with and dependency on electronic media is also now complicated by our growing awareness that our online activity leaves its own carbon footprint[29] and that our used computers being shipped to developing countries for disposal and reuse, which exposes the poorest, including children, in those countries to hazardous heavy metals and toxic contaminants (Kostigen, 2008).[30]

Conclusion

The purpose of this Introduction has been to set the stage for this anthology, and to promote consideration of some of the ways in which globalization, or global flows of resources, commodities, cultures, creativity, political systems, people, ideas, and technologies is/are of interest to art education. I have concluded with a commentary about technology because most of my work in art education these days relies on, utilizes, and is about how new technologies shape experience, creative expression, and education, and because I believe, like many of the media scholars I have consulted, that digital technologies are bringing about something quite new, quite important, and of global significance and scale—that is, global civil society (Delacruz, in press; Delacruz, 2009).

The many considerations offered throughout this anthology are important insofar as we are interested in the contexts and forces underlying artistic and cultural practices, productions, and patronages, and insofar as we want to think about how global flows influence and are influenced by local cultures and creative expression in different eras and locations. Understanding constructs and processes of globalization also informs our conceptualizations about multicultural, intercultural, and transnational identities, practices, and what that means for visual arts/visual culture education. And as the chapters in this anthology demonstrate, our work as educators now involves consideration of complex, dynamic, and contested practices and understandings. This includes the multiple directions and dynamics of the global flows of ideas, culture, and world views; processes and tensions of glocalization, creolization, bricolage, and cultural hybridization; the nature and impact of new global digital media; concerns about global mass culture and commerce; and concerns about empire, homogenization and hegemony, personal agency, and citizen polity emerging from a critical point of view.

In attempting to understand globalization, the ideology for the new millennium, the new world order, or whatever one chooses to call the current state of the world, comes into greater focus. It starts with the concept that "I am a citizen of the world," an active agent of global civil society, and it envisions a future in which the idealizations of imagination and creative cultural expression, social justice, citizen polity, honesty, and sustainability are firmly embedded in both our world view and daily practices at home.

Acknowledgments
Many thanks to Kristin Congdon and Doug Blandy for their thoughtful suggestions on an earlier draft of this chapter.

REFERENCES

Appiah, K. W. (1997). Cosmopolitan patriots. *Critical Inquiry, 23*(3), 617-639.

Appiah, K. W. (2001). Liberalism, individuality, and identity. *Critical Inquiry, 27*(2), 305-332.

Appiah, K. W. (2006). *Cosmopolitanism: Ethics in a world of strangers.* New York: Norton.

Barber, B. R. (1996). *Jihad vs. McWorld: Terrorism's challenge to democracy.* New York: Ballentine.

Barber, B. R. (2002). Beyond *Jihad* vs. McWorld. *The Nation* (January 21, 2002). Retrieved December 15, 2008 from http://www.thenation.com/doc/20020121/barber

Barber, B. R. (2003). Can democracy survive globalization? *Government and Opposition, 35*(3), 275-301.

Berger, P. L. (2002). The cultural dynamics of globalization. In P. L. Berger & S. P. Huntington, (Eds.), *Many globalization: Cultural diversity in the contemporary world* (pp. 1-17). New York: Oxford University Press.

Boli, J., & Lechter, F. (2002). Globalization and world culture. In N. J. Smelser & P. M. Baltes (Eds.) *International encyclopedia of the social and behavioral sciences,* (pp. 6261-6265). Oxford: Elsevier.

Brand, S. (1995). We owe it all to the hippies. *Time Magazine,* March 1, 1995. Retrieved December 15, 2008 from http://www.time.com/time/magazine/article/0,9171,982602,00.html

Carr, M. (2005). *Bioregionalism and civil society: Democratic challenges to corporate globalism.* Vancouver: UBC Press.

Delacruz, E. M. (in press). Visual arts: Technology pedagogy as cultural citizenship. In B. Cope & M. Kalantzis, (Eds.), *Ubiquitous learning,* (pp. 216-226). Urbana, IL: University of Illinois Press.

Delacruz, E. M. (2009). Art education aims in the age of new media: Toward global civil society. *Art Education, 62*(5), 13-23.

Delacruz, E. M. (2009). From bricks and mortar to the public sphere in cyberspace: Creating a culture of caring on the digital global commons. *International Journal of Education & the Arts.* Retrieved February 5, 2009 from http://www.ijea.org/v10n5/

Friedman, T. (1999). *The Lexus and the olive tree.* New York: Farrar Straus Giroux.

Friedman, T. (2007). *The world is flat, 3.0: A brief history of the 21st century.* New York: Farrar, Straus and Giroux.

Gunder Frank, A. & Gills, B. K. (n. d.). *The five thousand year world system in theory and praxis.* Retrieved November 15, 2008 from http://www.rrojasdatabank.org/agfrank/theory_praxis.html

Habermas, J. (1974). The Public Sphere: An Encyclopedia Article. (Translated by Lenox, S. & Lenox, F.). *New German Critique, 3,* 49-55.

Hardt, M., & Negri, A. (2000). *Empire.* Cambridge, MA: Harvard University Press.

Hardt, M., & Negri, A. (2004). *Multitude: War and democracy in the age of empire.* New York: Penguin Press.

Huntington, S. (1996). *The clash of civilizations and the remaking of world order.* New York: Simon and Schuster.

Kellner, D. (2002). Theorizing globalization, *Sociological Theory, 20*(3). 285-305.

Kostigen, (2008). The underbelly of globalization: Our toxic wastes exported to developing countries. *Toxic Trade News,* 25 September 2008. Retrieved December 12, 2008 from http://www.ban.org/ban_news/2008/080925_the_underbelly_of_globalization.html

Lancaster, L. C. (2003). The click and clash of generations. *Library Journal, 128*(17), 36-39.

Lenhart, A., & Madden, M. (2005). *Teen content creators and consumers.* Retrieved Feb 15, 2007 from the Web site of the PEW/Internet and American Life Project. http://www.pewinternet.org/

Ludden, D. (n. d.). *A quick guide to the world history of globalization.* Retrieved December 12, 2008 from http://www.sas.upenn.edu/~dludden/global1.htm

McPhearson, T. (2007). *Digital youth, innovation, and the unexpected.* Cambridge, MA: MIT Press.

Montgomery, K. C. (2007). *Generation digital: Politics, commerce, an childhood in the age of the Internet.* Cambridge, MA: MIT Press.

Oswell, D. (2006). Popular culture: From people to multitude. In D. Oswell, *Culture and society: An introduction to cultural studies* (pp. 74-102). London: Sage.

Rheingold, H. (2002). *Smart mobs: The next social revolution.* Cambridge, MA: Perseus.

Shirkey, C. (2008). *Here comes everybody: The power of organizing without organizations.* New York: Penguin.

Stiglitz, J. E. (2002). *Globalization and its discontents.* New York: Norton.

Tomlinson, J. (1999). *Globalization and culture.* Chicago: University of Chicago Press.

Tomlinson, J. (2003). Globalization and cultural identity. In D. Held & A. McGrew (Eds.) *The global transformations reader: An introduction to the globalization debate* (pp. 269-277). Malden, MA: Blackwell Publishing, Ltd.

Tomlinson, J. (2004). Globalised culture: The triumph of the West? In T. Skelton and T. Allen (eds), *Culture and global change* (pp. 23-31). Routledge: London.

Turner, F. (2006). Taking the whole earth digital. In S. Brand (Ed.). *From counterculture to cyberculture* (pp. 103-140). Chicago: University of Chicago Press.

Wallerstein, I. (2000). Globalization or the age of transition? A long-term view of the trajectory of the world system. *International Sociology, 15*(2), 251-267.

Yonge, C. D. (1893). Life of Diogenes. In The lives and opinions of eminent philosophers by Diogenes Laertius. *Diogenes Laertius.* (Trans. C. D. Yonge). Retrieved December 10, 2009 from http://classicpersuasion.org/pw/diogenes/dldiogenes.htm

ENDNOTES

1 Diogenes was a citizen of Athens during the time of Plato. See Yonge in references.

2 Regarding climate change, see information provided by the Intergovernmental Panel on Climate Change at http://ipccwg1.ucar.edu/wg1/FAQ/wg1_faqindex.html. See also http://www.climatecrisis.net/thescience/

3 See the National Solid Wastes Management Association report, *Modern Landfills: A Far Cry from the Past* at http://www.rumpke.com/pdfs/white%20paper%20landfill%20final.pdf. See also information about the U.S. Environmental Protection Agency superfund toxic waste and cleanup risk assessment program at http://www.epa.gov/oswer/riskassessment/risk_superfund.htm.

4 For a comprehensive report on the impact of globalization on world health see http://www.who.int/healthpromotion/conferences/hpr_special%20issue.pdf

5 For information about initiatives to reduce global threats from nuclear, biological, and chemical weapons see the website of the *Nuclear Threat Initiative,* chaired by Ted Turner and Sam Nunn at http://www.nti.org/index.php

6 See http://www.poverty.com/ See also the United Nations report, *The State of the World's Children 2009* at http://www.unicef.org/sowc09/docs/SOWC09-FullReport-EN.pdf

7 The concept of "whole earth" that emerged in the 1960s was linked to the environmental and peace (anti-Vietnam War) movements, and came together in *The Whole Earth Catalog* originated by Stewart Brand in 1968. Contributors to *The Whole Earth Catalog* have included Buckminster Fuller, David Brower, the Dalai Lama, Margaret Mead, Gregory Bateson, Ralph Nader, William S. Burroughs, Timothy Leary, the Black Panther Party, and Norman Cousins. See http://www.wholeearth.com/ The whole earth movement was motivated in part by early images of the earth taken from space in the late 1960s. For example see a copy of the original the June 1970 Earth Day Proclamation at http://www.wowzone.com/proclamn.htm.

8 The phrase "think local act global" is attributed to David Robert Brower, founder of the Friends of the Earth, the Earth Island Institute, and first Executive Director of the Sierra Club. See http://www.foe.co.uk/resource/press_releases/20001107132336.html and http://www.browercenter.org/node/17

9 Religion has played a significant and distinctive role in the construction of world culture, providing motivation and legitimizing the actions of some globalizers, contributing to the process of creolization (the creative and selective blending of religious and cultural practices and identities), and providing a vehicle for cultural expression (Boli & Lechter, 2002). In the contemporary era religious globalization has also been important in preserving indigenous cultures, contributing to heterogeneity in the world, promoting the civil rights of Third World citizens, and advocating for protection of the environment, while at the same time producing or perpetuating new forms of conflict, oppression, and rivalry (Barber, 1996, 2002).

10 See *Bioregionalism and Civil Society: Democratic Challenges to Corporate Globalism* (2006) by Mike Carr, *Cosmopolitanism: Ethics in a World of Strangers* by Kwame Anthony Appiah, and Appiah 1997 and 2001 cited in the references.

11 Negri was a student of prominent postmodern theorist Michael Foucault, and Hardt is a former student of Negri.

12 The term *supranational* refers to organizations and institutions comprised of members from several nations, and that are given higher levels of regulatory or juridical authority in world affairs than individual nations. Examples include the European Union, the Organization of American States, the African Union, the Association of Southeast Asian Nations, the United Nations, the World Trade Organization, the International Monetary Fund, the G8, and the Organization of the Petroleum Exporting Countries. Supranational institutions have become the target of intense criticism, protest, and resistance by anti-globalization activists. Activists also condemn the policies and practices of powerful transnational corporations (Coca Cola, Nike, Disney, Time-Warner, and so forth), and sometimes even NGOs, international and national non-government organizations and not-for-profit philanthropic foundations (such as the International Red Cross) whose annual budgets are now larger that the economies of some developing nations (Hardt & Negri, 2004).

13 Writings on the "new world order" and Empire are profuse, extensive, and largely negative, and owing much of their analytical framework to Marxist and postmodern critical theory.

14 In his well-known book and heavily disputed book, *Globalization and its Discontents*, Stiglitz (2002) criticizes the World Trade Organization, the World Bank, and the International Monetary Fund for their irrational logic, arrogance, heavy-handed strategies, and devastating effects on developing countries.

15 Some worry about the resulting loss of cultural identity and threats to democracy with people no longer see themselves as connected to particular cultures and nations. Barber (2003) and Tomlinson (2004) warn that that the erosion of national sovereignty and autonomy creates a world in which democracy has no home.

16 Violent protests staged by international alliances of individuals and groups from around the globe not normally in association with one another and in reaction to the concept of a new world order have emerged as powerful counter forces to globalization. Two well known and starkly contrasting examples of local resistance to globalization (or resistance to the ideology of Euro-American empire) that have had worldwide impact would include the terrorist guerilla tactics of Al Queda and the international alliance of civil society advocates, religious organizations, laborers, and environmentalists who shut down the meeting of the World Trade Organization in Seattle in 1999.

17 Globalization critics observe that current conditions lead to the weakening of nations-states, as multi-national corporations have moved their bases of operation from core states (industrialized nations) to peripheral states (developing countries) through practices commonly referred to as off shoring and outsourcing. These conditions include a large commodity base where everything is up for sale (land, water, agricultural products, and governmental policies, and ideas or inventions); labor costs are cheap and workplace, environmental, and public health protections are minimal or non-existent; and where there exist huge new untapped consumer markets. New technologies (advancements in production, communication, and transportation) accelerate these process as goods and services, policies and practices, and people, ideas, and cultural patterns traverse the globe with greater ease than any other time in human history.

18 In Friedman's (1999) optimistic view both the new global economy (the Lexus luxury car of the upwardly mobile capitalist leisure class) and pre-modern national aspirations and cultural identities (the gnarled olive tree on the banks of the river Jordan) are part of the *new global village*, now interlinked and in constant communication on the Internet. These metaphors of the Lexus and the olive tree (the title of his best selling book advocating a utopian vision of globalization) are Friedman's stand-ins for the hopes for a higher standard of living worldwide, now possible in the fast-paced Internet-hyped global marketplace (the Lexus), and (in the metaphor of the olive tree) the lingering need for a sense of intimacy and belonging to a particular family, tradition, community, and culture.

19 Lynne Lancaster is co-owner of a consulting firm that gives advice on bridging generation gaps. She describes *millennials* as people born 1982-2000. They are "globally concerned, collaborative, realistic, cyberliterate, media savvy, and environmentally conscious" (Lancaster, 2003, p. 7).

20 Discussion of the Shanghai eARTs festival and China's recent transformation may be found at See http://chinayouthology.com/blog/?p=355

21 Lisa Li, 2008, ¶ 4. See http://chinayouthology.com/blog/?p=412

22 See http://chinayouthology.com/blog/?p=3

23 For a description of *1 World Manga* see http://youthink.worldbank.org/multimedia/gallery/manga_passage2/index.php

24 The six books comprising *1 World Manga* are available for purchase at http://publications.worldbank.org/ecommerce/catalog/product?item_id=6361507

25 See http://youthink.worldbank.org/about/news_webbynomination.php

26 Schlain is quoted from http://youthink.worldbank.org/about/news_webbynomination.php

27 See http://www.youtube.com/watch?v=a5NjIcqfrhU

28 European superiority in ships and weaponry in the 1400s allowed it to traverse the world and impose its commercial and political goals throughout Asia, Africa, and the Americas. The transcontinental railroad in the US meant broken treaties, land grabs, and an escalation of atrocities toward the indigenous nations that already inhabited the "new world." 20th-century scientific discoveries have given us nuclear and biological weapons of mass destruction. The carbon-based energy technologies that fueled modernization have also brought about global warming, which is now said by scientists and politicians to be one of the world's most critical problems in terms of the long-term survival of humanity.

29 Research conducted by Harvard physicist Alex Wissner-Gross and sensationalized in a January 11, 2009 *Sunday Times* of London report, and now disputed by Google™ and others, raises awareness about the environmental impact of online activity (including the electricity required for all those servers involved in searching for information on the Internet). See http://www.technewsworld.com/story/Harvard-Prof-Sets-Record-Straight-on-Internet-Carbon-Study-65794.html. See also Wissner-Gross's startup company that encourages "green" searches, http://www.co2stats.com/.

30 See also the U.S. Government Accountability Office (GAO) finding that a substantial quantity of electronics exported for disposal and recycling ends up in countries where the items are handled and disposed of in a manner that threatens human health and the environment: http://www.gao.gov/new.items/d081044.pdf

CULTURAL IDENTITIES, CULTURAL HERITAGE SITES, & EDUCATIONAL PRACTICES

Introduction: Section I

Elizabeth Manley Delacruz

Globalization, Art, and Education opens with historical surveys, case studies, philosophical discussions, and critical analyses of the interconnections of globalization, governmental policies, and artistic practices in different places in the world. Each of the authors in this first section of the book considers creative cultural expressions (art, visual and material culture, and other cultural signifiers and traditions) as important indicators of contemporary and local cultural adaptations to globalization; and each of these authors offers unique insights from a variety of international vantage points, with particular interests in what this all suggests for education.

The first chapter comes from Taiwan, a country that emerged in the immediate post World War II era—one currently striving to maintain a sense of distinctiveness that takes into account both its long history of migrations, wars, military occupations, martial rule, and cross cultural infiltrations, along with its recent economic prosperity and its tenuous geopolitical status as a sovereign nation. In "Taiwanese Picturebooks and the Search for National Identity" Chien-hua Kuo explains that the island country of Taiwan was once inhabited by people of Malay-Polynesian descent who settled in the low-lying coastal plains but who never unified into a single cohesive cultural group. Taiwan is now a multi-cultural nation that includes immigrants who arrived from China in several waves, along with those left behind by its Spanish, Dutch, and Japanese colonizers. Importantly, Taiwan presently claims both a cultural identification with and (at the same time) independence from China. As Chien-hua Kuo observes, a *Neo-Taiwanese* self-consciousness has emerged over the past 20 years, resulting from a need to acknowledge and resist the hegemony of China. Notably, one strategy is through government-supported publications of Taiwanese children's picture books that emphasize and celebrate distinctly Taiwanese traditions.

In the following chapter, "Glocalization: Art Education in Taiwan," Li-Yan Wang and Ann Kuo also describe Taiwan's struggles, as they recount the attempts by Taiwan to reestablish with its citizenry a sense of the collective amidst ever-shifting regional and global political, economic, military, and cultural arrangements. Wang and Kuo explain how national identities and political and economic situations of different time periods in Taiwan have been translated, re-interpreted, and juxtaposed in Taiwan art education theory and practice. These two opening chapters reveal the multi-faceted, intertwined, and shifting impacts of global and regional developments on national identities, fears, and aspirations; and they demonstrate how the forces of globalization are interpreted and acted upon in localized value systems, cultural and governmental practices, and educational adaptations.

As noted by the next author, Hyungsook Kim, the interwoven relationships between the individual, the nation, and the unyielding forces of globalization are also of central interest in contemporary understandings about culture and art education in South Korea, a country Kim prefers to call, simply, Korea. In "Globalization and Cultural Diversity: Shifts in the Cultural Terrain in Korea" Kim builds her arguments on Western discourse about cultural diversity and multicultural education in her examination of South Korea's recent cultural, political, economic changes. As Kim observes, the myth of a monocultural national identity has long been the tradition in Korea, but a new awareness about South Korea's increasing cultural diversity is currently taking form in governmental policies and educational thought due to the influx of foreign migrant labor and international marriages in South Korea. At the same time, as Kim explains, the population of Korea is rapidly aging and birthrates are low. Consequently, South Korea is experiencing both a population decline and a dramatic shift in the demographic makeup of the people that now inhabit this nation. Of particular interest is Kim's discussion of recent changes in South Korean policies and thinking in the arts, and in art education in higher education, as Kim describes how contemporary art education in South Korea should commit to cultural democracy, and how Korean educational policy and practices might engage marginalized classes, handicapped people, border dwellers, and immigrants, as well as indigenous Koreans.

Effects of military occupations, wars, economic development, international trade, immigration, intercultural exchange, and subsequent local governmental and educational responses to these ever shifting circumstances are of primary concern in global studies, as are the ways in which complex multicultural community identities now exist within and are fostered by nation states through efforts to reinvent and promote traditional local, transplanted, and hybridized cultural practices. For example, in the next chapter in this section, "Effects of Globalization on the Arts Practices of the Bush Negro People of Suriname," Herman Jiesamfoek provides a rich ethnographic description of the hybridized arts and cultural practices of the Bush Negro people, descendents of escaped slaves of several different African cultures and one of the many distinct cultural groups that now inhabit the Republic of Suriname. Formerly known as Dutch Guyana and located in northern

South America, Suriname gained its independence in 1978. Jiesamfoek briefly recounts the history of the Bush Negroes of Suriname and the current disruptions to their environments resulting from over-farming, over-mining, and tourism industries. He then describes the arts traditions and cultural practices in their villages, in the isolated interior areas of Suriname, and in the urban centers, sharing recent concerns expressed by elders about the negative impact of global media/global culture on Bush Negro youth, and explaining how both elders and young people are now attempting to preserve their artistic traditions through apprenticeships, festivals, and new interpretations of traditional artifacts. These are familiar lamentations about the devastating effects of government-sanctioned environmental degradation on local peoples and their ways of life; as are nostalgic concerns about the disaffection of the youth with the cultural traditions of elders. Also familiar are the imaginative creative reinventions and strategies employed by local and indigenous people in attempts to reaffirm their cultural distinctiveness amidst the homogenizing pressures of globalization.

The opening chapters of this book explore shifting notions of ethnic-, cultural- and national-identities, taking into account historical, political, economic, cultural, and environmental forces of globalization as they play out at the local levels, and giving due regard to the role of the arts and education in shaping the self-affirmative tendencies and desires of individuals, cultural groups, and nations. In "'Parisianisme' and Local Cultures: Supra-national, National, and Infra-national Cultures" Frank Vigneron, a French art historian now living and teaching in Hong Kong, describes inconsistencies and contradictions about notions of cultural identity through his analysis of the tensions of globalization, nationality, and local community in Hong Kong, a dynamic international site and a contemporary global cross road. Vigneron deconstructs the narrative of national cultural unity in Hong Kong against the backdrop of economic and cultural globalization, migrations, hybridization, and the reemergence of notions of local culture there; and he compares these notions to understandings about how cultural developments in Europe (Paris, in particular) and China are also creating new types of cultural reactions, resistances, and representations.

Cultural representation is also the topic of

Yuehchen Wang's study, "Sculpting the Sky: The Art and Culture of Weifang International Kite Festival." Wang describes the city of Weifang's International Kite Festival in China, an event that attracts thousands of visitors annually from around the world. Her discussion includes a brief history of the development of Chinese kites; descriptions of kinds, styles, designs, and symbolic meanings in Chinese kites; the use of this festival to promote tourism and local economic prosperity; and the exporting of Chinese kites to millions of kite enthusiasts globally. The Weifang International Kite Festival exemplifies current practices employed in many places throughout the world, as national and local governments and public/private entities merge their commercial, historical, aesthetic, and political interests in the creation of objects, sites, and venues for both creative cultural expression and economic development.

The merging of the commercial, cultural, and political in ethnic arts programming in locations throughout the world produces a dazzling array of themes and sites for the study of globalization; and the diverse cultural backgrounds and experiences of the authors in this book are further evidence of the strength, reach, and ubiquity of globalization. Ryan Shin, in "Promotion of Ethnic and Cultural Identity through Visual and Material Culture among Immigrant Koreans," provides an intriguing case study of East Asian immigrants (Korean, Japanese, and Chinese) in Tucson, Arizona. Focusing on Korean immigrant culture in particular, Shin positions their vibrant ethnic arts, community programming, and cultural traditions within mainstream U.S. multicultural, visual, and material culture practices, and examines why and how Tucson Korean immigrants use their arts to maintain and transmit their Korean cultural heritage. Shin concludes that art educators need to understand and embrace immigrant ethnic cultural expressions as educational content in an effort to prepare their own students for the era of globalization, mass migration, and international trade and travel.

Martina Riedler, in "The Nature and Notion of Museums in the Age of Globalization," also asks how people maintain a sense of national identity and culture in response to the forces of globalization. She analyzes the challenges of national museum practices and policy formation when, rather than being seen as mere cultural centers of a particular geographical region, national museums now expand beyond the political and geographic boundaries of their nation states. Exploring these issues, Riedler provides insight into the changing relationships between large museums' local, national, and international role in knowledge and culture production at a time when globalization has led to reexamination of the role of culture and its relationship to nationalism and identity formation.

Karen Frostig, who self-identifies as a U.S.-born Jewish artist, scholar, activist, feminist, and educator who has traced her lineage to her Austrian roots, also problematizes notions of nationality. In "Transnational Dialogues Dealing with Holocaust Legacies," she shares her experience of her attempts to recover her family's tragic history as citizens of Austria, their stories as victims and survivors of the Holocaust, her forging of an independent relationship to Vienna, and her recent establishment of dual citizenship. Frostig also shares her own story as an artist engaged in international activism, explaining how she uses her art to create conversations with children of Holocaust perpetrators in an effort to heal years of estrangement. With thoughtful and persuasive logic, she then reframes this poignant discussion in a critique of contemporary trends in the US toward regimentation in public schooling. Although Frostig is herself hesitant to claim linkages between what happened in the Holocaust and the growing movement in the US toward standardization, prediction, and control of its citizenry through recent problematic educational policies of the federal government in their attempts to shape U.S. *national character* and increase U.S. *global competitiveness*; readers, on the other hand, may draw their own conclusions about such trends.

There can be no doubt that human rights atrocities and genocidal histories span the globe and continue to the present day. In "Never Again: A (K)night with Ben," Wanda Knight recounts an evening in conversation with Benjamin B. Ferencz, chief prosecutor of the Nuremberg trials, on a flight from the United States to Germany. Knight reflects with great sensitivity on the atrocities on the Holocaust, but then shifts the spotlight to U.S. atrocities: slavery, lynchings of African Americans, genocide of America's indigenous populations, recent demonization of Latinos, Muslims, and Arabs, and treatment of prisoners at Abu Ghraib and Guantanamo Bay. Knight asserts that by uncovering what she calls "difficult sites" and "hidden histories" and by interrogating with our students the visual culture practices of instilling hatred (propaganda, stereotypes, and cultural misrepresentations of "other"), we are in a better position to see people as individual human beings whom we otherwise perceive as unlike us. For Knight, the forces of globalization must now promote notions of global justice, civic engagement, and world peace.

In the final chapter to this section of the anthology, "A Policy Analysis of Formal Education in Modern Multiethnic Kenya: A Case for Cultural Hybridization," Kenyan-born scholar and art educator David Ogega Nyaberi provides a case study and critical analysis of contemporary educational policies, curriculum structures, and political practices in modern day Kenya. All eyes were on the Republic of Kenya in January of 2008, when violence erupted over a contested presidential election. Bordered on the north by Ethiopia, the northeast by Somalia, the west by Uganda, and the northwest by Sudan, Kenya currently had been considered most stable among east African countries. Nyaberi's insightful and timely analysis is conducted with respect to not only to Kenya's colonial past and its precariously peaceful present moment, but also with regard to Kenya's contemporary multiethnic composition, an artifact of the geopolitical partitioning of many parts of Africa during the European colonial era. Informed by a post-colonial theoretical framework, Nyaberi explicates how an arts-based multi-cultural/inter-cultural literacy curriculum, one informed by contemporary critical theory and that takes into account current facets of globalization, can be designed to both foster Kenyan national identity formation and at the same time empower and recognize the value and contributions of Kenya's many peoples. Nyaberi's intercultural educational model envisions a means by which Kenya, other African nations, and indeed nations everywhere might reorient their national multicultural educational practices and priorities in a globalized world.

Each of the chapters in Section I of *Globalization, Art, and Education* offers perspectives about the nature of and responses to globalization in specific localities in the world. Multicultural, intercultural, and transcultural themes pervade these chapters. Both embracing and interrogating emerging and shifting notions of citizenship, cultural identity and nationhood, they also raise questions about differential power relations, cultural hegemony, and resistance; and they focus our attention on the inseparability of culture, commerce, politics, ethnicity, race, religion, social class, and environment. Stories of the effects of imperialism are interspersed with equally compelling stories of cultural adaptation, invention, agency, and emergence, as the people of the world learn to live together in an increasingly interconnected world. As do the following chapters in this book, the authors in this section see artistic expression and education as central to the character and well-being of the many nations, cultural groups, and people of the world.

Taiwanese Picturebooks and the Search for National Identity

Chien-hua Kuo

Globalization impacts the cultural, economic, and political life of a nation. Forces of globalization include international migrations, wars and military occupations, cross cultural communication and exchange, international or transnational trade and commerce, and the impacts of expansionist tendencies of some countries (imperialism) that accompany these globalizing forces. Scholars differ on whether globalization is good or bad for a particular country. For Tomlinson, one of the major aspects of globalization is that "global culture is dominated by the commodifying practices of global capitalism" (1999, p. 80) and for this reason it has moved toward a homogeneous rather than a heterogeneous state. For critics and advocates alike, this movement toward homogenization is seen as a continuation of imperialism. In the non-Western world, debates about globalization often involve ideologies "in which globalization is viewed as either the cause or the cure of all local problems" (Grant & Short, 2002, p. 7).

With these considerations in mind, this chapter looks at the attempts of one country, the island state of Taiwan or the People's Republic of China, to define its own unique character in the late 20th and early 21st centuries. As is often the case as a people respond to homogenizing impacts of globalization, an emphasis on the local is increasingly engaged and a return to nationalistic traditional values and culture revival are, in turn, often used as a strategy to that end. Following a brief history of Taiwan's complicated history over the past four centuries, and a discussion of Taiwanese attempts to overcome centuries of domination by others, I provide a study of a recent concentrated effort in Taiwan as an example of localization; in this particular case, I examine the recent publication and proliferation of Taiwanese children's picturebooks, written by Taiwanese writers and artists, published by Taiwanese governmental agencies and companies, and designed to reaffirm Taiwanese culture and values as a form of resistance to globalizating tendencies.

The Search for Taiwan's Identity

Taiwan is a multicultural nation due to the different political powers that have ruled this territory and imposed their cultures here over the past 400 years. Originally, people of Malay-Polynesian descent settled in the low-lying coastal plains of present-day Taiwan. They were the ancestors of the present-day aborigine groups. They lived in different areas of Taiwan but never unified as one political group to control all of the island territories. It was not until the 16th century, when Portuguese navigators "discovered" Taiwan and called it *Ilha Formosa,* the beautiful island, that Taiwan was recognized in Western history. Since then, both the Spanish and Dutch have colonized parts of Taiwan because of their economic interests. In 1661, after being defeated by the Qing Dynasty Manchus in China, Cheng Chen-gong, the last general of the Han Chinese Ming Dynasty,[1] led 25,000 nobles, soldiers, and pirates to invade Taiwan and expelled the Dutch. In 1683, Cheng Chen-gong's descendents and soldiers lost Taiwan to the Manchus, which allowed the Qing Dynasty to take over western Taiwan. During the Qing Dynasty era (1683-1895), more and more Han Chinese settled in Taiwan. As a result, the Han Chinese became the major population in Taiwan.

The search for a Taiwan national identity is a long-standing concern. At its most basic levels, Taiwanese consciousness may be understood as a resistance discourse that has evolved first in resistance to Japanese colonialism, then in resistance to the Koumintang's monocracy, and now in resistance to the hegemony of Mainland China and the forces of Western globalization (Huang, 2000). Each of these forms of resistance are discussed in greater detail below.

Taiwanese consciousness as a resistance to the Japanese colonialism. The roots of Taiwanese consciousness can be traced back to the Japanese colonial era (1895-1945) and it has been evolving up to the present day (Huang, 2000). During the Cheng Chen-gong era (1661-1683) and the Qing dynasty

(1683-1895), Han immigrants rarely had a Taiwanese consciousness but developed a strongly different local consciousness based on where their ancestry originated.[2] But in 1895, the Sino-Japanese War ended and China ceded Taiwan to Japan. Then the Han immigrants developed a sense of togetherness as Taiwanese, which differed from the Japanese colonizers and from another colonized group, the aborigines.[3] Thus, Taiwanese consciousness arose as a resistance to colonialism (Huang, 2000).

Taiwanese consciousness as a resistance to the Kuomintang's monocracy. When Japan lost World War II in 1945, Taiwan returned to China and was ruled by the government of the Republic of China, which had taken over from the Qing dynasty in 1911. During the period from 1945 to 1949, Taiwan was ruled by a local government and governor was assigned by Chiang Kei-shek. His government was the Kuomintang (the Nationalist Party), which was involved in a civil war on the Chinese Mainland with the communists.[4] An important event occurred in Taiwan when a local investigation of illegal cigarettes turned into riots and massacres in the cities of Taipei and Kaohsiung on February 28, 1947.[5] It caused a political repression in which many innocent Taiwanese intellectuals and local people were killed or disappeared because they were suspected of being communist spies. This was called the "228 Incident" and it became taboo to talk about this under the Kuomintang government. After that, people in Taiwan learned not to become involved in politics, and families of the victims in the "228 Incident" kept silent. Accordingly, Taiwanese consciousness transformed from resisting the Japanese colonialism to resisting the Kuomintang's monocracy (Huang, 2000).

In 1949, the Chiang Kei-shek government and his followers fled to Taiwan after being defeated by the communists on the mainland. Later, Chiang Kei-shek was elected by senators, who were elected by the people in China, as the president of Taiwan, known as the Republic of China (ROC.), for the rest of his life. During the era of Chiang Kei-shek and Chiang Ching-kuo (the son and successor of Chiang Kei-shek), the Kuomintang represented Taiwan and controlled the national resources and the political, military, economic, and social aspects of Taiwanese society. According to Winkler, the objective of the Kuomintang was to reinforce "Chineseness" in Taiwan during the period from 1945 to 1960 (as cited in Chou, 1998). A strong ideology of patriotism for "Great China" was promoted in society and it limited free speech for those with criticisms about the Kuomintang. The myth of "Great China" was to emphasize that Taiwan

was the successor to a 5,000-year Chinese traditional heritage which followed orthodox Confucianism. It was intended to create a unified singular national narrative.

The island of Taiwan played a marginal role in this grand narrative. Thus, Taiwanese consciousness was oppressed by a Chinese ideology and a firm and strict political control. At first, Taiwanese intellectuals devoted their consciousness of Taiwan to literature rather than politics. These literary works encouraged the younger generation to resist the political repression. As a result, more and more Taiwanese intellectuals began devoting themselves to political movements for the right of free speech in the 1980s. The pressure from these groups led to conflicts, such as the "Mei-li Dao Incident,"[6] and eventually caused martial law to be lifted.

During the Kuomingtang era, the population in Taiwan was categorized as "wai-sheng ren" (which means Mainland Chinese, including followers of the Chiang-Kei-shek government from China), "ben-sheng ren" (which means the descendants of the early Han immigrants), "ping-di shan-bao" (which means plain aborigines living in cities), and "shan-di shan-bao" (which means mountain aborigines living in mountains). During this period, the term *Taiwanese* narrowly referred to state-residents.

Taiwanese consciousness as a resistance to the hegemony of Mainland China. According to Song (2003), the idea of localization originally came from resistance to the political oppression and invasion by Mainland China. Since the post-Chiang Ching-kuo era (during the late 1980s), the government of the ROC has gradually shifted its attitude from fighting for the legitimate position of representing old China to being an independent democratic nation. As a result, the concept of localization is now a means to identify with Taiwan itself rather than with the imagery of old China. As a result, many politicians born in Taiwan have been assigned the higher positions in the government body, which was impossible during the Chiang Kai-shek era. This indicates that the government has tended to indigenize its political power and public policy.

Recent demand for localization in Taiwan, the establishment of a Neo-Taiwanese identity, and tenuous relations with Mainland China. Vice president Li Deng-hui assumed the presidency following the death of Chiang Ching-kuo in 1988. After serving as Chiang Ching-kuo's successor until 1990, Li Deng-hui became the first president voted into power by the people under a democratic process. Since Li was a "ben-sheng ren," his identity gave the localization movement in Taiwan a significant political meaning. In the eyes of its people, Taiwan was finally ruled by a president born in Taiwan, although he was a leader of the Kuomintang. In Li's view, rather than using the name of "the ROC in Taiwan" to represent the island, the term "Taiwan" should be used alone to stand for this island nation. Since then and to the present, Taiwan has tried to present itself as an independent nation on the global stage.

The move in Taiwan toward independence has caused serious concerns in Mainland China—which still claims sovereignty over Taiwan—and analysis of the local, regional, and international consequences over the debate between Mainland China and Taiwan is beyond the scope of this chapter, other than to say that this debate is foremost in many Taiwanese people's thinking. In order to clarify confusions or political discussions over the definition of who is Taiwanese, President Li Deng-hui claimed that *all* people who live in Taiwan and are willing to devote their lives to this land are *Neo-Taiwanese*. The Taiwanese population body is now categorized as Hokklo, Hakka, "hsin-chu-min" (which means new residents or mainlanders, immigrants from China after 1945), and "yuan-chu-min" (which means aborigines). This new definition is meant to prove the idea of Taiwan's independence[7] and to unify Taiwanese consciousness as a means to resist the hegemony of Mainland China.

President Chen Shui-bian, who succeeded Li Deng-hui in 1996, has continually practiced Li's move toward localization based on a new Taiwanese consciousness. Like Li, he is a "ben-sheng ren" and his party, the Democratic Progressive Party (DPP), represents Taiwanese intellectuals who promote Taiwan's independence. As a result, the DPP has emphasized Taiwan as the national name on many important occasions, a strategy to promote the individuality of Taiwan.[8] During the DPP era, the government body has gradually become more indigenized. For example, "ben-sheng ren" have been promoted as administrators at higher levels and the use of everyday language has not been limited to traditional Chinese Mandarin. Moreover, it is obvious that Taiwanese consciousness has heavily influenced public issues and policy making. For example, recent cultural policy for strengthening Taiwanese consciousness consists of promoting an equal right for different native languages (including local dialects like Min-nan Hua, Hakka Hua, and various aboriginal languages), preserving and researching traditional Taiwanese cultural heritage (including historical buildings, local customs, and rituals), promoting cultural creative industries, and recruiting and training cultural volunteers and professionals

(Council of Cultural Affairs, 2004). All of these local cultural practices and political movements are part of a call for national identity based on Taiwanese consciousness as a means to resist the hegemony of Mainland China. Taiwanese consciousness is also a force used to strengthen local civil education in the current era of globalization.

Taiwanese Children's Picturebooks and the Promotion of Taiwanese National Consciousness

This section considers an example of how Taiwan public policies and private industries have come together to facilitate the establishment of a Taiwanese national identity, offered in this case through a study of the publication of children's picturebooks in Taiwan over the past 20 years. Children's picturebooks in Taiwan have increasingly emphasized the local over the global as a means to educate children about their cultural roots and to reinforce their identification with being *Taiwanese*. An analysis of publishing strategies of these Taiwanese children's picturebooks provides intriguing insights about competing pressures of globalization and national identity currently being played out in Taiwan.

Because the book market in Taiwan is limited and costs are less for publishing translated books, most children's books published in Taiwan have been imported from the United States, Japan, and European countries and then translated into Chinese. This has limited the availability of books for children created by and for the Taiwanese people. In response to this situation, and in light of Taiwan's interests in promoting its own national identity, since the 1990s there has been an increase in publication of children's picturebooks in Taiwan written and designed by Taiwanese authors. These picturebooks have been explicitly developed to educate children about their cultural roots and to reinforce their identification with being *Taiwanese*. In order to make picturebooks created by Taiwanese writers and illustrators more visible in the book market and in order to promote good sales, publishing efforts have become very important in Taiwan. A major strategy has been to publish Taiwanese picturebooks in sets, with central themes that emphasize Taiwanese lifestyles and culture. Publishing houses propose these Taiwanese themes and then invite local writers and illustrators to develop them. In doing so, these publishing houses receive financial support from the central or local governments because of current cultural and educational policies supporting localization. This government/private partnership in local publishing is seen as a means to cultivate children's identification with Taiwan, and indeed, children's picturebooks written by Taiwanese authors have grown rapidly in Taiwan's book market in recent years. Taiwanese children's picturebooks have been broadly adopted in school curriculums, book clubs, library activities, and the like (Bradbury & Liu, 2003).

Children's books convey implicit and/or explicit ideologies. As Stephens observes, "[p]icture books can, of course, exist for fun, but they can never be said to exist without either a socializing or educational intention, or else without a specific orientation towards the reality constructed by the society that produces them" (1992, p. 158). This applies well to the motives and intentions of the publishers of Taiwanese picturebooks created by Taiwanese writers and illustrators and published after 1990 in *sets* with themes reflecting Taiwanese local culture and traditions. In my analysis of kinds and subject matter of varying recently popularized sets of picture books, I have identified eight general themes or approaches. The following categories, listed below chronologically, reveal favored themes amongst publishers and governmental officials.

1. *Spring in the Countryside Series*—developed to introduce agricultural Taiwan products, culture, and future of agricultural development (100 titles in total, published by the Council of Agriculture from 1992 to 2000);
2. *The Beauty of Tainan County Series*—developed to introduce traditions and customs around Tainan County (100 titles in total, based on its publishing proposal, with 18 titles published by the Culture Affairs Bureau, Tainan County from 1999 to 2001 and 19 titles published by Children's Publication from 2005 to 2008);
3. *Firefly Picturebook Series: Taiwanese Folktales and Folk Lives*—developed to introduce six Taiwanese Han folktales and six different customs, including religious beliefs, traditional crafts, and traditional housing (12 titles published by Yuan-Liou Publishing in 2001);
4. *Taiwanese Children's Picturebook Series*—developed to introduce art, traditions, and the environment in Taiwan (10 titles published by the Council of Cultural Affairs and Children's Publication in 2002, with no limitation on future titles under this series);
5. *Genuine Youth of Taiwan Series*—developed to introduce six well-known adult writers' childhood memories about agricultural Taiwan during the 1950s to 1970s (6 titles published by Youn-Liu Publishing in 2003, no limitation on future titles under this series);
6. *Firefly Picturebook Series: Taiwanese Aboriginal Folktales*—developed to introduce aboriginal folktales from different tribes (6 titles published by Yuan-Liou Publishing in 2006);
7. *Taiwanese Folktale Series*—developed to introduce six Taiwanese folktales from both the Han and aboriginal traditions (6 titles published by Taiwan Mac Educational Company in 2006); and
8. *Cultural Taiwan Picturebook Series*—developed to introduce Taiwanese culture based on the four aspects of arts, folk life, history, and ethnic groups (100 titles in total, based on its proposal, with 10 titles published by the National Taiwan Museum of Fine Arts and Dong-Hua Publishing in 2006).

Three publishing models can be identified in these eight series of publications: (a) publication by the government, (b) government and private commercial publisher cooperative ventures, and (c) publication exclusively by commercial /private publishing companies. The first two models require that the content of the books reflect current government public policy, while the third one is more flexible. In all cases, the publications have the same goal, which is to reintroduce and preserve traditional local folk life and culture in Taiwan, and to emphasize Taiwan's purity and uniqueness. These picturebook sets can be seen as an attempt to construct a national identity within a more general demand for both recognition and localization in Taiwan and as a response to the crisis of blurred national identity caused by globalization and the threat of hegemony from Mainland China.

Professor Su Jeng-ming, an art educator and one of the major consultants involved in the development of four series of picturebooks,[9] believes that picturebooks are a powerful means to promote local cultures and strengthen children's identification with Taiwan, the major goal he has pursued and emphasized in the creation of these picturebooks (J. M. Su, personal communication, September 22, 2007). These government publications not only fulfilled Su's personal purpose but also met the government's particular expectations.

Agriculture, a major theme in many recently published picturebooks, once dominated social and economic life in Taiwan. In these picturebooks and in Taiwan more generally, agriculture has now become more of a nostalgic link to a nationalistic idea of the past. In response to the globalizing effect of Taiwan joining the World Trade Organization, *Spring in the Countryside Series* was published by the Council of Agriculture from 1992 to 2000. Interestingly, the *Spring in the Countryside Series* was an educational publication designed to teach children about the transformation of agriculture in Taiwan from being an essential industry that provided the food for the island into being an element of recreation and tourism and to set the stage for important social, economic, and lifestyle changes that have been in the making for many years. Taiwanese farmers have had to accept the fact that imported agricultural products with lower prices would soon occupy the Taiwanese market and they have needed to change the way they ran their farming businesses, including adapting their traditional income-producing farming businesses to accommodate a new economic emphasis on tourism and recreation. One main goal of the *Spring in the Countryside Series* project was to educate the younger generation about this transformation, in part because they would become potential future customers for this form of local tourism and recreation. In addition, these books illustrated the historical development of Taiwan agricultural industry. Local agricultural products and their original production areas are introduced in a narrative format within which local customs and lifestyles are embedded and explained.

In another series of picturebooks, the theme is appreciation and preservation of local customs. *The Beauty of Tainan County Series,* produced by the Culture Affairs Bureau of Tainan County, was designed to preserve those cultural heritages in a picturebook format. Tainan County, located in the south of Taiwan, was the earliest area where the Han people migrated and developed a centralized business and cultural area. It has retained rich traditional cultural heritages to this day. The content that *The Beauty of Tainan County Series* covers includes local customs, special products, and unique landscapes from different districts in Tainan County. This publishing strategy promoting local culture was adopted by other Culture Affairs Bureaus at the county level throughout Taiwan, and several individual picturebooks with local themes—such as oral folklore, local history, and famous local products and sights—have been published after *The Beauty of Tainan County Series* was published. Because these picturebooks contained specific local themes, they became teaching materials for the "native cultural education" movement introduced into the current elementary curriculum standards regulated by the Ministry of Education.

The *Taiwanese Children's Picturebook Series,* sponsored by the Council of Cultural Affairs, and the *Cultural Taiwan Picturebook Series,* sponsored by the National Taiwan Museum of Fine Arts, carry out similar publishing concepts. Visual artists, traditional costumes, aboriginal-related themes, life in the cities, and the like have become valuable subject matters. Although these subject matters are presented in a straightforward manner, they deliver specific kinds of messages to their readers about how to perceive Taiwan's identity. Three examples are discussed below.

First, Taiwanese senior artists, who were born and educated in the Japanese colonial period, are introduced in the picturebooks. Most of the paintings of these senior artists depicted the landscapes of Taiwan before it became industrialized or modernized. Their artworks have become the icon of "native" Taiwan since the localization movement evolved. The stories not only emphasize the great artworks they created but also their love for the land where they were born and lived. These stories invite child readers to identify with the artists and their land.

Second, speaking native languages or mother tongues in schools was prohibited and punished during the 1950s to 1970s, when standard Mandarin was enforced as an official language. People who spoke mother tongues were considered inferior and uneducated. In order to change this conception and preserve the beauty of traditional languages and cultures, mother tongue education became a required course in cultural curricula. This demand is shown in three books within the two series of picturebooks, where the texts of children's rhythms and songs are written with mainly Min-nan Hua, partly Hakka Hua, and one aboriginal language. This language proportion also illustrates the actual population of different mother tongue speakers in Taiwan.

Third, three particular titles of the *Cultural Taiwan Picturebook Series* reveal the historical events that shaped Taiwan in order to question, emphasize, or rethink the meanings associated with those events. *The Sculpture of Wai-Gong* (meaning matriarchal grandfather)—a story of the Taiwanese senior artist Cheng Chen-po (1895-1947), who was executed by the Kuomintong soldiers in the "228 Incident"—is the first picturebook dealing with such challenging political issues. The narrator in this story is the grandson of the artist who himself is a sculptor. He was invited to create a statue of his grandfather, which would be placed at the park in Chia-Yi, where the senior artist was born. This story depicts the sculptor's search for the memory of his grandfather artist with help from his grandmother. It conveys the family's pain and loss and shows the artist's love for his homeland, which explicitly emphasizes the artist's contribution to the art world and implicitly questions the reasons for the "228 Incident."

Mona Rudao is a story in memory of Mona Rudao (1882-1930), who was the leader of the Seedeq tribe and led the revolt of Wushe in 1930 against the

Japanese colonial authorities. This story shows Mona Rudao as a resistance hero against Japanese occupation and as a role model who fights for Taiwan's freedom and independence.

Taiwan Growing in the Maps presents maps of Taiwan in diverse historical contexts, including the Dutch and Spanish occupations, Ming and Qing Dynasties, the period of Japanese control, and the Kuomintang era. The maps serve to help the young viewer to perceive Taiwan in relationship to the rest of the world. The images indicate the idea of being an island situated in the center of a map (implying Taiwan's independence) or situated southeast of Mainland China (implying Taiwan as part of China). The book encourages children to take the view of Taiwan as an independent island in the Pacific Ocean.

The four series of picturebooks including *Firefly Picturebook Series: Taiwanese Folktales and Folk Lives*, *Firefly Picturebook Series: Taiwanese Aboriginal Folktales*, *Taiwanese Folktale Series*, and *Genuine Youth of Taiwan Series* were published by independent publishing houses, following their own publishing strategies. Folktales and folk lives are the common themes used in these picturebooks to illustrate and encourage cultural identification with people of Taiwan from the past to the present and from different regions. The publishing strategy of the *Genuine Youth of Taiwan Series*, however, distinguished itself from the others by building a collective memory of the agricultural period from the 1950s to 1960s. This is done by retelling six well-known Taiwanese writers' unforgettable childhood memories. The stories demonstrate diverse life experiences from different regions of Taiwan. Like different pieces of a puzzle, they come together to reveal an overarching Taiwanese culture. According to Lain, the editor of *Genuine Youth of Taiwan Series*, these picturebooks were designed for children and their parents. Through reading together, the parents could share and discuss their childhood memories with their children (T. M. Lain, personal communication, December 15, 2004). In this way, the conversations will keep old memories alive by passing them down to the younger generation.

Conclusion

This study places Taiwanese children's picturebooks in the context of the localization movement in Taiwan during the presidencies of Li Deng-hui and Chen Shui-bian (1990-2008). I consider relationships between the publishing of these picturebooks and the development of modern day Taiwanese consciousness, and against the backdrop of globalization. To strengthen Taiwanese national self-consciousness and to emphasize Taiwan's independence, the DPP government used strategies of "de-Chinese ness" and "re-Taiwanese ness," attempting to devalue the Chinese influence and emphasize the recognition of Taiwan as a nation.[10] When situating the eight series of picturebooks that I studied in the discourse of "Taiwan's identity," the representations in these picturebooks reveal a concern for a reconstruction of Taiwanese culture, as promoted by both the government, and, importantly, the publishing editors. These editors are the key individual persons who shape the publishing channels that carry out these strategies, including adoption of the title "Taiwanese Picturebooks." Specific writers and illustrators selected by the editors complete the mission of *representing* a Taiwanese consciousness. Their strategies are to focus on folktales and myths, agricultural traditions, local cultural practices, senior artists, and personal narratives from Taiwan's past, and all of these strategies are used to provide children with the idea of a unique Taiwanese culture.

The eight series of picturebooks labeled "Taiwan Picturebooks" are significant not only because they were made in Taiwan by Taiwanese people for Taiwanese people, but also because they are intended to promote a positive sense of Taiwanese national identity in children. As such, they both represent an example of how one country engages in a strategy of localization as a response to globalization. At the same time, they also convey both assertions and fears about their continued identity as an independent people, free of the complicated, uncertain, and hegemonic forces of Mainland China.

Acknowledgments
I would like to express my appreciation to Professor Su Jeng-ming for his kindness in sharing his insightful thoughts for this chapter.

REFERENCES

Bradbury, S., & Liu, F. (2003 March/ April). Everywhere a children's book: The view from Taiwan. *The Horn Book Magazine, 79*(2), pp. 239-48.

Chao, K. T., ets. (2002). Taiwanese nursery rhyme. In C. C. Lin. (ed.). (2002). *Taiwanese Children's Picturebook Series.* Taipei: Council of Cultural Affairs and Children's Publication.

Chen, Y. C., & Chang, C. M. (2006). The sculpture of Wai-Gong. In J. M. Su (Ed.). *Cultural Taiwan picturebook series.* Taichung: National Taiwan Museum of Fine Arts & Taipei: Dong-Hua Publishing.

Chen, Y. C., Lin, W. H., Huang, W. B., Chen, L. Y., & Mao, W. L. (Eds.). (1999-2004). *The beauty of Tainan county series.* Tainan: Culture Affairs Bureau, Tainan County.

Chen, Z. Y. (1998). *Taiwan literature and localization.* Taipei: Cheng-Chong Books.

Cheng, M. C., Tsao, C. Y., Lin, L., Ma, C. H., Su, J. M., & Chen, M. C. (Eds.). (1992-2000). *Spring in the countryside series.* Taipei: Council of Agriculture.

Chou, K. C. (1998). The Kuomintang's government and Confucianism after postwar. In J. J. Huang & J. P. He (Eds), *Cultural development of Taiwan toward the 21st century* (pp. 59-90). Taipei: Taiwan University Press.

Council of Cultural Affairs. (2004). *Cultural Taiwan: New century, new face.* Taipei: Yoan-Liou Publishing.

Deng, H. Y., & Chiu, R. L. (2006). Mona Rudao. In J. M. Su (Ed.). *Cultural Taiwan picturebook series.* Taichung: National Taiwan Museum of Fine Arts & Taipei: Dong-Hua Publishing.

Grant, R., & Short, J. R. (2002). Globalization: An introduction. In R. Grant & J. R. Short (Eds.), *Globalization and the margins* (pp. 3-14). New York: Palgrave Macmillan.

Hao, K. T. (Ed.). (2001). *Firefly picturebook series: Taiwanese folktales and folk lives.* Taipei: Yuan-Liou Publishing.

Hao, K. T. (Ed.). (2006). *Firefly picturebook series: Taiwanese aboriginal folktales.* Taipei: Yuan-Liou Publishing.

Hao, K. T. (Ed.). (2006). *Taiwanese folktale series.* Taipei: Taiwan Mac Educational Company.

Huang, J. J. (2000). *Taiwanese consciousness and Taiwanese culture.* Taipei: Cheng-Chong Books.

Lain, T. M. (Ed.). (2003). *Genuine youth of Taiwan series.* Taipei: Yuan-Liou Publishing.

Lin, C. C. (Ed.). (2002). *Taiwanese children's picturebook series.* Taipei: Council of Cultural Affairs & Children's Publication.

Lin, C. C. (Ed.). (2005 ~2008). *The beauty of Tainan county series.* Taipei: Children's Publication.

Liu, K. H., & Chiang, P. R. (2006). Taiwan growing in the maps. In J. M. Su (Ed.). *Cultural Taiwan picturebook series.* Taichung: National Taiwan Museum of Fine Arts & Taipei: Dong-Hua Publishing.

Lo, C. S. (1999). *Teaching philosophy of the grades 1 through 12 curriculum integration.* Retrieved February 15, 2001, from http://www.iest.edu.tw/issue/j1/v16n2/1.htm.

Song, K. C. (2003). Is this the indigenization we want? *Cyberbees.glog.* Retrieved October 7, 2003, from http://www.cyberbees.org/blog/archives/001353.html.

Stephens, J. (1992). Language and ideology in children's fiction. London and New York: Longman.

Su, J. M. (Ed.). (2006). *Cultural Taiwan picturebook series.* Taichung: National Taiwan Museum of Fine Arts & Taipei: Dong-Hua Publishing.

Sun, D. C. (2000). *Construction of minority: Taiwanese indigenous language, culture, and politics.* Taipei: Lian-He Literature Publishers.

Tomlinson, J. (1999). *Globalization and culture.* Chicago: The University of Chicago Press.

ENDNOTES

1   The Han Chinese are the majority population of old China. The so-called orthodox Chinese culture followed by the Han Chinese is based on Confucianism, which has become a dominant culture. As a result, the Han-centrism developed into a historical and political ideology.

2   The Han immigrants came from different regions of the Fu-chien and Guang-tong Provinces (south coast of China) and were mainly divided into three groups: Quan-zhou, Chang-zhou (both are Hokklo and speak Min-nan Hua, but with different accents), and Hakka (who speak Hakka Hua). Due to the use of different languages, the practice of different rituals and customs, and different time periods of immigrating to Taiwan, these Han immigrants competed with each other for Taiwan's natural resources. Because these three groups occupied most of the plains and mountainsides, aborigines were either forced to move into the mountains or assimilated to the Han Chinese.

3   These Han immigrants, the settlers, believed that they were superior to aborigines because they were proud of their Chinese culture and they thought that the aborigines were uncivilized. It was not until the Wushe Incident occurred—a violent resistance to Japan by a tribe of aborigines in 1930—that the Han Taiwanese intellectuals were aware of the fact that aborigines were part of the Taiwanese (Chen, 1998).

4   Modern China (the Republic of China) was established in 1912 by the Kuomintang, founded by Sun Yeh-shen when democracy was promoted to replace the traditional autocratic monarchy held by the Qing dynasty. Meanwhile, Sun Yeh-shen became the national father and the Kuomintang was the first and only legal political party in China. After the death of Sun, Chiang Kei-shek was the successor as the leader of the party.

5   The "228 Incident" that led to a riot was not accidental because the society was controlled by an unfair government system which made economic and social conditions worse after World War II.

6   Mei-li Dao means beautiful island, drawn from the word *Formosa* in Portuguese. It was a political magazine established in the summer of 1979, which often criticized the Kuomintang. During the martial law era, mass media were controlled by the Kuomintang. Any criticism of the government was excluded from the dominant media, such as TV and newspapers. Therefore, political elites who resisted the Kuomintang's monocracy formulated a political group and published magazines to criticize the government. According to martial law, it was illegal to organize any political party and collective demonstrations. Thus, these non-Kuomintang political elites attempted to fight for the removal of the martial law and to protect the right for free speech. On December 10, 1979, International Human Rights Day, the non-Kuomintang political elites organized a demonstration for supporting the declaration of international human rights in Kaohsiung. However, this demonstration was considered illegal by the local police. Unfortunately, physical conflicts occurred between the crowd and the police. As a result, it turned into a riot and later the major political activists were arrested and were put into jail due to this illegal collective activity. This summary is based on the information provided by the website of the Education Ministry, at http://content.edu.tw/local/kaushoun/dazen/country/38/index.htm. In 1986, the non-Kuomintang political elites organized their own party, namely the Democratic Progressive Party (DPP). Through constant resistance to the Kuomintang's monocracy during the 1980s, the martial law was finally lifted in 1987. In 1991, the DPP passed a program of proposing Taiwan's independence. And, the party won the presidential elections in 1996 and 2004.

7   However, Sun (2000), who is an aboriginal scholar, criticizes this definition because it is based on the Han-centrism and it is problematic.

8   However, the Kuomintang and its related parties have argued the existence of the ROC. in Taiwan. Although different parties hold their own interpretation toward the idea of Taiwanese consciousness, its common goal is to resist the hegemony of Mainland China (Chen, 1998).

9   Included amongst Su Jeng-ming's titles are *Spring in the Countryside Series, The Beauty of Tainan County Series, Taiwanese Children's Picturebook Series,* and *Cultural Taiwan Picturebook Series.*

10 The major concepts and political strategies of this localization movement during 1990-2008 shifted in a different direction after the change of presidency in May 2008. The Kuomintang political party has reacquired power and now emphasizes the recognition of traditional Chinese culture as an important aspect of Taiwan's heritage. In addition, the current president, Ma Ying-chiu, stresses that Taiwan should be devoted to economic development in order to seek opportunities in the global marketplace. In so doing, Taiwan should promote its advantages and seek to develop economic ties with China. However, Taiwan's independence is still a major concern when the Kuomintang government deals with the political relationship between Taiwan and China. Therefore, the evolution and transformation of the localization movement in Taiwan will require more study in the years to come.

Glocalization:[1]
Art Education in Taiwan

An earlier version of this article was presented at the 32nd InSEA World Congress in Osaka, Japan in August 2008.

Li-Yan Wang and Ann Kuo

Writing in an Ambiguous Time

As an island state, Taiwan[2] (Republic of China or ROC) has long been subject to globalizing influences. Under the Dutch and Spanish, the Chinese Ming Dynasty (1386-1644), the Ching Dynasty (1644-1911), Japanese colonial rule (1895-1945) and the Chinese Nationalist governance (1945-2000),[3] Taiwan has historically been influenced by outsiders and by large population movements. These migrations and changes in governing entities have created a nation of diverse interests and peoples and have contributed to a lack of consensus about Taiwan's national and cultural identity. In the past 20 years, the rapid development of information technology and increasing cross-cultural interactions have crystallized a new "global village" consciousness within Taiwanese educational thought, one which will have a deep, lasting, and reinvigorating impact on Taiwanese culture.

As citizens of a small "country/nation-state," the people of Taiwan have a fear of being left behind, so we are always quick to accept novelty. Education, "a site of struggle and compromise," has become both "cause and effect, determining and determined" (Apple, 2000, p. 58). Education policies interact with political, economic, social and cultural changes. Art, as a required course in the school curriculum, similarly undergoes directional changes. As Desai and Chalmers (2007) point out, "(s)chools have always been subject to an overwhelming variety of socio-political demands, which shift in response to the political climate—impacting art education in different ways" (p. 6). In Taiwan, the powerful influence of historical and political forces on education cannot be ignored. Taking into consideration that "one way to reexamine the apparent inevitability of globalization is to situate the contemporary debate in an historical framework" (Burbules & Torres, 2000, p. 3) we trace the evolution of art education in Taiwan within the context of globalizing forces, and then discuss our insights about this evolution.

Why is the Taiwan example important? Although we believe that the Taiwan example is unique, we also note that many aspects of what has happened here can also be observed in many other places in the world. With the collapse of centuries of European Colonialism throughout the world, the fall of the Soviet Union, and other events of great magnitude, newly emerging countries world-wide are establishing and reestablishing their own national identities, educational and cultural practices, and economic and political futures. And like nearly 100 new nations created at the end of World War II, Taiwan is also trying to work its way out of massive identity crises to fashion a future out of its tangle of historical legacies (Frazier, 2005).

The struggle of Taiwan for 'national' identity has been complicated by its past and present relations to the Mainland China. The future of Taiwan is yet uncertain just as the field of art education in Taiwan is continuing to unfold and change. Our uncertain future allows a sense of imagination but at the same time presents difficulty in drawing a final conclusion. With this uncertain future, this paper presents a view from the Asia-Pacific region. It reflects the current thinking of the authors who studied and worked for many years abroad before returning to Taiwan and working toward the advancement of its art education.

The History of Art Education in Taiwan

The following section will briefly explain the history of art education in Taiwan, before discussing the complexities of the present situation. Due to word limitation and for the sake of clarity, many details were omitted. It is important to know that the following is, therefore, not a complete detailed account of art education history in Taiwan.[4]

Educational Practices in Taiwan Prior to the Establishment of Public Schools

Evidence of human life in Taiwan dated back at least 15,000 years to the Paleolithic Age. "Taiwan's early aboriginal groups led a fairly insular existence and had no island-wide politically unifying organization. Naturally, there was no state" (Huang, 2007, p. 1). Although the original inhabitants of Taiwan left no written records of their origins, current archaeological research and linguistic analysis suggest that Taiwan's indigenous groups are Austronesian (Malayo-Polynesian) people.

In 1622, the Dutch East India Company established a base on the Penhua Island but was promptly driven away by Ming Dynasty forces. The Dutch then set up a base in the south of Taiwan in 1624 and extended their hegemony over the island's southwestern coast. Meanwhile, in 1626, a rival Spanish consortium occupied areas in northern Taiwan, but it was driven away by the Dutch in 1642. In 1662, Jheng Cheng-gong led an army of soldiers from southern China and ended four decades of Dutch governance. In other words, from 1624 to 1662, Taiwan was a Western colony, colonized by both the Dutch and the Spanish. A short span of self-rule under the Jheng family ended in 1683 and from 1683 to 1895, Taiwan was governed by China.

And beginning in the early 17th century, Taiwanese lowland indigenous groups were inexorably driven into the island's mountainous interior, "overwhelmed by alien conquerors from both Europe and Asian, and by wave upon wave of immigration of Han people fleeing poverty and war in China"(Government Information Office, Republic of China, 2008, p. 1). Desiring better lives, and seeking refugee from upheavals during the transition between the Ming and Ching dynasties, the ancestors of Taiwan's Han people began migrating from China's southeastern provinces to the island in the 17th century. "Over the centuries, many indigenes have been assimilated into Han-immigrant communities, and many Taiwanese have both Han and indigenous ancestry" (Government Information Office, Republic of China, 2008, p. 1).

Little is written about Taiwan's history of art educational practice in these earlier days, but starting from the 1630s, missionaries began to set up mission schools in Taiwan. Although music was part of the religious school curriculum from its earliest days. The role of visual art in these schools was less clear. In addition to the missionary schools, a traditional Chinese education system was also adopted in Taiwan.

One key feature of such a system was the competitive examinations at local, district, and national levels. "The competitive examination that all young men could take was the method for academic, social

and economic advancement" because passing these tests gave one the opportunity to seek appointment in government, education, or other governmentally controlled sectors of society (Smith, 1981, p. 32). To prepare students for the exams, at the local level, a group of parents would employ a teacher to work with the young men of the village—either in small groups or on a tutorial basis. Instruction in these private lessons focused on the writings of Confucius and Mencius, the poetry and literary arts...etc. The methodology of the teaching/leaning process consisted of copying the great texts of the past, interpreting them and memorizing those portions relevant to the times, and passing the inevitable district examinations (Smith, 1981). Teachers were often men, and so were the students. Wealthy families also hired artists and people who have passed the higher levels of examinations to teach their children Chinese painting and calligraphy. Children of lower socioeconomic classes could engage in traditional arts and craft-making through apprenticeships. After acquiring the necessary skills from their masters, young men could be employed or start their own business.

Japanese Period (1895-1945)

In 1895, Japan defeated China in the Sino-Japanese War (1894-1895). The Treaty of Shimonoseki ceded Taiwan to Japan. Taiwan, including Penghu Island, became Japan's first colony. Perhaps for this reason, Japan was determined to make the administration in Taiwan a success. Public education was an important means of Japanese state control and intercultural dialogue. Elementary schools and teachers' colleges were established; both male and female students started attending these modern schools. Courses in the visual arts and crafts gradually entered the public school curriculum. At that time there were no professional art schools in Taiwan. Because very few Taiwanese people were admitted to secondary schools and colleges due to educational inequity,[5] a new wave of young students started going abroad, especially to Japan, to earn higher degrees.

As traditional apprenticeships and private tutoring been replaced by Western style public schools, the teaching and learning of art changed drastically during the Japanese rule. For example, Japanese artists and teachers introduced to Taiwan new concepts of art and art education, most of which were developed in Japan and Europe. New ways of art making, such as gouache painting, watercolor, oil painting, and new training methods that emphasized drawing began to influence Taiwan artistic practices and fostered a new generation of Taiwanese artists. Lee Wuh-Kuen (2006) points out that:

> the influence of western painting came through a number of different channels, including the modernization of art education, the impact of art schools in Tokyo and the Japanese art community in general and the organization of exhibitions such as the Imperial Art Exhibition, Taiwan Art Exhibition and Governor's Art Exhibition. (p. 18)

Japan had a profound social and cultural impact on Taiwan. The direction and goals of art education were modeled upon those of Japanese schools. Japanese art education textbooks were modified and published for Taiwanese school children. Many recognized that under Japanese rule expanded educational opportunities were provided to school age children. But because of the attention that was devoted to transforming Taiwanese children into Japanese imperial subjects, Japanese colonial efforts also encountered resistance. Starting from self-organized armed resistance to cultural reform efforts led by the Taiwanese Cultural Association in the 1920s, Taiwanese people both embraced new changes and voiced their concerns using a variety of means.

After World War II (1945-1987)

After Japan's loss in World War II in 1945, the Nanjing-based Republic of China (ROC) government declared Taiwan a province of China, citing the Cairo Declaration[6] as its justification. Initially, Taiwanese people, who had been under Japanese rule for 50 years, welcomed the Chinese Nationalist forces. But the joy soon changed into sorrow and anger when the new authority appeared to be repressive and corrupt. The tension gradually burst out into the open in the February 28th Incident in 1947. The follow up military suppression led to arrest and execution of many Taiwanese leading figures and innocent students, lawyers, doctors, etc.

In 1949, the ROC Government led by Chiang Kai-shek and Kuomintang (KMT), also known as the Nationalists in China, after losing control of Mainland China to the communists, "retreat" to Taiwan and established ROC there. The lost mainland territories then became the People's Republic of China (PRC) established by the communist party.

The relocation of the KMT government from China to Taiwan brought a new influx of Han immigrants hailing from a variety of provinces in China, and significantly changed the ethnic makeup the people in Taiwan. On May 20, 1949, the Taiwan Military Garrison Command declared martial law on Taiwan. Although the imposition of martial law was justified on the basis of the civil war with the Communist and intended to be temporary, Taiwan remained under martial law for 38 years until 1987, marking the longest period of martial law in modern history.

The change of government thereby brought another wave of educational reforms. Building upon the public school system set up under Japanese rule, many additional new policies and structures were introduced into Taiwan public education. School curricula began to adopt the system developed in Mainland China. Instead of teaching students to become loyal Japanese citizens, the new school curricula placed heavy emphasis on Chinese language, culture and history, intending to infuse a new sense of Chinese cultural and national identity. In the national visual art standards, the teaching of Chinese painting and other traditional Chinese art forms were listed as major components in art education. Despite the fact that many Taiwanese people's native languages are Holo (Taiwanese), Hakka and aboriginal languages. For many years, only Standard Mandarin (Chinese) was taught in schools; students were forbidden and even punished for speaking their native languages in schools.

Particularly during the period of Martial Law (1949-1987), economic growth and a solid Chinese national identity were the top priorities of the KMT. Art and crafts courses, although still officially part of the school curriculum, were sometimes "borrowed" to teach other "core subjects". In addition to promoting Chinese culture heritage, art education was also considered as one of the ways to prepare students for their careers, and to instill a diligent work ethic. With the support of the government, mainstream Mainland Chinese values and practices came to dominate cultural life in Taiwan. However, increasing international trades and communication brought in other outside influences. The influences of the West were evident in many disciplines.

For example, art debates in Taiwan in the 1950s and 1960s focused on whether and how artists should incorporate traditional Chinese painting with new Western styles of artmaking. The profession of art education as a distinct discipline in the 1960s was just beginning to develop, and did not seem to be concerned with the possible conflicts between "East and West." For Taiwanese art educators and researchers who worked hard to establish their own journals and deliberated about the best ways of teaching art, particular theories of art education that were developed and promoted in other countries seemed to be good ways of stimulating new ways of thinking about art education in Taiwan.

Starting from the 1960s, Herbert Read and Victor Lowenfeld's ideas were translated into Mandarin. Children's drawing contests and exhibitions were held around the country. The importance of self-expression and education through the arts were advocated particularly by art educators.[7] This new approach echoed, to a certain degree, the "child-centered approach" developed in other countries. Although these drawing contests did successfully gain media attention and support among teachers, and help to promote the idea of not to judge students' works by adults standards, the concept of competition somewhat ironically contradicted the original ideas of child-centered approach. Regardless the interpretation (or possible misinterpretation) of Western ideology, in the second half of the 20th century, Taiwanese art field has learned much from Europe and the US, despite worries about "following in the footsteps of others."

In 1971, when Taiwan (ROC) lost its seat in the United Nations to the People's Republic of China (PRC), Taiwan also lost many of its traditional allies.[8] The lack of international recognition as a country as well as many other internal factors led the people of Taiwan to search for their local roots and to add "local" and "traditional Taiwanese" art forms in the schools. Since the 1980s, with the establishment of several large public museums in Taiwan, the development of art has entered a new era. The end of Martial Law opened up new possibilities of artistic creations and freedom of speech. The establishment of cultural centers, debates about the appropriate approach to art making, and development of new media have fostered the development of numerous art disciplines in Taiwan, which combine international influences and trends with special attention to localism. Large-scale and solo exhibitions in addition to international exhibitions have been launched in Taiwan over the past 25 years, elevating the development of art. Art education as a defined profession in Taiwan with an articulated theory, professional practices, goals, standards, and teacher professional preparation similarly has undergone dramatic changes during this time.

Contemporary Art Education (1987-2007)

The lifting of Martial Law in 1987 unleashed a new wave of political, educational, social and cultural reform. Issues related to Taiwan's national identity were openly discussed in public arena in educational venues, public forums, and through mass media. In addition to recognizing the rich cultures of Taiwanese aboriginals, the influences of Japan, China and the influences of other international countries were recognized as significant to Taiwan cultural, artistic, and educational practices. The process of adaptation—sometimes called Taiwanization or localization—signify how Taiwan is slowly developing its own identity.

On the one hand, new courses intended to help students learn more about local histories, folk art traditions and different dialects were added to the Grade 1-12 curriculums.[9] On the other hand, new ideas that were already popular in other countries such as postmodernism, feminism, and postcolonialism began to enter Taiwan's intellectual discussions and influenced many disciplines, including art education.

In art education, Discipline-Based Art Education (DBAE) was introduced to Taiwan in the late 1980s. Elliot Eisner's and other DBAE proponents' ideas were translated and became the focus of several studies. At the same time, other paradigms for art education were considered. Over recent years, Taiwanese art educators, after obtaining advanced degrees from other countries, especially from United States, came back to Taiwan with new ideas about DBAE, community-based art education, multicultural art education, computer-mediated art education, and visual cultural art education. All of these ideas have enriched the repertoire of art education theories under consideration in Taiwan. Large scale art education research projects were conducted and new curricular reforms were underway. Graduate degree programs and new professional art education journals have now been established in Taiwan.

Facing a new social-cultural climate, the knowledge-based economy, political uncertainty, and international competition, the Taiwanese government, under the push of several social groups, has taken new initiatives to address the effectiveness and relevance of the education system. Calls for school reform from parents and other social groups have inspired several of these new curriculum changes.

One of the major changes is the Grade 1-9 curriculum reform starting from 1997,[10] which re-organized previously separated subject and re-defined them as seven learning areas.[11] One of the seven learning areas is the Arts and Humanities curriculum, which comprises the visual art, music, and performing arts. It means that previously separated visual art and music courses need to be integrated while adding performing art to the curriculum. The change toward an integrated curricular approach in Taiwan brought serious concern and unprecedented debates among art educators (Wilson & Kao, 2003). As some scholars proposed and examined different ways of curriculum integration, many scholars and teachers held reservations toward the integrated approach between different subjects. Even appropriateness of the wording "Arts and Humanities" was questioned.

Nerveless, the push for school reform continues to be strong. 2008's "Education in Taiwan" report (http://english.moe.gov.tw/public/Attachment/8111017533671.pdf) states that:

> Taiwan's educational system has grown and expanded; now steps need to be taken to upgrade the quality of education. Globalisation has greatly influenced education, the economy and politics. Like other nations of the world, Taiwan is working zealously to improve national competitiveness. (Ministry of Education, 2008)

An overall education goal was summed up in "Creative Taiwan, Eye on the World". The Ministry of Education uses the following three core approaches to support the implementation of this motto: "adaptability in nature and ability, embracing globalisation and supporting the disadvantaged" (Ministry of Education, 2008, p. 10).

Conclusion

Over the past three decades we have witnessed, on the one hand, the success of Taiwan in creating an economic miracle and turning from a police state into a democracy, and, on the other hand, struggles for interethnic harmony, 'national' identity, and political setbacks in the international community (Law, 2003). "Few nations face a future more fraught with uncertainty than Taiwan. Even whether Taiwan is a nation is questioned"[12] (Copper, 2003, p. 227), what complicates the issue of Taiwan national identity and autonomy is that our future is not just in the hands of the Taiwanese people. The positions of the international community, particularly America and China, on the "Taiwan issue" will influence the future of the Taiwanese people. In the meantime, Taiwan's destiny will continue to be affected by its changing social, economic, and political conditions (Copper, 2003).

From apprenticeship to Western style art training methods, to post modern concerns for diversity and plurality, and finally to interests ranging from global culture to preserving local identities and practices, art education in Taiwan has changed and absorbed both Eastern and Western artistic and educational theories and practice. As Robertson (1995, p. 27) notes, globalization has seen cultural tendencies for both homogenization and heterogenization in "mutually implicative" tension. Taiwan's art education, although it has absorbed experiences and theories from other countries, raises questions about cultural colonialization and issues of autonomy and subjectivity, and

exemplifies how one country both navigates and contributes to global, regional, and local conditions.

Looking back on the history of art education in Taiwan, it is clear that the discipline of art education is shaped not only by what happens inside the profession of art education itself, nationally and internationally, but also by the political and economic contexts of different time periods. While some may see globalization as a recent phenomenon, in Taiwan, globalization started at least as early as the 17th century. Colonization has shaped Taiwan's economic, political and cultural life, and by extension, its art education theories and professional practices. If we define globalization broadly and not look at it simply as a recent phenomenon, we can also see how the development of the profession of art education in Taiwan also engages processes of change, adaptation, and resistance.

The Taiwan example suggests that that the concept of art education is semi-open and evolving. Education is not neutral or value-free. Art education is influenced not only by what happens inside the field but also by general educational policies which reflect national identities, political and economic situations. Ideas developed in a particular context were translated, re-interpreted, and juxtaposed with existing ideas. National boundaries today are no longer distinct, and cross-disciplinary collaboration is now accepted practice in education. As intellectual, cultural, artistic, and educational communities work side by side, the interaction and fusion of ideas is even apparent than ever. Although issues related to one's national and cultural identities are still important issues to ponder, it seems counter-intuitive to claim one's uniqueness within a context of cross-pollination, fusion, movements, and mergings. Despite our many uncertainties about the future, we believe that Taiwan's example will shed some light on the multiple-faceted nature of globalization, art and education. As our own "take" on globalization is local and localized, we maintain that "only through situated, local, and self-critical analyses can we begin to see the two-way, mutually constitutive dynamics of local-global flows of knowledge, power, and capital, or systematic as well as unsystematic and uneven 'effects,' and of local histories that always embed 'the new' in existing and generative material-economic and cultural conditions" (Luke & Luke, 2003, p. 276).

Acknowledgments
The authors wish to thank Drs. Michael Parsons and Elizabeth M. Delacruz for their valuable inputs during the process of writing this article.

REFERENCES

Apple, M. (2000). Between Neoliberalism and Neoconservatism: Education and conservatism in a global context. In N. C. Burbules, and C. A. Torres (Eds.), *Globalization and education: Critical perspective* (pp. 57-78). New York: Routledge.

Burbules, N. C., & Torres, C.A. (2000). Globalization and education: An introduction. In N. C. Burbules and C. A. Torres (Eds.), *Globalization and education: Critical perspective* (pp. 1-26). New York: Routledge.

Copper, J. F. (2003). *Taiwan: Nation-State or province?* Boulder, Colorado: Westview Press.

Desai, D., & Chalmers, G. (2007). Notes for a dialogue on art education in critical times. *Art Education, 60*(5), 6-12.

Frazier, D. (2005). Taiwan's post-post-coloniality: A talk with M.I.T. Professor Emma Jinhua Teng about new views on Chinese imperialism, Taiwan's colonial past, and how primary sources are now all online. Retrieved April 11, 2008, from http://web.mit.edu/fll/www/people/images/Teng%20Interview.pdf

Government Information Office, Republic of China (2008). *About Taiwan: People and languages.* Retrieved September 11, 2008, from http://www.gio.gov.tw/lp.asp?ctNode=4101&CtUnit=900&BaseDSD=7&mp=807

Huang, F. (2007). The periods of early inhabitants—The orphan of East Asian and a self-sufficient society, *A brief history of Taiwan: A sparrow transformed into a phoenix.* Retrieved May 1, 2008, from *http://www.gio.gov.tw/taiwan-website/5-gp/history/tw02.html*

Law, W. (2003). Globalization, localization and education reform in a new democracy: Taiwan's experience. In K. Mok and A. Welch (Eds.), *Globalization and educational restructuring in the Asia Pacific region* (pp. 79-127). New York: Palgrave Macmillan.

Lee, W. K. (2006). Preface. In C. Tsai (Ed.), *Macro vision, micro analysis, multiple reflections: Contemporary art in Taiwan in the post-martial law era.* Taichung: National Taiwan Museum of Fine Arts.

Luke, C., & Luke, A. A. (2003). *A situated perspective on cultural globalization.* In N. C. Burbules and C. A. Torres (Eds.), *Globalization and education: Critical perspective* (pp. 275-297). New York & London: Routledge.

Ministry of Education. (2008). Educational Reform; Creative Taiwan, Eye on the World. *Education in Taiwan 2008* (pp. 10-12). Taipei: Ministry of Education. Retrieved November 10, 2008, from http://english.moe.gov.tw/public/Attachment/8111017533671.pdf

Robertson, R. (1995). Glocalization: Time-Space and homogeneity-heterogeneity. In M. Featherstone, S. Lash, and R. Robertson (Eds.), *Global modernities* (pp 25-44). London: Sage.

Smith, D. C. (1981). *An island of learning; Academeocracy in Taiwan.* Taipei: Pacific Cultural Foundation.

Wang, L. Y. (2008). An overview of art education development in Taiwanese schools. In M. C. Cheng (Ed.), *Taiwan arts education history* (pp.106-163). Taipei: Wunan.

Wilson, B., & Kao, C. (2003). An integrated curriculum development in Taiwan for Arts and Humanities: Problems and Prospects. *Research in Arts Education, 6,* 1-19.

ENDNOTES

1. The term "glocalization" originated in the 1980s and was popularized by the sociologist Roland Robertson. Glocalization, a portmanteau of globalization and localization, is used in this article to emphasize the point that globalization and localization are actually complementary processes. The local is integrally tied to the global, and global to the local. Taiwan's art education, for example, has adopted the experiences and theories of other countries and assumed unique qualities based on its own politics, economics, society, and culture.

2. Taiwan, also known as Formosa or Republic of China, comprises Taiwan Island and other small islands including Penghu, Kinmen and Matsu.

3. Chen Shui-bian, who was elected in 2000, was the first non-KMT president of Taiwan. The 2008 election of President Ma Ying-jeou then marked the second peaceful transfer of power back to the KMT.

4. For a more detailed account, please see Wang, L.Y. (2008). An overview of art education in Taiwanese schools. In M.C. Cheng (Ed.), *Taiwan Arts Education history* (pp.106-163). Taipei: Wunan.

5. Glaring inequities of treatment between Taiwanese versus Japanese students persisted despite slogans such as "everyone treated equally," "ethnic coalescence" advocated by colonial authorities.

6. The Cairo Declaration was a result from Cairo conference at Cairo, Egypt, on November 27, 1943. President Franklin Roosevelt of the United States, Prime Minister Winston Churchill of the United Kingdom, and the Chiang Kai-shek of the Republic of China were present. Some argue that the document is simply a statement of intent and non-binding press release, which occurred without any presence or agreement of representatives of the Taiwanese people. The counterargument is that while the Cairo Declaration itself was a non-binding declaration, it was given legal effect (http://en.wikipedia.org/wiki/Cairo_Declaration).

7. Many of them taught in elementary schools. In addition to being school teacher, they also started their own studios to teach young children drawing outside of schools.

8. The number of Taiwan's allies dropped from about 80 in 1971 to 24 in 2007.

9. In addition to the required Mandarin and English courses, native languages such as Holo, Hakka and several aboriginal languages are now offered in the elementary schools. Although standard Mandarin is still the dominate language, there is an attempt not to loose the languages and artistic practices of the original inhabitants of Taiwan as a means of preserving Taiwan's cultural diversity and history.

10. Initial planning of Grade 1-9 Curriculum started in 1997. Experimentation in selected schools began in 1999. The Grade 1-9 Curriculum was officially announced in 2002.

11. Grade 1-9 curriculum includes the following seven areas: Language Arts, Health and Physical Education, Social Studies, Arts and Humanities, Science and Technology, Mathematics, and Integrative Activities.

12. The People's Republic of China claims that Taiwan is a province of China. Although there is an increasing percentage of people argue for Taiwan autonomy and even independence, there are also some in Taiwan see Taiwan's future as part of China or Chinese federation.

Globalization and Cultural Diversity: Shifts in the Cultural Terrain in Korea[1]

Hyungsook Kim

In the 20th century, globalization was carried along global channels of cultural flow, occurring with the rise of the West and impacting the rest of the world. Globalization extends the range of imagery, information, and tourism, which has effectively eaten away national boundaries. The phenomenon of globalization has created a shift in the cultural terrain of nations throughout the world. Giddens asserts that globalization is one of the fundamental consequences of modernity. "Globalization—which is a process of uneven development that fragments as it coordinates—introduces new forms of world interdependence, in which ... there are no others" (Giddens, 1990, pp. 174-175). Roberts, on the other hand, sees globalization as "a relatively independent source of ideas about the conception of postmodernity," in relation to what he terms "the modernity-globalization-postmodernity issue" (Robertson, 1992, p. 11). This reflexive aspect of the relationship between the individual and the global must be of crucial interest in the contemporary debate on culture and art education. Following Robertson's conceptualizations, I would argue here what we may miss in grandiose claims about the homogenizing tendencies of globalization is that when people draw global influences into their lives, there will always be an interplay between global and local influences. Interpenetration between global cultural flows and local cultural patterns are central to the continuing process of globalization.

With these conceptualizations in mind, this chapter draws attention to increasing cultural diversity in Korea and related social conditions created with the impact of globalization in Korea over the past 50 years. The central purpose of this essay is to examine how globalization has impacted both cultural policies and higher education discourse in contemporary Korea–how it has changed our notions of our own cultural diversity, higher education goals, and art and cultural policies and practices in Korea. I begin with a general discussion of globalization discourse.

Thoughts about Globalization

The expression *globalization* achieved terminological stardom in the 1990s and was soon embraced by the general public and integrated into numerous languages. Above all, globalization means that social, political, and economic activities cross and blur the borders of nations. Events, decisions, and activities in one region of the world have tremendous influence on individuals or communities in other regions of the world. In this sense, globalization expresses the trans-regional interconnection and expansion of social activity and power (Spybey, 1996). Ulrich Beck (1992, 1994) and Anthony Giddens (1990, 1991) have referred to globalization as *reflexive modernist*, which may be defined as a universalized form of life that touches on everyone and causes individuals to orient their actions towards it. In late modernity, intensified globalization provides individuals with increased information with which to engage in social interactions. People are faced with an extended range of imagery and information involving models of citizenship, forms of production, styles of consumption, modes of communication, principles of world order and, in addition, different ways of reacting to all of these. There is enhanced capacity for reflection as a result of the exposure to globalized social processes (Spybey, 1996). A main consequence is that under such conditions individuals cannot engage in any social interaction without consciously or subconsciously relating it to social interactions on a global scale.

The media of mass communication and travel bring the world to the individual and the individual to the world on a continuous basis, so that the motivation, rationalization and reflexive monitoring of social interaction routinely include global knowledge, awareness and experience. Air travel and electronic communication create *relative location*. Lash and Urry (1994) draw our attention to a form of cultural interpretation in which the universalization of air travel and electronic communication relegates other means of travel and communication to the level of the particular and the localized (Spybey, 1996). The flow of information on a global scale has effectively eaten away at national boundaries. The products of the electronic media of communication have particularly strong effects. Mediascapes are constructs with which people identify alternative to the nation-state or any other focus. Imagery projected through television, the cinema, or popular music becomes available as a body of knowledge, a style, which people identify with. This flow of information on a global scale is weakening national boundaries. Spybey asserts that globalization should be seen as a trend from the particular to the universal or the local to the global. The latter consists of institutionalized influences extended through time and space as globalized culture. The former consists of institutionalized aspects extended over a time and space that is much more bounded, as in a localized culture (Spybey, 1996).

> Global programmes ... are read differently in different countries and places ... Indeed in some respects there is an increasing contradiction between centralized production (at least in some respects) and more decentralized and fragmented reception. (Lash & Urry, 1994, p. 308)

Globalization is an influence, a trend, a cultural flow, but it can never be an absolute universal since, in order to be reproduced, it must impact on particularistic cultural influences. This reflexivity constitutes a continuing part of the globalization process (Spybey, 1996).

Additionally, the bounds of leisure travel of all kinds have been expanded far beyond the nation-state to the continental and the global (MacCannell, 1976, 1992). People also travel for work. Migrant labor has contributed significantly to large-scale transfers of people across borders. In the case of Korea, significantly, the number of migrant laborers has been increasing since the 1990s, as will be discussed later in this chapter.

Some scholars have argued that globalization was created along with the rise of the West and its impact upon the rest of the world during the 20th century. The outcome has been a world increasingly globalized and, in many people's eyes, *Americanized*. However, there is always an interplay between global and local influences. Roland Robertson (1992) refers to this as *interpenetration* between global cultural flows and local cultural patterns. In such a view, globalization is a characteristic of post modernity that overcomes the homogeneity stressed in modernist discourse. It rediscovers non-Western cultural traditions and specificity, and the voices of marginalized groups such as women, the handicapped, and others,

all of some scholars believe have been neglected in the process of modernity.

Like globalization, higher education is a highly controversial terrain. It is easy to assume that arrangements in higher education globally are pretty much the same as in the United States. But differences in the histories and political economies of the nations of the world have resulted in significant differences in higher education. This is true of questions of access, organization, programs and institutional variety, and of needs and goals of people living in different parts of the world. In the next session, I discuss the particular cultural situation of Korea, including changes impacting Korean national identity, aspirations, and cultural policies.

Addressing Changing Patterns of Cultural Diversity in Korea

In the West, cultural differences have been discussed in educational discourse for the past 40 years in relation to gender, nationality, race, culture, and social class. This discourse was raised in the context of the particular history of the United States and the idea of a melting pot influenced American public school policy for minorities such as blacks, women, the handicapped, and homosexuals. It could be argued that these aspirations were impacted by the 1960s U.S. Civil Rights Movement, which brought national attention to issues of educational and societal equity for America's diverse citizenry. Notably, more recent multicultural educational scholars such as James Banks (1997) and his many followers have been prominent in asserting that the diversity of the nation should be considered in the law, curriculum, and environment of U.S. education. In their view, students should have equal opportunities in education regardless of gender, social class, race, culture, nationality, disability, religion, or sexual orientation; and the educational environment should be adjusted for every student to reach educational equity. In the US, political and cultural democracy are now demanded within the context of this culturally diverse society, and excellence and equity are seen as key goals of U.S. higher education.

Since the myth of a unified nationality and tradition has been stronger in Korea than in the US, the discourse of cultural diversity is only now becoming a current issue here, as Korean society becomes more globalized. Historically, Korean educational scholars and policy makers seem not to have expressed much interest in issues relating to cultural diversity. Rather, since the provinces of Korea have been culturally homogenous for a long time, Korea has constructed its own national identity and tradition. In recent years, however, the country has encountered a more diverse cultural environment–through networking with other nations, the influx of foreign labor, international marriages, and so on. The development of transportation, human exchange, the Korean War of 1950-1953, and globalized electronic international communications have now created an atmosphere of internationalism in Korea. Yet, as mentioned above, in Korea, in contrast to the United States, the discourse of globalization and cultural differences has begun only recently. Influences responsible for this shift include the impact of recent trade negotiations,[2] migrant labor flows into Korea, international marriages, low birth rates, and other impacts, some of which are briefly explained here.

Currently, with the influx of foreign migrant labor and international marriages to Korea, Korean cultural and educational policies are encountering change. In the last decade, Korea has also experienced social changes resulting from low birth rate and an aging society. The population of Korea today is rapidly aging, as confirmed by several indexes, but the greatest contributing factor is the low childbirth, which fell rapidly in the late 1980s, arriving at its lowest point in 2004.

As indicated in Table 1, the population of the younger generation has decreased as the age of the older generation has increased, with an overall reduction of the total population. In 1970, the younger population in Korea was 13,710,000, 42.5% of the total population. This decreased to 9,240,000 in 2005, and is predicted to arrive at 380,000 in 2050, which will be 9.0% of the total population (Kim, 2006). In contrast, the population of elders was 990,000 in 1970, 3.1% of the total population, and 4,380,000 in 2005, 9.1% of the total population. It is expected to be 15,790,000, 37.3% of the total population, in 2050. It is clear that Korea has already become an aging society. These trends will reduce the working population to less than 50% of the total by the year 2016.

Relatedly, another factor contributing to the shift in the population demographics in Korea is migrant foreign labor. People travel to work in Korea; and this much needed migrant labor force, guest workers, constitutes a large-scale shift in Korean society. In the early 1990s, the number of foreign workers in Korea was just 50,000; it rose to 360,000 by 2005. The number of foreign workers is going up, while the number of native Koreans joining the workforce is dropping. Today, foreign labor is 2.2% of the working population. These foreign workers have frequent contact with Korean natives. With the growth of foreign labor, international marriages are also increasing in Korea. In our society, there were 35,000 international marriages in recent years, which were 11.4% of total marriages. In rural areas there were 27.4%, as shown in Table 2 (Kim, 2006).

Low childbirth, decrease of total population, growth of foreign labor, and international marriages all mean that Korean society is no longer one homogenous nation and no longer free from foreign cultures.[3]

In addition to the direct contact with foreigners, Koreans indirectly encounter numerous other diverse cultural experiences and information, through their travels and studies abroad. In all these ways, Korean society has already entered a global society, and the trend will intensify. This suggests important issues regarding social, political, and cultural policies. Additionally, the shifts of regional communities bring about issues regarding local as well as global identities.

These multiple phenomena have resulted in a new Korea, one that is no longer a homogenous nation. It has become evident that we now need revised educational policies that engage the increasing diversity of contemporary Korean society. Significantly, in Korea, current national policies regarding cultural diversity address differences between social classes rather than racial differences, and these policies are focused primarily on native Koreans. Cultural democracy is a key social goal and Koreans today are demanding it more than anything else. I would argue here that if Korea is to achieve its goals of cultural democracy, it must

Table 1

Childbirth

Year	1970	1980	1990	2000	2001	2002	2003	2004
Rate of Childbirth	4.53	2.83	1.59	1.47	1.30	1.17	1.19	1.16

Source: The Sum Total of Korea's National Statistical Office

Table 2

International Marriages

Year	Total Number of Marriages	Total Number of International Marriages	%
1990	399,312	4,710	1.2
2000	334,030	12,319	3.7
2004	310,944	35,447	11.4

Source: The Sum Total of Korea National Statistical Office, 2005.

engage its more complicated notions of its growing diversity, more adequately and with greater regard for individual, racial, and cultural differences. In such a framework, cultural and educational policies in Korea should include a commitment to educating previously overlooked and marginalized classes, the handicapped, and others, as well as native Koreans. If Korea's educational policy concentrates on education opportunities for some, while excluding many other groups, Korea will have ignored societal needs and failed to meet the needs of its increasingly diverse people.

Changing Cultural Values in Art and Education in Korea

Culture has its own value and specificity which forms within particular social and political contexts. Art has the same character, in that what are said to be outstanding artworks in a particular culture actually conveys local values and perspective in specific regions and nations. Art, in the end, has its own specificity and has no universal hierarchical organization or transcendent criteria for evaluation. This is a truism of the discourse of postmodernism, which coincides with the discourse of cultural diversity as well.

The notion of cultural diversity in U.S. art education discourse promotes the education of all students to become analytical and critical thinkers, capable of examining their life circumstances and social stratification (Efland, Freedman, & Stuhr, 1996). In other words, the discourse of cultural differences in the US can be understood as a cultural democracy approach. It promotes cultural pluralism and social equity (Efland, et al, 1996). However, understandings about cultural diversity in Korea are different from that occurring in the West.

In Korea the notion of cultural diversity has originated in response to the current needs of a contemporary global society, while in the US it developed as a basic human rights issue. At the practical level, the ideals of cultural diversity are applied to diverse races, nations, social classes, genders, and religions in the US, whereas in Korea it partly applies to the development of educational policy that recognizes that other cultures are no longer foreign but now part of Korean culture.

Particularly important in this discussion is the fact that many of the changes occurring in Korea and mentioned thus far have impacted Korean national identity, discourse about cultural practices, and policies regarding the arts. For example, as Koreans gradually came out of the shock of the Korean War, artists, art critics, and educators realized that Korea modern art lagged far behind the world's art scene.[4]

Their biggest concern about the country's art came to be known as *internationalism*. When Korea came to positively meet the West and the structure of culture and art education began to change, art, culture, and education in Korea each needed to be interpreted within the international context.

In the early 1990s, with increased acceptance of Western art and culture in Korea, methods of multicultural art education were also proposed in Korea's schools in an effort to search for Korea's own identity in art (Park, 1993). Eundeok Park (1995) also asserted that multicultural art education should be applied to our public school system in order to help learners better understanding their own culture. Meanwhile, a policy engaging cultural diversity was also addressed in Korea by the Ministry of Justice (MJ), the Ministry of Culture and Tourism (MCT), and the Ministry of Gender Equity and Family (MGEF). In particular, the Ministry of Culture and Tourism attempted to establish new policies for foreign labor and international marriages. In 2004 the Ministry of Culture and Tourism set up a long-term plan for culture and arts education.[5] Their concern for the quality of life had increased, and culture and art education were now considered significant means for improving the quality of life.

At the same time as these shifts have been taking place, numerous social problems and conflicts have also emerged in Korea as a result of rapid economic growth and globalization. Under these circumstances, attempts to engage various problems were strengthened by promoting the development of self-reflection and creativity in Korean citizens. Culture and arts education policies introduced by the Ministry of Culture and Tourism emerged amongst several other efforts to address problematic social conditions and to develop Korean society (Kim & Kim, 2004).[6] For example, in 2005 the Ministry of Culture and Tourism opened a festival for foreign labor, where participants could enjoy leisure activities. Cultural guidebooks were translated and published in ten languages, supporting the adaptation of foreign labor in Korea. Similarly recognizing the importance of changes in Korean society resulting from migrant laborers and international marriages, the Ministry of Gender Equity and Family also recently addressed the needs of families of international marriages. For example, in 2005, MGEF developed the program of support for international marriage, and the family program for international marriage (Kim, 2006). Significantly, in 2004, in order to establish Korean administrative systems and national culture & arts education policies, new laws that supported culture and arts education were enacted. The Culture & Arts Education Support Law supported culture and arts education in Korean schools and communities.[7] This law signaled increased understandings amongst policy makers of the role of the arts in fostering Korean identities and in promoting Korean cultural practices.

Although changes in official Korean cultural policy mentioned so far indicate movement toward engaging notions of internationalism and cultural diversity, I would argue here that the cultural policies of the MGEF, MCT, and MJ need to be further developed within the long-term context of Korean cultural diversity. First, I posit that the matter of diversity and unity should be considered simultaneously and not as separate issues to be addressed at the policy development level of Korean governance. The discourse of cultural diversity is not only meant to value diversity in society but is also related to how to unify Korean society. Second, any contemporary Korean policy for cultural diversity should be expanded to include the many other marginalized classes living in Korea, and not only developed for migrant labors or the family of international marriage. Current cultural policies in South Korea are limited to the families of international marriages; and such a cultural policy does not adequately engage the needs of our culturally diverse society. Finally, Korean policy for cultural diversity should focus not only on foreigners but also on Korean citizens currently occupying varying domestic sectors of Korean society.

Cultural Diversity and Higher Education in Korea

Higher education is central to any society's advancement in a globalized world. The ideology of multiculturalism and social justice in culturally diverse societies promotes access to higher education regardless of gender, socioeconomic class, or cultural and racial character. Since social and economic class also affects academic achievement, it is also argued that higher education should provide the same learning opportunities and foster the same successful learning outcomes for individuals, regardless their of economic, gender, or racial differences.

Building from this discourse of excellence and equity in higher education, Korean universities now need to consider how to understand, serve, and bring into full participation people from currently marginalized sectors of Korean society, and there is some encouraging evidence that this strategy is already underway. Currently, universities in Korea have a program for university students to teach youngsters from marginalized groups. They visit socially marginalized areas and teach language, mathematics, and so on. These activities occasionally are related to the cultural art education conducted by the government. Students earned college credits as their general education at a university, not credits for their major. As the future elite, students attending universities will be responsible for the future society. They need to consider how to serve people of marginalized areas.

University museums in particular play an important role in fostering community service, and Korean university students can also earn course credits in museum internship programs. Partnerships between universities and museums also occur through classes of exhibition planning and art administration (Solinger, 1990).[8] University museums can be considered the university's social institution in the community, and people living around a university can learn and experience the culture and visual arts through the museum's programs and exhibitions.

Additionally, there are some scholars in Korea who now argue that more culturally sensitive methods of teaching and learning should be practiced in Korean higher education. For example, some believe that the curriculum in higher education should include consideration of feminist perspectives and gender differences. In Korea gender difference is a serious issue in higher education. Most of the professors in Korean universities are male, and the academic environment is both directly and indirectly a political arena. In other words, teaching is a process of delivering a particular value, idea, premise, and knowledge. Simultaneously, it eliminates alternative values, ideas, premises, and knowledge (such as gendered studies or feminist perspectives) when those who control and disseminate knowledge are solely male.

As argued in this chapter, Korean policies for cultural diversity need to focus on exchange and communication between different cultures, so that there can be greater mutual social understandings in Korea. But one cannot balance diversity and heterogeneity by valuing diversity alone. This is where higher education is also needed. At the same time, whilst arguing for attention to diversity and contemporary perspectives in higher education in Korea, I would also argue here that in the higher education curriculum, Korean traditional culture also needs to be studied for carefully and fully in order to gain a clearer sense of Koreans' unique perspectives on the world. Since Korean culture and art have been so greatly influenced by Westernized culture in contemporary global society, some Korean scholars now believe that Korean higher education should have an emphasis on local culture in promoting traditional Korean culture and art.[9] Classes such as

Asian art history, Korean art history, calligraphy, seal carving, traditional painting, and oriental ink painting are now offered to university students so that they may build on Korean's traditional art techniques and values, while they also construct their own orientations toward the world. Criticizing the unconditionally accepted Westernized culture, critics argue that Korean learners need to construct their own ideas based on an understanding of their local culture. From there, Korean learners can then expand their perspectives to include other cultures.

Finally, as a visible feature of globalization, new Internet technologies have also created a revolution in higher education worldwide. Korean university educators and policy makers need to take better advantage of the wide variety of distance learning delivery methods currently available. These methods range from traditional correspondence courses to the use of TV and new online technologies. Korean universities have various e-learning systems but such systems currently remain marginal and underutilized. Although the pedagogical quality of e-learning remains contested amongst university scholars and educators; I would argue here that e-learning formats may be at least as good and possibly better than some face-to-face instruction—especially given the often large numbers of students in large lecture sections, and especially in high-demand vocationally oriented areas.

Globalization and a New Vision of Higher Education in Korea: Some Final Thoughts

Globalization is not a monolithic and static process but a dynamic one. It is comprised of highly differentiated phenomena, including various competing and complementary political, economic, educational, and cultural interactions and activities. With these realizations in mind, I have observed and briefly described here how both public policy and higher education in Korea are prime movers in developing both an individual's and a nation's character and destiny. In closing this chapter, I add some final thoughts about Korean higher education in particular, and in relation to impacts of globalization, cultural diversity, and Korea's national identity.

Our vision and strategies in higher education should now be focused on the creative and productive performance of knowledge. In this context, Korea is attempting to reform education and achieve both excellence and equity in education, recognizing however that current reforms and their resulting societal changes seem inadequate. It is not easy to reform the university system in Korea, due to the diverse and complicated administration and decision making procedures. At the same time encouraging changes are emerging, and flexible curricula and practices towards cultural diversity and community-based art education have been developed in the field of cultural art education in Korea. This was made possible with government support and concern for the role of cultural- and arts education. Education in arts and culture does not only promote people's self-expressive skills and creative activities, but also encourages their attitudes toward becoming responsible citizens by developing their self-directed activities. Therefore, cultural- and arts education is considered by Korean governmental officials and policy makers to enhance social conditions for a healthier and safer Korean society. The discourse of cultural differences in the context of globalization is also intended to provide a more equitable distribution of power, to reduce discrimination and prejudice, and provide social justice and equitable opportunities for all groups. Within this discourse, Korean universities must now further articulate those methods and models which can promote equity and pluralism in their practice and processes.

REFERENCES

Banks, J., & Banks, C. (1997). *Multicultural education: Issues and perspectives*. Boston, MA: Allyn & Bacon.

Beck, U. (1992). *Modern society as a risk society*. Berlin: W. de Gruyter (1994). *Reflexive modernization: Politics, tradition and aesthetics in the modern social order*. Stanford, Calif.: Stanford University Press.

Efland, A., Freedman, K., & Stuhr, P. (1996). *Postmodern art education: An approach to curriculum*. Reston, VA: National Art Education Association.

Held, D., & McGrew, A. (2002). *Globalization/anti-globalization*. Cambridge: Polity Press.

Giddens, A. (1990). *The consequences of modernity*. Stanford, Calif.: Stanford University Press.

Giddens, A. (1991). *Modernity and self-identity: Self and society in the late modern age*. Cambridge, U.K.: Polity Press in Association with Basil Blackwell.

Kim, H. S., & Koh, H. (2006). A Study on Curriculum Development of Department of Painting in College of Fine Arts in Korea. *Art Education Research Review, 2(1),* 343-364.

Kim, S. H. (2006). Multicultural Society and Cultural Policy. *Proceedings of the Korean Association for Public Administration*.

Kim, S. H., & Kim, H. S. (2004). *Long-term plan for culture & arts education*. Seoul: Korea Culture & Tourism Policy Institute.

Kim, Y. N. (2005). *20th century Korean art*. United Kingdom: Laurence King Publishing.

Lash, D., & Urry, J. (1994). *Ecomomies of signs and space*. London: Sage.

MacCannell, D. (1996). *The tourist: A new theory of the leisure class*. London: Macmillan.

McFee, J. (1998). *Cultural diversity and the structure and practice of art education*. Reston: National Art Education Association.

Osterhammel, J., & Niels P. P. (2003). *Globalization: A short history*. Princeton and Oxford: Princeton University Press.

Park, E. D. (1995). Multicultural art education in the United States. *Art Education Research Review, 5,* 5-14.

Park, J. A. (1993). Socio-ethnographic methods for multicultural art education. *Proceedings of Art Education Research Review, 3,* 3-29.

Robertson, R. (1992). *Globalization: Social theory and global culture*. London: Sage.

Schaeffer, R. K. (2005). *Understanding globalization: The social consequences of political, economic, and environmental change*. Littlefield.

Solinger, J. W. (1990). *Museums and universities: New paths for continuing education*. New York: National University Continuing Education Association.

Spybey, T. (1996). *Globalization and world society*. Cambridge: Polity Press.

Yang, H. M. (2004). *The administrative and legal system for culture & arts education policy*. Korea Culture & Tourism Institute.

ENDNOTES

1 Throughout this chapter, I refer to the name of my country as "Korea" rather than differentiating it as "South Korea." In some instances my summations include both North and South Korea. Since it is difficult to obtain reliable information about educational and social policies in the north, and current ideological differences between the south and north are substantial, in many other instances throughout this chapter my observations and claims refer to events and aspirations that are only taking place in Korea in the south. For example, the observations that I make in this chapter about increased international marriages, labor force migrations into Korea, and Korea's increased academic discourse and interests in embracing cultural diversity in its educational policies are currently taking place in the South Korea.

2 For example, in the arena of international trade negotiations, the reduction of the Screen Quota system in the process of trade negotiation between Korea and the United States was a particularly influential occasion that brought about this new discourse in Korea. The US demanded the reduction of the Screen Quota system, while the world of film in Korea wanted to maintain the Screen Quota system (Kim, 2006).

3 In the case of international marriage, generally, the wife is the foreigner in Korea. The nationality of the wife or husband in an international marriage was as follows in 2008: Japan (6,261); China (3,172); Philippines (1,938); Vietnam (574). Foreign workers moved into Korea with the Korean dream. According to the statistics of the Ministry of Education, Science and Technology in 2007, the nationality of foreign workers were as follows: Mongol (321); Japan (258); China (181); Philippines (69) (The Sum Total of Korea National Statistical Office, 2008).

4 For example, art critic Lee Kyoung-sung asserted that the issues confronting the Korean art world are first, rationalization, second, modernization, and third, globalization (Kim, 2005, 253).

5 Before setting up the plan for culture and arts education, Korean education system did not recognize the potentialities and nor appropriate them for better educational achievement. Those areas are generally approached from a leisure perspective, or understood in the regard of artistic excellence. As a consequence, culture and arts were often considered as marginalized areas in education.

6 In 2006, Kim and Kim suggested related art and cultural policy recommendations for Korea as follows: first, culture and arts education should promote people's cultural creativity by developing opportunities for cultural experience. Second, culture and arts education should develop people's communicative abilities by encouraging their use of culture and arts for communication. Third, it should extend its scope to cultural diversity in order to broaden people's cultural perspectives. Fourth, it should promote the cultural tradition of Korea and expand its meaning and uses in contemporary Korean society. Finally, culture and arts education should be provided on the basis of learning, not by educating.

7 This *Culture & Arts Education Support Law* consisted of five chapters and 30 Articles. The five chapters provided: (a) general provisions, (b) the mission of the central and the regional governments, (c) support for culture & arts education in the schools, (d) support for culture & arts education in the communities, and (e) training of educators specialized in culture & arts education (Yang, 2004).

8 Salinger (1990) asserts that the integration of community involvement and academic scholarship is no longer a project for the future, but is the pertinent issue confronting both museums and universities today.

9 Higher art education in Korea began with universities were established under the influence of U.S. higher education. Korean universities have developed quantitatively since World War II, and over the decades since there came to be established 138 painting major programs in Korean universities by the year 2006. In particular, during the 1980s and 1990s the painting major was established since the government went through the number of students for admission to the university and tried to establish diverse purposes for universities (Kim, H. S. & Koh, H., 2006).

Effects of Globalization on the Arts Practices of the Bush Negro People of Suriname

Herman Jiesamfoek

Art belongs to the daily life of the Bush Negroes. There is change, as I said before, there are few people remaining there [in the interior]...and one is influenced by Western ideas because nowadays one seldom builds a pina hut [traditional hut with grass roof]. Zinc roofs, everywhere you now see zinc roofs, and that is a big change.

(INFORMANT EL, 2002)

This chapter considers observed changes in the Bush Negro society of Suriname[1] within the context of how globalization currently impacts Bush Negro life and art. Referring to the Surinamese Bush Negro,[2] cultural anthropologist and leading African American Studies scholar, Melville Herskovits, observed that, "Bush-Negro art in all its ramifications is, in the final analysis, Bush-Negro life" (cited in Price & Price, 1999, p. 38). If that is so, what then are the consequences for how the arts of the Bush Negro can continue as their life changes in the 21st century? Following a brief discussion of the history the forced migration of the Bush Negro people of the Republic of Suriname, their subsequent establishment of social and communitarian identity in South America, and their evolving forms of transcultural and hybridized artistic practices, I consider this and related questions about how Bush Negro artistic traditions and cultural expressions are currently understood, valued, and changed by contemporary Bush Negro elders, youth, and outside forces and influences. These outside forces include a trend toward urbanization, media influences, and eco-tourism and do appear to have a negative impact on efforts amongst Suriname Bush Negro people to maintain their cultural identities and traditions. Contemporary strategies adapted by Bush Negro artists, elders, young people and others to reinvigorate the place of the arts in community life conclude this chapter.

Bush Negro Communities in Suriname

The forced migration of African slaves that occurred in Suriname between the 17th and 19th centuries brought to the new world individuals from tribal areas in the current African states of Ghana, Togo,

All Photos: Herman Jiesamfoek

Figure 1

Left: Modern zinc roof building next to traditional village huts.

Figure 2

Right: Zinc roof huts in the interior.

traditions from which their artistic actions evolved. Murphy (1989) posits that in an individuated, socially-driven civilization, kinship remains the principal source of its people's closest ties; but in simpler past and remaining primitive groupings, kinship provides more than individual love and support—in fact, it creates the structure of entire societies (p. 105). Residence among the *Saamaka* and *Ndjuka*, the two largest tribes in Suriname, may be patrilocal or matrilocal, but descent is matrilineal (Dark, 1973). However, the matrilineal line of descent should be considered loosely, according to Saunders-Williams (1996) and Price (1996), because not all Bush Negroes belonging to a specific matrilineal kin-line were actually born in the matrilineal system.

The *Granman* (paramount chief) has traditionally been the formal head of the tribe, with the most extensive and ultimate authority over his own village and the villages in his direct neighborhood. In villages too far removed from the *Granman's* seat, his authority is symbolic. He is assisted and represented by the *Edekabiten* (head captain), who supervises the affairs of a village or groups of villages. Next comes the *Kabiten* (captain), who acts out his authority in the village in the absence of the *Granman* or *Edekabiten*. The *Kabiten* is assisted by the *Basia* (assistant), whose responsibility is to maintain social order.

An important question is to consider how escaped slaves in their newly set-up villages came to cultural homogeneity and cohesion with artistic traditions unique to their society. In the case of the Bush Negro, the Dutch deliberately mixed captured people from different African cultures and languages to discourage communication among them (Weatherford, 1994). The resulting assembly of escaped slaves in the Surinamese rainforest then came from different African cultures and tribes, each with their own artistic and tribal traditions. Price (1996) states that although the Bush Negro tribes of Suriname's interior were formed under similar historical and ecological conditions, they each nevertheless displayed small but significant variations in language, culture, and expressions of art and dance. Some degree of consensus was reached in Suriname, notes Saunders-Williams (1996), that the Bush Negro people, while drawing heavily on their African origins, created a new culture out of recalled elements without becoming "merely a carbon copy of that found in West Africa" (p. 15). Their stylistic qualities came from African traditions and many of their material culture traits were adopted from native Indian and European Celtic traditions. This amalgam of South American, African, and European influences helped the runaway slaves form a unique culture with

Benin, Zaire, Angola, Sierra Leone, Liberia, Senegal, Dahomey, Nigeria, Cameroon, and Congo (Stephen, 1995; van der Hilst, as cited in Sankeralli, 1995) to work in Suriname's newly established plantation economy. Earlier periods of the English colonization of Suriname resulted in small groups of slaves who fled regularly from the plantations to settle in communities in the interior.

When the Dutch assumed colonial power in 1679, it was estimated that a quarter of all Africans in Suriname at that time—approximately 700 to 800 runaway slaves—were living in the jungle (Bakker, Dalhuisen, donk, Hassan Khan, & Steegh, 1998). Around 300 slaves escaped yearly, until by the end of the 18th century, about 7,000 runaway slaves were living freely in the rainforest. Their descendants, the Bush Negroes (*bosneger* or *boslandcreool* in Dutch, *Busi Nëngë* in Sranang, the language of Suriname) were estimated at 27,698 in 1964 when a fairly accurate census count was possible (Price, 1996). Vernooij (1996), citing statistical information from the 1980s, raised the number to 34,649 Bush Negroes in Suriname's interior. Their society is divided into six tribes: the *Saamaka* in the coastal area; the *Ndjuka* and *Paamaka* in the eastern regions; the *Matawai* in the central regions near the *Saamaka* settlements; the *Boni*, in the southeastern region bordering French Guiana; and the very small group of the *Kwinti*, who live in unspecified areas (Price, 1996).

Social Relations Authority Structure and the Arts

The Surinamese kinship and authority structure of the Bush Negro illuminates the social settings and vital arts traditions (Dark, 1973). Bakker (1998) concludes that the infrastructure they built was so strong that it still stands today largely untouched by outside cultures. Price and Price (1999) agree, observing that the Bush Negro arts traditions were virtually unaffected by the rapid diffusion of European art traditions, and instead continued to develop their own forms of artistic expression. However, growing evidence confirms that even the Bush Negro social structures and arts traditions are now being impacted by effects of globalization.

The Arts of the Bush Negro People

The Bush Negro people have traditionally dealt with almost every aspect of their life in diverse, imaginative, and artistic ways. Dark (1973), Hureault (1970), and Price and Price (1999) have all vividly described Bush Negro art and culture with key examples of their artistic variability and how art permeates life and life permeates art. The artistic works of the Bush Negro include objects from their material culture (e.g., spoons, combs, stools, paddles, and plates decorated with elaborate and typically symmetrical designs), as well as secular and non-secular dances, music, plays,

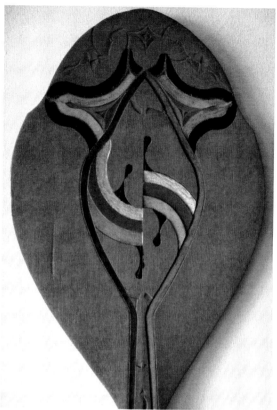

Figures 4, 5, 6

Left: Detail from Paddle.
Bottom Left: Paddles.
Bottom Right: Detail from Paddle.

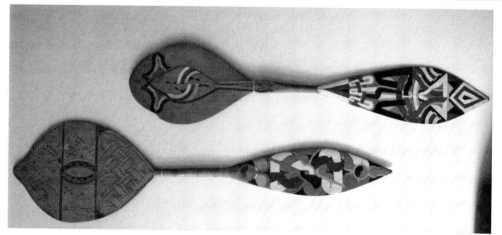

and architecture, although the focus of this paper will be mainly their material culture. Nearly all carved and decorated wooden objects are executed with artistic, aesthetic, and cultural forethought and deliberation. Some of these are gifts made by the husband for his wife as tokens of love given during courtship and from time to time to maintain her affections.

Although most of these carved works also have utilitarian value within the household, some of them are so intricately carved that they lose all utilitarian value and gain significance only in aesthetic and symbolic contexts (Dark, 1973).

It is important for the Bush Negro to achieve pleasant symmetrical harmony in their designs. On visits to the interior, I personally experienced this in something as mundane as baking cassava bread. With her bare fingers working cassava dough substance on a smoking red-hot plate, a Bush Negro woman expertly formed perfect designs in cassava bread. Noticing my fascination, she invited me to bake bread myself. During the baking process, she continuously guided, encouraged, and instructed me to make perfect circles in the dough, to maintain even thickness throughout, and to watch for symmetry in form and design. The instructions were given while my fingers—not used to the heat—were burning on the hot plate. Most outstanding, though, were the meticulous instructions for aesthetic designs in the patterns of cassava bread. The same attention to harmonious design pervaded the daily activities of men and women.

Effects of Globalization on Bush Negro Life
Impacts from Outside

To understand how globalization issues impact the arts traditions of the Bush Negro people, I focused specifically on adaptation, acculturation, change, and integration in my study of the cultural life of the Bush Negro. Doing so allowed me to discover signs of how their arts and cultural practices have adjusted to political and economic impacts on their traditions. Moreover, I had the chance to examine changes resulting from contacts with the Surinamese urban and global culture and to consider whether traditions in the Bush Negro arts were being replaced or modified by other newer traditions. Finally, I was able to consider how these impacts have altered Bush Negro art in ways that integrate their traditions into the arts of the dominant urban culture of the Suriname.

War impact. The devastating impacts of the interior wars in Suriname during the 1980s, triggered by the military overthrow of the democratically-chosen government, drastically accelerated the deterioration of traditional Bush Negro village life and village authority structure in the interior. The villages remain and the authority and hierarchical system exists in theory; however, in practice, these were hardly observable during my recent visits (Jiesamfoek, 2004). In an article in the Surinamese newspaper *De Ware* Tijd,

reporter Carla Tuinford (2002) confirmed my observations of the diminished authority of the *Granman*, *Kabitens*, and *Basias* and their difficulty in maintaining and administering justice and authority, especially among youth.

Eco-tourism. Tourism is currently being developed in Suriname as one of the economy's pillars, in addition to mining and agriculture. Eco-tourism was established by the Surinamese government in 1962. A Suriname Tourist Foundation (*Stichting Toerisme Suriname*) was founded in 1996 to market Suriname as a tourist site.[3] As a result of the tourist trade, the Bush Negro people have changed the artistic designs on the objects that are made and sold to tourists to reflect ordinary perceived exoticism without the symbolic meanings that were traditionally designed on their objects. Thus, Bush Negro artists and villages have become more focused on monetary accumulation—a development welcomed and supported by the central Surinamese government. Increased dependence on monetary exchange has altered the Bush Negro peoples' reciprocal tradition of trading skillfully and aesthetically-designed artistic objects. As well, the shift from a mostly non-monetary-based society with reciprocal traditions to a society reliant on money explains the growing trend toward occupational specialization in particular social trades that is evident today among the Bush Negroes, as Informant EL described:

> Later one started to specialize. For the gardens, for example, now you have specialists. They are being paid because most men remain in the city, they send money to their wives, the wife looks for someone who has specialized in clearing the grounds. And then you have others who now mainly make canoes. She can buy one, she can order one, and she gets it immediately.

Media influence. The new lifestyle in the city that money has made possible, combined with the exposure of Bush Negro youth to global culture via electronic media, continues to influence how Bush Negro people process and transform new impressions. Price (1999) described how in the past, the Bush Negro returned to the city, and processed and incorporated new impressions into surprisingly creative designs.

In a more negative observation, Carpenter (in Price & Price, 1992) claims, "We use media to destroy cultures, but we first use media to create a false record of what we are about to destroy" (p. 38). Media influences on the Bush Negro youth culture that today come from television and video clips show girls in string bikinis, performing vulgar hip movements with voluptuously perverse facial expressions (Informant HB). Bush Negroes, who are masters at imitation (Price & Price, 1999), have copied and incorporated such

Figure 7

Store in the interior.

facial expressions and movements into their dances upon witnessing them in the media and urban centers. This kind of transformation prompted by the media is undesirable, according to current local, urban, and communal morals, as Informant HB noted when discussing a "string" bikini worn by a young girl:

> Thus, such a string has become a beauty ideal for them. And then you have a group of young rappers with a girl, and the girl wears long pants with a string that is pulled up high. And then you have a long row of boys walking behind her pulling on her string. This is not good, this is not good.

Strengths from Within

The Bush Negroes continue to maintain and contribute to cultural cohesion and continuity in the arts by selling their arts and crafts on the streets of the capital city, Paramaribo. Motivations responsible for their drive and desire to perpetuate their arts and to express ideas in personally creative ways are very much embedded in the idea that art is their identity. This concept was presented by nearly all the Bush Negro people I interviewed. Informant JT (2002) said, "We are no artists, art is part of us." This thinking could be the single-most enduring creative factor for the cohesion and continuity of their arts in the face of outside challenges. I also found that this cohesion was supported by their informal indigenous education which assumes that children, who are included in artistic production, performance, and connoisseurship from a very early age, will all grow up to be active artists and assertive critics (Price & Price, 1999). However, the reality of the Bush Negro artists unable to make a living in the city from selling art was the most frequently articulated reason why Bush Negro people felt discouraged to continue making art. Traditionally, art permeated daily life on all levels of their society. Today, art has become more of an appendage to life (Informant JT, 2002). Furthermore, as JT explained, master artists regularly visited the city from their villages in the interior to sell their products in front of local stores. While some of them were highly regarded artists in their culture, they lost interest in making art once the police hindered their selling and chased them from the storefronts. As JT said passionately, "And then you sit along the Saramaka street, you sit in front of the market, and then the police come. 'Clear your stuff away!' Grrrrrr [sound of disgust as JT sweeps his hand over the table] all products are taken away. Precious people, museum pieces, walking museums."

Ancestral Arts Traditions: Cultural Identities in the Urban Community. Other feelings such as a sense of belonging, feeling at home, ease with community expressions, and positive identification with

like-minded people have also contributed to resiliency in cultural habits and upholding interests in the arts in traditional cultures. Brown (1989, as cited in Mintz & Price, 1992) attributed the resiliency of Cuban religious expressions to the powerful U.S. efforts to co-opt, control, and destroy them. Suriname's Bush Negro in the city have collaborated beyond tribal boundaries as a single larger group to, as Informant PA says, face the discrimination they experience in the city: "Yes, all things [art, music, dance] that we do are from the Saamaka tribe. But we are all Bush Negroes. We are all one Bush Negro [group]. And here [in the city] all Bush Negroes formed one group." Thus, the Bush Negro, collectively, have started new cultural institutions to perpetuate their ancestral traditions, ceremonies, and arts and to teach the younger generations. Such creative expressions assume a kind of institutional character that, as Muensterberger (cited in Jopling, 1971) observes, attributes to the deep connection between art and ceremony. I encountered two perspectives on the perpetuation of tribal traditions—an outer perspective from a city informant (HB) and an inner perspective from a village informant (EL).

> The Bush Negro people fight to spread their culture, because they are heavily discriminated. Bush Negroes [in the city] are often seen as criminals...a negative stamp is put on them. What indeed happens is that the young Bush Negroes who come to live in the city...realize how important it is to maintain their identity...they start to increasingly see the worth of their own culture, and organize themselves in clubs. They discover that it is the American, the European who come to plunder *their* [HB's emphasis] forest to claim patents. Thus the Bush Negro is now more conscious, and they make their people now conscious too. (HB, 2002)

EL, the villager, also suggested such re-awakened interest in identifying with the ancestral culture. When he lived in the city, he discovered increased interests among fellow Bush Negroes living in the city in the arts of their community, either because they were born and raised in the interior and remembered these ancestral arts traditions, or because strong family connections and traditions were maintained even in the city. Now, he said, as Bush Negroes realize the need to pass on their ancestral artistic traditions to their children, they join Bush Negro collective cultural groups in the city to hold informal meetings for the exchange of traditional arts.

> I do this as a hobby [drumming twice weekly at cultural institution gatherings]. I do not earn with it. Yes, [I do it] out of love, out of love for the culture. In the past I had become westernized. Yes, yes, it [my traditional culture] started to become diluted.

EL explained the Bush Negro concept of a *Kifoko*, which is a storage place for whatever is no longer of

Figure 8

Woodcarving
workshop outside
the capital city.

use. It is a dumping place in the corner of a village house that is cleared yearly or on a special day. EL thus concluded that the things from a *Kifoko* seldom come back into use with Bush Negroes. Everything from a Kifoko is ultimately thrown away. "The intention with us is to stop that,...yes, to stop that process from the Kifoko to the garbage can."

The Status Quo and Signs for the Future

Despite the efforts of the Bush Negro in the urban city, few in the traditional but changed village settings felt the incentive or even had the ability to perpetuate the arts traditions. Young men no longer want to stay in the villages to work and learn traditional communal ways. Convenient modernity and easier access to goods from the city through the accumulation of money have proved more attractive. Traditional roles of father, uncle, son, and mother, aunt, daughter as teachers of cultural and arts traditions and rituals have diminished in importance. The elders interviewed in the interior found this development most unsettling and confusing, but none could offer solutions. Their sighs, silences, and pensive moments during interviews were subtle and pained answers to questions on how they felt about these developments:

> *Elder KPA:* Everybody has a will and if the person does not want, then there is nothing you can do.
>
> *Dance master PA:* They [younger generation] go to dance at night. They have no time to learn. If they want to learn, they have to come here [his dance and music gathering in the city]. They say that it is tiring; we don't need it anymore. New fashion, fashionable dances, crazy stuff.
>
> *Elder KWG:* There is not much engagement in the arts anymore. The young think more about money. They have no time to make the traditional things. If they, for example, want a stool, they will not make it, they go and buy it.

Identity and re-awakened interests. Despite drastic changes in the Bush Negroes' traditional locations and social, cultural, and artistic environments, strong signs of identification with their Bush Negro culture emerge that manage to keep traditions alive mainly through the arts. Among young Bush Negro, increased awareness and interest in their ancestral culture have grown, especially since they have started to realize that the wealth of wisdom and cultural knowledge of their elders can produce arts that can be sold to generate cash income.

Some Bush Negroes in the city have started businesses to promote their culture, either as tour operators or as woodcarvers. Two owners of tour businesses to the interior villages told me that this engagement transformed their initial disinterest in the arts of their own village into great appreciation, admiration, pride, and positive identification with their ancestral culture.

They spoke of regrets and missed opportunities to learn from their village elders. As JT said, "It is now that I cry that my grandma has passed away. When she said, 'Come let me teach you,' I did not want to, but now I cry. Now I cry, because I need the information." While the elders are no longer with them, some youth in the city try to sustain the artistic and cultural traditions of their Bush Negro people with their businesses.

Decline of traditional values. Much of the current decline and changes in the arts and culture could be attributed to the lure of gold, as JT noted. Money earned in gold has changed people's values. They spend money on food and luxury and do not share it with their interior community (JT). The difficulty, then, is to continue the status quo in the arts, given the changed traditional social structures and circumstances in the villages. Art as a separate cultural expression, as perceived in the West, is not typically part of their cultural thinking. JT observed that communal cohesion in his village had indeed been disrupted and that practicing the arts has largely discontinued. This, he explained, becomes most visible when one considers needs. The village *Kabiten* is a knower, but no one needs his type of knowledge anymore: "What we need now is money. I do not anymore ask a person for help. Now I have money and buy the things I need" (JT). The times of helping another without expecting payment are gone. According to JT:

> I had not been there [in the interior] for three weeks and that thing [hut roof] started to leak. And the people just sat there. I arrived and they said that there were heavy rains. They did not even stand up to repair it. If I would say that I'll pay them they will do it, you know, it is very difficult...., and you would have to pay an awful lot.

Adaptation in the urban community. Specialization is also observable in the performing arts. The concept of a Western-style theater, for example, is mostly foreign to the Bush Negro people of the village. To perform in the city, they have to adapt to a Western theater space and consider lighting, choreography, sound equipment, and speech techniques. An important part of the *Pee* (a traditional Bush Negro playful, verbal, rhythmic interaction based on call and response) in the village is the interaction between player and audience. Dance also has a give-and-take, show-and-follow of actions format in the village, which is not possible in a Western-style theater in the city.

Traditional dances have changed to accommodate tourists' taste, according to Informant ML, and Informant PA noticed that dances have become superficial in their execution, much as the woodcarvings now comply with tourists' expectations of quality, portability, and attractiveness. Other illustrations of adaptation are the Bush Negro beauty pageant festivals that, according to Informant HB, are the latest craze in the urban community. Modeled after Western beauty pageants, they provide an opportunity to emphasize Bush Negro beauty values and promote Bush Negro cultural aspects. These are also examples of how influences from outside are adapted to the Bush Negro aesthetics in their arts.

They [the Bush Negro] say "we do not blindly copy the miss festival, we do not apply Western beauty criteria,"... thus their beauty criteria are large buttocks, bandy-legs and a hollow back. And that is funny. Because of these festivals we [in the city] learn about their culture. (Informant HB)

Some goals of these festivals in the city include teaching village norms and values to Bush Negro city youth. An article in the daily newspaper *De Ware Tijd* (Rijsdijk, 2002) highlighted the importance of reestablishing rituals that had been completely or partially forgotten. For arts and crafts, these festivals perpetuate traditions of crochet and cloth-making, especially the *kwé* (a loin cloth worn by teenage females to show she is not yet marriageable) and the *pagni* (a cloth an 18-year-old girl wears when the time for marriage has arrived). In such festivals, the girls wear different traditional Bush Negro cloths draped around their shoulders and hips.

The winner receives both money and traditional Bush Negro wood carvings. In this way, arts traditions (men carving wood pieces for women; women making cloths for men) are continued, albeit in a somewhat modern context.

Conclusion

The arts continue playing an important role in the contemporary culture and social life of the Suriname Bush Negroes in both interior and urban settings. Yet, interviews and observations revealed that modern conveniences and moneymaking activities are very attractive for village youth, and the traditional roles of elders as models and teachers of art and rituals have diminished. The elders have found this development

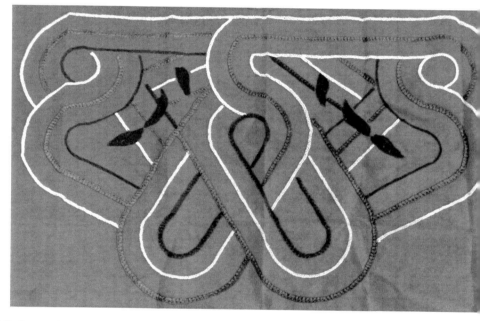

Figure 9

Pagni.

unsettling and confusing. At the same time, in the urban settings, Bush Negroes have showed increased interest in their own culture and have started organizations or joined existing cultural groups to express aspects of their ancestral culture.

Price and Price (1999) and Hureault (1970) suggest that after the Bush Negro society was formed in Suriname's interior in the 17th century, another century passed before they could establish their distinctive cultural and artistic ways. While they provide different theories and timelines for this development, these scholars agree that after another two centuries, numerous stylistic changes permeated the artworks of the Bush Negro. Change has always integral to the historical development of the Bush Negro people, but these changes were initiated within the cultural and artistic concepts of their society rather than from outside. Today, however, the strongest impacts of cultural changes are mainly triggered by outside influences. Notably, changes now occur with greater speed than in the past, and in village conditions that make it increasingly difficult to support, absorb, and adapt to these changes artistically, culturally, and socially. These changes deal less with explorations of new ideas and materials, meaning-making, and communication; rather, they are quick solutions to new social and economic problems for a people also struggling to maintain an artistic status quo or pre-serve cultural legacies. The increased availability and interest in Western goods, values, media, and social events, together with the loss of intact village social structures, have accelerated the rapid decline of art-making in the interior. Yet, as my study suggests, through a re-emerging collective idea that their life is art and through their renewed desire to express their culture and values imaginatively through the arts, the Bush Negro are finding innovative and contemporary ways to continue their unique artistic traditions, even in the face of adaptations to modern challenges.

Acknowledgments

This study relied heavily on interviews and observations in the Bush Negro community. I am therefore deeply grateful for the generosity of my informants who selflessly made themselves available whenever asked. Their passionate cooperation was testimony to the legendary hospitality of the Surinamese people and a great indicator of how much they all cared for the arts and artistic heritage of their people, whether in the interior of Suriname or its urban centers.

REFERENCES

Bakker, E., Dalhuisen, I., Donk, R., Hassankhan, M., & Steegh, F. (1998). *Geschiedenis van Suriname: van stam tot staat [The history of Suriname: From tribe to state].* Zutphen, The Netherlands: Uitgeversmaatschappij Walburg Pers.

Carrithers, M. (1992). *Why humans have cultures: Explaining anthropology and social diversity.* New York: Oxford University Press.

Communications and tourism of Suriname: Special advertisement supplement, (2001, September 20). *New York Times,* p.3.

Dark, P. J. C. (1973). *Bush Negro art: An African art in the Americas.* New York: St. Martin's Press.

Hureault, J. (1970). *Africains de Guyana: La vie matérielle et l'art des Noirs Réfugiés de Guyane [Africans in Guyana: The material life and the arts of the black fugitives of Guyana].* La Haye, Paris: Editions Mouton.

Jiesamfoek, H. F. (2004). Art making, aesthetic considerations and the formation of social and cultural homogeneity with the changing Bush Negro society of Suriname. *Journal of Intercultural Studies, 25*(1), 8-20. London: Taylor & Francis Group, Carfax Publishing.

Jopling, C. F. (Ed.). (1971). *Art and aesthetics in primitive societies: A critical anthology.* New York: E. P. Dutton & Co.

Mintz, S. W., & Price, R. (1992). *The birth of African-American culture: An anthropological perspective.* Boston: Beacon Press.

Murphy, R. F. (1989). *Cultural and social anthropology: An overture* (3rd ed.). Englewood Cliffs, NJ: Prentice Hall.

Price, R. (1996). *Maroon societies: Rebel slave communities in the Americas* (3rd ed.). Baltimore, MD: The Johns Hopkins University Press.

Price, R., & Price, S. (1992). *Equatoria.* New York: Routledge.

Price, R., & Price, S. (1980). *Afro-American arts of the Suriname rain forest: Museum of cultural history catalogue.* Berkeley: University of California Press.

Price, S., & Price, R. (1999). *Maroon arts: Cultural vitality in the African Diaspora.* Boston: Beacon Press.

Rijsdijk, E. (2002, April 9). Kwé-uma contest 2002. Show over begeleiding van meisje tot vrouw [Kwé-uma contest 2002. Show about the guidance from girlhood toward womanhood] *De Ware Tijd,* p. 4.

Sankeralli, B. (1995). *At the crossroads: African Caribbean religion and Christianity.* Trinidad & Tobago, West Indies: Caribbean Conference of Churches (CCC).

Saunders-Williams, C. E. (1996). *Protocol for visiting the Bushnegroes of Suriname's rain forest.* Paramaribo, Suriname: Vaco Uitgeversmaatschappij.

Stephen, H. J. M. (1995). *Winti en hulpverlening. Een bijdrage aan de gezondheidszorg in multicultureel Nederland [Winti and assistance. A contribution to healthcare in multicultural Netherlands].* Amsterdam: In eigen beheer.

Tuinford, C. (2002, July 19). Paramaccaanse goudzoekers claimen recht in concessie Suralco [Paramaka gold seekers claim rights in concession Suralco), *De Ware Tijd,* p. 6.

Vernooij, J. (1996). *Bosneger en katholieke kerk: Van confrontatie naar dialoog. [Bushnegro and the Catholic Church: from confrontation to dialogue].* Paramaribo: Stichting Wetenschappelijke Informatie.

Weatherford, J. (1994). *Savages and civilization: Who will survive?.* New York: Ballantine Books, Random House.

ENDNOTES

1 Suriname, officially the Republic of Suriname, formerly known as Dutch or Nederlands (Netherlands) Guiana and sometimes written as Guyana, is situated in South America and borders at the North on the Atlantic Ocean, at the south on Brazil, at the East on French Guiana, and at the West on Guyana (formerly known as British Guyana).

2 These people are also known as Maroons, a name derived from the Spanish word *Cimarrón,* first used in Hispaniola (Haiti). Because this term was used derogatorily by the Spaniards to refer to wild cattle that got lost in the hills, and later, to refer to enslaved Amerindians who escaped into the hills, and by the 1530s, mainly to refer to Africans who escaped from their plantations on the island (Price, 1996), I have decided to refer to these people as Bush Negroes. This is supported by my research findings in Suriname where, when addressing this topic, I was frequently reminded that the term Maroon does not evoke as strong a cultural identification, distinction, pride, and sense of self and belonging as that of the term "Bush Negro" [Busi Nёngё] (Jiesamfoek, 2004).

3 Mr. Guno H. G. Castelen, Minister of Transport, Communications, and Tourism of Suriname, in *The New York Times* special advertising supplement of Thursday, September 20, 2001.

'Parisianisme' and Local Cultures: Supra-national, National, and Infra-national Cultures

Frank Vigneron

Paris Ville-lumière

Living in Paris in the 1980s as a student, I worked part time for a small review specializing in poetry. While researching the work of a poet from the 1930s, my friends and I met a former medical doctor who had known intimately many painters and writers in Paris between the two World Wars. Many dinners ensued in the legendary brasseries of Montparnasse called La Rotonde which always followed a fixed ritual of eating and conversing. Talking to that fascinating old man, who lived in an old house in Montparnasse (where many artists of Paris used to live at least until the 1960s)—a house my friends and I came to call 'the house of Nosferatu' for its strange narrow shape and its red brick walls—and making him reminisce about the Paris of the 1920s and 1930s made us merge with our surroundings: a restaurant where all these figures had lived and talked and created the visual and literary works which are now part of what we call "modern art." Nothing could have made us more aware of how much we had become 'Parisiens.'

One day, we talked about a friend of ours who had decided to live in Brazil, a fashion designer who wanted to experiment a different lifestyle in the hope of creating more original garments. Although the founder of this review had himself been born in Brazil–but had been educated in Europe–and remained profoundly attached to his tropical birthplace, he was the first to say that he could not consider, as a poet, the possibility of leaving Paris. The conversation then continued on the superiority of Paris as a cultural capital and culminated in a joke that made us all laugh to tears: What if we all moved to Australia? I don't suppose our reaction to this comment would make any sense to someone who does not know about the old stereotypes of *Paris-ville lumière* ('Paris-city of lights'), its glorious literary and artistic past, and how much this old cliché is still alive in the minds of French intellectuals. Having lived in Hong Kong since 1990, I am not entirely sure whether this same comment would now make young Parisian intellectuals laugh as much as

we did in the late 1980s. There are now new frontiers available to these young urban elites and many of them consider carriers abroad as perfectly acceptable, but they still represent a minority, a very visible minority, but a minority nonetheless.

When I came to Paris in 1983 to study Chinese, I became part of a student population who had come to the capital to further their education. I was then very much a 'Provincial' and perfectly aware of what centuries of Paris-centered thinking had done to the psyche of French nationals: I was in Paris less than a full-fledged person, a mere embryo in a soup of cultural superiority. The roots of that idea are well-known and stem from the long history of centralization France has known ever since Louis the XIV established its frontiers. He then established Paris as more than the heart of the land, its veritable soul and the unique source of its cultural vitality. The rest of France has been known since then as the 'Province' and this word still maintains a large degree of repulsiveness in the mouth of the 'Parisiens.' No other population in Europe has established such a clear dichotomy and even the British, whose capital has also been the center of culture for a long time, would not reduce the rest of their island into a similar undifferentiated figure as the French 'Province.' Just like the 'East' has been invented to create a 'Western identity,' Parisian elites have been relying on the Paris/Province dichotomy to describe the superiority of life in the capital. In spite of nearly 30 years of political and economic decentralization, the 'Parisiens' are still convinced that they can command a mastery of everything 'cultural' much better than anyone else living in the 'Province.'

Misconceptions and stereotypes still form the basis of the old Paris-Province dichotomy which has existed for a long time. Balzac had already divided his *Comédie Humaine* into separate sections among which *'scenes from the life in Province'* and *'scenes from the life in Paris'* were two of the most important parts. 'Monter à Paris' (to go up to Paris), already the ambition and life goal of Rastignac, one of Balzac's most important characters, has been the motto of many French artists, poets and writers at least since the Enlightenment. This situation has probably made the renaissance of local cultures less visible in France than in Germany for instance, where provinces have always retained a great deal of cultural autonomy. A tendency towards a 'rediscovery' of local cultures and languages is also manifest in many other countries. What might appear as contradictory, i.e. the fact that economic globalization seems to be accompanied by an increase of cultural divisions, is only so on the surface.

The Return of Local Cultures

It is a fact that, in a world where exchanges of goods and ideas are increasingly frequent on an international level, people have become more aware of the unique characteristics of their local cultures. Similarly, and it is particularly obvious in the European Union, the disappearance of the old national frontiers when it comes to goods and persons, have made the artificiality of borders clearer: the creation of national identities, not so long ago after all, and the political desire to brand and localize them within artificial boundaries having far too often very little to do with any sense of local belonging. This was particularly obvious in the repression of local languages in the school system of the nineteenth century; in France, the positive creation of free, secular and compulsory schooling in 1882 was also accompanied by a ban on using one's own language in the classroom, and the near disappearance of languages like Gaelic or Provencal must be understood in that context.[1]

In fact, it is another aspect of globalization which has made the re-emergence of local culture possible very often on a personal level, as so many small personal epiphanies. Being displaced, voluntarily or involuntarily, has also made local cultures something of a portable item, something placed inside the individual. Personally, I have never felt more northern French than since I have moved to Hong Kong, even though it would be difficult to pinpoint how this manifests itself. I suppose there are millions of details in the attitudes of the people surrounding me in Hong Kong which do not match exactly the millions of details in the attitudes of the people who once surrounded me when living in France. It might be all these big and small discrepancies in the way people live and behave that are emphasizing the fact that my cultural and behavioral background is so different. These small personal epiphanies were helped by the rediscovery made by actors of local cultures of a variety of objects specific to their own cultural sphere.

According to many anti-globalization associations (most of them being actually in favor of globalization but not in its present form—which makes the French term of 'alter-mondialiste,' literally 'another kind of globalization,' much more accurate), economic globalization could only be viable if it encourages local cultures to be individualized and differentiated. Very few people nowadays would approve the idea of a cultural globalization relying on the leveling of traditions, evened out to the level of a Westernized popular culture that could be marketed to anyone in the world. Since there is a definite tendency for economically dominant cultures to spread their commodified cultural productions (as it is the case today with North American popular culture), there should be a counterreaction to stabilize what threatens to become cultural pauperization. In order to do so, cultural diversity should always be encouraged through projects like the education of human groups on their local culture.

Moreover, because cultures are mainly mediated through language, and since it has been proven by educators that multilinguism is beneficial to the development of children, there is actually no reason to discourage populations to use their local language as well as one or two other tongues (countries like Switzerland or Belgium, where the majority speak two or three tongues in addition to local ones are proof enough that this is a perfectly viable project). Hong Kong, with its own language and specific culture is an ideal laboratory to observe a 'local' culture and its relationship with globalization. The idea of multilinguism, and the persistence of what continues to be called dialects, are important topics when it comes to the revival of local cultures. In local cultures, the use of dialects is central in what can be called, to simplify, popular culture. In Hong Kong, there is an entire industry of music and movies relying on Cantonese, although this tongue, spoken by hundreds of millions of persons, could hardly be called a local dialect. Attachment to one's local culture through the use of local languages is more obvious in regions where an official language has long been the norm, even in popular culture. To take the example of the province where I grew up, there are now publications destined to let other French speakers become conversant in the specific type of French spoken in the North, a type now called 'Picard' although it was not given the right to a name not so long ago. The number of publications in Picard is growing and such gems of French-speaking popular culture, like the comic book *Lucky Luke* (created by two French-speaking Belgians), have been translated into Picard for a population limited to the

North of France, as no one else in the country would understand even half of its content.

This emphasis on the French-and-French-dialects-speaking cultures of Europe, but also of North America, are often construed as attacks on 'American culture,' but this is only true on the surface. What many actors of these cultures react against are the conditions created by dominant cultures, dominant because their techniques of dissemination are so commercially powerful that they do not leave much room for other modes of expression to coexist. For the moment, these dominant cultures are mostly English-speaking, and, among these cultures, there is no doubt that the *primus inter pares*, 'first among its peers,' is a certain type of popular American culture. It is a fact that commercial or popular American culture occupies that dominant spot and it is another fact that the pressure created by that overwhelming power has a tendency to eradicate the voices of minority cultures around the world. It is another universally acknowledged fact that many languages are on the verge of disappearing not only because the speakers of these tongues are getting fewer but also because the use of English is such an absolute necessity in a globalized market that there are very few incentives to continue using these languages.

Glocal

To avoid this cultural leveling, the dissemination of 'local characteristics' to other territories might be the only viable solution for globalization: instead of the assimilation of everything into a monstrous center, the deterritorialization of a multitude of local cultures into ever-growing peripheries. However, this emphasis on local culture would only be possible if it is accompanied by another, outbound movement: localization can only work in this new context of globalization, an idea expressed by the term *glocalization*. Within the confines of countries though, it is not possible to completely discriminate local culture and national culture: for instance, if the local culture is made up of elements like the language we use in family and close friends circles, as well as certain types of food or clothing, the national culture is made up of historical events and stories often associated to the 'nation building' movements of the past. There are however no clear limits between what constitutes local culture and national culture, in reality, the one simply gradually turns into the other.

Many elements belong in that grey area where local culture becomes national culture and vice-versa. What unfortunately happened quite often,

especially in periods of conflict, is that national cultures get surrounded by a sort of thick crust which stops any possible interactions with other cultures. That paralyzing crust is caused by an ossification of national culture, something I would call nationalism or patriotism. I suppose both of these feelings can be useful and honorable at times, but when they become ossified they simply cut a culture from outside influences, a situation that eventually leads to aggressive and destructive behaviors. A good example of such negative influences would be nineteenth-century style colonialism, an attitude caused as much by economic reasons as by the requirements of patriotism gone wrong. In extreme cases, the national culture is so developed that it stifles the core of local culture and turns into an extremely thick crust of nationalism/patriotism, a case that often leads to loss of identity, conflicts and violence.

For those who believe that promoting local cultures is the same as promoting national cultures but on a smaller scale, I would present two arguments. First, overgrown national cultures have usually been created forcefully, without the consent of the majority: the example of the local languages which were forbidden in the European schools of the late nineteenth century is a perfect illustration. The resurgence of these languages, and the customs that came with them, at the time many national borders are in effect dissolving—as in Europe or, more dramatically, in the former Yugoslavia—is ample proof that national cultures are always on the brink of dissolution and always relying on the powerful tools of centralized powers, i.e. schools and press in the past and television and mass media in the present, to continue to exist. Second, local cultures are much more profoundly a part of the individuals and, because of that deep feeling of possession, individuals feel they are less in danger of losing them. National cultures are not as deeply a part of the individual's psychological makeup as local cultures, and the reason why national cultures have been, and are, defended with such violence is because they are constructs whose artificiality has been less well internalized within the fabric of the Self. People do not feel they have to defend things that are essential parts of themselves, whereas they always have to defend what is always threatening to fall away.

It is possible to observe how new cultural elements, which do no belong to either local or national cultures or did so in a remote past, have been recently created in this 'glocal' context with a simple example: the re-invention of the old figure of Charlemagne, now dubbed a 'European' emperor (a name that would have meant nothing to that 8th-century ruler). Charlemagne has been looked upon at the beginnings of the European Union in the 1950s as the founder of European culture. Although he did create a distinctive culture by improving the administrative organization of his empire and by fostering a cultural recovery of the Roman heritage, these characteristics were limited to the upper layer of the society of the time and cannot be attributed to Charlemagne only. Anyway, for a time (a time that seems to have passed since the figure of Charlemagne does not make much sense to symbolize a European Union with 25 members), Charlemagne was construed as a European symbol mostly because his reign was so ancient and so absent from the memories of the inhabitant of the union that it could be transformed into any kind of cultural message. The example of Charlemagne illustrates perfectly what is meant by the creation of supra-national cultures: it is a symbol that does not fit in any of the discourses about national cultures created during the nation building periods of the past because the zone of existence of his empire did not correspond to the national borders created during these periods. The borders of Charlemagne's Holy Roman Empire covered most of what the European Union looked like in the 1960s, except England. If we can imagine the existence of supra-national cultures, it might be better to rename infra-national cultures what I have called until now 'local cultures.'

Another multi-purpose figure used in ideology and also nation-building discourses would be that of Mao Zedong. It is obvious that a portrait of Mao Zedong by an American artist of the 1970s and by a contemporary Chinese artist will not bear the same implications or even the same meaning. Such figures are quite literally floating signifiers and can be filled with a variety of implications. In Hong Kong, Mao Zedong does not have the aura of infallibility it has been granted in the People's Republic. In fact, the questions surrounding the problems of infra-national versus national cultures can be read in the works of a number of artists from Hong Kong where a very strong infra-national culture has developed. Starting in the late 1980s, particularly because of the signing of the treaty deciding the handover of the colony to the People's Republic of China (the Sino-British Joint Declaration on the Future of Hong Kong in 1984), there has been a great deal of talk about a Hong Kong cultural identity—usually involving terms like 'hybridity,' 'floating,' 'Diasporic,' and so on—even though this topic is not as hotly debated as it was before 1997.[2] The fact that identities are always defined in terms of limits (this is mine, that is yours), self-definition always rely on

the characterization of the 'others' which, in the case of Hong Kong, were in majority Chinese and British culture.[3] It is literally *against* the representations the Hong Kong people have of these two powerful cultures that they have defined their identity (we are talking only of representations here, there is no relation to a possible truth of what constitutes Chinese and British cultures). Neither here nor there, the actors of any cultural identity have to make hybridity their *raison d'être* and, although it was always true, as there is no 'pure' culture of any kind, some places have made this situation more visible than others. Hong Kong has been such a place for already a long time and will hopefully remain so.[4]

An excellent example of the attitude of many Hong Kong artists towards their culture, and especially their own language, can be seen in a work by Blue Puk Yuk-chun titled *English in Chinese*. It is a simple list of Chinese characters which, pronounced in Cantonese, are transcriptions of English words used in everyday life in Hong Kong. For example, she gives the two characters 'tea' and 'boiling pot' which, pronounced together, vaguely sound like the English word 'trouble'. This very simple work is in reality a complex statement on the linguistic, and therefore cultural, situation of Hong Kong: a place where everyday language is Cantonese, and therefore not the official language of the People's Republic; where Cantonese, once called a dialect, is the only non-official language of China that can be written down (to the extent that many new Chinese characters have been created); where this language itself can be hybridized with elements of the former colonial tongue.[5] These new words, created by actors of the Hong Kong infra-national culture over the last century, have been introduced in a written language prized by the defenders of the Chinese national culture for its great antiquity. These artworks, made by Hong Kong artists relying on their local culture, are ample proof that infra-national cultures have the potential to revive ancient national cultures, and, in this process, relate to the rest of the world. The international success of a film like *In the Mood for Love* by the Hong Kong director Wong Kar-wai shows very clearly that a work built on 'local' elements can successfully become 'glocal,' or even, more simply, 'global.'

The most pressing demand for art educators, art critics, and curators is therefore to establish bridges between artworks produced in infra-national cultures and an international audience. Clarification of the cultural background of such works is actually necessary for outsiders to understand at least part of their message. As Zheng Shengtian, the present managing director of the magazine *Yishu* specialized in contemporary Chinese art, once said during an art fair in Shanghai in September 2007, there is the need for three 'legs' to sustain such a rich environment: a healthy art market, productive artists who can feel free to use anything in their art making, and also well-informed art criticism and curatorship in order to give access to these works to anyone interested. As an art educator, I feel it is my duty to encourage my Hong Kong students to explore their own culture in order to inform and shape their artworks. I must add that, in view of the very lively local culture of Hong Kong, this has been a singularly easy task. Whether it would have been as easy in the north of France I will never know, but in view of the revival of the Picard culture, my guess is that the reactions might have been similar.

Hybridization

The new narratives of supra-nationality in the case of the European Union actually seem to work, and maybe because they are based on figures and discourses changing with the times as the situation of the Union is changing every time new members are being added. The fact that these narratives are working can be seen in the growing number of French, English, German etc. who are feeling 'European'. It is another fact though that it is easier to feel very strong feelings of being 'European' inside the many groups of European expatriates whose connection with Europe is more sentimental than with people actually living in the Union. Although one could argue that infra-national cultures are growing stronger and are given more and more institutional support in Europe at large, the narrative of a national cultural unity is still strong and widely believed in. As for the idea of a politically and economically unified Europe, it will be interesting to follow what will happen, in the near future, to that concept of 'Europeanity' still supported by such fictions as the 'European ambitions' of historical figures like Charlemagne, when the disappearance of Europe's internal frontiers will reveal more clearly the bewildering variety of its many languages and cultures. One could add that cultural variety has also emerged more clearly in China because of the impact of globalization on its national culture and that movement truly started in Hong Kong.

The way infra-national cultures tend to reappear in a globalized context, would be another way to encourage further cultural hybridization. Now, 'hybridization,' that is a word which is rapidly going out of fashion in historical and cultural studies but its present lack of popularity is also based on another misconception. In the context of Hong Kong, for instance, hybridization has become a buzz word that has somehow replaced the old, and now clearly unacceptable, concept of 'East meets West'. Although repeating the same word too often always turns that word into a meaningless sound, hybridization probably should not be rejected so easily since every culture is a hybrid of some sort. In fact, hybridization is how cultures are shaped and constantly transformed. The reason why it has become so tiresome for Hong Kong intellectuals is not an inherent irrelevance of the term but maybe just its painfully obvious visibility. When one is in Paris and speaks French, one is inadvertently using many Arab words like 'coton,' 'café,' 'sofa,' 'sucre,' 'carafe,' 'alcool,' etc. but they have been French for such a long time, that they pass for essentially French. What happens in Hong Kong, particularly in the constant use of English words local elites are making, is a simple situation of greater visibility. And it is that visibility that has turned the constant use of the term 'hybrid' into cultural nausea.

In Paris, France and the rest of the world in general, a process of hybridization into the creation of cultural identities has always been taking place but it turns into a topic of questions and questioning only when it becomes a problem. One can frequently see such patterns of identity creation in history: unless there is a deliberate policy of cultural eradication, in which case, it is nearly impossible to conserve it, the more difficult the conditions to preserve one's cultural identity are, the more vigorously the actors of that cultural identity will defend and cultivate it. It is now obvious that the creation of infra-national cultures is not any longer the privilege of the 'Province': these cultures can very well sprout in the old center of national culture with all the potency and independence one would expect from the culture of a geographically remote area. And this can be taken as probably the most obvious sign that the 'Paris-city of light' narrative is somehow weakening. Still today however, many 'provinciaux' in small and medium-sized cities, whose job or travel destinations are increasingly geared towards an international context, are often quite blind to the changes brought about by economic globalization and still believe in the power of the national governments to influence the economy. The possibilities of 'local cultures' are still very much in their infancy though, and their potential is only visible, and construed as desirable, seen in and from bigger cities. The possibility of a Picard language as usable in comic books, movies or broadcasting was made possible in the Northern Province of France by the development of the European Union while the Eurostar was putting Lille, the largest city of the region, at the crossroad between London, Brussels, and Paris. The same thing happened in Hong Kong because it has been an international financial center for many years.

It is in the permanent and always renewed definition of what constitutes infra-national, national and supra-national cultures that infra-national cultures have a chance to exist and grow more visible. In fact, they can only exist if they define themselves inside a narrative of oppositions: the reason 'Parisians' are still seen as 'non-Provincial' is because they both need one another to define who and what they are. The creation of supra-national narratives with the creation of Europe had the effect to reinforce infra-national cultures. As the ultimate supra-national narrative, globalization has already created its own 'hero,' but this new folklore did not take the form of an ancient flesh-and-blood figure—how could it? The Internet has been given the role of unifying element for this new narrative with as little reality as the invented figure of Charlemagne at the beginning of the creation of the European Union: 16.6% of the world population had access to the internet in 2006, and 19.1% in 2007 according to the website 'Internet World Stats' (www.internetworldstats.com/stats.htm). For some continents, it has as much reality as the 'stuff dreams are made of.'

For infra-national cultures to blossom again, and hopefully give back to individuals a stronger measure of confidence in their own cultural makeup, there is a need for the old national cultures to somehow shrink a little. Ideally, if national cultures do shrink, they would leave more room for essential elements of the infra-national cultures to take back some of their former significance: it is, for example, clear that the dialects of the past have more and more the right to be identified as languages. It is not making much sense to call Cantonese a dialect for instance when a province the size of a big European country relies on this language for its everyday operations. But this resizing of national cultures can only take place in an environment which accommodates other supra-national narratives, and these new narratives (which always tend to be replaced by other new narratives like any other element of a cultural identity) are already in place in the European Union for instance, with such heroes as the Eurostar and the new currency. In that new context, where infra-national and national cultures tend to share an increasingly equal amount of cultural space in the individuals, the reasons why the narrative of 'Paris-city of light' is showing some sign of weakening become quite clear.

Before the establishment of the European Union and the development of globalization, Paris was the most potent symbol of national culture in France and naturally forced in the actors of French culture coming from the rest of the country, the deletion of the local cultures they carefully left behind before 'going up to the capital.' The discourse of the 'other' applied without any niceties: one was either 'Parisian' or 'Provincial' and had to choose camp. If the dichotomy 'Parisian'/'Provincial' is still alive today, it has been weakening because this narrative cannot rely any longer on the old national culture that had created it. But it is still there in a sort of slightly diluted state and is slowly being shaped into a new form by the sometimes contending and sometimes collaborating influences of two forces: the revived infra-national cultures and the burgeoning new forms of supra-national cultures. In this new context created by different aspects of globalization, there might be, in the near future, a time when not even a Parisian poet would laugh at the idea of emigrating to Australia.

REFERENCES

Abbas, A. (1997). *Hong Kong. Culture and the politics of disappearance*. Minneapolis: University of Minnesota Press.

Calvet, Jean-Louis (2002). *Linguistique et Colonialisme*. Paris: Payot.

Chow, R. (1993). *Writing Diaspora : Tactics of intervention in contemporary cultural studies*. Bloomington and Indianapolis: Indiana University Press.

Clarke, D. (2001). *Hong Kong art: Culture and decolonization*. Hong Kong: Hong Kong University Press.

Hinterthür, P. (1985). *Modern art in Hong Kong*. Hong Kong: Myer Publishing Ltd.

Pennington, M. C. (Ed.). (1998). *Language in Hong Kong at century's end*. Hong Kong: Hong Kong University Press.

Zhu Qi (2005). *Xianggang Meishu Shi*. Hong Kong: Sanlian Publishing Ltd.

ENDNOTES

1   On this question of the imposition of certain languages, and many others attached to colonial domination by European countries, see Calvet, Jean-Louis (2002). *Linguistique et Colonialisme*. Paris: Payot.

2   On the issues of hybridity and Diaspora in relation with 'chineseness', see Chow, Rey (1993). Writing Diaspora: Tactics of Intervention in Contemporary Cultural Studies. Bloomington and Indianapolis: Indiana University Press.

3   Although the question of cultural identity has been treated by many writers in Hong Kong, one of the most celebrated books on this changing issue was published during the 1990s: Abbas, Ackbar (1997). Hong Kong. Culture and the Politics of Disappearance. Minneapolis: University of Minnesota Press.

4   Although the number of publications on art in Hong Kong is on the rise in the Chinese language, very few books in English have been dedicated to this issue. See Hinterthür, Petra (1985). Modern Art in Hong Kong. Hong Kong. Myer Publishing Ltd., as well as Clarke, David (2001). Hong Kong Art: Culture and Decolonization. Hong Kong: Hong Kong University Press. The most complete study in Chinese is Zhu Qi (2005). Xianggang Meishu Shi. Hong Kong: Sanlian Publishing Ltd.

5   On the relationship of a 'local' language with the official language of a country, and especially in the post-colonial context of Hong Kong, see Pennington, Martha C. (Ed.)(1998). Language in Hong Kong at Century's End. Hong Kong: Hong Kong University Press.

Sculpting the Sky: The Art and Culture of Weifang International Kite Festival

Yuehchen Wang

Every April, the sky fills with thousands of beautiful kites of all shapes and sizes in Weifang, China. The International Weifang Kite Festival has been held continuously every year, attracting thousands upon thousands of visitors from around the region, as well as kiting enthusiasts from all over the world. This chapter shares insights gained from my inquiry about how the Weifang Municipal Government has used traditional local kite art to develop local tourism and promote their cultural heritage. I describe how the International Weifang Kite Festival conveys multiple, local, and global facets of Chinese culture, tradition, and community through art. I also discuss how this form of engagement with artistic and cultural tradition fosters local community economic development. This study has the potential for increasing our understanding about how art educational endeavors become more meaningful by taking art education outside of the classroom.

The Origins and Development of Chinese Kites

China is the birthplace of kites, which have a history of more than 2500 years (Hart, 1967; Hiroi, 1978; Jue, 1968; Liu, 1994; Wang, 1989). According to historical documents, the earliest kite flying was used for military purposes and in scientific research. Kites first appeared in the spring and Autumn Period (770 B.C. - 476 B.C.) in China. It did not take long for kites to spread from China to the outside world (Ha & Ha, 1990; Hiroi, 1978; Liu, 2004; Wang, 1989). Early kites created in China for recreational and artistic purposes were often made of wood and bamboo in the shape of birds and hence were commonly called "wooden hawks" at the time. Later, kites were increasingly made of silk or paper. Kites were called by different names in different places, such as "paper hawks", "wind zithers", and "wind kites" (Liu, 1994; Wang, 1989). *Feng Zheng* means wind kite in Chinese: the *feng* means wind; the *zheng* means kite. During the late Han Dynasty (947-950 AC.), a person named Li Ye attached a bamboo whistle to a kite (Hart, 1967; Wang, 1989). When the wind blew into the whistle, it produced a sound like that of a Chinese instrument called a *zheng*. At that time, Chinese people began to call this kind of kite *Feng Zheng*, a name which was later applied to all types of kites (Ha & Ha, 1990; Wang, 1989).

Figure 1

Kite flying strengthens the integrity of families and the community.

By the middle of the Qing Dynasty, kite flying became closely related to the Chinese people's lifestyle and social customs. Chinese kites are highly colorful and decorative. Flowers, birds, insects, fish, beasts, and characters in fairy tales and legends can all be the subjects of kites. When flying in the sky, the vivid colors and ornate patterning contrast impressively with the blue sky and white clouds. Chinese kites, which have various modeling and lifelike designs, carry Chinese people's deepest feelings, artistic senses, yearning for the fine art, and their pursuit of future ideals (See Figure 1). One of the kite's most important contributions to Chinese science has been in the study of flight in the development of aircraft (Hiroi, 1978; Liu, 1994; Wang, 1989).

Traditional Chinese kites are currently made according to ancient practices and frequently incorporate hand made paper, silk, silk fabric, and bamboo (Ha & Ha, 1990; Tyrrell, 1978; Liu, 1994; Wang, 1989). Chinese kites come in every imaginable shape and size. For example, some mini-butterfly kites may be only 2.5 centimeters long and 2.4 centimeters wide and still fly very well. According to design, Chinese kites can be divided into several types: figures, objects, characters, flowers, birds, and insects. They all can be painted with abstract designs, figurative decorations, or both. Currently there are two commonly used types of Chinese kite construction: whole-piece frame and folding frame, and two types of structure: hard-winged and soft-winged (Liu, 2004; Wang, 1989).

After long and extended eras of kite use and development, the Chinese have incorporated kites into many important religious, social, and cultural celebrations, activities, and rituals. In 1980, the development of Chinese kites entered a new period of prosperity on the world stage and over the past three decades, kite artists have actively participated in domestic and international kite exchange and competitions.

The Weifang International Kite Festival

History tells us that the people of Weifang have been flying kites since 1368 A.D. Many believe Weifang to be one of the birthplaces of Chinese kites. On April 1, 1984, a memorable day in Chinese kite history, the first Weifang International Kite Festival was solemnly opened in the city of Weifang (Liu, 1994; Wang, 1989). Weifang City is in central Shandong province of China. The land area of Weifang City is 15,800 square kilometers and has a population of about 8.5 million. The city was well-known in history for its handicraft industry and is known as the World Kite Capital (Donovan, 2007; Gunn, 2005; Liu, 1994). Weifang is a modern city and offers numerous gift shops, including kite shops that sell many different kinds of both traditional Chinese kites and modern kites (see Figure 2).

From the 19th to 23rd of April, 2007, the Weifang International Kite Festival was held at the impressive stadium facility and recreation grounds 20 kilometers west of Weifang City. The theme of 2007 Weifang kite festival was: "Kites Fly Olympics." All of the International kiters were warmly welcomed by the people of Weifang and China. Steve Donovan, who has been active in kiting since the '70s, is a member of Team Kaos and the Queensland Kite Society, described the 2007 Weifang International Kite Festival, "All kite flyers around the world should take the time to visit, and see for themselves at least once in their lives. To also take in the enormity [big] of what kiting means to the people of Weifang, and China in their culture as a whole" (Donovan, 2007, p. 11).

One of the most impressive things about the Weifang International Kite Festival is the enormous amount of different styles of kites on display and flying together. Gunn (2004) described his first time attending and competing in the Weifang Kite Festival in 2004. After their team stopped several times along their 1/4-mile walk to the kite flying grounds, they

Figure 2

Traditional Chinese silk kites are very colorful and decorative.

Figure 3

In recent years, extra large kites have been a common sight in the Weifang Kite Festival. Dragonfly Kite pictured here.

Figure 4

Left: The Monster Kite floated placidly through the gale.

Figure 5

Right: International kiters and their wonderful kites.

gazed into a sky filled with thousands of kites of all shapes, styles, colors, and sizes, realizing how packed the sky was because there was literally zero open air space. Gunn commented that one could see any kind of kite one could imagine, from modern kites, to traditional kites to bucket-shaped palatial lantern kites to extra large soft-body kites to hand-made one-of-a-kind kites (see Figure 3). He observed at least 3 dozen one of a kind soft bodied, hand-made dragon kites in the sky during the local judging and was impressed by how much the Chinese love the dragon-head with centipede body kites (Gunn, 2004)!

In recent years, extra large kites have become a more common sight in the Weifang Kite Festival (see Figure 4). One dragon kite was so large that it had to be brought in on a flat bed truck. The head was about 5 feet tall (Gunn, 2005). As in 2004, a Chinese kite flyer launched a very large "Chinese missile" kite. Gunn (2004) described his experience of this kind of super kite, "After that mess was straightened out my eyes were drawn to a very large 800 square foot flow form style kite that had special appliqué sewn into it that was designed to look like Tianamen Square Rostrum" (p. 11). During that particular festival, International kite flyers from 40 different countries were greeted by thousands of spectators (see Figure 5). In addition to the international kiters, there were hundreds of kiters from all over China who displayed and flew their fantastic traditional kites. By 2005, approximately 500,000 people participated in the Weifang International Kite Festival. The venue was a huge soccer stadium that seats about 80,000 people. About one billion watched the ceremonies on television. The ceremony consisted of dancing, singing, traditional Chinese drummers, and an hour-long beautiful fireworks display. This is Weifang's version of an Olympic style ceremony (Donovan, 2007; Gunn, 2006).

Implications for Art Education

Weifang is now considered by many to be the kite capital of the world (Donovan, 2007; Gunn, 2005; Liu, 1994). As mentioned earlier, there are numerous kite factories and stores in Weifang City that make and sell traditional Chinese kites as well as modern kites. What makes this kind of international cultural expression and exchange so remarkable for art education theory and practice is not only its cultural and multicultural value, its growing international popularity, and it's artistic and aesthetic richness, but also its fascinating function as a site for global cultural, artistic, recreational, and economic activity and exchange. The Weifang International Kite festival is at the same time local and global. Local artists and kite makers create, exhibit, compete, and sell their kites in this festival, and residents look forward to and make extraordinary preparations for this event.

Community-Based Art Education: Linking Community-Based Art to Community Development

For the Weifang International Kite Festival, the Weifang Municipal Government uses local art to both develop tourism and to promote their cultural heritage. It provides an opportunity for all of the residents in Weifang City to revitalize their cultural identity and to re-examine their traditional heritage by sharing their culture and art with the kiters and visitors who come from all over the world. I find strong linkages between the now globalized practice of kite design and flying taking place at the Weifang International Kite festival and community-based approaches to art education, an orientation that has gained increasing popularity in the field of art education.

A significant participatory role of community residents in art making is often described as community arts. Celebrating and valuing local art is an important concept of community–based art education. Art educator June McFee (1991) noted that many art education approaches consider art forms hierarchically; in other words, high art as contrasted with low art. By participating in the kite Festival and looking at the various kinds of art activities as an educational endeavor for adults and children alike, the role of art education in communities is enhanced. Festivals of this sort, with their tendency to merge traditional, artistic, economic, and recreational facets of local culture challenges narrowly defined art categorizations and blurs the boundary between fine art and popular art.

Utilizing a model of community-based art education, the movement of art education into the community has important ramifications for our professional theory and practice (London & Briggs 1996; Marché, 1998). Art educator Peter London (1996) argues that the goal of community-based art education is to "shift the use of the community from its prevailing one as an interlude, a diversion, or an enrichment to one in which it is the primary educational resource" (p. 57). As London observes, community-based art education approach encompasses all people. It is "sensitive to individual differences, and promotes self identity and self esteem" as well as a "subjective, interpretive approach to the world" (p. 42). Similarly, according to art educator Flavia Bastos (2002), locally produced art study is at the core of educational practices. The process and study of making local art provides people with opportunities to reflect themselves in the art they produce. It creates and reflects one's culture and constantly alludes to renewal and change. In the example of the Weifang International Kite Festival and in community sites throughout the world, art making creates a space for individuals to both interpret and share their own culture; it can also increase and enrich an awareness of both local and global citizenship. Learning about indigenous and local art, culture, and traditions helps people understand the relationship of art, culture, and traditions to present and past localized value systems, as well as to globalize aesthetic and economic trends and tensions.

Community Art for Community Development

The Weifang International Kite Festival also provides an opportunity to help the city to develop and promote its traditional kite culture through a growing intercultural method of community development. As Seana Lowe (2000) notes, the community-art education process provides a ritualistic setting for social interaction and documents the construction of neighborhood community. "The social bonds of solidarity and collective identity that occurred as a result of bringing neighborhood residents together" provides an opportunity for people to develop a "shared goal and set a common mood for the purpose of designing a community symbol" (Lowe, 2000, p. 358). In the International Weifang Kite Festival, sponsoring organizations, local kite artists, and the Weifang community are affected by and interact positively with each other by using art as a catalyst for community development. The link between educational communities through local art is not only meaningful to residents and the community for artistic or cultural expression, but it is a facet of community development and social-reconstruction practice. It provides neighborhood residents with a shared interest in conveying to the world their own cultural heritage, an opportunity to interact socially, and a structure for community economic and cultural development. Troy Gunn (2006), in his third year of attending the Weifang International Kite Festival, describes his impressions of Weifang, "Every year that I come to Weifang, old buildings are being demolished, and new buildings are being built. The city is growing at an alarming rate!" (p.13). As the Weifang government promotes the kite culture, there have been an increasing number of kite factories and stores opened in Weifang. They all spread the seeds and traditions of Weifang and carry forth the mission of community development. By examining the relationship between local art and community development, one can learn how art becomes a tool for community change.

Community Art for Intercultural Art Education

Some have argued that there is a growing feeling of isolation and little community spirit in contemporary society. Researching and responding to community culture through art becomes a means for intercultural education. The Weifang International Kite invites kiters and visitors from around the world and from other ethnic backgrounds as well as China to construct new understandings and connections between the global and the local through encounters with their own and others' cultural contexts. As such, this Festival represents a form of intercultural art education.

Donovan (2007) pointed out that it was very fulfilling to be able to observe for the first time International kite visitors, taking in so much information about the history of Chinese traditional kite making, and how kiting is embroidered into the earliest fabric of Chinese culture. Another international kiter American kite–flying champion, Gunn made a similar statement. After he toured two or three kite-building shops, where he saw how traditional Chinese bamboo and silk kites were made, Gunn (2004) concluded, "This work looked very tedious and time consuming! It definitely gave us a better appreciation of what goes into making these hand crafted kites and what a great value these kites are to buy and collect" (p.11). For the Weifang people, they are able to share culture with people from within their community and people from all over world. By sharing culture through art, they are gaining insight into multiple and global aspects of their culture, tradition, and the life surrounding them.

Conclusion

For more then 2500 years, Chinese people have loved kites for their various shapes, beautiful painted pictures, and the pleasant music that they produce. Kites harmoniously merge with the natural surroundings. In the eyes of the connoisseur, a skillfully made, artistic kite is a work of art. Kite flying has become a popular mass sport and has attracted people of all ages. People not only exercise their legs and eyes, but also entertain themselves and strengthen the integrity of families and the community. In many ways the Weifang International Kite Festival represents a unique form of both community-based art educational practice, intercultural education, and community economic and cultural development. Community-based art education is an attempt to promote self-discovery through firsthand encounter between children and their world. The impact and benefit for adults is as much as for children. Participation in diverse cultural art activities like the Weifang International Kite Festival enhances visitors' abilities to understand diverse cultural practices, value systems, and increase diverse peoples' ability to understand, tolerate, and respect cultural and ethnic expressions. Cultural pluralism is essential to building a flourishing global perspective and a more peaceful world.

Acknowledgments

The author would like to thank Dr. Rachel Williams for her insightful editorial suggestions for this article and Dr. Steve McGuire for his suggestion and support. The author is also grateful to Mr. James Wright for permission to use images from his photo gallery.

REFERENCES

Bastos, F. M. C. (2002). Making the familiar strange: A community-based art education framework. Y. Gaudelius & P. Spears (Eds.). *Contemporary issues in art education,* Upper Saddle River, New Jersey: Prentice Hall.

Cleveland, W. (2001). Trials and triumphs: Arts-based community development. *Public Art Review*, *13*(1), 17-23.

Donovan, S. (2007).Weifang Kite Festival: International quests abound in China. *Kitelife Magazine,* Issue 54 May/ June. Retrieved January, 5, 2008, from http://www.kitelife.com/archives/issue54/weifang07/index.htm.

Gunn, T. (2004). Weifang International Kite Festival. *Kitelife Magazine*, Issue 36 May/ June. Retrieved January, 5, 2008, from www.kitelife.com/archives/issue36/weifang04/index.htm.

Gunn, T. (2005 July/August). 22nd Weifang International Kite Festival. *Kitelife Magazine*, Issue 43. Retrieved January, 5, 2008, from http://www.kitelife.com/archives/issue43/weifang05/index.htm.

Gunn, T. (2006 May/June). Weifang Kite Festival. *Kitelife Magazine,* Issue 48. Retrieved January, 5, 2008, from http://www.kitelife.com/archives/issue48/weifang06/index.htm.

Ha, K. and Ha, Y. (1990). *Chinese artistic kite.* Hong Kong: The Commercial Press.

Hart, C. (1967). *Kites: An historical survey*. New York: Frederick A. Praeger.

Hiroi, T. (1978). *Kites: Sculpting the sky*. New York: Pantheon Books.

Jue, D. F. (1968).*Chinese Kites: How to Make and Fly Them*. Japan: Charles E Tuttle Co.

Liu, C. (2004). *Chinese kites*. Beijing: Foreign Language Press.

Liu, Z. (1994). *Chinese kites*. Beijing China: Shandong Science and Technology Press.

London, P. & Briggs, C. (1996). Step outside: Community-based art education, *American Journal of Art Therapy*, *34*(4), 117-123.

Lowe, S. (2000).Creating community: Art for community development, *Journal of Contemporary Ethnography* 2000; *29*; 357-386.

Marché, T. (1998) Looking outward, oooking In: Community in art education, *Art Education*, *51*(3), 6-13.

Mcfee, J. K. (1991). Art education progress: A field of dichotomies or a network of mutual support. *Studies in Art Education*, *32*(2), 70-82.

Tyrrell, S.(1978). *Kites: The gentle art of high flying*. New York: Doubleday & Company.

Wang, H. (1989). *Chinese Kites*. Beijing: Foreign Languages Press.

Promotion of Ethnic and Cultural Identity through Visual and Material Culture among Immigrant Koreans

Ryan Shin

One of the common topics of discussion among Korean immigrants[1] in the United States addresses the following question: "Why did you come to live in America?" I have observed that many enjoy sharing their personal stories and are also interested in hearing from others. I have frequently shared my story and can remember speaking about the topic with other Koreans since coming to the United States in 1998. Discussion of this popular question commonly focuses on one of two main themes. Either you were looking for better economic opportunities and believed America to be the land of opportunity, or you sought a quality education for yourself and for your children, so that they too could have a better life. Thus, economic success and education constitute the top two priorities in managing one's immigrant life in America. To attain the two main goals, they are often willing to sacrifice their personal lives, working extended hours and taking on a second or third job. Some do not return to their native country for more than a decade and, therefore, maintain long-distance relationships with family members back home.

In Tucson, Arizona—as well as in the smaller towns where I lived in Florida and Wisconsin—I have encountered newly arrived Koreans each year. The new arrivals often work in low-income jobs and struggle for economic survival. Those who have lived in America for a while tend to be more financially secure and enjoy higher income jobs. They own small or mid-sized businesses, such as restaurants, laundries, retail stores, or accounting offices. Other popular and highly respected professions providing stable incomes include health care, education, insurance, real estate, biotechnology, manufacturing, marketing, pharmaceuticals, and government. Some immigrants have formed Korean organizations, schools, or churches that play central roles in their own community life and offer places where they can meet other Koreans and freely speak their native language.

As an art educator observing those with whom I share a common heritage and value system, I became curious about the role that visual and material culture[2] plays and has played in all of our lives. This would include the visual arts, music, recreation, food, domestic artifacts, dress, hairstyle, architectural styles, newspapers, magazines, and various expressions of popular culture—those things that had defined our cultural lives in Korea, but that are less accessible to us here in America due to our conditions as immigrants living in an adopted country with different social and cultural values than our own. I have often found myself wondering how or to what degree other Korean immigrants have become Americanized or embraced American forms of entertainment or visual and popular culture, what impact they feel this may have on maintaining their Korean ethnic identity, how aspects of traditional Korean cultural practices have remained stable within U.S.-Korean communities, and how Koreans now self-identify themselves in terms of nationality, culture, and ethnicity.

When I conducted a short survey on this topic, most of the Koreans that I polled in Tucson answered that they considered themselves to be Korean or Korean American, not merely "Americans," even though many have lived here for more than two decades and are established among the middle class.[3] Clearly, maintaining their Korean identity and ethnic heritage was important to them, and many felt that they were not fully integrated into American culture. Among the reasons some gave for not fully immersing themselves in or enjoying American culture, they listed the differences in language, food, belief systems, and lifestyle. The results of this casual survey motivated me to undertake a more scholarly study of visual and material culture among the Korean immigrant community in Tucson. First and foremost, I was interested in discovering whether a distinct visual and material culture that could be characterized as Korean truly existed in the US. And if it did, I was curious to identify what the basic characteristics of this visual and material culture might be. Among other interests, I sought to discover and define the social functions of visual and material culture in Tucson's Korean ethnic community life. In this chapter, I will provide a brief description of the Korean community in Tucson before then moving on to an examination of Korean visual and material culture and its role and characteristics. Once this has been accomplished, I will conclude with a discussion of the values and meanings of Korean immigrant visual and material culture and explore the broader application of my findings with regard to the field of art education.

The Tucson Korean Community and Its Ethnic Infrastructure

According to the 2000 U.S. census, about 2,000 Koreans live in the Tucson area. However, most Koreans I have met agree that the actual numbers are now between 3,000 or 4,000, indicating that in the last 8 years a significant number of new Koreans have moved into the Tucson metropolitan area, which hosts a population of around one million.[4] A fairly large percentage of the Korean population includes students enrolled in the universities and colleges in the city.

Relatively speaking, the Tucson Korean community is much smaller than those of Los Angeles, Atlanta, or New York. Nonetheless, Tucson offers many commercial services for Koreans, as well as ethnic programs or events hosted by Korean organizations. The Korean community in Tucson enjoys a well-established economic, social, and cultural support system, which constitutes a significant ethnic infrastructure (Stoller, 1996), and provides for the traditional and emerging needs of its people. This infrastructure includes grocery stores, restaurants, fraternal organizations, churches, ethnic cultural centers, language schools, newspapers, Korean cable or satellite channels, and some Korean Internet sites. Most immigrants highly value these services and activities. Here, I will broadly sketch the outline of the ethnic infrastructure in order to establish the social context to understand their community life.

First, Korean markets and restaurants are one of the most important components of the infrastructure. Although the relatively small Korean population in the Tucson area would not be enough to form a Korean neighborhood or town, many Koreans enjoy the several Korean markets and a Korean restaurant, which also serve as small Korean community centers, offering information about the local immigrant population. Often owners have a large circle of acquaintances and can offer a wealth of information relating to Korean organizations, schools, social groups, or churches in Tucson. They are one of the most popular social venues where Korean community newspapers or journals are freely available, which are essential resources for new immigrants who have difficulty in reading English, and provide important news directly related to their immigrant community life.

There are several nonprofit organizations that also serve Korean residents in Tucson. A Saturday morning Korean school is available for helping children learn Korean language, art, music, and dance. About 70 students from kindergarten to high school level are enrolled at the school. Most of the students are fluent English speakers, and their parents send them to learn Korean, believing that language is important in growing to be a Korean. The school opens every Saturday morning for 3 hours in a local Korean church. Children can also learn about their native traditions and culture at a couple of Taekwondo (Koran martial art and combat sports) schools, and from an Arirang folk dance group that teaches Korean dances. As for fraternal Korean organizations in Tucson, there are the Southern Arizona Korean Association and Tucson Korean American Woman's Association. Both help new immigrants adjust to the city and offer various social activities or events.

Korean churches play a very important role in the lives of many immigrants, serving as community centers where immigrants meet, exchange information, and share Korean foods—going well beyond the organization's basic religious mission. There are eight Korean churches that meet every Sunday. They often host Korean art and cultural events because there is no Korean cultural center in the city. Additional elements of the infrastructure that serve the need of the Tucson Korean community are a dozen Korean-owned Chinese or Japanese restaurants, a couple of beauty salons, several insurance agencies, a few real estate agents, a couple of clothing and wedding shops, a furniture store, an accounting office, and several Korean-speaking medical doctors.

Having undergone the experience of moving and adjusting to new towns several times in the United States, I have observed that most Korean ethnic infrastructures are very loosely connected, so it is not unusual for new members of the community to take several months in order to identify and become familiar with those aspects of the ethnic infrastructure that are available to them. The Tucson area Korean infrastructure is no exception. A Korean moving to Tucson will need some time to get adjusted. For me, it took a couple of months to learn about the community primarily through word-of-mouth because there was no official community guide or booklet. Most Koreans that I have talked to believe that this ethnic infrastructure is an essential part of their immigrant community life, and hope that their ethnic infrastructure will continue to grow and become well-established enough to one day be recognized by the mainstream American society.

Korean Ethnic Visual and Material Culture

In this section, I describe Korean ethnic visual and material culture in Tucson and its characteristics. I believe that this description provides a good example of the significance of studying aspects of visual and material culture when we study ethnic groups of people. This also shows how ethnic visual and material cultural practices play an important role in shaping an ethnic group's community life and identity in a new country. The following description of Korean ethnic visual and material culture is a summary of what I have learned from participation in Korean ethnic organizational activities, informal meetings or interviews with Koreans in Tucson, and my own reflections and observations as one who has lived the experience.

Sustaining and Strengthening Korean Identity

My observations about Tucson Korean ethnic infrastructure, organizational activities, leisure, media consumption, and lifestyle indicate that Korean visual and material culture in Tucson helps immigrants sustain or promote their native identity. Korean markets are places a person can easily be reminded of what life is like in Korea. Whenever I enter in a Korean market, for example, I feel as if I am crossing a cultural border from America to Korea. My thinking, acting, and attitude changes from that of an Americanized persona to that of a Korean. Right away, my ears capture Korean spoken language, and I am under pressure to speak Korean. The customs I learned as a boy living in Korea are revived in my mind. I remember how to act, greet, and talk. I often hear Korean music that I instantly recognize, or spend a few seconds watching a popular Korean TV show or news delivered by a Korean television channel. The visuals, including shop and restaurant signage, advertisement posters, fliers, decorations, newspapers, peoples' manner of dress, etc., make me feel as if I am in a Korean world (Figure 1). I am also naturally attracted to all the Korean words written on cookies, food, beverages, packaged meat, seafood, kitchenware, books, movie videos or DVDs, and cosmetic and beauty supplies.

Restaurants are another place to experience a rich Korean visual and material culture of symbols, characters, foods, music, voices, utensils, or interior decoration. Characteristics of the interior design of these restaurants typically reflect the style of traditional Korean culture by displaying Korean arts and culture that put one in mind of Korea (Figure 2). All these visuals capture my eyes, as I also see Koreans serving and being served. Typical Korean foods tantalize my nose and eyes. It is a place in which Korean is freely spoken. Hearing Korean transactions, music, and other noises made in the process of ordering, serving, and engaging in casual conversation make me feel that I am in a Korean world. As Bolin and Blandy (2003) noted, I use the five senses for hearing music, noises, voices, smelling and tasting the food, grasping the eating utensils, as well as being surrounded by all

Figure 1

Left: Decorated wall with posters or flyers to promote calling cards, a realtor, and Korean churches. Korean markets are one of the few places Koreans can see their native language publicly displayed in North America.

Figure 2

Right: A display cabinet in a Korean-owned restaurant entrance shows traditional wedding and children figurines.

the visual and materials. That kind of feeling of being in a Korean world quickly fades right after I leave that place, seeing all the signs and Western buildings in the street.

Another example of sustained Korean identity involves clothing and hairstyles of Koreans. Hair and clothes are one of the most popular topics discussed among Korean women in particular due to the difference of Korean hairstyles from those of Americans. Koreans often say that they can even distinguish among Korean, Japanese, or Chinese by hairstyle and the way they dress. Many times I have heard Korean women complaining about American beauty salons or clothes. If possible, they prefer to have their children wear Korean brands of clothes, not those found in Macy's or JCPenney because they believe that American brands are not as cute or pretty as those to which they are accustomed. Their favoritism to Korean style often is shown in the way Korean children dress or use a lot of "cute" hair ornamentation. I often observe parents bragging about their kids wearing clothes mailed to them from their family members or relatives in Korea for special occasions.

Their preference for Korean styles over American styles also applies to hair. Many Koreans like to have their hair cut or styled by a Korean beauty stylist. Even for those among the established middle class in Tucson, a visit to a Korean beauty salon is often a requirement whenever they visit a big city such as Los Angeles and San Diego. When they have returned home, you can expect to hear some comments about their changes among Korean friends. I also have seen trendy Korean styled hair and fashion on campus at my university, which is readily distinguishable from the more casual fashion of American students. In fact, it is common to see recently arrived Korean students whose hair and clothes are modeled after Korean actors or actress on television or in movies. Some of these students keep recent images of their favorite cultural icons on their own websites and study their hair and dress style for imitation.[5]

The Internet has played an important role in maintaining and strengthening ethnic and cultural identity for immigrants (Rios & Gaines, 1998; Soruco, 1996; Viswanath & Arora, 2000). It helps many Koreans in Tucson enjoy television programs, movies, and newspapers they would normally have had access to in Korea. The Internet also allows them to follow popular stars' stories, or connect with their Korean friends through on-line chatting, or to construct and update their personal web site to share their American life. Through the Internet, Koreans continually keep up with Korean music, jokes, sports, and news, which helps them sustain their native values, morals, or belief systems. Even though they are surrounded by and interact with Americans and people of other ethnic groups in their workplaces, their evenings or weekends remain to enjoy surfing the Internet looking for Korean sites.

Appropriation of Traditional Cultural Images
Another chief characteristic of Korean visual culture in the US is the appropriation of traditional visual imagery. Images of Koreans in traditional dress, historical sites, cultural heritage, artworks, scenic places, and symbols or maps of Korea are commonly used by merchandisers and restaurants to market their products and to make their patrons feel comfortable. An

Figure 3

The image of *Samtaeguk* is one of the most well-known and easily recognized Korean symbols.

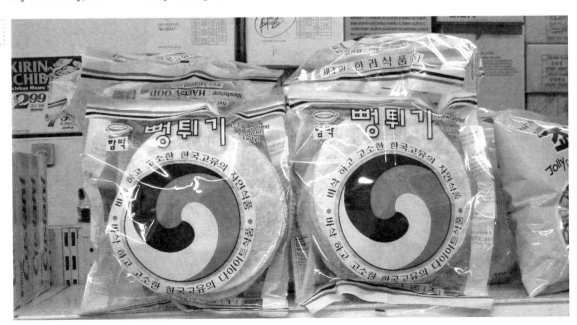

example of a familiar image that appears on various merchandise and media advertisements is the symbol called *Taeguk*, which is representative of the Taoist concept of *Yin* and *Yang* in Korea, and which also appears in the Korean flag. The two colors of blue and red in the *Taeguk* symbolize the world view of dualism. The image on the pop rice (Figure 3) shows a popular variant of the *Taeguk*, which is called *Samtaeguk*. By adding one more color, yellow, which symbolizes human, the three colored shapes are believed to represent the universe in emblematic form: that is, human with heaven and earth. The *Samtaeguk* symbol is commonly seen on Korean fans. A Tucson Korean restaurant also uses the symbol on its signboard.

Gift or souvenir items in Korean markets are another example that shows the appropriation of traditional cultural artifacts and imagery. They often occupy a large section that shows arts and crafts, or are displayed close to the entrance of the store, so most visitors cannot miss them. Some popular items sold are key chains, figurines, refrigerator magnets, chopsticks, fans, decorative masks, coffee mugs, memo holders, or other personal ornaments or accessories. I often hear Koreans discussing what type of gift would be appropriate as a present for American friends or their children's school teachers. The aforementioned gifts are popular choices because they feature traditional Korean motifs, colors, figures, or stories. Interestingly, I have not seen many of these items in the local supermarkets that I have visited in Korea. They are mainly sold at tourist sites, museums, or folk village gift shops, not even in popular department stores or local markets in Korea. However, it is notable that these kinds of artifacts have become very popular items displayed and sold in Korean or other Asian markets in North America. I assume that their popularity is due to their representation of Korean or Asian culture, their attractiveness and distinctiveness, their inexpensiveness, and their highly commercial portability.

Further examples of Korean popular visual culture items include kitchenware, upholstery, and interior decoration intended to imitate Korean traditional houses, which are commonly found in Korean restaurants. Most U.S. Korean homes also display those some sort of decorative objects or images. I have observed pottery, crafts, traditional Korean landscape painting, letter arts or calligraphy, Four Gracious Plants painting, masks, folk painting,[6] folding screens, and chests or cabinets in Korean homes in North America. These are visible indications of the ethnic identity of the house owner. He or she often presents them in a manner that highlights the relative socio-economic status of their household by reference to the quality of the Korean art and crafts.

Traditional Korean images are ubiquitous in commercial advertisements. Korean newspapers or cable, as well as satellite channels, are flooded with them. The websites of Korean organizations or commercial sites also show exclusive use of Korean images, characters, or symbols. Many Korean organizations use South Korean flag on their home page as a symbol. Internet banners on their sites also employ traditional Korean art and craft form to help visitors recognize the maker's nationality and promote a sense of national pride. Even though little research has been done on the commercial use of traditional Korean images in the US, my informal observation indicates that these images are more strongly represented in Korean community media in the US than in similar mass media in Korea. I believe that this appropriation of Korean art and cultural images in the visual media comes from a belief that the most effective advertising method for Koreans in the US is to employ Korean traditional images and, in so doing, to capture the eyes and hearts of Koreans who are surrounded by American visual images and popular media.

Centering Arts in Korean Immigrant Community Life

Koreans often express pride in the fact that Korea has a long history of 5,000 years, and they believe it is important that the second- and third-generation Koreans raised in America should be aware of and learn about their traditions. Along with the visual and material cultural appropriations and adaptations mentioned above, the expression of pride in one's native Korean ethnicity appears in almost every kind of promotional materials for Korean community events or programs in the form of invitational flyers, posters, and media advertisements and commercials. For example, a promotional advertisement I found in a newspaper promoting a party for a Korean immigrant community utilized images of Korean artisans and performance artists to draw the attention of Koreans in the community. The host organization eloquently described Koreans' pride by saying that a banquet had been prepared in order to share their brotherly love, and further stating that the party would present an opportunity for the next Korean generation to learn and enjoy the spirit of their fellow Koreans. Another example of a similar event involved a "Korean Night" that was being held for Korean War veterans who fought for the freedom of South Korea. A full-page invitational advertisement in a Korean community newspaper, called *Korean Today,* expressed great cultural pride by saying that this event would teach our next generation that Koreans are people who express thanksgiving for others' sacrifice, and who show dignity and pride in our beautiful culture and arts.

Most Korean community parties, events, or activities present Korean visual and performance arts rather than Western games or plays. Some typical examples include Korean folk songs, folklore, traditional dance, drum dance, Taekwondo demonstrations, or Korean dress shows.[7] In such Korean community events, Korean foods are usually served, and many Korean children or women wear traditional dresses, called *Hanbok*, which often attract the attention of non-Koreans (Figure 4). Organizers of those programs feel the need of offering those programs, and participants have also come to expect them. It is assumed that Korean community events will show something unique about Korea. The hosts of these programs are aware that people are looking for programs Koreans can enjoy that likewise offer some educational value by teaching the next generation the importance of Korean culture and history. These events or activities also serve to provide opportunities or gathering places where they release the stress of daily life and can forget momentarily their immigrant life far away from their home country by enjoying Korean art, culture, and food.

Here, a comparison of my personal experience and exposure to Korean visual culture in Korea and in the US might provide some further insight. I taught for about six years as a public school teacher in Seoul, before I came to the US. As a teacher I taught Korean traditions and culture, and remember depending on books, visuals, or videos. There simply were not enough opportunities for me as a teacher to watch and enjoy those performances. However, since moving to the US, I have been able to watch many of the cultural programs I had previously missed. When I ask myself why the Korean community in America has put so much emphasis on the arts, I have come to realize more than any other time in my life that the arts are essential carriers of social and cultural values, through which Koreans can "feel" their Korean identity.

Conclusion

In this study, I examined visual and material culture in the Korean immigrant community in Tucson as an example of immigrant ethnic culture in North America. Korean ethnic culture is viable, serving to promote Korean identity through the appropriation of traditional Korean art and culture and, it has been argued, is central to the ongoing sustenance of Korean community life. Many Koreans, at least those of the first immigrant generation, rather than being completely assimilated into American culture, have formed their own unique visual and material cultural practices as an important part of their American experience. They have protected and continued to share among Koreans many forms and expressions of Korean visual and material culture as valuable reminders and communicators of their Korean ethnic identity.

Introducing the study of ethnic and minority cultural practices in the art classroom would benefit students in this era of globalization, mass migrations, and international trade and travel. Considering that the world is getting smaller and future workplaces will become points of international exchange, art teachers can help students study diverse migrant cultures in preparation for engaging migrants as global citizens. Art teachers can take advantage of the fact that diverse ethnic cultural groups and their accompanying visual and material cultures are accessible in communities throughout the US. From being involved in directly studying those localized ethnic cultures, that is, learning by exposure to real settings and people in

Figure 4

The headline story in this popular Korean tabloid newspaper, *Korean Today*, promotes a local party for adopted Korean children.

their neighborhood, students have deeper and richer opportunities to learn about others' belief systems or values beyond the superficial description in textbooks or videos.

Although this study has focused on only one ethnic group, with whom I share a common ethnic and cultural heritage, it is hoped that my study will motivate one to study other ethnic groups—such as African Americans, Europeans, and other Asian groups—and will promote the exploration of other similar locations and contexts while sharing the author's interest in providing art educators with a richer and more unique body of knowledge and content with which they might develop their future art curricula. I believe that through ethnic minority culture studies art teachers and students will pay more attention to these neglected groups of people in the art curriculum, promoting the art and cultural expressions of diverse groups of people in schools (Delacruz, 1995b; Stuhr, Petrovich-Mwaniki & Wasson, 1992).

Lastly, I want to emphasize again that visuals and other materials produced by ethnic groups are expressions that reflect their values, beliefs, morals, and worldview. They often have been neglected in the art classroom, in particular when they are of non-Western origins. This seems due to the misconception that they are trivial or that teaching others about them takes time away from teaching about more highly valued Western fine arts (Delacruz, 1995b). As an extension of multicultural art education that advocates the teaching of art and cultural expression and practices of diverse groups of people in this country (Chapman, 1985; Delacruz,1992, 1995a; Cahan & Kocur, 1996; Garber, 1995; Chalmers, 1996; McFee, 1998, 1991), I hope that many art educators invite students to see the value of others' visual and material cultural expressions.

Acknowledgments
The author thanks the editors for their insightful comments and suggestions on an earlier draft of this book chapter.

REFERENCES

Bolin, P., & Blandy, D. (2003). Beyond visual culture: Seven statements of support for material culture studies in art education. *Studies in Art Education, 44*(3), 214-229.

Cahan, S., & Kocur, Z. (1996). Affirming diversity and humanizing education. In S. Cahan & Z. Kocur (Ed.). *Contemporary art and multicultural education*. New York: Routledge and The New Museum of Modern Art.

Chalmers, F. G. (1996). *Celebrating pluralism: art, education, and cultural diversity*. Los Angeles, CA: The Getty Education Institute for the Arts.

Chapman, L. H. (1985). Curriculum development as process and product. *Studies in Art Education, 26*(4), 206-211.

Delacruz, E. M. (1992). Reconceptualizing art education: The movement toward multiculturalism. In A. Johnson (Ed.), *Art education: Elementary* (pp. 55-76). Reston, VA: National Art Education Association.

Delacruz, E. M. (1995a). Multiculturalism and the tender years: Big and little questions. In C. M. Thompson (Ed.). *The visual arts and early childhood learning* (pp. 101-106). Reston, VA: National Art Education Association.

Delacruz, E. M. (1995b). Multiculturalism and art education: Myths, misconceptions, and misdirections. *Art Education, 48*(3), 57-61.

Garber, E. (1995). Teaching art in the context of culture: A study in the borderlands. *Studies in Art Education, 36*(4), 218-232.

Jung, E., & Lee, C. (2004). Social construction of cultural identity: An ethnographic study of Korean American students. *Atlantic Journal of Communication, 12*(3), 146-162.

McFee, J. K. (1998). Cultural diversity and the structure and practice of art education. Reston, VA: National Art Education Association.

McFee, J. K. (1991). Art education progress: A field of dichotomies or a network of mutual support. *Studies in Art Education, 32*(2), 70-82.

Rios, D., & Gaines, S. (1998). Latino media use for cultural maintenance. *Journalism and Mass Communication Quarterly, 75*(4), 746-761.

Shin, R., & Choi, C. (2006). The art of Minhwa: Korean folk painting as vital element in religion, life, and culture. *Journal of Cross-Cultural Research in Art Education, 24*, 121-134.

Soruco, G. R. (1996). *Cubans and the mass media in South Florida*. Gainesville: University Press of Florida.

Stoller, E. P. (1996). Sauna, Sisu, and Sibelius: Ethnic Identity Among Finnish Americans. *The Sociological Quarterly, 37*(1), 145-175.

Stuhr, P., Petrovich-Mwaniki, L., & Wasson, R. (1992). Curriculum guidelines for the multicultural classroom. *Art Education, 45*(1), l & 24.

Viswanath, K., & Arora, P. (2000). Ethnic Media in the United States: An essay on their role in integration, assimilation, and social control. *Mass Communication and & Society, 3*(1), 39-56.

ENDNOTES

1   According to the Library of Congress Country Studies, there are approximately one million Koreans living in North America, almost all of whom are from South Korea (http://lcweb2.loc.gov/frd/cs/kptoc.html). The North Korean government has prohibited N.K. citizens from obtaining U.S. visas. I have not seen a single Korean from North Korea since I came to the US about a decade ago.

2   In studying immigrant Korean culture, I have adapted an approach of *material culture studies* that advocate studying all human-made objects, forms, and expressions (Bolin and Blandy, 2003). This approach helps me focus on common or everyday objects and expression, and include various sensory experiences such as sounds, smells, and tactility beyond the visual sense alone. However, in this paper I use the term *visual and material culture* to highlight the significant impact of visuals on the experience of Korean immigrants and their culture.

3   In fact, some Koreans who are born in or came to the US at a very early age, prefer to accept being Korean as their ethnic identity rather than being called *American* (Jung & Lee, 2004).

4   Almost all Korean residents in Tucson have obtained legal status as U.S. citizens or permanent residents, or have a visa that allows them to live in the country as a student, worker, or visitor. This contrasts with those of other ethnic immigrant groups living in the city illegally, yet comprising a significant part of the city population.

5   Based on my observation of some Korean students, it is clear to me that they feel it is important to keep up with the hair and fashion trends of Korean popular stars, although this may vary from student to student and largely seems to be an extension of their personality.

6   For more information on Korean folk images in paintings or other decorative items, see Shin and Choi's (2006) article, "The art of *Minhwa*: Korean folk painting as a vital element in religion, life, and culture," *Journal of Cross-Cultural Research in Art Education*, 24.

7   Some examples of Korean arts and cultural events that one can see in Tucson and the Phoenix area, which are hosted by Korean community organizations, are the Arirang Festival, Korean Culture Night, Korean Night for Korean War veterans, feast in deference to the aged, Korean new year, the full moon harvest party, the party for Korean adopted children, and a Korean Independence Day concert.

The Nature and Notion of Museums in the Age of Globalization

Martina Riedler

Museums in their modern sense came into being during the Age of Enlightenment and have evolved through the politically significant and influential transformation of royal collections (Duncan, 1995). More specifically, royal collections were culled, amplified, and rearranged to construct a grand narrative that could present a universally valid and reliable world picture. Such institutions, according to Hooper-Greenhill (2000), "were established by proud city fathers or by nations newly celebrating their political identities [that] saw themselves as separate from the mundane world of the everyday, as standing for higher, purer values" (pp.14–15). As a result, national museums began to take on a vital role in the protection and preservation of the national patrimony, and the public museum, now conceived of as a pedagogical tool for the masses, became an instrument for advancing national character through education (Bal, 1992).

During the last two decades, however, international and global connections have led to a shift in the history of power of Western museums, and this transformation has become central to the current circumstances of museums and other display institutions. That is, because, in simple terms, *globalization* refers to contemporary phenomena like the worldwide flow of information, capital, people, goods, ideas, and culture that encompass all domains of life and permeate any boundaries (see Sassen, 2002), the concept of a globalized museum differs noticeably from more traditional museological perspectives. Most particularly, this shift in perspective has resulted in a series of rapid positive and negative changes in the ways that museums are constructed, experienced, and understood. Thus, additionally to the contribution of postmodern 'new museology' literature (see Crimp, 1993; Karp, Kreamer, & Lavine, 1992; Sherman & Rogoff, 1994), museums as classic centers for cultural production and representation deserve new attention, especially with respect to the policies and practices they develop in response to the effects, issues, and challenges of globalization. This paper examines these developments from three different theoretical perspectives: the utilitarian, the oppositional, and the transformational. The paper also throws light on the challenges of policy formation when museums are no longer understood as mere cultural centers of a particular geographical region but expand beyond the political and geographic boundaries of nation states. Exploring these complex issues from multiple stances should provide insights into the changing relationship between the museum's local, national, and international role in knowledge and cultural production at a time when globalization has led to a reexamination of the role of culture and its relationship to nationalism and identity formation.

Museums for Cultural Tourism: A Utilitarian Perspective

Those who argue for a utilitarian viewpoint support the idea that globalization provides marvelous new tools for changing the nature and policies of museums, tools that can have beneficial effects on a developing global culture and improve museum practices for global and local transformation. For example, Macdonald (1996) argued that

> museums occupy an intriguingly paradoxical place in global culture ... Bound up with much that is heralded to be nearing its end—stability and permanence, authenticity, grand narratives, the nation-state, and even history itself—their numbers are growing at an unprecedented rate. (p. 1)

This utilitarian perspective offers a useful lens through which to examine many key issues of globalization's impact, including the reinterpretation of national and regional collections for an increasingly multicultural society; conservation concerns related to the traveling of artifacts; the continuing debate over the ownership of international collections; and questions of identity and heritage, commoditization, historical and cultural representation, authenticity and ownership, neoliberalism, and homogenization.

Utilitarians have proclaimed that globalization can transform museums into global cultural tourism centers that can create authentic cultural experiences for tourists in the face of increasing globalization (see Kirshenblatt-Gimblett, 1998, 2006; Meethan, 2001; Smith, 2003). These exhibition centers can set in motion cultural tourism in local communities and aid in the development of the local economy. For instance, diasporic communities have returned to Ghana to visit sites associated with slavery (Kreamer, 2006), while community museums in Mexico are using cultural displays to affirm their solidarity with migrants in the United States (Camarena & Morales, 2006).

As these examples indicate, cultural tourism as a vehicle for cultural exchange and understanding can provide a visitor with a mix of educational and entertaining experiences of another community, region, or cultural group. A range of platforms, development-orientated activities and opportunities for discussions are offered. The fact that these experiences should be authentic in turn promotes the conservation and preservation of hereditary cultural values and rituals and traditional building and craft skills. By organizing these authentic events to attract high income educated travelers, cultural tourism can contribute significantly to a regional economy and redevelopment by bringing in more money spent per visit and encouraging longer stays.

As a result, some institutions are transforming themselves to reap the benefit of globalization, and global franchising has seemingly become an overriding determinant of exhibition content as defined by occidental art history. For instance, at the end of the 1990s, the Guggenheim, under foundation director Thomas Krens, was considered the defining force of the new contemporary art museum because of expanding the Guggenheim 'brand' in New York's Soho, Berlin, Las Vegas, and Bilbao and pursued additional satellite museums in Austria, Brazil, Taiwan, and Mexico in the same way that the Big Mac has been dispersed and made available to the world as a uniform commodity. Likewise, while local cultures and ethnicities around the world are increasingly repackaging themselves to meet the tastes and interests of consumers, global products are being repackaged to seemingly appeal to local markets. Accordingly, by dividing into several branches, the museum can lay claim to representing a world-class collection and exhibition program and producing a universally valid global art world.

By and large, however, many believe that the Guggenheim Museum Bilbao and other planned satellites involve so much real estate and architecture that they seem made more for tourism and corporate capitalism than the art world (Alberro, 2005; Werner, 2005). For example, even though Krens announced his retirement in early 2008, he will continue to serve as a consultant for the new Guggenheim in Abu Dhabi, the capital of the United Arab Emirates ("Progress on the Guggenheim Abu Dhabi," 2008). Similarly, in 2007, the French Ministry of Culture signed contracts for the Louvre Abu Dhabi, a branch of the Parisian museum to be built on the emirate state's Saadiyat Island ("Art in the Desert: 'Louvre Abu Dhabi' Gets Green Light," 2007). Such institutions almost always work with finished artifacts and tend to play it safe. Therefore they do not immediately draw interest of an art connoisseur or professional. Additionally there is little to no space for interaction or discussion with artists and critics.

As these Euro-American museums position themselves between the local and the global, the West and the East, the Self and the Other, the museum is perpetuating an imperialist notion at the expense of particular groups. That is, a gap in epistemological authority continues to exist between exhibition creators and their subjects, and between museum professionals and visitors, which raises the question of whether, as museums expand, capitalist culture might not replace local and indigenous forms of cultural expression.

Globalization's Impact on Museums: An Oppositional Perspective

Those who go beyond the utilitarian and neutral positions oppose or resist globalization, countering that the impact of global forces on museums will progressively destroy the last vestige of our humanity and cultural diversity (see Rothkop, 1997; Cowen, 2002). Most particularly, they fear that societies are becoming exposed to the homogenizing effects of global markets that provide a superficial new world of consumer choice and identity options (Skramstad, 1999). At the same time, those who feel that their identities are undermined hold on to and reassert their familiar traditional cultures and identities (see Welchman, 2006) with the danger of "retreat[ing] into fortress identities" (Robins, 1999, p. 22). Some have also argued that, in this materialistic and technologically driven world, a major function of museums is to support human values against the technical and economical which is mostly represented through mainstream media (Wu, 2006). Thus, in general, oppositionists have criticized the view of museums as sites for global cultural tourism and consumerism by identifying the potential negative effects of increased tourism to particular destinations, including environmental degradation, strain on local infrastructure, and the so-called Disneyfication or commodification of treasured cultural resources.

Among such oppositionists, Kirshenblatt-Gimblett (2006) claimed that globalization creates paradoxes and ironies in relation to the homogenization and universalization of the display world. Specifically, she analyzed the process by which the United Nations Educational, Scientific and Cultural Organization (UNESCO) chooses, codifies, and preserves tangible, intangible, and natural heritage in an effort to create global cultural commons. Criticizing the arbitrary nature of such authoritative and universalizing operations, she argued that the discourse of heritage prioritizes the rights of consumers to access global heritage over the needs of those whose habitus is transformed into heritage. Likewise, Bunn's (2006) investigation of border control in the South African Kruger National Park showed how colonial and apartheid era border control hid impoverished rural black communities from tourist routes or even incorporated them as model villages for tourist consumption, leaving descendents with no meaningful connection to their land and a feeling of emptiness.

At the same time, many critical theorists have argued for the importance of analyzing and revealing social justice problems like domination, alienation, and repression to create an equal and just representation in society through museums (see Garoian, 1999; Lindauer, 2007; Wexler, 2007; Young, 2002). Critical theorists have also argued that through the formal and hidden strategies and policies, many museums reconstructed through globalization are organized to produce and reproduce the dominant categories and values necessary for maintaining dominant global social and economic relations (Kirshenblatt-Gimblett, 2006; Lee, 2003). As a result, these museums provide no meaningful opportunities for visitors and local communities to generate their own meanings and personal knowledge. Rather, they continue to reproduce modernist museum messages that involve the passive absorption of isolated bits of information rather than supporting the active construction of knowledge through engagement with ideas in meaningful contexts. Indeed, according to oppositional theorists, despite the profound changes of the nature and contexts in which museums operate the issue of representation and voice still poses a particular challenge to the museum because they traditionally upheld the aura of the object and granted the viewer unmediated access to a frozen past and an elitist, Euro-American view.

A number of essays in *Museum Frictions: Public Cultures/Global Transformations* have identified globalization as an uneven process that results in new inequalities. For instance, in addressing the political,

economical, and social issues of the Guggenheim Bilbao Museum, Fraser (2006) made it clear that Bilbao residents, many of whom work in low-paying service sector jobs, rarely visit the Guggenheim. Admittedly, building this museum revived the Basques' hope and discussion of permanently transfering Pablo Picasso's *Guernica* (1937) to the new museum instead of the far-off Reina Sofía Museum in Madrid. However, officials of both museums rejected the transfer of this Basque icon because of its supposed fragility and thus disavowing the Basques' interest. Likewise, Witz (2006), in a careful discussion of the workings of a range of postapartheid South African museums, described the frustrations of the residents of the peripheral township of Lwandle (Cape Town) that the development of a local Migrant Labour Museum took precedence over their immediate need for housing. Similarly, in a case study of individuals and institutions left out of triumphalist accounts of globalization in Cambodia, Muan (2006) described a stale national museum showing no evidence of engagement with the reflexive museology of the 1990s. She concluded, given that most Phnom Penh residents have limited mobility and access to new media, the packaged meat aisle in a Lucky Market might create a greater sense of wonder and awe than Cambodia's National Museum.

Hence, theoretically, an oppositional perspective identifies museums as institutions that deconstruct the ongoing regime of global dominance and its hegemonic structures of regulation and control to give voice to the needs and expectations of unrepresented minority groups and local cultural communities. In reality, however, the small number of minorities and indigenous groups that have had solo exhibitions in past years makes it difficult to say that today's museums are successfully providing opportunities for unrepresented groups and communities. Accordingly, oppositionists argue, if contemporary art museums are to become sites for social justice and equality, certain political and ideological questions must be examined in the light of ideologies of globalization and the complexities of the nation-state: Whose knowledge is presented in museums? Why is it being presented to a particular group in a particular way? What are its real or latent functions in the complex connections between cultural power and control (Apple, 1990) These questions are central to the development of socially just art museums in the age of globalization because

the very nature of museums as repositories for knowledge and objects of value and visual interest makes them key institutions in the production of social ideas in many nations. Museum collections and activities are intimately tied to ideas about art, science, taste, and heritage. Hence, they are bound up with assertions about what is central or peripheral, valued and useless, known or to be discovered, essential to identity or marginal. (Karp, 1992, pp. 6-7)

At the same time, developing oppositional or critical museum practices requires a critical examination of the relationships among globalization (versus a national sphere), knowledge construction, ideology, and power in the museum context in terms of several dynamics:

- Developing an understanding of how the relationship between the museum's mission and the social and historical context of the museum community shapes visitors' views and understanding of museum collections and displays;
- Developing an understanding of how the relationship between the museum's context and social, political, and economic forces of globalization shape visitors' views and understanding of museum collections and displays;
- Examining the control of language and discursive practices linked to the existing and unequal distribution of power, goods, and services in museums.

Indeed, many critics have argued that globalization cannot be understood as a simple process of homogenization; instead, it must be seen more as a process of negotiation, hybridization, transformation, democratization, and/or glocalization (see Mayo, 2004; Robins, 1999).

The Museum as a Site for Democratic Empowerment: A Transformational Perspective

Beyond the utilitarian and oppositional perspectives lies the transformational view that the forces of globalization will replace or radically transform the basic definition of museums, which mainly valorize concepts from a Western perspective. However, even though this position envisions an essentially positive end result, the process itself is not without difficulties. According to transformationalists, the task is to understand and guide this transformation by identifying and establishing museums as sites for dialogue, conversation, negotiation, democratization, social participation, and community development undertaken through a global frame (see Borg & Mayo, 2006; Friman, 2000; Hooper-Greenhill, 1999; Sandell & Dodd, 2001). Consequently, from a transformational perspective, museums should aim to understand the needs of visitors, local communities, and underrepresented groups, develop more supportive, collaborative engaging learning scenarios, and become

more inclusively democratic. By doing so, museums can promote and support peace and the strengthening of democracy and good governance globally.

Indeed, some South African museums were supposedly founded on the ideas and principles of peace, social justice, democracy, and governance. However, it remains questionable whether museums have the power and ability to act on and deal practically with issues of race, peace, conflict, and reconciliation, instituting democratic processes, and working with diversity in the community. According to Karp (2006), despite substantial African collections, these so-called transformational museums have actually become cultural history museums organized essentially to display the superiority of European culture over African culture. Accordingly, they have changed their names and are now known as MuseuMAfricA or the African Window. Despite these problems, some of these museums' displays provide excellent examples of transformational and transformative museum practices. For example, in Johannesburg's MuseuMAfricA, a visitor can "become a mine worker going down into the mine, subject to the abusive language of [the] bosses" or attend "one of the major apartheid trials, in which photographs of all the participants who were charged in the trial were put up around the room..." (Karp, 2006, p. 5). After emphasizing the need for audience participation in a small society like South Africa, Karp described this latter experience as follows:

As people came in, they began to document what happened to these people, many of whom had just disappeared: so and so went into exile; him, he died in Tanzania; so and so disappeared; so and so was killed by the apartheid police. People turned the exhibit into a form of mourning for people lost and celebration of changes to come. It became a transformative and cathartic way of engaging with society. (p. 5)

In times of global change, the museum may shape the tension between tradition (museums as a nation-state's cultural tradition) and contemporary adaptation to new paradigms (like cultural diversity, democratic participation, spaces of cultural activity that exist in the non-Western world). Whereas 18th- and 19th-century museums may be seen as agents of nation-state construction, contemporary institutions are under pressure to adapt to an unidentified future that may already be past at the time of reaction. Nevertheless, museums and alternative display institutions (such as biennials) within a transformational framework must take on significant political and social functions to provide a common democratic bond that allows citizens to think of themselves as part of a local and global community.

A transformational perspective identifies museums as democratic and educational sites for a community of learners who construct museum practices as an interactive process between the community's present and future in the context of globalization. Such democratic museums encourage visitors to respond to objects not simply as art critics but as politically aware members of a community. They also provide opportunities for the museum community to move beyond the particularistic politics of class, ethnicity, race, and gender to develop an empowered democratic community that stresses difference within unity. Central to such empowerment is a notion of community developed around a shared conception of social justice, rights, and equality.

Another excellent example of a democratic-transformative museum is the District Six Museum, also in Cape Town, South Africa, established in December 1994 in a Black suburb destroyed by the White regime. According to its website (http://www.districtsix.co.za), the museum "is committed to telling the stories of forced removals, and assisting in the reconstitution of the community of District Six and Cape Town by drawing on a heritage of non-racialism, non-sexism, anti-class discrimination and the encouragement of debate." The museum also functions as a forum, a meeting place of conversation and dialogue; in which debate and policy development is initiated. Overall, as Karp (2006) pointed out, the transformational acts of the District Six Museum board

> involved revising history, providing voices for people to articulate experiences that had otherwise been silenced. They brought in new personnel. They altered the sense of who owned objects and how collections could be used. They created a kind of partnership between museum and community, [in which] the museum is the instrument of community development, a location of identification for the community, and as such a place for community debate about identity and the future. (pp. 5-6)

The District Six Museum and other transformative museum examples indicate that museums as institutions that operate on behalf of society and for the public good must use their knowledge and resources, their programs and collections, to relate to the more critical issues of their time on local, national, and global levels. By doing so, they can become institutions for social development and agents for change and thus highlight different topographies of power. On the other hand, the District Six Museum also exemplifies the role that global Western actors play in the transformation of the museum into a democratic institution in that for some time the museum was funded first by the Swedish African Museum Program and then by the Rockefeller Foundation. In recent years, an increased attention by Western museums to the contemporary arts of the non-Western world has resulted in new global relationships, which have changed the dynamics between centers and margins that predominantly structured the exhibitionary world. Transnational networks of scholars, artists, and museum professionals have formed to analyze these faces of globalization; for example the *Global Art and Museum Project* ([GAM] at www.globalartmuseum.de), which explored the impact of art globalization on art institutions, art history, and the art market through a global and comparative frame (Buddensieg & Weibel, 2007). Thus, if the goal is to develop a critical practice on a global scale the formation of new alliances, exchanges and structures may contribute to alter our art history maps. Accordingly, some oppositionist museum experts and researchers have questioned the role that global Western actors play in museum transformation in order to demonstrate how complex, complicated, and partial museum transformation is in the age of globalization.

Conclusion

Because new museum content and policies are continually emerging and co-existing as new forces of globalization are created, the nature and function of museums in the age of globalization will most certainly continue to change. As a result, future conceptions of the nature and function of museums in a globalized world will no doubt differ from today's perceptions. Nevertheless, to clarify these latter, this paper has examined globalization's impact on the nature and context of museums from three different theoretical perspectives, perspectives that, however, are not the only possible approaches. Further studies are needed to investigate other means of defining or identifying the characteristics and patterns of museums and exhibitionary functions that co-exist in the current globalized world. The three theoretical perspectives employed here assist this endeavor by suggesting a useful and consistent sequence of potential goals to guide research and practice in the field of museum studies.

REFERENCES

Alberro, A. (2005). *Museum highlights. The writings of Andrea Fraser*. Cambridge, MA: MIT Press.

Apple, M. W. (1990). *Ideology and curriculum*. New York: Routledge.

Art in the Desert: 'Louvre Abu Dhabi' gets green light. (2007, March, 7). *Der Spiegel*. Retrieved March 21, 2008, from http://www.spiegel.de/international/0,1518,470356,00.html

Bal, M. (1992). Telling, showing, showing off. *Critical Inquiry 18*(3), 556-594.

Borg, C., & Mayo, P. (2006). Museum education as cultural contestation. In *Learning and social difference: Challenges for public education and critical pedagogy* (pp. 75-89). Boulder, CO: Paradigm.

Buddensieg, A, & Weibel, P. (2007). *Contemporary art and the museum. A global perspective*. Osfildern: Hatje Cantz.

Bunn, D. (2006). The museum outdoors: Heritage, cattle, and permeable borders in the Southwestern Kruger National Park. In I. Karp, C.A. Kratz, L. Szwaja, & T. Ybarra-Frausto (Eds.), *Museum frictions: Public cultures/ global transformations (pp. 357-391)*. Durham: Duke University.

Camarena, C., & Morales, T. (2006). Community museums and global connections: The union of community museums of Oaxaca. In I. Karp, C.A. Kratz, L. Szwaja, & T. Ybarra-Frausto (Eds.), *Museum frictions: Public cultures/ global transformations (pp. 322-344)*. Durham: Duke University.

Cowen, T. (2002). *Creative destruction: How globalization is changing the world's cultures*. Princeton, NJ: Princeton University.

Crimp, D. (1993) *On the museum's ruins*. Cambridge: MIT Press.

District Six Museum in Cape Town: http://www.districtsix.co.za/

Duncan, C. (1995). *Civilizing rituals: Inside the public art museums*. London: Routledge.

Fraser, A. (2006). Isn't this a wonderful place? A tour of a tour of the Guggenheim Bilbao. In I. Karp, C.A. Kratz, L. Szwaja, & T. Ybarra-Frausto (Eds.), *Museum frictions: Public cultures/ global transformations (pp. 135-160)*. Durham: Duke University.

Friman, H. (2000). A museum without walls. *Museums Journal, 100*(8), 28.

Garoian, C. (1999). *Performing pedagogy: Toward an art of politics*. Albany, NY: State University of New York.

Global art and museum project [GAM] at www.globalartmuseum.de

Hooper-Greenhill, E. (1999). Education, communication and interpretation: Toward a critical pedagogy in museums. In E. Hooper-Greenhill (Ed.), *The educational role of the museum* (pp. 1–27). London: Routledge.

Hooper-Greenhill, E. (2000). Changing values in the art museum: Rethinking communication and learning. *International Journal of Heritage Studies, 6*(1), 9-31.

Karp, L., Kreamer, C., & Lavine, S. (Eds.). (1992). *Museums and communities: The politics of public culture*. Washington: Smithsonian Institution.

Karp, I. (2006). *Panel discussion: Transformation in the college museum. Conference transcript editing by S. Goodwin & K. Gallien* (2006, April 8). Retrieved February 23, 2007 from http://tang.skidmore.edu/documents/downloads/o-u/Transformation_in_College_Museum.pdf

Kirshenblatt-Gimblett, B. (1998). *Destination culture: Tourism, museums, and heritage*. Berkeley, CA: University of California.

Kirshenblatt-Gimblett, B. (2006). World heritage and cultural economics. In I. Karp, C.A. Kratz, L. Szwaja, & T. Ybarra-Frausto (Eds.), *Museum frictions: Public cultures/ global transformations (pp. 161-202)*. Durham: Duke University.

Kreamer, C. M. (2006). Shared heritage, contested terrain: Cultural negotiation and Ghana's Cape coast castle museum exhibition 'Crossroads of people, crossroads of trade.' In I. Karp, C.A. Kratz, L. Szwaja, & T. Ybarra-Frausto (Eds.), *Museum frictions: Public cultures/ global transformations (pp. 435-468)*. Durham: Duke University.

Lee, P. M. (2003, November). Boundary issues: The art world under the sign of globalism. *Artforum International, 42*, 164-167.

Lindauer, M. (2007). Critical museum pedagogy and exhibition development: A conceptual first step. In: S. Knell, S. MacLeod, & S. Watson (Eds.), *Museum revolutions: Museums and change* (pp.303-314). London: Routledge.

Macdonald, S. (1996). Introduction. In S. Macdonald & G. Fyfe (Eds.), *Theorizing museums: Representing identity and diversity in a changing world* (pp. 1-18). Oxford: Blackwell.

Mayo, P. (2004). Engaging with practice: A Freirean reflection on different pedagogical sites. In *Liberating praxis: Paulo Freire's legacy for radical education and politics* (pp. 125-150). Westport, CT: Praeger.

Meethan, K. (2001). Creating tourism spaces: from modernity to globalization. In *Tourism in global society: Place, culture, consumption* (pp. 16-40). Hamshpire: Palgrave.

Muan, I. (2006). Musing on museums from Phnom Penh. In I. Karp, C.A. Kratz, L. Szwaja, & T. Ybarra-Frausto (Eds.), *Museum frictions: Public cultures/ global transformations (pp. 257-285)*. Durham: Duke University.

Progress on the Guggenheim Abu Dhabi (2008, February). Retrieved April 11, 2008, from http://www.guggenheim.org/news/index.html

Robins, K. (1999). Tradition and translation: National culture in its global context. In D. Boswell & J. Evans, J. (Eds.), *Representing the nation: A reader – histories, heritage and museums* (pp. 15-32). London: Routledge.

Rothkop, D. (1997, June 22). In praise of cultural imperialism? Effects of globalization on culture. *Foreign Policy*. Retrieved September 26, 2007 from http:www.globalpolicy.org/globaliz/cultural/globcult.htm

Sandell, R. (2002). Museums and the combating of social inequality: Roles, responsibilities, resistance. In R. Sandell (Ed.), *Museums, society, inequality* (pp. 3–23). London: Routledge.

Sandell, R., & Dodd, J. (2001). *Including museums: perspectives on museums, galleries and social inclusion*. Leicester: Research centre for museums and galleries, University of Leicester.

Sassen, S. (Ed.). (2002). *Global networks, linked cities*. New York: Routledge.

Sherman, D., & Rogoff, I. (1994). *Museum culture: Histories, discourses, spectacles*. London: Routledge.

Skramstad, H., (1999). An agenda for American museums in the twenty-first century. *Daedalus, 128*(3), 109-128.

Smith, M. K. (2003). The impact of cultural tourism. In *Issues in cultural tourism studies* (pp. 45-61). London: Routledge.

Vergo, P. (Ed.). (1989). *The new museology*. London: Reaktion Books.

Welchman, J. C. (Ed.). (2006). *Institutional critique and after*. Zurich: JRP/ Ringier.

Werner, P. (2005) *Museum, Inc.: Inside the global art world*. Chicago, IL: Prickly Paradigm.

Wexler, A. (2007). Museum culture and the inequities of display and representation. *Visual Arts Research 33*(1), 25–33.

Witz, L. (2006). Transforming museums on postapartheid tourist routes. In I. Karp, C.A. Kratz, L. Szwaja, & T. Ybarra-Frausto (Eds.), *Museum frictions: Public cultures/ global transformations (pp. 107-134)*. Durham: Duke University.

Wu, D. (2006). *Cultural hegemony in the museum world*. Paper presented at the INTERCOM 2006 conference and annual meeting in Taipei, Taiwan. Retrieved April 26, 2008, from http://intercom.museum/documents/2-5Wu.pdf

Young, L. (2002). Rethinking heritage: cultural policy and inclusion. In R. Sandell (Ed.), *Museums, society, inequality* (pp. 203–211). London: Routledge.

Transnational Dialogues Dealing with Holocaust Legacies

Karen Frostig

As an educator and daughter of a Holocaust survivor, I am preoccupied with abuses of power and notions of relationship. Feminist criticism as a political orientation[1] informs my work as an artist, scholar, activist, educator, author and theorist. Feminism also sheds light on the development of this essay.

This past summer I assembled a large portfolio of archival documents, and met with officials from the Office of Immigration in Vienna to establish my father's Austrian citizenship, 69 years after his exile and 36 years after his death. The bureaucratic hoops that I had to jump through were significant. Since my father was born in Poland in 1911 and moved to Vienna as an infant, I had to find a number of documents that would substantiate his citizenship. Given that all the documents were written primarily in German, Portuguese, and Spanish (only a smattering of U.S. documents were in English), I could not decipher much of the content. As a result, the selection process was largely intuitive. I also had to meet with Austrian immigration officials and narrate my father's story of escape with adequate knowledge, so that his plight as a refugee would never be construed, at any point, as a situation where he had willingly forsaken his homeland. Having been arrested by the Gestapo in 1938, and having had his entire family, except his two siblings, murdered by Hitler's armies, I was now in the surreal position of defending my father's unwavering allegiance to Austria.

Immigration officials were required to make a legal case for my father's citizenship based on their review of 60 pages of his documents. They correlated specific dates representing changes in Austrian law, concerning policies for dealing with Jews, with actions that my father took on his own behalf, in an effort to rescue his family. Without recourse, he was expelled from Austria in 1938. When his German passport expired while in Cuba, the German consulate refused to renew it, all exquisitely documented in his records. Under these unusual circumstances, becoming a U.S. citizen and serving in the U.S. Navy did not refute his Austrian citizenship. In a discussion that extended over five pages, the officials concluded their arguments by asserting various dates and claiming that, as his descendant, I too am an Austrian citizen. Furthermore, according to detailed calculations, I have always been an Austrian citizen!

This fact is significant to me on many levels. As an artist searching for funds from the Austrian government in support of a public project dealing with Holocaust legacies, I am no longer perceived as an outsider, I am now an insider. In terms of language, schooling and a general affinity for Austrian culture, however, I remain at a distance, cautious, sustaining a fractured attachment to my father's homeland.

In 2006, prior to learning about my Austrian citizenship, I submitted a conference proposal, entitled "Austrian Funding Practices Regarding Post-War Projects Dealing with Holocaust Legacies" for the 2006 32nd Annual *Social Theory, Politics and Art* (STP&A) international conference.[2] The conference was to take place in Vienna, at the Academy of Fine Arts, (the very art school that had rejected Hitler as an aspiring artist in 1908).[3] By attending this conference, I was, in effect, breaking the code of silence that had encased my family for a half a century. The conference became the stage upon which I would begin the process of reclaiming my German Jewish heritage.

The paper for the conference presented research that tracked how I, as an artist and daughter of a Holocaust survivor, approached a nation for funding, while examining that nation's culpability and subsequent handling of past transgressions. I posed a series of questions: How does the process of reparation and the restoration of silenced Jewish voices back into mainstream culture relate to Austria's record of funding artistic projects by children of survivors? What is the nature of the interdependent relationship between children of perpetrators and children of survivors, moving toward a shared understanding of paired legacies? What is my relationship to my father's homeland? Finally, what is Austria's position regarding children of survivors of the Holocaust embarking on a journey of "return," both physical and metaphysical? In my discussion (Frostig, 2006), I noted how my own readiness to tackle family history paralleled Austria's willingness to address its troubled past, evidenced by a recent flurry of government-sponsored programs regarding Holocaust legacies.

The Vienna Project

In the process of interviewing various Austrian officials from the cultural ministry about Austria's holocaust history, I began to consider opportunities to exhibit a new body of work about my family's history in Vienna. Dr. Martha Keil, Director of The Institute for History of the Jews in Austria, expressed interest in my project and offered to partner with me so that I would be eligible to apply to the National Fund of the Republic of Austria for Victims of National Socialism for funding support.[4] She also had a contact at the University of Vienna School of Law, where my father earned a Doctorate in Law and Economics in 1936.

The Vienna Project entails the production of 18 memory panels. An exhibition of 12 "Erinnerung aus dem Exil/Exiled Memory" panels, were installed at the University of Vienna's Institute for Law and Philosophy at the Juridicum on November 25, 2008. An international conference "Vertriebenes Recht," hosted at the time of the opening, was designed to further contextualize the exhibition and also mark the start of a new body of curriculum dealing with the period of "lawlessness" between 1938-1945. The conference formally explored the question of "What happened to Austrian Jewish lawyers, graduates of the University of Vienna, after 1938?"[5] In addition, the exhibition encompassed a gallery talk with university students, providing new insights about art as a social means of stimulating critical discourse.[6]

"Transnational Dialogues Dealing with Holocaust Legacies" reflects my triple-edged experience of: (a) trying to recover my family's Holocaust history, while establishing an independent relationship to Vienna, largely to children of perpetrators; (b) negotiating Austrian receptivity and support for a new body of work aimed at stimulating fresh dialogue between children of survivors and children of perpetrators; and (c) examining how my status of Austrian citizenship complicates my relationship to Austria, the locus of my voice, and the criticality of my work.

The Letters as Evidence

Qualitative research methodologies resemble artistic practice in both spirit and scope. Analytic and associational processes trigger new ideas and observations that can prompt additional questions and produce fresh contexts. In *The Vienna Project*, I combine photography with autoethnographic practices to become a participant observer of contemporary Viennese culture. Embracing a feminist, self-reflexive model of investigation, the camera lens becomes my lens. In addition, I am interviewing numerous histori-

ans, archivists and museum curators, and use family archival documents to resurrect a portrait of Viennese culture in 1938. Situated as primary narrator and direct descendent of murdered Holocaust victims, I am both outsider and insider of contemporary Viennese culture. In *The Vienna Project*, I join cultural discourse with creative cultural production to develop a critical reading of historical events that inform my family's Holocaust legacies.

Each aspect of the research informs other components of the project. The project was initiated by the translation of 68 letters written to my father between 1938-1941 from my grandparents, before their deportation to Riga. The letters constitute primary source material[7] and serve to organize the various channels of research.

Figure 1

Karen Frostig, *Beile Samuely and artist*, 2005. Photomontage. Passport photos of my grandparents hung on the wall in my home growing up. Scanning the photo of my grandmother required that I remove the photo from the frame, disturbing the vacuum of silence that enshrined the two photos for 60 years. Posing as my grandmother, I insert my photo into the blank space, as background tile. For the first time, we share the same space.

Following the death of the last of three family Holocaust survivors in 2004, I received a packet of letters, held together by a simple band of elastic. These letters crossed the Atlantic three times. These letters traveled from Vienna to eight countries, five U.S. states, and 17 cities. They were passed between the three sole survivors of my family, given first to my aunt upon my father's death, then to my uncle upon my aunt's death, and finally to me. Becoming the latest guardian of these letters and filing claim for war-time restitution from the republic of Austria, I began the arduous process of reconstructing my family's history. Through this process, I became a secondary witness[8] to my grandparents' execution and considered anew my transnational identity as the daughter of a Holocaust refugee in exile.[9] (See Figure 1.)

The Vienna Project entails numerous forms of investigation. I am using a digital SLR to clinically document my emotionally charged encounter with Vienna, the city where my father grew up, and the outskirts of Riga, the city where my grandparents were murdered.[10] In addition to meeting with historians, archivists and curators, I am conducting a literature review and writing position papers and grant proposals, as well as delivering an assortment of papers at various international conferences. I also developed a series of paintings and digital photomontages and am working with digital production technicians to ensure that the work is produced according to specifications.

Scanning historical documents meant that I needed to locate low-light, archivally-sensitive scanners used by museums when recording light-sensitive material. The process of scanning the letters and turning them into digital files became a fascinating component of the project. No longer fixed entities,

the letters became incorporated into my world, my temporal reality. I was now able to engage in a virtual inter-textual dialogue, not constrained by language or distance, measured in time or space. I was free to integrate my experiences as outsider, time traveler, visitor to the forsaken homeland, into the insider space of text and page.

Analysis of the letters produced new information. My grandfather, Moses Frostig, and my grandmother, Beile Moskowitz Samuely, were the two primary speakers, with rare guest appearances from a few uncles and aunts.[11] Missing information was substantial and troubling.[12] This could be attributed to the fact that the Nazis censored all correspondence out of Austria. Each letter was numbered and checked off, and some words were blackened. Swastika stamps infiltrated the letters, communicating the regime's authority to control content and screen information that might otherwise trigger unwanted, international scrutiny.

The letters contained lots of repetitions. The focus was primarily about urgent plans for emigration, i.e. securing appropriate visas, passports, money for landing tax, and boat tickets with specified cabin numbers. My grandparents were trapped in a climate of fear, and the letters were punctuated by anxious questions regarding each child's safety, closing with a refrain of hope for the reunification of the family. References to the Jewish community and networks of escape were present in the earlier letters, slowly fading as time went on. Isolation mounted.

Yiddish syntax was prevalent throughout, and many letters contained passages written in Hebrew. The passing of time was expressed through the Jewish calendar, noting holidays, birthdays, and also evictions and moves to new addresses, and the exodus of

Figures 2, 3

Left: Letter written by my grandmother, Beile Moskowitz Samuely, to her son, Benjamin Frostig, 1938; Postcard written by my grandmother, Beile Moskowitz Samuely, to her son, Benjamin Frostig, 1940. My grandmother's hand is fairly shaky in the postcard.

Figures 4, 5

Right: Letter written by my grandfather, Moses Frostig, showing his embellished and buoyant handwriting; Later postcard written by my grandfather, Moses Frostig, showing his later cramped and angular handwriting. The numbers under the "A" indicate that the card was censored.

trainloads of children by the Kindertransports.[13] Brief mention of new taxes and restrictions on Jews was noted and surprisingly, not censored.

The physical appearance of the letters also changed over time. Early on, the script was graceful and fluid, embellished and hopeful. As the months passed, the make up of the text became increasingly constrained, cramped, angular, and shaky. The use of paper also changed, going from airmail stationery to scrap graph paper and small postcards, moving from private to public and from space to no space (Figure 5). The availability of international stamps diminished, as did the size of script and the amount of blank space per page. Writing would occur in the margins and even around the address. According to the dates, the frequency of the letters also decreased, indicating that

letters may have been lost or never arrived. The content of the letters corroborated these observations.

In the vibrant, cultural capital of Vienna,[14] 1938-41 marked a dark, pre-genocidal era filled with unbridled racism and hatred of Jews. Working as an artist and scholar, I juxtapose my seemingly benign encounters of Vienna with my grandparents' letters to create a more complete portrait of my father's homeland. The memory panels deliver a critical reading of how I, as the daughter of a Holocaust survivor, reconcile traumatic memory with the sweet yearnings to embrace the full complexity of my cultural heritage.

Memory Panels

The artistic component of this project deals with time travel and collaboration. I become an active participant as narrator of my grandparents' story.[15] The memory panels "Erinnerung aus dem Exil/Exiled Memories" become ancestral conversations, developed as digitized photomontage. I use three divergent layers of imagery: the letters, stills of Vienna, and paintings of open wounds, bruised patches, and

pools of carnage, scanned into a digitized format. The photos and paintings are located in the stratum below the letters, bleeding upward toward the surface, in effect, creating an interior dialogue, a text event, within the letters. At times, these inter-textual events appear to overwhelm the letters, shifting perspectives from the personal to the historical narrative and from foresight to hindsight.[16] Playing with different opacities, the layers collapse and fragment, recreating lost and imagined connections to my murdered ancestry across the great chasm of time.

From the thousand or so stills shot of Vienna, I selected a number of emotionally charged images that worked as metaphorical code, connoting acts of perpetration committed by the murderers, by-standers, and thieves of Vienna upon 65,000 of its Jewish citizens.[17] The blood from the "Carnage Series" seeps into work denoting widespread violence, bloodshed and murder, while connoting the "one drop rule" as a measure of racial selection (Saltzman, 2006, p. 62).

The letters appear as a veil or filter to the photos, which function as a disruptive presence to the letters. The images register as an unsettling fusion of tourist snapshots and a serious effort to document sites of past criminal activity. The images read as pilfered objects, compromised renderings of a time lost.

Haunting, animating, and informing the text, the images also shed light on a past by continuing the narrative into the present. My family's story unfolds in a double timeline, as a dual narrative: one strand historic, the other contemporary; one strand text, the other image; and one strand authentic and vulnerable,

Figure 6

Left: Envelope from one of my grandparents. The swastika occurred on many of the postcards and the envelopes, which were also covered with multiple stamps. The letters were also numbered and some of the sentences were blackened.

Figure 7

Karen Frostig, *Co-collaborators,* 2005. Photomontage.

the other critical and subversive. As a descendent of murdered victims, my voice is, by definition, a defiant voice, confronting murder with the jolt of survival. The hindsight of genocide situates me, as a post-witness, precariously positioned between memories of past atrocities and a peculiar form of hospitality, extended to me, in present day Vienna. Issues of trust permeate the work.

The panels function as memory-scapes, evoking a sense of place. Devoid of a horizon and vanishing point, the panels convey an empathic, meandering and encompassing space. The text serves as time portals, entry points.

The longing to populate the unknown with the known, to go to the edge of the abyss, is a reoccurring preoccupation, in the lives of many children of survivors. Mass murder dehumanizes people.[18] To retrieve my grandparents' voices from pending oblivion is to reclaim their histories as individuals, re-inscribing their lives with dignity. "Erinnerung aus dem Exil/Exiled Memories" recovers my grandparents' voices, while repudiating the intent to silence through murder. Speaking across barriers of time and language, my voice woven into the text as image, represents continuity in the face of finality.

Estrangement in Education

Current trends in education privilege the power of the system over the individuals that system is designed to serve. The common thread that bridges a discussion of my family's Holocaust history with a critique of the U.S. education system concerns the meaning of institutional to personal relationships such as that which exists between students and schools. Without an understanding of relational experience, human interactions divide along lines of power, privileging one group over another. I am particularly concerned about those human interactions that favor expediency and predictability over intimacy, complexity, and depth of meaning.

I use feminist concepts of "voice," grounded in ideas about relationship and inclusivity, to illuminate troubling issues brewing in today's schools. Voice and mutual regard are feminist concepts that impact classroom environments: "Our capacity to generate excitement is deeply affected by our interest in one another, in hearing one another's voices, in recognizing one another's presence," declares bell hooks (1994, p. 8). "Radical pedagogy must insist that everyone's presence is acknowledged" (hooks, p.8).

Finding voice sits at the center of feminist activist art and pedagogy, which has as its "long-term goal, the critique and dismantling of patriarchal systems

of power" (Flanagan, Gonzales, Girls, Machida, Meskimmon, & Rosler, 2007, p. 19). Voice, used interchangeably with ideas of empowerment, also conveys expansive notions of inquiry. Both terms imply crossing borders, transgressing limits, and moving beyond what is known.[19]

Cultivating deep inquiry in response to personally derived questions about a wide spectrum of topics is both congruent with artistic practice and constructivist pedagogy in the 21st century, as well as with democratic principles regarding ideas about choice and freedom. Constructivism is an inquiry-based pedagogy, which promotes deep understanding (not imitative behavior). Teachers are interactive, seeking the students' point of view, "posing problems that hold relevance to students' lives" (Brooks & Brooks, 1999, p. 35). Becoming active participants rather than passive consumers, inquiry-based models of investigation place students' ideas and questions at the center of learning. Favoring inquiry and critique as a method of engagement in visual arts education, many progressive thinkers talk about the power of education to liberate.[20] Kerry Freedman, a leading theorist in art education, insists that current concepts of freedom in education must "supersede old assertions that democratic education was to simply provide equal access to excellence... Contemporary curriculum [must tackle] the more complex systems of freedom, individualism, equity, and social responsibility" (2003, p. 106).

It is my contention, that in spite of or directly contrary to this progressive movement in educational theory, current U.S. educational policy and practice has disturbingly moved in the opposite direction with the ever-growing, accountability-driven standards movement. I am particularly concerned about the most recent permutation of this movement–the No Child Left Behind Act (NCLB)–and the misguided over application of standardized educational methods in this and related U.S. nationalized testing policies.[21] Such practices seriously compromise meaningful learning in the lived experience of the classroom, and place emerging concepts of social responsibility at risk. The underlying rationale for the national standards and testing movement rests on the belief that high expectations and the setting of predictable, measurable and reliable goals lead to strong schools and sound education. However, accountability must also recognize and support relational experiences between teachers and students, the need for development of personal and communitarian identities and connections, and an understanding of the value of imagination and the creative processes. These kinds of outcomes are not measurable by any reliable, repeatable, one-size-fits-all national test, and their fruits are seen both in terms of the quality of the relationships and bonds that form within classrooms and, ultimately, in terms of the kind of society that builds from such rich and rewarding educational experiences. Arts theorist, Peter Renshaw (2005), warns:

> ...higher arts education institutions [must] understand and respect the fundamental distinction between explicit knowledge, in which targets can be measured in quantifiable, mechanistic terms, and tacit knowledge which is more intuitive, reflexive and learned in very particular situations...Arts institutions and schools have to rise to this challenge and ensure that the intrinsic value of creative experience is not trivialized by simplistic forms of assessment (p. 112-113).

Imposing a prescribed and mediated set of objectives onto teachers and students ultimately impedes open-ended inquiry and filters voice. The formulaic, impersonal and authoritarian nature of nationalized standards categorically disregards student-initiated investigations. In standards-based educational formulations, students are expected to solve problems pre-determined by teachers, administrators, or state officials. At best, students can modify exemplars, not reinvent the problems. Rubrics, which represent a fixed evaluative scale, determined in advance by supposed curriculum or content experts, measure a student's ability to conform to preset expectations. In a standards-driven educational mindset, students are rewarded for following directions and are penalized for demonstrating independent thinking or too much voice. Control of classroom discourse and elimination of distractions from the agenda is central to the success of such a mindset. The fruitful reciprocity between discreet cognitive/affective/aesthetic/ perceptual processes—choosing, selecting, examining, interpreting, discovering and evaluating—is devalued in standards-driven authority-dominated classrooms.[22]

Teachers are often as much at a loss as their students in such a scenario, coerced by an authoritative educational system and a mindset that favors, again, predictability and control over nuance and complexity. Teaching in this system is regimented, limited to that which appears on the list of what is to be taught. The schedule and the agenda, and student performance on preset ideas and skill sets are all encompassing. The stakes are high in that teachers, schools, and communities are then reported to and judged by an increasingly impatient public, a public that has also been led to believe in the national myth of standardization and testing.

By emphasizing the need to follow directions over the need to ask questions, we all lose sight of one of the most profound lessons of the Holocaust: the breach of relationship.[23] We must reclaim open spaces in curriculum as legitimate arenas for new learning that validate independent thinking. Challenging regimented rules that disempower teachers and students alike must go hand in hand with the development of flexible and locally relevant standards that support student-centered initiatives and sustain relational experiences between teachers and students.

Conclusion

This chapter, entitled "Transnational Dialogues Dealing with Holocaust Legacies," pertains to my family's Holocaust history, the evolution of *The Vienna Project*, and concludes with a discussion about misguided authoritarian, educational practices and implications for relational and ethical development. *The Vienna Project* animates my voice as an active, relational, moral presence, bridging the past with the here and now. The project is as much about using the instrument of memory to create a visual field of protest regarding war and genocide as it is about longing for ancestry and wrestling with my German-Jewish transnational identity.

I have made linkages here between my own family history, my recent painful investigations into a past filled with trauma, suffering, and unspeakable human atrocities, and finally with speculations about how a nation originated around notions of democracy and social justice, the US, now sets forth its own aspirations through a heavy handed and ill conceived discourse about educational means and ends. Challenging the national discourse of high stakes standardized testing, I see evidence that the U.S. public at large seems to buy into this system uncritically. Lost in the national standardization movement is the impulse to question, to imagine alternate realities, and to create alternate futures.

How to engage students as active participants in a run-away world full of strife and moral complexity calls for the development of a receptive educational environment that invites questions and discourages passivity. I can only wonder had German and Austrian children been evaluated according to the quality of their questions and their relational capacity, rather than the extent of their obedience,[24] whether we, the children of survivors, would have inherited a different kind of legacy.

REFERENCES

Aagerstoun, M. J., & Auther, E. (2007). Considering feminist activist art. *NWSA Journal: A Publication of the National Women's Studies Association, 19*(1), vii-xiv.

Apel, D. (2002). *Memory effects: The Holocaust and the art of secondary witnessing*. New Brunswick, NJ: Rutgers University Press.

Brandauer, A. (2000). Practicing modernism: "...for the master's tools will never dismantle the master's house..." In N. Mirzoeff (Ed.), *Diaspora and visual culture: Representing Africans and Jews* (pp. 254-261). New York: Routledge.

Brooks, J. G., & Brooks, M. G. (1999). *In search of understanding: The case for constructivist classrooms*. Alexandria, VA: Association for Supervision and Curriculum Development.

Coining a word and championing a cause: The story of Raphael Lemkin. (October 5, 2007). Retrieved January 19, 2006, from http://www.ushmm.org/wlc/article.php?lang=en&ModuleId=10007050

Efland, A., Freedman, K., & Stuhr, P. (1996). *Postmodern art education: An approach to curriculum*. Reston, Virginia: The National Art Education Association.

Felshin, N. (Ed.). (1995). *But is it art? The spirit of art as activism*. Seattle: Bay Press.

Flanagan, M., Gonzales, J., Girls, T. G., Machida, M., Meskimmon, & M., Rosler, M. (2007). Feminist Activist Art, a Roundtable Forum. *NWSA Journal: A Publication of the National Women's Studies Association, 19*(1), 1-22.

Freedman, K. (2003). *Teaching visual culture: Curriculum, aesthetics, and the social life of art*. New York: Teachers College Press.

Frostig, K. (2006). *Austrian funding practices regarding post-war projects dealing with Holocaust legacies*. Paper presented at the Social Theory, Politics and the Arts (STP&A) 32nd Annual Conference, Academy of Fine Arts Vienna, Vienna, Austria.

Future Fund. Retrieved June 6 2006, from htp://www.zukunftsfonds-austria.at

History. Retrieved June 6 2006, from http://www.ikg-wien.at/static/etis/html/start.htm

hooks, b. (1994). *Teaching to transgress: education as the practice of freedom*. New York: Routledge.

Institute for the History of Jews in Austria. Retrieved June 6 2006, from http://www.injoest.ac.at/

Kindertransport, 1938-1940. Retrieved January 18, 2006, from http://www.ushmm.org/wlc/article.php?lang=en&ModuleId=10005260

Laqueur, W. (Ed.). (2001). *The Holocaust encyclopedia*. New Haven: Yale University Press.

McEvilley, T. (1991). *Art &discontent: Theory at the millennium*. New York: McPherson & Company.

Miles, M. (Ed.). (2005). *New practices—new pedagogies: A reader*. New York: Routledge.

Mirzoeff, N. (Ed.). (2000). *Diaspora and visual culture: Representing Africans and Jews*. New York: Routledge.

National Fund of the Republic of Austria. Retrieved June 6 2006, from http://www.nationalfonds.org/

No Child Left Behind. Retrieved January 20, 2008, from http://www.doe.mass.edu/nclb/

Renshaw, P. (2005). Connecting conversations. In M. Miles (Ed.), *New practices—new pedagogies: A reader* (pp. 99-116). New York: Routledge.

The Rise of Adolf Hitler: Hitler fails art exam. (1996). Retrieved June 6, 2006, from http://www.historyplace.com/worldwar2/riseofhitler/art.htm

Saltzman, L. (2006). *Making memory matter*. Chicago: University of Chicago Press.

University of Vienna, Department for Legal Philosophy, Law of Religion and Culture. Retrieved January 18, 2006, from http://www.univie.ac.at/recht-religion/en/index.html

Young, J. E. (2000). *At memory's edge: After-Images of the Holocaust in contemporary art and architecture*. New Haven, CT: Yale University Press.

ENDNOTES

1   Aagerstoun and Auther characterize feminist activist art as "simultaneously critical, positive, and progressive. By critical we mean work that seeks to explore underlying ideologies or existing structures that have a negative effect on women and their lives; by positive we mean work that takes a stand....by progressive we mean a belief in the feminist tenets of equality and inclusiveness, a better world free of sexism, racism, homophobia, economic inequality, and violence." (Mary Jo Aagerstoun and Elissa Auther. "Considering Feminists Activist Art" in Aagerstoun, M. J., & Auther, E. (Eds.), *NWSA Journal: A Publication of the National Women's Studies Association*, Bloomington, IN: Indiana University Press, 2007, p. vii).

2   "The conference on Social Theory, Politics and the Arts (STP&A) is an international and inter-disciplinary gathering of researchers, policy makers and practitioners that highlights [current and] conceptual and empirical issues concerning cultural policy, social theory, and arts administration practices in the U.S. and abroad." *STP&A*. (From http://stpa.culture.info/)

3   *The Rise of Adolf Hitler: Hitler fails art exam October 1907*. (From http://www.historyplace.com/worldwar2/riseofhitler/art.htm)

4   *Nationalfonds* was established in 1995, using Austrian government funding from the Ministry of Financing (not restitution funds), allocating 1-2 million euros per year to international artists dealing with projects concerning Austria's Holocaust history *during* the war. Another fund, the Reconciliation Fund, is an alternate fund that expired in 2003 and was closed in 2005. The new Future Fund was established in January 2006, in an effort to redistribute remaining funds. Additional money comes from Austrian enterprises, the Austrian government, and private contributions. The mission of the fund is to support scientific projects that have a connection to enforced slave labor. All application material must be submitted in German, which places applicants who do not speak German (such as some children of survivors) at a disadvantage. This fund is the only existing fund that I found, supporting cultural projects dealing with the Holocaust, that receives applications from non-Austrian citizens. *Nationalfond*. (From http://www.nationalfonds.org/; *Future Fund*. From http://www.zukunftsfonds-austria.at/)

5   Austria was annexed by Nazi Germany under the "Anschluss," in March of 1938. The Nuremberg Laws were immediately implemented, depriving Jewish citizens of their civil liberties. Jews were barred from attending school, the university, and could no longer own businesses or work. In the early months, large numbers of Jews, especially those regarded as the intelligentsia, were arrested and deported to Dachau. Many lawyers either fled or were arrested and expelled from Vienna at that time. (Walter Laqueur, (Ed.). *The Holocaust Encyclopedia*. New Haven: Yale University Press, 2001, p. 44-49).

6   Critical discourse, in this context, refers to naming the unspeakable silence that surrounds the childhoods of many children of survivors and children of perpetrators. This form of dialogue is akin to what Felshin describes as "'changing the conversation,' to empower individuals and communities." (Nina Felshin, "Introduction" in Nina Felshin, ed., *But Is It Art? The Spirit of Art as Activism*. Seattle: Bay Press, 1995, p. 26). The Vienna Project in its entirety, encompasses Felshin's discussion of [feminist] activist art: "Activist art, in both its forms and methods, is process- rather than product- or product-orientated, and it usually takes place in a public sites rather than within the context of art-world venues...A high degree of preliminary research, organizational activity, and orientation of participants is often at the heart of its collaborative methods of execution, methods that frequently draw on expertise from outside the art world as a means of engaging participation of the audience or community and distributing a message to the public....Whether the form of these activities take is permanent or impermanent, the process of their creation is as important as its visual or physical manifestation" (Felshin, 1995, 10-11).

7   These letters corroborate the tendency to equate evidence with text "the real thing, consisting of ink on paper." (Aline Brandauer, "Practicing Modernism" in Nicholas Mirzoeff, ed., *Diaspora and Visual Culture*. New York: Routledge, 2000, p. 259).

8 In the literature, I have come across a variety of terms referring to children of survivors, who vicariously witnessed the Holocaust through their parents: secondary witness, post-witness, belated witness, and vicarious witness.

9 The Vienna Project invokes Drewal's discussion of African theories of agency: "memory and agency" paired with "legacy and action." (Henry John Drewal, "Memory and Agency," in Nicholas Mirzoeff, ed., *Diaspora and Visual Culture.* New York: Routledge, 2000, pp. 241-43).

10 The memory panels invoke what Young refers to as "aesthetic interrogation of the Holocaust." (James E. Young. *At Memory's Edge: After-Images of the Holocaust in Contemporary Art and Architecture.* New Haven, CT: Yale University Press, 2000, p. 5). The work also speaks to the "postwar generation's preoccupation with not having been "there" but still being shaped by the Holocaust." (Young, 2000, pp. 9-10).

11 Translator: Ingrid MacGillis. In reading the translated letters I learned the names of three new relatives (and their addresses), who were among the 16 members of my family, murdered in the Holocaust.

12 In the first few weeks after the Anchluss, thousand of Jewish homes were looted, Jews were randomly arrested, beaten, publicly humiliated, even murdered without consequence. A number of transports took Jewish "prisoners" to Dachau. Applying for emigration, Jews were required to wait in long lines, were routinely attacked, thrown in front of moving trams; property was confiscated through eviction and Jews were relocated to cramped "Judenhausen" (houses for Jews easing deportation roundups). The letters also omitted mention of the Kristallnacht program, on November 9, 1938, when 42 synagogues and prayer halls were burned, 27 Jews killed and 6,547 persons arrested; and on September 21, 1941, when Jews were forced to wear the yellow star. Although the letters indicated that Jews were no longer welcome in Austria, specific facts about changing conditions were only intonated. (Laqueur, 2001, 46).

13 Kindertransports (Children's Transport) "was the informal name of a rescue effort, which brought thousands of refugee Jewish children to Great Britain from Nazi Germany [which included Austria] between 1938 and 1940." (From http://www.ushmm.org/wlc/article.php?lang=en&ModuleId=10005260)

14 In 1918 there were 300,000 Jews in thirty-three communities within Austria, including 185,000 in Vienna. By March 1938, Austria was annexed by Nazi Germany under the Anschluss. Soon after, the Nazis enacted the Nuremberg Racial Laws, whereby Jews lost all of their civil liberties. Nazis encouraged emigration, and as a result, nearly 130,000 Jews left Austria. Following the *Wanassee Conference* in January of 1942, invoking the resolution to completely destroy the Jewish race in Europe, more than 65,000 Viennese Jews were deported to concentration camps. Only 2,000 Jews survived the war, 800 by remaining in hiding. *History.* (From http://www.ikg-wien.at/static/etis/unter/html/gs_index.htm)

15 Apel refers to as *traumatic realism:* "Representations are chronologic, traversing time from then to now; artists retell the story while telling their contemporary conditions of the telling of the story, thus bringing the recognition of the present to bear not only on our understanding of the past, but also on the effects of the past in the present." (Dora Apel. *Memory Effects: The Holocaust and the art of secondary witnessing*, New Brunswick, NJ: Rutgers University Press, 2002, p. 7).

16 Completing the textual narrative with photographic images, delivering contextual information, is a variation on what McEvillery describes as the postmodern use of "quoting." Artistic quotes are riddled with irony and contradiction, providing new content: "Through quoting, the process of representation is simultaneously acted out and criticized: its cultural-conventional roots are laid bare at the same moment they exercise their effects upon us." (Thomas McEvilley. *Art & Discontent: Theory at the millennium.* New York: Documentext McPherson & Company, 1991, pp. 92-93).

17 The panels engage the audience as spectators, re-enacting the earlier stance of bystander. This strategy is consistent with Walker's formulation of audience "...prompt[s] us to consider not just history, but its legacy in the present...we are implicated as spectators, in the depicted scenarios." (Lisa Saltzman, *Making Memory Matter.* Chicago: University of Chicago Press, 2006, p. 71).

18 Genocide, a relatively new term coined by Raphael Lemkin in 1943, in the aftermath of the Holocaust, refers to the [systematic] "destruction of a nation or an ethnic group." *Coining a Word and Championing a Cause: The story of Raphael Lemkin.* From http://www.ushmm.org/wlc/article.php?lang=en&ModuleId=10007050. Genocide erases individual identities. Making genocide real and personal by developing individual narratives, counteracts the impersonal nature of mass murder. In The Vienna Project, I use my voice in the form of image production to reveal my grandparents' narrative, thus engaging my audience with the tragic legacies of genocide.

19 "The engaged voice must never be fixed and absolute but always changing, always evolving in dialogue with a world beyond itself" (hooks, 1994, p. 11).

20 Hooks differentiates between "education as the practice of freedom and education that merely strives to reinforce domination" (hooks, 1994, p. 4). For further reading on this topic, see John Dewey, Paulo Freire, Parker Palmer, bell hooks, Robert Fried, Karen Keifer-Boyd, Jonathan Kozol, Neil Postman, Audre Lorde, Paul Duncum, Olivia Gude, Deborah Meier, Ted Sizer, David Perkins, and many more.

21 The No Child Left Behind Act (NCLB) signed by President Bush in January of 2002, is the "principal federal law affecting education from kindergarten through high school. NCLB is built on four pillars: expanded local control and flexibility; doing what works based on scientific research; accountability for results; and more options for parents." The NCLB act called for the implementation of educational "standards" (formerly known as outcome-based education) designed to ensure quality education for all children enrolled in the public schools. (*No Child Left Behind.* From http://www.doe.mass.edu/nclb/).

22 Postmodern theorists, such as Efland, Freedman, and Stuhr contend that curriculum entails a "continual flux influences and shapes understanding, and that this flexibility of knowledge is vital because it enables creative thought" (see Arthur Efland, Kerry Freedman, & Patricia Stuhr, *Postmodern Art Education: An approach to curriculum.* Reston, Virginia: The National Art Education Association, 2006). According to Efland, postmodern curricula has a lattice or web-like structure, which invites the learner to pursue meanings in multiple directions along many routes of intellectual travel" (Efland, Freedman, & Stuhr, 2006, p. 115).

23 Murder represents the ultimate breach of relationship, the complete absence of empathic regard.

24 I am referring here, to intellectual unruliness.

Never Again:
A (K)night with Ben

Wanda B. Knight

Look carefully at the face of the enemy. The lips are curled downward. The eyes are fanatical and far away. The flesh is contorted and molded into the shape of monster or beast. Nothing suggests this [person] ever laughs, is torn by doubts, or shaken by fears. [The enemy] feels no tenderness or pain. Clearly [s/he] is unlike us. We need have no sympathy, no guilt, when we destroy her/him.

In all propaganda, the face of the enemy is designed to provide a focus for our hatred. [S/he] is the other. The outsider. The alien. [S/he] is not human. If we can only kill [her/him], we will be rid of all within and without ourselves that is evil.

—(KEEN, 1986, P. 16)

The above passage by social psychologist Samuel Keen illustrates how so-called *normal* people and war-justifying nations dehumanize particular groups of people, making them *enemies*, to rationalize ethnic violence or to justify war against them. A commonly noted example, in Nazi Germany, is Adolf Hitler's deliberate and systematic extermination of millions of European Jews and other alleged "Untermenschen."[1] To illustrate this deliberate and systematic extermination, the Nuremberg trials (1945-1946) of Nazi war criminals legally applied the term "genocide." Subsequently, the Genocide Convention (adopted by the United Nations in 1948) was intended to be a promise that the horrific crimes of the Holocaust would "never again" be repeated. However, since that time, the world community has failed to prevent similar atrocities around the globe (e.g., in Rwanda, Bosnia, Cambodia, and Northern Iraq). Considering these atrocities and human rights abuses, and the United States' history of the decimation of indigenous American Indian cultures, the lynching of African Americans and the internment of Japanese Americans in California during WWII, leading German artist Käthe Kollwitz's 1924 drawing, titled "Nie Wieder Krieg!" ("Never Again War!"), represents a cry that is as relevant today as it was following WWI (see Figure 1). If history serves as a guide, it should not appear alarmist to associate pre-genocidal societal behavior with the existing United States political and cultural climate. Particularly, in view of the United States' self-proclaimed global leadership on the *war on terror*, its current pervasive anti-immigration and anti-Arab sentiments, racial profiling, policies and practices of intense surveillance, unlawful detainment, and civil rights abuses at Abu Ghraib and Guantanamo Bay, a particular sector of humanity is seen as enemy, as inferior, as dangerous, as disposable.

In an age of globalization, how effective is education in awakening critical stances and enabling visions of global peace and social justice, and what strategies can be used to deal with human rights

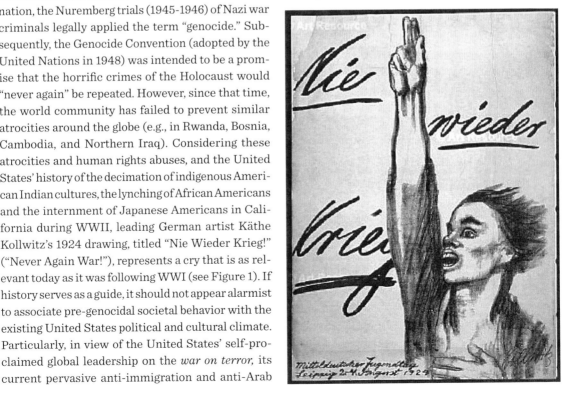

atrocities, genocidal histories and "difficult sites" such as concentration camps? Certainly, invisibility and epistemological ignorance should be never again! Some histories are perpetuated in education while other more "difficult" histories are avoided. Here, my focus is on the histories that have been ignored in art classrooms and how those histories are connected to issues today and relevant for art education content.

During July 2007, while on a flight from the United States to Germany to attend the Horizons International Society for Education Through Art (InSEA) Art Education Research and Development Congress, I had the great fortune to sit beside historical figure Benjamin B. Ferencz, chief prosecutor for the United States in the Nuremberg Trials. Our night together was filled with stories about our seemingly parallel efforts to eradicate oppressive systems that deny social justice in democratic societies. From our conversation, I learned that Ben[2] was the chief prosecutor in the Einsatzgruppen (special extermination groups) Case, characterized as the "biggest murder trial in history." In the Einsatzgruppen Case, 22 defendants were charged with murdering over a million people. All were convicted, and 13 were sentenced to death. Ben was only 27 years old, at the time. The Nuremberg trial was his first case.

While enlisted in the United States Army, Ben served under the command of General George S. Patton. Further, he fought in every campaign in Europe. Subsequently as lawyer, educator, and activist, Ben has devoted his entire life to combating genocide and crimes against humanity.

Ben was 88 years old at the time of our meeting, in 2007. Born in 1920, in Transylvania, Ben grew up in Hell's Kitchen in New York. A graduate of Harvard Law School, he founded the Pace Peace Center at Pace University, in New York City, where he is currently adjunct Professor of International Law.

Ben's work for global justice has evolved in phases. First, he worked hard to find the perpetrators and prosecute them. Next, he expended much time and energy to help restore victims to a state of wholeness through a concept he originated, known as reparations. Currently, he works towards preventing genocide and fulfilling the promise of "Never Again." Imagine the global impact if every child and teacher visualized this promise and was aware of the practices and policies that have kept it from being fulfilled. A thoughtful tracing of the use of images, slogans, and selective reporting leading up to the genocide of Jews–prior to and during WWII–provides one way to interrogate practices of instilling fear, anger, and hatred. This chapter weaves this history with contemporary times, looking for strategies to educate teachers and students (through art) to be agents of change for social justice.

To Create an Enemy	To Make a Friend	Figure 2
Start with an empty canvas. Sketch in broad outline the forms of men, women, and children.	Start with a complete portrait of humanity. Sketch in particulars that highlight the unique character of each individual.	To Create an Enemy, To Make A Friend.
Dip into the unconscious well of your own disowned darkness with a wide brush and stain the strangers with the sinister hue of the shadow.	Dip into the well of consciousness your own responsibility to self-enlightenment with a delicate brush and reveal the humanity of persons tarnished by decades of stereotypes.	
Trace onto the face of the enemy the greed, hatred, carelessness you dare not claim as your own.	Trace onto the face of one unlike yourself eyes of one who is generous, loving, considerate like others you know.	
Obscure the sweet individuality of each face.	Show the sweet individuality of each face.	
Erase all hints of the myriad loves, hopes, fears that play through the kaleidoscope of every finite heart.	Add the distinct myriad loves, hopes, fears that play through the kaleidoscope of every finite heart.	
Twist the smile until it forms the downward arc of cruelty.	Stretch the smile so that it forms an upward arc of kindness.	
Strip flesh from bone until only the abstract skeleton of death remains.	Add layers of flesh to bone until the concrete embodiment of life emerges.	
Exaggerate each feature until man is metamorphasized into beast, vermin, insect.	Enhance each feature until humanity is metamorphasized into friend, family, ally.	
Fill in the background with malignant figures from ancient nightmares—devils, demons, myrmidons of evil.	Fill in the background with reputable figures from ancient dreams—saints, guardians, myrimidons of good.	
When your icon of the enemy is complete you will be able to kill without guilt, slaughter without shame.	When your portrait of the friend is complete you will be able to embrace with sincerity, love without inhibition.	

The thing you destroy will have become merely and enemy of God, and impediment to the scared dialectic of history.

Keen, 1986

The individual you create will have become quite a friend, an ally and a contributing member to our global society.

Knight, 2008

How can we as teachers relate the lessons of the Holocaust to our students' lives today or to current world events? How can we integrate, throughout the curriculum and in other educational contexts, lessons learned from the Holocaust?[3] What conversation might you have with young people, or people of any age, in looking at images of difficult sites, like concentration camps?

Visual culture has great power to create enemies. Because enemies are socially constructed, an important first step is to examine how they are created. By interrogating visual culture practices of instilling hatred, we are in a better position to see people that we perceive unlike us as individual human beings.

In Figure 2, in the column on the left side, Sam Keen uses a template derived from a collection of over 300 political images to convey how an enemy is created. In the column on the right side of that same figure, I have re-visioned the template as opposite to humanize abstractions and to reflect upon ways to make a friend from the images of enemies drawn from the global spread of visual culture.

Art educators might use this parallel list to create or critique historical and contemporary images of propaganda and stereotypes. Consider how the faces of the enemy are created in relationship to how the faces of an ally are made. Analyze how the face of the enemy is designed to provide a focus for our fear, anger, and hatred. In what follows, I describe various selected factors that contribute to enemy making. In doing so, I consider parallels to the relevance in art education pedagogical practice.

Globalization, Ethnocentrism and the Perpetuation of Eurocentric Norms

Ethnocentrism is considered one of the United States' worst societal or pathological problems (Goodman, 2002). Ethnocentrism is the tendency to look at the world primarily from one's own culture and entails the worldview that one's own culture is superior and the base of normalcy from which to judge others. People who are ethnocentric tend to judge what they perceive as different or strange, as being backward, primitive, bad, or stupid. Creating and maintaining classrooms that affirm difference requires art educators to have an awareness of their own worldview. Worldview refers to the way in which one looks out on the universe (Spradley & McCurdy, 1990). It includes our values, beliefs, and assumptions, or the way in which we perceive "the Other" (Knight, 2006a).

Ethnocentrism is inextricably linked to globalization and Eurocentrism. Globalization means different things to different people. Some see it as a blessed state of global peace and prosperity, while others perceive it as a new form of chaos (Chandra, 2003; see Tavin & Hausman, 2004, for a discussion of Art Education and Visual Culture in the Age of Globalization). While I believe that globalization has some utility, my argument sees *globalization* as a euphemism for *Westernization,* which is a form of colonization and perpetuation of Eurocentric norms. Globalization of Eurocentric norms—particularly Westernization in an "Americanized" form—is ethnocentrism that attempts to wipe out pre-existent cultures and destroy local self-government to reinforce global dominance by those who hold political, economic, and social power.

In considering the interplay between ethnocentrism, globalization and Eurocentrism, it is important to note that my "critique of Eurocentrism is addressed not to Europeans as individuals but rather to dominant Europe's historically oppressive relation to its internal and external [*others*] (Shohat & Stam, 2004, p. 3). Moreover, my critique is not meant to imply that globalization does not have favorable aspects such as increased opportunity for free trade and travel, and interaction between cultures and societies; yet, globalization has created unprecedented wealth for some nations and left others mired in abject poverty. This imbalance in power and wealth distribution between industrialized nations and developing countries affects the rules of global engagement (Chandra, 2003). Further, my analysis of ethnocentrism is not intended to negate the fact that it is okay to be proud of one's heritage, country, and culture; nevertheless, ethnocentrism can lead to extreme nationalism. This nationalism can then be used to justify racism, violence, and war against those characterized as "the Other." Next, I interrogate selected practices of instilling fear, anger, and hatred.

Weapons of Terror and Terrible Weapons: Image Matters, Visual Culture Practices of Instilling Fear, Anger, and Hatred

We live in a culture increasingly dominated by visual imagery. The history and persistence of degrading images, used in propaganda and stereotypical representations of negative reference groups (e.g., Blacks, American Indians, Latina/Latinos), have served to normalize White/ness, reinforce social privilege and oppressive positions, naturalize prejudicial attitudes, and reinforce White supremacy.

Considering the gravity of race relations and negative racial stereotypes, of particular interest is today's *war on terror*. Whether it is the United States characterizing Arabs and North Koreans as incarnations of evil or Black men as dangerous, image matters as visual culture has great power in creating enemies. Among the various avenues through which visual culture circulates, television and the Internet are prime examples. Because of the global flow of visual culture, propaganda and stereotypes have been used as *weapons of mass dissemination.* Seen recurrently in all parts of the world, when left unchecked, visual culture practices of instilling fear, anger, and hatred have proven to be *weapons of mass destruction* (a lesson learned from the Holocaust).

As educators , we are in a position to challenge various forms of silence that maintain racial domination and subordination that result in inequities and injustices in personal, pedagogical, and political educational practice. Moreover, the art education classroom can serve as a site where attention is given to theories and practices that support antiracism (Vavrus, 2002). For example, art educators can facilitate discussions that examine how "[W]hite skin preference has operated systemically, structurally, and sometimes unconsciously as a dominant force" in various societies and cultures around the globe, particularly in the United States (Jay, 2005, p. 2). Further, since the majority of practicing and preservice teachers in the United States are White (Hodgkinson, 2002; Carignan, N., Sanders, M., & Pourdavood, R. G., 2005), we can view this as an opportunity to help them explore their own Whiteness or racial privilege. An art teacher who is able to deconstruct his or her own Whiteness is in a better position to challenge Eurocentric perspectives and dismantle White privilege.

Whiteness studies are antiracist and should not be seen as an attack on White people, nor should they focus on individuals. Instead, the focus should be on structures of social power and privilege, which carries with it a commitment to social justice and structural change (see Knight, 2006b for a discussion of Whiteness and racial privilege).

Propaganda

Propaganda can be designed to evoke feelings of fear, anger, hatred, pride, and patriotism. To cite an example, *Weapons of Mass Dissemination: The Propaganda of War,* a specialized collection of decorative and propaganda arts, consisting of posters, house wares, children's books, games, matchbooks, pamphlets, decorative items and ephemera,

held at the Wolfsonian–Florida International University, in 2004, presents a historic representation of visual culture propaganda that inundated the lives of ordinary citizens during the First and Second World Wars and the Spanish Civil War (Harper, 2004). Such an exhibition might be useful to art educators who want their students to gain practical insights into how propaganda can be integrated subtly into everyday life to normalize *weapons of mass destruction* and make war seem ordinary or routine (i.e., cigarette lighters in the shape of bombs, brass lamps with artillery tanks as a base, tea cups and dessert plates with pictures of military weaponry) (Harper, 2004). In this respect, they bear a resemblance to contemporary forms of visual propaganda (i.e., video games that play at war and war movies) that create subliminal influences on our thoughts, feelings and actions.

The Nazis believed that Germans were members of a *master race,* superior in mind and body to all others, and Hitler perceived racial mixture as a threat to the German nation. Underscoring his obsession with racial purity, he set out a full-scale propaganda campaign to make Jews the enemy, alleging that they hailed from a mixture of genetically inferior types such as Africans, Asians, and Middle Easterners. In other forms of visual propaganda (i.e., movies, plays, cartoons), Jews appeared as rodents that needed to be exterminated from German society.

Similarly, leaders throughout history and around the globe, have employed an arsenal of time-tested propaganda tactics, I call these "weapons of mass deception" to persuade the public to support their agendas for waging war (Alper, 2008). Moreover, many of the techniques used by past leaders bear a striking resemblance to those used in contemporary times, including the following:

- Invoking images of nationalism, and channeling fear and anger towards perceived enemies and threats.

Figure 3

Human"Bastards" Nazi Propaganda from the Dachau Concentration Camp Museum. Photo by author, 2007.

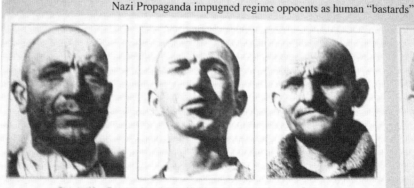

Nazi Propaganda impugned regime oppoents as human "bastards"

- Vilifying adversaries by framing the conflict as one of good versus evil and making comparisons to Hitler.
- Presenting a selective view of history.
- Portraying themselves as reluctant commanders-in-chief who wage war as a last resort and only with the noble intentions to spread freedom and democracy.
- Using the rhetoric of democracy to convince the public that war is a benign and altruistic act.
- Proclaiming commitment to peace and desire to avoid war, while simultaneously ordering the use of lethal violence.
- Using peace as a rationale to wage perpetual war.[4]

Stereotypes and Social Representations

Cultural and racial stereotypes stem from ethnocentrism. Toys, dolls, postcards, children's books, magazines, comics, and video games expose children and others to stereotypes and other social representations. Think about the imagery and narratives of video games that play at war and their cultural meaning and significance, particularly during a time in which the United States is still engaged in the "war on terror." What perspective is promulgated with these images? What information and/ or aspects of war do these images ignore or gloss over?[5] Who is the enemy?

Although the most extreme stereotypical characterizations are pretty much non-existent today, more subtle forms of racial stereotypes are plentiful. A recent highly publicized example relates to boxes of waffle mix sold at a conservative political forum that mocked Democratic presidential nominee Senator Barack Obama's race and religion. As a take-off of a widely recognized demeaning stereotype of Aunt-Jemima on pancake mix boxes, Senator Obama is portrayed wearing Arab-like clothing, with a shiny big-lipped smile, with bulging white eyes, gazing excitedly at a plate of waffles. This stereotype was intended to vilify Mr. Obama, to make him an enemy. The image can be found at www.obamawaffles.com.

In art classrooms, teachers can help students become more politically astute by using images of propaganda and other strategies of persuasion to examine negative stereotypes used throughout U. S. history. Analyze why the images and texts are so powerful or effective in evoking feelings of fear, anger, pride, and patriotism. Think critically about the imagery and narratives. Look at the color choices, symbolism, language, and design elements. Discuss slavery, the difficult history of racism in the United States and how it has lead to the inequalities that continue to pervade U.S. society today. What can we do to bring about change and social justice? In what follows, I discuss the concept of reparations as a means to bring about social justice.

Globalization and Reparations

Ben recognizes the importance of bringing about justice by prosecuting those who commit genocide and other crimes against humanity. Yet, equally important, he recognizes the need for reparations because they can also facilitate justice. As a result of Ben's leadership in the creation of an international criminal court, efforts to seek justice for victims through reparations are increasing globally. But some misunderstand the concept and think that monetary compensation is its only form. However, under modern international law, a range of different responses to atrocities and wrongdoings are available, including restitution, compensation, rehabilitation, and promises of "Never Again."

In the educational arena, educational professionals need to review the methods of discipline they use in schools and classrooms. Too often, teachers and administrators believe they need to punish children for their misbehavior and they, like others in the United States, equate discipline with punishment. However, art teachers could use the concept of restitution or reparations to move beyond punishment and redirect students, and restructure traditional methods of school discipline (Gossen, 1997). Teaching students to make restitution or reparations, rather than punishment, is a humane means of guiding students towards self-discipline. It helps them understand the responsibility of choices and consequences and helps them make an evaluation of what they can do to repair their mistakes. An example of punishment is to isolate the student from the group for misbehavior. This form of punishment gives the child no control over returning to the group. On the other hand, removing the child from the group until he or she is ready to return and correct the problem leaves the student with some control over when he or she returns. As a consequence, this may produce the long-term effects of good behavior because it is the student's choice to return to the group, and he or she has made a commitment to solve the problem (Gossen, 1997).

Bearing Witness: Dealing with Difficult Sites/Sights, Concentration Camps, and Genocidal Histories

The voices silenced during the Holocaust can never be restored; however, the greatest tribute that we

Figure 4

Wall Memorial
Commemorating
Prisoners
Exterminated
Between 1933-1945
at the Dachau
Concentration Camp.
Photo by author,
2007.

can pay to those who lost their lives is "countering a demonstrated will to historical amnesia" (Apel, 2004, p. 3). No matter how painful, we must take steps to never forget. Through "bearing witness," today, to concentration camps and other difficult sites/sights, "the traumatic history they represent is reframed through...shifted context[s]," of contemporary works of art, exhibitions, and memorials (Apel, 2004, p. 3). Further, "bearing witness" allows us to reflect upon the moral and spiritual questions raised by the events of the Holocaust as well as our own responsibilities as citizens in a democracy. (See Figure 4.)

Survivors, witnesses, communities, and individuals touched by genocide and other human rights atrocities have created countless works of art, ranging from small drawings to elaborate memorials, in an attempt to deal with difficult sites/sights, and to memorialize victims. (See Figure 5.)

Today, many towns and cities have dedicated Holocaust memorials. Some mark locations of actual events. Other memorials take a more general approach to honoring the victims. To cite a few examples, the *Homomonument*, by Karin Daan, in Amsterdam is a memorial dedicated to homosexual victims of the Holocaust. The memorial is defined by three large pink triangles. The *pink triangle* was the symbol the Nazis used to mark and humiliate homosexuals in concentration camps. Also, through student effort, under the tutelage of history teachers Kevin Daugherty and Jane Fisk in Illinois, The *Wings of Witness Project* uses 11 million pulled tabs from soda cans to numerically represent and commemorate those murdered by Nazi Germans during the Holocaust. A full

Figure 5

Bronze sculpture
of concentration
camp prisoners at
the Dachau Museum.
Photo by author,
2007.

description of the project is at: http://www.wingsof-witness.org/ProjectBackground.htm

Many former concentration camps are now memorials. In numerous instances, buildings have been preserved or reconstructed for visitors. After a night with Ben, I was inspired to visit Dachau, the concentration camp that incarcerated more than 200,000 prisoners from 27 nations. Dachau, built in 1933, the Nazi regime's first concentration camp, subsequently became the model for all others. The thought that I was standing on the grounds where thousands of people were murdered and, in Ben's words, "stacked up like cordwood," cremated, and subjected to slave labor,

Figure 6

Right: Crematorium
at the Dachau
Concentration Camp,
Photo by author,
2007.

Figure 7

Above: International
Memorial, at Dachau
Concentration Camp,
by Nandor Glid.
Photo by author,
2007.

not only evoked emotions of outrage and revulsion but reminded me of a very specific history that must never be forgotten (Apel, 2004). (See Figure 6.)

A central international monument, completed in 1968 by Yugoslav sculptor, Nandor Glid, at Dachau, is an abstract interpretation of twisted, screaming emaciated corpses, strung in a barbed wire fence. This monument commemorates the millions of Jews murdered in extermination camps. (See Figure 7.)

Signposts: Problems and Possibilities for Art Educators

There are lessons to be learned from the Holocaust and other human rights atrocities. Art teachers can explore historical and contemporary media representations, look at the roots and outcomes of prejudice, racism, and stereotyping, the dangers of indifference, and the importance of individual and civic engagement.

The Holocaust, slavery, lynchings, and other human rights abuses are not, as we would like to believe, accidents in history. They happened because individuals, groups, and nations made decisions and choices to act or not to act. As art educators, we must speak up when we see injustice and persecution of others. If not, silence and indifference can perpetuate the problem. We ought to challenge and correct conduct that foster hate and prejudice. Starting first with self, we should question our complicity in creating a climate of racial animosity or perpetuating racial stereotypes—through jokes, comments, and casual remarks, among other things.

When I consider Ben's life's work towards fulfilling the promise of "Never Again," I can't help but imagine the global impact, if every child could visualize that promise. Aside from the strategies already discussed, a way to empower conscientious generations

Figure 8

Dachau Concentration Camp Memorial with "Never Again" Written in Five Languages. Photo by author, 2007.

of democratic citizens committed to work toward peace and social justice is for educators to " imagine a process by which we might change our institutions and our psyches...to take seriously the nurturance of consciousness, conscience, compassion, and community" (Keen, 1986, p. 184). Never again should our actions foster racist policies of exclusion, dehumanization, and violence. And more importantly, never again should differences of race, religion, or ideology be permissible justification to massacre "the other."

Acknowledgments
I would like to thank Karen Keifer-Boyd for her feedback and invaluable insights.

REFERENCES
Alper, L. (2008). *War made easy: How president & pundits keep spinning us to death.* Massachusetts: Media Education Foundation.

Apel, D. (2004). *Imagery of lynching: Black men, White women, and the mob.* New Jersey and London: Rutgers University Press.

Carignan, N., Sanders, M., & Pourdavood, R. G. (2005). Racism and ethnocentrism: Social representations of preservice teachers in the context of multi- and intercultural education. *International Journal of Qualitative Methods, 4*(3), Article 1. Retrieved September 1 2008 from http://www.ualberta.ca/~iiqm/ backissues/4_3/html/carignan.htm

Chandra, N. (2003) . *Coming together: Globalization means reconnecting the human community.* Retrieved May 30 2008 from http://www.globalenvision.org/library/8/567/

Goodman, S. (2002). *Ethnocentrism.* Retrieved on August 23, 2008 from http://www.auburn.edu/~goodmsb/Papers/Ethnocentrism.doc

Gossen, D., 1997. Restitution: Restructuring school discipline 2nd edition. Chapel Hill, NC: New View Publications.

Harper, P. (2004). *The objects of war: An exhibition of propaganda posters and household furnishings bore timely lessons about the ways bellicose messages can infiltrate everyday life,* New York: Brant Publications.

Hodgkinson, H. (2002). Demographics and teacher education. *Journal of Teacher Education, 53*(2), 102-105.

Jay, G. (2005). Whiteness and the multicultural literature classroom. *MELUS: Journal of the Society for the Study of the Multi-Ethnic Literature of the United States, 30*(2), 99-121.

Keen, S. (1986). *Faces of the enemy: Reflections on the hostile imagination* New York: Harper & Row.

Knight, W. B. (2006a). Using contemporary art to challenge cultural values, beliefs and assumptions. *Art Education: The Journal of the National Art Education Association, 59*(4), 39-45.

Knight, W. B. (2006b). E(raced) bodies: In and out of sight/cite/site. *Journal of Social Theory in Art Education, 26,* 323-345.

Media Education Foundation (2008), Independent media in a time of war. Retrieved on September 1, 2008 from (http://www.mediaed.org/wp/study-guides

Media Education Foundation (2008), War made easy. Retrieved on September 9, 2008 from (http://www.mediaed.org/wp/study-guides

Spradley, J. & McCurdy, D. (1990). *Conformity and conflict.* Glenview, IL: Scott Foresman.

Shohat, E., & Stam, R. (2004). *Unthinking Eurocentrism: Multiculturalism and the media.* New York: Routledge.

Tavin, K., & Hausman, J. (2004). Art education and visual culture in the age of globalization. *Art Education, 57*(5), pp. 47-52. Reston: National Art Education Association.

Thomas, R. (1996). *Redefining diversity.* New York: Amacom.

Vavrus, M. (2002). Transforming the multicultural education of teachers. New York: Teachers College Press.

ENDNOTES
1   *Untermenschen* is a term in Nazi racial ideology used to describe inferior people (i.e. homosexuals, Blacks, Poles, disabled people, Jehovah's Witnesses, and Gypsies), specifically those not of Aryan descent.

2   Benjamin Ferencz asked me to call him "Ben," as he now considers me a friend.

3   The New Jersey Commission on Holocaust Education offers outlines for the development of a Holocaust and Genocide Curriculum for students in kindergarten through 12th grades. Go to http://remember.org/hist.root.holo.html.

4   These propaganda tactics were adapted, extended, or rewritten from the Media Education Foundation Study Guide, *War Made Easy: How President & Pundits Keep Spinning Us to Death,* retrieved from the Media Education Foundation website, at www.mediaed.org.

5   Questions related to video games were formulated from the Media Education Foundation Study Guide, *War Games: Thinking Critically About Video Games That Play At War,* retrieved from the Media Education Foundation website, at www.mediaed.org.

A Policy Analysis of Formal Education in Modern Multiethnic Kenya: A Case for Cultural Hybridization

David Ogega Nyaberi

In January 2008, inter-ethnic clashes broke out in Kenya. Hostilities were directed at people perceived to have voted for a particular political party during the December 27, 2007 presidential and parliamentary elections in which the main opposition political party accused the government of rigging. Several people died in the skirmishes, while others were displaced from their homes and sent seeking refuge in churches and police stations. Hostility escalated prompting the international community to step in to assist with food, shelter, and other essential needs. The former United Nations Secretary General, Mr. Kofi Annan, stepped in to broker negotiations[1] between the opposing sides. Although the disputed elections were blamed for the crisis, ethnic conflicts emanate from longstanding land disputes between various ethnic groups dating back to the colonial period.

While few accusations of wrongdoing against the British colonizers might be disputable, and many would argue that the British legacy of inequitable power relations, unequal distributions of resources and opportunities among Kenya's ethnically diversity communities, and an obsolete and inadequate educational system continue to limit Kenyan prosperity and threaten national unity, I argue here that it is time to move forward. I further argue that in post-independent Kenya, and against a backdrop of colonial domination, oppression, and marginalization, education is now one of the most important means to empower Kenyans with the knowledge necessary to understand, acknowledge, and define their own identity as a united country of diverse ethnicity. In this chapter, I discuss historical and contemporary contexts in which educational policies, curriculum structures, and educational practices in Kenya contribute to the current state of affairs in Kenya. I engage these contexts as a basis for which contemporary education in Kenya could be restructured and formulated as a model for envisioning a means by which Kenya might reorient itself in a globalized world. I show how the arts and art education are central to this goal.

Impacts of Colonial Partitioning and Post-colonial Independence on Educational Thought in Kenya

The present social, political, and economic conditions in Kenya are a direct consequence of the General Act of the African Conference signed at the Berlin Conference of 1885, and the Brussels Declaration of 1890 in which European nations[2] allocated themselves the vast land and resources in the continent of Africa (American Journal of International Law, 1921). The people of Africa were neither invited nor represented at the Berlin Conference and the Brussels Declaration. In 1919, the United States of America and the European powers ratified the Agreements made at the two forums under Article Eleven of the Act, which paved way for partitioning the African continent. As a result of the partition of Africa and subsequent establishment of British colonial rule in Kenya, the colonial power demarcated geopolitical boundaries and introduced British formal education. These developments destabilized and changed the lifestyles of more than 40 indigenous ethnic cultures in Kenya. Blanton, Mason, and Athow (2001) wrote, "When the European powers imposed formal territorial boundaries throughout the continent in 1885, the seeds for ethnic conflict in post-colonial Africa were sown. ...boundaries were drawn with little or no consideration to the actual distribution of indigenous ethno-cultural groups" (p. 473). In the struggle toward independence, Kenya's political landscapes were fragmented and divided along ethnic and religious affiliations foreshadowing a divide between different elements of the prospective ruling class. Blanton, Mason, and Athow noted, "With the demise of colonial rule, the former colonies, with their colonial borders essentially intact, were transformed into some of the most ethnically fragmented states in the world" (2001, p. 473).

After gaining independence from Britain in 1963, the newly independent nation of Kenya faced the enormous challenge of mapping out strategies for reconstruction, and laying a foundation for national unity from the existing cultural diversity. The limited availability or denial of formal education opportunities to Kenyan Africans during the colonial era generated a lasting demand for schooling after independence (Eshiwani, 1993; Sheffield, 1973). The new government formed the first education commission, the Ominde Commission,[3] to formulate a new education policy for Kenya. The commission established guidelines for the newly independent nation and initiated "a beginning of a continuous planning in Kenya" (Kenya Government, 1965, p. 10). A major theme that emerged from the first part of the Ominde report was that the political and social role of education in independent Kenya were made evident in the utilitarian, social, cultural, and personal goals of education. The Commission made 160 policy recommendations that stressed the role of education in nation-building and promoting national unity through emphasis on cultural and social values, and integrating education with national economic planning (Kenya Government, 1965; *see also* Eshiwani, 1993; Sheffield, 1973). The Ominde Commission was first among the many education commissions that would later characterize the way the Kenya government would deal with education changes.

There were numerous subsequent major reviews and official reports that came over the years, but the 1998 Commission of Inquiry chaired by Dr. Davy Koech performed the most intensive and extensive inquiry into the education system. The Commission visited all of the districts in Kenya between August 1998 and August 1999 and collected information from members of the public and specialized groups and individuals, including educationalists and representatives from the civil society, religious organizations, and politicians. Despite the intensive, extensive, and comprehensive nature of the Koech Report, the government of Kenya never implemented its recommendations. Instead, the Ministry of Education argued that the report was not implementable, citing cost, structural, and institutional limitations. The rejection of the Koech Report brought into question Kenya's respect for education planning, curriculum development, and recognition of professionalism in research (Amutabi, 2003).

Notwithstanding the rejection of the Koech Report, the Kenya government, under external pressure to implement Structural Adjustment Programs[4] (SAPs), indicated in a 2001 education report that "The development of education in general and providing quality for all in the country is difficult, if not impossible, under the implementation of the SAPs' requirements, for example, cost sharing and liberalization of the economy" (Kenya Ministry of Education, 2001, p. 10). However, the report also mentioned that inadequate policy based on the inherited education system and legal frameworks and statements have negatively affected the development of quality basic education. According to the Ministry of Education, education in Kenya "to a large extent still has a colonial orientation, promotes rote learning and is still elitist," and "the process of policy making, planning and implementation does not seem to be based on systematic evaluation of the education sector based on available information" (Kenya Ministry of Education, 2001, p. 12). The challenges in education are impacted by the multiethnic nature of Kenya's population, and any meaningful reforms in any sector including education must address the challenges of a multiethnic society.

Ethnic Inequalities

In pre-independent Kenya, minority non-Africans[5], mostly Europeans and Asians, held key positions in government and the private sector. Political independence was an opportunity for African Kenyans not only to receive sovereignty, but also to expect higher participation in the government. However, at independence, Kenya adopted a British-styled constitution and inherited a poorly trained work force responsible for a new nation faced with meeting the needs of the diverse ethnic groups with variegated interests (Sheffield, 1973). As a result, after independence, most of the non-Africans were retained in the workforce as expatriates. Nevertheless, expectations of African Kenyans were high, and for the new government, priorities established in expenditure patterns were of direct relevance to the opportunity for members of various ethnic groups to compete in the marketplace for political and economic positions. While the allocation of resources and provision of social services to the citizens were crucial issues, one area of concern that was never addressed was the geographically defined ethnic pattern (land distributions) that would later and periodically become a major source of ethnic conflicts.

The existence of ethnic and racial imbalances during the colonial era in Kenya emanated from the British colonial policy of *indirect rule*.[6] This was a tactical policy that provided for sharing of power between the colonial government and the local leaders to provide protection for the Christian missionaries and the British settlers from any potential local hostilities (Parker, 1950). The British colonial government held the view that through the system of indirect rule, the Natives would enjoy a significant share in their own government. At the same time, British settlers allocated themselves most of the fertile land in Kenya, while "restrictions on Native landholding, urging and even forcing the Natives to work, limitation on Native production of certain crops, and considerable racial discrimination in government services, education, and social life have had unfortunate effects, especially in Kenya" (Parker, 1950, p. 21). This manner of patronage was inherited by the African Kenyan leaders of the new government and resulted in the uneven distribution and re-distribution of national resources, especially the re-allocation of former white land[7] in the Rift Valley province, by Jomo Kenyatta, the first president of Kenya.

When Kenyatta, a member of the Kikuyu ethnic group, assumed office as president of Kenya, there seemed to be a notion held by the rest of Kenyans that the Kikuyu were in power, and it was apparent that the Kikuyu people exploited this notion to their political and economic benefit. During Kenyatta's rule, legislative elections enabled local and regional elites to move in and out of Parliament and power as the regime allowed competing leaders to vie openly for local supremacy under the one-party state. Orvis (2001) compared this style of administration to the late colonial period, where the central government, often using repressive tactics, largely limited politics to few selected ethnic groups, particularly in central Kenya, which included the Kikuyu, Embu, Meru, and Kamba. Similarly, President Moi,[8] who proved to be a far shrewder political operative than anyone had imagined, quickly set out to replace systematically the existing Kikuyu political elite with his followers from the Kenya African Democratic Union (KADU),[9] particularly from his own Kalenjin ethnic group.

In 1992, tribal groupings emerged with demands for equity and inevitably caused political tensions in various parts of Kenya, particularly in the Rift Valley Province where most of the land formerly belonging to British settlers had been re-allocated to the most affluent members of the Kikuyu community by the Kenyatta government (Orvis, 2001).

Although the issue of land has continued to be a sensitive issue in Kenya during the post-independence period, I view the most serious problem that has never been addressed since independence to be the boundary demarcations and political divisions between Kenya's ethnic groups. These were essentially British demarcations in their scheme of dividing and ruling Kenyans, and as subtle as this might seem, it is the crucial issue responsible for the ethnic clashes in 1992 and more recently in the 2007 post-election period. While ethnic and sub-ethnic factionalism has been the hallmark of elite politics, it is the British-orchestrated political tribalism that has taken a more grim turn on the ground (Orvis, 2001). It is no wonder that even several decades after independence, Kenya's ethnic groups continue to identify themselves by their so-called ancestral lands because political leaders, especially in the last 20 years, have maintained serious rifts by creating yet more ethnic-based administrative divisions. For instance, between 2004 and 2006, the president of Kenya, Mr. Mwai Kibaki, created new political districts for Kamba, Tugen, and Gusii communities in a move to solidify his political status. This is a practice that post-independent Kenyan leaders have often used to maintain status quo, while appearing to settle disputes among ethnic groups involved in power struggles to secure control of the nation's resources. It is evident that the ongoing struggle for resources, particularly land, among the various ethnic groups has created a destabilizing and volatile situation. Despite government efforts to unify all ethnic groups, ethnic considerations still dominate and the fight for equal access to resources results in such a precarious situation; it hampers progress and constantly creates a source of potential conflict. After the December 2007 presidential elections, the situation spilled over, degenerating into inter-ethnic violence.

Engaging the British Legacy in a Framework for the Future

As a post-colonial Kenya establishes and maintains a sense of civil cohesion and attempts to position itself for its future in an increasingly globalized world, I posit that it is crucial for Kenya to reconceptualize its educational framework to address three areas of concern:

1. Strengthening Kenya's national identity as a multicultural nation with a long, rich, and varied history, not only to be compatible with postmodern formulations of hybridity, syncretization, and pastiche, but also to consider the growing transnational movements of capital, labor, and culture as the material realities of globalization (Ashcroft, Griffiths, & Tiffin, 2002).

2. Redirecting Kenyan educational policy toward construction of a critical and culturally inclusive national curriculum, which is central to Kenya's vision of itself as a nation that affirms cultural

diversity from personal, social, historical, and political contexts (Nieto, 2004).

3. Engaging the study of the arts in education as a means of reaffirming both ethnic diversity and national unity.

Multicultural education has been stated as a concept that would be ideal if incorporated into education policy (Banks, 1993). Moving from but respecting multi-cultural orientation, one in which each ethnic or cultural group maintains a sense of identity, shared history, social cohesion, and opportunity, I embrace here an *intercultural orientation*, one that engages the notion of *cultural hybridity*. The notion of cultural hybridity, for Kenya, implies a fusion of legacies, ethnic practices, and aspirations amongst and across Kenya's 40 distinct ethnic groups and with due regard to their European and British historical legacy, value systems, institutions, and structures. Intercultural education is central to such a notion.

Various notions of *cultural hybridity* depend on their context of description. From a Media Studies perspective, Kraidy (2005) describes "hybridity" as a contemporary emblematic notion that "captures the spirit of the times with its obligatory celebration of cultural difference and fusion, and it resonates with the globalization mantra of unfettered economic exchanges and the supposedly inevitable transformation of all cultures" (p. 1). In the context of colonization and in the post-independent nations, Lunga (2004) describes hybridity as a survival strategy for cultures "caught between the languages of their colonization and their indigenous languages" and that hybridization is a process though which post-independence cultures "use colonial languages without privileging colonial languages" (p. 291).

From these perspectives, cultural hybridity is represented as the result of contact between and integration of cultures, but within the context of multiethnic post-independent nations, what would the notion of cultural hybridity really entail? I consider as a case in point the problem of language. During the colonial period, the establishment of the British colonial empire, demarcation of geopolitical boundaries, and introduction of British formal education undermined the indigenous cultural values and practices in Kenya. British influence was manifested in the notion that it was synonymous with modernity and civilization for a person in the colony both to receive British formal education and speak the English language. In this regard, the use of English language played a powerful role in subjugating the cultures of colonized countries. Some critics argue that the continued use of the colonial language in Kenya is a sign of continued

colonization of the mind (Ngugi, 1986), while others contend that the colonial language, in this case English, could be used without privileging or creating hierarchies across specific indigenous cultural identities (Lunga, 2004). Although some might consider it colonization of the mind, I find the English language to be an essential tool for weaving strands of cultural and ethnic diversity into the fabric of Kenyan national consciousness in a globalized world. Paradoxically, I therefore argue for the maintenance of the use of the English language as a means of furthering social cohesion amongst Kenya's diverse ethnic groups. Kenya, after all, is now a country of both blended and distinct cultures, situated within an increasingly globalized economy, and greatly impacted by political, environmental, religious, and ethnic issues, events, and aspirations throughout the world. A unified identity relies on, at the very least, a common language.

Other than the use of English and existence of geopolitical boundaries separating Kenya from other African nations as defined by the British, there exist internal geographical and cultural divisions demarcated largely on the basis of ethnicity. If the notion that "hybridity involves the fusion of two hitherto relatively distinct forms, styles, or identities, cross-cultural contact, which often occurs across national borders as well as across cultural boundaries, is a requisite for hybridity" (Kraidy, 2005, p. 5) is correct, then there is need to initiate and expand meaningful conversations across cultures. One of the most effective ways to cultivate meaningful interaction and understanding across cultures is through educating Kenyan people to understand and respect not only their own cultural heritage, but also to embrace their obligations to maintenance of a peaceful, prosperous, and unified multicultural nation.

Educational Policy Recommendations

As mentioned earlier, the education system inherited from the British was not adequate to make significant contributions to intercultural harmony in independent Kenya. Ntarangwi (2003) writes, "Many [Kenyans] receive an education devoid of the central ingredients that are crucial in making them active participants in their own socio-cultural existence" (p. 213). Furthermore, the government of Kenya acknowledges that "the education sector faces management problems which are occasioned by centralized bureaucratic structures and politicization of education at national, provincial and school levels" (Kenya Ministry of Education, 2004, p. 13). The obvious problems of centralization of management are administrative rigidity and lack of responsiveness, which normally result in delays in decision making and/or ineffectiveness in implementing recommendations made by various stakeholders in the education sector. In a politicized education system, other impediments would include lack of adequate resources, inefficiencies in policy execution, and lack of accountability, especially among the low-rank workforce. I recommend the following reforms in response to these conditions.

First, the government must restructure its system of the education management, initiate curriculum reform, and improve teacher education. This conclusion is already well understood amongst Kenyan policy makers. The Kenyan Ministry of Education acknowledges that while there should be no excuse for inefficiency, "Inadequate policy and legal frameworks and statements have negatively affected the development of quality basic education" (Kenya Ministry of Education, 2001, p. 12). The Ministry further acknowledges that Kenya's education system, to a large extent, has a colonial orientation, promotes rote learning, and is still elitist. According to the Ministry, "the process of policy making, planning and implementation does not seem to be based on systematic evaluation of the education sector based on available information" (Ministry of Education, 2001, p. 12), and the policies relating to education have in most instances been inadequate. There is urgent need for the government of Kenya to improve the management style of education by systematic research and evaluation of the sector by education and research experts. Subsequently, policy recommendations should be implemented by competent education officials and qualified teachers in the schools.

Second, the government should reform the national curriculum to serve effectively both the interests of diverse communities and those of a nation. While a reformed curriculum would provide all round education in the sciences in the humanities, I have emphasized the value of teaching the English language in Kenya. Driven by the need to respond to the challenge of engaging with one's language of colonization, several critics have discussed and explored the tenability and feasibility of using the language of colonization to express cultural identities (Lunga, 2004). While some may argue that as a language of imperialism, English remains potentially a hindrance for its African users because it alienates Africans from their own culture and languages, the use of English can also be liberating for diverse ethnic groups by providing a unified voice in which different cultures identify themselves as one nation (Lunga, 2004). Furthermore, in the globalized world, English language unites the ethnically diverse nation of Kenya while connecting the country to the rest of the world.

Third, for curriculum changes to be meaningful, effective, and successful in achieving intended goals, the country needs to improve teacher training programs, especially at the primary level. The Ministry of Education acknowledges, "Teachers are an important resource in the teaching/learning process and their training and utilization therefore requires critical consideration" (Kenya Ministry of Education, 2004, p. 18). The government should provide training for teachers and education department officials to ensure that both groups understand policy requirements. Training provided by the government should promote cooperation between curriculum development, teacher training, and the development of curriculum support materials.

Fourth, rather than including it as part of extra-curricular activities, *the government of Kenya should incorporate arts education as a central and an integral part of the school curriculum.* This move would benefit a wide cross-section of students who would gain knowledge and understanding of local and global trends in politics, culture and education. To promote intercultural unity and understanding, an arts education curriculum would incorporate visual arts from various ethnic groups in Kenya. The arts education curriculum should also incorporate the performing arts including oral tradition, music, drama, and dance. Through the oral tradition, which includes storytelling and poetry, children will be become aware of their cultural and material heritage that they will be required to safeguard and share with others. An arts education program will combine the listening to, making, and sharing of music from various ethnic groups in Kenya. These activities would provide a social-cultural context for promoting interethnic appreciation of music and the creative potential, which is an essential component the school curriculum. In addition to music, various communities have unique dance styles that could be shared by all cultures. It would be important to both students and teachers to understand the meaning of dance styles and formations of the various ethnic groups. For example, the Gusii and the Maasai—by tradition—each have dance performances for various occasions. However, each of occasions might have different meanings and interpretations for each ethnic group. For example, among the Gusii, initiation of boys into adulthood is through circumcision, but among the Maasai, it is the killing of a fierce wild animal, say, a lion; each of these initiation rites has a dance that accompanies a successful completion of the process, but differ in the meanings and interpretations attributed to each process. An essential aspect of learning about dances from these two ethnic groups would be to assist students to understand the meanings and interpretations of those dances from the perspectives of the respective cultural groups. The inclusion of music, dance and poetry would be vital in transmitting to children their oral tradition through stories, songs, simple poems, riddles, nursery rhymes and games. In addition to learning about the visual and performing arts, students need to understand how their artistic heritage is changing with trends of globalization. A major reason for students to learn to appreciate their own cultural diversity is that there is to counter the enormous external influences through popular culture that somehow overshadow the traditional arts of the various ethnic groups in Kenya. Rather than embrace popular culture especially from the West, students should learn to filter out only the relevant aspects for the good of their interethnic coexistence.

Some Final Considerations

Technology, commerce, and travel have turned the world into a global network of scientific, economic, political, and cultural exchanges, and what happened in Kenya now impacts other parts of the world. Despite its recent ethnic violence, Kenya has long been considered a model for post-colonial African nationhood. I have considered problems of Kenyan political and educational practices inherited from the British at independence in 1963 and have considered how multiculturalism, cultural hybridity, use of the English language, and arts education contribute to Kenya's potential as a unified and prosperous nation. I have argued that an education policy in Kenya should accentuate the interrelationships and diversity of cultural heritage in a globalized world. I also argue here, as have many others, that the education sector (governmental officials, policy makers, and educators) in Kenya needs to directly address the issues, however difficult, and formulate *and implement* a critical and culturally inclusive national curriculum that would strengthen Kenya's national identity as a multicultural nation. This includes discussions of remnants of colonial administration policies and reviews of forms of discrimination in local policies. Such discussions are fundamental to an understanding of policies and practices that have failed to redress racial injustice by maintaining existing inequalities and neglecting the cultural heritage of Kenyans. Colonial education created an effect that has made it difficult to differentiate between the new imposed ideas of the colonizers and the accepted former practices of the indigenous people. As a result, "postcolonial education has the enviable task of finding a way to speak to a community and a nation that is at one level marked by sameness and at another by difference" (Dei, 2000, p. 228). Dei argues, "If some forms of ethnic, religious, linguistic, gender, and class identities attain dominance, there is need to understand how it occurs, how students, educators, and communities interpret this occurrence and how individual subjects define their relations to the dominant identity (p. 228).

The task of establishing a successful post-colonial Kenyan national identity will not be easy, and even after 40 some years of independence the task is still incomplete and riddled with complex problems. In his critique of postcolonialism in relation to education and development, Ntarangwi (2003) finds that as a former British colony, Kenya continues to show strands of economic and cultural dependency to the extent that most of Kenya's political and economic policies are oriented toward European and American contexts. Kenyans view development as "a process of self-denial that constructs an imagined self devoid of the assumed cultural baggage of its own traditional social and cultural practices" (Ntarangwi, 2003, p. 213). Faced with this situation, Ntarangwi argues that many Kenyans have difficulty in deciding between assuming a British/Western and a Kenyan identity, invariably results in bearing the burdens of both. With this in mind, a reconstructed education system for Kenya should aim at boosting the identities of the people and uniting previously isolated individuals and cultural groups. I believe that the arts have an important role to play in this due to both their centrality to individual cultural identity and their power to communicate across cultural distinctions those most important common human aspirations.

REFERENCES

American Journal of International Law. (1921). Convention Revising the General Act of Berlin, February 26, 1885, and the General Act and Declaration of Brussels, July 2, 1890. *The American Journal of International Law*, Vol. 15, No. 4, Supplement: Official Documents (Oct., 1921), 314-321.

Amutabi, M. N. (2003). Political interference in the running of education in post independence Kenya: A critical retrospection. *International Journal of Educational Development 23,* 127-144.

Ashcroft, B., Griffiths, G., & Tiffin, H. (2002). *The empire writes back: Theory and practice in postcolonial literatures* (2nd ed.). New York: Routledge.

Banks, J. A. (1993). Multicultural education: Historical development, dimensions, and practice. *Review of Research in Education, 19* 3-49.

Blanton, R., Mason, D. T., & Athow, B. (2001). Colonial style and post-colonial ethnic conflict in Africa. *Journal of Peace Research, 38(4)* 473-491.

Dei, S. G. (2000). Social difference and the politics of schooling in Africa: A Ghanaian case study. *Compare, 35(3)* 227-245.

Eshiwani, G. (1993). *Education in Kenya Since Independence*. Nairobi, Kenya: East African Educational Publishers.

Kenya Government (1965). *Ominde Education Report*. Nairobi, Kenya: Government Printer.

Kenya Government (2000). *Koech Education Report*. Nairobi, Kenya: Government Printer.

Kenya, Ministry of Education, Science and Technology (2004). *Annual Report*. Nairobi, Kenya: Government Printer.

Kenya, Ministry of Education, Science and Technology. (2001). Report presented at the 46th Session of the International Conference on Education, Geneva.

Kraidy, M. (2005). *Hybridity, or the cultural logic of globalization*. Philadelphia: Temple University Press.

Lunga V. B. (2004). Mapping African postcoloniality: Linguistic and cultural spaces of hybridity. *Perspectives on Global Development and Technology, Volume 3*(3), 291-325.

Ngugi, T. (1986). *Decolonising the mind: The politics of language in African literature*. Portsmouth, NH: Heinemann.

Nieto, S. (2004). *Affirming diversity: The sociopolitical context of multicultural education*. Boston, MA: Allyn and Bacon.

Ntarangwi, M. (2003). The challenges of education and development in post-colonial Kenya. *Africa Development, 27*(3, 4), 211-228.

Orvis, S. (2001). Moral ethnicity and political tribalism in Kenya's "virtual democracy" *African Issues, 29*(1/2), 8-13.

Parker, G. G. (1950). A summary of British native policy in Kenya and Uganda, 1885–1939. *The Journal of Negro Education, 19*(4), 439-448.

Sheffield, J. R. (1973). *Education in Kenya: A historical study*. New York: Teachers College Columbia University Press.

ENDNOTES

1   Kofi Annan, the former United Secretary-General, brought the government and opposition parties together to resolve the disputed elections. Both parties agreed to form a government of national unity, which created a post of Prime Minister that was filled by the opposition leader.

2   The Berlin Conference was held under the German Chancellor Bismarck. European countries at the forefront of partitioning Africa were France, Germany, Great Britain, Portugal, Spain, Italy, Belgium, and Netherlands.

3   The Education Minister appointed a commission in 1964 headed by Dr. Simeon Ominde to review all aspects of education in Kenya. The Ominde Report was published in two parts; first at the end of 1964 to deal with policy, and the second in 1965 to provide quantitative recommendations and a plan of priorities (Sheffield, 1973).

4   During the 1990s, the World Bank and the International Monetary Fund (IMF) mandated the Kenya government to make certain policy changes for Kenya to receive new loans from those institutions.

5   As a British colony, the majority of Europeans were British nationals, but because of the Berlin Conference of 1885 and 1890 Declaration of Brussels declared Africa a free trade area for European nations; there were nationals of other European nations living in pre-independent Kenya. The Asian population was made up mainly of Indian nationals who moved to Kenya during the building of the Kenya-Uganda Railway.

6   *Direct* rule was an ideology by Sir Frederick Lugard, a famous British colonial administrator, who pioneered the idea into practical use in Nyasaland, Uganda, Kenya, and Nigeria.

7   This term refers to land that was previously occupied by the British settlers in the fertile Rift Valley province of Kenya.

8   Daniel Moi took over as Kenya's second president in 1978 after Kenyatta's death. Moi ruled for 24 years, leaving office after the second multi-party elections in Kenya in 2002.

9   KADU emerged as a coalition of smaller ethnic groups that feared Kikuyu and Luo domination of the newly independent country and fought for *majimbo* [federalism] for protection against central (Kikuyu and Luo) domination (Orvis, 2001).

ART, ARTISTIC PRACTICES, GLOBAL VISUAL CULTURE

&

Introduction: Section II

Elizabeth Manley Delacruz

Readers may recall from the introduction "Globalization, Art, and Education: Mapping the Terrain" that globalization and globalism are related constructs in global studies. Whereas *globalization* refers to processes and problems associated with structural changes in the production and dissemination of goods, information, culture, the concomitant rise of transnational and supranational entities and systems, and impact on and responses of individuals, cultural groups, and nations to such dynamics; *globalism* refers to a way of thinking, whereby association and allegiance with a particular ethnicity, cultural group, or nation state is complemented by a cosmopolitan mindset, a greater sense of interdependency. New technologies, movement of people, ideas, and cultural practices and products across the globe, and accelerated transformations of social, economic, and political arrangements underlie and complicate both *globalization* and *globalism*. In the second section of this book, authors examine how global phenomena, processes, and idealizations shape artistic practices, local and global visual culture, and art education in the 21st century.

In the first chapter in this section, "Globalization and Contemporary Art," Julia Marshall provides a densely packed exposé about how eight artists 'picture' personal, social and cultural life in the age of globalization. Marshall's analysis includes discussion of ways in which artists understand and engage forces of globalization (connectivity, polarization/differentiation, and accelerated change), utilize the mechanisms of globalization (collusion, fusion, and hybridization), and their own tactics (parody, satire, and iconoclasm) in which they reinterpret and reflect the icons and imagery of global visual culture. As Marshall observes, contemporary art frequently offers a critique, sometimes playfully and other times with subdued seriousness, of globalization.

The following chapter, "Border Theory, Nationalism, and Transnational Art Pedagogy," adds to our understandings of contemporary art practices. In this chapter, Rachel Bailey Jones describes how competing notions of national identity, community, and difference are reconciled in the work of border artist Emily Jacir, a Palestinian living and working in the US and who now claims a transcultural identity as neither one nor the other but both. For Jones, contemporary artists such as Emily Jacir also complicate our own understanding of issues of nationality, movement across national borders, differential power relations between cultures and nations in conflict, and the complicity of major world powers in longstanding and ongoing regional conflicts.

In a different vein but exploring similar themes of transcultural identity, in Alice Arnold's "Jan-Ru Wan: A Transcultural Journey" we find a compelling firsthand account of how the global flow of people, culture, and ideas is conveyed in the art of an artist who grew up in Taiwan and now lives, makes art, and teaches in the US. In a conversation between author and artist, we learn about the life and work of Jan-Ru Wan, who as a child longed for a means of finding a way of life as an artist, who traveled great distances to achieve such a goal, and whose work bridges her femininity, feminist sensibility, and dual-identity in an effort to navigate and make sense of both her culture of origin and her American experience.

For Marshall, *glocalization*, which she explains as localized adaptations that selectively fuse and alter global and local traditions and phenomena, is a central strategy for artistic expression and cultural engagement. For Jones, *border-dwelling* is a more apt strategy, as artist Emily Jacir resides not in one place or the other, but in the contested border area, which Jones describes as a contact area where nations, cultures, and people meet and clash and an important site for constructing and negotiating meaning. For Arnold, the story is that of the emergence in the mind of Jan-Ru Wan of a *transnational identity*, one in which the loving memories and traditions of Taiwan are contrasted with her realizations of the limitations on women and artists in her home country, and in which opportunities afforded by both serendipity and guidance from caring teachers resulted in Jan Ru's re-identification in her new home in North Carolina. In their descriptions of the strategies, works, and lives of these contemporary artists, each working in varied media and coming from different backgrounds, Marshall, Jones, and Arnold make these artists accessible to teachers and students of contemporary art. They provide a close-up glimpse at how contemporary artists invent, utilize, and reflect upon new aesthetic and transcultural artistic conventions and experiences; and they richly illustrate facets of the interrelated, complex mechanisms of globalization.

In the next three chapters, Courtney Lee Weida, Borim Song, and Karen Keifer-Boyd examine interactions of contemporary artists with relatively new global digital media. In "Subversively Discursive Digital Communities of Contemporary Craft" Courtney Lee Weida looks specifically at crafts, considering the impact of electronic communication technologies on the practices of traditional crafts worldwide, and examining the construction of counter-discourses, creative collaborations, and revised identities within e-forums

for ceramics, fiber arts, and other studio crafts. As Weida observes, although communities of artists working with traditional craft media would seem unlikely netizens, Wed forums, electronic bulletin boards, and Internet collaborations for craftspeople are growing rapidly.

In the following chapter, "Redefining Cultural Identities in Digital Art Practices: Artistic Journeys across Cultural Boundaries and Ethnic Borders," Borim Song considers the changing nature of cultural identity explored within the new artistic practices of digital art, and discusses implications for college-level art education theory and teaching. Extrapolating from her case study of an academic conference and exhibition of Korean computer-mediated art that took place in New York City in 2006, Song highlights the work of six contemporary artists who participated in this conference, exploring the potential of their work as agents of cross-cultural exchange in art education.

Next, Karen Keifer-Boyd describes her work with preservice teachers in the creation of cybernet art as a means of advancing a more just world in her chapter, "CyberNet Activist Art Pedagogy." For Keifer-Boyd, public pedagogy is a form of critical social praxis that uses public media such as the Internet to challenge racism, sexism, and other systemic prejudices. Here, Keifer-Boyd describes how she and her college students consider ways that online art activism (what she refers to as *cyborg border-crossings*) fosters participatory democracy, resistance to global capitalism and patriarchal systems, redefinitions of human identity, and revisions of human relationships to place/time. In these three chapters, Weida, Song, and Keifer-Boyd not only provide descriptions and analyses of emerging digital creative artistic practices—they also forecast what is yet to come in 21st-century art and art education theory and practice.

Looking at the visual culture of technology-mediated experiences, Michelle Simms and B. Stephen Carpenter II also describe the impact of emerging electronic media on art education theory and practice. Simms and Carpenter consider how new technologies influence art and image production worldwide and pose relevant questions about visuality, mass-produced representations of the world, and controlled sources of imagery. Their chapter, "Putting the World Together: Virtual

Globes and The Changing Nature of (Digital) Global Representations," reflects growing interests in strategies that engage the interdisciplinary study of global visual culture as a form of art education pedagogical practice.

In the following chapter, "Transnational Visual Culture: Indecipherable Narratives and Pedagogy," Charles R. Garoian and Yvonne M. Gaudelius consider complications that occur at the intersections of theoretical speculations about global visual culture, Empire, interdependency, and cultural specificity. Exploring the similarities, contestations, and self contradictory narratives and projects of both transnationalism and collage, Garoian and Gaudelius describe how the revolutionary, disjunctive strategies of collage invented by the 20th-century avant-garde now provide a contemporary pedagogical strategy (in art education programs of study) for exposing, examining, and critiquing the patriarchal and homogenizing ethos of globalization.

Finally, Anna M. Kindler thoughtfully questions many of the assumptions, practices and productions of the postmodern internationalized art world discussed in earlier chapters in this section. In "Art and Art Education in an Age of Globalization," Kindler considers varying currently popular philosophical positions about the nature and value of art, including art as language, art as social action, and visual culture art education; and she posits her own argument that art remains the center of inquiry in contemporary art education theory. As do some of the other authors in this section of *Globalization, Art, and Education*, Kindler also examines contexts and cultural relationships of art creation and dissemination in relation to the proliferation of new media technologies. The roles of new global digital media and technologies, considered in relation to artistic and visual culture production in these latter chapters, are more fully examined with due regard to youth culture and educational practices in Section III of this anthology.

Globalization and Contemporary Art

Julia Marshall

There is a billboard in my neighborhood. On it is the familiar round blue-and-white striped ATT logo strategically adorned with Mount Fuji, the Eiffel Tower and the Liberty Bell accompanied by the words "ATT works in more places, like Japaridelphia." When we stop to consider this sign we find a virtual encapsulation of a world. Devoid of geography, this is a zone where time and distance are conflated and compressed by instantaneous connection. It is a transworld territory far removed from physical space. This is, in fact, a corporate vision of our globalized world—simple, accessible, homogenized, unified, and flat. The ATT billboard is significant for its vision of reality in our age of globalization. Moreover, the way the image conveys this reality is equally notable.

This chapter explores both topics: reality in an age of globalization and the ways visual images, especially art, portray that reality or realities. To do this, it provides examples of art and an analysis of the conceptual strategies art uses to generate and convey ideas. The ATT logo provides a springboard for this discussion because of the traits it shares with art as well as the way it differs from it. First, the ATT logo demonstrates so clearly the power of visual imagery to distill and create reality. Second, it employs two basic visual strategies used by artists and designers to do this: juxtaposition of images (collage) and, because the logo resembles the earth, the representation of an idea in terms of something else (metaphor). In this way, it gives us simple direct clues to how meaning is constructed through familiar symbols and visual imagery, clues we can also use to understand art. Third, the ATT image with its vision of reality stands in stark contrast in its message and meaning to those we usually discern from art.

Globalization and Art

What, then, is global reality? Berger (2002), Hopper (2007), Pieterse (2004) and Tomlinson (1999) argue that our globalized world and its dynamics are far more complex than the one portrayed in the ATT icon or in any corporate logo. In fact, globalization consists of multiple globalizations and creates many different realities. Since globalization affects our lives every day, understanding it is critical for all of us. This is especially true for young people who undoubtedly will be affected by increasing globalization and who have never lived without it. Hopper (2007) argues that to truly understand globalization we need to focus less on broad abstract concepts or generalizations and examine specific instances. This is where art comes in. Art zeroes in on the specifics. It also goes beyond and beneath corporate images/logos because it tells us about the many layers and corners of globalization (the personal and the local), and the side effects of it. Foremost, art emerges from personal experience and thought and provides the perspective of an individual. While corporate logos sell a simple vision, art portrays a complex and lived reality. This is the reality or realities we want our students to penetrate and understand.

The scholarship around globalization is extensive. A few key concepts from the anthropology of globalization are germane to our discussion here of contemporary art. The first is *connectivity*. Tomlinson (1999) describes this phenomenon as *complex connectivity* and argues that it is the critical force behind globalization. Complex connectivity generates collision and fusion; on one hand, it creates cultural homogenization that is heavily American and commercial in flavor and, on the other hand, it incites cultural differentiation and local resistance to it. However, the simple fusion/collision dichotomy is an inadequate explanation of the dynamics of complex connectivity. Pieterse (2004) argues that reality lies somewhere beyond fusion and collision, in *hybridity*—in the dynamics that create forms that maintain elements of the original forms but are distinctly new. He maintains that hybridization is and has always been the primary process of globalization.

Furthermore, Pieterse argues that accelerated hybridity is the creative force behind our age of monumental cultural innovation. Pieterse's notion of hybridity is central to our discussion of contemporary art. It not only characterizes the creative mechanisms that animate and shape global art and the environment that allows it to thrive, it also describes the collaged nature of much of this artwork. Also, contemporary global art addresses hybridity itself. At times it celebrates it but more often it critiques it; cultural differentiation, resistance to global standardization and critical commentary on globalizing forces characterize much contemporary art. Above all, global art helps us to understand the hybridity and complexity of today's world; it is in the images of art (not in corporate visual culture) that the nuances of complex connectivity are mined and revealed.

Glocalization is a key concept directly related to hybidity. Robertson (1992,1995) coined the word to describe the intermixing and interpenetration of global and local phenomena, which involve the imposition of the global onto the local and/or local adaptations of global trends and entities (Hopper, 2007). Glocalization is a factor in contemporary art as well; much of it represents the local or personal adaptation of global trends in art. These global trends include using forms that emerged from Western contemporary art such as installation and performance, the use of non-traditional materials and technology, and employment of devices such as humor, iconoclasm and irony.

Contemporary Art Responds to Globalization

The art discussed in this chapter responds to globalization in three ways. The first is in the content of the work; these artists address and interpret the critical issues and realities that global change and connectivity have generated. In their works, the primary themes of connectivity, polarization (local/global, traditional/new), and accelerated change are brought to life, most often in ancillary themes such as identity, home and mobility, dislocation or migration, difference and similarity, alienation and conformity, war and peace, politics and power. The second response lies in these artists' use of imagery from a common global visual culture. The images can be familiar icons of international commerce, politics or entertainment but often they include (or contrast with) local historical and/or traditional images. The third is in the visual conceptual strategies these artists use to convey their ideas and generate surprise and insight. Their strategies

mimic many of the mechanisms of globalization (collision, fusion and hybridization) identified by Pieterse (2004). They include ironic juxtapositions/collage (collisions), synthesis (fusion), layering, superimposition, re-contextualizing, adaptation and repackaging (hybridization). All of these strategies are common postmodern art practices that contemporary artists use to make meaning (Gude, 2004).

What follows is not a comprehensive recounting of all the images, subjects, and strategies contemporary artists use. It is, however, a condensed description of some important trends in the art world and some artists who work within them. The intention here is to illustrate some of the central themes and strategies of this artwork to make them accessible and useful to teachers and students of contemporary art. The themes are many but the strategies remain somewhat simple (strategies so simple we can see them in corporate logos). Therefore, this discussion is organized according to conceptual visual strategies. It is by no means meant to reduce these strategies to formulas. It should be remembered that globalization is a complex topic and art does not make ideas simple; it makes them more complex. Ironically, it often does this in deceptively simple ways.

Artists and their Conceptual Strategies
Fusion: Takashi Murakami

In globalization theory, fusion is understood as blending. This involves crossing boundaries and glossing over differences (Hopper, 2007). In art, fusing is a strategy of blending art forms and ideas and crossing borders. Often this involves combining art and popular visual culture and/or merging art with commerce. This strategy animates the work of Japanese artist Takashi Murakami. Indeed, Murakami takes fusion to new heights; his work grows out of a rich matrix of Tokyo pop culture (*Otaku* subculture images and *ani-manga*), pornography, American Pop Art (Warhol), science fiction (particularly robots and technology), and Japanese traditional art (the manga of Katsushika Hokosai) (Hebdige, 2007). The most prominent of these influences is Japanese popular culture. Murakami takes the style and flavor of pop-culture images, which teeter on the supremely mundane (like cartoon mushrooms, round-faced daisies and bunnies, wide-open eyes with flowing eyelashes, and wide-eyed, hyper-sexualized manga girls), and either blows them up into monumental objects or repeats them endlessly in patterns like wallpaper. He also invents his own characters. Perhaps his most famous is *DOB*, a post-manga spoof of Mickey Mouse, who Murakami

Figure 1

reincarnates in multiples, prints, paintings and inflatables with each avatar becoming ever more sinister (See Figure 1). Hebdige, (2007) describes Murakami's figures and style as "sado-cute". This "sado-cute" style has infiltrated the art world. While highbrow aesthetics might condemn the "cutesy", cartoony, kitschy and common, Murakami has lifted them out of lowbrow culture and given them acceptability in art (Hebdige, 2007).

Crossing the divide between contemporary culture and art is one part of Murakami's approach; another is blending art with commerce. Many artists have made this leap, but Murakami does it with particular flair, audacity, and relevance. He understands his art as a business and an industry and he revels in the corporate-style branding of his works. This shows in his marketing of his signature figurines, posters and other collectables, which are produced in his three factories. His 2003 collaboration with Louis Vuitton exemplifies his merging of art and consumerism. His rainbow-colored adaptations of the famous "LV" patterns were exhibited as paintings, further blurring the line between art and fashion design. An example of this is *Eye Love Monogram* (2003) (Siegel, 2005). The subsequent marketing of Murakami/Vuitton line of handbags in Murakami's first major US retrospective, *c. Murakami* (2007) at the Museum of Contemporary Art in Los Angeles is another case in point (Hebdige, 2007).

So what is Murakami up to? On the surface, the "sado-cute" style, the cartoon pop culture figures, the mass-production and marketing may look like

a wholesale acceptance of global (read American) culture. On the contrary, Murakami is fighting back against it. In the many manifestos that accompany his exhibitions, he has voiced his intent to redeem Japan, to cast off the humiliation inflicted on it after World War II, and challenge American cultural hegemony (Schimmel, 2007). His is an effort to celebrate and promote Japanese culture, and to infiltrate the world. Murakami's work, therefore, is an act of differentiation and resistance and, because its forms and styles are so popular globally beyond the art world, it is a case of what Berger (2002) calls *alternative globalization*—the global spread of forms from sources outside Western culture.

Layering: Saira Wasim

Another strategy for addressing globalization is *layering*. This usually involves using a traditional form or style to tell a contemporary story. In *layering*, the genre or style is a critical *productive* factor; it generates meaning. For a style or genre to be productive, it must have cultural resonance; it must evoke a host of values, behaviors and concepts. It also must be recognized, understood and powerful. Often this means stylization and use of familiar icons. Contemporary artists who use this strategy often come from places with strong iconic traditions that they can naturally use. Rather than adhere to tradition, these artists harness the depth and power of these traditions and use their visual tropes as tools to zero in on contemporary issues. This strategy packs a punch.

Artist Saira Wasim is one such artist. She is a keen observer of global politics, especially as they play out in her native Pakistan and its volatile neighborhood. Wasim has lots to say and she does it by mixing biting wit with visual opulence. In her *New World Order* (2006) (see Figure 2), Wasim depicts George W. Bush, Hamid Karzai, Tony Blair, and Pervez Musharraf perched gleefully on or around a globe. Musharraf sits like a ventriloquist's puppet on Bush's lap while his 'boss' waves to the world and the Blair-Karzai twins are all smiles. In another painting, *Mission Accomplished* (2004), Wasim depicts Bush and his cohorts frolicking with bow and arrow across Asia on the back of a cow. In these depictions, Wasim takes issue with the pacts and exploits that shape the post 9/11 Muslim world. To amplify her perspective on these players, Wasim takes their images from contemporary media and depicts them in the traditional Indian miniature style of the Mughal Dynasty (1526-1857) (Ali, 2006). In doing so, Wasim, dips into the rich store of meaning that this style and genre possess, thus connecting

the hubris, exploits, and follies of today's rulers to that of past royals. This layering of contemporary content onto an historical style becomes Wasim's finely honed instrument of satire and irony as she cuts her protagonists down to size and 'miniaturizes' them. The effect is augmented ironically by the delicacy, intricacy and sheer beauty the miniature style brings to these images. The result is an exquisite political cartoon with disquieting overtones. Wasim's work demonstrates how style and genre are inextricable from content and how critical both are to meaning. Secondly, her work is a clear example of placing the contemporary and international into a historical and local frame—a frame that a global art audience can decipher and understand.

Employing the Meaning of Materials: Wang Jin and Do-Ho Suh

When some sculptors discarded bronze, marble and wood in favor of modern materials, they found a new vehicle for conveying meaning: the material itself. The medium became an integral part of the message. Some contemporary artists make exceptional use of this

idea. They choose materials that not only have an aesthetic presence but also have meaning or resonance in themselves. Two materials come to mind that have a universally recognized character, meaning, and sensory qualities and are, therefore, common mediums for manifesting ideas connected to globalization. One material is plastic because it is new, and the other is silk, because it is old.

Plastic. No other material evokes the contemporary and new quite like plastic. It speaks of many factors in contemporary life—technology, artificiality, the commonplace and the mass-produced. We saw this in the work of Takahashi Murakami. However, plastic has other associations. On one hand, it conjures the concept of permanence; plastic does not degrade. On the other hand, plastic acts as a metaphor for impermanence, instability and things we discard. Perhaps that is why artists often use it to embody their ideas about contemporary life and its tensions between permanence and tradition, immutability and change.

One such artist is Wang Jin. Wang's *A Chinese Dream* (1997) (see Figure 3) is a set of Chinese opera costumes. The costumes are a potent symbol

Figure 2

Left: Saira Wasim, *New World Order* (2006). Courtesy of the artist.

Figure 3

Right: Wang Jin, *A Chinese Dream* (1997). Courtesy of the artist and Pekinfinearts Gallery, Beijing.

Figure 4

Do Ho Suh, *Seoul Home/LA Home/New York Home/Balitmore Home/Seattle Home* (1999), Museum of Contemporary Art, Los Angeles. Purchased with funds provided by an anonymous donor and a gift of the artist. Courtesy of the artist and Lehmann Maupin Gallery.

of Chinese civilization; the opera is a venerated art form—a jewel of Chinese culture. Instead of the colorful embroidered silk of which these costumes are usually constructed, Wang reinterprets them in translucent plastic. The translucency of Wang's costumes gives this highly stylized ornate attire an ephemeral quality; they have the feeling of a gauzy dream or memory. However, for Wang this dream is a nightmare brought on by the onslaught of global tourism and its catering to Western tastes, which he sees as bastardizing genuine Chinese culture and making it inauthentic. Wang's perspective is reflected in his choice of such an artificial material as plastic. For him, replacing the authentic silk of the original costumes with clear embroidered plastic creates the perfect materials-based metaphor for an artificial spectacle that is now the Chinese culture that most outsiders see (Hung, 1999).

Silk. Silk, on the other hand, is a natural material with ancient roots. For his *Seoul Home/LA Home/New York Home/Baltimore Home/Seattle Home* (1999) (see Figure 4), Korean-American artist Do Ho Suh created an exact replica of his traditional Korean home in Seoul. For this he chose translucent silk, an airy, milky fabric with deep cultural resonance and practical versatility. Because his *Home* is translucent (like Wang's costumes) it alludes to memory and dreams. Here the memories and dreams are of home in Korea. However, the artist does not dwell in nostalgia and homesickness; he takes his home with him and this transportability of home is the subject of this piece. Silk is the perfect medium for this message as it makes for a 'tent' that is easily rolled up, packed away and

transported. Suh also made a replica in silk of his New York apartment. These 'tents' are apt metaphors for the life and spirit of the new global nomadic set, the artists who live with a lingering sense of displacement, detachment and freedom because they are always in transit. The artist elaborates on this idea. He finds that his displacement gives him the creative space and critical distance to see things clearly and make the art that conveys his vision (Suh, 2003). This detachment seems to work. Do Ho Suh is a consummate observer. He is also a master at distilling his observations into simple statements of great import, power and transcendent beauty. Coupling the physical presence of a material with its metaphorical meanings is one of his most potent strategies.

Tapping the Global Image Bank: Marian Heyerdahl

Easy universal tourism, artist mobility (grants and residencies), and the explosion of information technologies (books, the Internet, movies) have made images from all cultural traditions part of a global visual cultural experience and, therefore, part of our shared human 'image bank.' Therefore, artists now have a rich storehouse of visual imagery (and the meanings associated with them) with which to construct and convey their ideas. Also, artists now can reach a global audience and capitalize on an image's original cultural meanings and any new meanings it may have acquired in this globalized environment. The expansion of imagery has also expanded artists' thinking—allowing them to see their concepts in new ways.

eyes) and different hand positions (praying, hiding in sleeves, out-stretched in offering).

Because the original Xian figures embody warlike masculinity, invincibility and power, they are the perfect foil and medium for Heyerdahl's contrasting message—the suffering and inner strength of women in times of war (Terkaoui, Reder, McHugh, Coe, & Craig, 2007). However, the original figures are legendary not only as icons of a past era and exemplars of masculine power, but also as icons of contemporary Chinese culture with its growing global presence and marketability. The Xian *Terracotta Army* is one of the biggest tourist spectacles in the world. Reproductions of the figures are common and they often border on kitsch. Although the associations with contemporary China, tourism, and souvenirs tend to overshadow the original significance of these figures, Heyerdahl's women benefit from this notoriety; we all recognize the warriors. The power of Heyerdahl's work, however, lies in her restoration of the original meaning of these figures and the way she uses that meaning to make her statement.

Collage of Cultural Icons: Sui Jianguo, Yinka Shonebare, and Jean-Ulrick Desert

Collage involves the juxtaposition of two powerful iconic images. The positioning of these icons creates an ironic collision of imagery that conveys a new concept, which does not exist in either of the individual icons alone. In the artwork discussed here, the icons come from contrasting cultures—East and West. The work of Chinese artist Sui Jianguo employs this strategy. In his *Dying Slave* (1998) (see Figure 6), Sui clothes a classical icon from Western art history, Michelangelo's original *Dying Slave*, in iconic clothing of China—a Mao uniform. In a simple juxtaposition, Sui makes his point: the Mao uniform is a slave shackle. Equally important, Sui conflates the classicism of Western European culture with Mao, thus implying that the aesthetics and icons of Maoism are the new classical forms of China (Kelley, 2005). Sui Jianguo's work fits in with our theme of globalization in this

We find a clear example of this strategy in the work of Norwegian artist, Marian Heyerdahl. In *The Terracotta Women's Project* (2006) (see Figure 5), Heyerdahl presents 57 life-size female versions of the famous Han Dynasty warriors of Xian, China known as *The Terracotta Army*. At first glance, these figures seem very similar to the heroic warrior figures they mimic; they are of the same size and material (ceramic) with similar dress, facial features and hair designs. However these new figures are female and each figure is different; they have various expressions (some are crying, some screaming, some with closed way: he uses images from Western art that are part of a global visual vocabulary, thus making a statement that is discernable to a global audience. It is critical to his message that the images he uses are cross-cultural and resonate with cultural and historical significance. The collision between these two loaded icons delivers the new meaning. Another reading of this piece delivers a related message. The slave could represent a Westernized China enslaved in a communist straightjacket or perhaps a straightjacket of history. This looks to be Sui's comment on the new Westernized capitalistic spirit of China imprisoned in Maoism—his take on Mao-dernization.

Anglo-Nigerian artist, Yinka Shonibare uses the collage strategy too, juxtaposing cultural icons to great effect in his installations. His primary icon is *wax print* fabric, a brightly colored cloth printed with various patterns and images, which is popular among African women. This cloth signifies African identity; to wear this cloth is to announce that one is authentically African (Diawara, 2004). Shonibare picks up on the notion that in Africa clothes express identity. He collages this iconic wax print cloth to non-African icons. One such icon is Victorian fashion. He makes Victorian-style costumes out of wax print fabric and displays his crossbred attire on headless mannequins. These figures are often arranged in groupings that suggest power relationships. It is apparent in these installations that Shonibare is addressing colonialism; Victorian costumes are emblematic of colonial rule. For Shonibare, colonialism is a dialogue (although uneven); each party puts its stamp on the other. Addressing colonialism sets the stage for Shonibare's primary subject: stereotypes in a contemporary postcolonial world. For Shonibare, stereotypes do not hold; nothing is quite as simple as it seems. The wax print fabric exemplifies this complexity. It has come to signify authentic Africa but it is made in Holland. The icon itself has a hybrid heritage. In drawing on this fact, Shonibare zeros in on a universal truth: there are no pure cultural products or identities today.

Shonibare takes collage of iconic images and forms a step further in his re-creation of renowned paintings from Western art history. One such painting is Thomas Gainsborough's *Mr. and Mrs. Andrews* (1750), which Shonibare restages in *Mr. and Mrs. Andrews Without Their Heads* (1998). Here Shonibare replaces the rigidly upright inhabitants of the English countryside portrayed in the original painting with his wax cloth-dressed mannequins. Shonibare's hybridized figures have entered a foreign, once unattainable world. Another painting mimicked by Shonibare is Jean-Honore Fragonard's 18th-century genre painting, *The Swing*. Shonibare's restaging of this work in

Figure 7

Yinka Shonibare, *The Swing (after Fragonard)* (2001), Courtesy of The Stephen Friedman Gallery and The Tate Gallery, London.

The Swing (2001) (see Figure 7), with its buoyant central figure blithely floating through the air, also places a hybridized figure in an old iconic Western frame. This framing suggests that an African-diasporic identity can defy the gravity of racial and cultural stereotypes to play in a Western postcolonial world (Diawara, 2004). In both works, the conveyance of Shonibare's message about the fluidity of identity today depends on the viewer recognizing the referenced paintings and the social worlds they depict. This recognition sets the stage for the collision of images and the resultant expression of Shonibare's ideas. It also generates irony and humor.

Other striking examples of collage of cultural icons occur in the work of Jean-Ulrick Desert. Born and raised in Haiti and of African descent but now living in Berlin and New York, Desert lives a bi-cultural life and this gives him a special perspective on living between cultures. Ironic juxtapositions of icons serve his message of collision and tension well. In a series of performances in which he donned a traditional German outfit, complete with a feathered cap and lederhosen, and strolled the streets of German cities, Desert juxtaposed the symbolic uniform of German identity with himself (an iconic figure) to challenge the notion of German homogeneity. This work bears a strong resemblance to Shonibare's installations in which apparel acts as an emblem of national and cultural identity, and entrenched habits of mind are challenged through the juxtaposition of icons.

Iconic juxtapositions that involve attire are equally effective in Desert's *The Burqa Project: On the Borders of My Dreams I Encountered My Double's Ghost* (2001) (see Figure 8). In it are four figures wearing burqas, the traditional head-to-toe garb of Muslim women. This iconic dress of the East collides with icons of the West; each Burqa is made out of a flag from a Western power (Germany, France, the USA and the UK). Here Desert comments on the clash of cultures and the complex relationship between the West and the Arab world, which he observes as a citizen of the world (Ramirez, 2007).

In the Art Classroom

It is important that our students understand two things: globalization and art. As for learning about art, the artwork discussed here is particularly educative. The first lesson it provides concerns iconic images. In this work, icons are central and critical to the artworks' meanings. The prominence of icons provides opportunities for students to examine how iconic images evoke associations and have meanings that stretch way beyond their visible form. This is especially critical knowledge in a world where many

Figure 8

Jean-Ulrick Desert, *The Burqa Project: On the Borders of My Dreams I Encountered My Double's Ghost* (2001), Courtesy of the artist.

images are universally used, recognized and understood, and where some images can carry ideological weight and incite strong reactions.

Using icons is one central strategy of art; connecting them to other visible forms (images, materials or style) is another. As we have seen in the artwork discussed here, connection making, whether it comes in the form of collage, layering, combining or metaphor, generates new meanings by reframing or reinterpreting existing images. The artwork examined here could be especially useful in studying these strategies because it makes these devices visible and accessible. This accessibility can help students understand how connective strategies trigger ideas and catalyze critical insights. If students grasp the dual message about icons and connective strategies they can use this knowledge to inform and shape their own artwork.

In regard to globalization, Mansilla and Gardner (2007) contend that to fully grasp the dynamics and impacts of globalization, students need to go beyond absorbing information to developing *global consciousness*, which they define as, "a mindful way of *being* in the world" (p. 48). Mansilla and Gardner see global consciousness as the ability to place oneself and ones life within the context of the entire planet—to see things globally. As we have gleaned from the examples discussed above, contemporary art that addresses global realities provides fresh insights into the world and how others perceive and live in it. This art, therefore, can be a powerful tool for seeing issues from others' perspectives, thinking more deeply and diversely about planetary concerns, and for fostering the global consciousness Mansilla and Gardner encourage.

There are also insights into global consciousness to be gleaned from the lives of the artists discussed here. As players in the international art world, these artists are highly transient and their transnational lives give them first hand experience of dislocation and change as well as unusual vantage points on culture and humanity. All of them are scholars in their own right, steeped in their own traditions and aware of global trends. They also enjoy the freedom that art affords. Art is a domain with open structures and no borders and it thrives on critiquing orthodoxies and breaking rules. These artists are respondents to and critics of culture but also creators of culture. All of them contribute to the global conversation: they raise questions, make observations and bequeath images to our collective visual vocabulary. In the work they make and the lives they lead, they show us how ambitious, thoughtful artists can be proactive, how they can personally influence or change culture. It is important for students to see that this can be done and how it is done. For these reasons, the artists presented here offer good role models for our students as *beings in the world* with the sensitivities, wisdom, knowledge and vantage points that can lead to global consciousness. Reading their images, learning from their strategies, following their examples, these are some ways to achieve this.

REFERENCES

Ali, A. (2006). Saira Wasim. In M.Chiu, K. Higa, & S. Min (Eds.), *One way or another: Asian American art now* (pp. 120-125). New Haven: Yale University.

Berger, P. (2002). Introduction. In Berger, P. & Huntington, S. (Eds.), *Many Globalizations: Cultural diversity in the contemporary world.* Oxford, UK: Oxford University Press.

Diawara, M. (2004). Independence cha cha: The art of Yinka Shonibare. In *Yinka Shonibare: Double dutch* (pp. 18-23). Rotterdam: NAI.

Gude, O. (2004) Postmodern principles: In search of a 21st century art education. *Art education, 57*(1), 6-14 .

Hebdige, D. (2007). Flat boy vs. skinny: Takahashi Murakami and the battle for "Japan". In P. Schimmel. c *Murakami* (pp. 14-51). Los Angeles, CA: The Museum of Contemporary Art, Los Angeles.

Hopper, P. (2007). *Understanding cultural globalization.* Cambridge, UK: Polity.

Hung, W. (1999). *Transience: Chinese experimental art at the end of the twentieth century.* Chicago, Ill: University of Chicago.

Kelley, J. (2005). *Sui Jianguo: The sleep of reason.* San Francisco, CA: Asian Art Museum.

Mansilla, V. B. & Gardner, H. (2007). From teaching globalization to nurturing global consciousness. In M. Suarez-Orozco (Ed.), *Learning in the global era: International perspectives on globalization and education* (pp. 47-66). Berkeley, CA: University of California.

Pieterse, I. (2004). *Globalization and culture: Global mélange.* New York: Bowman & Littlefield.

Ramirez, N. (2007). Jean-Ulrick Desert. In T. Mosaka (Ed.), *Infinite island: Contemporary Caribbean art* (pp. 100-105). New York: Brooklyn Museum.

Robertson, R. (1992). *Globalization: Social theory and global culture,* London: Sage.

Robertson, R. (1995). Glocalization: Time-space and homogeneity-heterogeneity, in M. Featherstone, S. Lash and R. Robertson (Eds.), *Global modernities* (pp. 25-44). London: Sage.

Schimmel, P. (2007). Making Murakami. In c. *Murakami* (pp. 53-79). Los Angeles, CA: The Museum of Contemporary Art, Los Angeles.

Siegel, K. (2005). In the air. In T. Murakami (Ed.), *Little boy: The arts of Japan's exploding subculture* (pp.269-289). New York: Japan Society.

Suh, D. H. (2003). Interview with Susan Collins. In *Art 21: Art in the twenty-first century, season 2* (pp. 48-59). New York: Harry N. Abrams.

Terkaoui, S., Reder, G., McHugh, S., Coe, A., & Craig, C. (2007). Marian Heyerdahl. In. C. Hanaor (Ed.), *Breaking the mould: New approaches to ceramics* (pp. 114-117). London: Black Dog.

Tomlinson, J. (1999). *Globalization and culture.* Chicago, Ill: University of Chicago.

Border Theory, Nationalism, and Transnational Art Pedagogy

Rachel Bailey Jones

With all the recent focus on the implications and effects of globalization, the border has become an important site for constructing and negotiating meaning. As the boundaries that mark the separation between countries, borders play an essential role in policing the movement of people and the creation of categories and identities. Many artists have used the border as a metaphor in their work, challenging the rigid physical borders by subverting the ideas of separate cultural identities; for many border artists, it is the mixing, melding, and reforming of multiple cultures at the border that is of interest. The border is the literal and metaphorical space in-between and has the power both to police and exclude, but also the power to create space for transcultural and inclusive pedagogy. Artistic expression of hybrid and transnational experience functions in this global border space created by the movement of capital and people. As a response to increased movement and the supposed breakdown of the nation-state, there is increased xenophobia and contraction. In many countries, political parties that advocate a restriction of immigration and a more narrow definition of national citizenship have been winning supporters and elections. Reactionary parties play on a fear of difference that seem to be increasing as the distance between various forms of difference gets smaller. Cultural producers who create works of art and media across boundaries can call this fear of difference into question.

Transnational feminist theorist Ella Shohat (1998) calls for a "transnational imaginary" (p. 46) to add life to what she calls "inert, static maps chartered by ethnic studies, area studies, women's studies, and gay/lesbian studies." The current neo-imperialism of global capital requires imaginative acts that go beyond traditional boundaries of nation. This "transnational imaginary" is a space that is created by artists who work across borders; they question the flow of capital and the Western hegemony of meaning and knowledge. Such imaginative acts create liminal spaces of inquiry. This chapter considers how art creates space for such inquiry, focusing on how one artist, Emily Jacir, questions and repositions those multiple and imagined border spaces conditioned by American/Israeli/Palestinian political, historical, cultural, geographic, and economic interests, disputes, and settlements.

The Border Writer

The meaning of images and words is culturally determined through complex processes of negotiation and mediation. Semiotic codes, generally used to describe the cultural meaning of words, can also be applied to visual forms of communication. The border space provides for the mixing of cultural codes and for the creation of new meaning. Emily Hicks (1991) writes of the border writer as someone who is the product of two sets of referential codes, "The reader of border writing may experience the deterritorialization of signification; to read a border text is to cross over into another set of referential codes" (p. xxvi). Border artists create images/experiences that draw on the visual semiotic codes of multiple cultures. Border space exists not just at the physical, legal border between two nation-states; it is a space that exists metaphorically and culturally wherever there is an overlap or negotiation of cultural codes.

Artist Emily Jacir's border space exists literally on the Israeli/Palestinian border, and figuratively in the meeting of American/Israeli/Palestinian codes of representation and her visual negotiation of these codes. Her work cannot be viewed as a product of any pure, distinct culture or regime of representation. It is both rooted in the distinct geography of Palestine and uprooted in the crossing of cultural borders and her own physical travel between lands. "When one leaves one's country (deterritorialization), everyday life changes. The objects that continually remind one of the past are gone. Now, the place of origin is a mental representation in memory" (Hicks, 1991, p. xxxi). This "place of origin" that exists in the memory of the border crosser is detached, fragmented, and reconfigured in relation to the location of displacement.

Cultural codes are both reified and deconstructed in one's memory; the fragments of origin are reassembled with fragmented cultural codes of the new location.

Emily Jacir in Context

Emily Jacir is an American-born artist living and working in multiple geographic locations, specifically New York City and Ramallah in the Palestinian territory. Born in New York, her family has geographic and familial ties to the disputed land known as Palestine. Jacir's Palestinian family origin has deeply affected her art and her sense of home. Her connection to the imagined community of Palestine can be framed by the discourse of diaspora, a way to theorize the global connection of people who share emotional and psychological ties to a region or an adopted homeland. Though not the location of her birth, the disputed land that lies at the center of Israeli/Palestinian conflict is the home that exists in Jacir's artwork, a mental space without geographical place:

> Between the mutually perpetuating fanaticisms of the suicide bombers and the militant Israeli right, Jacir hollows a tentative aesthetic space in which it's possible to sense, without feeling obliged to make excuses for the savagery of either side, the bitterness of exile.
>
> (Breidenbach, 2003, p. 188)

The artwork is about the relationship between a traditionally Muslim culture, the displacement of this culture through the creation of Israel, and the conflicts of a Western-born woman artist living and working between cultures. Although several of her pieces deal with gender, the artist is clear in her belief that the work cannot be flattened into a commentary on women's oppression or liberty within culture or religion. Nor can the artwork and longing of Jacir be analyzed or examined separately from the history, culture, and political events of the region and the ongoing conflict that has sustained the focus of much of the world. Though the importance and history of this land traces far back, and it has importance for three major monotheistic religious traditions, the event that is at the core of discussions of the area occurred after World War II with the creation of the Israeli state.

Of course, there are many sides to every historical event, and the Israeli/Palestinian conflict has proven to be particularly divisive and controversial. In writing about the conflict, I sought source material for the artwork of Jacir, who identifies with Palestine and therefore focuses on the issue of identity and belonging from that perspective. The 1947 United Nations declaration partitioned what was formerly known as Palestine into separate Arab and Jewish states. Israel was created as a Jewish homeland and was intended to exist with an independent Palestinian Arab state. Feelings of displacement and tensions over the creation of the Jewish state built after its creation and led to direct military engagement between Israel and its Arab neighbors. In addition to the multiple military conflicts that resulted from the creation of Israel, the settlement of a new national population of Israelis meant that others were removed and relocated from their original homes. Many Palestinians felt a loss of identity. Despite living in the same general geographic location, they were no longer allowed a national or group identity that was separate from the Israeli occupation. Beginning in 1987 and existing in varying degrees and intensity, the *Intifada*, or Palestinian uprising, has been a mass response to years of living with uncertainty (Llewellyn, 1998, para. 5). While uprisings against Israeli rule have drawn international attention to the situation, the Israeli response to the daily effect of the Intifada was an increasingly regulated and policed form of living imposed on the Palestinians. "Palestinians are frequently under curfew and, as stateless refugees, they are often forbidden to work or travel. They are besieged, their houses demolished for the third or fourth time" (Said, 2003, p. 48). Many Palestinians now have to go through Israeli checkpoints in order to get to school or work in the morning, and waiting in long lines and having personal documents examined are commonplace. These checkpoints are borders within the nation-state of Israel; they regulate and restrict the movement of Palestinians. Another function of the checkpoints is to intensify the feelings of dislocation and confusion of not being a citizen of the nation in which you live and work.

Despite many internationally organized attempts at peace agreements, there has been no lasting peace or solution to the problem that is agreeable to all parties. Continuing attacks that kill civilians on both the Israeli and Palestinian sides have exacerbated tensions and hindered negotiations. Violence and threats of violence are the daily reality for all concerned. For many Palestinian artists who have ties to the occupied territories, the creation of visual and multi-media pieces cannot be separated from the political realities of daily life under Israeli rule. "'Palestine' has become a worldwide metaphor for trouble, unrest, violence: for Palestinians, that combination of words evoking fact, memory, and aspiration and the images associated with them stands in for citizenship or passport" (Said, 2003, p. 47). Perhaps the most politically charged geography in the world, the land of Israel, Palestine, and the countless checkpoints and borders surrounding Palestine create opportunities for artists to create meaningful expressions that can capture the reality of living in the borderlands. Border artists can address the uncertainty and negotiation symbolized by the crossing through guarded stations. Art can take the intractable fear and violence of the real border and create forms of expression that can allow others to experience the border vicariously.

Crossing Borders

Emily Jacir's body of work is varied in its intention and form; some works are conceptually based documentation of performance, others are carefully hand-made objects that are more traditionally sculptural. The work explores the tension of the exile who has lost citizenship and cannot travel and the artist who identifies as an exile but who also carries an American passport. The dislocation of living between worlds, for Jacir, also includes the violence of fragmentation and lives split into pieces by the forced movement and resettlement of people. Uncertain spaces open up between traditional centers; in these spaces, postcolonial identity formation begins to occur based not on fixity but on movement, migration, and negotiation. For artists who migrate, the lack of fixed center and the loss of home are expressed in their art as a question of mythical fixed ideas of self and other. Sets of referential codes, cultural markers that convey meaning, are deterritorialized (Hicks, 1991) when physical and mental borders are crossed. Meanings from both sides of the border are fragmented and reconstructed in the border zone. Jacir's multiple border zones exist in her work as an attempt to reconstruct—or reterritorialize—meaning between cultural locations. There is a tension between the transnational artist who is defined by her movement and the subjects of her work who are defined by their confinement. Just as unequal relationships of power can be analyzed and expressed through the ability to see and control who is seen, dominance can also be asserted through the ability to move and control who can and cannot move.

Jacir uses mixed media, photography, video, installation, and performance that speak to her longing for a home that cannot exist in Palestine. While the postcolonial identity is predicated on movement, Jacir turns this around in her work that questions the uneven availability of movement. She creates pieces that center on the inability of the Palestinian exile to return home, on the control of movement through checkpoints, and on a longing to travel that is denied. All of the work has in common a sense of unease, of longing for something that is physically absent but present in memory, an inability to be at home and yet powerless to move.

Jacir has split her adult life living between New York and Ramallah, identifying with the Palestinian longing for home but also as an American citizen able to do what a Palestinian cannot do: travel freely. In one of her stays in the occupied territory, Jacir had to pass through an Israeli military checkpoint to go work every day. Upset by the intrusion of the armed guards at the checkpoints, she began to bring a video camera through the crossing. "I was walking across this checkpoint every day to get to Birzeit University from my home, and I just wanted a recording of it for myself" (Jacir, 2004, p. 18). One day Israeli soldiers caught her filming and they "held me at gunpoint for three hours, they confiscated my tape, they threw my passport in the mud" (p. 18). A casual decision to record her own experiences led to this traumatizing experience and in turn led to the creation of a video installation entitled *Crossing Surda.* Jacir hid a video camera in her bag, with a hole cut for the lens. The result is a disorienting video, shot at knee-height, of the repetitive daily crossing through the checkpoint. It is the documentation of an event that is ordinary and banal to the Palestinian who walks to school or work, but it is an uncomfortable experience for others to witness the waiting, the crossing, the automatic weapons, and to realize that this is a lived reality. The line between the Occupied Territory and the state of Israel cannot be described as a border in the strict sense of a dividing line that separates two national groups who mutually agree upon the terms of the separation. The area is better understood in terms of the psychological border described by Irit Rogoff (2000):

> In reality this is, however, a far more complex and nebulous entity, traversed on both sides, a constant leakage of hostile bodies, never able to sustain the separations and protect the inhabitants in the way that its huge military mobilization set out to do. (p. 137)

These psychological borders function to reinforce the power, control, and citizenship of one group while simultaneously fortifying the powerlessness of the other. While Israeli guards hold automatic weapons and control access, the Palestinian worker or student must supplicate to Israeli authority. While the zones of contact at checkpoints assert the legal Israeli national identity and power to enforce, they place the Palestinian in the floating identity of proving one's status as a non-entity.

In *Where We Come From* (Said, 2003), Jacir asked exiled Palestinians what they would do if they could return to their homeland and see their family and friends. She then visited the named territories using her American passport, fulfilling the wishes of the exiles and photographing the act to later exhibit.

"That work is so autobiographical in the sense that it is coming from my experience of spending my whole life going back and forth between Palestine and other parts of the world" (Jacir, 2004, p. 9). *Where We Come From* is exhibited in pairs of objects: the first is a framed piece of text, in both English and Arabic, that describes the wish of the exiled Palestinian, and the second is a photograph of Jacir completing the wished-for task. One of the pairs displays the wish of a son separated from his mother for Jacir to visit the mother and hug and kiss her; the accompanying photograph shows the artist embracing an older woman:

> Her compositions slip through the nets of bureaucracies and nonnegotiable borders, time and space, in search of not grandiose dreams or clotted fantasies, but rather humdrum objects and simple gestures like visits, hugs, watering a tree, eating a meal—the kinds of things that maybe all Palestinians will be able to do someday, when they can make their way home peacefully and without restriction. (Said, 2003, p. 49)

In using the power of her American passport, Jacir fulfills the wishes and dreams of these Palestinian exiles. She also highlights the inequity of the situation, and the incomprehensibility of how mundane tasks such as kissing one's mother or eating a family meal have been made illegal through the policing of borders and the controlling of movement by authorities.

From Paris to Riyadh (1999, 2001) is Jacir's piece that deals specifically with gender issues, and it does so in a subtle but haunting manner. Visually, the piece appears to consist of floating solid black shapes on a background of vellum. The description that accompanies the piece lends meaning to the black forms, "marker on vellum, documenting the illegal sections of *Vogue* magazine" (Jacir, 2004, p. 19). After reading this description, body parts start to appear, truncated pieces of arms, legs, torsos that had to be marked out in order for the French fashion magazine to be brought into Saudi Arabia:

> Most people kept interpreting it was about the repression of Middle Eastern women when it wasn't ... Being back and forth between these two spaces—one of commodification and the other of banning the image of the female body—which was equally repressing and equally discomforting. (p. 19)

It is interesting, and predictable, that Western critics and viewers of *From Paris to Riyadh* would assume it be about the repression of Muslim women. That is the meaning that is appropriate to much Western cultural discourse about gender and Islam. But Jacir bristles at such an uncomplicated reading of the piece. She stresses that repression cannot be so easily defined and assigned to one culture and counter argues that both the marketing of women's bodies for profit and the denial of the body are repressive in different ways. With her assertion of the complexity of this work, Jacir is challenging the reading of visual codes through Western cultural lenses; covered body parts, blacked out with marker, are not to be automatically equated with repression. Without stating it in these terms, she is asking for a *border reading* of her work, where visual codes are the result of cultural negotiation that must be read through transnational lenses. There is also an ambivalence that Jacir has for the use of the woman's body as cultural code; in fact *From Paris to Riyadh* is the only piece that deals directly, through its covered absence, with the female body. As a woman artist who deals with issues of (traditionally Muslim) Palestine, Jacir avoids being associated with the veil as the only visual cultural code available to her for the expression of difference.

In more recent work, Jacir deals directly with the question of difference and the shrinking distances of difference that are brought about through global movement. She juxtaposes daily experiences and seemingly ordinary events, crossing and blurring boundaries and binaries. *Ramallah/New York*, a video installation from 2004-2005, juxtaposes everyday scenes from Palestinian communities in the two geographically distant cities that are rendered indistinguishable in the video installation. Western viewers are accustomed to being affirmed in the cultural superiority of their modern, rational societies through news media who show the foreign as generally traditional, violent, dirty, and hungry. We have the commercials for Christian Children's Fund that play on our guilt while reaffirming our ideas about how "other people" live and treat their children. When we are shown scenes from Islamic countries, the images usually support this idea of inferior difference; we see the veiled women and the faceless men bowed in ritualized prayer. When viewing *Ramallah/New York, a* video installation that shows almost identical scenes of daily life in the United States and the Occupied Territory of Palestine, the Western viewer is not given the familiar relationship to the foreign. The lack of physical space between the two screens and the similarity of the action does not leave room for cultural or moral superiority. Here, the artist is not equating experience of the citizens but creating a loss of center in the viewer, a space of uncertainty, a mental border space. For Jacir, the lack of fixed center and the loss of home are expressed in her art as a question for the viewer of mythical fixed ideas of self and other. Bhabha (1994) names this space as the hybrid, the liminal, and the interstitial that break with essentialized colonial discourse. "This interstitial passage between fixed identifications opens up the possibility of a cultural hybridity that entertains difference without an assumed or imposed hierarchy" (p. 5). This construct of hybridity posed by Bhabha is very similar to the space of the border artist, an ambiguous area where fixed notions of identity and meaning are disturbed and reconfigured.

Creating Border Knowledge

In viewing and writing about the art created by Emily Jacir, the concept of deterritorialization and the work of Emily Hicks help to frame the production and reception of the work. The artist is a form of border writer who uses a combination of image, text, and experience to create and translate meaning. It is both rooted in the distinct geography of Palestine and uprooted in the crossing of cultural borders and her own physical travel between lands. The reception of this border creation can also be grounded in the concept of deterritorialization. When signification and connections are drifting between geographic and cultural locations, the meaning of the work is always a negotiation between the artist, the art, and the viewer. Cultural codes can cross borders, but they are still rooted in the specificity of location. Meaning, therefore, is subject to a process of deterritorialization; the signification of the work is both tied to original intention of the artist and simultaneously displaced through interaction with the viewer's cultural codes and history.

This concept of the deterritorialization of meaning is important in conceptualizing the move from viewing artwork to the creation of pedagogy. Every experience with text or image can be mediated through understanding the intention of the artists, but the construction of meaning is made possible through interaction with previous exposure to dominant cultural codes.

The concept of the border writer, or the border artist, relies on an understanding of physical and psychological lines of demarcation that can be crossed. Distinctions must be made between the culture, people, and beliefs that exist on differing sides of these borders. Border space is privileged in the work of Jacir through juxtaposition of cultural meanings and the blurring of clear, unified identities. At the same time the space where the cultural and psychological borders exist is always shifting. In place of a clear, demarcated borderline these border artists are working to create border zones where new meanings are co-constructed between artist, art, and viewer. Irit Rogoff (2000) writes of these areas:

> While a national geographic entity produces and policies identity, the notion of a 'zone' is one suspended between various identities—a site of evacuation in which the 'law' of each identity does not apply, having been supplanted by a set of contingent 'rules.' (p. 120)

Identity is contingent upon experience in these border zones, which can function as starting points for the creation of inclusive community identities and sites of pedagogy.

The work of border artists, such as Emily Jacir, can inform a border pedagogy that is firmly based in a postcolonial critique of Eurocentric and imperialist ideas of a static hierarchy of civilization. The border artist highlights the zones of cultural hybridity and contest; the myth of "pure" countries and cultures fall away within the work of the border artist. The contingency of the border zone can offer a pragmatic way to educate about the spaces open for reshaping identity and notions of difference.

Border Art Pedagogy

My own pedagogy is built on the theoretical work of postcolonialism, pragmatism, border theory, and critical art pedagogy. Postcolonial theory provides an analysis of global relationships of power and displaces the West as center of all knowledge and creativity. Pragmatism, as a philosophy, adds to postcolonialism an acceptance of ambiguity and a focus on learning and changing through experience. Pragmatists, like William James and Charles Sanders Peirce, advocated a constant questioning of assumptions and habits through the lens of experience. Border theory is in many ways a contemporary form of pragmatic philosophy that roots ambiguity in the traveling between cultural and geographic borders. Border theory, then, is the connection between postcolonialism and pragmatism; it celebrates uncertainty and the doubting of assumptions that is embedded in imbalanced relationships of power and privilege.

My focus on the use of contemporary, border-crossing artists necessitates a form of critical art pedagogy that questions Eurocentric, modern myths that are entrenched in traditional art pedagogy. The border is an ambiguous metaphorical space where knowledge and meaning can be created through experience and the dislodging of accepted truths. By studying the work of artists like Emily Jacir, we can create a form of pedagogy that encourages critical questioning of calls for national purity and the restriction of movement for people across mental and physical borders.

REFERENCES

Bhabha, H. (1994). *The location of culture*. New York: Routledge.

Breidenbach, T. (2003). Emily Jacir. *Artforum, 41*(10), 188.

Hicks, E. (1991). *Border writing: The multidimensional text*. Minneapolis: Regents of the University of Minnesota.

Jacir, E. (2004). Stella Rollig: Emily Jacir interview. In E. Jacir & E. Said (Eds.), *Emily Jacir: Belongings works 1998-2003* (pp. 6-19). Austria: O.K. Books.

Llewellyn, T. (1998, April 20). *Israel and the Intifada*. Retrieved from the BBC News website: http://news.bbc.co.uk/2/hi/events/israel_at_50/history/82302.stm.

Rogoff, I. (2000). *Terra infirma: Geography's visual culture*. New York: Routledge.

Said, E. (2003). Emily Jacir: *Where we come from*. In E. Jacir & E. Said (Eds.), *Emily Jacir: Belongings works 1998-2003* (pp. 46-49). Austria: O.K. Books.

Shohat, E. (1998). Introduction. In E. Shohat (Ed.), *Talking visions: Multicultural feminism in a transnational age* (pp. 1-64). Cambridge, MA: MIT Press.

Jan-Ru Wan:
A Transcultural Journey

Alice Arnold

This chapter explores the early life of Jan-Ru Wan, a young fiber artist who grew up in Taiwan and now calls the United States her home. My dialogue with my colleague Ms. Wan explores the intricacies of life in her birth country of Taiwan and her many transitions needed to assume the position of artist/teacher in the US. Our conversation considers Jan-Ru's early years of being nurtured by a large and loving family and uncovers the teachers who played critical roles in her important early years of rapid growth and character formation. Stories of her father's "meditating Buddhism" practice and the importance of the temple and prayer are viewed as anchors for Wan's mystical imagery and labor-intensive work—work necessary for the creation of her on-site installations. Memories of her mother and grandmother and of Taiwan's rich textile industries and beautiful fabrics also form the basis of her contemporary fiber artwork. The place of work, as modeled within her large family, is seen as the heart of a life of fulfillment. Difficulties and challenges are uncovered and posed against the exhilaration of the discovery of a personal voice and a personal aesthetic stance that finally allows her to reconsider the culture of both her country of origin and her new home in the US.

Jan-Ru Wan is a fiber artist currently living and working in Durham, North Carolina; she is an assistant professor of art at North Carolina State University. This dialogue and reflection are an exploration of her early life in Taiwan, her migration to and work in the US, and the formative and transcultural experiences that inspire her current art.

Our Conversation

Alice: *Today I'd like to talk about your life and your transition from Taiwan to the US. I'd like to talk about your artwork, how it's changed over time, and the meaning of your art to you now … what you're thinking when you're making it, what images come from your early days in Taiwan, and what images come from your current life here in the US.*

Jan-Ru: Thank you. Thank you for having me. I would say I was a very, very shy kid. I usually didn't talk to people in kindergarten years, and my mom was worried until one day I called to my teacher loudly: "MY MOM IS HERE" and the teacher was so shocked and started to cry and said, "She finally spoke!"

My parents found out I enjoyed painting, not because I was good at it, but because I was happy when I did finger painting and made everything really messy. So they sent me to classes during the weekends. My father thought maybe I could be an artist one day, but when I went to elementary school—first grade, second grade—all my teachers said, "No, she cannot be an artist. She's too messy" and "she cannot do Chinese calligraphy; she cannot draw things realistically." Partly they were right, because every time I was in my calligraphy class, I put more black ink on my shirt than on the paper.

During that time, art education in Taiwan had no room for other kinds of arts except for classical. My mom still sent me to private school during the weekends, not because she expected me to be an artist, but she knew that made me happy.

Alice: *Oh, that's wonderful that you look back on those very early elementary years with such fondness both for your mom and your dad because they encouraged you in the field of art.*

Jan-Ru: They didn't encourage me as an artist. In Taiwan, the priority during those years was passing the national exam to go to a good high school and college one day. That was very stressful to kids and families. I was okay on the average but sometimes I had a hard time remembering things—especially Chinese history. China had 5000 years of history … and a lot of my history teachers … just recited the whole book. I mean, there's no storytelling with Chinese history. It's so confusing with who had a war against whom and why … it's very, very frustrating.

Then one day, I decided to draw a little picture, so I drew a picture of this country fighting that country and after I finished the picture I understood the whole thing, so I guess it was the first time I realized that I ... did better if I could visualize things—better than when people tell me things in words. I used this method to go through my junior high years.

And after I finished my junior high I got so frustrated because if I didn't do that well in high school, I would have to stay one more year and go to cram school to pass exams. You have to pay money for special education. So after my exam, I was really frustrated and at the same time relieved that was over. I cut up my backpack from school out of frustration.

Alice: *You cut your backpack ...*

Jan-Ru: Old canvas. It was an old canvas backpack so I cut it into pieces.

Alice: *How many pieces?*

Jan-Ru: Many pieces. My parents weren't home. Then I realized, "Oh, no, what had I done?" It was uncharacteristic of the sweet, gentle, and obedient daughter like me. So I decided to sew it together to make a garment for my doll—a really funky one. And then my parents saw it and said, "Oh! She is going into fashion design! She made an interesting garment for her doll! Let's send her to fashion design school!"

Alice: *Did you like school?*

Jan-Ru: I think so. At the time my feelings were not very strong for anything, but I guess you have no choice. Nobody asks you if you like school if you are in Taiwan and no one asks what you like or don't like. You just have to go. I learned to deal with it the best I could. And that's how I ended up at fashion school, not because I say, "I Jan-Ru will be a fashion designer."

It's because my parents say, "Oh, maybe we shouldn't send her to high school. It would be too much pressure on her," so I went to a special community college, a school just for fashion design. So, that was how I started my training as a fashion designer. During that time I liked learning things. I liked making things, so I really enjoyed sewing with different machines, hand sewing, and all the techniques. But still, I felt so limited within the school because most people went to fashion school wanting to decorate themselves, and I was not like most of them.

Alice: *And this is during your high school years.*

Jan-Ru: Yes, it was 3 years of high school and 2 years of college—5 years total. And I was miserable because I had not found my passion yet. For 5 years I never made any garments for myself. I only sewed for the model or more related to fiber art during that time. I had no ideas what the fiber art was; I just knew I was not happy.

I did try to work for a fashion design company for one year, and I just didn't see that as my path, but I didn't know what my path was.

Alice: *Sounds confined, actually.*

Jan-Ru: Yes, nobody told me there is another world. I only knew one way and that's how people had been telling me, but I told myself there must be another way. Even my parents thought I was worried about a job. "Oh don't worry when you get your degree; we will try to find you a job, a nice job, find you someone to marry and you'll be nice and happy." But I was not happy and I wanted more. I decided to study English harder and apply to school in US.

Alice: *Sounds like a real crisis in your life. Now, then did you get accepted to the Art Institute of Chicago?*

Jan-Ru: Well, after 2 or 3 years of fighting with my parents, we came to a mutual agreement. First, I wanted to go to Paris and they said no, the only country I could go to is the US. And so I had a couple of choices. I had an American teacher from Illinois and he suggested that I go to the Art Institute in Chicago, and I had no idea what or where the Art Institute of Chicago was and I said, "Okay" and I got in.

Alice: *That was a very good choice.*

Jan-Ru: Yes, yes, it actually opened my eyes during those years. The first day I went to class . . . after the teacher saw my sketches, she took me to the museum privately and talked with me for one hour. We looked at each painting and she said, "You have great potential. Your eyes are different from the rest of the people in the class." And I thought, oh, for the first time people think I'm good at something.

Alice: *So you had not really received a lot of special attention.*

Jan-Ru: No, no ... I didn't get encouraged before to be different. So the environment of the Art Institute of Chicago was a critical turning point for me.

Alice: *Oh, that's wonderful that you had that opportunity and that teacher back in Taiwan. Why did he recommend the Art Institute of Chicago? Do you know?*

Jan-Ru: I don't know. He actually taught English but he traveled a lot, and he wrote many poems about the political situation in Taiwan, so maybe he saw the Art Institute of Chicago as a little bit controversial from time to time. And he knew I wanted more.

Alice: *That's wonderful. When I was a little girl in Bloomington, Illinois, my grandmother would take me up to the Art Institute in Chicago, and I remember seeing the paintings of Renoir and Monet in the galleries and how beautiful they were. She took me at Christmas time, and then we went down to see the beautiful windows and the animations in the store windows; then we went to Berghoff's Restaurant for lunch and we went shopping and bought our Christmas presents. But the Art Institute of Chicago was an icon of excellence during my life.*

Jan-Ru: It was. I enjoyed all 3 years I stayed there because even during lunch I could walk in to see any masterpiece and have discussions with my classmates or critique the masterpiece because we could go to the museum all the time. The school is connected to the museum so we could just go, take a lunch walk, and see the art. It was really special.

Alice: *You're so fortunate that you made that leap.*

Jan-Ru: Yes, it was really, really lucky.

Alice: *Were there other aspects of your early life in Taiwan that you think were important experiences to your transition to the US or to your work now?*

Jan-Ru: Yes, there are a couple of areas. I have thought more about it later in life. The community in Taiwan, and my religion of Buddhism and Taoism, and the idea of balance has played an important role in my life. My father, he's a believer in meditating Buddhism. So growing up we just talked and discussed life and trained ourselves to meditate daily.

I have a wonderful relationship with my father. We just discuss things, anything, so he is really special for me in life. Growing up in Taiwan, I feel he loved me too much and he tried to hold onto me. The more he wanted to hold onto me, the more I wanted to leave because I wanted to search more in life. But when I'm in the US now, I feel more connected to him and also more connected to my culture because while you're out of the society and you start looking back at all your culture, your roots, everything becomes clearer. But when you're in your own environment you don't question things. So a lot of my culture and my roots become my inspiration more while I live in the States. I feel closer to home. We went to a lot of temples on special holidays. You have many rules to follow, and no one questions. In Chinese society, you respect the elderly and the past, and we don't ask questions. Now that I live in the US I realize there are so many different cultures, religions and rules, and we are all products of different cultures and societies.

Alice: *That's wonderful!*

Jan-Ru: Yes, it's this environment, which is full of wonderful opportunities, that allows me to look back at my own culture and education.

Alice: *Well, speaking of the Art Institute of Chicago, what do you feel you pulled away from that experience?*

Jan-Ru: Oh, I think most of it is teaching. My English was okay to pass the exam, but when people talked about art history, they used a lot of adjectives which I could not find in the dictionary, so every day I was sitting in the auditorium of 200 people, and daily I had to record the whole lecture with my tape recorder, and then I went home, rewound the tape one word at a time and tried to figure out which words she was saying—with a dictionary in one hand. Even though I might not get the whole class 100%, I was very impressed with those art history professors who were always very alive and talked about the story behind the art and other aspects of the work. There was more than just the formality of the art. I have felt much more connected with art since then.

And those art history courses were a turning point because I started to realize the power of art and how it related to the artist, and how it related to the society and to the people at the time, and how artists respond to the environment of their time.

Before, in Taiwan, we had to memorize the history for the test. So in those courses it was truly an eye-opening experience, and after that everything became more meaningful. Later, I also learned a lot during critiques during studio courses, and those were huge learning steps for me at that time, but great experiences.

I still remember the first time I was introduced to Robert Rauschenberg's collage works; in my mind I screamed, "Oh, my God, you can do that? Am I allowed to do that?" and "Hmm ... I guess I can do that."

Alice: *Yes, I remember my very first art history classes at Illinois Wesleyan. I was in sheer bliss, looking at art history for the first time. The images were so incredibly wonderful to me—complex and wonderful. I must have had a parallel experience to yours.*

So your ideas were really starting to formulate at the Art Institute of Chicago. Why do you think you gravitated toward the fibers?

Jan-Ru: I think mainly the fibers give me a lot of potential to create and a lot of techniques to work with. This media carries a lot of memories and everyone knows fibers and living with them. Everyone has ideas about quilts or stories about them. Everybody has had a grandma knitting something for them, so it holds a wonderful memory for everybody. Even though the material is very labor intensive, people can appreciate ... this "labor of love" which is very important in my work. I cannot find any other media that carries so much weight, and I can still find excitement every time I play with them ... It has been good for me to find fiber art.

Alice: *It's interesting that fiber arts were a real important part of your early life because I share that. My father's mother had a lot of fibers in her home, and I used to love to play with them.*
Were there other things about your early life?

Jan-Ru: Well, if you look at my work, most of the scale is big. It's about 20 ft by 20 ft or larger, and so the scale is an important element in my work. The material is important. The intensive labor aspect is very important. And I think one more thing influenced my work growing up. My grandma owned a shop to make mosquito nets.

Alice: *Oh, my word! Your grandmother owned a shop ...*

Jan-Ru: Owned a shop. So every holiday when we went home to my mom's hometown, I guess my aunt-in-law and my aunt all had to help to make mosquito nets from gauze. And the kids just played with the fabric—just rolls and rolls of ... translucent gauze. At the time it was a mix of cotton and polyester, but it was different colors and they were translucent. In Taiwan the style of a mosquito net covered the whole room. It connected to the corner of your room. There was a hook in each room so you had to construct it into a sculpture.

Alice: *Wow!*

Jan-Ru: I guess when I was little I just played with the material and my mom and my aunt were constantly making the net.

Alice: *In the house?*

Jan-Ru: In the house, downstairs, so they were downstairs making the nets, and the kids played upstairs. We have a huge house, and we had all the fabric to play with and see suspended in space over my head. Those experiences must have made an imprint in my mind.

Alice: *Oh, it must have... it really must have.*

Jan-Ru: Yes, and today my grandmother is 99 years old, and we are very close still.

Alice: *Your mother's mother?*

Jan-Ru: Yes, my mother's mother.

Alice: *I was also very, very close to my [other] grandmother, my father's mother, and she let me play with all of her velvets and silks. And she had a large drawer in her home where all of her silk scarves and fabrics were. I would also get them out of the drawer and tie them end-on-end-on-end and wrap them around my body and play with those silk scarves.*

Jan-Ru: Wow! So you would do a performance?

Alice: *I would definitely do a performance! But I remember the beauty of the scarves, the feel of the scarves, and how gorgeous they were when they were wrapped and draped. I think she was probably a very permissive woman to allow me to play with her scarves like I did.*

Alice: *So, coming back to the US, you had sort of a quest for place, a quest for home, for your career, your new life. How did that transition happen?*

Jan-Ru: Well, I think most of it happened after I finished my MFA at the University of Wisconsin in Milwaukee. I met my husband—my boyfriend at the time—in Milwaukee. He's a scientist. Then after we graduated we decided to get married and moved to Washington, DC.

During the school year, I tried to save money so I didn't go home often, and then one summer I went home, and I started to realize I had culture shock with my own country. I was a little bit disconnected with my family's daily life, even though we talked on the phone. It still seemed different. People had gone in different paths, and my brother was married and had kids. One day, my niece and nephew in Taiwan asked me, "So, when are you going home?" I said, "This is my home." "No, you were here before, and you are from America," she said, and I kept saying, "This is my home."

Then I started to question where my home was. I got married in the US, and his family was in China. The reason we stayed in the US was for our careers, but my culture and connections are 50% here and 50% in Asia.

I started to look for my own culture. Most Chinese families have an ancestor shrine in their home, usually to pray for the eldest son. So in Chinese culture if a woman never gets married or doesn't have a son, they have no one to carry on and pray for them after they pass away. So the idea of home and continuation of the family even after you pass away is reinforced in religion and society. And if someone didn't marry and she passes away, her name cannot be in the family book, family shrine, or family grave. So I used my works to question that system.

Alice: *Yes, yes.*

Jan-Ru: So in Chinese this word means female and this word means home. And these two together, it means *married*. So I started thinking, "OK, so you're female plus home equal married. OK? So if you're married minus home equals female. So I start to play a little game, so if a female is not married and has no home…"

Alice: *Oh, dear!*

Jan-Ru: Yes, and I go back and look at my culture and how I was trained to think about these things. In the meantime to try to find my home, but I guess art is such a wonderful way to express your own feelings and culture. So one of my works is in Chinese:

女 + 家 = 嫁   女 = 嫁 - 家
Woman + Home = Marriage   Woman = Marriage - Home

Alice: *Yes, that sounds right. Where you're living, where you're staying, where you found happiness could be your home. So are you feeling more at home now that you've been in North Carolina for a few years?*

Jan-Ru: I think so. I think teaching helps. When I look back at my life, the teachers played such an important role for me. I mean the style of teaching and the different ways of teaching made a huge impact in my life, so when I started to teach, I realized that I had found my second passion. I mean my first passion is to create my work. I have always loved ideas in my mind, and I am so happy to share them with students because I cannot do it all.

Alice: *Right!*

Jan-Ru: And I'm so happy to see some people find their own voice.

Alice: *… to help people find their own voice? I like that too, and it can take many years.*

Jan-Ru: There was a moment I realized what kind of artist I was. At that moment, I was able to examine my own culture like an outsider; I started to look at all things freely. In Taiwan, you see those religious settings intensely and you can see the performances happen on the street. During one of those ceremonies, there were these giant puppets, probably two or three stories high, and people standing inside holding the structure. On the surface, it is highly decorated, and beautiful except for the scary face, and they would be swinging the long arms back and forth. When I was growing up, I loved to see those performances, but I was always scared to see them at the same time. It gave me a sense of power, attraction, and repulsion— the feeling of beauty and danger!

So even now when I go back to Taiwan, I can still feel that power over me. One time while those people who perform under those puppets were taking a break, I went over to see all those sitting puppets.

They were beautiful painted wood and embroidered textile, and I dared to touch them. I asked myself why they were so powerful if they are just wood and textile?

At that moment, I realized while they performed they made people believe those materials have certain important meanings and certain power by their scale and "unsettledness" or "non-static" form which created power for their audience.

Just like me! I take fabric, found objects, and re-texture them to create new life and then assemble them in this enigmatic form and suspend them in the air to make people believe there are many meanings and stories within. That realization was very important for my works and my teaching because now I can analyze them in much clearer ways and teach my students to find their tools as designers and artists.

Alice: *You're like that too. You can come to rest, but you can also be powerful and assume power.*

Jan-Ru: Or just taking the very common material and making something unordinary.

Reflections: Moving from East to West

Jan-Ru's journey has many stories to tell, many narratives to uncover. We see a young girl searching for a sense of place in the world among a large and loving family, steeped in a culture struggling with its own identity as an autonomous nation wanting at the same time to foster its centuries-old traditions. We see what at times seems like an overly protecting father, a man of great wisdom and caring, discussing all sorts of worldly topics and concerns with his young child. He takes her to the temple to worship and give thanks for a life of blessings and thus teaches his child to exist in the realm of wonder and not-knowing, a realm that will permeate her mature artistic style and remain a source, a touchstone, of her artistic expression. We see also the mother's role as one of providing for the young child at school as well as at home, of making things with her hands, to "keep the hands busy at all times" with useful work and diligent service—and thus, a role model of dedication to work. And we see a large and extended family (Noddings, 2002) who all provide *attentive love* to the "obedient" child and her curious nature, while at the same time encouraging her to find her own way, which in this case meant leaving her home and eventually calling another place "home." And we see teachers, sometimes restrictive and critical, other times encouraging, and still other times, opening up previously unfathomable new doors of possibility for the aspiring young artist.

For Jan-Ru, her early journey of searching for self in a multicultural and globalized world was a struggle. Her memories of schooling in Taiwan were that national exams were more important than her budding interests in art, that her teachers found her artistic work (calligraphy, for example) "too messy," and that she was not happy as a young "fashion designer" in her high school years or her first and final year in the fashion design industry in Taiwan. She enjoyed learning the techniques of the designer but was not a good fit for a fashion design career, lacking the desire to make clothing for herself or others. She knew she was not fulfilled and wanted so much more. Her lifelong quest had begun, and it included coming to the US to study. She had no idea at the time that this decision would impact her later life so dramatically. The choice of the School of the Art Institute of Chicago, at the suggestion of an American teacher she had in Taiwan and who happened to be from Illinois, was serendipitous.

It was only when Jan-Ru finally convinced her parents that she should attend the School of the Art Institute of Chicago, in the US, that she now believes her personal freedom and personal voice were permitted. Her life in Taiwan was governed by norms of cultural history and tradition, but also provided a broad experience with textile methods and materials that were essential for her work as a fiber artist to eventually expand. Her parents, supportive from the beginning of her interests in art, were also foundational to her sense that she could be an artist.

It then was that "wonderful teacher," the art historian at The Art Institute who took the young student under her wing and explained art in such great depth that Jan-Ru's vision as an artist flourished. The mastery of technique had been established, but the final language of form was becoming resolved with the daily walks through the storehouses that were the galleries of the Art Institute. Just the right amount of freedom was given for the highly motivated international art student to perform at peak skill. Jan-Ru had come into a state of *flow* at the Art Institute, and would work with little sleep for days to complete her assignments. Her personal voice was being nurtured by her mentor/teachers and her own drive to learn. Harvard psychologist Csikszentmihalyi, in his book *Flow: The Psychology of Optimal Experience* (1990), discusses the state of "timelessness" that he calls flow when someone is functioning at optimum potential. Like the traditional, multicultural, international, and contemporary cosmopolitan art she found in her surrounds at the Art Institute, Wan knew intuitively that she too could have "artistic license" with her art, which then permitted and propelled her exploration of issues of cultural identity. In her case, it was her transcultural identity and voice that was allowed to surface in her art at the School of the Art Institute and to mature at the University of Wisconsin, as her work began to attend to broad themes of her Chinese cultural history and tradition, memories of home, and Chinese women's traditional roles—all reinterpreted in contemporary installations that made use of silks, gauzes, and a variety of other fibers.

In *Educating Citizens for Global Awareness,* Nel Noddings maintains that it is imperative to explore biography and narrative with students (2005). She further asserts that it is incumbent upon educators to uncover the mythology that is engrained in our culture and to question the stereotyped belief systems that students hold close. Even controversial issues such as war, violence, or betrayal can be explored in classrooms with students of all ages and can be used to debunk the narrow myths of popular culture. Only with authentic dialogue about important narratives can this method of uncovering prejudice and wrong-mindedness exist. As Noddings observes, there are novels, biographies, poetry, and essays relevant to all school subjects, and these could be used to encourage habits of mind and heart (2005). The habits of mind desired, in such a view, require *critical pedagogy*, a higher-order analysis of subject matter that allows students to see the moral and ethical dimensions of life. My conversation with Jan-Ru Wan, similarly, allowed us to think and talk about the mythologies of her own cultural experiences, both in Taiwan and in the US, to talk and think of cultural stereotypes and expectations, and explore some of the moral and ethical dimensions of her own life. Themes that emerged in our conversation and that seem important to me now include Wan's experience of living between and navigating two cultures (Taiwan and the US), her search for her own artistic identity and eventual creation of a body of work that brings together traditions from both cultures, recognition of the power of love and caring, and a disposition that allows Jan-Ru to identify her "home" based on her ability to re-envision or re-create a sense of self in the world on her own terms.

Figure 1

Left:

女 + 家 = 嫁
Woman + Home = Marriage

女 = 嫁 - 家
Woman = Marriage - Home

Figure 2

Top: *The Ripple of Resonance*

Figure 3

Left: *Everyone Praying for Good Life*

Figure 4

The Unbearable Lightness of Being

REFERENCES

Csikszentmihalyi, M. (1990). *Flow: The psychology of optimal experience*. New York: Harper & Row Publishers.

Noddings, N. (2002). *Starting at home: Caring and social policy*. Berkeley, CA: University of California Press.

Noddings, N. (Ed.) (2005). *Educating citizens for global awareness*. New York: Teachers College Press.

Subversively Discursive Digital Communities of Contemporary Craft

Courtney Lee Weida

There is no doubt that the future belongs to the virtual spaces of craft.

—SANDRA ALFOLDY, 2007 IN
NEOCRAFT: MODERNITY AND THE CRAFTS

How do online networking sites for crafts define themselves, and how do they compare to physical communities of contemporary crafts? This chapter analyzes constructions of subversive speech and counter-discourses within digital forums for ceramics, fiber art, and other studio crafts. Communities of people working with studio craft media might seem unlikely netizens, however, Internet forums for craftspeople are growing rapidly. In many ways, web forums such as message boards and tutorials offer alternative social and teaching spaces. Web dialogues, exchanges, and collaborations also provide participants with opportunities to reclaim and/ or revise artistic identities and conceptions of past and present craft communities. To explain some relevant vocabulary in the context of this chapter, I am using the term "digital communities" to refer to groups of people who learn, share, and discuss their work in the crafts online, and the often problematic category of "crafts" to categorize objects described as such by their makers.

Figure 1

Image of lawn mower cozy by Jennifer Marsh, 2007. Permission granted by the artist.

Crafts (as I have seen it defined [as a category] online) encompasses a range of traditionally-created works from embroideries, to quilting, to knitting, to handmade cards, to crochet, to ceramics, to jewelry. While craft contextually extends to a variety of art projects and products, this chapter will primarily address (a) my own experiences as a ceramicist, (b) fiber crafts and my involvement and knowledge in that area via projects such as Jennifer Marsh's International Fiber Collaborative, and (c) jewelry as craft within the context of my correspondence with jewelry artist and researcher Sarah Kettley. The subversive aspect in this chapter title stems from shocking or rebellious objects, messages, inscriptions, and the notion that making one's own day-to-day objects thoughtfully contests consumer power structures in contemporary society. Meanwhile, the discursive nature of these crafts addresses written dialogues between a range of topics and objects that interweave traditional objects and contemporary messages.

Personal Craft Connections

Being a potter and ceramic sculptor affords me an extended liminality not only within ceramics, but also in art and craft; for ceramics typically engages the real and imagined borderlines of the two areas. Although I have studied and taught at five universities, I also have been a student at Haystack Mountain School of Craft and become engaged in craft traditions and digital spaces of contemporary craft. My own role as a ceramic artist gives me the flexibility and indeterminacy of being a craftsperson and/or an artist, while my dual roles as ceramicist and doctoral student/professor also engage some tensions and hierarchies of traditional forms of education (such as those ceramics techniques passed down through families and workshops) with more standardized and formalized ones of the universities (such as formalized studio and methods courses). For this reason and others, my writing on the area of craft speaks from within and without various communities.

As a ceramic artist, I have come to believe that the earthy, physical processes in the ceramic studio can be oddly parallel to those undertaken in the virtual, digital realms of my computer. I might sculpt, burnish, and glaze ceramics during the same hour, engaging with different works of art at different stages of completion. Meanwhile, at my computer, I find myself using my word processor to plan out my ideas; dabbling in Photoshop to format images, and keeping several "tabs" open in my web browser to look at ceramic art history, pottery quotes, and/or other possibilities to inspire making processes. My studio and

computer projects are often undertaken simultaneously, with many various parts evolving with different paces, places, and phases. This is similar to what Sherry Turkle (Director of MIT's Initiative on Technology and Self) calls an enlargement of the "thinking space" through the "dynamic, layered display" of the computer (1995, p. 1). For many craftspeople, the social networking of the computer is fluidly linked with more physical artistic processes.

Technologist and philosopher, David Weinberger, (2002) comments on the relationship between the physical and the virtual in relationship to corporeality, "the bodiless Web reminds us of the bodily truths we have always lived." (p. 142). While the Web does not connect us with tactile spaces of a ceramics studio, knitting circle, woodshop, or other physical craft places directly, it does reflect and reference materials and spaces of craft continually. Although the studio itself is often a quiet and tactile place with unspoken poetry, the web communicates itself with a wide array of words and images. In other words, it expresses visually and discursively. However, the language with which we express ourselves online may be casual, personal, lengthy or short, and the space is perhaps more democratically communal and communally expressive than a traditional studio craft workshop. Malcolm McCullough (1998), a researcher of craft and digital technology, also notes the repetitive movements of the computer as comparable to craft. I have often found myself similarly soothed by the repeated motions of weaving baskets as those of following threads of thought online. In this way, the relationships between weaving a basket and making one's way through craft sites become more apparent.

Crafting Spaces

When weaving through the digital cultures of ceramics and other crafts with which I both observe and take part, I am always intrigued by the conceptualizations of space and community that exist among groups. Space is a key aspect of web communities as defined by their titles. I went from Craft Ark to Craft Church to New Orleans Craft Mafia. The look, feel, and function of a Craft Church in your web browser can be very different than that of a Craft Mafia–and this naming allows the digital forums important distinctions in the same way that university studios may differ from casual workshops. Words, fonts, backgrounds, colors, and images can give each communal space a very different feel. While some of these communities do not continually or solely exist socially in physical space (rather the connection is found online), groups may still perceive their socialization as taking place in a space and defend their rights to define and delineate their space. The Church of Craft website elucidates some of its many (and changing) roles as place, concept, and object:

> The Church of Craft could be seen as a giant piece of art. Performance art of the very best kind, where the people involved don't always know that they are making art. The kind of art that is endless and endlessly meaningful, that generates discussion and prompts action. Art that is deeply personal and yet rooted in the world. And if you see the Church that way I wouldn't argue with you, and neither would many of its members or, indeed, its ministers. But the Church is also real—the kind of real that doesn't need quotes or capital letters. The Church of Craft is, without irony or disclaimer, a church. (www. churchofcraft.org, 2006)

It may be noted that this mission statement has since changed. Indeed, the mission of groups such as these are more frequently subject to change than real-time organizations such as schools and arts centers. This perhaps suggests the fluidity and freedom of an online space in comparison to a physical one. Other groups alter their name or mission to reflect the specific identities of the members, such as listings of crafts by men, or explorations of the connections of feminism and women's work in the craft.

There is sometimes a gendered aspect of engaging with webspace that persists from earlier times. Sherry Turkle (1995) writes that in the recent past, some folks "identified being a woman with all that a computer is not, and computers with all that a woman is not." She goes on to argue that "the emerging culture of simulation becomes increasingly associated with negotiational and nonhierarchical ways of thinking" (p. 56). In digital craft communities, the assertion of female identity is often prominent in declarations of space such as the "craft grrl community" or "knitter girl community." From my perspective, this sometimes reflects a certain revision of women's historical membership in arts and crafts communities as well as an honoring of tradition, for it asserts women's presence in the crafts as in the past, but does so in a technology rich forum not always historically available to women.

While individual artists and craftspeople may certainly benefit individually from exposure and learning environments online, there are a variety of unique social situations created around web communities of craft pertaining to the process of making itself that redefine social hierarchies. From web theorists Michael Hauben and Ronda Hauben's (1997) perspective, the Internet offers both a "bottom up" redesign of social frameworks as well as inviting more "intellectual activity" than is typically encouraged offline. Certainly some digital forums may serve as counter-culture for art studio spaces, providing different kinds of time and space for personal reflection and inquiry than might be encouraged in a studio. I have observed some hierarchy of craft that exists between crafting sites that cater to those who create crafts as hobbies and sites that identify as relating to "professional" craft. Sites like the Center for Craft, Creativity and Design are more academically-focused and approach the sociological, art historical, and other research-related aspects of craft practice. Such university-affiliated sites can also seem comparatively ambiguous about their membership and goals, addressing both academic researchers and craftspeople working outside of university settings.

Contextualizing Crafts

Some craft communities view themselves as antithetical to historical notions of craft and aim to redefine themselves artistically and socially. One site, Craftster.com, boasts that it is intended for visitors who "love to make things but who are not inspired by cross-stitched home sweet home plaques and wooden boxes with ducks in bonnets painted on." Other articles, found on Almostgirl.coffeespoons.org, addressed "Renegade Crafters," as web-savvy craftspeople who employ unexpected or unconventional craft techniques such as embroidering a skateboard, creating an illuminated ("light-up") tank top, and/or weaving an iPod cozy. There is also an important linguistic concern in the terms we use to describe craft, from "studio craft," to "fine craft," to "craftsmanship in art," to "artisan crafting," and on to other derivatives. These definitions imply and engage hierarchical relationships and varying levels of status, but digital crafts communities perhaps uniquely re-define, re-create, and even newly create different categories.

Craft objects have utilitarian meaning, as a potholder or quilt does, but the functionality is updated along with changing day-to-day needs. Additionally, these craft items often have personally relevant, subversive, ironic, and/or political messages within their forms or shapes. For example, we find knitted dolls that are monsters instead of more neutral cuddly figures or embroideries include messages like "I have my period." These objects are not uniform alongside items of the same function and traditional stitch, but individually express the personality and opinions of the maker. Additionally, they often merge traditional objects with popular and consumer culture, suggesting a critical awareness of consumption.

Given that the crafts do not occupy the space they once did in family homes and workplaces, the web also offers a revised and altered space for learning and

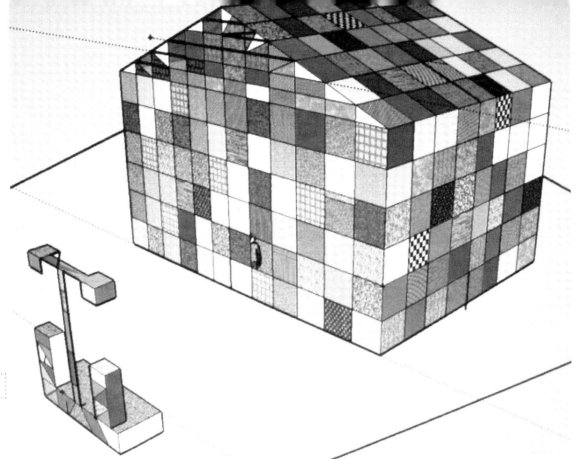

Figure 2

Image of planned
gas station covering,
created by Jennifer
Marsh, 2007.
Permission granted
by the artist.

display of this traditional work. Critic Charles Bern-stein (2000) asserts,

> I want to contrast the solitary conditions of viewing a work on a computer screen, my posture fixed, my eyes ten inches form the image, with the physicality of look-ing at a painting or sculpture in a large room, moving around it, checking it out from multiple views, taking in its tactile surface, its engagement with my thoughts. (p. 183)

There often is, on the other hand, a contextual enlargement of the craft object itself when a scarf or piece of pottery can be viewed alongside the biography of the maker, a tale of its creation, and the commentary of the artist's peers. Although the computer can be a limiting screen or lens of vision and some network-ing sites allows us to disclose our identities in limited, imaginative, or even false ways; craft communities are often spaces to engage us with the person who makes a craft item and a variety of supplementary information not typically included when purchasing or viewing a hand-made utilitarian item. This might include nar-ratives about the use of a scarf or piece of furniture, images of the maker and their homes, and additional commentary that links the object and its design with the identity of the craftsperson. As Turkle (1984) writes, computers can "play an important role in human development ... allow[ing] us to see ourselves from the outside, and to objectify aspects of our-selves we had only perceived from within" (p. 155). In

this way, both the artist and the viewer can engage in ongoing dialogue with the work, with contextual infor-mation online, and with one another, from different spaces and times that would be difficult to accomplish within a particular physical space and time.

McCullough (1998) argues "Networks make arti-facts more transmissible, and provide more settings for comparisons and discussions of practice, than do their grassroots traditional craft counterparts" (p. 270). Echoing this notion, some of the folks I have met who work within online knitting groups mentioned that they know crafting podcast personalities (those who produce Internet radio shows about crafts) better than television celebrities. This is accomplished via crafting podcasters' shared techniques, images, and other information published through the Web. This information engages viewers with an array of dif-ferent contexts of the objects and emphasizes the maker perhaps as much as the art object. In contrast, is rare for a gallery show or exhibit to invite and host such extensive information and discussion of artistic process as the Web enables.

Other craft communities go beyond revising of craft traditions in their practices, to physically deconstructing traditional discarded craft items. The International Fiber Collaborative gathers fiber panels that are knitted, woven, crocheted, or even recycled from older quilts and other textiles to be re-made into

Figure 3

International Fiber
Collaborative
founder Jennifer
Marsh working on
fiber panels with
school children.
Photographed by
Cathryn Lahm, 2007.
Permission granted
by the artist.

new works. Over the past few months, I have followed this interesting project, a collective open to all fiber artists, inviting participants to create 3 square foot fiber panels to be connected into a large covering for abandoned gas stations throughout the United States (Figure 2 is a plan for this covering). Engaging public school classrooms (as seen in Figure 3), fiber artists from universities, and more traditional crafts communities within this online forum allows them to dialogue with one another about how the crafts interplay with contemporary dependencies on oil. Craft researcher Bruce Metcalf (2007) notes "craft retains one crucial opposition stance [in that] the hand-made object is widely understood as the antithesis of mass-produced anonymity" (p. 21). While the Fiber Collaborative project is open-ended and includes many diverse opinions and experiences pertaining to the politics of oil usage, the contrast between the resources and processed involved with hand-made crafts and resources and processes involved with oil as fuel communicate themselves clearly.

To further define crafters in terms of their identities online, Hauben and Hauben (1997) specify that not all Net users are netizens: "Netizens ... are people who decide to devote time and effort into making the Net, this new part of our world, a better place." (p. x). I have found that there is indeed a notable outreach, or community-based element to many online craft communities. For example, craftzine.com features outreach projects for community service. Ceramic artists in particular may be familiar with the Craft Emergency Relief Fund, which has come to the aid of artists whose pottery studios have been destroyed by fire or natural disaster. Similarly, Craft Alliance Community features a website and states its program goal as bringing arts to "everyone, regardless of economic circumstance." Internet theorist Judy Breck (2006) muses on the connection of virtuality and such visionary thinking, theorizing the word virtual as "something ... that is imaginary or hypothetical" (p. 11). Similarly, Sandra Alfoldy (2007) asserts, "The idea of utopia remains central to our understanding of the crafts" (p. 157). There is an openness to these online sites that is imaginative, visionary, and full of possibility because these sites are always comfortably unfinished and evolving.

Crafting Communication; Communicating Craft

While ceramics communities and other craft communities are on the one hand simply social groups where artistic sharing, technical conversations, and critiques occur, the social interaction may be uniquely asynchronous and visitors may even "lurk" or visit a site without making one's presence known as in the physical world. This provides an interesting individuality within the community. McCullough (1998) observes that "operating a computer may then seem less like sitting alone with a machine and more like entering a world of action in which you are the narrator" (p. 136). In this way, one's journey as an observer is not self-conscious in the same way physical journeys through art or craft environments may be with observable presence. A protagonist in the realm of online crafting may experience greater autonomy, creating individual pathways and processes where the amount of feedback and input from others is self-selected (as opposed to some studios and galleries of the physical world in which critique can be difficult to avoid.) On the other hand, the anonymity that is easily obtained may not always be desirable. As a craftsperson who exhibits artwork in web galleries, seeks professional development online, and teaches online art classes, reconstructing my persona and representing my work

real-world community gatherings. Additionally, As Malcolm McCullough (1998) writes "in the unusual event that a master takes time out to articulate a craft, the result seldom takes a well-established literary form" (p. xvi). Certainly, the image-heavy and conversational tone of shared patterns, themes, projects, and other creative expressions is unorthodox in format and yet may be approached with interest and usage extending possibilities of traditionally-published text with specific expectations such as those relating to language, length, and content.

While craft communities are transformed and re-created by web communities, craft forms themselves may reflect both computer technologies and the craft communities they enable. Sarah Kettley, a jewelry artist, has been interested in how jewelry wearing is experienced as a researcher and a maker. Her work engages the concept of a wearable computer, using

Figure 4

Left: Detail of Sarah Kettley's design-led interactive jewelry. Permission granted by the artist.

Figure 5

Right: Detail of Sarah Kettley's design-led interactive jewelry. Permission granted by the artist.

in each space can be at times more tiring and repetitive than appearing physically and speaking verbally. Balancing community and individuality seems to be a skill that those learning crafts techniques online are apt to pursue. From my perspective, this may suggest that a new skill set of identity construction and reconstruction is engaged within digital forums.

The unified theory of the Web argues that such "web conversations ... aren't just multi-threaded; they're hyper-threaded" (Weinberger, 2002, p. 67). This interweaving of conversational time and space allows us to ask basic questions or go on craft tangents without breaking the etiquette and flow of real-time conversations. In this way, the web can offer both a unique space and a new approach to craft education. Broader definitions of teaching and learning may embrace the fluid nature of craftspeoples' work in interactions in which a diverse group of crafters of can share all sorts of information through questions, answers, and comments difficult to maintain through

LEDs and radio transmissions to alter the appearance of the jewelry. (Figures 4 and 5 show parts of this jewelry, while Figure 6 demonstrates the necklace being worn.) A sort of trace of meetings with other jewelry wearers is revealed in the light display, bringing about a visual representation of social interactions.

Conclusion

Within various sites of craft explored here, a merging of the cultures of traditional craft makers and those of new technology users are taking place. While the Web may often be a space that reflects and represents (re-presents) personal and communal visions of craft practice, it is also its own locale for creative forms of publication in craft as well as an enlarged view of the craft process and contexts in contemporary society. Given that the crafts do not occupy the roles and locations that they once did, the Web also offers a distinctive and contemporary space for learning and display of this traditional work. Within research

Figure 6

Sarah Kettley's design-led interactive necklace modeled. Permission granted by the artist.

here, it becomes important to think about the fluidity in which craft's identity, along with the identity of the maker is both reclaimed and revised in exciting and problematic ways within digital spaces. Metaphorically, dialogues taking place between tradition and innovation are parallel to the interplay of craft and digital technology.

REFERENCES

Alfoldy, S. (2007). Introduction, In S. Alfoldy, (Ed.). *Neocraft: Modernity and the crafts*. Nova Scotia: the Press of Novia Scotia College of Art and Design.

Bernstein, C. (2000). I don't take voice mail. In S. Bee and M. Schor, (Eds.). *M/E/A/N/I/N/G: An anthology of artists' writings, theory, and criticism*. New York: Duke University Press.

Breck, J. (2006). *109 Ideas for virtual learning: How open content will help close the digital divide*. Oxford: Rowman & Littlefield Education.

Crabe, G. (2002). *Crafter's Iinternet handbook: Research, connect and sell your crafts online*. Cincinnati, OH: Musca and Lipman Publishing.

Gremley, K. (2002). In *The nature of craft and the Penland experience*. New York: Lark Books.

Hauben, M., & Hauben, R. (1997). *Netizens: On the history and impact of Usenet and the Internet*. Los Alamitos, CA: IEEE Computer Society Press.

John-Steiner, V. (2000). *Creative collaborations*. New York: Oxford University Press.

Metcalf, B. (2007). Replacing the myth of modernism, In *Neocraft: Modernity and the crafts*. Nova Scotia: the Press of Novia Scotia College of Art and Design.

McCullough, M. (1998). *Abstracting craft: The practiced digital hand*. Cambridge, MA: MIT Press.

Robertson, S. (1961). *Craft and contemporary culture*. London: United National Educational, Scientific, and Cultural Organizations.

Stafford, B. (2001). *Visual analogy: Consciousness as the art of connecting*. Cambridge, MA: MIT Press.

Turkle, S. (1995). *Life on the screen: Identity in the age of the Internet*. New York: Simon and Schuster.

Turkle, S. (1984). *The second self: Computers and the human spirit*. New York: Simon and Schuster.

Weinberger, D. (2002). *Small pieces loosely joined: A unified theory of the Web*. Cambridge, MA: Perseus Books.

WEBSITE RESOURCES

The New Orleans Craft Mafia is a group of several independent artists working in a variety of media: jewelry, clothing, accessories, home decor, and others. This website showcases artists' works and events. http://www.neworleanscraftmafia.com/

The Church of Craft is a community of crafters with chapters throughout the world. While this is not a religious organization per se, the website is structured like the rhyme with "doors" to networking, a "steeple" of wisdom, and "people." http://www.churchofcraft.org/

The Craft Alliance is an organization committed to community outreach, working with hospitals, schools, and agencies. The Craft Alliances offers classes and workshops, with a mission that everyone should have access to arts learning. http://www.craftalliance.org/outreach.htm

The Craft Relief Fund helps artists in times of need. Grants and awards are given to artists in the events of emergencies that affect their art-making and livelihood. http://craftemergency.org/

The Center for Craft, Creativity, and Design is a North Carolina based center that supports craft research and craft programs. As an affiliate of the University of North Carolina, the CCCD also curates exhibitions and provides educational programs. http://www.craftcreativitydesign.org/

Haystack Mountain School of Crafts is a Maine-based international craft school. A variety of artists teach workshops in craft media for beginners and experienced artists/craftspeople. http://www.haystack-mtn.org/

Jennifer Marsh's International Fiber Collaborative is a project inviting artists and craftspeople to create a 3 square foot panel of their choice. These panels are connected and assembled into a gas station covering, pointing out and interrogating contemporary dependencies on oil energy. http://www.internationalfibercollaborative.com/

Knitgrrl is Shannon Okey's fiber art website, complete with a blog and resources for schools and teachers. Shannon is an author, editor, columnist, and TV personality of various media relating to fiber and fabric. http://www.knitgrrl.com/

Sarah Kettley is a jewelry artist exploring human-centered design with interactive technologies. Her work includes a range of research projects with jewelry as well as published articles. http://www.sarahkettley.com

The Craft Ark is a collection of projects and videos for craftspeople. The website includes galleries, glossaries, and a variety of resources for making crafts. http://www.thecraftark.com/

Redefining Cultural Identities in Digital Art Practices: Artistic Journeys across Cultural Boundaries and Ethnic Borders

Borim Song

During the past several decades, globalization has blurred the borders among cultures, to some extent. The development of computers and the Internet has accelerated the collapse of cultural boundaries and changed the way people experience cultures; thus, defining one's cultural identity is now a more complicated process. These changes imply that approaching the concept of cultural identity in the new artistic practice of digital art cannot be based only on a traditional understanding of what culture means in society and how it interacts with art.

A number of art educators and cultural theorists have pointed out the changes in cultures in the digital age and the artistic implications of these shifts (Ballengee-Morris & Stuhr, 2001; Bolter & Gromala, 2003; Burnett, 2004; Freedman, 2003; Langer & Knefelkamp, 2001; Ndalianis, 2004; Paul, 2003). In particular, Burnett (2004) states that traditional "cultural distinctions" need new definitions and require a more complex view. He insists that we should reconsider the idea of community in computer-based communication and states that there is a big "difference between traditional forms of community development and what happens in digital spaces" (p. 159). For example, in the words of Burnett, communities created in the virtual world only exist as long as they are in need or as long as community members want to keep communicating with one another.

This chapter critically examines the changing roles of cultural identities in artistic practices in the age of globalization and digital technology and their implications for higher education. This study is based on the following research questions: Given that cultural boundaries and ethnic borders are collapsing and new theories and practices of cultural identity are apparent in the digital era, how do artists understand their cultural contexts and what are the implications for art education? Furthermore, how are critical perspectives and practices used to negotiate artistic and pedagogical identity within these changing cultural contexts?

Critical Inquiry into the Changing Roles of Cultural Identities in the Age of Globalization and Digital Technology

This study mainly focuses on the conceptual and artistic outcomes of a conference/exhibition project entitled Virtual Conversations Across Visual Cultures: Cultural Identity in Korean Computer-Mediated Art, which was presented at Teachers College, Columbia University, in New York City in 2006. Highlighting the theme of cultural identities in Korean digital art, this project consisted of a 2-day academic conference and three concurrent exhibitions, one of which took place at Macy Gallery, Teachers College. In order to explore the ideas and responses of conference presenters and participating contemporary artists, this study investigated the verbal presentations and written statements of the seven conference presenters, e-mail-based interviews with six participating artists, and their artists' statements and artworks. The conference participants were people of diverse backgrounds, including college professors, art critics, artists, art educators, and graduate students with various education majors. The six contemporary artists who participated in the Macy Gallery exhibition and interviews included YOUNG-HAE CHANG HEAVY INDUSTRIES (two group members), Sung-Dam Hong, Soonok Jung, Shin il Kim, and Taejin Kim.

The conference/exhibition project took 3 years of planning. One goal of the project was to explore the potential of art ideas as agents of cross-cultural change in art education. While organizing this project, I, to some extent, conceptually depended on a conventional definition of cultural identity based on ethnic distinctions. However, as a variety of ideas, perspectives, and opinions were exchanged through the conference programs and in the digital artworks created by Korean artists on view, it seemed to be apparent that we needed to go beyond the ethnic and geographic background of the country and to use a filter of critical perspectives to fully understand the concept of cultural identity in digital art. Consequently, the project explored diverse ideas about what cultural identity means in current society, and the kind of role it plays in digital art practice.

Personalizing Cultural Identities: Artists' Perspectives

The capacity of artists to transcend physical and conceptual boundaries in exploring cultural identity was described by a presenter, Graeme Sullivan, as a "migratory" process because "artists, after all, are migratory as they explore physical traces that navigate pathways across cultural places and conceptual spaces" (Sullivan, 2006, p. 2). He described the way artists often personalize their cultural experiences through artistic journeys:

> The image of the artist as a migratory individual who moves purposefully within and between cultures has

a particular resonance these days. This is especially so with artists who reside on both sides of the mythical East-West divide, and even more so with artists for whom their Asian heritage is the core experience from which they launch their artistic journeys. Whether traversing physical places around the globe, or traveling within virtual spaces, there is a dual sense of critical distance and embedded engagement that characterizes much of contemporary art. (Sullivan, 2006, p. 2)

Through e-mail-based interviews, the participating artists revealed how they explored and traveled back and forth across cultural and geographical boundaries and how they internalized the concept of cultural identity through their digital art practice. For example, artist Sung-Dam Hong pointed out that "self-reflection" is an important factor in his art. Through his artistic practice, he critically examines social issues and political events in his country and reveals hidden problems and violence on the part of the government. Hong claimed that, without his constant self-reflection, he would resemble the target that he had been criticizing, which he described as a monster.

Except for Sung-Dam Hong, whose artistic goal is a search for his cultural identity in a sense, most of the participating artists did not purposefully present

Figure 1

Sung-Dam Hong, *Breakaway, the Century of Sound and Fury*, video installation, 1999. Used with permission from the artist.

CHAPTER 16 | Redefining Cultural Identities in Digital Art Practices: Artistic Journeys across Cultural Boundaries and Ethnic Borders

119

their interest in cultural identity. In fact, while selecting artists for the Macy Gallery exhibition, as curator I focused on finding artists whose artistic journeys were spontaneous, flexible, and free—exploring their culture and society through a self-reflexive process and incorporating the findings into creative artwork. This is because it can be argued that presenting/representing one's cultural identity through artmaking or, finding it while viewing a certain artwork, is not a process forced by cultural, societal, or political factors. Rather, it is a more personal and organic process of incorporating what artists encounter in their everyday lives from critical perspectives and a creative mindset. Artist Shin il Kim also shared these ideas in his interview comments:

> I do not try to show my cultural identity in my artwork. In the process of artistic practice, a Korean cultural identity or a certain mixed cultural identity can spontaneously emerge. But, I tend to avoid leaning on one side and, as a result, try to mix the East and the West. However, my Korean sense is stronger, so, in many cases, my works are visually viewed as those with strong Eastern cultural values. I think that, in this process of repeated mixing, I can find another cultural identity of me. (personal communication, March 7, 2007)

At the conference, YOUNG-HAE CHANG HEAVY INDUSTRIES, an artist group with two members who create Net art, presented their Net art pieces exploring the conference topic, instead of giving a regular lecture. They provided their critical views on being forced to form a united national character under the name of cultural identity. The following is the text featured in one of the Net art pieces by YOUNG-HAE CHANG HEAVY INDUSTRIES (2007) that were introduced at the conference, entitled *CULTURAL IDENTITY AND NOTHINGNESS*:

> Cultural identity and nothingness. Or perhaps we are not. And that is the theme that we would like to address briefly today. Who we are, where we live and work, and what we do. In other words, cultural identity, or perhaps, a lack of cultural identity. Nothing. People who have no identifiable culture. People whose culture is a mishmash of odds and ends. People, we hope, like ourselves, lucky people who don't have the burden of representing a given cultural identity...What, though, does this world have to do with so-called cultural identity? And, in particular, Korean cultural identity? Nothing, we hope. We have no idea what Korean cultural identity is. Or is not. And frankly, we don't care if we are creating it or working against it. This, we might add, is perfectly normal.[1]

During their interview, the members of YOUNG-HAE CHANG HEAVY INDUSTRIES stated that, as artists, they consciously put themselves into their work but did not try to think what it meant to them and their art. Given my question about the revelation of themselves in their work, the group members answered, "We don't really know...In fact, we're not trying to reveal so much as to hide ourselves in our work" (personal communication, April 12, 2007). The artists' responses offer important implications for how we can understand the roles of cultural identities in artistic practice in this ever-changing society that is full of digital technologies and virtual communications. As artists who work on Net art—mostly in a virtual format—the members of YOUNG-HAE

Figure 2

Shin il Kim, *The Transubstantiation*, 2880 pressed line drawings on paper, sound, 8 video scenes, 8 rear projection screens (the size of each screen: 234x177cm), 8 DVDs, 8 video projectors, 4 speakers, a sound from Dalai Lama's collection of talks, "Live in a better way," playing backward, loop, sound, 2005. Used with permission from the artist.

CHANG HEAVY INDUSTRIES considered the presentation and representation of cultural and societal components to be a "burden," viewing them as aspects in opposition to art.

However, it can be argued that the reason why viewers are excited about the works of these artists is that, to some extent, the viewers find some linkage between what the Net art pieces present and their own lives. And this linkage may be, at some point, closely related to society and culture. For example, one conference participant reflected on the Net art pieces, focusing on her cultural learning:

> YOUNG-HAE CHANG HEAVY INDUSTRIES emphasize the negative aspects of cultural identity that breed, "nationalism, oppression and demagoguery," but we are still able to learn about modern Korean life from them. From their work I found out that Seoul is crowded, has traffic jams, movies, and cell phones. People are very much engaged in the corporate life-style. There is little cultural diversity. I learned that foreigners feel like outsiders, Korean food is very spicy. (personal communication, February 28, 2006)

It seems that cultural and societal factors are not opposed to art, at least for viewers who try to appreciate and communicate with artworks. Interestingly, the YOUNG-HAE CHANG HEAVY INDUSTRIES artists also stated that finding those cultural and societal connections and implications in their work is "your job"—what viewers or interpreters should do (personal communication, April 12, 2007).

In contrast, artist Shin il Kim, who stated that he did not attempt to intentionally reveal his cultural identity in artwork, viewed cultural and societal contexts as an integral part of his art making: "I think that the main function of art lies in communicating with others through visual languages, so it is imperative to think about society and culture to expand the scope of communication" (personal communication, March 7, 2007). As shown in these statements, the artists whom I interviewed were constantly negotiating their cultural identities—consciously and unconsciously—in personal, spontaneous, and artistic ways.

Negotiating Cultural Identities and the Role of Art

Through their interviews and conference presentations, the participating artists described how they negotiated their cultural identities in art making, and the main issues that emerged were the roles of art and artists in society and their freedom and responsibility in artistic practice. To artist Sung-Dam Hong, communicating with other people through cultural exchanges is a critical role of artistic practice. In his view, the computer's capability that makes it easier to copy things and to communicate with others may promote a uniqueness of each culture, rather than blurring boundaries among diverse cultures.

So, So Soulful, a Net art piece that YOUNG-HAE CHANG HEAVY INDUSTRIES created for the conference, is an insightful example of redefining cultural identities in today's world. This art piece was created for the conference on cultural identity in Korean digital art but presented hardly any Korean cultural symbol or context. Instead, the main geographical and cultural backgrounds of the narratives in the art piece were Japan and the US. To my question about this choice of cultures, the artist group replied:

> ...we thought it would be interesting to show that 'Korean cultural identity' isn't always what it seems to be. That a good part of that identity can be intertwined with Japanese cultural identity and American cultural identity. That 'Korean cultural identity' is what one makes of it. That 'Kenji' might be Korean, or that the nameless female narrator might be Korean. That appearances are deceptive. That life is complicated, oftentimes in a good way. That the global mixing of cultures and identities, although tragic in a purist sense, is a source of hope for many. (personal communication, March 21, 2007)

The artist group's statement suggests that, in the age of globalization and digital technology, cultural identities cannot be understood and interpreted based only on conventional distinctions among cultures and nations.

Artist Shin il Kim expressed a similar idea about cultural identity in contemporary society, pointing out the mixing of cultural values. According to him, cultural identities are changing to a great extent due to globalization and the expansion of the Internet technologies, and these changes blur cultural and philosophical boundaries among countries. But, he also noticed the continuous impact of conventional ethnic boundaries on the understanding of cultural identities today. Thus, Kim focused on the hybridization of diverse cultural identities and insisted that cultural identities should be understood within the contexts of the past, the present, and the future.

CHAPTER 16 | Redefining Cultural Identities in Digital Art Practices: Artistic Journeys across Cultural Boundaries and Ethnic Borders

121

Experiencing Virtual Identity

People's interest in *virtuality* has increased with the development of digital technology. This concept of virtuality has also changed the way we understand our identities, to some extent. During his conference presentation, Graeme Sullivan defined digital technology as a "place," not a thing or a tool. In this context, the YOUNG-HAE CHANG HEAVY INDUSTRIES artists create Net art in a new place that is virtual. As they actively use this virtuality of their art medium, their artists' talk was presented in the form of Net art—an online presentation through the Internet network. Even though the artists participated in the conference physically, their presentation was narrated by their virtual spokeswomen, Victoria and Lola.

What was apparent in the Net art presentations of YOUNG-HAE CHANG HEAVY INDUSTRIES was the interaction between the virtual and the real. All the ideas in the presentation were provided through the *virtual* narrators, not by the artists. However, *real, physical* conversations with the artists that took place at the conference's panel discussion and during their interview implied that the ideas were those of the artists themselves. At the conference, some of audiences were not familiar with the form of Net art and looked confused about the artists' virtual presence. Therefore, in the panel discussion, topics such as virtuality, communication between artists and viewers, and the role of art were addressed and shared in light of the works by YOUNG-HAE CHANG HEAVY INDUSTRIES.

Interacting in Between Cultures: Artistic Journeys Within and Beyond Cultural Boundaries

This study was based on an assumption that in this era of digital technology and globalization, artists often explore cultural contexts beyond cultural boundaries. This collapse of cultural borders in artists' free and flexible journeys was demonstrated in the cases of YOUNG-HAE CHANG HEAVY INDSTURIES, Soonok Jung, and Shin il Kim. According to the data, these artists believe that traditional boundaries among countries and cultures do not play as important a role as they did in the past. After their critical and reflexive examination of conventional cultural distinctions, they emphasized the need for new theories and practices that facilitate the changes in the current era. This result resonates with what Ecker (1990), Ballengee-Morris and Stuhr (2001), and Burnett (2004) insist upon regarding the changes in cultures, communities, and artistic practices due to the development of computer technology. While Ecker (1990)

emphasizes the infusion of cultural diversity and its educational implications for cross-cultural art education, Ballengee-Morris and Stuhr (2001) highlight the complexity of cultural identity in today's world by maintaining, "there is no such thing as 'an' African American culture or 'a' Native American culture or 'a' Jewish culture" (p. 7). The research findings in this study also reaffirm Burnett's (2004) ideas about the changes in how culture and community are interpreted in a digital-based society.

However, concurrently, the data indicate that there were also artists who did not agree with the idea of blurring conventional cultural boundaries. In the case of these artists, culture and cultural identity are explored mostly within traditional distinctions among nations and ethnic groups. For example, artist Sung-Dam Hong believed that cultural exchanges happen within cultural boundaries. He insisted that the advancement of digital technology can increase the uniqueness of and enrich the cultural heritage of each culture, rather than blurring the borders among cultures.

The data indicate that the participating artists find mixed cultural values in their societal environment. During their interviews, they often focused on cultural hybridization and collisions that are apparent in current societies. While some participants understood cultural identity beyond their own ethnic distinctions, others still remained within these boundaries. While some participants interpreted cultural identity as related to a certain national character within the context of homogenized culture, others focused on the need to explore cultural contexts beyond conventional ideologies from the past, particularly because of the digitization in artistic practice and, in general, in the lifestyles of today. One common pattern emerging from the results was an emphasis on the will and role of artists as free and open-minded creators in the high-tech age of cultural changes. The ideas of educators such as Carr-Chellman (2005) and Ballengee-Morris and Stuhr (2001) are examined as part of this discussion.

Artistic Freedom in Mixing: The Will and Role of Artists within Cultural Collisions and Hybridizations

The issue of mixed cultural values was raised by many participants, and this concept is shown to be important in interpreting cultural identity in the digital era. This context of mixing in cultures was particularly apparent in the cases of YOUNG-HAE CHANG HEAVY INDSTRIES and Shin il Kim. These artists presented thoughtful ideas about their role in this

digital age, when diverse cultures crash into each other and are hybridized to some extent. Particularly, the concepts such as cultural *collision, hybridization*, and *mixing* were highlighted by these artists.

Most participating artists focused on presentation and expression. They seemed to believe that the way in which their works might serve as a representation of current cultures and societies was beyond their discipline. The data reveal instead that the primary consideration of the participating artists is to express what they think and feel while living their everyday lives. During their interviews, the notion of artistic freedom was addressed by most of the participating artists. In many cases, incorporating artists' cultural identities into their artwork accompanies the presentation of certain cultural symbols, involving representation and interpretation. This was apparent in the case of artist Sung-Dam Hong, who focused on the topics of Korean political, societal, historical, and cultural events and their meanings. But some artists in this study found that to intentionally present certain cultural symbols to represent their cultural identities went against their will and freedom to express themselves in their art making, to some extent.

This appears to be why many artists in this study, including YOUNG-HAE CHANG HEAVY INDUSTRIES, Soonok Jung, and Shin il Kim, stated that they did not intend to consciously show their conception of cultural identity in their artworks. But this does not imply that they are not aware of their culture and cultural identity in artistic practice. In this study, all of the participating artists expressed their personal interest in the ever-changing culture of today and showed their deep understanding of the process of cultural changes. Rather, they seemed to view their freedom and will to express their artistic interests as their goal. The artists considered the interpretation of their cultures and identities as represented in their works of art to be a function for the viewers. Thus, most artists in this study were interested in communications and interactions with their viewers and audiences.

The data suggest that computers play a primary role in artists' processes of presentation and expression. Also, computers sometimes serve as guidance for viewers' interpretations of and interactions with digital artworks. The findings concerning artists' digital art practices resonate with Bolter and Gromala's (2003) theory of "window and mirror." In their view, computers serve as a window and a mirror—tools for presentation and representation. Through a digital interface, artists view the world—both physical and virtual—and reflect on themselves. In this way, the digital interface serves as a window to see the other side of the world and a mirror to reflect on their own

CHAPTER 16 | Redefining Cultural Identities in Digital Art Practices: Artistic Journeys across Cultural Boundaries and Ethnic Borders

123

Figure 5

Taejin Kim, *Art, Market,* video installation, 2005. Used with permission from the artist.

appearance and environment. Many ideas of the participating artists about their culture and self support this theory of "window and mirror." The artists' focus on their artistic freedom and will to choose their own subjects and express them in very personal ways also parallels Goodman's (1996) view of the computer as "a filter that selectively screens, colors, and constructs a new reality" (p. 19).

Digitization in Artistic Practice: Cultural Exploration beyond Homogenization and Nationalism

Another important issue raised from the data is whether cultural identity can be understood within the context of national character. This finding was particularly apparent in the responses of participants with a Korean cultural background. Some participants agreed with this idea, while others emphasized the need to go beyond this view of cultural homogenization. The research participants often related the notion of cultural identity to tradition and history, because they thought that they could find Korea's unique character in its traditional culture. Many of the Korean presenters at the conference emphasized striking a balance between traditional culture and Western practices and theories to preserve their unique cultural heritage. On the other hand, this tendency to focus on building a certain national character under the name of cultural identity was criticized by some artists in this study.

This critical view on nationalism and cultural homogenization was particularly apparent in the ideas and artworks of participating contemporary artists. These artists seem to be flexible, open, and adaptable

when personalizing the concept of cultural identity. While creating digital artworks, they often explore the notions of culture and cultural identity beyond ethnic and national boundaries. Therefore, many artists in this study explore cultural identity beyond the country's homogenized culture and nationalism. As seen in the case of YOUNG-HAE CHANG HEAVY INDUSTRIES, even the artists' cultural background hardly impacts their artistic experiences. The use of digital technology, which enables artists to experience cultures in virtual spaces and communities, seems to expand and deepen their flexible cultural exploration beyond ethnic borders and national boundaries. These findings confirm the theory of Ballengee-Morris and Stuhr (2001), who highlight the conceptual "fluidity" of geographical boundaries in national and global cultural identities.

In addition, some conference participants' view of computer technology as a shortcut for the country's development reflects the "technological determinism" that Carr-Chellman (2005) criticizes in relation to technology-based education. In Carr-Chellman's view, technological determinism is dangerous as "social systems are by their nature non-determinist" (p. 129). Therefore, the data suggest the importance of understanding, interpreting, and defining cultural identity beyond the traps of nationalism and homogenization. Also, it can be argued that art educators and students who conceptualize cultural identity in a limited context can learn from the digital art practice of contemporary artists, who are conceptually flexible in adjusting to the cultural hybridization and collision that are happening in the current time.

Redefining Cultural Identities: Tradition and Transformation

According to the research findings, the artistic journeys of artists using digital technology take place both within and beyond traditional cultural boundaries. A collapse of cultural boundaries that often happens in interactions in digital-based societies today does not necessarily result in unifying or homogenizing cultures. The data indicate that, instead, cultural changes create an increase and enrichment of diversity. Through cultural hybridization, the scope of cultural diversity has been expanded, and this goes beyond just a mixture of diverse ethnic groups. As a result, new theories and practices regarding cultural identity formation, which is a more subtle and profound process, are required.

This chapter reveals that the ideas of tradition, transition, and transformation play a main conceptual role when the artists and art educators in this study explore cultural identities in digital art. Their cultural exploration and self-examination in artmaking is, in a way, a process of negotiation within the cultural changes apparent in today's cultures, societies, and communities. In addition, the process of negotiating artistic identity and pedagogical identity is, in many cases in this study, based on the concepts of presentation, representation, and expression in digital art practice. This interactive process of artmaking and meaning-making based on the participants' understanding of cultural collision and hybridization as well as cultural transformation and change suggests the existence of intercultural and trans-cultural movements in today's tech-based society (Burnett, 2004; Mesa-Bains, 1996).

Thus, the data revealed in this study reaffirm the importance of challenging cultural assumptions that are embedded in our understanding of interactive relationships among technology, art, and culture (Garoian & Gaudelius, 2004). This means that, by going beyond the boundaries between the traditional and the present, the old and the new, and the known and the unknown, contemporary artists who create digital artworks negotiate their cultural identities, and this creative and critical process offers implications for art educational practice. According to the findings, it can be argued that the transformative and transitory characteristics that are apparent in digital art practice should perhaps be fully understood by art educators through open and flexible instructional approaches. This will be particularly important for higher education, where students' learning can be directly connected to the art practice of contemporary artists.

Acknowledgments

I am greatly indebted to Professor Graeme Sullivan and all the participating artists and educators who made possible the Virtual Conversations Across Visual Cultures conference at Teachers College.

REFERENCES

Ballengee-Morris, C., & Stuhr, P. L. (2001). Multicultural art and visual cultural education in a changing world. *Art Education, 54*(4), 6-13.

Bolter, J. D., & Gromala, D. (2003). *Windows and mirrors: Interaction design, digital art, and the myth of transparency.* Cambridge, MA: The MIT Press.

Burnett, R. (2004). *How images think.* Cambridge, MA: The MIT Press.

Carr-Chellman, A. A. (Ed.). (2005). *Global perspectives on e-learning: Rhetoric and reality.* Thousand Oaks, CA: Sage Publications.

Ecker, D. W. (1990). Symposium on K-12 art education: Cultural identity, artistic empowerment, and the future of art in the schools. *Design for Arts in Education, 91*(3), 14-20.

Freedman, K. (2003). *Teaching visual culture: Curriculum, aesthetics, and the social life on art.* New York: Teachers College Press and Reston, VA: the National Art Education Association.

Garoian, C. R., & Gaudelius, Y. M. (2004). Performing resistance. *Studies in Art Education, 46*(1), 48-60.

Goodman, S. (1996). Media education: Culture and community in the classroom. In S. Cahan & Z. Kocur (Eds.), *Contemporary art and multicultural education* (pp. 18-23). New York: The New Museum of Contemporary Art and New York: Routledge.

Langer, A. A., & Knefelkamp, L. L. (2001, November). *Forms of literary development with technology in the college years: A scheme for students, faculty, and institutions of higher learning.* Paper presented at the Association of American Colleges and Universities Conference on Technology, Learning, & Intellectual Development, Baltimore, MD.

Mesa-Bains, A. (1996). Teaching students the way they learn. In S. Cahan & Z. Kocur (Eds.), *Contemporary art and multicultural education* (pp. 31-38). New York: The New Museum of Contemporary Art and New York: Routledge.

Ndalianis, A. (2004). *Neo-Baroque aesthetics and contemporary entertainment.* Cambridge, MA: The MIT Press.

Paul, C. (2003). *Digital art.* London: Thames & Hudson Ltd.

Sullivan, G. (2006, February). *Artful inquiry across braided boundaries.* Paper presented at the Virtual Conversations Across Visual Cultures conference at Teachers College, Columbia University, New York, NY.

YOUNG-HAE CHANG HEAVY INDUSTRIES. (2007). Cultural identity and nothingness. Retrieved October 18, 2007, from http://www.yhchang.com/NOTHINGNESS.html

ENDNOTES

1   http://www.yhchang.com/NOTHINGNESS.html

CHAPTER 16 | Redefining Cultural Identities in Digital Art Practices: Artistic Journeys across Cultural Boundaries and Ethnic Borders

125

CyberNet Activist Art Pedagogy

Karen Keifer-Boyd

The Gonzalez Goodale Architects, the firm in charge of designing a new school on the site of the demolished Ambassador Hotel, argued that she was using too much "content" rather than articulating more "universal" themes with her piece: "'Universal' has been a euphemism for a dominant culture which is historically Anglo," Baca told the students in the classroom, "at this particular moment 'universal' is Latina/o. I'll keep you posted as to this process but I wanted you to know what it is like for a public artist."

— SANDOVAL & LATORRE, 2008, P. 102. RECORDED FROM JUDITH BACA'S TEACHING SESSION ON OCTOBER 24, 2006, AT SPARC, SOCIAL AND PUBLIC ART RESOURCE CENTER IN VENICE, CALIFORNIA

As public pedagogy, or *public spheres of influence*, cyberNet activist art facilitates participatory critical democracy.[1] This takes many forms and directions. Critical public pedagogy of cyberNet art, as an educational and artistic practice, is a critical stance concerning socio-pervasive artifacts, processes, and interfaces that acculturate and assimilate values, beliefs, and sensitivities. Critical cyberNet art is designed to enable diversity of participation. Howard Becker's (1982) account of *spheres of influence* radiating from art reshapes into a multidirectional layered "matrix of sensibility"[2] when the art's medium is Internet communication technologies. This is because (inter)action is perpetuated through cultural interfaces such as humans, technologies, localities, and politics. Such cyberNet artworks are performed networks of relations.

CyberNet activist art, such as the work of Electronic Disturbance Theatre (EDT) and Critical Art Ensemble, includes virtual sit-ins, tactical media practices, and virtual grassroots projects. Other collaborative art teams, such as The Yes Men (1999), use communication technologies to disrupt capitalism, often through duplication, impersonation, or reversals. Judith Baca's Digital Mural Lab is a collaboration between Baca, youth of color, and specific communities such as the Estrada Housing Project in East Los Angeles (Sandoval & Latorre, 2008). Baca's critical feminist pedagogy has empowered youth, and toppled stereotypes. CyberNet activist art often crosses borders between physical and virtual realms in ways that are not clearly differentiated; yet such local activism can have a global reach.[3]

When violence, homophobia, and bigotry expressed through racism, sexism, and other systemic prejudices transform into critical social praxis, cyberNet activist art is at its best, as I will show with the examples discussed here. This chapter on cyberNet activist art pedagogy explores critical cyberNet art practices in four areas: (a) participatory democracy, (b) interventions that challenge capitalism and other patriarchal systems, (c) cyborg border crossings, and (d) re-visions of place and time. I guide students in my university courses, whose goals are to become art educators, to investigate the public pedagogy of cyberNet art as a medium of communication that can contribute to a more just world. Public pedagogy is the use of a public medium such as the Internet to influence behaviors and beliefs. Public pedagogy enacts societal curricula that are easily consumed because of its ubiquitous nature. Awareness of consumption of public pedagogy via the Net is important because of its global reach. Consumers change to producers when participating in the public pedagogy of the Internet. Educators need to be versed in how to facilitate investigations of public pedagogy in virtual global landscapes and how to guide students to develop critical Net art practices. It is this combined curricular emphasis that I refer to as cyberNet activist art pedagogy and discuss in this chapter.

Virtual Landscape Curricular Emphasis: Public Pedagogy Investigations and Critical Net Art Practices

Many people are global consumers, not producers. Those who are global producers often make decisions based on individualistic gains rather than social justice and on the impact of information and capital traversing the world via communication technologies. I prepare art teachers to become producers of a socially just world by becoming critical public pedagogues in Internet extensions of classroom teaching. Simulation, interactivity, collaboration, and intertextuality are characteristics of cyberNet activist art pedagogy with which I familiarize students through experiences of Net art and through projects that lead up to and include the creation of Net art. The MacArthur Foundation Series on *Digital Media and Learning* describes the type of education needed: "As professional educators, we have the responsibility to design learning environments and institutional practices that foster the acquisition of foundational skills that students will need for a lifetime of network navigation, information synthesis, social participation, and creative knowledge production" (Anderson & Balsamo, 2008, p. 245). As a professor in a university art education program, I prepare preservice teachers for social responsibility in their future teaching and learning.

In a junior-level university course about visual culture and technology, for those pursuing art education careers, which I have been teaching almost every semester since the mid 1990s, students create Net Art. Characteristics of students' Net art are that their work has palimpsest traces, perpetually displaces stagnate categories, has an interplay of surface and depth, has no prescribed path, presents a multifaceted critical pastiche, and enables others' participation in shaping the work. Students use image hotspots, anchors to direct to specific places, animations, blogs, wikis, motion sensors, audio and video recording and remixing, among other strategies to create a layered matrix of sensibility in cyberspace. Multivocal participation built into the design of their Net art encourages production of public pedagogy.

Students and I evaluate their work based on the characteristics of Net art set forth as criteria by them. To prepare students to develop criteria, they need to experience, study, and critique Net art.[4] Their familiarity grows through dialogue that I facilitate, as well as from conversation in small groups when experiencing Net art, and from the readings about Net art that we discuss together. Figure 1 is an example of student-generated criteria for Net art. Students meet in groups of about five members to develop criteria based on the course readings, discussions, and experiences. They then share these with the class as I type, using their words, for large screen projections of the text under discussion. Students ask each other for clarification and argue until all ideas that all understand and agree with are included. I give them a couple of days to review what they had produced for final changes prior to use as the assessment criteria for their project. Each semester consensus is reached. While specific language changes, students' criteria involve interactive engagement, metaphor, and intertextuality.

Each semester, I vary the themes for organizing Net art for students' critical explorations. For example, in fall 2007, the four areas were: identity (i.e., self in relationship to others), representation through visual metaphor, intertextual palimpsests, and real-time social networking. In spring 2008, the areas included various ways to consider environment: global warming, safe environments, ownership rights and shared environmental resources, and personal/public environments. Therefore, the four areas discussed in this chapter are one organizational scheme in developing familiarity with cyberNet activist art pedagogy. In this case study of cyberNet activist art pedagogy, I selected four student works of the 20 created in my fall 2007 course, along with Net artworks students experience as part of my teaching. My purpose is to provide ideas on how to facilitate cyberNet activist art pedagogy in global extensions of art classrooms via Internet medium.

CyberNet Art Participatory Democracy

According to Wikipedia® (2001), which is a Web 2.0[5] example of participatory democracy in knowledge formation, "participatory democracy is a process emphasizing the broad participation (decision making) of constituents in the direction and operation of political systems" (¶ 1). Virtual sit-ins,

Figure 1

Criteria developed by students in fall 2007 to evaluate their Net Art creations.

Criteria for Net Art Developed by Students in Fall 2007

Design layout criteria: Imagery, fonts, and color scheme are unified and relate to the theme, concept, and/or visual metaphor. The Net artwork is inviting to enter and keeps viewers actively engaged with one another and the artwork.

Concept, theme, and/or visual metaphor: The work exists on the Net and functions as a piece of artwork using the Internet as a medium. "Function as an artwork" is further defined as a view of art in which metaphors for life are communicated and stimulate viewers to think creatively, and the Net art introduces a concept in a unique way rather than as factual reporting.

Intertextuality: The Net artwork encourages deep levels of thinking, in which meaning is thoughtfully and thoroughly constructed.

Figure 2

a powerful form of cyberNet art activism for participatory democracy, close down websites or redirects cyber traffic. For example, Electronic Disturbance Theatre (EDT),[6] "recircuits agitprop actions to mobilize micronets to act in solidarity with the Zapatistas in Chiapas by staging virtual sit-ins online" (Dominguez, 2000, p. 284). EDT jams a URL with a computer script FloodNet that reloads a targeted website several times a minute. This shuts down the site when masses of people access the site simultaneously. Postings of upcoming sit-ins and an archive of the purpose and impact of previous ones are listed at the Electronic Civil Disobedience (2007) website. This Net activism has drawn the attention both online and offline of the Mexican government and the U.S. Department of Defense (Electronic Civil Disobedience, 2007; Kartenberg, 2005; Shachtman, 2004).

Operación Digna, cyberfeminist activism in solidarity with the women of Juarez and Chihauhua, Mexico, also use FloodNet for virtual sit-ins. Operación Digna lists the names on the Web of murdered women, provides protest posters for community rallies, and initiates petitions to the Mexican government. The protest posters and petitions express a demand for thorough investigations of the murders. Their cyberNet art is intended to provoke and influence officials to find the perpetrators of the crimes, to end the harassment by agents of the Mexican state against families of the victims, and to enact laws to responsibly and quickly investigate missing persons reports (Justicia Para Nuestras Hijas, 2003; Operación Digna, 2003a, 2003b).

Critical Art Ensemble (2002) is known for their use of tactical media,[7] with a range of projects such as broadcasting to denounce fascist news items, and CD-ROM distribution on such things as hacking GameBoy® to free male youth from limiting norms of what it means to be a man. Historically, tactical media referred to quick tactical infiltration of dominant media practices for critique of dominant social systems, and has roots in such arts movements as Situationalists, Dada, and Surrealism (de Certeau, 1984). It is a group action, in which individuals are not identified, creating a spectacle from existing elements within society (Lovink, 2002; Meikle, 2002). Today it sometimes involves the critical use of mobile technologies to reach communities that have limited access to technology, and places the media in the hands of the community, or provides distribution avenues that counter media power centers (MediaShed, 2006; Mongrel, 2006).

A team in my fall 2007 course, Lorielle Ressler and Emily Sylvia, collaborated in creating their Net

art project, *The Ripple Effect*[8] (see Figure 2). This piece concerns how everyday actions impact the future. A rock gallery provides nonlinear interaction. A click on each rock in a pile of rocks reveals stories the students collected concerning consequences of one's actions. A video narrative in which one action creates the next action, and a blog encourages viewers to think about how their past actions shape the future. This work can be considered critical participatory democracy in bringing awareness of consequences of one's action as well as consequences when one does not take action as some of the rock gallery and blog testimonies express.

CyberNet Art Interventions that Challenge Global Capitalism

Cyberactivist artists concerned with the *not-so-free market* of capitalist *free markets* provide open access, and often develop or use *open source* software or provide DIY (do-it-yourself) alternatives to corporate products as a form of intervention to global capitalism. They seek to provide and promote equal access, as both a move toward participatory democracy within and beyond national borders, and to disconnect capitalist global economies from the rhetoric of democracy.

Open source could be defined as free distribution of the source code of functional software so that others can modify the computer program without restrictions or copyright penalty. Additionally, open source code is not proprietary or "predicated on any individual technology or style of interface" (Open Source Initiative, 2005, ¶ 10). For example, Emitto (2002), the Latin word meaning "to send out," is a collaborative publishing network providing an online cultural art resource, conceived by new media artist, Carlos Rosas. The Emitto community aspires to promote democratic values that transcend nationhood, and to make art accessible.

The proliferation of the Creative Commons

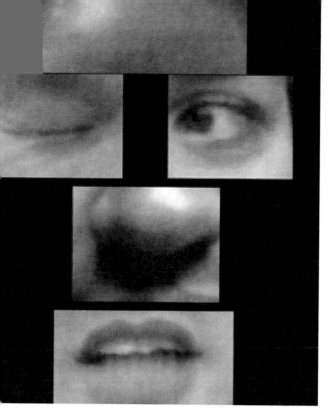

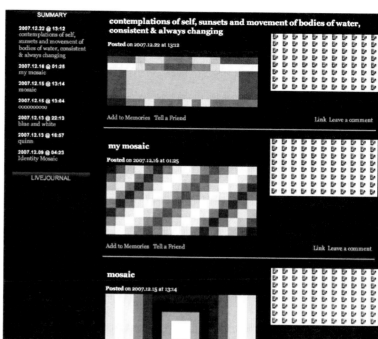

symbol on Net activist art is an intervention into capitalist economics. Creative Commons (CC) is "devoted to expanding the range of creative work available for others to build upon and share" (2001, ¶ 1). The animation, *Reticulum Rex* (n.d.) is a playful artwork that describes Creative Commons. The animation creators encourage others to remix and develop their own creations from any aspect of their animation, including the fonts they have developed. The Creative Commons "human-readable summary" of their copyright code stipulates for the animation and other CC works that you must give the original artist or author credit, you must not sell your work that remixes CC works, and the "share alike" symbol needs to be placed on the work if distributed.

The open source cinema movement involves "peer-to-peer information sharing and the support of a participatory culture" (Anderson & Balsamo, 2008, p. 248). Sharing of films and other creative artworks as well as open source programs is the purpose of organizations such as Creative Commons (2001), the Electronic Frontier Foundation (1990), Internet Archive (1996), Open Source Initiative (2005), and Participatory Media Literacy (2007).

In their online and offline media tactics, the Danish artists SUPERFLEX (Rasmus Nielsen, Jakob Fenger, and Bjørnstjerne Christiansen) challenge corporate market practice through large-scale DIY projects. By revealing and making processes freely available, they usurp the proprietary practices of major corporations. For example, the appropriation of logos and provision of recipes for

Star & Buck Cafe draws attention to consumer culture and offers prosumer (production and consumption) DIY alternatives to large corporate monopolies (COPYSHOP, 2007).

Other critical cyberNet art strategies include the use of communication technologies as interventions to capitalism through duplication, impersonation, or reversals. For example, in 1993, Mike Bonanno (who founded The Yes Men with Andy Bichlbaum), switched the vocal audio boxes in Barbie *dolls* and G.I. Joe *action figures* and returned them to the store shelves to disrupt the capitalist enterprise that perpetuates gender stereotypes (Yes Men, 1999). Corporate law protects The Yes Men, who are supported by a corporate brokerage (®™ark, 2000), since corporations cannot be held legally responsible for corporate actions. Thus ®™ark's corporate veil is key to the success of The Yes Men and others who sabotage corporate control. Such cyberNet activist art redefines the nature of artworks.

Becca Brittain's Net art, *Identity Mosaic* (2007)[9] that she created in my course, is a DIY disruption to capitalism. Becca found a simple solution to enable identity mosaics created at her website to be shared by providing the password to her blog. This changes the nature of a blog from ownership by the initial creator of the blog to ownership by all who participate. Her Net artwork encourages people to think about the shifts and reconfigurations of their identity as they move from context to context. Figure 3 is a screen shot of the page for creating mosaics, and Figure 4 is the blog where the mosaics are posted.

Figure 3

Left: This entrance screen shot to Becca Brittain's Net art, *Identity Mosaic* (2007), captures frames from the five videos assembled to make a whole face. The videos play simultaneously to show close-ups of different parts of a face in motion.

Figure 4

Right: This participatory visual blog screen shot, which is part of Becca Brittain's Net art *Identity Mosaic* (2007), also includes the grid of colors each used to create a mosaic.

CyberNet Art Interventions that Challenge Patriarchal Systems

Several new media cultural theorists (Manovich, 2001; Ihde, 1990; Sofia, 2003) have argued that digital technologies are cultural interfaces. Sofia posits that "questions concerning technological futurity can be translated into questions about who—or what—are the agents of cultural change" (2003, p. 503). Thus, to change the patriarchal world involves feminist activism in cyberspace. María Fernández (2002) reminds us that cyberspace is primarily occupied by and for those who have the economic means to have electricity, computer equipment, and Internet connection; as well as have the life experiences with technology to develop interest and confidence to be active in technological developments—primarily White males younger than 50 years of age. Therefore, socio-economic class, race, age, and gender are factors in who has power and controls the cultural interfaces of digital technologies.

Cyberfeminist art pedagogies[10] create aesthetic-expressive forums to disrupt patriarchal inscriptions, practices, and structures. subRosa, founded by Faith Wilding in 1991, is a cyberfeminist collective that combines performance and Web work. subRosa defines itself as "a reproducible cyberfeminist cell of cultural researchers committed to combining art, activism, and politics to explore and critique the effects of the intersections of the new information and biotechnologies on women's bodies, lives, and work" (¶ 2).[11] The website and exhibition, *Cell Track* (subRosa, 2004) is a visualization of the "global dispersal, patenting and privatization of human and animal embryonic stem cells" (¶ 5). The goal is to investigate the feasibility of a public, non-patented, non-proprietary embryonic stem cell bank. *US Grade AAA Premium Eggs* involved a performance at Bowling Green State University, in Ohio in April 2002, in which students were invited to donate egg and sperm cells that were then assigned a flesh market value. Website visualizations of the flesh market of selling gametes (cells), tissues, and organs were integrated in the performance to defy global bio-Web markets that prize human bodies monetarily.

Computer source code writing is a powerful way to challenge patriarchal inscriptions of the cultural body. For example, Ka-Ping Yee (2005, 2007) launched a website on July 30, 2005, that reverses gender pronouns and other gendered terms on any website that one enters in the search engine, thus calling attention to socially constructed gendered perspectives in the English language. Regender.com produces high-speed revisionist texts of the *New York Times*, the *Book of Genesis*, and other worldview representations. Reading a regendered text reveals assumptions about gender roles. For example, one preservice art educator in my course wrote in response to an assignment to critique Net art:

> *Regender* ... can be a tough idea to wrap your mind around, so by using this device that does something as simple as changing "he's" to "she's" and names like "George" to "Georgia" allows us to see [the] impact [of] this genderization ... I wanted to do something more personal that forced me to look at gender roles in our everyday life. ... I spent a class period taking notes and switching proper nouns and pronouns from masculine to feminine and vice versa. ... With my roommates I tried to talk as if this switch was normal. ... I even referred to our friends using opposing gender words. "Oh my god, Christopher looked so hot in his sundress and pink heels last night!" I got some strange looks and questions but once I was done conducting my little experiment I realized just how much gender factors into our world. (K. Evanosky, September 13, 2007)

Another student describes her experience of *Regender*. One article she regendered was on polygamy and the other on Britney Spears. "I took all of the articles I looked at from CNN.com. ... [One] article describes [men] as "second-class citizens" to the women. But why did I find this more shocking than the original article?" (A. Fell, September 13, 2007). These student responses show how each translated experiences with *Regender* into her life from face-to-face conversations to reading the news on the Internet.

CyberNet Art Identity Redefinitions with Cyborg Border Crossings

While globalization describes current socio-economic situations, nations increasingly fortify political borders. The Internet, often viewed as borderless, is not a border easily entered by those who are economically disenfranchised, and *dedicated* sites oust posters through social pressures (Byrne, 2008). CyberNet activist art involves border crossing in varied ways. In her cross border communication Web-based project, *Looking for a Husband with an EU Passport*, Slovakian artist, Tanja Ostojic (2000-2001), selected potential husbands from e-mail exchanges, married, immigrated, and divorced.

Some artists have used cyborg border crossing and masquerade (e.g., Andreja Kulunčić, Sandy Stone, and Helen Varley Jamieson) in simulated worlds on the Internet—such as *Cyborg Web Shop* and *UpStage*—to disrupt global media portrayals of what it means to be human.[12] *Cyborg Web Shop* (2004), created by Andreja Kulunčić, with a production team, is a mock e-shopping site for purchasing hi-tech body enhancements. Similar to shopping from a catalogue, one browses through pages of technological enhancements to select body improvements. Chats with other cyborg enhancement shoppers on the website tend to focus on seeking immortality with the prosthetic body revisions. In *Cyborg Web Shop,* the Net art critiques consumerism, and through trajectories of speculative fictions about constructions of virtual selves redefines what it means to be human.

Avatar Body *Collision* (2002), a precursor of other globally distributed performance troupes using *Upstage,* perform personally shared global concerns such as *Dress the Nation* (2003), which protested the portentous U.S. invasion of Iraq. The four *colliders,* i.e., women "who live (mostly) in London, Helsinki, Aotearoa/New Zealand, Australia and cyberspace," meet, devise, rehearse, and perform online (2007, ¶ 1). *Upstage*[13] is a free-downloadable software developed for cyberformances that also enable impromptu audience participation. Creators "encourage you to use it for creative, educational and social purposes" in performances for global audiences (*Upstage,* Download, ¶1).

Second Life (SL) is a programming system Web platform, in which a downloadable client server is freely accessed on the Internet. SL's in-world is vast with much diversity of activity in building worlds and events in those worlds. For example, in August 2006, students at the University of Texas in Austin in Sanchez's (2007) class created avatars based on their personal role-models, which included Malcolm X, Ellen DeGeneres, Mother Teresa, Shakespeare, and Teddy Roosevelt. In SL, in their cyborgian self, they held discussions with each other in character about the role of leadership and compassion, leadership and creativity, and leadership and morality.

Some *Second Life* residents merge SL with other programming systems. For example, machinima, a process for rendering computer-generated imagery (CGI), uses real-time, interactive (game) 3D engines such as SL.[14] Through programming border crossing, avatar and world creation with machinima outside of SL can be brought into SL.

A student in my course, Morgan Reightler,[15] created a Net artwork that presents animated, inanimate objects from her home to suggest how these objects are extensions of self. Her work shows the fluid nature of how we know self in that when one clicks on an object word, an association appears, and then the word and association disappear (see Figure 5). Attention to the double-codes of objects as prosthetics of herself, Morgan's Net art evokes mutual articulation between humans and objects.

CyberNet Art Re-visions of Place and Time

Cyberspace has become so integrated into our life that for some it has become a real space (Dodge & Kitchin, 2001). Geographer David Harvey (2001) attributes spatiality to cognitive maps and suggests that hyperlinked knowledge on the World Wide Web is a re-envisioning of human relationship to place. We conceptualize from the spatial forms that knowledge occupies. Simulations are "a kind of map-in-time, visually and viscerally" (Friedman, 1999, ¶ 20). Friedman suggests that simulations have the potential to create what Fredric Jameson calls "an aesthetic of cognitive mapping: a pedagogical political culture which seeks to endow the individual subject with some new heightened sense of its place in the global system" (1991, p. 54).

The compression of space-time in cyberspace impacts our understanding of each other and our relationship to local geographies. It enables networking and sharing of local concerns for gathering diverse perspectives and mobilizing political actions. However, if the Web replaces face-to-face discussions of small local groups, than immediate and site-specific concerns may be inadequately addressed. An example of the dissolution between cyber and physical locations is in the work of a loose-knit art collective, *The Department of Space and Land Reclamation* (2002-2008). They use the Web to plan weekend campaigns to reclaim public space in Chicago, San Francisco, and Los Angeles. This cyberNet activist art pedagogy revisions human relationship to place.

CyberNet artworks function pedagogically in the global public spheres of the Internet, and impact embodied personal experience of self and place. Artist team Sawad Brooks and Beth Stryker have explored socio-spatial relations in cyberspace, the

Figure 5

A click on *stairs,* one of the object words in Morgan Reightler's (2007) Net artwork, reveals a poem of actions associated with stairs as the word *stairs* disappears from the Web page.

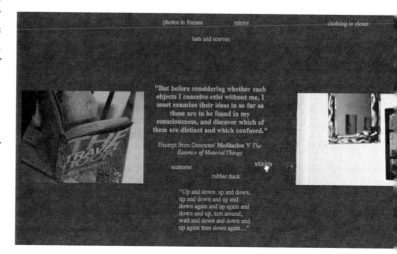

Figure 6

This is the second image in a sequence of photographs by Quinn Dwyer (2007) created for her Net artwork.

tree branches, interrupted with sped up cuts of noisy machinery, and then back to calmness with the word "Progress?" constantly visible through the duration of the video. Quinn's Net art explores human relationship to physical place in the ephemeral cyberspace of her site, which includes a blog in response to her question, "What direction will you go to change where we are headed?"

CyberNet Public Art Pedagogy

The concern that there is "too much content," which targets art with controversial or anti-establishment content, still influences the public art of U.S. cities, as we learn from Baca's 2006 experience quoted at the beginning of this chapter. However, Baca and other artists have found that Net art can bypass influential gatekeepers who control economic dispersion. And, instead, the content is visibly shaped by multitudes of participants experiencing and (inter)acting in the cyberNet artwork. Such access is particularly important for those who may not have opportunities to participate in offline public spheres (Byrne, 2008). Critical cyberNet activist art pedagogy involves a relationship between collective voice and social change, as well as embodied learning through social (inter) actions of global and local scale with communication technologies. The spheres of influence of such public pedagogy do not stay in cyberspace but impact the material world.

interplay between public and private concerns, and how these intersect with geographic space, Diasporas, and community formation. *DissemiNet* consists of the testimonies of those driven from their homes yet connected in cyberspace by the stories they share. Physical movement of the cursor displaces elements of the stories, like the private lives presented in this public forum. Their *RadarWeb* (1999) project calls attention to social injustice that has been occurring for many years in Okinawa, Japan. Okinawa residents post photographs and descriptions of their experiences of abuse by soldiers stationed at the nearby U.S. military base. By clicking on the date of the occurrence, people throughout the world can read these site-specific reports.

Quinn Dwyer's Net art, created in my course, is a series of photographs in which natural landscapes are severed by human occupation (see Figure 6).[16] The photo series culminates in a video that begins with a slow beautiful scene of the sun coming through

Acknowledgments

I wish to thank Christine Liao, graduate teaching assistant in fall 2007 and spring 2008; students in my courses since the mid 1990s who have explored Net art with me; and I give special appreciation to the fall 2007 students who gave permission for me to quote from their class papers and present their Net art as examples in this chapter. Further, I thank cyberNet artists for their important work, and the Penn State Gender and Technology Writing Group, especially Irina Aristarkhova, Wanda Knight, Christine Liao, and Eileen Trauth, for feedback on a draft of this chapter.

References

Anderson, S., & Balsamo, A. (2008). A pedagogy for original sinners. In T. McPherson (Ed.), *Digital youth, innovation, and the unexpected* (pp. 241-259). Cambridge, MA: The MIT Press.

Ars Electronica Center (2008). *The archive of the Prix Ars Electronica* (jury statements). Retrieved January 28, 2008, from http://www.aec.at/en/archives/prix_einstieg.asp

Avatar Body *Collision* (2002). Retrieved January 15, 2008, from http://www.avatarbodycollision.org/

Becker, H. S. (1982). *Art worlds*. Berkeley: University of California Press.

Brooks, S., & Stryker, B. (1998–2001). *DissemiNet*. Retrieved January 15, 2008, from http://disseminet.walkerart.org/

Brooks, S., & Stryker, B. (1999). *RadarWeb*. Retrieved January 15, 2008, from http://www.thing.net/~sawad/radarweb/

Byrne, D. N. (2008). The future of (the) "Race": Identity, discourse, computer-mediated Public Spheres. In A. Everett (Ed.), *Learning race and ethnicity: Youth and digital media* (15-38). The John D. and Catherine T. MacArthur Foundation Series on Digital Media and Learning. Cambridge, MA: The MIT Press.

Bureau of Inverse Technology (1991). Retrieved January 15, 2008, from http://www.bureauit.org/

Creative Commons (2001). Retrieved January 15, 2008, from http://creativecommons.org

Critical Art Ensemble (2002). *Digital resistance explorations in tactical media*. Brooklyn, New York: Autonomedia.

Critical Art Ensemble (n.d.). Retrieved January 15, 2008, from http://www.critical-art.net/

COPYSHOP (2007). Retrieved January 2, 2007, from http://copy-shop.org/knoxville/

de Certeau, M. (1984). *The practice of everyday life* (S. Rendall, Trans.). Berkeley: University of California Press. (Original work 1974)

Department of Space and Land Reclamation (2002-2008). Retrieved January 15, 2008, from http://www.counterproductiveindustries.com/tour/

Dress the Nation (2003). An international cyberformance protest against war by Avatar Body *Collision* with Lysistrata Project. Retrieved January 15, 2008, from http://www.avatarbodycollision.org/lysis/lysis.html

Dodge, M., & Kitchin, R. (2001). *Mapping Cyberspace*. New York: Routledge.

Dominguez, R. (2000). Electronic Disturbance Theatre. In C. Fusco (Ed.), *Corpus Delecti: Performance art of the Americas* (pp. 285–286). New York: Routledge.

Electronic Civil Disobedience (2007). Archive of e-actions. Retrieved January 28, 2008, from http://www.thing.net/~rdom/ecd/ecd.html

Electronic Frontier Foundation (1990). Retrieved January 15, 2008, from http:eff.org

Emitto (2002). Retrieved January 15, 2008, from http://www.emitto.net/

Fernández, M. (2002). *Is cyberfeminism colorblind?* Retrieved January 15, 2008, from http://www.artwomen.org/cyberfems/fernandez/fernandez1.htm

Friedman, T. (1999). Semiotics of Sim City. *First Monday: Peer reviewed journal on the Internet*. Retrieved January 11, 2008, from http://www.firstmonday.org/issues/issue4_4/friedman/index.html

Geertz, C. (2000). Art as a cultural system. In C. Geertz (Ed.), Local knowledge: Further essays in interpretative anthology (3rd edition) (pp. 94-120). New York: Basic Books. (Original work published 1983)

Giroux, H. A. (1999). Cultural studies as public pedagogy: Making the pedagogical more political. *The encyclopedia of philosophy of education*. Retrieved January 10, 2008, from http://www.vusst.hr/ENCYCLOPAEDIA/cultural_studies.htm

Harvey, D. (2001). *Spaces of capital: Towards a critical geography*. New York: Routledge.

Humanfuture (2008a). *sk-interfaces: Exploding borders–creating membranes in art, technology and society* (Exhibition catalogue). Liverpool: FACT (Foundation for Art and Creative Technology) and Liverpool University Press.

Humanfuture (2008b). Retrieved February 1, 2008, from http://humanfutures.fact.co.uk/

Ihde, D. (1990). *Technology and the lifeworld: From garden to earth*. Bloomington, IN: Indiana University Press.

Institute of Applied Autonomy (n.d.). Retrieved January 15, 2008, from http://www.appliedautonomy.com/

Internet Archive (1996). Retrieved January 15, 2008, from http:archive.org

Jameson, F. (1991). *Postmodernism, or, the cultural logic of Late Capitalism*. Durham: Duke University Press.

Justicia Para Nuestras Hijas (2003). *Justice for our daughters document (Extensive analysis of the killings)*. Retrieved January 18, 2008, from http://www.thing.net/~rdom/ecd/JuarezAction2003/JusticeforOurDaughters

Kartenberg, H. P. (2005). *An interview with Ricardo Dominguez*. Retrieved January 28, 2008, from http://post.thing.net/node/304

Keifer-Boyd, K. (2007). Cyberfeminist activist art pedagogy (Park, Jeong Ae, Trans.). *Journal of Research in Art & Education*, *8*(1), 29-89. [KoSEA: English 29-59 & Korean, 61-89]

Kuluncic, A. (2004). *Cyborg Web Shop*. Retrieved January 2, 2008, from http://www.cyborg.com.hr/about.php

Lovink, G. (2002). *Dark fiber: Tracking critical Internet culture*. Cambridge, MA: MIT Press.

Manovich, L. (2001). *The language of new media*. Cambridge, MA: MIT Press.

MediaShed (2006). Retrieved January 15, 2008, from http://www.mongrelx.org/About/

Meikle, G. (2002). *Future active: Media activism and the Internet*. New York: Routledge in association with Pluto Press.

Mongrel (2006) Retrieved January 28, 2008, from http://www.mongrel.org.uk/

Morgan, W. (2000). Electronic tools for dismantling the master's house: Poststructuralist feminist research and hypertext products. In E. A. St.Pierre & W. S. Pillow (Eds.), *Working the ruins: Feminist poststructural theory and methods in education* (pp. 130–147). New York: Routledge.

OBN (1997). Retrieved January 15, 2008, from http://www.obn.org/

Open Source Initiative (2005). Retrieved January 15, 2008, from http://www.opensource.org/docs/definition.php

Operación Digna (2003a). Retrieved January 15, 2008, from http://www.thing.net/~cocofusco/dignaeng1.html

Operación Digna (2003b). *An open letter to the Mexican Government in the State of Chihuahua*. Retrieved January 28, 2008, from http://operationdigna.typepad.com/

Ostojic, T. (2000-2001). *Looking for a husband with an EU passport*. Retrieved January 15, 2008, from http://www.cac.org.mk/capital/projects/tanja/

Participatory Media Literacy (2007). Retrieved December 15, 2007, from http://www.socialtext.net/medialiteracy

Reticulum Rex (n.d.). Retrieved January 15, 2008, from http://mirrors.creativecommons.org/reticulum_rex

Sanchez, J. (2007). *Sanchez social media: Connecting people, places, and spaces*. Retrieved December 15, 2007, from http://sanchezsocialmedia.com/secondlife.html

Sandoval, C., & Latorre, G. (2008). Chicana/o activism: Judy Baca's digital work with youth of color. In A. Everett (Ed.), *Learning race and ethnicity: Youth and digital media* (pp. 81-108). Cambridge, MA: The MIT Press.

Shachtman, N. (2004). Hackers take aim at GOP. *Wired.* Retrieved January 28, 2008, from http://www.wired.com/politics/law/news/2004/08/64602

Sofia, Z. (2003). Contested zones: Futurity and technological art. In J. Mallory (Ed.), *Women, art, and technology* (pp. 502–522). Cambridge, MA: The MIT Press.

subRosa (2004). *Cell track: Mapping the appropriation of life materials.* Retrieved January 5, 2008, from http://www.cyberfeminism.net/

®™ark (2000). Retrieved January 15, 2008, from http://www.rtmark.com

Tonella, K. (1994-2005). *Border crossings: Cyborgs.* Retrieved January 8, 2008, from http://www.uiowa.edu/~commstud/resources/bordercrossings/cyborgs.html

Upstage (2004). Retrieved January 15, 2008, from http://upstage.org.nz/blog/

Wikipedia (2001). *Paticipatory democracy.* Retrieved January 13, 2008, from http://en.wikipedia.org/wiki/Participatory_democracy

Yee, K.-P. (2005). *Regender: A different kind of translator.* Retrieved January 15, 2008, from http://regender.com/index.html

Yee, K.-P. (2007). *Wolog.net.* Retrieved January 15, 2008, from http://zestyping.livejournal.com/

Yes Men (1999). Retrieved January 15, 2008, from http://www.theyesmen.org

ENDNOTES

1. Giroux describes that public pedagogy is located in a "spectrum of public spheres in society" (Giroux, 1999, p. 1). It involves the "understanding of how the political becomes pedagogical; that is, how the very processes of learning constitute the political mechanisms through which identities are shaped, desires mobilized, and experiences take on form and meaning" (Giroux, 1999, p. 2).

2. Geertz, 1983, p. 102

3. See, for example, Baca's Digital Mural Lab at http://www.sparcmurals.org/, which is part of the non-profit SPARC (The Social and Public Art Resource) that Judith Baca with Christina Schlesinger and Donna Deitch founded in 1976.

4. The project assignment with resources is at http://explorations.sva.psu.edu/322/projects/2_critique.htm. Presentations include introduction to Ars Electronica Center in Linz, Austria, and their annual competition, *Prix Ars Electronica*, which since 1987 has served as a "barometer for trends in contemporary media art" (Leopoldseder, Schöpf, & Stocker, 2008, ¶ 4). An archive of jury statements is at http://www.aec.at/en/archives/prix_einstieg.asp.

5. Web 2.0 refers to second-generation Web use, which favors open source participatory activity.

6. EDT was formed in 1998.

7. There are several other artist groups, such as the Bureau of Inverse Technology (B.I.T., 1991) and the Institute for Applied Autonomy (n.d.), who use tactical media.

8. See http://explorations.sva.psu.edu/322/visualculture/netartf07/Sylvia-Ressler/home.html

9. See http://explorations.sva.psu.edu/322/visualculture/netartf07/Brittain/netart.html

10. See Keifer-Boyd (2007) and Morgan (2000) for further discussion of cyberfeminist activist art pedagogy.

11. Also see the collective Old Boys Network (OBN, 1997) for further examples of cyberfeminist activism.

12. Further examples of border crossing Net art are compiled by Karla Tonella (1994-2005), and at Humanfutures (2008a, 2008b), which presents artwork that "transcend the borders between the physical, virtual, biological and digital" (2008b, ¶ 1).

13. *Upstage*° was first launched on January 9, 2004, funded by the Community Partnership Fund of the New Zealand Government's Digital Strategy, and is a collaborative project of CityLink, MediaLab, and Auckland University of Technology. It is open source and licensed under a dual-license: Creative Commons Attribution-NonCommercial-ShareAlike 2.5 License and GNU General Public License (GPL).

14. There are other virtual worlds in which to create oneself and to use machinima to cross programming borders including free to download programs: *Active Worlds*°, *There*°, *Entropia Universe*° and *Dotsoul Cyberpark*°.

15. http://explorations.sva.psu.edu/322/visualculture/netartf07/Reightler/index.html

16. See http://explorations.sva.psu.edu/322/visualculture/netartf07/Dwyer/home.html

Putting the World Together: Virtual Globes and the Changing Nature of (Digital) Global Representations

Michelle Simms and B. Stephen Carpenter, II

Seeing is Believing?

Scholars in visual culture studies increasingly agree with the idea that Americans currently live in a media and image saturated society (Freedman, 2003; Mirzoeff, 1999). An analysis of the resulting cultural effects of mass media images reveals insight into its homogenizing effects on world cultures, specifically through constructed images. Such effects are seen in the rapidly developing digital experiences of virtual worlds, social networking, and communication technologies. These digital experiences function as substitutes for direct person-to-person communication and often include real world images and video. As an extension of such mediated communication, virtual globes provide entry into an era of unprecedented access to real world images.

Virtual globes like Google Earth™ provide "virtuality" (Mirzoeff, 1999), whereby what is not *real*, but rather *realistic*, appears as real. That is, virtual globes present a constructed world where the resulting global image is a mosaic, tessellation, or quilt of smaller images stitched together to form a composite whole. In a virtual globe such as Google Earth™, each of the smaller images is obtained from several satellite image providers who themselves may have altered the image previously to satisfy security concerns from various local and national governments whose buildings and other strategically important landmarks might be "compromised" through such visibility. The composite image functions in much the same way that pixels align to form a larger digital whole built on the sum of the parts. Read as composite texts, virtual globes function as hypertextual representations of the world that render explicit issues and questions about time, place, power, voice, and subjectivity that are otherwise absent from traditional myopic depictions of the world.

While such constructed visual representations may now be embedded within the traditions of visual image production and consumption, what may be less obvious for many users is the disparity among the smaller individual visual texts themselves and the *metadata* they contain and represent. That is, the various smaller images that construct larger representations of the world in virtual globes may each differ in terms of acquisition date, service provider, and resolution. Users enjoy cloud-free views of the Earth captured from various points in time that produce an "ideal" image of the world. Virtual globes constructed with such carefully selected cloud-free images lack these obstacles that could be considered the "Achilles heel" of remote sensing. Users can zoom in on these idealized images of the world to see their own car parked in their own home driveway, navigate to the top of Mount Everest, fly through the Grand Canyon or hover above the Great Wall of China.

This act of merging imagery from various chronological and perspectival points in the past while enabling users to imagine future journeys in the present exemplifies the "proleptic" moment (Slattery, 2006)—a clarification about one's view(s) of the world in which past, present, and future combine into a single moment or event. While users may interact with global imagery in captivating ways through virtual globe technology, they may raise numerous critical questions about visuality, reality, and representation. In what ways are virtual globes manifested? How do these manifestations serve to homogenize the user's mental image of the world? Whose "world view" do they represent? What types of mass production are at work? How current are current representations of the world? What consequences for mental images arise due to controlled sources of imagery? One example of such consequences might be found in Google Earth's™ use of pre-Katrina images of New Orleans two years after the devastating storm and subsequent flood. The company returned to more current imagery only after public outcry and Congressional scrutiny. This example calls into question the reliability of virtual globes as providers of current depictions of the world. Less critical viewers may remain oblivious to such manipulations.

Virtual globes empower educators and private citizens with a mechanism to freely access and share topographical and geographical information and imagery of any part of the world with websites such as Juicy Geography (Jenkins, 2008), Google Earth Lessons ("Google Earth Lessons: An Educational Resource for Teachers," 2006), and Ogle Earth (Geens, 2008). Virtual globes also facilitate information sharing that builds upon hypertextual approaches to interpretation and meaning-making most commonly used in wikis, blogs, and hypertext authoring software. Through such collaborative, public-generated knowledge, also known as "crowd sourcing," a variety of implications for educational practice become evident. In fact, crowd sourcing might be evidence that our world is entrenched in an age of globalization.

Globalization is difficult to define in a singular, concise manner and its definition depends on what is being emphasized (Bloland, 2005). According to Bloland (p. 127), for some, "globalization involves the flow of money, goods, people, information, knowledge, technology, and culture, as well as disease and terror, across a networked world" (Castells, 1996, cited in Bloland; Lechner & Boli, 2000, cited in Bloland). Bloland adds, "Globalization is expanding, but it is so complex in its implications, ambiguous in its in meaning, and fraught with political conflict that it is difficult to understand and to know where it is

going" (p. 127). Globalization as a concept and site of inquiry resembles Pinar's (2004) notion of curriculum as "complicated conversation." Similarly, because of their integration of technology, imaging, and collaborative data production, virtual globes also function as complicated conversations when considered as interdisciplinary educational experiences worthy of meaningful interpretation and scrutiny. In the remainder of this chapter we argue that virtual globes demand critical analysis from various perspectives informed by and through critical practices in visual culture and art education. Such analysis helps to explicate these implications and thereby embodies a critical pedagogy of virtual representations of the world in an age of globalization.

What are Virtual Globes?

Since 2005, free software applications such as Google Earth™ (Google Inc., 2006), Microsoft's Virtual Earth™ (Microsoft Corporation, 2007b), or NASA's World Wind (Maxwell, Kim, Gaskins, Lam, & Hogan, 2007) have sparked a kind of revolution and created a new category of technology called virtual globes. With this technology, users have developed sophisticated social networking interfaces, communicated data on global human and environmental crises, and developed new modes of entrepreneurship (Roush, 2005; C. Taylor, 2006; F. Taylor, 2007c). Such enterprises are made possible by access to satellite imagery and high-resolution aerial photography of every part

Table 1

Locations to explore in Google Earth

Example	Location	Latitude and Longitude	Eye Altitude	Google Earth details
1	Al Jadidah, Iraq	33° 36 49.84 N, 44° 22 32.98 E	21.90 km	Toggle on the "More" layer to delineate the edges of the individual images stitched together to form the seamless mosaic. The dates of images will appear above image borders.
2	Darfur, Sudan	12° 52 10.26 N, 23° 51 10.31 E	250 km	Toggle on the "Global Awareness" layer to view sponsored data from organizations such as the United States Holocaust Memorial Museum.
3	New Orleans' Superdome, Louisiana, USA	29° 57 02.87 N, 90° 04 51.86 W	1 km	Google displays current imagery through Google Earth. Later, the controversial imagery was published at http://earth.google.com/katrina.html, however, it is no longer available.
4	Chicago, Illinois, USA	41° 52 33.19 N, 87° 36 58.94 W	485 m	Differences in imagery quality can be seen by comparing it with a location such as Maamoura, Tunisia.
5	Maamoura, Tunisia	36° 27 34.25 N, 10° 48 26.70 E	485 m	Differences in imagery quality can be seen by comparing it with a location such as Chicago, Illinois.

of the world. Virtual globes serve preprocessed satellite images and aerial photographs directly into the user's computer. These high-resolution images are captured in sections and stitched together into a seamless mosaic to provide what *appears* to viewers as a single image of the globe (see Table 1, Example 1: "Al Jadidah, Iraq").[1]

What makes this technology exciting is the ability for users to see their backyards from various altitudes, dynamically and virtually in three-dimensions. Virtual globes facilitate dynamic interaction with imagery and allow users to position their views based on location (latitude and longitude) as well as altitude (from several hundred meters above the Earth's surface down to as close as a tree top). Users can also change the angle of incidence and animate their perspective to simulate a view as if from the window of a landing airplane. The integration of digital elevation models—mathematical representations of the Earth's surface—provides a virtual three-dimensional skeleton over which the imagery is draped and provides the illusion of elevation and topographic relief.

In the same way that a photograph can support a newspaper article, location-based information can be better communicated through virtual globes as they provide the visual representation of context. "Google Earth provides an experience where users understand remote, large-scale events as collections of individual, small scale incidents with which they can relate and empathize, as well as possibly be inspired to action" (Jones, 2007, p. 11). It is one thing to read about wide-scale genocide on the other side of the world, but quite another to see the locations of each atrocity and all of the locations *in situ* from local, national, and global scales (Table 1, Example 2: "Darfur, Sudan").

Virtuality of Virtual Globes

If, in fact, seeing is believing, then spying one's backyard, one's neighborhood, or one's world through the lens of a virtual globe can be a powerful learning experience. Virtual globes allow viewers to obtain a bird's eye view of a location of interest to see its relationship with surrounding areas and compare its characteristics with similar or dissimilar nearby or distant locations. Many newcomers to the technology assume mistakenly that the images they are seeing were taken that same day or even during that same hour.

Virtual globes convey the quality of *virtuality* as they are examples of "an image or space that is not real but appears to be" (Mirzoeff, 1999). Users of virtual globes essentially see cloud-free, sun-bathed images of the world. It is impossible to photograph every portion of the earth at the same time. Half of the earth is shrouded in the darkness of night and one of two seasons at any given time. Simultaneous variations in climate and clouds are associated with monsoon seasons, blizzards, and summer thunderstorms that constantly obscure some part of the world. In explicit contrast to these realities, virtual globe imagery offers users scenes of perpetual sunshine, one season year round in all locations, and almost weather-less landscapes. The ubiquitous clarity virtuality provides simultaneously obscures realities of nature.

Moving from national to regional or local views, users are subjected to further false depictions of where they live. At locations where two or more image tiles have been stitched together, users may find themselves straddling two different moments in time which could vary by time of day, month, year, or decade.[2] Google Earth™ may be considered the front runner in virtual globe technology with over 350 million users reported in early 2008 (F. Taylor, 2008), increasing from 200 million in 2007 ("More Google Earth users than people in Brazil," 2007). This situation helps underscore multiple aspects of the technology and ways that users access and engage the technology. On one hand, virtual globe providers present the world with free access to otherwise expensive satellite imagery and aerial photography. Virtual globe producers are facilitators who either license the satellite imagery and aerial photography from the satellite providers or generate it themselves. In the latter case, they process pieces of imagery into a single mosaic and make it available to the users. What used to be a cost-prohibitive endeavor for most computer users can now be accessed free of charge by anyone with a computer and a high-speed connection to the Internet. That said, virtual globe providers also control what images the public can access, and thereby control views presented of and to the world. The implications of such control constitute meaningful content for critical inquiry.

Unmasking Imagery in Virtual Globes

We have established that virtual globe users experience a caricature of Earth and decisions about which images are used for this purpose rest with the virtual globe provider, not the user. While providing free access to global imagery is arguably a great public service, a critical eye might ascertain the hidden costs. The ultimate result may have serious literal, symbolic, and pedagogical implications for worldviews, global education, and a geographically literate society.

Google Earth's™ imagery is licensed from companies such as DigitalGlobe™ as well as generated by photographic technology installed on Google's own airplanes (Aubin, 2006) that capture aerial photographs of many American and European cities. NASA augments its own imagery with that of Microsoft™-owned TerraServer-USA™ (NASA, 2005). Microsoft™ combines its TerraServer™ imagery with imagery from GlobeXplorer™ (Microsoft Corporation, 2007a). While anyone willing to pay the price can obtain imagery from these providers, virtual globes take on the role of gatekeeper as few private individuals would ever pay for this service. This role of gatekeeper has major implications illustrated by a recent event. After Hurricane Katrina, and the subsequent flood that devastated New Orleans in 2005, people around the world looked to Google Earth™ for pictures of the aftermath. Google Earth™ was quick to upload current imagery just days after the storm. A year later, the imagery depicted on Google Earth™ reverted to pre-Katrina images[3] (Table 1, Example 3: "New Orleans' Superdome, Louisiana"). These images from the past caused public outcry and Congressional inquiry (Associated Press, 2007; Geens, 2007; Noyes, 2007). Google™ later responded by uploading current image data to Google Earth™. Without first-hand knowledge of a location and its current weather and surface conditions, to what degree can users rely on imagery in a virtual globe as current and accurate? As in the New Orleans example, principles of crowd-sourcing, where members of the general public function to perform a task, might aid in policing virtual globe providers in much the same way as wiki contributors edit and monitor the latest entries. With so few image providers and even fewer virtual globe providers, the average user has a limited ability to independently verify what they see with a virtual globe.

Although virtual globe users enjoy access to vast amounts of information, they are equally limited by this same information. To what degree are views provided by virtual globes controlled by a handful of people, whether intentionally or unintentionally, and to what ends? To what degree do users access the same visual information from the same sources? How do these limited views from a small number of image providers in effect homogenize our collective view of our world? We suggest that the globalization of imagery provided by virtual globes creates a crisis of sorts in what Goodman (1978) calls "worldmaking." That is, the visuality of virtual globes—how we see and how what is seen informs how we look—has the potential to greatly expand or limit our views of the world.

Visuality of Virtual Globes

Mirzeoff (1999) points to the "visual event" as the defining embodiment of the concept of visual culture. Manifested through "the interaction between the viewer and viewed" visual events incorporate "the visual sign, the technology that enables and sustains that sign, and the viewer" (p. 13). Through virtual globes (technology), users (viewers) interact with satellite imagery (visual signs) and construct knowledge about the world that they assimilate and share in some meaningful way (culture). As educators consider visual events through these four lenses, they can explore with their students broader concepts such as power and voice. For example, how do virtual globes encourage or discourage voice? How do virtual globes give, take, or limit power? How do virtual globes function as worldmakers? Who controls how we see the world and to what ends?

Current virtual globes possess inherent characteristics that cooperate to deliver the appearance that Earth is always as it appears due to (a) imagery of varying age and resolution joined together to form a whole view, and (b) an underlying topographic form creating the physical relief of the landscape. As might be expected, virtual globe providers have worked to provide access to high resolution imagery of certain locations around the globe—national capitals, highly populated cities, national landmarks and natural wonders—but limited access remains for other locations—less populated areas, locations with limited international political power, and Vice-President Cheney's house. For example, in January of 2008, we compared Google Earth™ imagery for Chicago, USA (Table 1, Example 4: "Chicago, Illinois") with imagery of the much smaller town of Maamoura, Tunisia (Table 1, Example 5: "Maamoura, Tunisia"). When viewed from the same eye altitude, the difference in image resolution (visual clarity) is striking. We believe the act of comparing the visual representations of locations in virtual globes demonstrated by this simple exercise can lead to questions worth exploration in classrooms that go beyond purely visual information. Questions exploring the perceptions that lower quality imagery convey, such as lower value of the subject or unworthiness to be imaged in higher resolution (speaking to voice and power), can be a rich area of classroom discussion.

With increased use of Google Earth™ and other virtual globes by schoolteachers around the world, we wonder what messages their students interpret about these differences in high resolution and low-resolution images. When students encounter low resolution and/or outdated imagery of their hometown for example, might they conclude that their home is somehow less important or less desirable than areas depicted with higher resolution images? Conversely, how do people who live in higher-resolution areas view their place in the world? In what ways are users' opinions of the areas, and their people, represented by low-resolution imagery shaped by such visual events? As virtual globe use increases and if the belief persists that the visual events presented by virtual globes offer credible visual representations of the Earth, the result may be a singular, homogenized, globalized yet inaccurate worldview.

The development of a collective worldview reveals the potential for *transculturation*, a term used by Fernando Ortiz and others as a process of acquiring a previous culture while uprooting and loosing it (Mirzoeff, 1999). Such potential for transculturation is amplified when one considers the authority and visual impact of virtual globes. This impact is so large that few members of the general public may ever question the accuracy of what is depicted in virtual globes. While the data (imagery) in virtual globes may offer a limited, single view of the world, the technology itself provides opportunities for worldmaking (Goodman, 1978) whereby meaning is made, not acquired. Such active knowledge construction about the world serves to counterbalance potential singular lens, homogenized views of the world that virtual globe data make possible. Worldmaking can take a variety of forms in virtual globes, but mainly manifests in the addition of new data such as three-dimensional models of buildings or landforms (De Paor, 2007; F. Taylor, 2007d), time series data representing natural or human-made changes in the landscape (F. Taylor, 2007b), or even visualizations of future events (F. Taylor, 2007a). These new data become an empowering layer of information generated not by virtual globe *providers*, but rather by virtual globes *users*.

Empowerment

For educators, virtual globes provide a new way to engage students in the study of science (Lisle, 2006; Tooth, 2006), literature (Google Earth Lessons, 2007), history (De Lorenzo, 2006; "Google Earth Community: Viewing forum: History illustrated," 2007; Google Earth Lessons, 2007), geography, and visual culture. Whether presenting a learning experience on the geographic distribution of the world's population ("Adriaan," 2005), natural resources (Harrison, 2007; World Wildlife Federation, 2007), or political and military conflicts (Kansas Event Data System Project, 2007), virtual globes offer a geographic context for inquiry by enabling students to tie events to their physical locations on Earth. Students can move between global and local scales and contexts as they visually explore the relationships among location and the chronology of events, objects, or concepts.

Literature teachers have used virtual globes to map locations of fictional and real events in classic stories as well as the lives of their authors ("LuciaM", 2006; Badger, 2007; Burg, 2007). With the recent development of time series in Google Earth™ version 4 (Google Inc., 2006), users can now watch animations of data changing over time. Examples of such data may be found in tracking historic hurricanes ("Mikey", 2005), flooding events ("Google Earth Hacks: Hurricane Katrina and Flooding 2005," 2007), or even prediction of effects of sea level rise on coastal cities (F. Taylor, 2007a). Indeed, many activist organizations are developing "placemark" data files for Google Earth™, technically referred to as KML files.[4] Users can access some of this information when they launch a virtual globe. Google Earth™ provides access to "sponsored data" that users can toggle on and off at will. This interaction with online data and resources exemplifies a form of Web 2.0 technology in which users become actively engaged in the construction and production of content. Such collaborative interaction with virtual globes changes the role of the user from mere consumer and reader to an active contributor and producer of visual representations of the Earth. Further, we believe that with the advent of more interactive and collaborative virtual globes and roles for users comes the necessity to develop a pedagogy of virtual globe representations that takes into account and encourages critical readings of how they are produced, consumed, and function as conveyors of meaning and representations of the world.

Toward a Critical Pedagogy of Virtual Globe Representations

As we work toward a critical pedagogy of virtual globe representations, we might consider numerous questions about visual events as cultural and curricular discourse. We believe a narrowly constructed critical pedagogy for virtual globes would be limiting, confining, and contradictory. Based on our discussion in this chapter, below we offer a few points of departure for educators interested in engaging critically with virtual globes.

Encourage Learners to View Virtual Globes with a Critical Eye

Careful viewers of virtual globes can identify a variety of discrepancies between what virtual globes depict and how they appear to the human eye. Such discrepancies suggest that learners may be well advised to develop a critical eye toward imagery they encounter in virtual globes. Learners might ask questions about the sources from which the visual data are taken; the age of the data; the relationships between the economic, political, social, or historical importance of low resolution areas in comparison to high resolution areas of Earth.

Position Virtual Globes as Tools for Worldmaking

Learners should develop understandings about the ways in which virtual globes function as constructs. Simply, because virtual globes are created as composite images of Earth as opposed to a single image, learners might develop understandings about how, why, and for who such constructed worlds function. Whom do these virtual globes serve? As learners become more aware of this aspect of virtual globes they can begin to imagine and construct their own representations of their world while remaining conscious of the various ways their world view can be interpreted and have influence over other viewers.

Consider Virtual Globes as Curriculum

Educators should recognize that virtual globes function as curriculum in that they contain information that can be discussed, studied, and examined. Virtual globes also provide a context in which learners can interact over a span of time, seek further information about what they see, and build a knowledge base about various geographical locations depicted in these representations as well as historical, political, economic and other related events and issues. The investigative journey learners take as they explore the visual and related content of virtual globes is a form of *currere*—the Latin root of the infinitive of curriculum—as an active form of running the course (Pinar, 2004) of content, inquiry, and learning.

Consider Virtual Globes as Metacurriculum

Learners should come to the awareness that what is depicted in virtual globes is an invitation to discover implicit and symbolic meanings. That is, they should take the visual images they see in virtual globes as opportunities to uncover underlying meanings and hidden curricula within the larger curriculum of the virtual globe. For example, what do lower resolution images mean? What relationships exist between populated areas and the accompanying metadata? When users view areas of a virtual globe depicted in lower resolution, are they to believe that these lower resolution areas are less important than higher resolution areas? If the locations or specific details of a structure or location are important to matters of national security for a country, that area might be depicted in low resolution in a virtual globe for protection. Users might consider the economic and political significance of such degraded imagery with respect to the global economy. As users make these comparisons they might consider how their visions of these locations are perpetuated or disrupted by such virtual global depictions.

Conclusion

Our intention has not been to condemn Google Earth or any virtual globe and we hope our discussion will not be misinterpreted as such. Rather, our intention has been to encourage the examination of this and any digitally-mediated visual technology with a critical eye to illuminate unintended consequences that may result from its use in society, especially in educational contexts.

Virtual globe technology can lurk in the background of our lives while allowing others to have more active interactions with who we are, where we live, and what we hold important. As Rick Anthes observes, users will access "on demand, climate, or any other information for any place on the planet, on the land, in the oceans, or in the atmosphere, at any time, past, present and future" (Butler, 2007). Where else this technology might take us remains to be seen, as do the ways in which educators will engage with it. Because of their reliance on visual qualities, virtual globes will remain part of the scholarly and pedagogical domain of educators who embrace visual forms of knowing and learning, practices central to the field of visual art education.

Dikovitskaya (2005) reminds us, "...visual studies is not limited to the study of images or representations but extends to the everyday practices of seeing and showing, especially those that we take to be immediate or unmediated" (pp. 119-120). As virtual globes become more immediate and embedded within our everyday lives we will have at our disposal meaningful and effective ways to make sense of and use these virtual representations of an ever expanding, shifting, and globalizing world.

REFERENCES

"Adriaan." (2005). Google Earth Hacks: World Population. Retrieved December 29, 2007, from http://www.gearthhacks.com/dlfile499/World-Population.htm

Associated Press. (2007). Google replaces New Orleans map with pre-Katrina images. *FoxNews.com* Retrieved March 16, 2008, from http://www.foxnews.com/story/0,2933,262621,00.html

Aubin, M. (2006). Google Earth: From space to your face ... and beyond. Retrieved August 16, 2007, from http://www.google.com/librariancenter/articles/0604_01.html

Badger, B. (2007). Google LatLong: Google Book Search in Google Earth. Retrieved December 29, 2007, from http://google-latlong.blogspot.com/2007/08/google-book-search-in-google-earth.html

Bloland, H. G. (2005). Whatever happened to postmodernism in higher education?: No requiem in the New Millennium. *The Journal of Higher Education, 76*(2), 121-151.

Burg, J. (2007). Google lit trips. Retrieved December 29, 2007, from http://www.googlelittrips.org/

Butler, D. (2006). Virtual globes: The web-wide world. *Nature, 439*, 776-778.

Butler, D. (2007). Earth monitoring: The planetary panopticon. *Nature, 450*, 778-781.

De Lorenzo, R. (2006). Teacher toolkit: Using Google Earth to teach Canadian history. Retrieved December 29, 2007, from http://canuckhistory.wordpress.com/2007/12/18/teacher-toolkit-using-google-earth-to-teach-canadian-history/

De Paor, D. (2007). Google Earth science. Retrieved December 29, 2007, from http://web.mac.com/depaors/Site/KMZs.html

Dikovitskaya, M. (2005). *Visual culture: The study of the visual after the cultural turn.* Cambridge, MA: The MIT Press.

Freedman, K. (2003). *Teaching visual culture: Curriculum, aesthetics, and the social life of art.* New York: Teachers College Press.

Garfinkel, S. (2007). Google Earth: How Google maps the world. *Technology Review, 110*(6), 20-21.

Geens, S. (2007). Ogle Earth: Google's New Orleans update gets US govt scrutiny. Retrieved December 29, 2007, from http://www.ogleearth.com/2007/04/googles_new_orl.html

Geens, S. (2008). Ogle Earth: A blog about Google Earth. Retrieved December 28, 2007, from http://www.ogleearth.com

Goodman, N. (1978). *Ways of worldmaking.* Indianapolis, IN: Hackett Publishing Company.

Google Earth Community: Viewing forum: History illustrated. (2007). Retrieved December 29, 2007, from http://bbs.keyhole.com/ubb/postlist.php/Cat/0/Board/EarthHistory

Google Earth Hacks: Hurricane Katrina and Flooding 2005. (2007). Retrieved December 29, 2007, from http://www.gearthhacks.com/dlcat72/Hurricane-Katrina-and-Flooding.htm

Google Earth Lessons. (2007). GELessons submitted lessons. Retrieved December 29, 2007, from http://www.gelessons.com/cgi-bin/lessoncatssearch.cgi?ccategory=Language+Arts

Google Earth Lessons: An Educational Resource for Teachers. (2006). Retrieved December 28, 2007, from http://www.gelessons.com/lessons

Google Inc. (2006). Google Earth (Version 4). Mountain View, CA: Google, Inc. http://earth.google.com.

Harrison, M. (2007). Boom town/Gold rush lesson plan. Retrieved December 29, 2007, from http://www.gelessons.com/lessons/newlessonfiles/boomtown.html

Jenkins, N. (2008). Juicy Geography's Google Earth blog. Retrieved December 28, 2007, from http://www.juicygeography.co.uk/blog/?page_id=7

Jones, M. T. (2007). Google's geospatial organizing principle. *IEEE Computer Graphics and Applications, 27*(4), 8-13.

Kansas Event Data System Project. (2007). Data: Political Instability Task Force worldwide atrocities dataset. Retrieved December 29, 2007, from http://web.ku.edu/keds/data.dir/atrocities.html

Lisle, R. J. (2006). Google Earth: A new geological resource. *Geology Today, 22*(1), 29-32.

"LuciaM." (2006). Jane Austen's Life & Works. *Google Earth Community* Retrieved December 29, 2007, from http://bbs.keyhole.com/ubb/showflat.php?Cat=0&Number=411188

Maxwell, C., Kim, R., Gaskins, T., Lam, B., & Hogan, P. (2007). World Wind (Version 1.4). Moffett Field, CA: National Aeronautics and Space Administration. http://worldwind.arc.nasa.gov.

Microsoft Corporation. (2007a). Microsoft enhances Virtual Earth platform imagery with GlobeXplorer Aerial Imagery. Retrieved December 29, 2007, from http://www.microsoft.com/presspass/press/2007/jan07/01-09GlobeXplorerPR.mspx?source=rss&WT.dl=0

Microsoft Corporation. (2007b). Virtual Earth (Version 6.0). Redmond, Washington: Microsoft Corporation. http://www.microsoft.com/virtualearth.

"Mikey." (2005). Google Earth Hacks: Lots of Hurricane Information. Retrieved December 29, 2007, from http://www.gearthhacks.com/dlfile10073/Lots-of-Hurricane-Information.htm

Mirzoeff, N. (1999). *An introduction to visual culture.* New York: Routledge.

More Google Earth users than people in Brazil [Electronic. (2007). Version]. *InfoNIAC.com, 05 June 2007.* Retrieved December 29, 2007, from http://www.infoniac.com/hi-tech/more-google-earth-users-than-people-in-brazil.html

NASA. (2005). World Wind. Retrieved December 29, 2007, from http://worldwind.arc.nasa.gov/download.html

Noyes, K. (2007). Google Earth gets real again with post-Katrina imagery [Electronic Version]. *Technology News World, April 2, 2007.* Retrieved December 29, 2007, from http://www.technewsworld.com/story/56652.html

Pinar, W. (2004). *What is curriculum theory?* Mahway, NJ: Lawrence Erlbaum Associates.

Roush, W. (2005). Killer maps. *Technology Review, 108*(10), 54-60.

Slattery, P. (2006). *Curriculum development in the postmodern era.* New York: Routledge.

Taylor, C. (2006). Google moves into virtual worlds [Electronic Version]. *CNN Money.com, December 14, 2006.* Retrieved December 29, 2007, from http://money.cnn.com/2006/05/11/technology/business2_futureboy_0511/

Taylor, F. (2007a). Google Earth Blog: Animation roundup: Rising sea levels, filling Grand Canyon, global clouds. Retrieved December 29, 2007, from http://www.gearthblog.com/blog/archives/2007/04/animation_roundup_ri.html

Taylor, F. (2007b). Google Earth Blog: Arctic ice melting animation in Google Earth. Retrieved December 29, 2007, from http://www.gearthblog.com/blog/archives/2007/11/arctic_ice_melting_animation_in_goo.html

Taylor, F. (2007c). Google Earth Blog: Crisis in Darfur. Retrieved December 29, 2007, from http://www.gearthblog.com/blog/archives/2007/04/crisis_in_darfur_the.html

Taylor, F. (2007d). Google Earth blog: DOE energy efficient buildings in 3D Google Earth. Retrieved December 29, 2007, from http://www.gearthblog.com/blog/archives/2007/11/doe_energy_efficient_buildings_in_3d_google_earth.html

Taylor, F. (2007e). Google shows pre-Katrina photos for New Orleans. *Google Earth Blog* Retrieved February 12, 2008, from http://www.gearthblog.com/blog/archives/2007/03/google_shows_prekatr.html

Taylor, F. (2007f). New Orleans pre or post-Katrina. Retrieved February 13, 2008, from http://www.gearthblog.com/blog/archives/2007/04/new_orleans_pre_or_p.html

Taylor, F. (2008). New stats for Google Earth - Over 350 million downloads. Retrieved February 16, 2008, from http://www.gearthblog.com/blog/archives/2008/02/new_stats_for_google_earth_over_350.html

Tooth, S. (2006). Virtual globes: A catalyst for the re-enchantment of geomorphology? *Earth Surface Processes and Landforms, 31*(9), 1192-1194.

World Wildlife Federation. (2007). WWF on Google Earth. Retrieved December 29, 2007, from http://www.panda.org/about_wwf/where_we_work/project/google_earth/index.cfm

ENDNOTES

1 In a series of e-mails dated March 10, 2008, Google, Inc. denied our requests to use screenshots or images obtained from their product stating, "Google Earth is used as an exploration tool for geographic information and the license does not permit larger-scale reproduction/re-distribution of the imagery. Please note that Google licenses these images from imagery providers and does not own the imagery in Google Earth." While Google Earth (GE) suggested that we "may want to contact the imagery owner(s) named in the bottom center of the Google Earth interface directly," obtaining the referencing information the image provider needs proved difficult for us to determine since multiple bounding boxes overlap any one location. We were not able to differentiate between bounding boxes for image sections to reference when contacting the imagery provider. However, with the information provided in Table 1, the reader will be able to interact with the examples on his or her own, and thereby create a more robust and first-hand experience. To download GE, go to http://earth.google.com.

2 For a more detailed depiction of the full process used by Google™ to produce virtual globes see Garfinkel (2007) and Butler (2006).

3 For more information and discussions about pre- and post-Katrina imagery, please see blogs such as Google Earth Blog (F. Taylor, 2007e, 2007f)

4 KML stands for Keyhole Markup Language and is similar to hypertext language associated with web page development. In 2004, Google, Inc. purchased Keyhole becoming the application known today as Google Earth.

Transnational Visual Culture: Indecipherable Narratives and Pedagogy

Charles R. Garoian and Yvonne M. Gaudelius

...politics is about concentrating power...and art is about dispersing it.

—PAUL CHAN (IN TOMKINS, 2008, P. 41)

...we have come to a moment in history when playing in closed systems of our own devising reinforces dangerous habits of mind.

—SHERRY TURKLE (2004, P. 112)

Prologue

...a shoe, it was just a simple, ordinary running shoe, the kind that one wears when running or walking long distances, or when engaged in particular athletic events...

...upon inspecting the shoe, its feel, its look, whether or not its construction was flawed, its materials substantial, to check out its design, to inspect it in full, ensure a sound purchase, the customer held the shoe in the one hand, then in the other, tossing it to-and-fro, feeling its weight, turning it over, and around, to examine the tread patterns on its sole, the lines of design on the shoe's side panels, on its toe and heel, its bright colors, and its stitching...

...the tip off, it was the shoe's label that was the tip off, its provenance raising questions, suspicion about its origin, where it came from, facts about its record of export and import, its pattern of migration, the several countries of its manufacture, the trajectory of its travels...

...evidently, the shoe had journeyed around the world prior to its arrival for purchase...

...a nomad without a human body, it had traversed the globe long before being worn by any customer...

...an immigrant upon its arrival at the shoe store, it had accumulated an impressive, comprehensive global itinerary...

...it was obviously *not* "made in the U.S.A."...

...the chemical processing and production of the shoe's white synthetic thread took place somewhere in Malaysia...

...its shoe string was made somewhere in mainland China...

...the synthetic fabric of its body was processed, spun, and dyed somewhere in Thailand, then shipped to somewhere in India where it was woven...

...synthetic rubber from somewhere in the Philippines and, a strange gel produced somewhere in Germany, were sent to a place in Taiwan where the former, the synthetic rubber was used in fabricating the sole of the shoe and the latter, the gel, imbedded within its sole as extra cushioning...

...the glue for attaching the sole was imported from Brazil and the leather patchwork and logo on its side panels were made in Mexico to provide stability and ensure its corporate identity...

...finally, before shipping to the U.S.A. for sale, all the fragments of the shoe, its component parts, were sent to a destination in France where its tongue was manufactured and sewn onto the upper part of its toe...

...there, in its final stages, it was assembled and affixed with the corporate logo from Mexico and the label that initially raised suspicions, which read "Assembled in France"...

This description of a globe trotting shoe, a traversing of conjoined printed words that you the reader are

reading   from   one   side   to   the   other...

and

down

this

page...

...these journeying words, like the ruins of memory traveling through history, ambiguous and incomplete fragments assembled in the form of a collage narrative,[1] a textual hybrid like that of the transnationality of the shoe, constituted by oblique and obtuse juxtapositions, a curious arrangement suggesting random component parts, a faltering construction, the shoe, appearing as if it were an amalgamation of territories, a composite map...the text fragments on this page, the patchwork of the shoe, their transnational voyage constituted by collage mappings, like Baudrillard's simulacrum, this text is the shoe is the map is the collage traversing the terrain of transnationalism.

Introduction

One of the challenges inherent in writing about art, visual culture, and transnationalism lies in the set of new terms that are introduced into the critical lexicon, including 'hybridity,' 'multiculturalism,' 'diaspora,' 'translation,' 'transnationalism,' 'nationalism,' 'internationalism,' 'globalization,' 'glocalization,' 'cosmopolitanism,' 'exile,' and 'postcolonialism.' All of these terms point to a shift in art language, a shift that encompasses the social and the political in far more explicit ways since they point to the conditions under which contemporary art and visual culture is produced. Our aim in this chapter is not to provide definitions of these terms but to engage in an exploration of the slippages between them, the production of visual culture, and pedagogy.

At first glance, transnationalism appears to be the antithesis of what we art educators might consider important about teaching art in the schools. Given that *globalization* is most often understood as the transnational distribution of cultural capital,[2] and *art* as individual self-expression, these two concepts seem to have nothing to do with one another. Upon closer examination, however, there exist common attributes between the two that are worthy of consideration. In this chapter, we will explore the globalization trope from the perspective of collage narrative, with the former, *globalization*, regarded by scholars as the paradigmatic shift of late 20th- and early 21st-century international politics (Jameson & Miyoshi, 1998), while the latter, *collage narrative*, believed to be the most significant contribution of the 20th century to the history of art (Ulmer, 1983, p. 84). While both globalization and collage have complexity and contradiction in common, these very attributes have contributed to scholars' contestations about their respective theoretical definitions (Ratnam, 2004; Kuspit, 1983). Nevertheless, as cultural theorist Sherry Turkle (2004) claims, in the reality of today's messy and grey shaded world "we need to be comfortable with ambivalence and contradiction" (p. 112), which we will argue constitutes the ethos of collage narrative. We will argue that regimes of power that

are not comfortable with Turkle's characterization of today's world are bound to impose strategies of binary conflict.

Collage/Transnational Narrative

Disjunctive fragments of visual, textual, and material culture constitute the indeterminate and indecipherable narrative of collage/transnationalism, and the dialectical associations and understandings that occur in its empty, in-between spaces represent possibilities for cognitive and hermeneutical navigations that enable critical interventions and challenge totalized cultural assumptions. We will show how the complex social, political, and economic networks of transnationalism share these attributes of collage while differing in how globalization deploys critical interventions as corporate forms of management and control guised as democratic practice.

The narrative economy of globalization "flows freely" across borders, writes *The New York Times* columnist David Brooks (2008), which also applies to the border crossings of collage/transnational narrative. Just as the historical narrative of international politics was "secured within borders," so too was the narrative of visual arts confined within the historical assumptions of art and culture, the framing edge of rectilinear pictorial space, and the white, antiseptic spaces of art galleries and museums. While some form of international exchange of visual and material culture has been going on since the early stages of capitalism in the 15th century, it was the advent of industrialization in the 19th century, mechanization in the early 20th century, and the digital age in the late 20th century that rapidly destabilized the historical assumptions and regimes of art, politics, and culture. This resulted in slippages of knowledge whereby new associations and conceptualizations of modern art and market economics could occur.[3] Art historian Robert Hughes (1991) refers in biblical terms to this historical environment from which the uncanny narrative of collage evolved, as "the mechanical paradise... [where] the speed, at which culture reinvented itself through technology in the last quarter of the nineteenth century and the first decades of the twentieth, seems almost preternatural" (p. 15). As the 20th century progressed, technological advances increased exponentially—from the mechanical to the electronic, from analog to digital systems, and from national to global networks of communication. The harnessing and exploitation of these technological advances by the oppressive regimes of corporate capitalism led to the failing of the modernist myth of progress by the end of the century.

The genre of collage evolved soon after the invention of photography when its mechanical representations fragmented and decontextualized optical and perceptual understandings of time and space; and it evolved as previous conceptions of human labor were brought into question and managed as components parts of industry to achieve greater efficiencies in production. Within this complex and contradictory historical context, collage evolved as the representative form of contemporary art and culture when the old world order of monarchies dissolved and fragmented into the independent nation states that engaged in the technologically advanced combat of World War I. The Dadaist artist Hans Richter (1965) refers to the international scale and intensity of Dadaist art as the "storm that broke over the world of art as the war did over the nations" (p. 9). In the spirit of Dadaism, one of its leading artists, Hans Arp declared:

> Revolted by the butchery of the 1914 World War, we in Zurich devoted ourselves to the arts. While the guns rumbled in the distance, we sang, painted, made collages and wrote poems with all our might. We were seeking an art based on fundamentals, to cure the madness of the age, and a new order of things that would restore the balance between heaven and hell. We had a dim premonition that power-mad gangsters would one day use art itself as a way of deadening men's minds. (In Richter, 1965, p. 25)

Ironically, Arp's premonition came to pass in the form of the propaganda art of the totalitarian regimes of the Third Reich and the Soviet Union; a premonition that still deserves attention, given the machinations of corporate conflict and control that are producing global economies of genocide and war under the guise of global democracy. Indeed, the evocative, compelling characteristics of collage and transnationalism are similarly constituted insofar as the slippages, border crossings, and migrations of their socially constructed assumptions occur within the interstitial spaces of their constituent fragments. While the flexibilities of meaning and understanding that occur interstitially in collage/transnationalism invite open, democratic discourse, within the business and politics of global capitalism they invite the cunning and opportunism of institutional and corporate control.

Social Morphology

In a 1999 article, Steven Vertovec outlines six premises that ground the concept of transnationalism: as social morphology, as a type of consciousness, as a mode of cultural reproduction, as an avenue of capital, as a site of political engagement, and as a reconstruction of 'place' or locality" (p. 447). The first of these, "social morphology," represents the formation of social networks across national borders. In many cases, these networks are virtual and exist among people who have never met each other and who are unlikely to ever to do so. These social networks are often seen as positive manifestations of culture. The Barack Obama campaign provides one telling example of the efficacy and reach of such virtual transnational networks. As *New York Times* columnist Roger Cohen (2008) writes in a recent article, "Obama has been a classic Internet-start-up, a movement spreading with viral intensity ... As with any online phenomenon, he has jumped national borders, stirring as much buzz in Berlin as he does back home."

However, as Vertovec points out, transnational organizations are not an inherently positive phenomenon. For example, the United States Department of Defense identifies, "terrorists, insurgents, opposing factions in civil wars conducting operations outside their country of origin, and members of criminal groups" as transnational organizations of people who are engaged in "cross-border activities involving such things as trafficking in drugs, pornography, people, weapons, and nuclear material, as well as in the laundering of the proceeds" (Vertovec, pp. 448-450).

Diaspora Consciousness

The second premise is described as "'diaspora consciousness' marked by dual or multiple identifications," which indicates a collective, yet often fragmented, memory; hence, "diaspora consciousness produce a multiplicity of histories, 'communities' and selves – a refusal of fixity often serving as a valuable resource for resisting repressive local or global situations" (Vertovec, pp. 450-451). Transnationalism also has emerged as a form of cultural production and "is often associated with a fluidity of constructed styles, social institutions and everyday practices. These are often described in terms of syncretism, creolization, bricolage, cultural translation and hybridity" (Vertovec, p. 451). Such a conception of transnationalism locates it as an in-between space in stark contrast to a universalizing conception in which everything is located within one system of meaning making. In this sense, globalization has simply replaced the universalizing ideals and aesthetics of the Enlightenment with a new, catchier term that has the same impulses toward homogeneity and sameness and leaves little room for difference.

Whereas the mode of address of collage/transnationalism enables performances of subjectivity, creative and political agency, and critical citizenship, the subjectivity of globalization aspires to Empire;[4] a world order that exploits human and natural resources, instigates fierce competition among and control of market economies, perpetuates the commodity fetishism of corporate capitalism, and instigates global warfare. Contrary to the cultural heterogeneity of collage/transnationalism, art theorist Georg Schöllhammer (1999) describes "economic globalization as a homogenizing, universalizing model which absorbs cultural differences and therefore rejects them" (p. 1). In support of cultural difference, the liminality and contingency of the narrative of collage/transnationalism allows for the co-existence of disparate ideas, images, and understandings. Contrary to the universalizing, relativistic materialism of corporate capitalism, art curator and critic Nicolas Bourriaud (2002) theorizes a "relational aesthetics and random materialism" similar to the liminal and contingent narrative of collage/transnationalism. Bourriaud espouses relationality that is interdependent and interconnects people through differing social forms. He writes:

> Being "materialistic" does not mean sticking to the triteness of facts, nor does it imply that sort of narrow-mindedness that consists in reading works in purely economic terms....this particular [random] materialism takes as its point of departure the world contingency, which has no pre-existing origin or sense, nor Reason, which might allot it a purpose. So the essence of mankind is purely trans-individual, made up of bonds that link individuals together in social forms which are invariably historical (Marx: the human essence is the set of social relations). (Bourriaud, p. 18)

Hence, when comparing the relativism and materialism of collage/transnationalism's narrative with that of globalization, there exists an interdependence among cultural fragments in the former, while the latter erases regional identities and markets through the establishment of homogeneous transnational corporate frameworks. Political philosopher Paolo Virno (2008) argues that the corporate ethos of globalization long ago "ceased to be the science of good government and has become, instead, the art of conquering and maintaining power" (p. 57).

Art's Dispersal of Power
Video artist Paul Chan's differentiation between politics and art cited in the epigraph of this chapter corresponds with the single most distinguishing characteristic between collage/transnationalism and globalization: power politics. Chan suggests that the politics of globalization concentrates power, while the politics of art disperses it (Tomkins, 2008, p. 41).

An example of art's dispersal of power is evident in the visual and conceptual play of images, ideas, and the meanings in the collage/transnational narratives of Chan's art installations, of which *The 7 Lights* (2005-2008) is one.

In the seven parts of this compelling installation,[5] Chan literally sheds light by projecting his digital videos and animations onto the gallery walls and floors of The New Museum in New York City and, in doing so, metaphorically sheds light on "contemporary tragedies such as 9/11, the war in Iraq, and the ongoing eruptions of terrorist violence around the globe" (New Museum, n.d.). Unlike art that is stationed within rectilinear frames and galleries, the dark spaces into which Chan projects his videos render gallery walls invisible,[6] and his video images, which suggest light falling through windows into a dark room (a parody of the historical framing of art), engage viewers to freely move in, around, and through his installations and to physically and personally experience them.

The collage/transnational narrative in Chan's video projections contain silhouettes of large familiar objects like a tree or a utility pole to provide a stationary counterpoint to smaller silhouetted objects that float upward as the silhouettes of human bodies "plummet" to the ground (New Museum, n.d.). The politics of war, terrorism, and violence are evident through the floating yet clashing signifiers in this dynamic collage narrative. While the beginning of *The 7 Lights* projections suggest peaceful and serene conditions, they crescendo into horrific, nightmarish imagery, then decrescendo back to the peaceful and serene. Considering the disjunctive character of the projections' imagery, they "convey a narrative

Figure 1
Paul Chan, *1st Light*, 2005, digital video projection, 14:00. Photo: Jean Vong, Image courtesy Greene Naftali, New York.

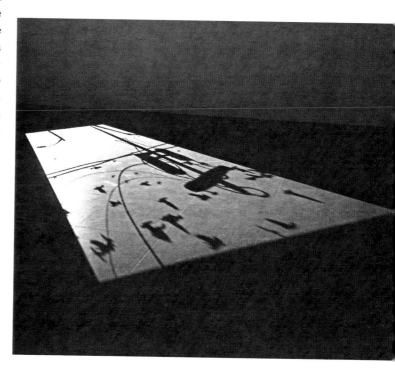

that is inevitably incomplete yet rich with historical [and contemporary] references" (New Museum, n.d.). Thus, the ambiguity and incompleteness of Chan's installations resist concentrations of power politics by enabling the creative and political agency of individuation.[7] Chan's notion that art disperses power is made evident as viewers are empowered through their performances of subjectivity.

Avenue of Capital

Vertovec's fourth location of transnationalism is an avenue of capital, which is comprised of transnational corporations [TNCs]. He argues that this is "due not least to the sheer scale of operations, since much of the world's economic system is dominated by the TNCs" and the "systems of supply, production, marketing, investment, information transfer and management often create the paths along which much of the world's transnational activities flow" (1999, p. 452). As we might expect, media and visual culture travel along these same lines of capital. However, this does not mean that there is a unified structure that manages this delivery of media for, as media theorist Kai Hafez (2007) argues; transnational media systems do not yet exist. For example, he points out that CNN, which is often referred to as a global media company that offers transnational programming, is a problematic case since the programming on CNN, "is no uniform programme, but consists of numerous [collage-like] continental 'windows' ... and is now merely a decentralized variant of an American television programme, whose country of origin remains easily recognizable in its agenda and framing" (p. 13). Hence, while TNCs do control much of the world's capital, they also offer locally specific frameworks for the creation of visual culture through media.[8]

Such in-between movements, slippages of global capital, are examples of what literary critic Frederic Jameson (1998) refers to as "an *untotalizable totality* [italics added] [a paradoxical condition] which intensifies binary relations between its parts—mostly nations, but also regions and groups, which, however, continue to articulate themselves on the model of 'national identities' (rather than in terms of social classes, for example)" (p. xii). Considering the utopian implications of intensified binary relations, Jameson insists on dialectical, collage-like interventions such as "antagonism and tension" in order to create an "intellectual space of 'globalization'" where critical discourses can occur (p. xii). Political philosophers Michael Hardt and Antonio Negri (2004), and Paolo Virno (2008) refer to such a network of criticality as the "multitude," which they conceptualize

as the necessary alternative to globalization's spread of Empire. Virno further characterizes the multitude as resistant to unity, "a network of *individuals*... [where] the many are a *singularity*" (2008, p. 76). In characterizing the relationship of the multitude with globalization, Hardt and Negri write:

> On one face, Empire spreads globally its network of hierarchies and divisions that maintain order through new mechanisms of control and constant conflict. Globalization, however, is also the creation of new circuits of cooperation and collaboration that stretch across nations and continents and allow an unlimited number of encounters. This second face of globalization is not a matter of everyone in the world becoming the same; rather it provides the possibility that, while remaining different, we discover the commonality that enables us to communicate and act together. The multitude too might thus be conceived as a network: an open and expansive network in which all difference can be expressed freely and equally, a network that provides the means of encounter so that we can work and live in common. (p. xiii-xiv)

Hence, for Hardt and Negri, and for Virno, the multitude represents a collage of individuation where subjectivities resist synthetic closure and totalization; a transnational multiplicity of individuals' differences based on their culture, labor, ways of living, views of the world, and desires. It is by way of the critical discourses across and among the differences and commonalities of the multitude that the coexistence and interdependence of a cultural democracy is possible.

Driving Forces in Globalization

Art historian and curator Niru Ratnam (2004) conceptualizes three teleological characteristics of globalization: technology, homogenization, and migration. He argues that while the predominantly American corporations' new communications and information technologies "maximize profits," their impact has a homogenizing effect on regional cultures and identities, which, in turn, arouses anti-American sentiments, resistance, and finally terrorist acts that then compel "the flows of migration that mark the contemporary global economy" (p. 288). The potential for volatility in Ratnam's conception of globalization is evident in the way that resentments about the homogenization of the Middle East through U.S. institutional, corporate, and military interventions gave rise to the ideological collage of terrorism in groups like Al Qaeda[9] whose suicide bombings and other horrific brutalities incited the U.S. military forces' retaliation in Afghanistan after 9/11 and preemption in Iraq, which resulted in the loss of thousands of civilian and military lives, and the mass exodus and displacement of Afghanis and Iraqis from their homelands into Europe and other countries in the Middle East, Asia, and the Americas.

Like Ratnam, Brooks (2008) also points to technology and homogenization as driving forces in globalization. He argues that technology has "leveled the playing field," suggesting an expansive relativism of transnational economies that is facilitated by widespread high-speed communications and fierce competition. This conception of expansive relativism suggests a cyborgian body politic that is wired and interconnected via "mobile phones, satellite television, and the Internet... bring[ing] the epochal happenings around the globe into the domestic orbit of those to whom they would once have appeared remote, exotic or irrelevant" (Ratnam, 2004, p. 286). Vertovec supports this point arguing that our "high degree of human mobility, telecommunications, films, video and satellite TV, and the Internet have contributed to the creation of translocal understandings" (1999, pp. 455-456). While cultural forms of meaning-making may be grounded in local traditions and culture, the technologies of transnationalism have enabled these forms of meaning to traverse the globe at ever increasing speeds.

Political Engagement

New technologies also have created a space for new sites of political engagement, the fifth characteristic of transnationalism that Vertovec identifies. This space is often occupied by non-governmental organizations [NGOs] that represent interests and issues that exceed any one country's or corporation's geo-political boundaries.[10] Joseph Nye, Dean of the Kennedy School of Government at Harvard and a former US Assistant Secretary of Defense, points out that during the 1990s there was a tremendous increase in the number of formally recognized NGOs,[11] "jumping from 6,000 to approximately 26,000," an increase that was largely the result of new technologies of communication (Nye, n.d.). Nye argues that NGOs do not, in and of themselves, make world politics more democratic since "most are elite organizations with narrow membership bases" and that "some act irresponsibly and with little accountability;" but he does argue that NGOs "pluralize world politics by calling attention to issues that governments prefer to ignore, and by acting as pressure groups across borders" (Nye, n.d.).

The question is whether this electronic facilitation constitutes the colonizing impulse of expropriation or the "new circuits of collaboration and cooperation" of the multitude described by Hardt and Negri. Contrary to the expansive relativism of globalization, the argumentative associations among

images, texts, and materials in collage narrative initiate liminal and contingent conditions that signal "an expanded sense of the possibilities and effectiveness of art—an expanded sense of the meaning of creativity and of art's world role," according to art historian, critic Donald Kuspit (1983, pp. 125-126). Kuspit suggests that the relativism of collage is enabled through collaboration and cooperation in-between and among its cultural fragments, and resists the limiting assumptions and understandings of binary thought.

Collage/Transnational Cognition

The evocative force driving transnational competition, according to Brooks, "is not globalization...[instead] we're moving into a more demanding *cognitive age* [italics added]. In order to thrive, people are compelled to become better at absorbing, processing, and combining information" (2008). To ensure that learning and the processing of knowledge include reflexivity and criticality, collage/transnational cognition sets in motion a dynamic process of critique, similar to Virno's process of individuation, where its "many [fragments] become one, with the one never fully resolved because of the many that continue to impinge upon it...[suggesting that] concrescence is, in effect, never finished, however much there may be the illusion of completeness" (Kuspit, 1983, p. 127). Similarly, Ratnam (2004) argues, "an adequate account of art and globalization needs to acknowledge the interweaving of art with wider social, economic and political issues, while not reducing any one of these terms to the others" (p. 286). Hence, the cognitive and narrative slippages of collage/transnationalism enable complex and contradictory understandings and performances of subjectivity to coexist, which are imperative in the education of a diverse global community of critical citizens (Suárez-Orozco, 2004, 174).

Comparable to the cognitive slippages of the narrative of collage/transnationalism, systems of information technology have enabled the free exchange of cultural capital across geographic, cultural, and conceptual borders. Yet, for Brooks (2008),

> the most important part of information's journey is the last few inches—the *space between a person's eyes or ears and the various regions of the brain* [italics added]. Does the individual have the capacity to understand the information? Does he or she have the training to exploit it? Are there cultural assumptions that distort the way it is perceived?"

Ironically, while Brooks is addressing the critical and creative understandings that are necessary in coping with globalization, his conception of embodied spaces—between a person's "eyes," between a person's "ears," and the various regions of a person's "brain"—corresponds with collage/transnational cognition, namely its in-between spaces where critical interventions, multiple interpretations, and understandings are possible. It is within its interstitial spaces where performances of subjectivity, personal memories and cultural histories challenge academic, institutional, and corporate assumptions.

To resist the relational hegemony of globalization, film theorist Noël Coward (2007) suggests that we instead consider "transnational relations...where it is understood that there are many different, often very unalike, kinds of transnational relations, and that these do not add up to a cohesive global network playing the same tune in different registers" (pp. 135-136). This notion corresponds with Bourriaud's theory of relational aesthetics and the relativistic associations among the coexisting cultural fragments within the narrative of collage/transnationalism where, as Kuspit suggests, concrescence remains incomplete. Rather than homogenizing cultural diversity, the relational aesthetics and random materialism of collage/transnationalism encourages evocative associations among differing cultural perspectives.

The Globalization of the Art World

Citing the cultural homogenization of the art world as an example of globalization, Coward describes an "emerging transnational institution of art" where much of the new work being exhibited "is involved in what is called institutional critique—critiques of the institution of the museum, of the system of biennales,[12] of the commodification of art, and of the art world in general" (2007, p. 140). Art critic and theorist Jon Bywater (2008) describes the system of biennales as a new form of the grand tour: "the 2008 Biennale of Sydney [Australia], which open[ed] in June...was connected to the recently developed Yokohama Triennale (founded 2001) and the Shanghai (1996), Singapore (2006) and Gwangjou (1995) biennials through a Grand Tour-style promotional collaboration, Art Compass 2008." Such packaging of biennials enables art professionals and curators to maximize the results of their efforts the way corporations maximize their profits—one trip can encompass several different biennials, extending the global reach of the curator.

Carolyn Christov-Bakargiev, who was the artistic director for the Sydney 2008 biennial, terms this "'biennial syndrome,' acknowledging that while the proliferation of this kind of show may plausibly 'have decentralized art and created multiple art systems,' it has also invented 'new possibilities of disempowerment'" (in Bywater, 2008, n.p.). While critical reflexivity is imperative for the attainment of creative and political agency in a cultural democracy, Coward finds the predominance of film, electronic media, video, and photography in the exhibitions of this emerging art system as embodying and being complicit with the message and power politics of globalization—a significant factor that Jameson refers to as "the sense of an immense enlargement of communication" (Jameson, 1998, p. xi; Coward, 2007, p. 140). While communications mediums have indeed enabled the homogenizing affects of globalization, they have, nonetheless, played a significant role in an anti-globalization movement of artists and, in doing so, "the proponents and opponents of globalization are using the same tools to create different versions of global consciousness" (Ratnam, 2004, p. 306). The strategies of anti-globalization implemented in the communication mediums mentioned above correspond with those of the artistic avant-garde in the 20th century, namely the Dadaists, the Situationists, and Conceptual Artists. These artists' explorations, experimentations, and improvisations with collage, montage, assemblage, happenings, installation art, and performance art resulted in the critical narratives that disrupted the socially and historically constructed assumptions and boundaries of art in their time.

Coward further characterizes the transnational institution of art as a new media aesthetic comprised of recurring themes, which are commonly understood and appreciated by an elite cosmopolitan corps of well-traveled international artists, critics, presenters, and other art world aficionados who organize, frequent, and patronize its exhibitions around the world. Many scholars agree with Coward about the correspondences of this artistic cartel with the goals of corporate capitalism, where diversity is understood in terms of supply and demand in the market system. For example, art historian Pamela L. Lee (2003) argues that "something of a colonial logic underwrites the expansion of the art world's traditional borders, as if the art world itself were gleefully following globalization's imperial mandate," which constitutes a patriarchal aesthetic reminiscent of previous "period styles" (p. 164). Ratnam (2004) agrees with Lee's assessment of the art world's "colonial logic." He argues that the inclusion of artists from "diverse geographical locations" in these transnational biennales "seems like a analogue for the process of globalization itself (p. 285).

This radical chic, in-the-know public shares rarefied knowledge and the "sense-making strategies" of interpretation "for advancing those themes, including radical juxtaposition, de-familiarization, and the de-contextualization of objects and images from their customary milieus" (Coward, 2007, p. 140). Ironically, these are the same cognitive strategies of collage/ transnational's narrative that we have been espousing in this chapter, which goes to show how easily strategies for critical discourse can be co-opted and reified yet appear to represent democratic values in a globalized network; an important point for us art educators to remember when considering pedagogies of resistance. Skeptical about the insularity of the art world and its ability to address the complexities of the global problematic, Lee asks: "But just how precisely has the art world addressed the conditions of 'multiplicity, diversity, and contradiction'...[which are coextensive with the processes of globalization]?" (2003, p. 164). Lee finds that much of the hoopla about transnational exhibitions is merely the emperor's new clothing in that their constituents and aesthetic are predominantly western European or players who have been recruited from nations around the world into their fold.

Collage/Transnational Pedagogical Strategies

We end this chapter by identifying some pedagogical strategies for art educators to consider in challenging and resisting art practices that end in academic and institutionalized outcomes. These strategies are predicated on understanding the narrative of collage/transnationalism as both a critical pedagogical process as well as the material outcome of students' research and creative work. Each strategy stands on its own yet is interdependent with the others. In other words, students' individual collages can be used as introductory projects to discuss how the relational aesthetic between and among their collage fragments can suggest ways in which a relational aesthetic might emerge between and among students with differing cultural perspectives[13] when working together collaboratively and as a community similar to Hardt and Negri's concept of the multitude.

Hence, the scope and complexity of a collage curriculum may begin with students' individual collages;

then lead to projects involving two students working collaboratively; then to projects involving the entire class; then between classes in the school; and then involving classes collaborating between differing schools. Pedagogically, the disparate discussions, decisions, and interpretations that will occur between and among students will be constituted by the liminal and contingent interactivity of collage/transnational narrative. Using a thematic approach, students' critical discussions and brainstorming in this collaborative, local, community-based art making process can lead to transnational literacies through explorations, experimentations and improvisations into ways of exposing, examining, and critiquing the hegemonic practices of globalization and their egregious effects on the depletion of natural resources, ecological devastation, rising levels of poverty, world hunger, the increasing scarcity of food in many countries of the world, and global military conflict. While assigning such controversial topics as academic exercises can limit students' understandings of the Empire building ethos of globalization to stereotypical representations, students' in-depth explorations in-between and among the fragments of a transnational collage of power politics can enable students' individual and collective creative and political agency within the multitude as they challenge its ideology of Empire and "create an alternative global society" (Hardt & Negri, 2004, p. xvii). Postcolonial theorist Diana Brydon (2004) argues that such

> transnational literac[ies] expand critical literacy into a more empathetic mode of reading that Spivak calls 'critical intimacy,' which must then be directed to the task of understanding new modes of globalizing power and the ways in which they have easily co-opted certain forms of now-established postcolonialism, including celebrations of hybridity and resistance, to their agenda. (Brydon, p. 62)

This then has the potential to open spaces of resistance and reclamation for teachers and students. Such spaces are critical for engagement if we are to move beyond our local understandings and reclaim agency within a transnational world.

REFERENCES

Bernanke, B. (2004). Financial access for immigrants: The case of remittances. [Electronic version]. Retrieved May 28, 2008, from <http://www.federalreserve.gov/boarddocs/speeches/2004/200404162/default.htm>http://www.federalreserve.gov/boarddocs/speeches/2004/200404162/default.htm

Bourriaud, N. (2002). *Relational aesthetics*. S. Pleasance & F. Woods (Trans.). France: Les Presse Du Réel.

Brooks, D. (2008, May 2). The cognitive age. *The New York Times*. [Electronic version]. Retrieved May 10, 2008, from http://www.nytimes.com/2008/05/02/opinion/02brooks.html?_r

Brydon, D. (2004). Cross-talk, postcolonial pedagogy, and transnational literature. In C.C. Sugars (Ed.), *Home-work: Postcolonialism, pedagogy, and Canadian literature* (pp. 57-74). Ottawa: University of Ottawa.

Bywater, J. (2008). 16th Biennale of Sydney. *Frieze (112)*. [Electronic version]. Retrieved May 10, 2008, from http://www.frieze.com/issue/article/16th_biennale_of_sydney

Coatsworth, J. H. (2004). Globalization, growth, and welfare in history. In M. M. Suárez-Orozco & D. B. Qin-Hilliard (Eds.), *Globalization: Culture and education in the new millennium* (pp. 38-55). Berkeley: University of California.

Cohen, R. (2008, May 26). The Obama connection, *The New York Times* [Electronic version]. Retrieved May 26, 2008, from http://www.nytimes.com/2008/05/26/opinion/26cohen.html?em&ex=1212033600&en=64f3a76fa9f17880&ei=5087%0A)

Coward, N. (2007, Winter). Art and globalization: Then and now. *Journal of Aesthetics and Art Criticism* 65(1), 131-143.

Garoian, C. & Gaudelius, Y. (2008). *Spectacle pedagogy: Art, politics, and visual culture*. Albany: State University of New York.

Hafez, K. (2007). *The myth of media globalization*. Cambridge: Polity Press.

Hardt, M., & Negri, A. (2004). *Multitude: War and democracy in the age of empire*. New York: Penguin.

Hughes, R. (1991). *The shock of the new*. New York: Alfred A. Knopf.

Jameson, F. (1998). Preface. In F.Jameson & M. Miyashi (Eds.), *The cultures of globalization* (pp. xi-xvii). Durham: Duke University.

Kuspit, D. (1983). Collage: The organizing principle of art in the age of the relativity of art. In B. J. Craige (Ed.), *Relativism in the arts* (pp. 123-147). Athens: The University of Georgia.

Lee, P. M. (2003, November). Boundary issues: The art world under the sign of globalism. *Artforum 42* (3), 164.

Lotringer, S. (2008). Forward: We the multitude. In P. Virno (Author) *A grammar of the multitude: For an analysis of contemporary forms of life*. I. Bertoletti, J. Cascaito & A. Casson (Trans.). Los Angeles: Semiotext(e).

New Museum (n.d.). *Paul Chan: The 7 ~~Lights~~*. Retrieved on May 31, 2008 from http://www.newmuseum.org/paulchan/index.html

Nye, J. S. (n.d.). *The rising power of NGO's* [Electronic version]. Retrieved May 28, 2008, from http://www.stwr.net/content/view/126/37/

Ratnam, N. (2004). Art and globalization. In G. Perry & P. Wood (Eds.), *Themes in contemporary art* (pp. 277-313). New Haven: Yale University.

Richter, H. (1965). *Dada: Art and anti-art*. New York: McGraw-Hill.

Schöllhammer, G. (1999). *Art in the era of globalization*. [Electronic version]. Retrieved May 10, 2008, from http://republicart.net/disc/mundial/schoellhammer01_en.htm

Suárez-Orozco, C. (2004). Formulating identity in a globalized world. In M. M. Suárez-Orozco & D. B. Qin-Hilliard (Eds.), *Globalization: Culture and education in the new millennium* (pp. 173-202). Berkeley: University of California.

Suárez-Orozco, M. M. & Qin-Hilliard, D. B. (2004). Globalization: Culture and education in the new millennium. In M. M. Suárez-Orozco & D. B. Qin-Hilliard (Eds.), *Globalization: Culture and education in the new millennium* (pp. 1-37). Berkeley: University of California.

Tomkins, C. (2008, May 26). Shadow player: The provocations of Paul Chan. *The New Yorker LXXXIV*(15), 40-45.

Turkle, S. (2004). The fellowship of the microchip: Global technologies as evocative objects. In M. M. Suárez-Orozco & D. B. Qin-Hilliard (Eds.), *Globalization: Culture and education in the new millennium* (pp. 97-113). Berkeley: University of California.

Ulmer, G. L. (1983). The object of post-criticism. In H. Foster (Ed.), *The anti-aesthetic: Essays on postmodern culture* (pp. 83-110). Seattle: Bay Press.

Vertovec, S. (1999). Conceiving and researching transnationalism. *Ethnic and racial studies, 22*(2), 447-462.

Virno, P. (2008). *A grammar of the multitude: For an analysis of contemporary forms of life*. I. Bertoletti, J. Cascaito & A. Casson (Trans.). Los Angeles: Semiotext(e).

Wright, L. (2008, June 2). The rebellion within: An Al Qaeda mastermind questions terrorism. *The New Yorker, LXXXIV*(16), 37-53.

ENDNOTES

1. We use the concept of "collage narrative" in this chapter to refer to the disjunctive strategies of the avant-garde in the 20th century in challenging social and historical assumptions of art making. While many art educators have relegated the avant-garde's movements to the junk heap of Modernism, our intent is to re-visit and re-present their strategies as possibilities for exposing, examining, and critiquing the patriarchal and homogenizing ethos of globalization.

2. Ratnam, 2004, p. 281.

3. For a broader historical characterization of globalization, read "Globalization, Growth, and Welfare in History," by historian John H. Coatsworth (2004).

4. The creative and political agency of globalization is predicated on a criticality that "never stops provoking resistance to its own rule" in order to attain power and control of capital (Lotringer, 2008, p. 18).

5. For digital video and still images of Chan's *The 7 ~~Lights~~* installation at the New Museum, see http://www.newmuseum.org/paulchan/4thlight.html

6. Chan's strikethrough of the word "~~Lights~~" in the title represents the absence of light in all seven installations.

7. Virno differentiates between "people" and "individual" arguing that the use of the former term assumes the masses, the synthesizing of individual's subjectivities into a totalized body politic. Instead, Virno calls for a politics of the personal, "as the ultimate result of a *process of individuation*...a progressive differentiation, [through which] the 'many' do not postulate an ulterior synthesis" (p. 76).

8. It is also important to note that many of the smaller transnational communities control a great deal of the world's capital. While not so easily located in the balance sheets of a few large TNCs, "the relatively small amounts of money which migrants transfer as remittances to their places of origin" (Vertovec, 1999, p. 452) make up a substantial part of the transnational economy. It is estimated that in 2003 these remittances amounted to "approximately $90 billion world-wide" (Bernanke, 2004).

9. According to Pulitzer Prize winning author Lawrence Wright (2008), Al Qaeda's transnational network was "constructed from rotten intellectual bits and pieces—false readings of religion and history—cleverly and deviously fitted together to give the appearance of reason" (p. 53). Considering its lack of geographical territory and its reliance upon new global communications and transportation systems, Al Qaeda itself is a "paradigm of globalization," claim education theorists Marcelo M. Suarez-Orozco and Desirée Baolian Qin-Hilliard (2004, p. 13).

10. Transnational corporations often are constrained by the politics of the countries in which they operate. For example, as Hafez describes, "Rupert Murdoch's impact in China, his political agreements with the communist leadership, which induced him, for example, to remove the critical BBC news from the Cantonese Star TV, show that Western capital is willing to come to commercially driven political arrangements to stabilize the authoritarian state" (Hafez, 2007, p. 165).

11. It is important to note that there are, in addition, many local and national NGOs that are not formally constituted and therefore are not counted in these figures.

12. To name just a few, there is the Whitney Biennial in New York City, the Venice Biennale in Italy, the Biennale de Paris in France, the Istanbul Biennale in Turkey, the Singapore Biennale, the Cairo Biennale in Egypt, the Sao Paulo Biennale in Brazil, the Moscow Contemporary Art Biennale in Russia, the Caucuses Biennale in Tibilisi, Georgia, the Melbourne International Biennale in Australia, the Pittsburgh Biennial in Pennsylvania.

13. For a detailed discussion of these ideas, see *Spectacle pedagogy: Art, politics, and visual culture* (Garoian & Gaudelius, 2008).

Art and Art Education in an Age of Globalization

Anna M. Kindler

In July 2006, I attended a UNESCO World Art conference in Lisbon[1] that had a more powerful impact on my recent scholarship than I ever expected. It happened when the organizers changed the theme for the block of presentations to which I was invited to contribute. I was now asked to address a theme: *Art as a language of communication and critical awareness*. My initial frustration with having to adjust my paper to conform to this new focus quickly turned into a sense of gratitude for forcing me to think more deeply about assumptions about art and art education that we often take for granted, and their fit with 21st-century art and art education in our increasingly global world.

I emerged from the conference perturbed by the discontinuity between the dominant rhetoric of that event and what I have understood to be the world of contemporary art. The talk about art as a means of effective interpersonal and intercultural communication, a vehicle promoting creativity, or a preferred medium of social awakening to urgent global concerns sounded very appealing. Yet it also seemed to have very little to do with the reality of the art world that I and my contemporaries currently experience. In this chapter, I problematize some of these assumptions and suggest alternative ways of construing a relationship between art and "art education" to enable our field to be more responsive to the realities of the global world.

Art as Language?

I would argue that art[2] today has become more obscure than ever before to the wider audience and that, because of its obscurity, it has rendered the long-used metaphor of "art as a language" both misleading and useless. To be sure, the obscurity of the message that much of the art of today purports to convey, and the obtuse means of conveying it, have marked the work of many modernist artists, but I would argue that our contemporaries have further pushed the boundaries of this incomprehensibility.

Consider, for example, Michel Blazy's *Fountaine de bonne volonté* (*Fountain of good will*). It features a red bucket turned upside down with a straw inserted through its bottom, sporadically spurting droplets of foam. I would challenge the readers to arrive, without help of an informed critic, at the (intended) understanding of this work's meaning. According to art critic François Piron (1999), the artist communicates in this case his "poverty and ingenuity, the self-sufficiency of a household activity and the poetic expression of savoir-faire in support of an absurd cause" (p. 99)—in my view, an unlikely interpretation for most spectators.

Similarly, I am sure many of those exposed to Damien Hirst's *A Thousand Years,* consisting of a rotting cow's head, sugar solution, fly eggs, and a fly zapper, have interpreted it as nothing more than a rotting cow's head, despite the artist's claim of "recasting the fundamental questions concerning the meaning of life, the existence of god and death as the final limit, in paradoxically the most factual and unorthodox way."[3] These examples, and many others including exploding works of Cai Guo-Qiang,[4] installations by On Kawara,[5] or presentations by the 2002 Turner Prize winners Keith Tyson[6] and Fiona Banner[7] at the Tate Gallery, clearly question the notion of art as an effective vehicle of interpersonal (never mind intercultural) communication—a hallmark of language in the "post-Babel" world.

An additional difficulty with the language metaphor is that any language has a structure with replicable elements and patterns of its use. These elements and patterns become acquired by members of a society through cultural and social mediation and are applied to make shared meaning possible. Wilson and Wilson (1985) noted that language can be seen as a "cultural path of symbols, that has been blazed long before any individual hiker walked along it, and one that will remain beyond the lifetime of those who will follow it, will continue to refine its main course, and sometimes will alter its direction a bit or chart new "shortcuts" (p. 92). While the Wilsons made a case for drawing to be considered as a language (or more precisely a family of languages), they did so by demonstrating how drawing meets the requirements of a symbol system. They set two criteria in this process: first, that as other symbol systems, it "provides the symbols that individually adopt, place in combination, and sometimes extend"; and second, that "the graphic configurations of a culture are as conventional, regular and predictable as the words of a given language" (p. 92). While the notion of a graphic language or languages can perhaps be defended at the level of it being a vehicle of pictorial representation, it would be problematic to make this argument for art in the light of the second criterion. Not only is the category of art itself ill-defined, to the point that "no two people will spontaneously define it in the same sense" (Read, 1969, p. 24), but also the very requirement of art, at least since art has abandoned its academic tradition, has been to generate novelty at all cost. This has placed the onus on artists to move beyond existing conventions, with results being often "unintelligible to the multitude" and requiring "philosophers and critics to interpret his message" (p. 24).

Although, as Goodman (1978) noted, works of art can function symbolically, "no inherent properties distinguish aesthetic from non-aesthetic symbols: the same symbol can function in and out of the arts" (Wilson & Wilson, 1985, p. 93). This suggests that although art can employ languages of graphic conventions (at least in the case of artistic drawings), it does not constitute a language in its own right—not even in the case of two-dimensional works created with the use of drawing tools—and certainly not when one considers the multitude of media and forms of expression that art has at its disposal. Unlike drawing conventions that can be culturally mediated in early childhood, allowing children to acquire and adapt for their use diverse graphic repertoires (Kindler, 1999; Kindler & Darras, 1994; 1997; Wolf, 1994; Wolf & Perry, 1998), art does not have its own language shared through relevant cultural practices. Furthermore, while art is a manifestation of a human desire to represent and thus may have a communication potential, it is important to note the distinction between art as a form of representation free from the mandate to communicate a shared meaning and the visual imagery specifically destined for communication purposes. The latter, in most cases, would not fit the category of art and yet is remarkably efficient as a "visual language"—once the convention through which it operates has been learned. Examples of such imagery include road signs, maps, visual icons, logos, and the like (Kindler & Darras, 1997; 1998). It is precisely the freedom from the structures, rules, and conventions of a language that has been one of the

distinguishing characteristics of art in the second half of the 20th and (so far) the 21st centuries.

As Tom Wolfe (1975) noted, art of the modern era has increasingly relinquished its traditional dependency on the visual interface in connecting with the audience and has instead engaged theory as its main vehicle to carry meaning. Unlike in the past, where "art theory had merely been something that enriched one's conversation in matters of Culture. Now it was an absolute necessity. It was no longer background music. It was an essential hormone in the mating ritual" (p. 39). In other words, for art to communicate it requires a translation into spoken or written text—and more often than not such text is accessible (and understandable) only to the "insiders" of the world of art. To quote Wolfe, "Frankly, these days, without a theory to go with it, I can't *see* a painting" (p. 6).

Consider Philippe Parreno's 1998 installation, *AD/DC snakes #3*. The artist, who was quoted as saying that "we can no longer look at an image as if it were superficial" (Parreno, 1999, p. 182), presents in this installation an arrangement of 16 electric plugs and adapters, all connected together with some extension cords stretching out on the ground. I have to admit to getting lost in my search for the work's meaning, despite the words of Eric Troney, which place this piece in its proper context by explaining that "In his personal works, he (Parreno) seeks the faults in imagery systems and infuses them with poetry and a critical conscious by creating new hierarchies: predominance of language, a reassessment of time and an affirmation of the narrative" (Troney, 1999, p. 184). In this case, I would require even more words to overcome the superficiality of my experience with *AD/DC snakes #3* and to override the visual message that reaches my brain to signal that I am contemplating a random arrangement of electrical equipment.

Art as Vehicle Promoting Creativity?

We are so used to this claim that it is almost impossible to problematize it. It is also difficult to challenge because the meaning of "creativity" has been so diffused. When approached from a systems perspective (Csikszentmihalyi, 1988, 1999) it is even harder to argue that what much of contemporary art offers has little to do with the advancement of human creativity, because "the field" of art has passed a positive judgment on it and integrated it within the domain. One can still ask, however, a question about the merits of contemporary artistic creativity and whether art today contributes to the development of creativity that is worthwhile. There is no doubt that late 20th- and early 21st-century art has provided us with an

abundance of unusual, weird, revolting, disgusting, repulsive, profane and shocking artifacts. How much depth, however, has it contributed to our understanding; how much has it moved us toward resolutions of problems; how much has it enlightened us to create a better world; how much it enriched our lives on societal or personal levels? I have to confess, that for all the "novelty," diving into the depths of much contemporary art (even with the help of theory), I have found myself touching the bottom of astounding triviality.

Let me offer an example of an artwork nominated for the 2005 Le Prix Marcel Duchamp: Gilles Barbier's *l'Orgue à Pets* (Fart Organ). It features a resin sculpture of a middle-aged man dressed in a black suit, slightly bent forward with a long, twisted crystal tube attached to his anus. Although art critics have praised this work for its insightfulness in "denouncing the ambivalence of the glory of artists and the grotesqueness of their stance," I agree with Bernard Darras who used one succinct word to capture the merit of this installation, calling it "minable" (Darras, personal communication, 2006).

Too often what has been described by critics as a creative idea has been in my view simply one step further up the predictable scale of shocking the public by an unconventional or out-of-place arrangement. While I have no difficulty accepting that at the onset of the Pop Art movement the notion of such displacement and interpretation of everyday objects within the

discourse of art was a creative idea, it hardly seems to be so decades later. This pursuit of the "never before" without serious consideration of the actual merits of such novelty seems to have trivialized the enterprise of art—and the "creativity" that it engenders.

As an art educator I am not sure how useful it would be for me to encourage students to come up with a yet more shocking use of human excrement (see Damien Hirst, *Politics and Power,* 1997) or the Hollywood sign (see Maurizio Cattelan, 2001), or to eloquently describe the significance of an empty room—give or take a piece of furniture (see Jorge Pardo, *Untitled,* 1999)—as a testimonial to their creativity. And I am certainly not keen on suggesting to my students that they should follow Thomas Hirschhorn's approach to artmaking, consistent with this obsessive pursuit of creativity through novelty and contradiction: "I spend all my energy fighting against the quality of the work. You shouldn't aim for improvement, but for deterioration. You shouldn't be better—but always less good." (1999, p. 142).

Interestingly, this association between creativity and something novel or unusual (especially at all cost) does not seem to be universal in the global context. This understanding of "creativity" has a very Western twist to it and explains why, for example, for a Western eye much of traditional Chinese art seems to be devoid of a creative spirit while it had been considered as very creative in its local cultural context. Chinese conceptions of creativity, as Cheng Ming Kai (2006) reminded the UNESCO conference audience, have much more to do with the sense of "effectiveness" of a creative idea than with the degree of its departure from what has been proposed before. In other words what is creative does not need to be "new"—and certainly not new at all costs. I have to admit that in the context of the direction taken by the world of art in the past two decades or so, I am particularly attracted to this notion of creativity. Yet in the era of globalization, artists around the world face pressure to conform to Western notions of creativity in order to successfully penetrate the world art markets.

Art as Social Action?

Finally, let me address the issue of art's social impact and the claim that art can be a prime medium for raising social awareness and shaking the fabric of the societal consciousness. Despite a long-standing tradition of art having an "eternally disturbing, permanently revolutionary" mandate (Read, 1969), particularly reinforced in the "after the end of Art" era (Danto, 1997), this has not been a consistent prerogative for art throughout most of art history and it still is not today, in the global context. It is true that raising critical awareness has been one of a long list of art's purposes and utilities—which included, among others, shamanic significance, mediation of religious beliefs, commemorative function, decorative utility— but, in actuality, one of the least fulfilled. It could be argued that an artist as "*ein Ruttler*, an upsetter of the established order" (Read, p. 4) may be particularly well placed to exercise an impact on critical awareness within a society and some artists of today clearly like to see themselves in this role. However, with a few notable exceptions of some moderate societal influence (e.g., Picasso's *Guernica* or murals by Diego Riviera), artists have been rather ineffective in their attempts to raise social consciousness among the masses. Although they have added, at times, to the power of a political or social message—the phenomenon particularly well illustrated in the Bolshevik era by production of Soviet artists who defined socialist realism—their contribution has been minimal relative to that of politicians, journalists, or social activists who chose to raise critical awareness through more direct means.

Twenty-first-century artists face another significant challenge in their ambition to contribute to the development of social consciousness due to the multiple alternative means of raising social awareness and the proliferation of technology-enabled global communication. They also have to face the reality of the "deja-vu" of much of today's "avant garde" message. Concerns about the societal effects of consumerism-obsessed societies; racial, gender, and sexual orientation-based inequities; poverty and social injustice; and environmental threats caused by human recklessness—as significant as they are—have been already extensively explored by artists over the past decades and the message conveyed again, at best, reminds us of importance of these issues, but it does not reveal them.

For example, the work of Ann Lumbye Sorensen, *Turning Points,* which presents a collection of used syringes displayed on a white podium, arguably intends to address the issue of drug abuse and perhaps attempts to alert us to the AIDS crisis. However, I would argue that an article in a local paper reporting yet another tragic death from a drug overdose, a photograph in the community pages section depicting a discarded syringe on a local school's playground, or a blog entry contributed by a person afflicted with addiction relaying a story of his/her tragic deterioration are much more effective in bringing the drug crisis to the forefront of consideration. These alternative forms of outreach are not only more effective in reaching a wide audience (as few will ever see Sorensen's work) but they also convey the message with precision and drama that Sorensen's work seems to lack. It would certainly be an over-claim to say that *Turning Points* contributed to a social awakening.

There seems to be a conflict between the ambition of art to be the innovator and the catalyst of change and the reality of the contemporary positioning of the world of art. Contrary to its traditional reactionary stance, art has found itself increasingly on the side of "political correctness." This sentiment was well captured in an article by Peter Whittle in the *Sunday Times Culture Supplement* (March 5th, 2006), who observed that "Any kind of real dissent is currently at a low ebb in the arts" (p. 25), because there is such an overwhelming consensus over the need to dissent.

I have also suggested that art faces strong competition in its ambition to exert a powerful social impact. Even within the realm of communication through the visual means, photo-journalism or television have been significantly more effective and prompt in raising critical awareness than art. This has been made possible through the power of immediacy and disturbing iconicity of images disseminated through these media, the scope of their distribution, and the timely fashion in which the images can be publicly shared.

For example, images of the destruction caused by the 2004 Christmas Day Tsunami released within minutes of the calamity have been extremely effective in raising critical awareness of the inequities between the developed and developing worlds and the disturbingly inefficient means of global sharing of information that could prevent such disasters.[8] Even more importantly, the impact was not limited in this case to raising critical awareness—it actually extended to a worldwide relief effort mobilizing millions of people around the planet to contribute their support to the victims. This example illustrates the power of images in stimulating critical awareness and prompting socially responsible action—and it also demonstrates that art has a serious competition in its role as an advocate for social justice.

Furthermore, the disturbing events which followed the publication of cartoons of the Prophet Mohammed in a Dutch newspaper, which were deemed offensive by some followers of Islam, remind us of the sensitivity and potential high societal costs of raising critical awareness through art.[9] The publisher of the cartoons had been quoted as saying that his purpose in commissioning the work was to raise critical awareness about the issues of self-censorship of the press. Needless to say, this exercise of raising awareness—by employing the "language of art"—triggered disastrous and unintended consequences.

This incident further problematizes the idea of art as an effective language of cross-cultural communication, as in this case, despite his intentions, the artist effectively conveyed very different messages to the various audiences, with serious negative societal consequences of this miscommunication. It also raises the issue of the scope of the moral responsibility of artists who choose to act as agents of social debate and change for the unintended consequences of their art. It further brings to light the responsibility that we have as art educators when we encourage artistic expression concerned with matters of critical awareness with respect to the cultural and religious sensitivities of the global world. The legacy of Picasso's dove has perhaps inadvertently contributed to the development of yet another art-related myth—namely, that art and peace always go hand in hand. We seem to have forgotten what the Danish cartoons have recently so powerfully demonstrated: artistic expression can also incite unrest.

Quo Vadis?

I have argued in this chapter that much of art, in its contemporary manifestations, has lost the capacity to deliver on art's long standing societal expectations. To be clear, my message is not that *all* art created in the 21st century lacks the ability to speak directly to the audience or does not have a potential to have a profound social impact. I have, however, argued that disturbingly too little of it does for us to continue to make these claims.

Consequently, I believe that it is timely to raise some fundamental questions regarding the relationship between art and an educational enterprise that we have for decades called "art education." What about art and in art—as art has defined itself at the onset of the 21st century—ought to be a concern of "art education?"[10] Are there still any skills, competencies, and abilities necessary (and worthwhile?) to be nurtured in order to achieve artistic success? Can they be identified? Can they be taught? Is it still relevant for us to aspire for some of our students to achieve artistic success? Or should we perhaps look at redefining our field in ways that would allow it to fit a long-standing rationale for its inclusion in public schools on the grounds of its intrinsic good and identify those aspects and attributes that have allowed us to make the claims of its unique, important merit—whether or not they reflect or are relevant to the world of art today? Or should we look for an even more profound change in direction?

To be clear, I firmly believe in the importance of nurturing the qualities of mind that we tend to associate with the category of art, but I am acknowledging the reality that much of art today lacks interest in these qualities. The qualities and attributes to which Elliot Eisner refers in *The Arts and the Creation of Mind* (2002), for example, seem to be missing from much of the celebrated artistic production at the turn of the 20th and the 21st centuries. We have found ourselves in a paradoxical situation where the sets of values that have characterized and justified the existence of art in education have almost disappeared from the domain of professional art, or at least had made it to the list of "endangered species."

Let me offer some examples. One of the strong anchors of the "intrinsic" rationale for art education has been a reference to the value and uniqueness of aesthetic experience. This rationale posits that there is something special and profoundly worthwhile in engaging with the world aesthetically—and that this engagement is qualitatively different for the intellectual, physical, or even spiritual interface. This notion of aesthetics is related to the concepts of beauty, harmony, and delight as powerful sources of pleasure and contentment—not very relevant anymore to much of mainstream art, as I have argued above.

Similarly, Eisner refers in his book to nuances and subtleties that art has traditionally embedded and operated through in its vocabulary of visual expression—yet, art often operates today in anything but subtle and nuanced fashion. Quite the opposite, much of art seems to be hitting the audience hard on the head. If art now requires dead flesh to reflect on mortality (see, for example, works of Damien Hirst[11]) or has to resort to using trash to depict chaos (as depicted in 1996 *Uno Momento* installation by Jason Rhoades[12]), then the subtle, the nuanced, the ambiguous that used to provide an engaging challenge is not anymore in the picture. In such cases, the visual interface makes attending to any nuances impossible because the visceral reaction that it triggers in the spectator prevents the possibility of a more refined engagement.

This shortcoming also marks many works of art that do not operate through the "how can I shock the audience" mechanism and are more subtle in their visual expression but which are so conceptually driven and entangled in theory that they do not lend themselves to the discernment of the intended nuanced meaning (often even despite the help of an art critics' verbal or written explanation). *The Nature Document* by Finish artist Pekka Nevalainen presented at the 23rd International Art Biennial in Sao Paulo exemplifies this concern. A TV screen positioned high on the wall projects a video showing images of hatching bugs in a bark of a tree, with a large white grid positioned vertically against a gallery wall and a small pile of dirt in front of this installation. According to the exhibition curator Minna Törmä, this piece "calls into question the prevailing image of what nature is in its pure state" (1996, p. 164). She notes, with reference to this artwork, that "Alienation is not necessarily a negative mark of degeneration or the product of urbanization. It may actually be essential to our survival: the structure of human consciousness has to cope with the need to comprehend longer temporal sequences, for example, in order to bring up family." I have to admit that I am intrigued by the narrative offered by Törmä but experience profound difficulty linking it to the presented artifact.

Even if the world of art today has distanced itself from these values, should our field also abandon interests in aesthetic concerns and catering to the dimension of humanity that many art educators have historically found so fundamentally enriching? I raise this question in the context of recent discussions about the possible shift in the direction of our focus towards visual culture. Much of what I have said earlier in this chapter suggests the merit of educating students about visual worlds more broadly conceived than only those situated within the world of art. Several art education scholars have argued in recent years the value of such focus (e.g., Boughton, Freedman, Hausman, Hicks, Madeja, Metcalfe, Rayala, Smith-Shank,

Stankiewicz, Stuhr, Tavin & Vallance, 2002; Duncum, 2001; Freedman, 2003; Freedman & Stuhr, 2004; Tavin, 2000, 2005). I have long believed that imagery that is relevant to the students and that impacts on our daily lives—whether it belongs to the category of art or not—should become a subject of study (e.g., Kindler, 2003). Especially in the context of the proliferation of visual imagery afforded by the technological advances that have allowed not only for sharing visual imagery worldwide but also greatly facilitated production of self-satisfying pictorial imagery, it is important to provide students with opportunities to engage with this rich visual world in the context of structured learning. It is also worthwhile to challenge them to move beyond the superficial, the misleading, and the trivial in this engagement.

Where my position differs from that of some of the advocates of the study of visual culture is that I am still keen on engaging with *the visual* for the value and unique experience that it affords. I see this engagement in the category of concerns that have long made art valuable in education—for the sake of enriching one's sensory experience and ability to understand, learn and express to oneself through the use of pictorial repertoires. While I acknowledge the potential in this process to tap into socially important matters, I also see value in students acquiring and refining the means of relating to the world through a visual interface, in visually commenting on issues and experiences that are not necessarily problematic, unresolved and troubling—but also those that are satisfying, delighting, and relaxing. I believe that the visual world continues to hold a potential to meaningfully impact human lives without the need of theory and that our role in education is to help students develop abilities to engage with this world without an addictive dependency on words to interpret it.

The world of visual culture in which I am interested in education is relevant to students on at least three grounds: first, because it belongs to a cultural, artistic heritage of the world and thus allows us to see ourselves in relation to our human ancestry; second, because it allows for a personal aesthetic and cognitive enrichment through the engagement of the visual brain; and third, because of the role that visual imagery plays in our lives—as it communicates and mediates ideas and values, invites reflection and commentary, prompts action and response, and even provides opportunities for gainful employment.

Art, as a segment of visual culture, has an opportunity to penetrate the curriculum at any one of these three levels, but it does not remain a sole focus. We are also invited in this context to select from the art instances that particularly lend themselves to consideration within this framework and leave aside those that do not support it. This approach incorporates study of visual imagery and learning of pictorial repertoires that have no ambition to ascend to the heavens of art but which have aesthetic and pragmatic value in everyday life and allow us to be more intelligent and comfortable participants in the visual world.

In conclusion, I believe that art education has not lost the capacity to contribute to the "creative growth" which was of so much concern to Viktor Lowenfeld (1943) and which has long been highlighted in our advocacy efforts. However, in the context of the dramatic changes in the world over the past half of a century it may be wise to reconsider this mandate in the broader context of our students' needs in visual/cultural/aesthetic education. I believe that this mandate can be reconfigured and reconciled within the realities of today without us losing sight of some of the values that have made many generations of our ancestors turn to what we used to call art: the sphere of thoughtful, intense, and satisfying visual engagement with the world.

REFERENCES

Aitken, D. (1999, December 15). *Beaux Arts Magazine,* 78.

Boughton, D., Freedman, K., Hausman, J., Hicks, L., Madeja, S., Metcalfe, S., Rayala, M., Smith-Shank, D., Stankiewicz, M., Stuhr, P., Tavin, K., & Vallance, E. (2002). *Art education and visual culture.* NAEA Advisory. Reston, VA: National Art Education Association.

Cheng, Ming Kai (2006, March 6-9). The importance of arts education. Panel presentation at the UNESCO World Conference on Arts Education. Lisbon, Portrugal.

Csikszentmihalyi, M. (1988). Society, culture and person: a systems view of creativity. In R. Sternberg (Ed.), *The nature of creativity* (pp. 325-339). Cambridge: Cambridge University Press.

Csikszentmihalyi, M. (1999). Implications of a systems perspective for the study of creativity. In R. Sternberg (Ed.), *Handbook of creativity* (pp. 313-335). Cambridge: Cambridge University Press.

Danto, A. C. (1997). *After the end of art. Contemporary art and the pale of history.* Princeton, NJ: Princeton University Press.

Duncum, P. (2001). Visual culture: Developments, definitions and directions for art education. *Studies in Art Education, 42*(4), 101-112.

Eisner, E. (2002). *The arts and the creation of mind.* New Haven: Yale University Press.

Freedman, K. (2003). *Teaching visual culture. Curriculum, aesthetics and the social life of art.* New York: Teachers College Press. Reston, VA: National Art Education Association.

Freeman, K., & Stuhr, P. (2004). Curriculum changes for the 21st century: Visual culture in art education. In E. Eisner & D. Day (Eds.), *Handbook of research and policy in art education* (pp. 815-828). Reston, VA: National Art Education Association.

Goodman, N. (1978). *Ways of worldmaking.* Indianapolis & Cambridge: Hackett.

Hirschhorn, T. (1999, December 15). *Beaux Arts Magazine,* Special Issue, 142.

Kindler, A. M. (1999). "From endpoints to repertoires:" A Challenge to art education. *Studies in Art Education, 40*(4), 330-349.

Kindler, A. M. (2003). Visual culture, visual brain and (art) education. *Studies in Art Education, 44*(3), 290-296.

Kindler, A. M., & Darras, B. (1994). Artistic development in context: Emergence and development of pictorial imagery in early childhood years. *Visual Arts Research. 20*(2), 1-13.

Kindler, A. M., & Darras, B. (1997). Map of artistic development. In A. M. Kindler (Ed.) *Child development in art* (pp. 17-44). Reston, VA: National Art Education Association.

Kindler, A. M., & Darras, B. (1998). Culture and development of pictorial repertoires. *Studies in Art Education, 39*(2), 147-167.

Lowenfeld, V. (1943). *Creative and mental growth.* New York: Macmillan.

Parreno, P. (1999, December 15). *Beaux Arts Magazine,* Special Issue, 182.

Piron, F. (1999, December 15). La Fontaine de bonne volonté. *Beaux Arts Magazine,* 99.

Read, H. (1969, December 6). The necessity of art. *Saturday Review,* 24-27.

Tavin, K. M. (2000). Teaching in and through visual culture. *Journal of Multicultural and Cross-cultural Research in Art Education, 18*(1), 37-40.

Tavin, K. M. (2005). Opening re-marks: Critical antecedents of visual culture in art education. *Studies in Art Education, 47*(1), 5-22.

Törmä, M. (1996). Finland. Pekka Nevalainen. *23. Bienal Internacional São Paulo.* (pp.162-165). São Paulo, Brasil: Fundação Bienal de São Paulo.

Troney, E. (1999, December 15). *Beaux Arts Magazine,* Special Issue, 184.

Whittle, P. (2006, March 5). *Sunday Times Culture Supplement.* 25.

Wilson, B., & Wilson, M. (1985). The artistc tower of babel: Inextricable links between cultural and graphic development. *Visual Arts Research, 11*(1), 90-104.

Wolf, D. (1994). Development as the growth of repertoires. In M. B. Franklin & B. Kaplan (Eds.), *Development and the arts* (pp. 59-78). Hillsdale, NJ: Laurence Erlbaum.

Wolf, D., & Perry, M. (1988). From endpoints to repertoires: Some new conclusions about drawing development. *Journal of Aesthetic Education, 22*(1), 17-34.

Wolfe, T. (1975). *The painted word.* New York: Farrar, Straus & Giroux.

ENDNOTES

1   http://www.mundiconvenius.pt/2006/unesco/en/program.htm

2   I refer here to art that is internationally acclaimed and held in esteem of the art establishment.

3   http://www.whitecube.com/html/artists/dah/dah_frset.html

4   http://www1.uol.com.br/bienal/23bienal/universa/iuascg.htm

5   http://www.davidzwirner.com/artists/13/work_1298.htm

6   http://www.tate.org.uk/britain/exhibitions/turnerprize/2002/tyson.htm

7   http://www.tate.org.uk/britain/exhibitions/turnerprize/2002/banner.htm

8   http://www.pbase.com/hockkai/tsunami
    http://www.photoduck.com/photos.aspx?gid=1815&pxo=0
    http://www.photoduck.com/photo.aspx?id=18161

9   I am referring to these cartoons as art, consistently with the ways in which cartoons as a pictorial genre are viewed by the contemporary art world.

10 I am leaving aside here consideration of the obvious merits of studying art from a historical perspective as a way to become acquainted with the cultural heritage of the world.

11 http://ca.youtube.com/watch?v=4voYZg1r8io&feature=related

12 http://www.hauserwirth.com/artists/37/jason-rhoades/images-clips/

GLOBAL AND LOCAL YOUTH CULTURES & SITES,

ONLINE AND ON-SITE EDUCATIONAL PRACTICES WITH YOUNG PEOPLE

Introduction: Section III

Elizabeth Manley Delacruz

The third section of this book draws closer attention to global and local youth cultures and sites, and to the online and on-site educational practices of young people in different parts of the world. In the opening chapter, "The Global and the Local: The Hybridity of Children's Culture," Christine Marmé Thompson observes how the impact of globalization on children is often characterized as largely negative, casting children as victims of manipulations they are powerless to resist. Challenging such a view, Thompson analyzes children's and adults' interactions in contemporary culture, noting the unprecedented mobility of children today; their access to information, global media, and material culture; and their interest in art created just for them. Considering how the canon of Western fine art and the critique of visual culture have all but eliminated considerations of young people as *active learners*, Thompson poses an alternative vision of children's culture—one in which children exert agency, choice, discrimination, and discretion in constant dialogue with the adult world.

The next few chapters provide fascinating examples of Thompson's observations about the creative ways young people assert their own interests and create new forms of art. In "Creating Parallel Global Cultures: The Art-Making of Fans in Fandom Communities" Marjorie Cohee Manifold shares her study of youth interests in anime, Cosplay, and cultural/media heroes. Manifold's findings are derived from her participatory observations, conversations, and interviews with hundreds of youth from 17 different countries, whose creative expressions are based on media-conveyed phenomena such as role-playing games, comics, manga, animations, and popular literatures. Manifold considers how the symbolic functions of these youthful expressions constitute a kind of neo-teatrum mundi—or "life as theater and theater as life"—as young people from diverse nations adopt masks of universal archetypes and replay the realities of their everyday lives.

Michelle S. Bae, in "Glocal New Femininity in Mediascape: Korean Teenage Girls' Popular Cultural Practices," provides yet another provocative example of how young people are creating their own forms of art, in her study of the online practices of teenage Korean immigrant girls' participation in *hanryu*, an emergent south Korean popular culture movement that provides Korean girls with an opportunity to create their own particular meanings about Korean ethnic femininity. Bae examines how these girls are both producers and consumers of global culture, observing how their digital imagery conveys a strong Korean-ethnic femininity in contrast to a Westernized standard of feminine beauty, and how they simultaneously both embrace and contradict traditional Korean values and expectations of women. Bae challenges conventional understandings of cultural globalization, which posit global media's cultural imposition over local, ethnic culture, and she illustrates how spheres of cultural influence move instead from the "periphery" to the "center."

In "Art Education and Cybermedia Spectacles in the Age of Globalization," Sheng Kuan Chung explains how new media and communication networks are now ubiquitous to contemporary youth culture, and offers cautionary insights for educators and policy makers who may be prone to over reactions to perceived dangers within these new networked worlds. Chung examines the aesthetics of the virtual world, online gaming, media violence, and pornography in particular, and describes their consumption by contemporary youth. Considering influences and protectionist measures by adults and schools and highlighting implications for a critical approach to media education and global visual culture art education, Chung, like Thompson, Manifold, and Bae, understands youth not simply as market-determined consumers of commercial culture, or as innocent prey in an online world of predators and corporations, but rather as tech-savvy, new-media-abled, and knowledgeable participants in and co-creators of new forms of art and cultural expression.

The following chapters, "Facilitating Intercultural Competencies in Cyberspace" by Nancy S. Parks and "Beyond Visual Literacy Competencies: Teaching and Learning Art with Technology in the Global Age" by Ching-Chiu Lin, each share additional and complementary findings about the nature of new media and online sites for interaction, young people's affinity for these new media and sites, and what such findings suggest for art education. Parks provides a description of two youth empowerment online virtual communities, *100 People* and *Second Life's Global Kids*. She explains their connections to the virtual global citizenship initiative, and finds resonance with Kerry Freedman's well-known and oft-cited principles for visual culture education and with Kristin Congdon's and Doug Blandy's concept of a *sixth world*. For Parks, new technologies are being used to create new educational practices that facilitate intercultural understandings and engage youth in imagining solutions to serious problems affecting their lives.

With notable exceptions, claims about the role of new digital global media in K-12 art education are largely speculative, prescriptive, and untested. In an in-depth school-based site-specific ethnographic study of teachers and students who use new digital media as a regular component of the secondary art curriculum, Ching-Chiu Lin shares findings about three high school art teachers' views about and praxis with new media technologies. Importantly, she uncovers, analyzes, and explains these teachers' firsthand perspectives about students' technology-related educational needs in a globalized world of digital media. Based on these findings, and through the lens of practicing art teachers, Lin describes youth competencies for today's technology-saturated world. She also challenges and realigns traditional academic notions of visual literacy education with a pluralist, multilayered, and ecological pedagogical vision; and she calls for shifts in thinking about the preservice education and professional development of art teachers.

Re-examining interrelationships of art, culture, and education in the context of globalization, many of the authors in this book have identified new forms of local adaptations, or *hybridization*, in cultural practices and productions. The next three chapters provide in-depth studies of cultural hybridization in three different locations in the world. In "Embracing a Predicament: Folk, Applied, Avant-Garde, and Singapore School Art," Koon Hwee Kan describes the strength of aesthetic association between the emerging Singapore Secondary School Art Style and three genres of art: regional-based folk art, function-based applied art, and issues-based avant-garde art. Although converging within the Singapore secondary art curriculum, each genre has its own historical antecedent, unique from the fine art movements customarily recorded in Western art history and typically adapted for public school art program in many postcolonial countries. Kan speculates on the future of this hybrid school art style within the context of globalization.

Next, Jae-young Lee analyzes the impact of globalization on South Korean art educational theory, identifying a continuum of adaptive, proactive, and hybridized approaches developed there. In "Globalization and Art Education in South Korea: Changes and Complexity of Art Curriculum Research and Practice," Lee describes these approaches as local adaptations to Western hegemonic forces. These approaches range from reactionary and assimilationist strategies at the extremes, and a critical, adaptive, pro-global but self-reflective approach to the left of center in Lee's continuum, an approach that privileges *inquiry*. Lee then shares a case study of this approach in a social reconstructionist-oriented curriculum that he designed and implemented with adolescents in South Korea. For Lee, such an approach has the capacity to facilitate amongst these Korean students critical self-reflection about their own emerging sense-of-self in an image-saturated world of global media.

Mary Stokrocki, Fernando Hernández, Magali Kivatinetz, Eneritz López, and Jordi Macián, in "A Social Constructivist Study of Metaphoric Portrait Drawings and Identity in a Barcelona Secondary School," also address how young people worldwide construct identities of both self and others, sharing a study of Barcelona middle school youth constructions of portraits of others. They examine how adolescence in a global world is a materialistic and hybridized social construction of mixed images, merging codes, and multiple selves. The authors also observe these adolescents' confusions and an inability to project a future self. Like Jae-young Lee, these authors call for teaching

with more dialogical and reflective strategies, and teaching with clearer understandings of influences on adolescents of a world of global media.

Tom Anderson, in the final chapter to this section, affirms the power of making art *together with* young people, with all due regard for the now globalized world of both epic tragedies and new possibilities for intercultural collaboration. Anderson's chapter, "The Kids' *Guernica* Peace Mural Project: A Paradigm for Global Art Education," describes an international project in which teachers, children, and community members have engaged in the development of more than 200 *Guernica*-sized murals in more than 60 countries. Anderson uses this project to demonstrate that art can be communication between human beings about things that count both in locally specific and global terms, and he addresses art and visual culture as projections of locally specific, intercultural, and global values. Anderson poignantly concludes that those values include social justice and peace education in a multicultural world, a concern that pervades many of the writings in this book.

The Global and the Local: The Hybridity of Children's Culture

Christine Marmé Thompson

When I was a kid growing up in New York City without too much access to outside information, in that age of the 1950s before 200-channel televisions and Internet porno, faith healers, dial-a-psychic, MTV, endless and largely banal news-programming, et cetera, the ideas I had about the world came mainly from three sources. The first was my own family, Cubans who had come to the United States by the mid-1940s, for whom life, unbookish, and uncluttered except by work and relationships, was largely a mystery to be unraveled, bit by bit, day by day. And then there was what I learned from the neighborhood: tales of tragedy and love passed about in its scatological language. My third source came from the Catholic church and school, where the Old and New Testaments were taken quite literally.

(HIJUELOS, 2000, P. 343)

Janus-faced, we look backward with affection to the conditions of our own childhood, and forward with perplexity to the childhoods being lived by "kids today." This seems to be a privilege of adulthood, a practice with almost ritual status. There may be reason in every generation to wonder at how quickly and how thoroughly life has changed. But the specific and recent changes that Hijuelos detects in the cultural experience of childhood do seem to be exceptionally radical and far-reaching. In a world in which various forms of mediated experience flood the child's world, where realities far beyond home, school, and neighborhood are there to be seen and sampled, children experience the world quite differently than those of us who came before. The directly experienced, the first hand, and the face-to-face are liberally supplemented by the vicarious, the second hand, and the distanced. As Kincheloe (1998) observes, the impact on the nature of childhood cannot be underestimated: "In the context of childhood education the postmodern experience of being a kid represents a cultural earthquake" (p. 172).

Postmodern childhoods in the Minority World—that portion of the world with ready access to media and wealth (Dahlberg, Moss, & Pence, 1999)—are increasingly privy to unfiltered information of many kinds. This is not an entirely unprecedented situation, insofar as the separation of childhood from adulthood is a more recent and more culturally specific phenomenon than we assume it to be (Aries, 1962; Cannella, 2002). The contemporary world is distinct in many respects, however, including the mobility of children themselves across cultural settings, and the global availability of products made for and marketed to them. In effect, the culture manufactured by adults for children, in the form of picture books and novels, films and television, clothing and accessories, toys and games, has become a universal language. To a considerable extent, childhood itself has become globalized by the proliferation of "art [and material culture] for children" (Bresler, 1998), the accumulation through which children pick and choose in order to construct their own cultures.

The conviction that children's image making was shaped by universal, predictable, and relatively invariant developmental processes was central to research and theories of child art since this everyday practice of children and youth (Gustavson, 2005) came to the attention of artists and scholars late in the 19th century. The nurture of child art, and the international exchange of children's images in blockbuster shows, catalogues, and archived collections, was meant to demonstrate the familial relationship of diverse cultures and to encourage recognition, empathy, and solidarity across borders. Arguably more than other aspects of children's growth and development, the capacity to create and apprehend visual images and objects was believed to be innate and biologically programmed to unfold in a predictable sequence, almost regardless of the provisions made for art practice. It was the similarity of children's images, rather than their differences, that fascinated and inspired their appropriation (and exploitation) in the cause of world peace and understanding.

Viktor Lowenfeld (1957) urged art teachers to offer motivations for art making that facilitated children's memories of "primary experiences," those shared and basic encounters that all children in the classroom were thought to have had. It was possible to circumvent incorrect assumptions regarding what constituted "normal" experience by providing fresh and immediately shared experiences in the classroom. Yet the focus was on the directly experienced, the vividly remembered, and only occasionally the imagined. Self-expression—or, more accurately, the autobiographical, the immediate, lived experience—was clearly favored in classroom practice. Despite retrospective criticism of the circumscribed world that Lowenfeld's child seemed to inhabit, the world he shared with the children he described was, quite objectively, a smaller and more personal place.

In the 1970s, however, Brent Wilson and Marjorie Wilson (1977) and others alerted art educators to the significance of the cultural contexts and idiosyncratic meanings of children's drawing. Increasingly, those who study child art recognize how decisive cultural influences and personal choices are to the experience and outcomes of the process of image making, even in earliest childhood. Almost from the moment that minimally communicative representations of humans emerge from the meander of scribbles, they don masks, costumes, and props that identify them as characters, and announce the beginning of a process of appropriation of source material from the culture at large that characterizes so much of contemporary children's drawing.

The relationships between children's culture and children's interest in producing images are complex and multiple. In this chapter, I focus on defining aspects of contemporary children's culture that are relevant to art education practice and research, and intertwined with issues of globalization and its impact on children and childhoods throughout the world. The text that follows is based in the recognition that, for good or ill, "Popular culture and mass media play a significant role in the way the contemporary child obtains information, forms perceptions, and acquires values" (Kasturi, 2002, p. 43). While many adults–art educators included–are quick to condemn children's infatuations with the latest media craze, there may be more to recommend the shared experience of commercial culture in childhood than we readily admit. At the very least, we must recognize our responsibility to examine the preconceptions that guide our interactions with children and to understand more clearly the conceptions of childhood, art, and culture that shape our teaching and research.

Defining Children's Culture

At least two forms of children's culture influence the theory and practice of art education. Perhaps most universal is the peer culture that emerges whenever people of similar age find themselves together, for an afternoon or an extended stretch of time. This is the recognition that passes between toddlers strapped into shopping carts navigating supermarket aisles, or inspires children to inject themselves into games already in progress, or to invent new ones on the spot. Peer cultures such as this exist throughout the world. As Corsaro (1985, 1997) and others note, in the West, at least, children's peer cultures often exclude adults, and exist in opposition to adult culture, helping children to define themselves as individuals and as members of a distinctive social group. No matter what our own childhood experience has been, adults tend to view children's participation in peer culture as essentially benign. Our own experience tells us how central to well-being the experience of finding oneself among friends (Dyson, 1989) truly is.

A second, distinct but closely related form of children's culture exists in the artifacts and practices created by adults for children, or appropriated by children from material intended for more mature audiences. Webkinz,™ the small stuffed animals tied in to elaborate online worlds ready to be furnished and accessorized, are an example of a cultural phenomenon created for children by adults that is wildly popular among children of elementary age. The classics of children's literature and other forms of "art for children" (Bresler, 1998) were also created with children in mind, or recognized by adults as appropriate childhood fare. Television shows such as *Dancing with the Stars* or *American Idol* or *CSI Miami*, not explicitly tailored to a child audience, are nevertheless popular among children who have discovered their pleasures. The recently released film, *Kung Fu Panda*, like much successful children's media, is accessible and appealing to multiple audiences simultaneously, thus ensuring that parents will not only tolerate but enjoy accompanying their young children to the film (and subsequently invest in the Kung-Fu-Panda-related merchandise that is sure to follow).

Kincheloe (2002) suggests that contemporary peer culture is different from the types of communal play described by Opie and Opie (1959), more closely tied to commercial children's culture than ever before: "The covert children's culture of the past ... was produced by children and propagated via child-to-child interaction. Twenty-first century children's culture is created by adults and dispersed by television and other electronic sources for the purpose of inducing children to consume" (pp. 104-105). Ruth Zanker, academic coordinator of the New Zealand Broadcasting School, commented, "The best research on children's culture at the moment isn't being done in the universities, it's being done by places like Nickelodeon, Disney, Hasbro, and Coca-Cola" (in Yano, 2004, p. 118).

Commercial Culture and Childhood

As Kincheloe's critique suggests, commercial children's culture can easily be caricatured as an Althusserian apparatus, beset by the least desirable aspects of globalization. These concerns are amplified by the stridency of moral panic that so often accompanies adult discussions of the predilections of younger human beings. Because the intended or actual audience for these seductive commercial productions are young, they are seen as extremely vulnerable to interpellation, readily seduced by images, ideas, and calls to buy, or buy into, the next new thing. As Mitchell and Reid-Walsh (2002) note, "Popular culture, especially mass media culture, is often constructed as a monolithic giant, while the child is depicted as a powerless object who is about to be consumed" (p. 1). Our pervasive aversion to the sinister effects of globalization—the homogenization and erasure of cultural distinction, the imposition of values, the mass commodification and colonization that occurs as goods and services and assumptions sweep across the globe (Duncum, 2001)–are magnified when we anticipate or observe their effect on younger human beings, those we perceive as least able to resist. Our protective impulses are mobilized almost involuntarily. Implicit in this reaction is an image of the child that "effectively separate[s] them (children) from us (adults)" (Yano, 2004, p. 133), that sees children as weak in mind and spirit, in need of constant guidance and protection from their own unchecked impulses.

Cross and Smits (2005) point out how readily Western adults jump to plausible, yet unwarranted, conclusions in regard to the global popularity of children's toys:

> The phenomenon of dark-haired girls in East Asia selecting blond-haired Barbie dolls might suggest the remarkable marketing power wielded by Mattel. It may even be a reflection of U.S. cultural imperialism, with girls in Korea or Japan concluding that European blond hair is more attractive or even superior to their own dark hair. But there is no evidence of this view, and instead this case may illustrate a more complex dynamic of globalization of children's culture that has been developing for several decades.

While adults tend to view each succeeding wave of commercial culture with increasing alarm, the phenomenon of commercial kinderculture has been with us for some time. As Cross and Smits (2005) suggest, none of those reading this chapter avoided the incursion of commercial culture into their own childhoods:

> the linkage of modern children's consumer culture with the globalization of the design and manufacture of innovative products. It is not merely that the American makers of Barbie have swept away traditional dolls and local culture, but the plaything industry across the world has become integrated, with design centered in the U.S. and Japan and production based in China. This particular configuration may be of recent origin, but dolls and toys have long been objects of international trade. Playthings have long roots in local folk cultures and crafts, and regional and national traditions of toy and doll making have long reinforced ethnic and local identities in children. But the construction of modern childhood over the past century especially has paralleled the decline of these craft traditions and the emergence of a global children's commercial culture. (n.p.)

Commercial children's culture is open to critique on multiple grounds, but a measured assessment suggests the possibility that it plays a significant role in helping children to amass social and cultural capital, facilitating social life, enriching imagination, and enhancing understanding of a world beyond the confines of circumscribed childhood experience (see Thompson, 2006). Moreover, the phenomenon of children's culture calls into question fundamental assumptions about the nature of childhood and the agency and critical capacities possessed and exercised by children. As Tobin (2004) observes, "Children may be prone to consumer crazes, but they choose which crazes, and they decide when a craze is over" (p. 10). Much as every generation of American schoolchildren seems to rediscover the same stash of knock-knock jokes and ghost stories, the appeal of cartoon characters and superheroes and *Where the Wild Things Are*, contemporary children choose from an ever-changing array of possibilities those things that are personally appealing and rich in potential for fueling improvisations on a theme. In whatever forms they assume, cultural practices favored by children contribute substantially to their imaginative lives (Fleming, 1996).

A particularly intriguing example of the phenomenon of global children's culture is found in "the rise and fall of Pokémon" (Tobin, 2004), the Japanese "pocket monsters" that captured the financial and imaginative commitment of children worldwide in the late 1990s. As Buckingham and Sefton-Green (2004) observed, brilliant marketing strategies played a considerable role in Pokémon's reach and longevity; however, "the global success of Pokémon is partly a result of its ability to 'speak' to shared aspects of childhood experience, and of the ease with which it can be integrated within the context of children's everyday lives" (p. 13). They continue:

> The appeals of Pokémon cross significant boundaries of age, gender, and culture, and, for those who have access to the Internet, they also transcend the limitation of geography. To a greater extent than many similar phenomena, Pokémon can be said to have created, or at least to have facilitated, a common culture among children. In the process, it can also be seen to develop their social and communicative competencies–skills in negotiation, self-confidence, and even tolerance for others. In terms more familiar within media and cultural studies, it would be argued that Pokémon fosters the development of new "interpretive communities" ... that in turn allow for more fluid and negotiable identities among their members. (p. 25)

Agency and Choice in Children's Culture

Zurmuehlen, Sacca and Richter (1984) pointed out that the ability to identify, draw, and discuss significant contemporary icons is a potent source of cultural (and cross-cultural) cachet, one which children routinely use as a mode of access to peer culture. Command of popular culture positions the "child-as-expert" (Mitchell & Reid-Walsh, 2002, p. 2), countering the belief in the intrinsic helplessness of children that too often stands as the corollary of a belief in childhood innocence:

> even very young children can and do participate in decisions about themselves that seem to call into question the idea that by definition as children, they are innocent and unknowing. This is also something that is acknowledged when it comes to the actions and experiences of children during extreme conditions of poverty or war, say in terms of the children who marched in the 1976 riots against apartheid in South Africa, the bravery of Anne Frank, and the labors today of children, especially girls, in sub-Saharan Africa to contribute to the family income, by working on the streets, and so on ... contesting the idea that children are not capable of caring for themselves. (p. 7)

As Mitchell and Reid-Walsh (2002) acknowledge, "Children possess an expertise about their own popular culture that is theirs by virtue of their being the intended audience and/or consumer, but it is also theirs by their willing and sometimes passionate engagement with the show, book, or toy" (p. 9). The social value of this commitment to a character, a game, a practice, or a phenomenon, whether it is Doraemon, drawing, or dinosaurs, cannot be overstated: "The sharing of common knowledge is crucial to children's peer groups" (Brougere, 2004, p. 193).

Popular culture, as part of what interests children and sets them apart as individuals and members of their own generation, is essential to peer culture as well. Considering the recent unprecedented global popularity of Pokémon, for example, Buckingham and Sefton-Green (2004) note that,

> Pokémon is centrally about acquiring *knowledge* ... to commit to Pokémon is to commit to a long-term engagement, which poses some significant changes in terms of finding, processing, remembering, and applying info. In interpersonal terms, this level of complexity also provides Pokémon enthusiasts with a great deal to talk about ... other forms of children's culture prior to Pokémon undoubtedly encouraged his kind of trade in informal knowledge, but not to the same extent, and certainly not on the same global scale. (p. 22)

Continuing their analysis of the allure of Pokémon to children across the globe, Buckingham and Sefton-Green (2004) remark on the phenomenon's "*portability,* the ease with which it crosses media and social contexts ... at the height of its popularity, Pokémon facilitated interaction in a wide range of children's social spaces, providing a ticket of entry to play, a pretext for negotiating friendships, as well as a vehicle for competition and conflict" (pp. 22-23). The games were explicitly "designed to generate activity and social interaction" (Buckingham & Sefton-Green, 2004, p. 23). Allison (2004) suggests that the social imperative is a matter of design, intended to counteract the situation of "children who live in urban, overprotective settings where they are deprived of contact with nature and social interactions with peers" (pp. 41-42):

> In designing the Pokémon game, Tajiri Satoshi had two motivations. One was to create a challenging yet playable game that would pique children's imaginations. The other was to give children a means of relieving the stresses of growing up in a postindustrial society ... in an environment where everyone moves fast to accomplish more and more every day, the human relationships once so prized have begun to erode. Increasingly, people spend more time alone, forming intimacies less with one another than with the goods they consume, and the technologies they rely upon ... Children are particularly susceptible to atomism, or what some have called 'solitarism.' One study reports that most Japanese ten- to fourteen-year-old children eat dinner alone, 44 percent attend cram school, and the average time to return home at night is eight. For such mobile kids, companionship often comes in the form of 'shadow families': attachments made to imaginary characters, prosthetic technologies, or virtual worlds. (p. 41)

Globalization and Glocalization: Children's Culture in Translation

Contradicting a discourse focused exclusively on Western imperialism, "The flow of toys across the Pacific Ocean is not unidirectional" (Cross & Smits, 2005, n.p.). Iwabuchi (2004) defines *global commodities* as "things of universal or transcultural appeal that bear the creative imprint of the originality of a producing nation" (p. 54): e.g., animé, computer games, and other recent inventions, many of them originating in Asia. Several authors suggest that curiosity about other cultures is satisfied, and respect cultivated, through the exchange of products and the absorption of cultural references that occurs when children delve into the worlds of Pokémon or graphic novels (Cross & Smits, 2005; Wilson, 2002). Iwabuchi (2004) writes hopefully of the influence of Pokémon on American perceptions of Japanese culture:

> Kamo Yoshinori (2000), a U.S.-based sociologist, observes that American children who love Pokémon believe that Japan is a very cool nation that produces wonderful characters, imaginary worlds, and commodities. He sees in Pokémon's success a very hopeful sign that American audiences are becoming more open to Japanese cultural values and that they are changing their image of Japan from a land that is strange and workoholic to someplace that is humane and cool. (p. 61)

Allison (2004) suggests that the contemporary Japanese aesthetic is exported along with these games: "With hits such as Pokémon, Japan is becoming recognized not only for its high-tech consumer goods but also for what might be called postmodern play aesthetics ... Products (*shohin*) are the currency by which Japanese culture enters the United States" (pp. 36-37). As Lemish and Bloch (2004) suggest,

> It is increasingly the case that children around the world share similar leisure activities and interests, as well as media references ... Children live in a world of cultural hybridity, including the multiple cultures they experience within their own locales. Our thesis is thus that contemporary global consumption is less a matter of cultural opposition than a process of coexistence of differences. (p. 166)

As Duncum points out, the appropriation and use of cultural goods from abroad is a creative endeavor, for "Cultural goods are not transmitted; they are translated" (Duncum, 2001, n.p.). If the products of commercial children's culture have become increasingly global in their availability and appeal, interpretation and appropriation of those products remains a local project, carried out by children acting in specific cultural circumstances. The term "glocalization" refers to "the way in which children confer local meaning on foreign content" (Lemish & Bloch, 2004, p. 166), as well as the intentional modifications made to retrofit commercial products such as the Power Rangers to ensure their capacity to speak to a range of international audiences. Lemish and Bloch (2004) point out that products intended for a global market are often designed to be as culture-free and universal as possible, to appeal to children worldwide; however, even these products tend to be adapted and modified to suit the tastes and circumstance of local players. Additionally, as Iwabuchi (2004) suggests,

elements of commercial culture that seem exotic at first tend to acquire an aura of familiarity with time and exposure:

> Images and commodities tend to lose their cultural odor as their original meanings and purposes are recreated by processes of local appropriation and negotiation ... Through local practices of appropriating and hybridizing images and commodities of 'foreign' origin, even the central icons of American culture are conceived of as 'ours' in many places. McDonald's is now so much a part of their world that to Japanese or Taiwanese young consumers it no longer represents an American way of life. (p. 73)

Just as the formula for Coca Cola is modified to cater to regional preferences, manufacturers of other cultural commodities may engage in a preemptive process of glocalization. Allison (2004) describes ways that "localizers" in the United States modified the original Pokémon prior to its introduction to American audiences:

> The convention in U.S. children's media is to feature clear-cut heroes with a moral dynamics that sharply differentiates good from evil. By contrast, ambiguity, in the sense of a murkiness that blurs borders (good/bad, real/fantasy, animal/human), is a central part of cuteness as generated by the cute business in Japan. This cuteness and ambiguity get muted a bit by its U.S. importers. But even in its exported version, Pokémon retains a gentleness, cuteness, and ambiguity that is characteristic of Japanese children's media culture. (p. 39)

Yet, as Katsuno and Mamet (2004) point out, new and uniquely Japanese "televisual and discursive codes" (p. 82) are introduced to American audiences via Pokémon and other forms of animé which employ a "more stark" aesthetic style and a more continuous and complex narrative structure than typical American cartoons, and tend to appeal across generations.

Critiquing the Culture of Contemporary Childhoods

It is important to acknowledge that critiques of children's commercial culture are culturally specific, often unconsciously so, related both to prevailing images of the child (Malaguzzi, 1993) and convictions regarding the morality of consumption (Yano, 2004). As Yano (2004) points out, "Pokémon panic" is a peculiarly Western phenomenon, emerging from "a moral order fearful of capitalism in both its productive and consumptive dimensions. Many critics, from school principals to child psychologists and parents, adopt a Frankfurt-school approach, alleging that consumers are helpless dupes of a cunning, manipulative culture industry (p. 115).

Issues of class and inequalities of privilege are raised by the commercial culture of childhood, and children experience their impact dramatically within communities (even in the nominally privileged Minority World) and across the globe. Disposable income is needed to consume this culture conspicuously, through display of its accoutrements on T-shirts and backpacks. Iwabuchi (2004) admits that "many parts of the world are still excluded from enjoying the fruits of participation in global cultural consumption" (p. 74). This exclusion can be particularly painful for children living in classrooms and communities where the spectacle of consumption is staged in full view, just beyond their reach. Often, in these instances, children can and do craft forms of participation for themselves, collecting photographs, memorizing characters and plots, and creating drawings in order to gain entry to the realms of "the kid cognoscenti" (Tobin, 2004, p. 9): A DIY (do-it-yourself) culture emerges as an adjunct to commercial culture.

Conclusion

Corsaro (1997) wisely observes that "Children are always participating in and part of two cultures— children's and adults'—and these cultures are intricately interwoven" (p. 26). Adults' attitudes toward children's participation in the cultural practices of their own generation are decisive, and all too frequently unexamined, sources of bias in research and teaching, as well as parenting.

As professionals whose expertise resides in an understanding of children and of imagery (Duncum, 2002), it is critical that art educators understand the complexities of children's culture, both global and local, lived among peers and within a world of objects, images, and technologies that invite children to navigate virtual and imaginative spaces. As Duncum (2001) suggests, adults must cultivate a balanced yet critical view of contemporary children's culture, recognizing its multiple manifestations, and the possibilities and the problems it presents: "An acceptance that students are active in their choice, consumption, and interpretation of global culture should be balanced with the recognition that these activities are framed an limited by the logic and dynamics of corporate capitalism" (n.p.)

REFERENCES

Allison, A. (2004). Cuteness as Japan's millennial product. In J. Tobin (Ed.), *Pikachu's global adventure: The rise and fall of Pokémon* (pp. 34-49). Durham, NC: Duke University Press.

Aries, P. (1962). *Centuries of childhood: A social history of family life.* New York: Knopf.

Bresler, L. (1998). "Child art," "fine art, and "art for children": The shaping of school practice and implications for change. *Arts Education Policy Review, 100*(1), 3-10.

Brougere, G. (2004). How much is a Pokémon worth? Pokémon in France. In J. Tobin (Ed.) *Pikachu's global adventure: The rise and fall of Pokémon* (pp. 187-208). Durham, NC: Duke University Press.

Buckingham, D., & Sefton-Green, J. (2004), tructure, agency, and pedagogy in children's media culture. In J. Tobin (Ed.), *Pikachu's global adventure: The rise and fall of Pokémon* (pp. 12-33). Durham, NC: Duke University Press.

Cannella, G. S. (2002). Global perspectives, cultural studies, and the construction of a postmodern childhood studies. In G.S. Cannella & J. L. Kincheloe (Eds.), *Kidworld: Childhood studies, global perspectives, and education* (pp. 3-18). New York: Peter Lang.

Corsaro, W. (1985). *Friendship and peer culture in the early years.* Norwood, NJ: Ablex.

Corsaro, W. (1997). *The sociology of childhood.* Thousand Oaks, CA: Pine Forge Press.

Cross, G. & Smits, G. (2005). Japan, the U.S., and the globalization of children's consumer culture. *Journal of Social History, 38*(4), 873-890. Retrieved December 10, 2007, from FindArticles database.

Dahlberg,G., Moss, P. & Pence, A. (1999). *Beyond quality in early childhood education and care: Postmodern perspectives.* Philadelphia: Routledge Falmer.

Duncum, P. (2002). Children never were what they were. In Y. Guadelius and P. Speiers (Eds.), *Contemporary issues in art education* (pp. 97-106). Upper Saddle River, NJ: Prentice Hall.

Duncum, P. (2001, June 10). Theoretical foundations for an art education of global culture and principles for classroom practice. *International Journal of Education and the Arts, 2*(3). Retrieved January 16, 2008.

Dyson, A. H. (1989). *Multiple worlds of child writers: Friends learning to write.* New York: Teachers College Press.

Fleming, D. (1996). *Powerplay: Toys as popular culture.* New York: Manchester University Press.

Gustavson, L. (2005). *Youth learning on their own terms: Creative practices and classroom teaching.* New York: Routledge.

Hijuelos, O. (2000). Endings. In *Three minutes or less: Life lessons from American's greatest writers* (pp. 343-344). New York: The PEN/Faulkner Foundation

Iwabuchi, K. (2004). How "Japanese" is Pokémon? In J. Tobin (Ed.), *Pikachu's global adventure: The rise and fall of Pokémon* (pp. 53-79). Durham, NC: Duke University Press.

Kasturi, S. (2002). Constructing childhood in a corporate world: Cultural studies, childhood, and Disney. In G.S. Cannella & J. L. Kincheloe (eds.), *Kidworld: Childhood studies, global perspectives, and education* (pp. 39-58). New York: Peter Lang.

Katsuno, H., & Mamet, J. (2004). Localizing the Pokémon TV series for the American market. In J. Tobin (Ed.), *Pikachu's global adventure: The rise and fall of Pokémon* (pp. 80-107). Durham, NC: Duke University Press.

Kincheloe, J. L. (1998). The new childhood: Home alone as a way of life. In H. Jenkins (Ed.), *The children's culture reader* (pp. 159-177). New York: New York University Press.

Kincheloe, J. L. (2002). The complex politics of McDonald's and the new childhood: Colomizing kidworld. In G. S. Cannella & J.L. Kincheloe (eds.), *Kidworld: Childhood studies, global perspectives, and education.* New York: Peter Lang.

Lemish, D., & Bloch, L-R. (2004). Pokémon in Israel. In J. Tobin (Ed.). *Pikachu's global adventure: The rise and fall of Pokémon* (pp. 165-186). Durham, NC; Duke University Press.

Lowenfeld, V. (1957). *Creative and mental growth* (3rd ed.). New York: Macmillan.

Malaguzzi, L. (1993, November). For an education based on relationships. (L. Gandini, Trans.). *Young Children, 49*(1), 9-12.

Mitchell, C., & Reid-Walsh, J. (2002). *Researching children's popular culture: The cultural spaces of childhood.* New York: Routledge.

Opie, P., & Opie, I. (1959) *The language and lore of schoolchildren.* Oxford: Clarendon Press.

Thompson, C. M. (2006). The "ket aesthetic": Visual culture in childhood. In J. Fineberg (Ed.), *When we were young: New perspectives on the art of the child.* Berkeley: University of California Press.

Tobin, J. (2004). *Pikachu's global adventure: The rise and fall of Pokémon.* Durham, NC: Duke University Press.

Wilson, B. (2002). Becoming Japanese: Manga, children's drawings, and the construction of national character. In L. Bresler & C. M. Thompson (Eds.), *The arts in children's lives: Context, culture, and curriculum* (pp. 43-55). Dordrecht, The Netherlands: Kluwer.

Wilson, B., & Wilson, M. (1977). An iconoclastic view of the imagery sources in the drawings of young people. *Art Education, 30*(1), 5-11.

Yano, C. R. (2004). Panic attacks: Anti-Pokémon voices in global markets. In J. Tobin (Ed.), *Pikachu's global adventure: The rise and fall of Pokémon* (pp. 108-138). Durham, NC: Duke University Press.

Zurmuehlen, M., Sacca, E., & Richter, I. (1984). Images and concepts Brazilian, Canadian, and U.S. art teachers interpret as stereotypes in their students' art. *Journal of Multicultural and Crosscultural Research in Art Education, 2*(1), 45-71.

Creating Parallel Global Cultures: The Art-Making of Fans in Fandom Communities

Marjorie Cohee Manifold

My curiosity about young people's fascinations with characters and stories of popular culture began when I became aware of my adolescent daughter, Josephina, and her friends' love of Japanese manga (comics) and animé (animation). As ardent *fans*, they were not content to simply read or watch and discuss manga and animé. These young people relentlessly copied images of their beloved characters, developed new storylines and illustrated them, created costumes and improvisational plays based on the characters, photographed themselves in costumed poses, and posted their written or illustrated adaptations of their favorite stories on the Internet to be shared with other fans of manga and animé around the world.

Later, as a young adult, my daughter's interests in popular narratives expanded to include fantasy literatures by Rowling and Tolkien, along with science fiction comics, films, and television shows about superheros. Like her earlier interests in Japanese manga and animé, fascination with these phenomena of popular culture resulted in Josephina's engagement with like-interested others in globe-spanning conversations, collaborations, and exchanges of appropriated stories, illustrations, flash videos, and costume plays adapted from and inspired by the favorite texts. Observing how she and her friends embraced and manipulated popular narratives, led me to wonder what sense adolescents and young adults made of these activities and what might be the consequences of engaging in fan-based artmaking with others globally.

Visual and textual narratives are omnipresent in the life-worlds of people living in technologically advanced cultures. Thus, being able to critically interpret explicit and tacit messages of graphic stories should be a concern of art educators (Freedman & Stuhr, 2004). Also, because migrations and immigrations of large groups of people from one geographic region to another are changing the demographic make-up of classrooms across North America (Banks & Banks, 2006), knowing how youth come together to share aesthetic ideas across national and cultural borders, and understanding what meaning young people make of shared popular culture may inform art educational practices appropriate to students from diverse cultural backgrounds. My curiosity about these matters led me to initiate a 4-year study of fan youth's artmaking activities and interactions related to their interests in several genres of popular narrative.

In this chapter, I report some findings from a study in which I explored reasons why adolescents and young adults might be drawn to and might create artworks based on popular narratives, how and with whom they share these interests, and how these activities might affect or be affected by local and global aesthetics. As these issues are examined, an image emerges of how fan-based artmaking permits youth of diverse cultures to transcend barriers of cultural stereotype and come to know one another, and how local cultural differences may serve as inspirational sources of individual artistic style. Questions arise about disconnections between youths' fans feelings of competence within fan communities and lack of agency in real local and global communities. The findings may have implications for the art education of contemporary youth.

A Conceptual Framework

The framework constructed for exploration of why and how youth create and share art based on narratives of popular culture in fan communities takes into account developmental stages of psychological and mental growth as suggested by Erikson (1950/1993), who explored how people develop psychologically and learn to exist with others in communities. Erikson describes adolescence as a time during which youth strive to construct coherent self-identities. Construction of self identify occurs through processes that involve conscious and unconscious responses to inner psychological and exterior social environments. Erikson's theory might be situated within larger theories of social construction, such as Giddens' (1991)

Structuration Theory. Giddens understands self as thoughtfully constructed through the creation and continual revision of a biographical narrative or story based on a personal interpretation of one's life, actions, and influences. Personal narratives take shape as individuals link to communities of people who are like themselves or "who, at least, have made similar choices" (Gauntlett, 2002, p. 103). The narratives are affirmed through social interaction as members of a group mark themselves in relation to others, practice particular attributes or skills, and explore effects and consequences of possessing these attributes or skills

When people construct new narratives of themselves and share these with one another, there is a corresponding change in social structure. Individual self-identity formation and social structure become locked in a dance of balance and counterbalance (Giddens, 1991). Young fans from diverse cultures, who embrace specific phenomena of popular culture (Fiske, 1989, p. 59), might become creators of new, overlaying cultures (Jenkins, 1992), which influence the aesthetic environments of future generations of youth. Shields that mark group differences may be pushed aside (see Figure 2), while cultural and

Figure 1

Left: Sharing a similar cultural/ national narrative permits members of a group to form self and role identities within that cultural/ national group. The identities created, however, might shield outsiders from easily coming to know individual members of the enclosed cultural group.

Figure 2

Right: When individuals from diverse cultural backgrounds share interests in a common narrative from popular culture, each person may come to know and be known by others through the mediation of shared story. Differences of culture, which might otherwise prove obstacles to people from different backgrounds coming to know one another, are pushed aside. Culture-specific aesthetic sensibilities may be drawn upon for developing personal styles of fanart or cosplay.

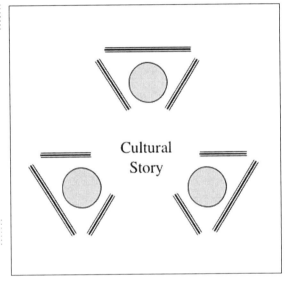

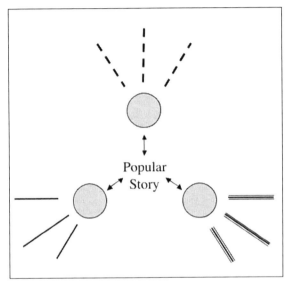

in relation to others (Sennett, 1994). These kinds of role or 'story' plays can be a way of making sense of and situating self within specific cultural environments (Sennett, 1974).

When grounded in local culture, biographical stories work to distinguish, differentiate, or insulate members of one cultural group from outsiders (see Figure 1). Curiosity, however, may compel youth to seek more enclusive narratives as models for transcending limiting, locally-specific identities (Egan, 1997). Large patterns, which both underlie and rise above unique cultural texts, are present in universal archetypes of classic stories and myths that affect people of all cultures and ages (Campbell 1949/1972). Thus, adolescents seeking narratives of self that are capable of functioning across cultural contexts might borrow and play with storied archetypes (Gauntlett, 2002). Stories that include archetypes as characters may serve not only as maps to self-discovery and cues for being known by others who 'are like us' by virtue of having made 'similar choices' in literature, but also, consequently, may serve as vehicles for *changing* our perceptions of who we are or want to be.

national differences may contribute to the individual fan's uniquely personal style of expression.

Methodology

For this inquiry I researched expressions, practices, and art making activities by adolescents and young people who identified themselves as fans of various popular visual and textual narratives and shared these interests with like-minded others in online or real life communities of fans or *fandom*. Favorite narratives included genres of Japanese manga/animé written for girls (*shôjo*) and boys (*shōnen*), Euro-American fantasies, and science-fiction stories, comics, films, and television shows. The study focused on two forms of artmaking in response to fans' appreciation of these narrative genres—*fanart*, or art based directly or indirectly on characters or settings from popular media-conveyed narratives, and *cosplay*, or dressing and posing or performing as characters derived from these sources.

Data about youths' fanart making and cosplay activities and interactions were gathered from (1) observing and conversing with *fanartists* and *cosplayers* at fan conventions[1] held in the United States and Asia, (2) perusing websites featuring fanart or cosplay photo galleries, forums, and fan blogs,[2] and (3) the responses of 101 fanartists and cosplayers to a survey instrument of 12 questions that addressed specific themes which emerged from the convention and website observations and conversations. I considered only the four following questions as having direct relevance to the topic of this chapter.

• When and how did you become interested in fanart or cosplay?
• What interests you about this fandom and expressive activity and how do you experience this interest?
• With whom do you share your interests?
• Do you think fanart or cosplay has affected the way you experience thinking about life?

The survey questions were emailed to 300 fanartists and cosplayers selected from the three large online fan-interest sites: *deviantArt*,[3] *Elfwood*,[4] and *Cosplay.com*.[5] These sites attract members from many parts of the world, who join in order to share their creative expressions with like-interested others. Of the 300 contacts (100 from each of three sites), 101 people—including 69 fanartists and 32 cosplayers—responded to my e-mailed questionnaire by answering the survey questions. Neither age nor national origin was taken into consideration when selecting potential subjects for the survey. Nevertheless, all but four who responded to the survey were between the ages of 14 and 24, and the sampling represented individuals from 21 countries or principalities, including: the US (51), Australia (5), Belgium (1), Canada (9), Chile (1), El Salvador (1), France (3), Hong Kong (1), Indonesia (1), Italy (1), Japan (1), Korea (1), Lebanon (1), Mexico (2), the United Kingdom (7), the Philippines (2), Portugal (1), Puerto Rico (1), Spain (2), Sweden (2), and Taiwan (1).

In spite of an attempt to select subjects who created art based on subject matter that might appeal to both female and male fans, 86% of the survey respondents were female. This is a limitation in that the results of the study may be skewed toward the girls' and young women's responses. Other limitations were that over half of the participants were from the US, and all needed to correspond in English.

Awakening to Fan Phenomena

Children from very early ages and across cultures have been found to spontaneously draw images inspired by characters from narratives of popular culture (Thompson, 2003; Wilson, 1974). In these cases, the creation of art may be a way of extending the texts of narrated,

animated, graphic or written stories into children's symbolic language of play (Egan, 1997; Winner, 1985). Nearly 66% of the adolescent and young adult participants of this study indicated that the event of becoming a fan of a particular subject occurred during or after early adolescence. These youth also made distinctions between the nature of the art they had made during childhood play with characters from popular stories and the art they make after adolescence in response to being fans of popular stories and characters. The differences between simple childish infatuation and the adolescent's devotion to a phenomenon were evident in the language used by subjects to describe the exact moment when, as adolescents, they became enamored of a fan subject. It "took my breath!" wrote one teenager (Darin, personal communication, June 26, 2006); it was "a turning point in my life" wrote another (Linnéa, personal communication, July 25, 2006). Several fanartists and cosplayers described intense desires to 'get inside the skins' or 'experience the souls' of adored characters in order to engage in deep understanding of traits or qualities they wished to know in an intimate and integrative way.

The experience of copying favorite characters' appearances and experiences through art provided fanartists and cosplayers pleasures that were attributed to recognition of likenesses between real or desired self and a projected character. Over 64% of the survey respondents reported having being drawn to specific characters of popular narratives that were like them in terms of physical features or emotional responses to everyday situations, while 70% percent of the fans described being attracted to characters that exhibited physical or personality traits, which they found desirable but believed they personally were lacking. Through copying the ideal character models as fanart or cosplay, fan youth discovered or developed aspects of themselves about which they were curious. For these youth drawing fanart and cosplaying represented a virtual donning of desired aspects and a simulation of experiences they had been unable to enjoy in reality.

Bettelheim (1976) gives explanation for youths' identification with fictional stories and characters by asserting that fairy tales and fantasy myths educate, support, and liberate emotions of young people. The heroes and villains of stories serve as archetypes of human agency and also as instructive models of ways-of-being in the world. Trinity, a 20-year old fanartist and cosplayer agreed:

Every character has to have a bio or historic background. That's the loose map of who the character is and might become. Then we play with characters and improvise on how they would act in this or that situation with other characters, in order to know them. Everything has to fit together, if someone plays out of character, the play won't fit together logically. (Trinity, personal correspondence, February 14, 2006)

Figure 3

Cosplaying youth at AnimeExpo, 2006 in Anaheim, California. Photograph by M. C. Manifold.

Knowing and Being Known by Others

Apart from meeting and making friends at fan conventions, only 26% of the survey respondents reported knowing other fans within their local communities with whom they could interact. The remaining 73% of the subjects of this study reported they sought the friendship of like-minded peers predominantly or exclusively through online sites. This attests to the social realities of life in contemporary technologically advanced cultures. Parents' changes in jobs or careers, divorce, or displacement due to natural disasters or human conflict mean many young people experience changing communal landscapes during their journeys from childhood to adulthood. Those living in small towns or rural areas may be unable to find local peers with whom to share their fan interests; those living in urban environments may feel lost in crowds of strangers with whom they are uncomfortable about confiding their interests.

If it is difficult for some youth to make connections with like-minded others in their real communities, how can adolescents and young adults meet and become known to one another within the vast nebulous realm of cyber-space? For the fanartist and cosplayer projecting an image of self, that might be recognized and known by hundreds of like-interested others around the world, solves this problem.

Sociologist Goffman (1959) explains a concept of 'impression management', whereby the presentation of self in the everyday world is not unlike a theatrical performance before specific audiences. Through dress, pose, and mannerism, people place themselves in roles appropriate to particular social situations. Metaphorically, for Goffman, 'all the world's a stage'. This reiterates a notion of *teatrum-mundi*, a view of life prevalent throughout much of Western history until the early18th century. *Teatrum mundi* held that every person is an actor playing out a role assigned to him or her by divine design (Denton, 2000). Everyday life is ordered, every person can always be assured of being recognized according to his or her role in the hierarchy of society, and is able to interact appropriately with others so long as every person is dressed in the appropriate costume and character of his or her assigned role. Young fans, who participated in this study, indicated they made contacts with other fans and became known to other fans through displaying images or donning costumes of characters that were immediately recognized by others of the fandom (see Figure 3). They avoided creating original characters and stories for fear that 'no one would know' them if they projected a non-canonical self.

Fans from all over the world were able to make contact with and come to know one another through the mediation of favorite narratives. Yet, this might not have happened without fans' willingness to expand provincial paradigms and open themselves to finding common grounds for communication across cultures and nations. Crossing into unfamiliar cultural territory required deciphering conventions of graphic narrative form, whether a manga, illustration, comic, or film, and negotiating unfamiliar culture-specific cues and nuances. Western fans of manga, for example, were obliged to recognize Japanese ideas about grade-level hierarchies in the educational system, and negotiate story-arcs or characters and themes grounded in intricately complex Shinto mythology; non-British readers of Rowling's saga of Harry Potter became familiar with concepts of the British boarding school 'house system' and a pantheon of Western mythic and folk traditions. The intellectual challenge of decoding narrative, cultural, and aesthetic referents rendered popular narratives appealing and enticing to fans.

Local Style in Fan Expression

The majority (79%) of fanartists and cosplayers from the study, claimed to learn basic skills of art making by copying source materials; however, 89% of the study participants agreed the ultimate goal of the fanartist

from knowing one another at personal levels became friends as they engaged in genuine dialogues through mediation of the common fan interest. Rather than allowing themselves to be pigeonholed by the invented stereotypes of cultural or national hegemonies, these non-mainstream youth were able to choose images of self by which they wished to be known. This seemed a significant effect of fan participation.

Sharing Ideas and Ideals through Global Fandom

Popular stories and images seemed to inspire some adolescent fans to question the ways things appear in their own cultures or the larger world. For example, on an *AnimeWebTurnpike* forum (see Bakadesu, 2003) fans publicly discussed issues of exclusivity, intolerance, and racism with others from diverse regions of the world. They expressed curiosity about local histories of conflicts, and resisted xenophobic attitudes of their parents and other adult members of their local communities.

Many popular narratives embraced by fan youth challenge dualistic world-views of good and evil. On interactive blogs, many fans expressed understandings of evil as the result of a culmination of many minor choices. For example, one fan reiterated an episode of *Smallville* (a television series based on Superman stories) in which a young Lex Luthor, who would one day become the nemesis of Superman, stated, "The road to darkness is a journey, not a light switch."[7] Several fans, who grew up reading the Harry Potter series, recognized moral instruction in Professor Dumbledore's admonition that every person must decide between what is 'right' or what is 'easy.' Like Harry, they agreed that every person must bear responsibility for his or her choices. These stories, which warn readers the sorrows they selfishly or intentionally inflict upon others can never be fully repaid even by the penance of a life lived well, are expressed visually in images of fanart and cosplay. Indeed, although there are many genres and stylistic renditions of fanart and cosplay—from lighthearted *chibi* cartoons such as drawings of Pokemon characters, to Gothic Lolita cosplays or fan-based illustrations done in ornate manga or pre-Raphaelesque styles—two underlying aesthetic characteristics across many genres suggest universal themes of chthonic nature.

Visual Evidences of Aesthetic Ideals

Fantastica is a realistic presentation of the impossible. Rooted in images of the imagination throughout history and in recent advances in cinematic special effects, the true importance of *fantastica* is that "it

Figure 4

Ryan Quizon, a Filipino fanartist, calls upon his knowledge of the Spanish colonialist rule of the Philippines in creating his unique interpretation of *Felisa Guardia Sibil,* a character inspired by a story by Modesto de Castro.

or cosplayer was to become skillful enough to develop a personal style. Because, local aesthetic influences could provide unique personal style accents, fans were encouraged to share their own cultural backgrounds and were praised and found themselves valued for the different aesthetic interpretations they brought to fan subjects (see Figure 4). Survey respondents wrote they appreciated seeing stylistic differences of others' fanart or cosplay presentations. Young people from non-mainstream cultures, such as Indonesian high school student Jia-Ling (who posted her illustration of a local folk puppet play, *wayang kulit*, in a manga-style[6]) were pleased that others accepted and showed laudatory interest in their cultural interpretations of a fan phenomenon. Thus, knowing one another through characters and stories that are appropriated as archetypes yielded a wide diversity of expressions and interpretations, and brought fans from diverse cultures to mutual appreciation.

The *teatrum mundi* projection actually served to break down barriers of prejudice and resistance. It allowed *entré* to the 'real' or desired self without the distraction of stereotypical cultural or national appearances. As a result, individuals whose cultural differences have historically hindered them

Figure 5

Right: *Death Be Not Proud*, by Erin McAuley, presents a notion of *awful beauty*.

Death, be not proud, though some have called thee
Mighty and dreadful, for thou art not so:
For those who thou think'st thou dost overthrow
Die not, poor Death, nor yet canst thou kill me.

From rest and sleep, which but thy pictures be,
Much pleasure: then from thee much more must flow,
And soonest our best men with thee do go,
Rest of their bones and soul's delivery.

Thou art slave to fate, chance, kings, and desperate men,
And dost with poison, war, and sickness dwell,
And poppy or charms can make us sleep as well
And better than thy stroke; why swell'st thou then?

One short sleep past, we wake eternally
And death shall be no more;
Death, thou shalt die. - John Donne

Figure 6

Bellow: Gallery Twenty Eight. *The River Session ~ Loss and Hope #3*, Nathalie Mineault, Canada. Photographed by Diane Blanchard. Natalie's cosplay of Professor Severus Snape demonstrates psychodramatic *fantastica*, as well as a sense of *awful beauty*.

makes obvious that the tale's concern is not useful information about the external world, but the inner processes taking place in an individual." (Bettelheim, 1976, p. 25). Children's book author C. S. Lewis stated that the most fantastic visible forms are actually most life-like since they reveal, "human life as seen, felt, or divined from the inside" (Lewis, 1936, quoted in Bettelheim, 1976, p. 24). Fantastica iterates this potential insofar as it supports fanartists' or cosplayers' attempts to expose psychological conflicts, motivations, desires, and deepest longings of story characters (see Figures 5 and 6) through exaggerated pose or dramatic gesture.

The aesthetic concept of *awful beauty* draws from ancient Greek notions of *pathos* and a Japanese aesthetic that is most evident in the presentation of the *bishōnen*, an effeminately beautiful male warrior, torn by internal conflict, loyal to a cause, regardless of whether that cause be noble or ignoble (Levi, 1998). Loveliness of image is often presented in direct proportion to the depth of tragedy indicated by the story. The result is not that deeply sorrowful events be presented as glamorous or desirable, but that life is revealed as a journey of ambiguous choice and possibility, with sorrow inevitably attending the journey's end.

Seeking the Spiritual Core of the Tale

The presentation of *awful beauty* in the imagery of fanartists and cosplayers suggests movement away from romantic or dualistic paradigms about the world to more philosophical understandings (Egan, 1997) and thoughtful, compassionate ways of making meaning of life events. Indeed, several theorists of participatory engagements with popular culture suggest fans may be seeking and responding to some spiritual undercurrent or subtext to stories (Hills, 2002; Jenkins, 2006; Levi, 1998). "There is a spiritual relationship to a text or a spiritual relationship to a character, and there are spiritual truths revealed to them," writes cultural theorist Jenkins (2006, p. 21).

The most dearly embraced popular texts "articulate a set of ethical or moral values through stories and people are deeply invested in those stories. They retell them, they circulate them, they see them as revealing some deeper truth about human experience" (p. 17) which is common to people across cultures. Sharing these stories across cultures may bind diverse peoples together in communities with common beliefs regarding tolerance and caring for the Other as urged by specific storied messages.

Revisiting the Conceptual Model

Up to this point the findings of this study align with the framework laid out at the beginning of this chapter. Adolescent and young adult fanartists and cosplayers, who were observed or who responded to the survey, acknowledged they were drawn to stories that supported or assisted the construction of desired or desirable self-identities. Interactions with other fans around the world reinforced those self-images and permitted youth to transcend their provincial cultural or national identities. This resulted in the formation of communities of like-interested fanartists and cosplayers, whose interactions formed loose webs that circumvented the globe. Members of fan communities or fandom came to share similar feelings and emotional responses to core values, ethics, and morals inherent in the messages of their favorite stories. Real cultural and nationally differences were pushed aside or transformed into elements of individual fans' personal styles.

Furthermore, these youth described creation of art based on beloved narratives and their interactions with other fanartists and cosplayers within a fandom as deeply pleasurable and self-fulfilling activities. The experiences allowed some youth to 'make sense of the world,' 'put life in order,' or 'balance life.' Others indicated profoundly personal and intrinsically self-satisfying reasons for enjoying fan-based art making. Nearly all the fanartists and cosplayers (98%) reported that they hoped or expected to continue creating art for their own pleasure and in response to their fan interests well into their adult lives. In this regard, descriptions of benefits of creating and sharing fanart and cosplay suggest these activities engage the senses and emotions in a kind of flow (Csikszentmihalyi, 1991) that is intrinsically satisfying but might not otherwise be experienced in the respondents' everyday lives.

Escaping to a Parallel Culture

Yet, there also was evidence that fanartists and cosplayers might become too enamored with pleasures of fantasy play. Nearly 70% of these youth admitted that fanart making and cosplay activities were satisfying because they presented opportunities for escape from the realities of life. Patrick wrote, for example,

> I've had the same crumby job since high school. I can't afford to go to college so I can get a better job. But I can go home at night, whip up a piece of fanart and post it on the web. I'm famous on the web. I can escape to a place where I'm important. (Patrick, personal correspondence, May 13, 2006)

Whereas fans may feel that they can act effectively and with empowerment at fan conventions and within virtual environments of online fandom, the real world may be perceived as a place where they have little agency for change. As such, fanart and cosplay activities that engage and satisfy youth emotionally and intellectually may permit fan youth to disassociate or disengage from the circumstances of their real—albeit sometimes difficult or unpleasant—lives. Contrary to Giddens' notion that collective actions of individuals affect structural changes in the larger society, these findings suggest that fan youth may be creating parallel cultures that satisfy needs for belonging to a community of others who share profound beliefs about universal truths; yet, these youth may see themselves as existing outside or disconnected from their own real cultural or national communities. Fanartists and cosplayers potentially may become so satisfied by images of themselves as competent agents within their fan communities as to eschew active roles in their real world communities.

Implications for Art Education

While a rich fantasy life is characteristic of the healthy mind (Maslow, 1962/1998), escapism into fantasy worlds suggests lack of integration of self into society. By escaping into imagination worlds, fan youth deprive the real world of their individual and collective creative energies, which are necessary to effecting change in society. Finding ways to help students bridge disconnects between competent self within the realm of imagination and competence of self in a real world may be the onus of 21st-century art education.

Alvermann, Moon, and Hagood (1999), suggest an aggregate approach to engaging students with issues of popular narratives. The approach would "recognize popular culture as a real authentic and influencing part of students lives" and acknowledge "the expertise that [fan] students bring to the learning environment, the pleasures that popular culture produce for students, and the multiple readings that students produce from popular culture" (p. 28). Art teachers could invite classroom discussions about the many archetypical ways of being and interacting with others in community that popular narratives provide, encourage individual and collaborative art making based on these themes, and guide students to consider how messages of popular narrative present possible models for solving real problems in a real world. Also, because many fanartists and cosplayers seem drawn to consider the deeply spiritual aspects of popular stories, these moralistic messages may provide gist for classroom discussions. Such discussions might engage all students to consider potentials for stories and images that shape them individually, culturally, nationally, and globally, and assist them in integrating powerful agency in fantasy worlds with competent actions in real local and global communities.

REFERENCES

Alvermann, D. E.; Moon, J. S.; Hagwood, M. C. (1999). *Popular culture in the classroom: Teaching and researching critical media literacy.* Newark, DE: International Reading Association.

Bakadesu. (2003). Racism and Xenophobia in Media and Society. *AnimeWebTurnpike.* Available online at: http://forum.anipike.com/showthread.php?t=6639.

Banks, J.; & Banks, C. A. (2006). *Multicultural education: Issues and perspectives* (6th ed.). San Francisco: Jossey-Bass.

Bettelheim, B. (1976). *The uses of enchantment.* New York: Knopf.

Campbell, J. (1949/1972). *The hero with a thousand faces.* Princeton, NJ: Princeton University Press.

Csikszentmihalyi, M. (1991). *Flow: The psychology of optimal experience.* New York: Harper Perennial.

Denton, J. (2000) *Orders and hierarchies in late medieval Europe.* Toronto: University of Toronto Press.

Egan, K. (1997). *The educated mind: how cognitive tools shape our understanding.* Chicago: Chicago University Press.

Epstein, E. J. (2005). *The big picture: The new logic of money and power in Hollywood.* New York: Random House.

Erickson, E. H. (1950/1993). *Childhood and society.* New York: W. W. Norton.

Fiske, J. (1989). *Understanding popular culture.* London: Unwin Hyman.

Freedman, K.; & Stuhr, P. (2004). Curriculum change for the 21st century: Visual culture in art education. In E. Eisner and M. Day (Eds.), *Handbook of research and policy in art education* (pp. 815-828). Mahwah, NJ: Erlbaum Associates.

Gauntlett, D. (2002). *Media, gender, and identity: An introduction.* New York: Routledge.

Giddens, A. (1991). *Modernity and self-identity: Self and society in the late Modern Age.* Cambridge: Polity.

Goffman, E. (1959). *The presentation of self in everyday life.* London, Penguin.

Hills, M. (2002). *Fan cultures.* New York: Routledge.

Jenkins, H. (1992). *Textual poachers. Television fans and participatory culture.* New York: Routledge.

Jenkins, H. (2006). *Fans, bloggers, and gamers: Exploring participatory culture.*

Jenkins, H. (2007). *The wow climax: tracing the emotional impact of popular culture.* New York: New York University Press.

Levi, A. (1998). *Samurai from outer space: Understanding Japanese animation.* Chicago: Open Court.

Manifold, M. C. (2005) Life as theater-theater as life: Spontaneous expressions of Information-Age youth. *Journal of Cultural Research in Art Education, 23.* 1-16.

Maslow, A. H. (1962/1998). *Toward a psychology of being* (3rd ed.). Indianapolis, IN: Wiley.

Sennett, R. (1974). *The fall of public man.* New York: W. W. Norton and Company.

Sennett, R. (1994). *Flesh and stone: The body and the city in Western Civilization.* New York: W. W. Norton and Company.

Thompson, C. M. (2003). Kinderculture in the art classroom: early childhood art and the mediation of culture. *Studies in Art Education, 44*(2), 135-146.

Wilson, B. (1974). The superheroes of J. C. Holz: Plus an outline of a theory of child art. *Art Education, 27*(4). 2-9.

Winner, E. (1985). *Invented worlds: Psychology of the arts.* Cambridge, MA: Harvard University Press.

ENDNOTES

1. These were AnimeExpo (Anaheim, CA), Comic-Con International, (San Diego, CA), The Witching Hour (Salem, MA), Phoenix Rising (New Orleans), and Animé Expo (Tainan, Taiwan).

2. These were Cosplay.com (http://www.cosplay.com/), deviantArt.com (http://www.deviantart.com/), Elfwood (http://elfwood.lysator.liu.se/elfwood.html), Leakey Cauldron (http://www.the-leaky-cauldron.org/fanart/), Epilogue, http://www.epilogue.net/index.php, and Fan Art Central (http://www.fanart-central.net/).

3. Available at: http://www.deviantart.com/

4. Available at: http://elfwood.lysator.liu.se/elfwood.html

5. Available at: http://www.cosplay.com/

6. See http://www.elfwood.com/art/j/i/jialing/wayangkulit.jpg.html

7. *Smallville*, Episode #29, "Ryan", written by Phillip Levens.

Glocal New Femininity in Mediascape: Korean Teenage Girls' Popular Cultural Practices

Michelle S. Bae

This chapter explores how a teenage Korean girl's image production (re)creates an ideal of Korean ethnic femininity through Korean popular cultural experiences. In the face of global media culture, this process constitutes a complex and contradictory resistance against U.S. cultural imperialism. After briefly sketching Korean popular culture, an emerging periphery power that is challenging U.S. media dominance in the global cultural field, I explain how Korean popular culture is producing a new construct of Korean ethnic femininity, a mélange of contemporary notions of feminism and traditional Korean views about femininity. I then illustrate this dynamic using a case study of a Korean teenage girl's image production as a (re)play of her Korean ethnic femininity as informed by Korean popular cultural experiences that resists U.S. cultural homogenization. This exploration takes a dialectic approach based on the interplay between how this girl's image production is shaped and informed by ideology, and how ideology necessitates that girls seek and utilize useful information selectively in order to both blend into the dominant culture and express their own individualities

Hanryu (Korean Wave): The Dynamics of Korean Teenage Girls' Cultural Practices

South Korean popular culture is a dynamic arena in which contemporary Korean girls actively participate in both consumption and production. Since the late 1990s, emergent South Korean popular culture has been known as *hanryu*, the *Korean Wave* (Kim, 2000; Park, 2006; Yi, 2003; Yu, Chung, Kim, & Chung, 2005). This movement provides Korean girls with both a sense of cultural pride and power and an opportunity to maintain and reproduce their own particular meanings about Korean ethnic femininity through image consumption and creation. These girls' dynamic practices in the *hanryu* movement epitomize Korean's active participation in local cultural production that is in competition with dominant U.S. popular cultural

productions.[1] How then has *hanryu* been viewed in the context of globalization? And how has *hanryu* motivated Korean girls to participate in the movement as a personal endeavor that suggests their emerging agency as creators of their own identitites?

Hanryu has greatly influenced East and South Asia since the late 1990s. *Hanryu* began with Korean melodrama and popular music, which brought about Asian consumers' unprecedented craze for Korean culture, and it has now expanded to include various cultural productions, such as movies, music videos, TV programs, fashion, food, accessories, and mobile phones. This phenomenon, by sharing desires and cultural motifs has created a new cultural meaning that crosses the boundaries of culture, geography, and politics in Asia. Simultaneously, its increasing local productivity and economic growth have challenged the unidirectional cultural flow from the U.S. to Asia. According to Park (2006), *hanryu*'s popularity and success, and the easy acceptance of Korean popular culture by other Asians.[2] is an outcome of emotional and "cultural proximity" (p. 253) that comes from sharing meanings within a Confucian cultural tradition. Other aspects of *hanryu*'s success, Park suggests, are the sophistication of its products and its depiction of luxurious modern lifestyles and stylish fashions. Hence, even though the movement retains Western consumerist cultural meanings, it also invokes traditional Confucian elements which revive Asian peoples' nostalgic sentiments and desires. These elements refer to proper social behaviors in relation to authorities, the elderly, parents, and spouse, all with a strong sense of duty. They include filial piety, loyalty, and individual development to achieve social harmony. Such contradictory qualities of hanryu result from its resistance to global homogenization by maintaining and recreating the local cultural identities.

Such a phenomenon challenges the view of globalization that sees it as cultural homogenization. Most scholars writing from the perspective of cultural homogenization believe that the US is the center of cultural hegemony and that globalization equates with Americanization. They have argued for the impact of American cultural imperialism on local populations (Beck, 1992; 2000, Hamelink, 1983, James, 1993). However, this view regards the local people as "passive consumers of the cultural meanings which supposedly flow directly and straight-forwardly from the commodities they consume" (Storey, 2003, p. 155).

The assumption that indigenous people are victimized and destroyed by American capitalism is contradicted by *hanryu,* understood as a local response to U.S. cultural hegemony. Such an alternative discourse defies the idea of the US as the center of cultural power and its influence on the rest of the world (Huntington, 1993; Classen & Howes, 1996; Lash & Urry, 1987; Tomlinson, 1991). A counterdis-course claims that there are many emerging centers of cultural power in other parts of the world, particularly in Southeast Asia, in which the emergence of localized economic, technological, and cultural powers contra-dict the previous notions of U.S. cultural superiority in the world. This indicates a countercultural flow with resulting changes in power relations because of national and regional efforts to maintain and reproduce cultures and identities (Held, Mcgrew, Goldblatt, & Perraton, 1999). From this perspective, the South Korean popular cultural practices of *hanryu* represent such a countercultural flow (Cho-Han, 2002; Park, 2006) that opens a new way of crossing boundaries between center and periphery, the center as U.S. culture and the rest of the world as peripheral.

In the landscape of *hanryu,* Korean girls have a great potential as local cultural producers that con-tinuously accommodate, negotiate, and resist the meanings of femininity in popular culture. These girls are not necessarily pursuing so-called authentic ethnicity. Rather they appear to be seeking to integrate their own ethnic values with dominant U.S. cultural ideas to produce an alternative ethnic femininity. For example, in their process of image production, elements that superficially appear to be mere copies of Korean popular culture actually constitute acts of exploration of imagined ethnic femininities that resist U.S. cultural hegemony. Their resistance lies in recreating an ethnic femininity. How then is that ethnic femininity portrayed in South Korean popular culture, and what social contexts contribute to how it is created? Answering such questions first requires a better understanding of the cultural arena in which Korean girls engage, along with insights into the connection between their viewing and production.

The Korean Wave and a New Ethnic Femininity

Since the late 1990s, in an unprecedented move, contemporary Korean popular media has begun to proliferate alternative femininities as an adaptation to the times. Motivated by the national catchphrase *han-kuk-eul se-gae-hwa-ro* (Korea to the global-ized world), South Korean popular culture has been formed "in the ebb and flow of both homogenizing and heterogenizing forces" (Storey, 2003, p. 158) that are both global and local. In 1997, particularly, South Korea faced a devastating economic crisis that required IMF (International Monetary Fund) restructuring of the economy (Cho-Han, 2002; Yi, 2003) and brought an enormous number of layoffs and social unrest. The economic crisis called for a construct of women as strong and powerful figures. Yet at the same time, the globalization suggested that Korean girls should pursue a high quality of life including a cosmopolitan lifestyle. Both influences propelled Korean women to pursue a better education and a profession. In this context, contemporary Korean popular culture produced an alternative portrayal of femininity as an unavoidable commercial strategy. Since then, both globalization and the economic crisis have greatly impacted the content of South Korean melodramas and films and the portrayal of femininity in these media forms.

The dominant image in the newly created ideal of Korean femininity is the capable woman with economic power who still adheres to a traditional view of femininity that is obedient and chaste (Kim, 2000). This portrayal of power femininity oscil-lates ambiguously between the traditional notions of Korean femininity and contemporary ideas about feminism without hinting at any contradiction. Many feminist scholars have viewed this ambiguity between traditional femininity and contemporary feminism as a condensed form of postfeminism that signifies recognition of a new kind of femininity (Brooks, 1997; Lazar, 2006; McRobbie, 2006). Brooks (1997) views much of the discourse about feminism as essentialist, self-evident, and hence outmoded. While some femi-nists (mostly second wave feminists) criticize the ambiguous and multifaceted quality of postfeminism as the silencing of feminism or the absence of any feminist political content or purpose, she interprets it as potentially subversive to the binary concept of femininity and feminism.

Such postfeminist attributes are illuminated in Korean popular culture. Korean popular culture takes qualities like sassiness, assertiveness, independence, and self-determination as signifiers of contemporary feminism, to which women's professional success adds significant meaning. These qualities are apparent in emergent[3] representations of young women in the Korean media, images that may indicate young women's empowerment. However, one residual[4] aspect remains in a form of hyperfemininity, which is attributable to traditional notions of Korean femininity, which has historically been influenced by Confucian traditions and is overromanticized by the media as chaste, pure, obedient, and strictly heterosexual. Such residual femininity caters to nostalgic sentiments for traditional female roles and relations in which the Korean female is frequently the object of male desire. These two different qualities of femininity, together with young Korean women's sophisticated contemporary urban life styles and appearance, weaken the boundaries between contemporary feminism and traditional views about femininity.

Such a contemporary blended notion of Korean femininity has been vividly portrayed in some melodramas and films—including *Full House, My Sassy Girl, Paris Lover, Love in Harvard, Good bye Solo,* and *A Fantastic Couple*—in which empowered, bold, and independent girl heroines exemplify the modern sophisticated young woman but at the same time adhere to traditional feminine qualities like purity and chastity. The active feisty representations appearing in such productions both define girl power and coexist with images of innocent and pure girls who are still the objects of male desire. It should also be noted that innocence here refers not only to the girls' appearance but also to the idea of their uncontaminated mindset, sexuality, and moral sense, a traditional Korean value of femininity that is intricately merged with the politics of postfeminism as a component that elevates girl heroines to empowered subjects. In fact, most Korean melodramas and films highlight the way that lively girl heroines fall back on a more conventional feminine script of romance. For example, in the melodrama *Coffee House,* a young heroine whose behavior and identity initially appear gender neutral, on falling in love with a young man gradually transforms into a being who fits the traditional romantic model. Thus, Korean popular media perpetuate this romanticized innocence of femininity and romance as the ideal.

This new femininity in contemporary Korean melodramas and films also challenges the distinction between modern and traditional femininity. For instance, Griffin (2004) disputed the conception that the modern girl is associated with an Anglo-Western context, while traditional femininity is tied to non-Western contexts, a view that serves to marginalize young women of other races and cultures. Rather, the ambiguity of new femininity in Korean melodramas and films provides evidence of a loosened distinction between the modern and the traditional that disrupts racialization and possibilities to diversify women's roles and lives. In line with the trend in global media—the convergence of contradictory modes between femininity and feminism—South Korean popular media has recreated a unique power femininity based on Korean social demands. Whereas U.S. media largely emphasizes women's sexuality as the empowerment of young women, the Korean media accentuates young women's purity and innocence in an intricate blend with independent sassiness as the empowerment of young women. Hence, what I will call the new Korean femininity in Korean popular culture subverts the normal Western version of feminism by preserving a traditional form of ethnic femininity. This term, coined especially for this study, infuses feminism into traditional Korean femininity. I developed it based on other postfeminist scholars' frequent use of the term *new femininity*, which refers to a representation and lived experience of femininity that is changing in a contemporary cultural context marked by unprecedented globalization and the hegemony of neoliberal forms of governance. This *new Korean femininity* also takes on the essence of postfeminism; however, although based on postfeminism, which centers on the West, the new Korean femininity references Asian ethnic sentiments in the postfeminist framework examined here.

To examine this idea of contemporary ethnic femininity in a Korean context, the next section reports the results of a pilot study that scrutinized one Korean girl's production of images and related narratives, which can be viewed as a local cultural production of Korean femininity. These findings indicate that the recreation of such femininity could represent a form of cultural resistance to Western indigenization.

The (Re)creation of an Ethnic Femininity as Resistance against both U.S. Cultural Homogenization and Traditional Korean Femininity: A Case Study

Korean melodramas, films, and popular songs offer Korean girls the opportunity to maintain and reproduce meanings associated with Korean ethnic-specific gender identities. Such image making, contained within and informed by Korean popular culture, leads to the (re)creation of a Korean ethnic femininity that is complex, contradictory, and fluid. However, such image creation is not merely a replica of these girl's lives and identities or a confessional depiction

Figure 1

Kyuri, Untitled, March 2004, digital image in Photoshop.

여우별

상처받는 일에 익숙해졌어.
헤메더라도 난 나인채로 좋아...

as I am; my mind wanders, though." This statement implies an emotional idealism, an ironic blend between endurance and pain that is complexly juxtaposed with the girl's acceptance of who she is. Such a contradictory message equates to the essence of postfeminism in that it points to the girl's empowerment in the tangle of feminism and traditional ethnic femininity. Thus, although a description of the emotional modes helps readers better understand how the meanings are embedded, these opposing modes are actually blended almost unnoticeably.

Regarding traditional ethnic femininity in Korean culture generally, women are expected to remain calm in a heterosexual relation even when their emotions are stirred; keeping emotion private is a socially learned behavior for Korean women. From this perspective, this girl's silent endurance of the pain caused by male rejection is an ideal virtue of the strong woman, one that symbolizes maturity. The tear-stained face also signifies an ethnic femininity that is tightly associated with emotional fragility—Korean tradition accepts women as fragile or delicate but not expressive of anger. Thus, tears belong to the woman, not the man. However, ironically, the image mixes the tear with a smile and the comment "I like myself" to boost the girl's ego and make her feel better. This strategy not only implies a feminist response that fights back against male oppression but points to a subtle conjunction of feminism and traditional ethnic femininity.

Such a new ethnic femininity is projected in a self-disciplinary script in which self-appreciation is a strategy for overcoming a broken heart. That is, the girl (re)creates self-appreciation as a cultural code in reaction to and as a struggle against the male partner. Not only does such a ploy suggest liberation from the male power but, in a feminist sense, the self-appreciation leads to a new ethnic femininity. Kyuri explained that "a girl should not show a guy sad emotion although she has pain from a guy. Instead, if I were her, I would smile at or be angry with him and show that I am OK with it." Such a comment clearly indicates a reversal of traditional ethnic femininity.

Another image created by Kyuri (Figure 2) differs from the previous one in that it is more pervaded by the ideology of traditional Korean femininity. The image shows a young woman who is not looking back at her male partner as he retreats into the distance, an image completed by the caption, "After the break-up, do not look at his back, because you may not see him any more [i.e., it could be the last meeting]." Therefore, although the man has left, the image implies the girl's longing for him. However, Kyuri tried to beautify

of their minds, but rather a playful performance that (re)creates imagined realities and identities. This case study illuminates how the construct of contemporary Korean ethnic femininity is revealed in one girl's cultural productions.

The girl studied, Kyuri, [Pseudonym used for the purpose of anonymity] was 15 years old at the time of study and an ardent fan of a famous teenage Korean girl singer named BoA, whose widespread fame across Asia has gained her recognition as a *hanryu* star. Kyuri admired BoA not simply for her appearance, songs, and dance, but also for her professional success at an early age (the same age as Kyuri). Most particularly, Kyuri greatly respected BoA's enormous efforts and devotion to becoming a distinguished entertainer, and she avidly collected BoA's albums, commercial images, and music videos. This consumption motivated Kyuri's image production: she drew on this collection to (re) create images for fun during her leisure time.

Whereas Kyuri's first image (Figure 1), a single tear trailing down BoA's smiling half face, suggested ambivalent emotions and attitudes, the poetic statement written below, translated, explained the context as follows: "I got used to being hurt. But I like myself

the separation in an over-romanticized manner and, when asked what she would do if a boyfriend left her, she responded, "I would not look at his back, because my ego would be hurt. I would not wait for his return, not like the image portrays. I would not let him claim to break up first." Hence, even though she had not yet experienced a break-up in her life, she had created this imagined reality to explore a real-life experience that had not yet happened but was possible. Moreover, as her unyielding response indicated, her image creation did not necessarily correspond to what she was currently experiencing in the real world. Such contradiction indirectly suggests that her appropriation of images is a play in which she can explore and perform different identities (Bloustein, 2003).

As the two images indicate, her productions commonly portray a young Korean woman's desperate romantic yearning for her heterosexual partner. However, her (re)creation of over-romanticized heterosexual images and content also reflect multilayered meanings of contemporary femininity. For example, on one level, her images—informed by the traditional romantic Korean ethnic femininity—do not mean that she has uncritically absorbed the message of Korean popular culture. Rather, her production must be understood as the imagined role play of Korean ethnic-specific gender through which she can also explore and critique this message. In other words, her playful image making of Korean ethnic femininity offers her an arena for feminist critique, one in which she resists ideas of male-dominated romance. Not only does her image play with the notion of Korean ethnic femininity, her self-placement helps her determine what she must do to deal with femininity: it provides her with a chance consciously to reflect what aspects of femininity inspire her resistance or accommodation. In this way, she has the freedom to traverse the boundaries between contemporary feminism and the traditional notion of Korean femininity.

Such a strategy can be viewed as a "conformity mode of resistance" (Driscoll, 2002), a term that

Driscoll applied to Currie's (1999) idea of selective, purposeful interpretation, which, rather than being a simple act of assimilation into the dominant hegemonic structure, is instead a strategy for coping with the reality on a conscious level. Kyuri's appropriation of a new ethnic femininity in Korean popular culture exemplifies how ideology requires girls to seek useful information from the dominant culture in order to appropriate their realities. That is, because their selective reading indicates partial conformity to the dominant hegemonic force in which resistance is embedded, Kyuri's appropriation of certain traditional aspects in her search for a femininity that fits her reality can be viewed as a method of resistance to traditional Korean ethnic femininity.

On another level, while traditional Korean ethnic femininity is seen as something to resist in the Korean context, in the global context it also serves as an essence of local culture that challenges U.S. cultural hegemony. From this perspective, this girl's appropriation of traditional Korean ethnic femininity can represent a local response to U.S. cultural homogenization, one of maintaining and recreating a distinctive ethnic femininity amidst Western idealizations of the feminine. Thus, the appropriation of traditional Korean ethnic femininity is a counter hegemonic tool employed in search of past continuities attributed to the local. Hence, this girl's appropriation of traditional Korean ethnic femininity can be equated with nostalgia[5] for the past. Indeed, nostalgia has been used as a contemporary media strategy by which people maintain their local culture (Jameson, 1998) during cultural homogenization. Kyuri's image production illustrates this, in that the image of Korean ethnic femininity is well elaborated and expressed in a sentimental form that arouses nostalgia for the traditional Korean femininity of heterosexual romance, as portrayed in Korean popular media.

However, the nostalgia in Kyuri's image production is a misplaced nostalgia, one in which the origin of the past object or event that evokes nostalgia either does not exist or is outside the context of her actual experience. That is, Kyuri is a member of contemporary generation living at a time when many issues related to the gender inequalities combated by a previous generation of feminists have, to a great extent, already been resolved. As many current feminist scholars have observed, feminist ideas have naturally permeated the minds of the current generation of young women (Harris, 2004; Heywood & Drake, 1997). Therefore, Kyuri's playful desire to go back to the nostalgic past—hinted at in her image production by her portrayal of traditional ethnic femininity—indicates

Figure 2

Kyuri, Untitled, March 2004, digital image in Photoshop.

an alternative resistance that young Korean girls adopt as a countermeasure against U.S. cultural hegemony. Thus, to this girl, traditional Korean ethnic femininity is desirable to experience and represents authenticity. Her recreation of traditional ethnic femininity is an act of rediscovery through contacts with representatives of the past that she has never experienced but can imagine. Given that this nostalgia exists for something she never experienced, it may represent more than a sentimental fascination; it may be an expression of potentially subversive power against U.S. cultural hegemony.

In addition, many current feminist media scholars have claimed that U.S. global media employ postfeminist elements to depoliticize power femininity, thereby producing a global sisterhood of women (Lazar, 2006). However, scholars have questioned the notion of such a sisterhood on the grounds that it eliminates the differences between women of different cultures, ethnicities, and nationalities. These critics argue instead for multiplicity, complexity, and intersectionality (Bhavnani, 2001; Gunew & Yeatman, 1993; Valdivia, 1995). The first, multiplicity, values local qualities and pays attention to traditional ethnic femininity by explaining its intersection with ethnicity, nationality, and race. From this perspective, a Korean girl's adoption of past representations in her cultural production can be construed as counterhegemonic to the politics of global sisterhood. Thus, in spite of its ironic form, Kyri's imagery is intricately bound to both postfeminist ideas of local differences and the ideology of Korean traditional femininity that invites feminist critiques. Overall, Kyuri's cultural productions are a product of playful ethnic-oriented gender practice that leads to engagement in cultural resistance against both Korean national and global media power. This engagement in individual media production manifests her role as an active agent in the construction of her own identity and as a cultural producer who contributes to cultural heterogeneity. Such production supports the countercultural flow within the landscape of globalization.

Art and Media Education: An Afterthought

Feminism has figured prominently in discourse on media culture, power, and identities in the era of globalization. Feminism has acknowledged that each period demands different sets of feminist paradigms and agendas and has engendered an alternative approach that meets the demands of situated places and times, opposed to the universalistic notion of sisterhood (Chakraborty, 2004; Sandoval, 2000). In the belief that each female—being subject to the intersection of class, culture, ethnicity, nationality, and race—responds differently to the media, contemporary feminist media scholars are endeavoring to seek out and illuminate a multiplicity of situated female subjectivities in response to contemporary local and global media. This reception-oriented approach offers significant possibilities for understanding that young women of different cultures, races, and nations are neither empowered nor assimilated by the global media, but rather they (re)create, negotiate, and resist it in their own local contexts.

To date, feminist discourse in art and media education has paid little attention to the contemporary feminist ideas and agendas required in this period of globalization, or to the experiences, production, and education of girls coming of age in diverse contemporary contexts around world. This void calls for an understanding and knowledge that goes beyond that of the Western-centered essentialized paradigm based on young, heterosexual, White, middle-class females' educational experiences, which is remarkably uniform and hierarchical. This realm of understanding and knowledge, the space of heterogeneity, must embrace diverse cultural interpretations of young women, and offer freedom for expression and critique. This is the realm to which feminism and media studies in art education should aspire.

Acknowledgments

I am greatly indebted to Dr. Elizabeth Delacruz, Dr. Michael Parsons, and Dr. Paul Duncum for their encouragement, intellectual insights, and support in the course of my writing.

REFERENCES

Beck, U. (1992). *Risk society: Towards a new modernity*. London: Sage.

Beck, U. (2000). *What is globalization?* Cambridge: Polity.

Bhavnani, K-K. (2001). *Feminism and race*. Oxford: Oxford University Press.

Bloustein, G. (2003). *Girl making: A cross-cultural ethnography on the processes of growing up female*. New York: Berghahn Books.

Brooks, A. (1997) *Postfeminisms: Feminism, cultural theory and cultural forms*. London: Routledge.

Chakraborty, M. N. (2004). Wa(i)ving it all away: Producing subject and knowledge in feminisms in color. In S. Gillis, G. Howie, & R. Mumford (Eds.), *Third wave feminism: A Critical Exploration* (pp. 205-215). New York: Palgrave Macmillan.

Cho-Han, H. (2002). Modernity, popular culture and east-west identity formation: A discourse analysis of Korean Wave in Asia. *Korean Cultural Anthropology*, *35*(1), 3-38.

Classen, C., & Howes, D. (1996). Epilogue: The dynamics and ethics of cross-cultural consumption. In Howes (Ed.), *Cross-cultural consumption: Global markets, local realities* (pp. 178-194). London: Routledge.

Currie, D. H. (1999). *Girl talk: Adolescent magazines and their readers*. Toronto: University of Toronto Press.

Driscoll, C. (2002). *Girls: Feminine adolescence in popular culture and cultural theory*. New York: Colombia University Press.

Griffin, C. (2004). Good girls, bad girls: Anglocentrism and diversity in the constitution of contemporary girlhood. In A. Harris (Ed.), *All about the girl: Culture, power, identity* (pp. 29-44). New York: Routledge.

Gunew, S., & Yeatman, A. (1993). *Feminism and the politics of difference*. Boulder, CO: Westview.

Hamelink, C. J. (1983). *Cultural autonomy in global communication*. London: Longman.

Harris, A. (2004). *Future girl: Young women in the twentiy-first century*. New York: Routledge.

Held, D., Mcgrew, A., Goldblatt, D., and Perraton, J. (1999). *Global transformations: Politics, economics and culture*. Cambridge: Polity.

Heywood, L., & Drake, J. (1997). *Third wave agenda: Being feminist, doing feminism*. Minneapolis, MN: Minnesota University Press.

Huntington, S. (1993). The clash of civilizations. *Foreign Affairs*, *72*(2), 22-49.

James, J. (1993). *Consumption and development*. New York: St. Martins.

Jameson, F. (1998). *The cultural turn: Selected writings on the postmodern, 1983-1998*. London: Verso.

Kim, S-N. (2000). Midioŭ *sok ŭi yŏsŏng ilkki* [*Reading femininity in media*]. Seoul: Ilchinsa.

Lash, S. and Urry, J. (1987). *The end of organrized capitalism*. Cambridge: Polity.

Lazar, M. M. (2006). Discover the power of femininity! Analyzing global "power femininity" in local advertising. *Feminist Media Studies*, *6(4)*, 505-517.

McRobbie (2004). Postfeminism and popular culture. *Feminist Media Studies*, *4*(3), 255-264.

Pack, W–D. (2005). *Hallyu: Tong Asia ŭi munhwa sŏntaek* [*Hanryu: A cultural choice in East Asia*]. Seoul: Pentagŭraem.

Park, J–S. (2006). The Korean wave: Transnational cultural flows in Northeast Asia. In C. A. Armstrong, G. Rozman, S. S. Kim, & S. Kotkin (Eds.), *Korean at the center: Dynamics of regionalism in Northeast Asia* (pp. 244-256). New York: M. E. Sharpe.

Sandoval, C. (2000). *Methodology of the oppressed*. Minneapolis, MN: University of Minnesota Press.

Storey, J. (2003). *Cultural studies and the study of popular culture*. Athens, GA: University of Georgia Press.

Tomlinson, J. (1991). *Cultural imperialism: A critical introduction*. Baltimore, MD: The Johns Hopkins University Press.

Valdivia, A. N. (1995). *Feminism, multiculturalism, and the media: Global diversities*. Thousand Oaks, CA: Sage.

Williams, R. (1977). *Marxism and literature*. Oxford: Oxford University Press.

Yi, S–Y. (2003). *Hanguk hyŏndae munhwa ŭi ihae* [*The understanding of Korean contemporary culture*]. Seoul: Hyŏnsil Munhwa Yŏngu.

Yu, S., Ahn, H., Chung, H., Kim, J., and Chung, K. (2005). *Hallyu DNA ŭi pimil: sopŭtu pawŏ, sopŭtŭ Koria ŭ hyŏnjang ŭl chajasŏ* [*The secret of hanryu DNA*]. Seoul: Saenggak ŭi Namu.

ENDNOTES

1. U.S. popular cultural productions refer to media products such as megazines, movies, music videos, and TV shows.

2. Other Asians refer particularly to people from Japan China, Taiwan, Thailand, Singapore, Indonesia, and Vietnam.

3. This term is borrowed from Raymond Williams (1977), who defines emergent as new cultural elements opposing or being alternative to dominant culture but at the same time beginning to incorporate to it.

4. This term is also borrowed from Williams (1977), defining residual as cultural elements of the past being still active in the cultural process.

5. According to Fredric Jameson (1998), nostalgia, together with pastiche, is a central feature of late capitalist image production. Specifically, in the postmodern age, it has become the appropriation of the past through stylistic connotation.

Art Education and Cybermedia Spectacles in the Age of Globalization

Sheng Kuan Chung

Globalization, Technologies, and Cybermedia

The availability of new-age communication devices is affording people increasingly diverse and efficient interactions with others across the globe. Not only are technological innovations shaping a global cultural landscape, but they are also driving globalization, playing a key role in transporting and transmitting commodities, services, and information among people in greatly varying geographical locations. Kellner (2000) views globalization as both a vehicle of progress and diversity and a force of homogenization and domination. Globalization involves technological revolution in pursuit of global technocapitalism,[1] which has a tremendous impact on local economies, polities, societies, cultures, education, and individual experiences (Kellner, 2000).

Globalization can be articulated by looking at how the technological revolution is laying down a networked infrastructure that enables systems of global communication, transportation, and exchange of goods, services, and other cultural forms. Kellner (2002) theorized globalization to be a condition resulting from "technological revolution and the global restructuring of capitalism in which economic, technological, political, and cultural features are intertwined" (p. 286). Indeed, technological innovations accelerate the transnational flow of images and capital, which in turn expands the global economy and creates a globalized visual culture in cyberspace in which the aesthetics of the virtual world are in full operation, amalgamating into what I call a globalized dis-location of visual spectacles. A product of global technocapitalism, the visual/media spectacles of cyberspace challenge our understanding of often taken-for-granted engagements with art and instead posits art as a cultural site of continuous contestation, both inter- and intranationally.

With a computer connected to the Internet, children have access to the cybermedia world in which they play virtual computer games, visit multimedia websites, browse adult materials, and construct their own communities in cyberspace. Unsurprisingly, the technologically savvy digital generation is immersing itself in these types of cybermedia activities as its everyday aesthetic sites/sights. The proliferation of visual spectacles in cyberspace is bound to pose new challenges to art education while at the same time heralding the importance of a critical approach to media literacy art education that guides students to examine and confront their immediate, if not controversial, visual spectacles. This chapter articulates the cybermedia as a globalized dis-location of visual spectacles, explores cybergaming and Internet pornography, and highlights their implications for a critical approach to media literacy art education.

Cybermedia as a Globalized Cultural "Dis-location"

Globalization is forcing culture to continuously borrow, restructure, and produce alternative cultural sites and practices. Culture is a floating variable, and a nation's cultural identity, even the dominant one, can never be as homogenous as depicted. This means that globalization is more likely to produce alternative cultural sites than to realize cultural imperialism. In the discourse of cultural imperialism, Tomlinson (1991) maintained that one of its conceptual problems arises from thinking of culture in "an exclusively spatial-synchronic mode" and ignoring the essentially historical nature of culture in process (p. 90). Accordingly, any given culture can never be conceptualized as fixed because it contains traces of foreign borrowings and influences that have then been naturalized and become an integral part of the often taken-for-granted everyday culture. Tomlinson (1999) asserted that a culture that does not change is a dying culture. Globalization not only helps to articulate culture as always mobile, constantly adapting, evolving, and seeking new outside influences and ideas, but more importantly also creates new globalized cultural spaces and locations that are connected, and at the same time disassociated, from one another.

Transnational capitalism has created hybrid cultural technoregions that are replacing geographic borders with technological borders. Kellner (2000) has pointed out that "global cultures permeate local ones and new configurations emerge that synthesize both poles, providing contradictory forces of colonization *and* resistance, global homogenization *and* new local hybrid forms and identities" (italics in original, p. 305). For example, the cybergame environment is such a cultural hybrid technoregion in which Japanese culture continues to dominate and influence the American video game industry (Consalvo, 2006). Transnational conglomerates understand that the key to a successful global business is to overcome local language and cultural barriers and to develop a line of cultural hybrid products to which the local consumer can relate. The cybermediascape manifests an increasingly hybrid globalized culture that challenges our perception of culture as a fixed variable.

Thus, globalization disrupts our typical association of culture with location and affects how we identify ourselves. According to Elteren (1996), globalization produces "simultaneously, new 'global' and new 'local' identifications. In this context the 'local' is defined by reference not to a specific geography or community but rather to a shared sense of place that is, itself, part of the global picture" (p. 58). Thus, an individual can simultaneously belong to the local and the global. In the context of a global society, the notion of locality is no longer an expression of geography-bound places tied to distinctive cultural traditions, but is instead perceived as one's sense of difference from the global (Frith, 1991 as cited in Elteren, 1996). Conceptually, a cultural location need not be situated in a geography-bound community but in fact can exist in the virtual world.

To express it another way, globalization produces what Abbas (1996) termed a "dis-location" of culture, that is, the transformation of place as a symbolic structure with definable physical characteristics into a conceptual space, which is characterized by a dis-location of cultural memories. Globalization presents us with a cognitive dilemma because culture is no longer defined in relation to place and tradition. Unlike the material-based cultural sites, the cybermedia culture exists only in cyberspace or in an imaginative cultural location as a "changing field of tensions and contradictions, where the physical is imbricated and competes with social, political and cultural dimensions" (Abbas, 1994, p. 442). The commodification of aesthetics driven by global technocapitalism is in full operation in cyberspace in the cybermedia arena. Undeniably, the cybermedia world, with its Internet multimedia capacity, provides children with multimedia, sensory-stimulating aesthetic experiences as increasing numbers of them indulge in cybermedia visual spectacles such as computer gaming and sexually explicit images.

Aesthetics of the Hyperreal: Multimedia Computer Gaming

William Gibson coined the term *cyberspace,* inspired by his observation of children playing computer games who seemingly believed there was an actual space behind the computer screen, someplace they knew was there (McCaffery, 1992). Perceived realism is a key factor in enticing children to the video game arena (Wood, Griffiths, Chappell, & Davies, 2004).

Postmodern theorist Baudrillard (1988) views the postmodern world as filled with simulations of realities transmitted through mass media and computer technology. An image on a computer monitor no longer serves as a representation of an object because it replaces the thing it represents and eventually possesses more power than the object itself. The image therefore takes on an "extra" reality, which Baudrillard terms "hyperreality." He argues that what people believe to be real is actually a simulation of the real—in his terminology, a "hyperreal construct"—and describes this situation as "an aesthetics of the hyperreal, a thrill of vertiginous and phony exactitude, a thrill of alienation and magnification, of distortion in scale, of excessive transparency all at the same time" (Baudrillard, 1983, p. 50).

Modern children of technologically rich nations enjoy multimedia computer gaming because such hyperreal experiences fulfill their aesthetic gratifications. Studies have consistently indicated that school-aged children use home computers mostly to play games (Roberts, Foehr, & Rideout, 2005), although boys tend to do so more than girls (Cole & Griffiths, 2007). A recent U.S. study confirmed that 83% of teens have a video game console at home and that 41% play console video games every day. Specifically, 65% have played the explicitly violent *Grand Theft Auto* video game (Roberts, Foehr, & Rideout, 2005). Game preferences based on gender essentially replicate gender stereotypes, that is, boys prefer games that are action based, competitive, and violent, while girls prefer games involving a higher degree of fantasy and make-believe (Wood, Griffiths, Chappell, & Davies, 2004).

Cybergaming is a global phenomenon and has been the subject of social debate because of its sexual and violent imagery. The compulsion to play electronic games varies from seeking entertainment, excitement, and challenge to coping emotionally and escaping from reality. The impact of cybergaming on children has been discussed mostly in terms of the negative psychological effects of violent exposure. For example, Grüsser, Thalemann, and Griffiths (2007) associate game addiction with the key elements of addiction. Generally, game addicts seek relief of dissatisfaction rather than the pursuit of satisfaction. In contrast, some have argued the positive aspects of computer gaming, for instance, the desire to challenge, compete, and accomplish, as well as socializing, discovery, and escapism (Yee, 2006). Moreover, computer gaming enhances problem solving, communication, and team building skills, all of which contribute to a player's psychological well-being (Bessiére, Seay, & Kiesler, 2007).

Cybergaming creates a networked sociality where the social bond is created and based on an informational project-by-project basis of exchanging data (Wittel, 2001). It is also a new form of social networking, and social interaction is the strongest motive for the time spent on cybergaming (Jansz & Tanis, 2007). The anonymity of the online gaming environment allows players to be more themselves without being judged by their physical appearance or characteristics. They can safely discuss sensitive issues that may be difficult to share with family and friends in real life. Most players participate in interactive virtual games as an outlet for making friends (Cole & Griffiths, 2007).

The contribution of cybergaming to one's psychological well-being has also been noted. Online multiplayer role-playing games such as *World of Warcraft* allow players to create a virtual character by choosing its appearance, profession, and personality. Bessiére, Seay, and Kiesler (2007) found that players usually assign more favorable attributes to their virtual characters (the ideal self) than they perceive in their actual selves, especially those with a lower psychological self-image. The anonymity of the game offers players a safe place to escape real-world norms and expectations and to act out virtual roles that embody enhanced versions of their real-life self. According to the authors, enacting an ideal self may reduce discrepancies between the actual self and the ideal self, increase feelings of self-confidence and self-worth, and link to one's physical or psychological well-being.

Additionally, cybergaming is a channel for participating in cultural production both locally and globally. Online game sites such as *The Sims* and *Velvet-Strike* provide a networked social environment in which players have the opportunity to reshape, modify, and recontextualize game modes, contexts, and content in the play arena. In this arena, the game-authoring agency is redistributed from the game creator to the player. This type of interactive and participatory mode of online gaming instantiates player agency by creating new game artifacts, contexts, and meanings that carry tremendous potential for cross-cultural exchange and production, which in turn ensures a constant, vibrant flow within the overall gaming community (Poremba, 2003).

But the virtual game site is also more a site of technocapitalism than of entertainment. Transnational corporations sponsor online game sites as promotional tools to connect their products directly to consumers around the world (Scherer, 2007). Corporate-sponsored online games not only engage consumers in interactive visual spectacles, but more importantly transform their cyber-experiences into a part of their everyday identities (Scherer, 2007). Online game sites such as *Neopets* allow children to participate in creating and sharing their own cultural artifacts. To engage in the variety of interactive activities these game sites provide, young users must first sign up for a free membership and create a profile disclosing personal information. Corporate-sponsored game sites gather enormous amounts of personal data on consumer habits, preferences, and online activities. Media surveillance such as data mining is pervasive in children's online game sites, playing a considerable role in developing and marketing children's products.

Aesthetics of the Forbidden: Internet Pornography

Unlike the institutionalized art world protected by security guards, access to the cybervisual world, including the forbidden, is effortless, being just a computer mouse-click away. According to Buckingham and Bragg (2004), the public display of naked human bodies in the art institution is mediated by its presentation as art and supported by a philosophy of beauty, nature, and purity that justifies such display. In contrast, the display of human nudity in the popular media is generally regarded as sexually charged material. This discursive distinction is becoming more difficult to sustain in the postmodern art arena where artists have blurred such distinctions by appropriating pop culture and using pornographic images in their work. Sexualized images are increasingly prevalent in cyberspace and can be easily brought up on any Web search engine. The Internet is becoming a notorious channel for pornography exposure and child sexual solicitation (Lo & Wei, 2005).

In the past the adult industry remained underground and was prohibited by law in many nation states. How pornography has become an everyday aesthetic site for youngsters is too controversial an issue for most educators to tackle. Images of sexually explicit human bodies now permeate cyberspace through various channels such as Web sites, unsolicited e-mail, Web cameras, and chat rooms. It is estimated that 70% of American children have viewed Internet pornography (The Henry J. Kaiser Family Foundation, 2001). Ybarra and Mitchell (2005) believe that the behavior of most youth who seek out pornography is simply a matter of age-appropriate curiosity about sex. They argue that the increase in children's sense of a sexual self is driven by interplay of biological changes and social experiences as they get older. Expression of sexual curiosity can range from talking about sex and looking at sexual materials to actually engaging in sexual activity. Recent studies have reported that technology-savvy boys are more likely to seek cyberporn while girls see it mostly by accident (Cameron, Salazar, Bernhardt, Burgess-Whitman, Wingood, & DiClemente, 2005). A U.S. national survey revealed that one in four of American youth reported an unwanted exposure to sexual material (Ybarra & Mitchell, 2005). Alarmingly, 31% of children have pretended to be older to get into an adult website (Roberts, Foehr, & Rideout, 2005).

While no study has been able to prove a link between pornography exposure and psychosocial effects or the influence of pornography exposure on sexual attitudes and behavior, Lo and Wei (2005) correlated pornography exposure with greater acceptance of sexual permissiveness and therefore a greater likelihood of engaging in sexually permissive behavior. Pornography may serve as a source of knowledge or teach children a distorted picture of sexuality. Children learn about human sexuality by observing what is depicted in pornography. Pornography may encourage adolescents to have sex earlier or develop recreational attitudes toward sex (Peter & Valkenburg, 2006). Moreover, most pornographic scenarios perpetuate and reinforce gender stereotypes that subject women to a subordinate role.

Additionally, Internet-based interaction with strangers can lead to transmitting sexually explicit material and further to face-to-face contact. Near 30% of teens contacted online by a complete stranger respond to find out more about the stranger (Lenhart & Madden, 2007). Moreover, one in four online American adolescents uses social networking sites to make friends, and most of these users post photos to their personal profiles such as on MySpace and Facebook.

Alarmingly, teens publicize actual personal information about themselves in their profiles, including their name, school, town, e-mail address, and even cell phone numbers.

This controversy over sex and violence in cybermedia has triggered calls for greater parental control, censorship, and surveillance. Two-thirds of American parents regulate the kinds of Internet sites and video games their children can access (Macgill, 2007). In 1998, the U.S. Congress requested the National Research Council to study tools and strategies for protecting children from pornography (Thornburgh & Lin, 2002). It recommended several protectionist initiatives based on law, technology, and education to eliminate inappropriate online materials. The recommendations include the initiation of public policy, media campaigns, adult supervision, and Internet safety education.

The perception of children as victims of the media is apparent in the recommendations of the National Research Council. Overwhelmingly, most technologically rich societies uphold protectionist approaches and attitudes toward Internet pornography by closely supervising children to avoid such exposure or by using a technological or religious approach. But a protectionist approach to censoring adult materials raises many serious questions about its effectiveness in protecting the media-savvy digital generation.

Implications for Art Education

Globalization has created a new terrain of aesthetic consumption that calls for rethinking art education theory and praxis in order to unravel the interconnected nexus of contemporary life, visual culture, and education. Art education must recognize the economy-dominated global forces, the new technologies, and the new location of global visual culture, and in response develop new pedagogies to advance "the project of human liberation and well-being" (Kellner, 2000, p. 317).

Globalization raises public anxieties concerning national identity, language, cultural traditions, and media consumption, and children are often the target of these anxieties. Cybermedia censorship is an expression of these anxieties that projects children as powerless victims incapable of shaping their own fate and speaking in their own defense (Jenkins, 1997). Most advanced societies uphold the myth of "childhood innocence" and deploy censorship to preserve the purity of the child. Jenkins (1997) maintained that such myths "empty children of any thoughts of their own, stripping them of their own political agency and social agendas so that they may become vehicles for adult needs, desires and politics" (p. 31). The innocent child is a universalized child existing outside the real-world conflicts of race, class, gender, and sexuality (Rose, 1984). This notion of childhood innocence, Jenkins further argues, presumes children to be merely passive receptacles, easily seduced by cultural images and in need of adult protection from the harmful. The myth strips children of active agency, of being capable of any thoughts of their own, or of having the ability to decode and process media materials themselves. It projects children as potential victims of the adult world in need of paternalistic protection.

Media protectionism is contradictory to a critical art pedagogy that empowers children and validates them as active participants in the real world. How does education equip children with a critical faculty if it prevents them from analyzing or from exposure to controversial materials in cybermedia? How do educators engage children in critical thought if they deny them access to challenging or provocative images? Protectionist approaches that impose adult moral authority on children are questionable because children do not see themselves as victims of cybermedia programs featuring extreme sex and violence (Cameron et al., 2005). Consequently, children are unlikely to take protectionist approaches and attitudes toward media education seriously (Buckingham, 2000; Chung, 2007). Cybermedia censorship is an attempt to circumscribe the rights of youth to obtain entertainment and information and create their own subcultures (Best & Kellner, 2003). It threatens the very existence of the Internet as a means of creative expression, education, and political discourse. Regulating Internet use is bound to silence youth from analyzing controversial information and isolate them from democratic participation in cybersociety. Computer devices that block access to media violence and online sexual material are "more an expression of adult hysteria and moral panic than genuine dangers to youth which certainly exist but much more strikingly in the real world than in the sphere of hyperreality" (Best & Kellner, 2003, p. 11).

Modern children define their cultures in opposition to adult restraints, values, and taste hierarchies (Jenkins, 1997). Specifically, "boy culture" exists in a space away from adult supervision and domestic restraints (Rotundo, 1993). Oftentimes, children are excluded from participating in mainstream media production and politics, whereas cyberspace is a discursive and political location in which they can empower themselves and construct their identities; interfere with, create, and disseminate their own cultural forms; and engage in public discourse and socio-political activism (Best & Kellner, 2003). Cyberspace is where youth can access information, entertainment, interaction, and connection through which they gain valuable skills, knowledge, and the power necessary to survive the postmodern adventure.

To function in a technoeconomy and the rapidly changing cybersociety, children need a critical faculty, media literacy, and technoliteracy to become critical consumers of cyber-aesthetics. All these are essential for them to understand and counter globalization, particularly of corporate domination, and to engage in technopolitics for cultural emancipation and democratization (see Kellner, 2000). Engaging children in technopolitics[2] opens new terrains of political struggle for voices and groups excluded from the mainstream media and thus increases the potential for promoting a democratic and anticapitalist social transformation (Kellner, 2003).

A critical approach to media literacy art education thus positions children as active agents within a global media culture "in the process of deconstructing injustices, expressing their own voices, and struggling to create a better society" (Kellner & Share, 2005, p. 382). This approach validates and utilizes children's existing knowledge and skills as media users by further empowering them to critically reflect upon their everyday aesthetic experiences and cultural consumption. Children need to think critically about the pleasures and politics of visual spectacles in cybermedia and analyze how these visual spectacles are created, shaped, and embedded with specific values and points of view. To reach this end, an unpoliced area of popular culture is necessary for children to learn to think for themselves, develop autonomy from their caretakers, and participate in political discourse/activism within cybersociety (Jenkins, 1997). The transnational imagery in cyberspace can serve as a site of inquiry where educational participants collectively investigate its cultural/political meanings, struggle with dominant discourses, and create alternative readings to make sense of their everyday visual surroundings. Critical media literary art education teaches children to appreciate the aesthetic qualities of media, critically negotiate meanings and analyze media culture as products of social struggle, engage with the problems of visual representation and misrepresentation, and use media technologies as instruments for creative expression and social activism (Kellner & Share, 2005).

Conclusion

Globalization facilitated by technological revolution is drastically changing a socioeconomy into a global platform of technocapitalism (Kellner, 2003). Sociologically, globalization is transforming the sovereignty of nation states into boundary-crossing cultural arenas. The social that used to deliver action tied to place and tradition is being displaced by the cultural, where digitalized products, services, and ideas circulate freely in the global mediascape.

As culture continues to evolve and transform, a reconceptualization of art education is needed for meaningful practice. Art educators should not ignore the fact that global capitalism has created transnational technoregions within which the cybercultural arena, a globalized cultural dis-location of aesthetic commodification and consumption, is situated. The cybercultural arena is an everyday aesthetic site for the digital generation and an invisible form of pedagogy that teaches children proper and improper behavior, gender roles, values, and knowledge of the world (Kellner & Share, 2005). It is also where 74% of American school-aged children explore the world, entertain themselves, and construct their identities (The Henry J. Kaiser Family Foundation, 2004). As long as cybermedia continues to dominate the life of the digital generation, it is important that art education be one of the educational forces that foster in children a critical faculty to survive in the postmodern world. A critical approach to media literacy art education is thus concerned with cultivating student skills that will enhance democratic participation and cultural emancipation through such projects as critically analyzing and evaluating media content, investigating media effects and uses, challenging dominant values and ideologies, and constructing alternative media (Kellner & Share, 2005).

The cybermedia is a commoditized cultural jungle saturated with pleasurable, if not violent or sexual, visual spectacles. It is thus essential for art education to employ critical pedagogy to engage students in projects of resistance so that they develop a critical understanding of how globalization changes or hybridizes local visual cultures, and how globalizing conditions affect their everyday cultural/aesthetic consumption in the mediascape. Art education must prepare students for the emerging cybersociety, equipping them with the techno-visual and media literacy necessary to process and resist the vast number of value-conflicting visual spectacles, such as Internet games and pornography, in the age of globalization.

REFERENCES

Abbas, A. (1994). Building on disappearance: Hong Kong architecture and the city. *Public Culture, 6*(3), 441-459.

Abbas, A. (1996). Cultural studies in a post-culture. In D. Gaonkar & C. Nelson (Eds.), *Disciplinarity and dissent in cultural studies* (pp. 289–312). New York: Routledge.

Baudrillard, J. (1983). *Simulations.* New York: Semiotext(e).

Baudrillard, J. (1988). Simulacra and simulation. In M. Poster (Ed.), *Selected writing* (pp.166-185). Cambridge, UK: Polit.

Bessiére, K., Seay, A. F., & Kiesler, S. (2007). The ideal elf: Identity exploration in World of Warcraft. *Cyberpsychology & Behavior, 10*(4), 530-535.

Best, S., & Kellner, D. (2003). Contemporary youth and the postmodern adventure. *The Review of Education/Pedagogy/Cultural Studies, 25*(2), 75-93.

Buckingham, D. (2000). *After the death of childhood: Growing up in the age of electronic media.* Cambridge, UK: Polit.

Buckingham, D., & Bragg, S. (2004). *Young people, sex and the media.* New York: Palgrave Macmillan.

Cameron, K., Salazar, L., Bernhardt, J., Burgess-Whitman, N., Wingood, G., & DiClemente, R. (2005). Adolescents' experience with sex on the web: Results from online focus groups. *Journal of Adolescence, 28*(4), 535-540.

Chung, S. K. (2007). An exploration of media violence in a junior high art classroom. *International Journal of Education Through Art, 3*(1), 57-68.

Consalvo, M. (2006). Console video games and global corporations: Creating a hybrid culture. *New Media & Society, 8*(1), 117–137.

Cole, H., & Griffiths, M. (2007). Social interactions in massively multiplayer online role-playing gamers. *CyberPsychology & Behavior, 10*(4), 575-583.

Elteren, M. (1996). Conceptualizing the impact of US popular culture globally. *Journal of Popular Culture, 30*(1), 47-89.

Grüsser, S., Thalemann, R., & Griffiths, M. (2007). Excessive computer game playing: Evidence for addiction and aggression? *CyberPsychology & Behavior, 10*(2), 290-292.

Jansz, J., & Tanis, M. (2007). Appeal of playing online first person shooter games. *CyberPsychology & Behavior, 10*(1), 133-136.

Jenkins, H. (1997). Empowering children in the digital age: Towards a radical media pedagogy. *Radical Teacher, 50*, 30-35.

Kellner, K. (2003). Globalization, technopolitics, and revolution. In J. Foran (Ed.), *The future of revolutions: Rethinking radical change in the age of globalization* (pp. 180-194). London: Zed Books.

Kellner, D. (2000). Globalization and new social movements: Lessons for critical theory and pedagogy. In N. Burbules & C. Torres (Eds.), *Globalization and education: Critical perspectives* (pp. 299-321). New York & London: Routledge.

Kellner, D. (2002). Theorizing globalization. *Sociological Theory, 20*(3), 285-305.

Kellner, D., & Share, J. (2005). Toward critical media literacy: Core concepts, debates, organizations, and policy. *Discourse: Studies in the Cultural Politics of Education, 26*(3), 369-386.

Lenhart, A., & Madden, M. (2007). *Teens, Privacy & Online Social Networks.* Retrieved from Pew Internet & American Life Project: http://www.pewinternet.org/pdfs/PIP_Teens_Privacy_SNS_Report_Final.pdf.

Lo, V.-H., & Wei, R. (2005). Exposure to Internet pornography and Taiwanese adolescents' sexual attitudes and behavior. *Journal of Broadcasting & Electronic Media, 49*(2), 221-237.

Macgill, A. R. (2007). *Parent and teenager Internet use* [Data memo]. Retrieved from Pew Internet & American Life Project: http://www.pewinternet.org/pdfs/PIP_Teen_Parents_data_memo_Oct2007.pdf.

McCaffery, L. (1992). *Storming the reality studio: A casebook of cyberpunk and postmodern fiction.* Druham, NC: Duke University Press.

Peter, J., & Valkenburg, P. M. (2006). Adolescents' exposure to sexually explicit online material and recreational attitudes toward sex. *Journal of Communication, 56*, 639–660.

Poremba, C. (2003). *Patches of Peace: Tiny Signs of Agency in Digital Games.* Retrieved November 7, 2007, from http://www.digra.org/dl/db/05150.24073

Rose, J. (1984). *The case of Peter Pan: The impossibility of children's fiction.* London: Macmillan.

Roberts, D., Foehr, U., & Rideout, V. (2005). *Generation M: Media in the lives of 8-18 year-olds* (Report No.7251). Retrieved from The Henry J. Kaiser Family Foundation: http://www.kff.org/entmedia/upload/Generation-M-Media-in-the-Lives-of-8-18-Year-olds-Report.pdf

Rotundo, E. A. (1993). *American manhood: Transformations in masculinity from the revolution to the modern era.* New York: Basic.

Scherer, J. (2007). Globalization, promotional culture and the production/consumption of online games: Engaging Adidas's 'Beat Rugby' campaign. *New Media & Society, 9*(3), 475–496.

The Henry J. Kaiser Family Foundation. (2001). *Generation RX.com: Teens and young adults surfing the Web for health info.* Retrieved from http://www.kaisernetwork.org/health_cast/uploaded_files/kff121101.pdf

The Henry J. Kaiser Family Foundation. (2004). *Survey snapshot: The digital divide* [Survey snapshot]. Retrieved from http://www.kff.org/entmedia/upload/Survey-Snapshot-The-Digital-Divide.pdf

Thornburgh, D., & Lin, H. (Eds.) (2002). *Youth, pornography, and the Internet.* Washington, D.C.: National Academies Press.

Tomlinson, J. (1999). *Globalization and culture.* Chicago, IL: University of Chicago Press.

Tomlinson, J. (1991). *Cultural imperialism.* London: Pinter Publishers.

Wittel, A. (2001). Toward a network sociality. *Theory, Culture & Society, 18*(6), 51-76.

Wood, R., Griffiths, M., Chappell, D., & Davies, M. (2004). The structural characteristics of video games: A psycho-structural analysis. *Cyberpsychology & Behavior, 7*(1), 1-10.

Ybarra, M., & Mitchell, K. (2005). Exposure to Internet pornography among children and adolescents: A national survey. *Cyberpsychology & Behavior, 8*(5), 473-486.

Yee, N. (2006). Motivations for play in online games. *Cyberpsychology & Behavior, 9*(6), 772-775.

ENDNOTES

1   Kellner (2002) uses the term *technocapitalism* to describe the synthesis of capital and technology or the changes in capitalism brought about by technological revolution.

2   For example, involve students in using media technologies to create digital videos or e-banners that address important social issues, and then have them disseminate their work to cybersocieties such as YouTube and MySpace to raise social awareness.

Facilitating Intercultural Competencies in Cyberspace

Nancy S. Parks

Globalization is transforming society. Some scholars believe that economic practices are at the core of globalization. However, as Tanneeru (2006) and Kellner (2002) point out, globalization involves more than economics. Kellner (2002) argues that "Globalization is a highly complex, contradictory, and thus ambiguous set of institutions and social relations, as well as involving flows of goods, services, ideas, technologies, cultural forms, and people (see Appadurai, 1990)". Included among these complexes of global relations, flows, and economic practices, and of interest to visual artists and educators are contemporary digital mediated experiences, ever present and proliferated in an endless array of electronic communication networks, websites, online games, and virtual communities. The ubiquitous nature of digital mediated experiences in everyday life is now affecting how young people learn about art and culture, both in and out of art classrooms. Online digital media today are part of their everyday life, as they are part of visual culture, multi-culture, and global culture. Understanding the nature of and addressing the globalization of online digital media in contemporary life is now a critical aspect of art education. I argue here that these digitally mediated experiences also provide a means of teaching *interculturality*, and that teaching interculturality is an equally critical aspect of contemporary art education theory and practice in a globalized world.

In part in response to globalization, art education theorists, such as Freedman (2003), Tavin (2003), and Duncum (2001), propose conceptual frameworks for teaching art in a visual culture in a global world. Freedman (2003) identifies a number of concepts that provide a foundation for teaching visual culture. Several of Freedman's principles are particularly appropriate to learning the kinds of intercultural competencies that I consider important in today's world, namely attending to: *meaningful aesthetics*, which requires visual forms to be understood through their context; *social perspectives*, which concern "the educative power of positions and opinions expressed by individuals and social groups through visual forms is a new emphasis in the curriculum" (Freedman, 2003, p. 21); *cultural response*, in that "multicultural, cross-cultural, and intercultural issues concerning the visual character of our social lives and environments are often the critical issues in art and the most important aspects of art to teach" (Freedman, 2003, p. 21); *technological experience*, in that new technologies are transforming what it means to be educated; and *constructive critique*, including understanding that knowledge comes from a range of sources and that "these fragmented, often contradicting, multi-disciplinary, and intercultural references may have more to do with student understanding of a school subject than does curriculum based on a discipline" (Freedman, 2003, p. 22).

New Worlds

As the world becomes increasingly visual and global, and as educators recognize the need for *global and intercultural competencies*, the potential for cyberspace to shape intercultural understanding becomes more prominent in our thinking. *Cyberspace* refers to the whole range of information resources accessed through computer networks (Gibson, 1984). Art educators, such as Gregory (1997) and Stankiewicz (2004), examine the implications of new technologies for art education and recognize that they require new ways of knowing and instruction, and Duncum (2001) likens the Internet to a rhizome, based on the notion of multiplicity and rupture, with many makers and communities where connections start, stop, and restart. New technologies allow for images and visual/aesthetic experiences to be created that are both seductive and contradictory, and it is increasingly apparent that entirely new worlds—alternate realities—are created, inhabited, and maintained in cyberspace. Indeed, throughout history, human beings have been concerned with reproducing reality, and new technologies only further blur the lines between what is real and what isn't real. Understanding the blurring of reality and fakery in human consciousness, Condgon and Blandy (2001) identify four worlds for understanding human experience, and add a fifth, the world of transnational or global experience, "Worlds one through four consist of administrative domains, geo-political limbo lands, communities of color, ex-underdeveloped countries, and conceptual places for indigenous peoples, exiles, immigrants, and deterritorialized people. The Fifth *World* is virtual space, mass media, the U.S. suburbs, art schools, malls, Disneyland, The White House and La Chingada" (p. 245). The Fifth World, in Condgon and Blandy's view, is where the fake and the real collide and this is also where many of today's youth spend their time. Congdon and Blandy urge art educators to "work with students to develop the courage to cross socio-political borders for the purpose of increased understanding, helping them to learn multiple ways of participating in discussions associated with public interest" (p. 276).

In addition, Congdon and Blandy suggest a *Sixth World*, as the space for critique. Their intent is not simply to encourage students to become involved in a search for "good or bad fakes," but to discover "personal and communal authenticity within the multiplicity of images and objects that constitute, converge, and mutate within the Fifth World" (2001, p. 273). The authors propose *critical pedagogy* as a tool to best aid youth in crossing from the Fifth world into the Sixth or *libratory world*. It is in that proposed Sixth World of critical understanding and social interaction that the kinds of intercultural competencies I envision are honed.

Interculturality

As mentioned above, society is increasingly shaped by a transnational flow of ideas, culture, and capital. New technologies not only create new worlds, they also can collapse borders and bring people of all ages, races, genders, and classes together to discuss, interact, and respond to a variety of issues. I refer to understandings resulting from such interactions as *interculturality*. UNESCO (n. d.) describes interculturality in the following way:

> Interculturality is a dynamic concept and refers to evolving relations between cultural groups. It has been defined as 'the existence and equitable interaction of diverse cultures and the possibility of generating shared cultural expressions through dialogue and mutual respect.' Interculturality presupposes multiculturalism and results from 'intercultural' exchange and dialogue on the local, regional, national or international level. (p. 15)

Changing demographics, new technologies, globalization, the Iraq War, and other world events have moved conversations about intercultural understanding to the forefront of public policy, communications, and education. Interculturality includes understanding concepts such as racism, which Holmes Norton (2008) sees as a problem of the international community in the 21st century, rather than just a problem of the 20th century.

Importantly, educational institutions and organizations are now exploring ways to prepare students to develop intercultural competencies. Travel abroad and exchange programs are popular types of experiences that expose young people to new places and face-to-face, cross-cultural contact. Cyberspace offers additional possibilities for facilitation of cross-cultural exchange, intercultural understanding, and bridging cultural differences and today, *intercultural perceptions* are socially constructed by youth through online discussions, social networks, websites, virtual communities, and video games, and it is here, in the interface of education and cyberspace that I make my arguments.

In the discussion that follows, I examine *cyberspace communities* that reflect Freedman's principles for visual culture art education, embody Congdon and Blandy's call for a space for critical pedagogy, and at the same time provide for the development of *intercultural competencies*. I look at two specific Web-based communities to provide some insight into their unique character, engagement of state-of-the-art digital media, breadth, and goals: 100 People: A World Portrait,® and Global Kids.® Both of these cyber-communities exemplify Blandy and Congdon's libratory Sixth World and they rely on and reflect Freedman's foundational principles for visual culture art education.

100 People: A World Portrait®

100 People: A World Portrait® is an educational, aesthetic, and cultural online site/community initiated in 2005. The premise behind this community is explained on their website:

> Imagine a world where each person is measured by nothing more than the frame of a camera. Our relationship to our neighbors depends on how we cultivate and value our membership in the international community. How does each of us see the world? How does it see each of us? As individuals, how can we better understand our unique roles in the world? What if the global population of 6.5 billion was reduced to only 100 people and all the statistics used to describe them remained proportionally accurate? What would those 100 people look like, and where would you fit in? (http://www.100people.org/projects_curriculum.php)

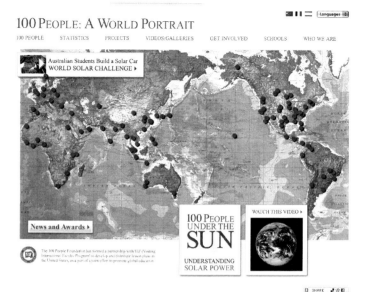

Figure 1

100 People.

100 People: A World Portrait® recognizes the necessary interdependence of the world for survival and hopes to educate people about art, culture, geography, and other attributes that shape how we see the world. The arts and new technologies play an essential role in this site and its communities.

> When technology allows us to immediately communicate with far away cultures and individuals, facilitating face-to-face introductions to the 100 people that represent our world population is our act towards global citizenry and towards progress. It is our hope that many others will continue this work far into the sustainable future. (http://www.100people.org/onehundred_history.php)

In its namesake project, a "snapshot" of 100 people, selected from 10,000 people who represent the world's 6.5 billion population, nominated by 500 schools from 100 countries, will be produced as a documentary film. The selection of the 100 people to be depicted in the film are based on specific criteria, and students participate by filling out a community profile and send in their nominations about an individual they wish to be included. An installation of 100 portraits will incorporate audio, still and video images, and a book with selected portraits.

The 100 People® website also provides curriculum materials for interaction and youth involvement, and notably, the curriculum project is guided by an advisory team that includes, notably, Dr. Deborah B. Reeve, the current Executive Director of the National Art Education Association (NAEA). Although the visual arts are not a specifically defined curricular area on which the 100 People® curriculum "modules" will focus, visual images and "artistic products" will be interwoven into the educational materials and curricular activities. It should be noted that much of the curriculum project is still in the planning stages at the time of the writing of this chapter.

The development phase of 100 People: A World Portrait® is key in understanding its potential. Print materials, podcasts, and streaming media are being considered as access points. A wiki will be used to allow participants to provide feedback about content. School participation is identified through school profiles, community profiles, and photographs. Geographic locations now include Mexico, Pakistan, Spain, Australia, Poland, Singapore, Indonesia, Niger, South Africa, and the United States; and indications are that young people around the world are engaging in the project. For example, in the video from the Shekou International School in China, the art teacher explained the 100 People® project and students began interviewing members of their community. In another example, the International School of Manila currently includes student artwork that represents a range of themes inspired by the 100 People® project, such as "religion," "one dying of starvation," and "clean, safe water." Links to educational resources include websites for organizations like ODT,[1] which offers consumers maps that provide alternative representations of the world to challenge assumptions about location and identity (i.e., maps like the *Waterman Butterfly* map that minimize distortion or maps that represent the world upside down).

The student-centered character of The 100 People: World Portrait® community is evident throughout the website. Remarks, like the following, reflect this orientation: "We are asking the children of the world to introduce us to their people of the world" (Sadurni, 2005). Sustained communication and exploration of art and social issues over time are required to engage students in deep learning, with critical analyses to avoid virtual tourism; therefore, assessment should play a key role in understanding the effectiveness of this project.

Global Kids®

Global Kids,® a digital media initiative begun in 2006 in New York City and an occasional resident in *Second Life*,® explores digital media and serious contemporary issues with urban youth.[2]

In Global Kids® students engage in online communication, are encouraged to become leaders through an online leadership program, connect in virtual worlds, participate in interactive and experiential learning, develop critical thinking skills and participate in school and community affairs. The Virtual Video Program engages youth in creating *machinima*,

Figure 2

Second Life's Global Kids.

Global Kids®

a type of filmmaking that integrates animation and video gaming techniques in a real time 3-D environment, about global issues related to digital media. A Digital Youth Advisory group provides opportunities for youth to express their voices, online youth dialogues offer avenues for young people to consider alternative points of view, and podcasts pertain to digital media and viewpoints of young people. Global leadership skills are developed in *Second Life®* through workshops where youth around the world learn and discuss global issues. In fact, collaborations between Global Kids® and organizations such as UNICEF have taken place. Holy Meatballs of Divine Spongiform blog, a flat-web technology, provides public access to Global Kids® activities. In March 2006, Global Kids® sponsored an essay contest where young people took a stand about a range of critical themes such as online race and gender.

Discussion and Conclusions

According to a report prepared by Arreguin (2007) that focuses on *Second Life®* best practices, the desirability or benefits of virtual environments include:

- A familiar online environment for game savvy users;
- "Possibility space," where real and imagined solutions can be tried out without real world constraints;
- A common space to imagine and create collaboratively;
- Both a unique virtual space and a society;
- Image-based content; persistent content; the ability to create and to tailor avatars' identity and virtual space; and
- Creation tools that are powerful and accessible to most learners.

The attractiveness and benefits of virtual environments such as Global Kids® and 100 People® to teachers, youth, and to citizens and community members worldwide may be in their creative adaptations of new digital media, visual richness, possibility, and interactivity. Their attractiveness may also be in their aims to make the world a better place, and one cannot but be inspired by the ease of intercultural interactions, connections, and pro-social and critically informed educative experiences afforded to young people by these digitally mediated sites.

Cyberspace is depicted as the great equalizer on the one hand, and on the other, is criticized for making cultural, ethnic, and racial differences invisible. Arreguin (2007) subscribes to the former position and views the ability of users to change appearances as a way to focus on ideas rather than appearances, which can lead to stereotyping. "The ability to change appearance also means students are free to be evaluated based on the quality of their ideas rather than by real world constraints and stereotypes" (Arreguin, 2007, p. 14). Merryfield (2003) similarly notes that online discussions can prevent American teachers, as well, from perpetuating stereotypes through "triggers of difference" that occur during face-to-face interactions. "I have found that American teachers interact differently online with people of other cultures than they do face-to-face. When they hear a Chinese accent, see a Jordanian woman's head cover, observe a Brazilian's body language, smell curry on an Indian's breath, some Americans automatically register a consciousness of difference that may trigger discomfort, stereotypes, xenophobia, or recognition of their own ignorance of other cultures" (Merryfield, 2003, para 56). The triggers of visual and aural differences often subconsciously make people uncomfortable or otherwise constrain people's abilities to listen, interact, and learn from others. But is it possible that these "triggers of difference" may affect youth differently because their assumptions are not fully formed? I believe that it is possible, and that digital environments such as the two I have discussed in this chapter are powerful learning tools that may reduce the possibilities for solidifying such triggers. These two sites certainly provide a space for youth to connect with young people across the globe and to identify and grapple with critical issues that both distinguish humanity and those issues that unite all of us, which are essential to development in adolescence, and to developing intercultural competencies.

The world has become increasingly visual, and new technologies are fast transforming our lives, including the ways in which we get information, communicate, conduct business, and spend our leisure time. Young people solidify their values and their understanding of the world through personal and sociocultural experiences with peers, groups, schools, and religious and secular-based organizations. As the world also becomes increasingly global, educators recognize the need for intercultural competencies and the potential of cyberspace as a tool for teaching and facilitating intercultural understanding. Innovative educational programming, such as 100 People: A World Portrait® and Global Kids,® is clearly shaping perceptions, knowledge, and interaction with global cultures; and embedded within the aims, directives, motivations, interactions, and the visual and virtual interface of Global Kids® and 100 People® are elements of Congdon and Blandy's liberatory Sixth World, critical pedagogy, and facets of Freedman's principles of meaningful aesthetics, social perspectives, cultural response, technological experience, and constructive critique. I believe that 100 People: A World Portrait® and Global Kids® support desired learning and provide important models for art educators to teach in a global, multimodal world. As globalization continues to shape our world, and youth continue to be "plugged in," we need to look closely at these kinds of digitally mediated communities, the dialogue and experiences they are having, and ways that cyberspace can support teaching and learning. Insofar as the role they play in mediating relationships between participating young people (rather than empowering some while marginalizing others), these sites will contribute to increasing intercultural competencies among youth. In this way, the cyber world indeed provides a global medium for transforming society in ways many art educators have hoped for.

REFERENCES

100 people: A world portrait. (2005). Retrieved May 15, 2007 from http://www.100people.org/projects_film.php

Appadurai, A. (1990). Disjuncture and difference in the global cultural economy. *Explorations in Critical Social Science, 7*(2), 295-310.

Arreguin, C. (2007, Fall). Reports from the field: Second Life community convention 2007 education track summary: The first in Global Kids Series on Virtual Worlds. Retrieved December 22, 2007 from http://www.holymeatballs.org/pdfs/VirtualWorldsforLearningRoadmap_012008.pdf

Congdon, K., & Blandy, D. (2001). Approaching the real and the fake: Living life in the fifth world. *Studies in Art Education, 42*(3), 266-278.

Duncum, P. (2001). Clarifying visual culture art education. *Art Education, 55*(3), 6-11.

Freedman, K. (2003). *Teaching visual culture: Curriculum, aesthetics, and the social life of art.* New York: Teachers College. Freedman, K., & Liu, M. (1996). The importance of computer experience, learning processes, and communication patterns in multicultural networking. *Educational Technology Research and Development, 44*(1), 43-59.

Gibson, W. (1984). *Neuromancer.* New York: Ace Books.

Globalori: http://globaloria-wv.blogspot.com/

Global Kids: http://www.globalkids.org

GlobalSchoolNet: http://www.globalschoolnet.org/

Gregory, D. (1997). *New technologies and art education: Implications for theory, research, and practice.* Reston, VA: National Art Education Association.

Holmes Norton, E. (2008). State of the Black union 2008. Smiley Group, [Television] C-SPAN.

Kellner, D. (2002). Theorizing globalization. *Sociological Theory, 20*(3), 285-305.

Merryfield, M. (2003). Like a veil: Cross-cultural experiential learning online. *Contemporary Issues in Technology and Social Studies* [Electronic Version], *3*(2). Retrieved on January 16, 2007 from http://www.citejournal.org/vol3/iss2/socialstudies/article1.cfm

ODT (http://www.watermanpolyhedron.com/)

Sadurni, I. (2005). *100 people.* [Video Trailer.] Retrieved January 10, 2008 from http://www.100people.org/videos_trailer_long.php

Stankiewicz, M. (2004). Notions of technology. *Studies in Art Education, 46*(1), 88-91.

Tavin, K. (2003). Wrestling with angels, searching for ghosts: Toward a critical pedagogy of visual culture. *Studies in Art Education, 44*(3), 197-213.

Tanneeru, M. (2006). *Globalization, technology changing the art world.* Retrieved January 18, 2008 from http://www.cnn.com/2006/SHOWBIZ/11/26/art.globalization/index.html

UNESCO (n.d.). *Guidelines on intercultural education.* Retrieved February 1, 2008, from http://unesdoc.unesco.org/images/0014/001478/147878e.pdf

ENDNOTES

1   ODT is a consulting firm turned innovative map-maker that creates and shares visual representations of the world through unique maps. They pioneered the use of the Peters Projection map materials in a variety of corporate culture change, leadership, and diversity diagnostic projects, and were catapulted to national recognition when one of their maps appeared in an episode of the TV series *West Wing* (http://ODTMaps.com/about_us/). See also (http://www.watermanpolyhedron.com).

2   *Second Life*®, created by Philip Rosedale, is a 3-D virtual world where residents create *avatars* that can socialize, conduct business, listen to music, attend events on college campuses and engage in a myriad of other activities. Global Kids® is an independent organization that interacts within, but not exclusively, *Second Life*®.

Beyond Visual Literacy Competencies: Teaching and Learning Art with Technology in the Global Age

Ching-Chiu Lin

Profound changes in the Internet, computer-based imaging, creative expression, cultural production capabilities, and in global computer-based communication networks now provide unprecedented avenues for creating, sharing, and consuming global culture, as well as influencing the ways in which individuals experience the world. The proliferation of digital information and the pervasiveness of electronic visual imagery have motivated educators, both within and beyond the profession of art education, to ask what learners should learn in the age of electronic globalization. Central to such inquiry is the construct of *literacy*, a dynamic concept that changes according to social conditions and society's expectations of what constitutes a literate individual (Lankshear, Snyder & Green, 2000; Leu, Kinzer, Coiro, & Cammack, 2004). In academic discourse, educational policy documents, and nationally standardized frameworks for learning, the question seems to be, "What skills do students need in order to be *literate*?" Complicating this question is the fact that a construct once almost exclusively concerned with reading and writing competencies, notions of literacy now move beyond a single focus on linguistic proficiency to highlight multiple forms and purposes of communication (linguistic, visual, cultural, and computer, for example), include varied recommendations for equipping individuals with the kinds of multiple competencies needed in contemporary society, and now articulate multiple list of skill sets to be put into place in schools today.

What is Visual Literacy?

Visual literacy is a construct that has been accorded many parameters (and whose origins and concepts remain diversely interpreted from one discipline to another (Debes, 1968, Avgerinous & Ericson, 1997; Elkins, 2008). Historically, the concept of being visually literate has been associated with an underlying hypothesis about the existence of a visual language. This notion of visual language can be traced to philosopher Nelson Goodman's (1968) *Languages of Art*, which uses the metaphor of art as language and works of art as symbols in a symbolic system. In Goodman's view, the representations and expressions in works of art, just like those in language, are conveyed within a structure (or grammar) and carried semantic meanings. In an early definition of visual literacy, educational technology scholar John Debes observed that visual literacy is a group of vision-competencies that humans develop by engaging their multiple sensory systems with images in their surroundings (1969). Soon after, Fransecky and Debes established guidelines for teaching visual literacy by defining a visually literate child as one that has "a basic understanding of the grammar of visual language and some realization that it parallels verbal language" (1972, p. 7). By visual language, they meant the "symbols, message carriers, [and] body language" (p. 7) delivered by mass media.

Over the three decades since the work of Debes, Goodman, and their followers, mainstream discussions of visual literacy have assumed the existence of a visual language as an avenue for learning and understanding images and have argued that interpreting visual images is as important as learning verbal language. Scholars of visual literacy who have privileged the study of visual language grammars consider the composition and design of images to be the syntax of visual communication. For example, Donis Dondis (1973), a public communication scholar, viewed all visual experiences as expressed in and drawn from the basic graphic elements and the compositional source. In a more detailed explanation, Australian art educator Anne Bamford (2003) observed that "Being visually literate is a combination of syntax and semantics. Syntax is the form or building blocks of an image" (p. 3), while "semantics refers to the way images relate more broadly to issues in the world to gain meaning" (p. 4). According to Bamford, the syntax of images suggests that visual composition refers to how elements and principles are organized and created, while semantics, the study of signs, explores how the visual form is communicated and how meaning is constructed by the viewer. In art and aesthetic education discourse, an individual's ability to communicate visually, also generally identified as visual literacy, has been advocated as one of many important forms and practices of literacy skills in society.

How has the Age of Global Media Impacted Discourse about Visual Literacy Art Education?

More recently, both visual literacy and art education scholars have considered how dynamic influences of the evolution of electronic technologies and the globalized proliferation of mass media have led to an accelerated dissemination of image production and reproduction that both creates and reflects expansive visual forms of contemporary culture. This phenomenon has drawn increased educational attention to the individual's ability to understand, interpret, create, and consume images, including but not limited to those in art works, material and visual cultural artifacts, and everyday life.

A visual language approach discussed in the previous section corresponds to art educator Doug Boughton's (1986) communication-oriented view of visual literacy in which the understanding of visual images means developing the individual's visual communication skills along with verbal literacy skills. Such an orientation has generated a large amount of scholarly attention in response to the impacts of pervasive electronically generated visual communication (Flood & Bamford, 2007; Metros & Woolsey, 2006; Spalter & van Dam, 2008). This ability to communicate visually is said to have become imperative in a digitally mediated society, not only because people's lives are conditioned by the visual but because electronic technologies accelerate the use of visual and multimedia communications globally, in ways that necessitate attention to student skills in critical thinking and meaning-making.

Scholars have also observed the inadequacies of visual literacy discourse in the age of global digital media, drawing attention to the increasingly important concept of multimodality, an ability to construct and communicate meanings through an intersected combination among multiple perceptional systems (Cope & Kalantzis, 2000; Kress, 2003; Bolin & Blandy, 2003, Duncum, 2004). These scholars argue that the significance of the multimodal nature of communication in the current digital environment is challenging the system of literacy categorization developed from the separation of various sign systems and skill types.

That is, if meaning is made and communicated cohesively through the global communication network using a combination of multiple perceptional systems—including linguistic, visual, aural, and spatial modes—is it appropriate to focus on one singular literacy form in framing literacy discourse and evaluating student competencies?

Today, the notion of visual literacy in art education generally refers to student comprehension of works of art and other visual forms of expression and related cultural productions, as well as student ability to express and communicate ideas and experiences through various visual forms, including but not limited to new electronic media. That is, based on the broad theoretical discourse in art education, the visual literacy concept alludes to a set of concepts, practical skills, and dispositions that enable communication, thinking, learning, and visual construction of meaning to develop and strengthen an individual's social engagement and ability to meet communication needs. Because the field of art education is associated with visual communication and production, it is now argued that creative and critical inquiries in the age of global media must engage a sophisticated understanding about how meaning is constructed through the intersections of communicative multimodality and interdisciplinary expertise. At the same time, it is argued that art educators must recognize that the interconnectedness of the senses—sight, hearing, taste, smell, and touch—occurs together with the process of learning with multimedia to create meaning that is more complex than visual experience alone.

The remainder of this chapter further examines the construct of *visual literacy* in relation to teaching and learning art with technology. Based on findings from my study of three technologically-engaged high school art teachers working in dramatically different Midwestern high schools, I problematize academic discourse concerned with visual literacy education, and I reposition questions and conceptualizations about visual literacy with the hope of leading to a more insightful and robust approach to understanding and facilitating art teaching and learning in an age of global electronic media.

Does Visual Literacy Actually Matter to Art Teachers?

Scholarly interpretations of the notion of visual literacy across disciplines have described values and possibilities associated with visual literacy learning in the age of global digital media. Despite intriguing advancements in thinking about the expansive nature of literacy in the global electronic era, the questions remain constant in visual literacy discourse. Those constant questions are: What skills and dispositions constitute visual literacy in an age of globalized electronic media, and how should teachers teach such skills and competencies? Notably, currently little empirical evidence exists to reveal how this type of learning occurs in regular, day-to-day technology-enriched classrooms. Embracing the excitement of global electronic media and culture exchanges, and also interested in questions about literacy, I wonder if we may now ask some alternative questions regarding art teaching, learning, and literacy: *To what extent do purportedly desirable forms of literacy actually prepare individuals for the era of global electronic media, or to become socially responsible citizens? What do we gain or lose if we follow the current literacy discourse to frame our thinking about the experience of learning in an art room?* The scholarly community in art education does not know how or why (or why not) art teachers are engaging inquiry processes and multimedia opportunities in the provocative and innovative manner described in the art education literature on the possibilities of technology (Delacruz, 2004). To find out how practicing art teachers equip their students with visual literacy skills in the age of global electronic media, I recently conducted a case study of three secondary art teachers' conceptualizations of and practices related to visual literacy in the context of their teaching practice with technology (Lin, 2008). I deliberately selected three highly respected, experienced, and technologically-sophisticated art teachers, all with masters degrees in art education, and all utilizing electronic media in innovative ways with their students.

Although my study began with an attempt to seek correspondence between these technology-savvy teachers' practical insights about visual literacy and the related academic discourse on the topic, surprisingly, my findings indicated that the academy's notion of visual literacy had little influence on these three teachers' art teaching praxis. That is, these teachers neither used the term *visual literacy* in their conversations with students, colleagues, or myself nor read or applied visual literacy academic discourse, constructs, or prescriptions in framing their curricula and executing their teaching practice. They interpreted *visual literacy* broadly, to mean a context-bound assembly of dispositions and practices related to what students should learn in their classrooms, but they derived their own conceptions about visual literacy from their individual practical experience and their knowledge about their specific students and communities, but not from scholarly texts. Additionally, although these

teachers believed that student knowledge transformation and media analysis are revealed through a correlation between creative and critical inquiry, they did not describe this learning experience as visual literacy or media literacy, the common terminology used in academic discourse for such learning activities. In arriving at these findings, I couldn't help but wonder what all this academic discourse about visual literacy was intended for, if not for teachers such as the ones who participated in my study.

Closer examination of my data also revealed that although not engaging scholars' writings about visual literacy, these three teachers have nonetheless accomplished similar goals that visual or media literacy theorists would expect. In art and aesthetic education discourse, an individual's ability to communicate visually, also generally identified as visual literacy, has been advocated as one of many important forms and practices of literacy skills in society. These teachers arrived at their conclusions mirrored in scholarly discourse, but without the help of educational theorists, media specialists, or policy makers. Importantly, these teachers' understandings of the notion of visual literacy went well beyond ideas about developing students' visual competencies and skill sets, to embrace instead a more comprehensive view about their teaching and learning experience—one that incorporates goals and strategies like empowering student voices, building a trusting relationship with students, making connections with their students' real lives, considering the unique demands and contexts of their particular teaching praxis, and drawing from the richness of their own professional knowledge. For these teachers, the process of learning through encounters with visual images and technology is a unified practice that is not limited to the creation and analysis of visual messages or the learning of specific skills for particular tasks, but is strongly connected to and with students' lived experience in their specific circumstances. Overall, my research suggests that these teachers' art teaching and learning with technology embraced a situational, inquiry-oriented, and holistic approach rather than a predetermined visual literacy agenda with particular skill sets and guidelines that must be followed, delivered, and evaluated.

Discussion: Is Literacy a *Means to* or an *End* in Learning?

In a world immersed in and mediated by proliferating electronic technologies and media, literacy forms and practices are changing so rapidly that new and varying approaches to literacy pedagogy literacy are emerging continually. However, whereas literacy has become a popular term in academic discourse to identify new skills now to be learned, terms like *visual literacy*, *media literacy*, or *digital literacy* seemingly make little sense to the art teachers that I studied. These teachers' disengagement from academic literacy discourse invokes further questions about uses of the literacy construct in academia: *Should the notion of literacy or visual literacy be seen as a means to or an end goal of learning in the face of the growing development of global media and communication? If visual literacy were envisioned as a means and not an end in education how might we reconceptualize and describe those means?*

In a culture of standardization and accountability, the U.S. K-12 educational system is dominated by a national discourse on how to improve learning using standardized curricula, instructional delivery mechanisms, and evaluation procedures. Students' learning is understood through nationally standardized assessments for their purported mastery of systematically prescribed sets of skills and abilities, and teachers are told to instruct students toward these intended learning outcomes in order to prepare them for life. The utilization of technology in education is seen in national discourse as having great potential for teaching and learning enhancements, and predetermined sets of discrete technology skill sets are commonly set forth both as models for technology implementation in the classroom and desired end points (or benchmarks) for assessing students' technology learning achievements. Standardizing visual, linguistic, and technology literacy skills have become an efficient way to simplify and encapsulate the learning process and are assumed to prepare the individual for a bright future in the face of the growing development of electronic technologies.

In contrast, I would argue here that what it means to be visually or digitally (or in any other way) literate in the global age is much too vague and complex a concept to be understood, described, or assessed in any objective, standardized fashion. The problem with attempts to standardize the construct is that when literacy (visual or otherwise) is seen as an expression or assembled term to describe concrete skill sets, standardized learning criteria, and prescribed expectations, the experience of learning is drawn out of its human context and disconnected from both the self and the world. Moreover, by describing a desirable end state of being literate in particular learning areas in such reductionist and decontextualized ways, education scholars and policy makers overlook the richness and unpredictability of *inquiry*, which I believe to be central to the processes of learning in any domain. As I reframe this argument, it is important to recognize that "Inquiry is not simply a process of accumulation of knowledge, but rather, a process; that is, a story involving recognition of a problem, physical and mental actions to address it, and a repeated cycle of evaluating and further transforming a situation" (Bruce, 2007, p. 211). Bruce's notion of an inquiry cycle reminds us that the significance of continuing exploration in the learning process is the key to fostering individuals' social and cultural development as "a unified whole" (p. 211), rather than as discrete parts. Learning, in such a view, is emergent, dynamic, and communal.

As early as 1938, Dewey, in *Experience and Education*, criticized the confusion between means and ends in education, one by which educators overemphasize the predetermined ends of learning achievements and ignore the significance of the learning experience itself. In contrast, Dewey proposed that the *means* of learning should be considered part of the *ends*, with learning being both about preparing for the future and engaging in present life. Dewey's view implies that teaching and learning art with technology in contemporary society should respond to a changing world, engage students fully at the moment they learn, and consider how to connect their lived experience with the world around them. As Dewey argued, "preparation for a more or less remote future is opposed to making the most of the opportunities of the present life" (p. 256). Building on Dewey's notions about education, and similar to Bruce's conceptions about the importance of inquiry, Delacruz posits that the basis of learning *is* inquiry and that central to an inquiry-based educational approach is "a reemerging interest in the personalistic nature of knowledge construction within a meaningful context" (1997, p.78), a fundamental belief in the power of constructivist educational strategies, and what Delacruz calls a *holistic model* for instructional design (1997). A holistic approach stems from a concern for the realities of young peoples' lives, a belief that learners are the makers of their own knowledge, and an interest in thinking about and solving the societal problems we all face. In this orientation, learning is seen as complex, embedded in lived experience, and puzzling; subjects are interrelated, thematic, and problem-centered; curricular structure is fluid, intertwined, and organized around real-world situations and simulations; and assessment is on-going, embedded in classroom activities, and authentic (Delacruz, 1997).

Indeed, for the three teachers that I studied, their engagement, presence, and means of learning are both context-bound and continuously cumulative as part of the ends of learning, with specific outcomes, ultimately, impossible to desegregate into discrete skills of units of knowledge and therefore unquantifiable. The learning that occurs in these teachers' art classrooms is not a collection of competencies or possessions that can be described in advance by scholars and policy makers; rather, it is "a coevolution of individual, society, literacy, and technology, given coherence by the processes of construction" (Bruce, 2003, p. 337). Numerous studies of exceptional teachers reinforce such a value system, that is, their belief in the embeddedness of learning in lived experience rather than segregated skill sets, their resistance to the mythologizing language of top down educational reform initiatives, and a sense of trust in their own moral landscapes as a guide for curricular and instructional decisions (Delacruz, 2004).

Implications and Recommendations for Art Education

The fact that the three technology-knowledgeable, experienced, dedicated high school art teachers that I studied are neither interested in employing a literacy agenda to frame their curricula nor in categorizing student learning outcomes as some type of "must learn" set of skills is illuminating; and it behooves scholars, theorists, policy-makers, and teacher educators to better understand how real-world master teachers connect their students with the moments of learning and these transform learning encounters into preparation for life. Having recognized that the construct of literacy indicates only one way to frame the structure of learning art with technology, this chapter suggests the need to emphasize *the processes* and *contexts* of learning instead of focusing so heavily on particular predictable results. The rationale underlying this proposition is that learning with, through, and about new media in the age of globalization is an interactive, multimodal, and interconnected social practice. Focusing on independent predetermined skills or abilities limits the richness of the learning experience and ignores the fact that human learning involves more than simple machine input and output. Based on this conclusion, I also offer further recommendations for art education theory and policy formation that attends to the potential new electronic media, reflects changes in the learning environment, and concerns student preparation for global citizenship.

First, we need more real-world, grounded research in regular classrooms if we are to bridge the current gaps between academic theory and K-12 teachers' praxis with new technologies and global media. Because scholars in both literacy education and art education are now inquiring into the definitions and meanings of literacy in relation to electronic technology development, there is a need for empirical research on teachers' perspectives, given in their own contexts and voices. My recent findings suggest that practicing teachers' situated viewpoints on visual literacy highlight the complexity and problematic nature of the construct. Indeed, these teachers' disengagement from theoretical discourse on visual literacy may generate a debate about the value and role of visual, technology, and media literacy constructs in the practical sector of education in contemporary society, open a wider discussion about the disconnections between academic theory and teachers' practices, and encourage scholarly research on underlying factors that influence this disconnection.

Second, art educators and scholars should further investigate and engage the changing landscape of new forms of engagement and modes of communication brought about by globalized electronic media, as well as their impacts on teaching and learning art with these new media. In particular, how might an interest in the multimodal, multi-purposed, and globalized nature of electronic technology-based experiences among young people further encourage art teachers' own investigations and insights about how art should be taught with new media? Changing electronic technology developments open further avenues for examining and questioning the possibilities and challenges of the emergent theories and practices. Further research potential lies in the investigation of how new media practices can be implemented in real-world art classroom settings, and what teacher knowledge and human and technology infrastructures are necessary for their implementation.

Third scholars and preservice educators may consider the strength of considering more holistic and contextualized conceptualizations about learning across subjects area, including those involving new media, in the public school system. As art education scholars herald the need for and significance of engagement with technology in teaching, consideration the notion of classroom learning experiences occurring across varied human interests, modes of communication, and disciplinary lenses would offer an alternative pedagogical perspective for examining relationships between visual arts and technology. Such a perspective would also suggest the need for a learning model that connects students' lived experience with the world in which they live, and offers insights on the actions that teachers might incorporate into their praxis to facilitate such learning.

Fourth, an important avenue for future research would include the exploration of individual experience with technology beyond the use of artistic tools for personal creative self-expression. If we are to promote a holistic learning model in learning art with/through/with technology, technology functions as a means for development of the individual's imagination, personal growth, *and social action.* It is important to understand that "holistic education is oriented toward humanistic notions of learning, a concern for the integrity of children's realities, and an interest in thinking about and solving the social problems children face" (Delacruz, 1997, p. 79). Therefore, because ever-evolving electronic technologies continually impact young people's lives, especially in the areas of education and recreation, further research might emphasize the implementation of technology in art education to help learners understand how technology influences their world and everyday lives and assist them to take action on issues of concern. In particular, "technological changes invoke issues such as empowerment, equality, access, speed, efficiency, liberation, and the development of a global community in support of a pro-technology agenda" (Bruce, 1998, p. 269). Such issues can be explored through art education by examining how global networks shape social relations around the world, and how technology contributes to the learning development of civically engaged citizens. Connecting art education and technology in a digital media-saturated world would also now aim to develop learners' public engagement and participatory citizenship. This means that "art educator's best strategy may be to embrace the challenge and complexity of contemporary life and to redefine teaching as the creation of meaningful opportunities for inquiry by students, individually and communally" (Delacruz, 1997, p. 87). Indeed, as, many art education scholars have suggested, teaching art with technology should engage social responsibilities and incorporate emerging technological issues like online collaboration and networking, cyber identity, innovative art forms, virtual communities, and virtual reality through art (Colman, 2005; Keifer-Boyd, 2005; Roland, 2007, Stokrocki, 2007).

This chapter suggests that art learning in the age of global electronic media should move beyond mere technical understanding of discrete electronic devices and dissociated acquisitions of favored art, cultural knowledge, or skill sets, and toward, instead, connecting to individuals' lived experience locally and globally. Learners' achievement of distinctive visual literacy competencies only makes sense when educational theory embraces a holistic view of the learning experience that sustains such facets of experience as empowering student voices, facilitating trusting relationships among teachers and students, community engagement, lifelong aspirations, and connections with the lives and contexts of particular teaching praxis. Such an approach moves beyond the ability to encode and decode the meaning of visual images and experiences, and interweaves the complexity of visual communication in the age of globalization into the relationships with and among learners, learning content and environment, and pedagogy.

REFERENCES

Avgerinous, M., & Ericson, J. (1997). A review of the concept of visual literacy. *British Journal of Educational Technology, 28*(4), 280-291.

Bamford, A. (2003). The visual literacy white paper. Retrieved October 9, 2007, from http://www.adobe.com/uk/education/pdf/adobe_ visual_literacy_paper.pdf

Bolin, P., & Blandy, D. (2003). Beyond visual culture: Seven statements of support for material culture studies in art education. *Studies in Art Education, 44*(3), 246-263.

Boughton, D. (1986). Visual literacy: Implications for cultural understanding through art education. *Journal of Art & Design Education, 5*(1), 125-142.

Bruce, B. (1998). The disappearance of technology: Toward an ecological model of literacy. In D. Reinking, M. McKenna, L, Labbo, & R. Kieffer (Eds.), *Handbook of literacy and technology: Transformations in a post-typographic world* (pp. 269-281). Hillsdale, NJ: Erlbaum.

Bruce, B. (2003). In closing: What is literacy in the information age? In B. Bruce (Ed.), *Literacy in the information age: Inquiries into meaning making with new technologies* (pp. 327-338). Newark, DE: International Reading Association.

Bruce, B. (2007). Communities of designers: Transforming a situation into a unified whole. In P. Mishra, M. Koehler, & Y. Zhao (Eds.), *Faculty development by design: Integrating technology in higher education* (pp. 205-220). Greenwich, CT: Information Age.

Colman, A. (2005). Net. art and net. pedagogy: Introducing Internet art to the digital art curriculum. *Studies in Art Education, 46*(1), 61-73.

Cope, B., & Kalantzis, M. (2000). Design for social futures. In B. Cope & M. Kalantzis (Eds.), *Multiliteracies: Literacy learning and the design of social future* (pp. 201-234). New York: Routledge.

Debes, J. (1968). Some foundations for visual literacy. *Audiovisual Instruction, 13*(9), 961-964.

Debes, J. (1969). The loom of visual literacy. *Audiovisual Instruction, 14*(8), 25-27.

Delacruz, E. (1997*). Instructional theory, research, and practice in art education: Design for inquiry*. Reston, VA: National Art Education Association.

Delacruz, E. (2004). Teachers' working conditions and the unmet promise of technology. *Studies in Art Education, 46*(1), 6-19.

Dewey, J. (1938). *Experience and education*. New York: Macmillan.

Dondis, D. (1973). *A primer of visual literacy*. Cambridge, MA: The MIT Press.

Duncum, P. (2004). Visual culture isn't just visual: Multiliteracy, multimodality and meaning. *Studies in Art Education, 45*(3), 252-264.

Elkins, J. (2008). Introduction: The concept of visual literacy, and its limitations. In J. Elkins (Ed.), *Visual literacy* (pp. 1-10). New York: Routledge.

Flood, A., & Bamford, A. (2007). Manipulation, simulation, stimulation: The role of art education in the digital age. *International Journal of Education through Art, 3*(2), 91-102.

Fransecky, R., & Debes, J. (1972). *Visual literacy: A way to learn—A way to teach*. Washington, DC: Association for Educational Communications and Technology.

Goodman, N. (1968). *Languages of art: An approach to a theory of symbols*. Indianapolis, IN: Bobbs-Merrill.

Keifer-Boyd, K. (2005). Technology interfaces with art education. *Visual Arts Research, 31*(1), 1-3.

Kress, G. (2003). *Literacy in the new media age*. New York: Routledge.

Lankshear, C., Snyder, I., & Green, B. (2000). *Teachers and technoliteracy: Managing literacy, technology and learning in schools*. St. Leonards, NSW, Australia: Allen & Unwin.

Leu, D., Kinzer, C., Coiro, J., & Cammack, D. (2004). Toward a theory of new literacies emerging from the Internet and other information and communication technologies. In R. Ruddell & N. Unrau (Eds.), *Theoretical models and processes of reading* (5th ed., pp. 1570-1613). Newark, DE: International Reading Association.

Lin, C. (2008). *A qualitative study of three secondary art teachers' conceptualizations of visual literacy as manifested through their teaching with electronic technologies*. Unpublished doctoral dissertation, University of Illinois, Urbana-Champaign.

Metros, S., & Woolsey, K. (2006). Visual literacy: An institutional imperative [Electronic Version]. *EDUCAUSE review, 41*(3), 80-81 from http://www.educause.edu/ir/library/pdf/erm0638.pdf

Roland, C. (2007). 2nd annual Internet survey for art teachers: Summary of the results. Retrieved March 7, 2008, from http://www.artjunction.org/atgi/teachers/Internet_survey07.html

Spalter, A., & van Dam, A. (2008). Digital visual literacy. *Theory into Practice, 47*(2), 93-101.

Stokrocki, M. (2007). Art education avatars in cyberspace: Research in computer-based technology and visual arts education. In L. Bresler (Ed.), *International handbook of research in arts education* (pp. 1361-1380). Dordrecht, The Netherlands: Springer.

AUTHOR'S NOTE

This chapter is derived, in part, from my dissertation, A Qualitative Study of Three Secondary Art Teachers' Conceptualizations of Visual Literacy as Manifested through their Teaching with Electronic Technologies (2008), University of Illinois, Urbana-Champaign.

Embracing a Predicament? Folk, Applied, Avant-Garde, and Singapore School Art

Koon Hwee Kan

Teaching and learning a single monolithic transcultural and ahistorical art in schools worldwide is archaic, and imposing one all-encompassing theoretical framework upon international arts education research is problematic. A hybrid aesthetic is currently under construction in schools, blending local social, cultural, economical, and political values with psychological and cognitive justifications of arts education. To better understand how such a hypothetical aesthetic embraces localization and globalization, an amalgam of research methodologies is needed. Through multiple perspectives—(a) art programs in operation, (b) students' learning in action, and (c) pedagogy in transformation—my research (Kan, 2004) untangles the nexus of sociocultural ramifications underlying the Singapore Secondary School Art Style to recontextualize its aesthetics and pedagogy.

Overview and Conceptual Framework

Globalization has a long, unrecognized history. Global interaction and exchange began when traders, preachers, adventurers, and warriors initiated, forced, and created bonding among human civilizations (Chanda, 2007). Geographic separation never guaranteed forever the self-sufficiency of nations and states or the eternal sovereignty of cultures and societies. Material culture permeates living and lives. Consumption of goods and services always affected the making and exchange of artifacts and ideas, thus, influencing the manifestation of the arts in cultures and indirectly impacting local aesthetics.

Historically, the philosophy and psychology of art typically defined art in terms of the Western fine arts canon. Hence, originality and self-expression in conventional art education were stipulated as intrinsic humanistic virtues and commonly promoted as universal educationally desirable outcomes. Of late, social and anthropological studies (R. Anderson, 1990; Dissanayake 1992; Freeland, 2001) have provided a more persuasive definition and evidence to confront what art is and what constitutes good art. In their

view, this human endeavor varies according to society, culture, time, and even among different cultural groups within one society during the same era. Consequently, art and art education serving universal values and judgments no longer hold true.

Continental institutional theorists (Bourdieu & Passeron, 1977) have observed that, typically, culturally embedded social hierarchies predetermine the reproduction of conventional aesthetic tastes within particular cultural groups. Mass education provided by schools, communities, and museums have succumbed to these social hierarchies, reflecting and maintaining the inherited power of elite social classes and enterprises, and perpetuating social conformity and customized criteria for artistic distinction. In the United States, in public and private K-12 art education programs of study the germinating aesthetic of the school art style (Efland, 1976) has its protection within a legitimate social institution—school—ultimately satisfy the proviso of another Danto's *artworld* (1981) and Dickie's *art circle* (1984). Variations of school art like fine arts become a kind of institutional art. It proliferates across international borders with the unchanged denominator—schooling—because

> education is not simply a technical business of well-managed information processing nor even simply a matter of applying "learning theories" to the classroom or using the results of subject-centered "achievement testing." It is a complex pursuit of fitting a culture to the needs of its members and of fitting its members and their ways of knowing to the needs of the culture. (Bruner, 1996, p. 43)

An equivocal approach to art education as investment to reproduce different tiers of cultural capital has facilitated Stankiewicz's (2007) mapping of histories for international arts education. Such an approach was found in the Israeli kindergarten (Toren, 2004) and in my own work. My research scrutinized the Singapore Secondary School Art Style with qualitative inquiry methods. A specially designed research methodology was adopted, blending ethnography and curriculum inquiry with narrative. Sources of

CHAPTER 27 | Embracing a Predicament? Folk, Applied, Avant-Garde, and Singapore School Art

205

data included prolonged *in situ* observations with extensive photo-documentation, triangulated interviews (i.e., semistructured interviews with teachers involved, open-ended interviews with students, and photo-elicitation interviews with recent graduates), and document analysis. In data representation and writing I experimented with photocollage-cum-essay to explore visual metaphors along with written stories of what happened at four sites over 2 years.

This chapter highlights cross-site analysis "via a simple descriptive matrix to form conceptual combinations and new insights" (Miles & Huberman, cited by Stokrocki, 1991, p. 43). I invented my own matrix, adopting "thinking" for creativity and artistic expression, and metaphorically confine the notion of schooling to "the box." The following discussion explicates how thinking inside, outside, and beyond "the box" takes on different degrees of significance when recognizing their relative positions as stages of a process within the transformation of school culture.

Thinking *Inside* the Box: Conservative Acceptance of Common Fate

The national scholastic assessment system in place in Singapore, based on criteria set forth by the Cambridge–Singapore General Certificate of Education (GCE), has preset artistic distinction, highly regarded in its secondary schools, and indirectly guides pedagogical practice and conditions adolescent students' artistic learning. This standard undergirded education credentials in many Commonwealth countries but often became localized when imported from Britain as in the case of Zimbabwe (Abraham, 2003). I hypothesize that the impact of these sorts of testing requirements may create an even wider sphere of influence, manifested in an almost identical but overlooked international style of school art.

In my case study, I have found that three art genres[1] have been agglomerated within contemporary Singapore Secondary School Art Style, namely *folk art, applied art, and avant-garde art.* Notably, aspects of folk, applied, and avant-garde art were designated national art exam components in addition to the usual fine arts concentration in Singapore; although I also observe that art teachers in individual Singapore schools have the leeway to interpret this nationally prescribed art curriculum and decide on the concentration for their specific art programs. But more to the point, inclusion of these three genres in the secondary art curriculum is by no means incidental but entails complex interwoven social, cultural, political, and economic forces. I have to abbreviate historical and cultural antecedents, simplifying also

their causality in the following discussion. Assuming a conservative perspective below, I briefly introduce how the status quo of each genre is preserved and maintained within Singapore schools.

Regional Folk Art

Determining what constitutes folk art in a particular geographical region has become increasingly challenging. The manifestations of Southeast Asian folk art in Singapore Secondary School Art Style, namely, batik painting and printing, paper-cutting, pyrography, tie-dye, and woodblock printing, could accommodate only a part of each medium's close associations with Singapore's two dominant ethnic cultures—Chinese and Malay (Kan, 1999). A brief look at the historical developments of these folk art forms is useful here.

First and foremost, *batik* is an Indonesian word and traditional art form referring to the traditional use of wax to resist dyes. Such resist-decoration on fabric was known in Africa, China, Japan, and the Middle East with cassava, rice paste, or mud as resistance; and Eastern European egg decoration is a variation of the process (Robinson, 1969). Moreover, indigo dyeing, fashionable in both the East and West, had spread widely via the Silk Road. Western Europeans came into contact with batik when the Dutch colonized Java in the 17th century. Subsequently, factories proliferated in Holland to manufacture imitations (Fraser-Lu, 1986). Today, many Southeast Asian national costumes showcase elements of batik in their designs. Similarly, tie-dye, one of the oldest and simplest manual method of patternmaking on cloth, has been connected to aborigines on almost every continent (Schoeser, 2003). Tying, knotting, and stitching fabric before soaking it in dye was eventually replaced by fabrication through modern machinery. Interestingly, tie-dye symbolized the free spirit of bohemians and hippies in the US and Europe during the 1960s and 1970s.

Originating as a well regarded and commonly found form of household ornament and utensil decoration in rural China, paper-cutting has a counterpart—the Mexican *papel picado* used to celebrate the Day of the Dead. Widely associated with Chinese Communist propaganda art in the 1970s, this paper craft was nevertheless selected as a gift to former U. S. President Clinton on his 1998 visit to China. Conversely, pyrography, or the craft of wood or leather burning, originated elsewhere because the necessary tool, the soldering iron, was invented after the Industrial Revolution. Gift shops worldwide now sell souvenirs made with this technique. Claims of this handicraft belonging to any local cultural heritage may now be verified only by examining the incorporated pattern and subject matter. Finally, woodcut printing, a Chinese invention predating 220 BCE, was used to embellish ritual ceremonies and special occasions, including weddings and funerals, and later, to reproduce inexpensive prints. The medium was better known in the world of fine arts after the French Impressionists' stylistic adoption of Japanese *ukiyo-e* and the German Expressionists' daring fin-de-siècle application.

In both my schooling as a student in Singapore, and my recent research experience I have observed that Singapore art teachers and students rarely adhere to their ethnic roots when choosing artistic media, and traditional folk art is given little serious attention. The decisive factor indeed appears to be the national assessment, which does not include folk art as an important category of information to be learned in Singapore. More about how Singapore secondary art teachers deal with folk arts will be expounded later in this chapter.

Functional Applied Art

Applied art, an ambiguous genre, has historically and technically encompassed a wide variety of decorative arts and crafts, including ceramics, jewelry metals, glass, textile, and wood. Its initial productions and creations catered to spiritual or religious purposes but were later characterized by distinctive functions to meet secular needs and wants (Dormer, 1997). Craftworks were executed with clear intention in their makers' minds: to protect or to transport, to provide bodily comfort or living necessity, or to function as ornament or utensils for serving or storage. Applied art later required an entire labor force for mass production, dissemination, and promotion of goods and services. Incorporating fashion, product, and structural and packaging design as well as graphic and multimedia advertising, this genre has evolved into many disciplines and trades. In the applied arts in Singapore, at the time of this writing, a highly developed network of professionals are engaged in this form of visual communication, including technicians using cutting-edge technology in the entertainment and media industries, specializing in visual effects. The works of crafters are regaining recognition with the reevaluation of the aesthetics of applied art today (Greenhalgh, 2002; Sennett, 2008). A new series of documentaries titled *Crafts in America*, broadcast on PBS, reframed craft with themes such as memory and community, inviting practitioners of this genre to rejoin the discourse of contemporary art.

Figure 1

Some regional folk art. All photographs by the author.

Divisions of labor have ultimately led to the emergence of visual specialists in modern times. Historically, guilds were established in Europe and workshop trustees protected their interests and designated the educational credentials and certified training necessary for these professionals (Efland, 1990). As such, architects, draftsmen, and sculptors rose to status above lower-class landscaping workmen after the Renaissance. The Industrial Revolution, however, completely transformed their fate. Artisans involved in the production of functional artifacts, were relegated to lower social status and received unfair monetary compensation for their work/art in most postindustrialized cultures. School art at one time took over such manual training for young people in preparing for jobs in the factories (Stankiewicz, 2001). Crafters were marginalized even more in classical Chinese societies where scholar–artists dominated social and political discourse. Often regarded as manual laborers who made a living reproducing superficial artifacts instead of originating sophisticated art for the pure joy of expression, the Chinese fine art world is exclusive of craftspeople. In Singapore's 40 years of struggle for modernization, local crafts had become a largely diminished trade; however, an increasing attraction to various design professions has enlarged the pool of contemporary applied artists, large enough to overtake the number of fine artists in the Singapore art scene (Cocks, 2007).

CHAPTER 27 | Embracing a Predicament? Folk, Applied, Avant-Garde, and Singapore School Art

207

Ironically, the term *craftsmanship* has been widely adopted as a term for judging the artistic skill and technicality involved in the creation of fine art both in the East and West. Moreover, Rococo, Art Nouveau, and especially the Bauhaus movements had rippling effects beyond this art genre, shaping our educational axiom today. A Bauhaus-influenced art curriculum was widely disseminated in U. S. public schools, following the successful restructuring of art foundation courses at the college level in the mid-1900s (Efland, 1990). In the case of Singapore, the British arts and crafts movement that took place earlier had more apparent impact on Singapore's school art curriculum. An emphasis on proficiency in executing formal qualities of art and design was established as the basis of its sequential national art curriculum. The practice of design or applied art maintains a firm position in Singapore secondary schools throughout the mid- to late-20th century. Reflecting upon my formative education in Singapore, I recall simple graphic design assignments, such as poster, book cover, brochure, single-motif repeat patterns, and calligraphy, as standard art homework. Regrettably, I could retrieve no meaningful craft-making recollections.

Issues-Based Avant-Garde Art

Avant-garde art is now widely accepted as contemporary art at large. Notoriously radical in concept, content, form, method, and practice to expand the notion of art for art's sake, issues of the avant-garde were transgressive and charged with controversy. Often alarming, images were sometimes disgusting, profane, and obscene, aiming to complicate, problematize, and defamiliarize, instead of please the audience, engage the senses, and normalize art. Avant-garde artists emerged from an epoch of inflated individualism and optimism, self-proclaimed prophets of their time with new taste and new social orders. With an implicit mission to make the world a better place for the rest of the populace, their explicit erratic expression and creativity suited the idealized existential heroes and heroines struggling to find viable *strategies of being* (Fineberg, 1995).

After several reincarnations in the West, avant-garde art arrived at the backdoor of many non-Western countries, struggling for modernization with large-scale urbanization, fast-paced lifestyle changes, and the erosion of traditional values. A sense of displacement and maladjustment among many indigenous people in colonized non-Westernized countries led to a quest for identity in the midst of contention, oppression, and struggle. When most of the present postcolonial countries gained independence after WWII, economic growth and political stability did not occur overnight but took several decades to take off. Overseas art students returned home to less than perfect native lands. Deeply influenced by their international educative experience, and self-charged with the democratic and progressive mindset of social activists, Asian avant-garde artists used their art to debunk established norms, hoping to advance society in the direction of their vision (Clark, Peleggi, & Sabapathy, 2006).

In Singapore, reputable pioneering artists were abruptly joined by returning junior artists from overseas (usually Europe and the US), who imported new art forms and concepts to challenge the established canon. Much of their experimentation with multimedia, such as happenings, installations, and performance art, were issues-based and sought to provoke viewers' active responses (Sabapathy, 1991), resulting in a striking contrast with the previous generation of artists who eagerly created a *Nangyang* (tropical) art style using traditional fine art mediums like oil and watercolor subtly to stimulate viewers' contemplation. Interestingly, in 1994, the Singapore government restricted performance art in public venues (Cocks, 2007). Nevertheless, an avant-garde-like orientation found in Singapore Secondary School Art Style can be considered the result of the transformation of the local art scene effected by this genre. Those profoundly influenced by the wave of novelty and advocacy for change included homegrown artists, art-school faculty members, and school-art teachers, who were the recipients of government teaching scholarships for overseas studies. Idealistic and uncompromising, I once fit the latter profile, expecting my art students to be equally enthusiastic when encountering the latest art forms and concepts. As a novice teacher I was in fact grappling with the complexity of multiple art genres and school art.

Thinking *Outside* the Box: Liberal Encounter With the Multiplicity of Art Worlds

My liberal stance, like that of Zwier & Vaughan, "moves away from traditional values and conventional ideas about the need to preserve and maintain established institutions at all costs" (1984, p. 269). This stance was strengthened by the expansion of most national art museums with detached wings or the dedication of entirely new facilities to display contemporary art worldwide. At the same time as new spaces for the exhibition of contemporary art emerged in Singapore and elsewhere, separate folk art museums have been established to redefine the roots of local tradition and preserve heritage bound by locale. Additionally, applied artists now create and introduce new art forms, with their accompanying brand names in chain boutiques, channeling billions in capital annually. Commercial galleries in global megacities now exhibit pseudo- or truly controversial works, including but not limited to ready-mades, installations, and conceptual art–objects fashioned exclusively for an art market but that are often seen as nothing more than worthless junk to an ordinary citizen not privy to aesthetic conventions and inside conversations of art world elites. Yet, connoisseurs and collectors compete to purchase these works at astronomical prices and routinely break records at public auctions. Such paradoxical cultural phenomena and aesthetic systems mirror the inconsistencies and discord within Singapore Secondary School Art Style.

Exoticizing Folk Art

Folk art is a genre scorned by many Western progressive liberal nations during the Cold War Era because it was adopted to promote nationalism by many formerly Communist countries. China (Berliner, 1986), Hungary (Karpati, 1995), and the former Soviet Union had during one stage of their recent national history embraced this genre openly to support the ideology and advocacy of learning from the working class. Its contemporary remixed version shows a wider range of positive traits, rewritten as part of invisible history in need of inclusion into mainstream art education (Bolin, Blandy, & Congdon, 2000). Typically tied to

the folklore, traditions, and heritage of places, folk art is an art form for and by the people; hence those promoting multicultural and intercultural understanding through art have become its closest allies. Formerly associated with rites and rituals surrounding seasonal celebrations or major food-gathering activities, folk art is sometimes intimately connected to cultivation and hunting ceremonies or other aspects of living and survival. Uniqueness is built into the art form because materials and mediums were often bounded by local flavor and regional characteristics; whereas skills needed for handling the media for expression were

Figure 3

Some issues-based art.

passed on through intergenerational apprenticeships instead of formal education with standard curriculum and instruction. Because its meanings are often intertwined with local sites and stories, folk art readily became a form of community art (Congdon, 2004).

A colonial past has propagated the objectifying of the practice and pedagogy of the folk art genre in Singapore schools, where art teachers involved in the teaching of regional folk art seldom practiced art of this genre themselves. Although they were unconcerned about promoting community connections, these teachers were self-trained experts who had mastered the look of and accompanying technical methods inherent in the particular craft of certain folk art forms and able to harness enormous success in coaching their students to produce "excellent" work

CHAPTER 27 | Embracing a Predicament? Folk, Applied, Avant-Garde, and Singapore School Art

209

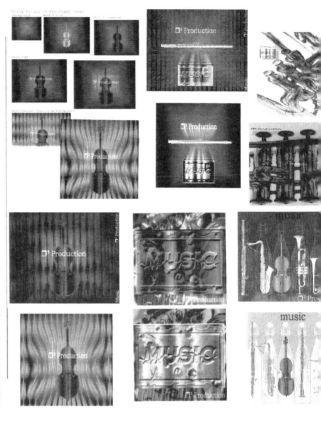

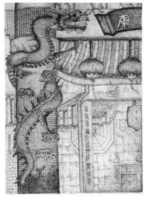

Figure 4

Left: Students'
artworks with folk
art influence.

Figure 5

Right: Students'
artworks with
applied art influence.

that met art exam requirements. Hence, exoticized folk artworks created by secondary students were exquisite and spectacular, but utterly lacking a deep connection to the meanings and cultural values associated with these forms of artistic expression.

Silencing Applied Art

Contemporary applied art has taken on a new spin with the recent shift in art education towards visual culture interests.[2] The applied art genre has almost become synonymous with commercialism, and visual culture advocates and others now condemn commercialized applied artists as the envoys of excessive capitalism. Open market capitalism promulgated the production and distribution of inexpensive merchandise affordable to all, yet mass production exploiting cheap labor and available raw materials shifted the interest of entrepreneurs, seducing them into concentrating industries in a few strategic locations on the globe. Aggressive commercial advertising and promotion has conditioned patterns of consumption with little consideration of environmental devastation, labor exploitation, or local values. Branded franchise outlets have increasingly threatened the unique characteristics associated with particular practices in specific locales, and have overwhelmed or overshadowed the pride and dignity of the citizenry.

Instead of educating students to reflect critically on the process of commercial aesthetic persuasion and cultivate resistance to hedonism, Singapore school art loyally trails market forces. Improved design and research development mean greater value-added output and indirectly promote the Singapore national economy. With more postsecondary educational opportunities available and greater recognition promoted by large-scale competitions, applied artists have triumphed in the system. Students have little opportunity to explore this genre in any alternative manner, such as one that offers an array of educational sites for further study of material culture (Bolin & Blandy, 2003), semiotics (Smith-Shank, 2004), and the media. Instead, applied art practice quietly pervades Singapore secondary art classrooms, aiming to establish a foundation and pave a direct vocational path for students who may eventually follow this direction to embark on a career. The rationale for training people in school as future investments is implicitly and explicitly validated. Metaphorically, the voices of distinctive and successful applied art practitioners (designers) echo triumph of the marketplace in Singapore schools, while the voices of those (crafters) not adhering to new globalized and commercialized venues and practices remain silent, nullified, and devoid of economic earning power.

Diluting Avant-garde Art

The chronic eccentricity and rebelliousness of the stereotypic artist held during the Romantic Era have dominated the conventional paradigm (Gergen, 1990); however, contemporary artists embody the spirit of the avant-garde and beyond. They were more likely schooled within certain traditions and held to specific expectations. According to Pollock (1992), avant-garde art evolved in three stages: (a) seeking reference in conventional style, form, concept and standard; (b) deferring these conventions; and (c) making a totally different claim to start a new trend or paradigm. Avant-garde artists must be adequately informed about art and cultural history, tuned in to the latest development of technology, and in possession of a substantial understanding of the interdisciplinary paradigm in order to appropriate themes and materials effectively in their work. Their artfulness injects new meanings by making ideas happen.

As such, this genre has inspired many contemporary art education advocates to focus on enduring ideas (Steward & Walker, 2006), issues (Gaudelius & Speirs, 2002), and themes (Anderson & Milbrant, 2002) as a means of restructuring K–12 curriculum to provide meaningful connections between students' lives and their living communities. Deeper engagement to such degree in this genre has been impossible inside Singapore public secondary schools because of some obvious impediments: (a) a lack of focus on historical, cultural, and aesthetic dimensions in its public operational art curriculum; (b) a shortage of time and supporting resources; and (c) a stratified education system that privileged students who could pursue this genre in autonomous, private schools. Although the exceptional schools possess the means and resources to encourage individualistic creation and artistic expression, ordinary Singapore public schools must cope with practical issues, such as surviving the national assessment or preparing students for an income-producing vocation. The kind of creativity and artistic expression that cater solely to the criteria preset by the exam board pervades the educational system. Supervised by a highly disciplined, conservative, and affluent middle-class society, an avant-garde point of view in Singapore public school can only remain diluted and mild.

Regrettably, even designated art textbooks, planned and written by appointed art specialists from the Singapore Ministry of Education in recent decades, could not provide adequate up-to-date background information on art genres. An acute shortage of scholarly studies in the local developments of varying genres is to blame; moreover, because art history is not required in the national prescribed curriculum, inattention in the operational art curriculum in Singapore seems justifiable to teachers. Neither the necessity nor the opportunity to delve into cultural and historical meanings of art in the school system exists. With busy schedules, big classes, ever-increasing duties, additional responsibilities, and rising expectations, many local art teachers could only conveniently consider the distinct characteristics of the art genres discussed in this chapter as delineated in art material catalogues. Annual budgeting and ordering of new art supplies perhaps exists as the only reminder that Singapore Secondary School Art Style is loosely related with art outside the school.

Thinking Beyond the Box: Radical Vision of the Future

For the last 20 years mandatory prolonged education has been the trend in all 10 Southeast Asian countries (Santa Maria, 2002), where receiving education

Figure 6

Students' artworks with avant-garde art influence.

CHAPTER 27 | Embracing a Predicament? Folk, Applied, Avant-Garde, and Singapore School Art

211

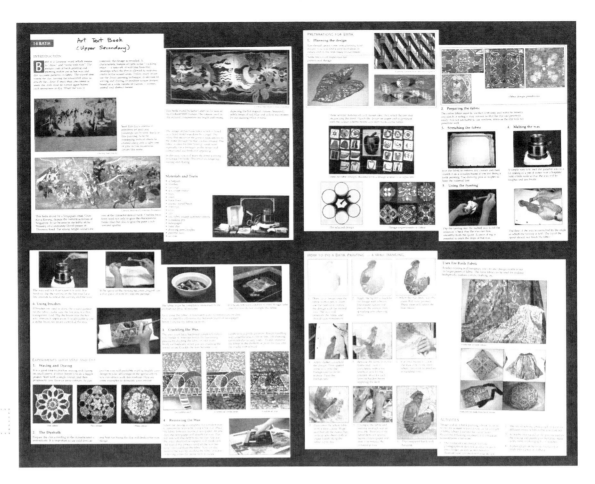

Figure 7

An analysis of Singapore art text books.

in a formal school setting is both a necessity and a virtue. From an economic standpoint, education is a vocational investment to meet the increasingly complicated demands of the job market. Cultural traditions in this region (Buddhism, Confucianism, Hinduism, Islam, and Taoism), dictate that learning is a most noble and valuable activity for youth (Reagan, 2000). Education becomes a social enterprise, an economic assurance for a better future, and also an integral part of cultural beliefs and practice, especially in newly industrialized countries, including Hong Kong (China), Singapore, South Korea, and Taiwan. People in these four locations have relied heavily on education to ensure their place in global economic competition in recent decades while facing a shortage of natural resources. Impacted by Confucian ideology, which emphasizes nurturing and training as self-improvement (Tu, 1985), postsecondary and tertiary diplomas will remain serious objectives or *goals* in these four locales. In order to contribute to the widening global conception of public art education and fostering interconnections of multiple art worlds, more research conducted on school art in this region is imperative.

Researching the interplay of various genres of art with Singapore Secondary School Art Style helped me gain critical insights into Singapore school practice, policy, and ideology. The following brief speculation on how Singapore Secondary School Art Style style may eventually manifest entering this millennium is based on the radical assumption that "the existing social system, of which the school is part, is in some way debilitating and therefore must change" (Zwier & Vaughan, 1984, p. 270). I hope the change will be for the better. Building on Kuhn's proposition (1970), the future-oriented purpose of knowledge lies in envisioning and finding new problems, not merely searching for solutions to existing problems. Identifying new issues inherent in old problems begins by formulating new questions from within. My purpose is not to propose another meganarration but to project a futuristic outlook for this amalgamated school art style.

Regional folk art that once occupied a significant portion of the Singapore secondary school art curriculum is disappearing as educational reform advocates rally for the more appealing new technology of computer art. Art teachers who can demonstrate techniques and impart knowledge of folk art and craft are declining in number, yet the easy availability of hobby art and craft materials outside the school milieu has had profound impact on students' artistic learning. Craft was deemed uninteresting and noncreative as an art assignment in school art (Bresler, 1998), but many female participants in my research confessed that it was the only kind of artistic creation in which they would personally be involved after leaving school. Hobby art (e.g., sewing, embroidery, and knitting) represented the closest relationship between art and life for them, reiterating how material culture has more direct impact on artistic learning and living. Student artistic learning requires more inquiry, especially with the recent push for understanding Asian art through its use and the manner in which it is experienced (Mrazek & Pitelka, 2007).

Contemporary applied art presently thriving in the educational system as "value-added" instruction will continue to prepare resourceful and disciplined students to become efficient workers in Singapore, especially as the small island-nation transitions into tertiary economic foci. Integrating art and design showcase the versatility of artistic learning, thus making art programs more defensible for inclusion and retention during economic crises; however, the need to address conflicting values and to acknowledge the multiplicity of meanings in a pluralistic world is still essential at educational sites. For example, with the promotion of both critical thinking skills and critical pedagogy, avant-garde art it offers various avenues to explore identities and purposes; hence, its status in Singapore secondary school will also be assured.

Envisioning its constantly changing primacies, I can only anticipate multiple directions of growth for Singapore Secondary School Art Style in our shrinking global village. I challenge art educators around the globe to recontemplate the context of school art, how to embrace and honor varied art pedagogies in schools where multiplicity of art genres are likely to already manifest. With limited time and inadequate resources, those who teach art in schools face constant challenges. Art educators promoting particular approaches, methods, and art genres in schools will need to reconsider all the demands of teaching and all dimensions of school practices in this millennium. Only by doing so can teachers capitalize upon their interests and capabilities to improve school art, and possibly also leading to concrete suggestions for the improvement of teacher preparation programs.

In addition, recent research about Singapore adolescents' experiences with artistic schooling (Kan, 2008) has shown students tactfully negotiating multiple layers of meanings from an ever-expanding school art milieu. Because of the immense popularity of unconventional teenage cultural practices around the world poses a threat to local community values

and cultures, I urgently call for a research agenda in our field that can offer an array of possibilities for young learners around the globe to accrue, construct, and shape personal meaning through school art.

Figure 8

The changing Singapore secondary school art style.

Coda

Invisible boxes (in addition to schools) may be ubiquitous in human society, yet as an artist recently converted to educational researcher, I sincerely and stubbornly hold a more idealistic outlook when considering the purpose of the arts in school. Their most profound contribution to education in fact embodies my confidence in their unique abilities to consolidate multiple layers of meaning to extend our ephemeral life experiences. As playful mindfulness in which skills, discipline, spontaneity, critical inquiries, interpretations, and connections to life can all become part and parcel of school curricula, the arts should be treated differently from other school subjects. Although other academic subjects continue to cultivate a strong allegiance to their own disciplinary structure with attainable goals, established instructional rules and set standards, the arts might be better off to attend to the deepest and wildest of human dreams.[3]

After all, dreams are so vital to being. And *being matters.*

CHAPTER 27 | Embracing a Predicament? Folk, Applied, Avant-Garde, and Singapore School Art

213

Acknowledgments

I am indebted to Professors Liora Bresler, Julia Kellman, and Christine Marmé Thompson for their advice, suggestions, and encouragement on earlier drafts. My special thanks to Shu-Chun Chen, Jung-ah Choi, Linda Meixner, and Barbara Poss for their excellent editorial assistance.

REFERENCES

Abraham, R. (2003). The localization of 'O' level art examinations in Zimbabwe. *Studies in Art Education, 45*(1), 73–87.

Anderson, R. (1990). *Calliope's sisters*. Englewood Cliffs, NJ: Prentice Hall.

Anderson, T., & Milbrant, M. W. (2002). *Art for life: Authentic instruction in art*. New York: McGraw-Hill.

Berliner, N. Z. (1986). *Chinese folk art: The small skills of carving insects*. New York: Graphic Society.

Bolin, P., & Blandy, D. (2003). Beyond visual culture: Seven statements of support for material culture studies in art education. *Studies in Art Education, 44*(3), 246–263.

Bolin, P., Blandy, D., & Congdon, K. (Eds.). (2000). *Remembering others: Making invisible histories of art education visible*. Reston, VA: National Art Education Association.

Bourdieu, P., & Passeron, J. C. (1977). *Reproduction in education, society, and culture*. Beverly Hills, CA: Sage.

Bresler, L. (1998). "Child art", "fine arts", and "art for children": The shaping of school practice and implications for change. *Arts Education Policy Review, 100*(1), 3–10.

Bruner, J. (1996). *The culture of education*. Cambridge, MA: Harvard University Press.

Chanda, N. (2007). *Bound together: How traders, preachers, adventurers, and warriors change globalization*. New Haven, NJ: Yale Press.

Clark, J., Peleggi, M., & Sabapathy, T. K. (2006). *Eye of the beholder: Reception, audience, and practice of modern Asian art*. New South Wales, Australia: University of Sydney.

Cocks, A. S. (2007). Focus on Southeast Asia: Joining up the dots. *The Art Newspaper 16*(182), 19.

Congdon, K. G. (2004). *Community art in action*. Worcester, MA: Davis.

Craft in America. Retrieved November 30, 2008, from http://www.pbs.org/craftinamerica/

Danto, A. C. (1981). The artworld. *Journal of Philosophy, 61*, 470–481.

Dickie, G. (1984). *The art circle: A theory of art*. New York: Haven Press.

Dissanayake, E. (1992). *What is art for?* Seattle: Washington University Press.

Dormer, P. (1997). (Ed.). *The culture of craft*. New York: Manchester University Press.

Duncum, P. (2001). Visual culture: Developments, definitions, and directions for art education. *Studies in Art Education, 42*(2), 101–112.

Efland, A. (1976). The school art style. *Studies in Art Education, 17*(2), 37–44.

Efland, A. (1990). *The history of art education: Intellectual and social currents in teaching the visual arts*. New York: Teachers College Press.

Fineberg, J. (1995). *Art since 1940: Strategies of being*. Englewood Cliffs, NJ: Prentice Hall.

Fraser-Lu, S. (1986). *Indonesian Batik*. New York: Oxford University Press.

Freeland, C. (2001). *But is it art?: An introduction to art theory*. New York: Oxford University Press.

Gaudelius, Y., & Speirs, P. (Eds.). (2002). *Contemporary issues in art education*. Upper Saddle River, NJ: Prentice Hall.

Gergen, K. J. (1990). *The saturated self: Dilemmas of identity in contemporary life*. New York: Basic Books.

Greenhalgh, P. (2002). (Ed.). *The persistence of craft: The applied arts today*. New Brunswick, NJ: Rutgers University Press.

Kan, K. (1999, March). *The Singapore Youth Festival Art Exhibition: An elevation and conservation of Southeast Asia crafts and folk art*. Poster session presented at the National Art Education Association Annual Convention, Washington, DC.

Kan, K. H. (2004). *Multiple manifestation of the Singapore Secondary School Art Style: A story told visually*. Unpublished doctoral dissertation, University of Illinois at Urbana-Champaign.

Kan, K. H. (2008). How Singapore adolescent students cruise the expanding school art milieu. *Visual Art Research, 34*(1), 16–28.

Kuhn, T. (1970). *The structure of scientific revolutions*. Chicago: University of Chicago Press.

Karpati, A. (1995). Arts education in post-communist Hungary: Policies, curricula, and integration. *Arts Education Policy Review, 97*(1), 11–17.

Mrazek, J., & Pitelka, M. (2007). *What's the use of art? Asian visual and material culture in context*. Honolulu: University of Hawaii Press.

Pollock, G. (1992). *Avant-garde gambits 1888/1893: Gender and the color of art*. London: Thames & Hudson.

Reagan, T. G. (2000). *Nonwestern educational traditions: Alternative approaches to educational thought and practice*. Mahwah, NJ: Erlbaum.

Robinson, S. (1969). *A history of dyed textiles*. Britain: Studio Vista.

Sabapathy, T. K. (1991). *Sculpture in Singapore*. Singapore: National Art Museum Gallery.

Santa Maria, M. (2002). Youth in Southeast Asia: Living within the continuity of tradition and the turbulence of change. In J. Brown, R. Larson, & T. S. Sarawathi (Eds.), *The world's youth: Adolescents in eight regions on the globe* (pp. 171–205). Cambridge, UK: Cambridge Press.

Schoeser, M. (2003). *World Textiles: A concise history*. New York: Thames & Hudson.

Sennett, R. (2008). *The craftsman*. New Haven, NJ: Yale Press.

Smith-Shank, D. L. (Ed.). (2004). *Semiotics and visual culture. Sights, signs, and significance*. Reston, VA: National Art Education Association.

Stankiewicz, M. A. (2001). *Roots of art education practice*. Worcester, MA: Davis.

Stankiewicz, M. A. (2007). Capitalizing art education: Mapping international histories. In L. Bresler (Ed.), *International Handbook of Research in Arts Education* (pp. 11–22). Dordrecht, Netherlands: Springer.

Steward, M. G., & Walker, S. (2006). *Rethinking curriculum in art*. Worcester, MA: Davis.

Stokrocki, M. (1991). A decade of qualitative research in art education. *Visual Arts Research, 17*(1), 42–51.

Toren, Z. (2004). Art curriculum, learning materials, and cultural capital in the Israeli kindergarten. *Studies in Art Education, 45*(3), 206–220.

Tu, W. (1985). *Confucian thought: Selfhood as creative transformation*. New York: State University of New York.

Zwier, G., & Vaughan, G. M. (1984). Three ideological orientations in school vandalism research. *Review of Educational Research, 54*(2), 263–292.

AUTHOR'S NOTE

This article is based on the author's doctoral dissertation, *Multiple Manifestation of the Singapore Secondary School Art Style: A Story Told Visually* (2004), University of Illinois at Urbana-Champaign.

ENDNOTES

1 *Art genres* denotes separation of style and kind, comparable with music genres, such as classical, jazz, or rock. It is not to be confused with *genre painting*, the portrayal of scenes from everyday life in 17th-century European art.

2 In light of such practices, visual culture advocates now position art education with the goal of bettering civic notions and eschew the temptation of visual culture (or reincarnation of applied art) with critical thinking (Duncum, 2001) and critical pedagogy. Educating informed consumers and responsible citizens is essential to such a view.

3 *Dreams* is used here as metaphor to include vision, perception, imagination, and aspiration, and all the in-betweens and beyond.

Globalization and Art Education in South Korea: Changes and Complexity of Art Curriculum Research and Practice

Jae-young Lee

With heightened awareness of the role of images in a global society, art educators are trying to ascertain impacts of globalization on visual arts education. Images, widely understood as innovative forms of representation, are seen as an essential part of international trade that accelerates globalization and cross-cultural amalgamation in our technologically advanced era. In other words, cultural globalization is intensified by increased international traffic in images and symbols and the spread of culture worldwide (Macdonald, 2006). By considering images and culture as the core of global exchange, art educators are now exploring the impact of globalization at the level of individual students' lives (Tavin & Hausman, 2004). Many art educators focus on the expressive, symbolic, metaphoric, reflective, and critical power of art to highlight the overwhelming forces of globalization that the economy, politics, media, aesthetics, and culture present in our lives (jagodzinski, 2008; Macdonald, 2006; Rectanus, 2006; Tavin & Hausman, 2004). These inquiries lead us to consider how economic and political exchanges become cultural exchanges, thus emphasizing the cultural impact of the proliferation of images and the increase in global cultural exchanges.

Taking a cultural studies approach to globalization reveals ways in which art education can play a key role in elucidating just how the process of globalization is embedded within the production, proliferation, and consumption of images that shape our identities—thoughts, feelings, desires, knowledge, behavior, and attitudes. We have already experienced how the distinctive and dominant roles of commodification and the consumption of images in daily life bring inevitable changes and impact our lives (Tavin & Hausman, 2004). Transnational commodities and commercial products, which include images of these commodities

and their representative symbolic visual representations and logos, configure the style of our daily lives and the patterns of our social lives.

With these considerations in mind, this chapter considers how art education in South Korea responds to particular forces of globalization. Such issues include but are not limited to the complex arrangements of and dangers inherent in cultural appropriation and subordination that come colonization, international commerce, and local adaptations. Although the goals of neo-liberalism with its vision of a global society (or marketplace) may be seen as highly attractive to some, I argue in this chapter that art education in South Korea should take on a more self-reflective and urgent social responsibility and engage complex issues that relate to the impact of globalization on Korean educational and cultural practices. Following a brief history of South Korea's traumatic past, I identify and describe five different approaches to art curriculum research practices in South Korea—conservative, relative, liberal, reliant and subordinate—each of these approaches representing a response to particular facets of globalization and now useful as lenses through which we can understand the cultural and ideological impact of globalization on Korean art educational thought. Based on this analysis I describe and recommend a hybridized, critical-reflective approach for South Korea, one that embraces, resists, and critically engages globalization and Western cultural hegemony, and that at the same time creatively and selectively merges with Korean conservative traditional values and cultural practices. The historical lessons learned from Koreans' understandings about the Westernization of South Korea—including a crisis of tradition and sovereignty—figure deeply into these considerations.

CHAPTER 28 | Globalization and Art Education in South Korea: Changes and Complexity of Art Curriculum Research and Practice

215

Globalization and Art Education in South Korea

As in the US and elsewhere, the impact of globalization, from a cultural and ideological standpoint, is currently in the mainstream of academic discourse in art education in South Korea. According to Lee (2004), globalization in South Korea is a kind of "reminiscent" (p. 28), if lamentable, historical lesson in many respects. In order to understand the unique impact of globalization in South Korea, we need to first consider the fact that globalization there is not especially recent, and the response to globalization in South Korea can best be understood when situated within a larger historical context.

From an historical point of view, the political singularity and linguistic autonomy once thought to be unique to Korean society were possible for a very long time because of its racial homogeneity, isolation, and geography. Korean purported cultural uniqueness was based on a specific cultural orientation strongly influenced by traditional Korean folk beliefs and religions, including animism, shamanisms, Buddhism, Taoism, and Confucianism. These beliefs remain part of the Korean psychic identity today, and are the foundation for contemporary South Korean nationalism and patriotism.

Many Koreans resisted opening of the Korean ports to Western society in the late 19th century because they feared Korean national integrity and independence would be jeopardized. Korean national integrity and independence was in danger also because of modernization that occurred in Korea after the opening of its ports and the influx of outside influences. A tragic consequence of the opening of Korean ports was attributed to Japanese expansionist colonialism. Korea was subjected to Japanese imperialism from 1901 until 1945. During this time, Korea lost its Mother language and even Korean citizens' traditional personal names. Japanese colonial policy worsened during WWII. The entire population was victimized, women were forced into prostitution for the Japanese military, and men were subjected to a compulsory draft.

Once Japanese colonization ended with the defeat of Japan at the end of WWII, there were new forces to contend with. Although opening ports originally brought modernization in Korea via Japan, modernization after the era of Japanese colonization ended included a gradual Westernization of Korean traditions. In mid 20th century, the Korean peninsula was victimized by the burgeoning Cold War, the Korean War, and finally, the tragic division of the Korean peninsula at the 38th parallel. Western aid was necessary to reestablish a national foundation—economic, political, cultural—of what became the nation of South Korea after the Korean War. However, during this time, a more suspicious attitude amongst Koreans toward modernization, Westernization, and even globalization throughout this cataclysmic period was strengthened. Nationalistic protectionists resisted Westernization and globalization in order to maintain South Korea's sovereignty and traditional culture. Issues of industrialization, modernization, Westernization, internationalization, and globalization thus created numerous different tensions between the forces of these social phenomena and a crisis of national identity that was political, socio-cultural, and socioeconomic.

These bitter historical events seem to be among the many reasons South Koreans currently resist the continued movement toward globalization. Their primary concern is that globalization threatens the sovereignty and autonomy of Koreans. In accordance with this increasing doubt about the benefits of globalization, intense Korean resistance to the impact of globalization can be traced back to the Uruguay Round of World Trade Organization from 1993 that aimed to establish lower duties imported products imported to Korea. Because of this and subsequent Free Trade Agreements with other countries as late as 2007 that appeared to Koreans to protect other countries' lesser competitive power in the global market, South Korean society has recently contended with more radical, illegal violent local protests in response to globalization, during which policemen were harmed and their equipment broken in clashes with demonstrators. In an extreme act of resistance, in 2007 one laborer set fire to himself in response to political pressures and the economic temptations of globalization. At the same time, many contemporary South Korean artists have also become social activists in the past 15 years, expressing their concerns about globalization in concert other protesters. Protesters' arguments have concerned the political and economic ramifications of globalization on Korean values and traditions, and their concerns about the long-term, potentially negative consequences of Korean cultural transformation and subordination.

With such a painful history of globalization, traditional South Korean society is today faced with both pessimistic and optimistic prospects of globalization. While the export-oriented economic structure of South Korea welcomes the driving forces of globalization for greater profits and economic prosperity, there is continued and increased anxiety that traditional Korean society and national sovereignty will be subjected to new forms of neo-colonialism as South Korea moves toward economic and cultural adaptation to Westernized ideological frameworks.

Relationships of Contemporary South Korean National Art Education Theory and Practices to Korean Social, Cultural, and Political Thought

It seems to me that South Koreans need a better understanding of the historical contexts of globalization in order to grasp not only how the traumas of the past and present conditions impact contemporary Korean economics, politics, culture, and political thought, but also how to now move forward decisively and proactively in an era of globalization. As Bydler observes, "To Koreans, globalization is no longer a fantasy or paradox. It is a reality to simply accept" (2004, p. 132). So the question becomes not merely how to respond to such a conflicted reality, but what kind of future we now envision for South Korea. I would argue here that an important strategy for such a task involves consideration of the role of education, and in particular, art education, as South Korea reestablishes a contemporary cultural, political, and philosophical framework for the future. On a fundamental and practical level, South Korean National Art Curriculum research and practice parallels the current responses, both positive and negative, to globalization in South Korea. Issues within South Korean National Art Curriculum discourse reflect what is at stake in contemporary Korean culture at large.

My analysis of recent changes in orientations to South Korean art curriculum research and practice reveals a spectrum or continuum encompassing two extremes, namely *ethnocentrism* as an extreme example of reactionary responses to globalization and *neo-colonialism* or utter subordination that follows as a consequence of extreme pro-globalization forces (Eder, 2006; Ritzer, 2006). A *liberal* approach occupies the middle of the spectrum, and *relativistic* and *reliant* approaches are situated between this central point and the two extreme poles of the spectrum. These two approaches differ only in the degree of their tendency toward the extreme poles.

Ethnocentrism: A Reactionary-Conservative Approach

Currently, some South Korean art programs and practices have touted nationalistic ethnocentrism as a pessimistic and reactionary response to globalization. The perception that traditional Korean culture is in crisis has resulted in a reexamination and promotion

Table 1

Changes and Complexity in Art Curriculum Research and Practice in South Korea in Response to Globalization

	Conservative	Relative	Liberal	Reliant	Subordinated
Influenced by	• Nationalism • Predominant Cultural Exclusivism • Ethnocentrism	• Cultural Relativism	• Cultural Liberalism • Cross-cultural & International understanding	• Cultural Toadyism	• Neo-Colonialism • Capitalism • Post-Industrialism
Characteristics	• Regional Uniqueness • Succession of culture • Resistant • Preservation • Transcendent • Extreme seclusionism		• Global Hybridization • Evolution & Recreation of culture • Reciprocal Interconnection • Interconnection • Diversity • Balance		• Transnational • Homogeneity • Exploitation of culture • Irresistible • Indiscreet Adoption • Extreme dominancy
Art curriculum research & practice in South Korea	• Discovering uniqueness and excellence of Korean culture		• Discovering cultural pluralism		• Critical discovering— a critique of Western ideology hidden in Korean cultural practice

of traditional Korean values and cultural practices in South Korean schools, rather than embracing a broader diversity of cultural practices and values resulting from globalization. Yi and Kim (2005) represent the essence of this approach:

> We realize that we are attached too much to the Western or European ethnocentric method of art education and thus ignore [the] techniques of East Asian art education ... In order to discover and know the traditional art of Korea, Korean traditional artworks should be included in...art curricula...[S]tudents will [then] learn to understand and enjoy the art and culture of Korea in the future. (pp. 18-20)

They describe one of the recent, mainstream trends in Korean art curriculum research and practice. Art curriculum research and practice in this framework focuses on traditional Korean art and culture as a means of protecting national identity and solidarity (Kim & Yi, 2005; Yi & Kim, 2005). To reinforce the excellence and uniqueness of traditional Korean artwork and culture that is "intuitive, natural, simple, pure, humorous, and meditative" (Kim, 2000, p. 44), these conservative approaches include the study of traditional Korean philosophy and aesthetics, traditional painting, folk painting, architecture, materials, subject matters, and traditional art education as a way to protect Korean society from globalism. Following this approach, globalization is thwarted in favor of learning about Korean tradition. Kim and Yi (2005) observe that more consideration of art education pedagogical methodology is needed to encourage students to have a better understanding of traditional art, culture, and philosophy to improve students' understanding of Korean culture. This awareness promotes further research into new pedagogies and the content of traditional Korean art in art textbooks to rebuild the characteristics of Korean art education in a modern global society.

Relative Approach

Cultural relativism refers to a partially self-protective interpretation and adoption of multicultural art education theory that insists on constructing a better society through further understanding and the development of cultures (McFee & Degge, 1977). A contemporary social reconstructive approach has been partially adapted in South Korean art educational thought as a catalyst to achieve cultural reconstruction and at the same time communicate the excellence of Korean tradition in the context of a global society. This approach seeks to discover a mutual interchange, blending, and alteration of Korean tradition to achieve the succession and evolution of Korean tradition (Yi

& Kim, 2005). Art educators believing in such an approach are studying foreign cultures with more active, selective, and open attitudes when that study produces positive influences on Korean society. One way this objective is being met is by including more images from foreign cultures in national art textbooks. Art classes thus put more emphasis on how to analyze the artistic achievements of foreign culture and learn how to adopt foreign culture to improve Korean traditional cultural practices. Research on traditional culture-based pedagogy now focuses on developing lessons, using field trips, worksheets, websites, and visual resources that are related to museum and cultural sites, cultural events and artistic festivals. The pedagogical methodology focuses mostly on exploring different techniques and materials.

Although accompanied by discourse about multiculturalism and social reconstruction, it is important to note that the main goal of this approach is to further develop Korean traditional values, to explore Korea's place in the context of global movements, and to promote an international understanding of Korean culture and traditions rather than focusing on the merits of cultural pluralism itself (Kim, 2000). The recent 7th National Korean Art Curriculum and the research related to that art curriculum partially reflect this approach, insofar as it aims at a better understanding of the Korean tradition in order to maintain Korean sovereignty through comparative cultural studies with other cultures in a global society (Gyoyookbu, 1998). In my view, the superficiality of the explorations of diverse cultures in this framework is substantively flawed in that it lacks intellectual rigor or historical depth in the manner in which it engages the study of other cultures. Moreover, it also reveals the limitations of research and practice aimed at promoting a better understanding of the Korean tradition through exploring other cultures. The correlation between studying other cultures and understanding Korean traditional culture has not yet been clearly understood or articulated. This correlation assumes transferability—that an understanding of other cultures will facilitate a better understanding of our own culture and its philosophical and aesthetic achievements. The transferability is an aspect that is assumed, but uncertain, in my view.

Liberal Approach

A liberal position assumes an idealized approach to globalization and international understanding in art education. Its aims are to achieve a balanced perspective in a pluralistic society (Jeong, 1996). The virtue of liberalism is its emphasis on art education for cross-cultural, reciprocal understanding, and its sense of a global village or global civil society. The liberal approach assumes that globalization brings mutual respect, harmonious international relations, shared values, and a neo-liberalistic, cosmopolitan life.

As the liberal view has become more widely held among South Koreans, the government has responded by creating the Globalization Promoting Committee, an advisory committee proposed in 1995 by South Korean President, Young-sam Kim. During this time, the South Korean Culture Ministry worked to establish a cultural infrastructure to ensure a balanced perspective between global pluralism and nationalism. Reconceptualizing the inter-relationship of global cultures within the traditional Korean culture thus became a national project.

Such an inclusive and open vision provides an impetus to contemporary art education in South Korea, and traditional Korean artists and art education scholars have been responding to the global interplay of cultures. New experimental initiatives to achieve a balanced cultural interplay have resulted in cultural diffusion, hybridization, mixing, displacement, and crossing borders as common topics for art and education (Eder, 2006; Erickson, 2000; Lippard, 1990; Pieterse, 2006). Several international art biennales held in South Korea and supported by the Culture Ministry and metropolitan cities are examples of this experimentation. These globally focused cultural festivals have strengthened the role of art in cultural exchange, cultural hybridity, and cultural reorganization (Bydler, 2004). New art subject areas have also expanded the scope of the traditional content of South Korean art textbooks and also the direction of art curriculum research. The influence of pluralism, deconstructivism, and postmodernism is accelerating this trend of art curriculum research in South Korea (Park, 2002). Several approaches explore transfused new ideas and techniques from different cultural perspectives, while others involve comparative research on cross-cultures.

However, as Eder (2006) notes, there is ongoing conflict between the inclination toward universalism or hegemonizing tendencies of globalization and increasing interests in preserving and promoting differences among countries and cultures. The conflict centers on how global interaction facilitates either homogeneity or heterogeneity of cultures in a global society (Eder, 2006). The ideological circumstance and the power struggle surrounding the mixing of different cultures is part of the debate (Pieterse, 2006). People are concerned that Korean tradition is endangered by recklessly adapting to other cultures because of globalization.

Reliant Approach

The reliant approach places great emphasis on the benefits of Western cultures in South Korea, conflating Westernization with modernization and economic prosperity for South Korea. It is easy to understand how the ideological implications of globalization yield a reliant attitude toward leading Western cultures. The hegemonic impact of Western culture on South Korean values is enabled by the rapid development of technologies and media that bombard Koreans with Western images and values. Through the proliferation of images in the mass media and cyberspace, the Western standard of beauty has brought Western fashion style and a boom in plastic surgery to Korea. Western cultures depicted in comics, animations, and TV dramas swamp domestic entertainment markets, culture, and websites. Commercial products and computer/video games also reflect this social trend. Assimilation into Western culture thus becomes a desire and the social trend in South Korea.

But a reliant approach has been sharply criticized in South Korea as reckless pro-Westernism. According to its detractors, a reliant approach embraces Westernism uncritically, fails to consider ideological implications of Western-oriented globalization, and does not give adequate consideration to the negative impact of the pervasiveness of Western culture on Korean identity and values. It is as if Western culture charms people into forgetting their ability to think critically about the undesirable impact of Western influences on their own traditions and value systems.

This same trend toward Westernization is also evident in art education theory and practice. The inroads of new Western art education theory has brought about an historic change to the National Korean Art Curriculum. Over the past 30 years or so, the National Korean Art Curricula have been based on Self-expressionism, Discipline-Based Art Education (DBAE), and multicultural art education. More recently, South Korean art educators are engaging in art curriculum research to adapt yet another Western framework for visual arts education, in their attempts to translate visual culture art education theory emanating from the US to Korean art educational practices. This continued reliant approach in Korean art education theory marginalizes art curriculum research in that it not only fails to take into account the importance of traditional Korean values and practices to

Korean citizens; in its uncritical adoption and incorporation of Western imagery, media, and visual culture productions into Korean art educational programs of study, and insofar as it misses an important feature of globalization, which in actuality functions in multiple directions, rather than uni-directional.

The Subordinate Approach

A subordinate approach is a variant of the reliant approach, and no Korean National Art Curriculum research has pursued subordination. In fact, South Korean educators are now noticing an increased tendency toward rejection of subordinated responses, in which Korean students lose their critical vantage point toward globalization, and recent Korean art curriculum research responds to the negative consequences of subordination to Westernized ideology and cultural practices in a globalized world.

Toward a Critical-Reflective, Hybridized Approach

Korean art educators have only just begun to recognize the need for a kind of critical lens through which students can investigate globalization as a form of neo-colonialism, neo-imperialism, capitalism, and post-industrialism. Thus, globalization in South Korea can be described either as a complicated power relationship or as blind subordination to a dominant Western ideology that accelerates global homogenization. Rather than adopting one particular approach over another, recent art curriculum research in South Korea has engaged a variety of visual culture art education, culture studies, media studies, visual literacy, multicultural, and social activist approaches in art education, each with increased sensitivity to and acknowledgement of the importance of strengthening Korean cultural practices and identities (Kim, 2005; Hwang, 2001, 2006; Park, 2006). For example, current research in Korea is intended to identify and investigate methods that encourage and empower Korean students' critical thinking through art, so that students can denote the invisible, but prominent, power of images in a global society (Hwang, 2006; Park, 2006). The goal of this research is to develop an approach to art curriculum development that encourages students to see how images are constituted, and how globalization often masks the ideology and hegemony of Westernization. Another significant aspect of recent art curriculum research in Korea highlights the hidden meanings behind images that are embedded in our daily lives. There is an increased concern for a deeper understanding of the nature of students' lives in a global society (Bigelow & Peterson, 2002; Tavin &

Hausman, 2004). Additionally, there is an increased awareness of the importance of understanding and engaging the popular culture that Korean students actually encounter (Park, 2006). The rationale behind these changes is the recognition that educators need to teach students to be aware of the global influences in their daily lives, providing them with models for being consciously, reflectively, and critically engaged in self, images, and society.

Summary

Although differentiated for purposes of this chapter, the five orientations discussed in this chapter in fact occur together in varying degrees in South Korean art educational thought and practice, but I believe that a critical-reflective approach has recently gained more attention. Although I still observe continued reliance on Western ideological orientations, many progressive Korean art educators are now exploring ways of balancing adoption of new Western art education theories against a renewed regard for the history, culture, traditions, and contemporary cultural values of South Korea. I also note an emergence of varying blends of educational orientations in art education in South Korea that are complex, interrelated, and at the same time both reciprocal and resistant to Western hegemony. Finally, I have argued here for the viability of an emerging paradigm in Korean art educational theory and practice, one that is *responsive, hybridized, and critically self-reflective.*

Exemplifying a Responsive, Hybridized Critical Self-Reflective Approach in South Korean Art Education Curricular Practice: A Case Study

Seeking to test the viability of my conceptualization of a responsive, hybridized, critical self-reflective curricular approach, I recently constructed and implemented a curricular model based on such an approach and conducted a case study with 6th grade (12 year-old) Korean students. The study examined how these students responded to and interacted with the theoretical conceptualizations that formed the basis of a 10–week curriculum intervention that I developed, adapting selected constructs of visual culture theory and inquiry-based learning theory to a Korean educational setting. The purpose of my curriculum model was to facilitate students' thinking as informed by critical theory, and to facilitate their insights about how images influence their understandings about their own values and identities in an increasingly globalized world.

An especially persuasive finding about the

efficacy of this emerging approach was exemplified in the case of a female student participant in this study whose interest in Japanese comics was a significant part of her life, so much so that she wanted to be a comic book artist. She had spent considerable time visiting blogs and websites to read comics and upload her own drawings. The Internet was one primary source that introduced this student to foreign artists and their comics. In the process of imitating her favorite Japanese comic in her own artistic productions, she had developed her own version of a stereotypical image of a female character. She had so internalized this stereotype that she tried to modify her own personality and appearance to be like her favorite comic character. Over the course of my curriculum, through studio explorations, examinations and discussions of selected imagery, and through my inquiries and interviews with her, she began to understand her use of this imagery *as a stereotype,* and to develop a facility for critical engagement with her favorite comic. Below, the student compares how she perceived her favorite comics before she participated in this art curriculum to how she later felt about those same comics:

> Before I took our classes, I thought that all beautiful characters had long hair, beautiful eyes, big eyes, and small noses. I also thought that all of them wore beautiful clothes and they were nice … I felt that main characters in comics should be nice and beautiful. The idea took all my heart … I had a bias for beautiful people. I did not realize why having the bias could be problematic. However, I knew that the stories and images from my favorite comics were related to my idea of what is beautiful. I also knew how the bias can destroy our society. Then, I could think I was doing something that destroyed our country…I think comics can be bad because they make me think a bias like this is beautiful, a slim woman is beautiful, and long hair style is beautiful … I think why do people try to imitate others in our country, so I made my work of art saying that our individuality is important. I really regret that Arina [Her favorite Japanese comic artist] has gotten the bias firmly into my head regarding what the standard of beauty is. (III: 6, 8; IV: 2, 12)

This passage shows how this student's standard of beauty—not traditional or particularly Korean, but globalized—was shaped by Japanese comics obtained through the Internet. It also shows how a contemporary responsive art curriculum may facilitate a student's capacity for self-reflective and critical thinking. This student was able to conceptualize and articulate her own thoughts about the problems of cultural homogenization, alluding to the cultural impact of the ideology behind images. Her response also suggested that she developed a willingness to challenge not just the original assumptions she had about beauty, but also what she perceived as her own

betrayal of traditional Korean values. Moments such as this provide an opportunity for critical insight—in this case, a chance for this student to consider how her bias had been shaped by Arina's comics and to reconsider her own individual beauty.

Conclusion

This chapter has considered selected forces of and responses to globalization in South Korean cultural and art educational theory, research, and practice. I have described varying art education approaches that have emerged in South Korea's response to globalization, and have suggested a contemporary adaptive, hybridized approach, one that both embraces and critically engages globalization. As an example of emerging Korean art curriculum research, I tested my approach with 6th grade students in South Korea as part of my dissertation study. My curricular approach was intended both to address the consequences of an extreme reliant approach to globalization in students' personal lives and to empower students' critical engagement with their favorite images in order to gain insights about subordinate tendencies that appear to accompany their consumption of global media and imagery.

For the better part of the late 20th century and into the present time, complex challenges of and changes within art curriculum research and practice in South Korea have reflected an interest in the ongoing local/global dynamics. This process of *glocalization,* in Ritzer's (2006) terms, not only provides us with the unique understanding of the particulars regarding the impact of globalization in South Korea, but also proposes the need for continuing to redefine globalization as an evolving concept within local contexts.

These dynamic processes suggest what, and how, art educators must endeavor to teach as they consider the impact of globalization in both local contexts and within a global society. The role of art education in global society is then both to share new partnerships with other disciplines and to satisfy social demands, either local or transnational, thus making the processes and ideologies of globalization transparent. Given the degree to which art curriculum researchers understand the impact of globalization—its historical origins and current ramifications—we can assume that new curriculum designed to respond to globalization will be rich and viable, making its processes and tendencies transparent to students who might otherwise never question the ideologies embedded within the images they encounter on a daily basis.

CHAPTER 28 | Globalization and Art Education in South Korea: Changes and Complexity of Art Curriculum Research and Practice

221

REFERENCES

Bigelow, B., & Peterson, B. (2002). *Rethinking globalization: Teaching for justice in an unjust world*. Milwaukee, WI: Rethinking Schools, Ltd.

Bydler, C. (2004). *The global art world, Inc: On the globalization of contemporary art*. Uppasla, Sweden: Uppsala University.

Eder, R. (2006). Eternal Mexico: Between nationalism and globalization. In J. Onians (Ed.), *Compression vs. Expression: Containing and explaining the World's art* (pp. 120-138). Dalton, MA: Studley Press.

Erickson, M. (2000). Crossing borders in search of self. *Art Education, 53*(2), 46-52.

Gyoyookbu [Ministry of Education]. (1998). *Je chilcha misoolgwa gyoyookgwajeong* [*The 7th national Korean art curriculum*]. Seoul: Daehan gyogwaseo jusikhwehsa.

Hwang, Y. J. (2001). Youngsang jeongbowha sidae'ei daeturehanun misoolgyoyook'eseo'ui visual literacy gyoyook [Visual literacy in art education in media information era]. *Misoolgyoyooknonchong* [*Art Education Research Review*], *12*, 137-156.

Hwang, Y. J. (2006). Sigakmoonwhagyoyook'gwa guggakyungjangyeok'e daehan gochal [Study on visual culture art education and national competition]. *Chodeunggyoyookyeongu, 17*, 155-168.

jagodzinski, j. (2008). Postmetaphysical vision: Art education's challenge in an age of globalized aesthetics (A mondofesto). *Studies in Art Education, 49*(2), 147-160.

Jeong, J. S. (1996). Damoonwhagyoyook'e gichohan minsokmisooljidoeul yihan gicho yeongu [A foundational study on multicultural art education based on teaching folk art]. *Sawhangmisoolgyoyooknonchong, 4*, 225-244.

Kim, H. S. (2000). Hankook juntong mi'ui'shik'ul batanguro han 21saegi misoolgyoyook'ui churhakjuk mosack [Philosophical approach toward 21 century's art education relating Korean traditional aesthetics]. *Misoolgyoyooknonchong* [*Art Education Research Review*], *9*, 41-61.

Kim, H. S., & Yi, S. D. (2005). The importance of Korean traditional art education and development of its lesson mode. *Journal of Educational Research, 22*, 137-160.

Kim, J. S. (2005). Maeche'e daehan sigakmoonwhagyoyookjuk jupgun [The approach of visual culture art education regarding media]. *Misulgyoyooknonchong* [*Art Education Research Review*], *19*(3), 65-82.

Lee. I. H. (2004). Peace, security and cultural understanding in the Korean context. In K. B. Bergquist (Ed.), *Images of Asia: Cultural perspectives on a changing Asia* (pp. 25-32). Copenhagen: Danish Center for Culture and Development.

Lippard, L. (1990). *Mixed blessings.: New art in a multicultural America*. New York: Pantheon Books.

Macdonald, S. (2006). Introduction to part V: Globalization, profession, practice. In S. Macdonald (Ed.), *A companion to museum studies* (pp. 378-380). Malden, MA: Blackwell Publishing.

McFee, J. K., & Degge, R. M. (1977). *Art, culture and environment: A catalyst for teaching*. Belmont, CA: Wadsworth Publishing.

Park, J. A. (2002). *Postmodern misool, misoolgyoyookron: Hankook'ui hyundaemisool, 21saegi misoolgyoyook'eiui dojeon* [*Postmodern art, art education: Korean contemporary art, the challenge of the 21 century art education*]. Seoul: Sigongsa.

Park, J. A. (2006). Popular visual culture and critical thinking in art education. In P. Duncum (Ed.), *Visual culture in the art class: Case studies* (pp. 135-141). Reston, VA: National Art Education Association.

Pieterse, J. N. (2006). Globalization as hybridization. In M. G. Durham & D. M. Kellner (Eds.), *Media and cultural studies: Keyworks* (3rd ed.), (pp. 658-680). Malden, MA: Blackwell Publishing.

Rectanus, M. W. (2006). Globalization: Incorporating the museum. In S. Macdonald (Ed.), *A companion to museum studies* (pp. 381-397). Malden, MA: Blackwell Publishing.

Ritzer, G. (2006). Art, McDonaldization and the globalization of nothing. In S. Dasgupta & R. Kiely (Eds.), *Globalization and after* (pp. 228-240). Thousand Oaks, CA: Sage.

Tavin, K., & Hausman, J. (2004). Art education and visual culture in the age of globalization. *Art Education, 57*(2), 47-52.

Yi, S. D., & Kim, H. S. (2005). A movement toward Eastern ethnocentric art education: The values of Korean art and cultural heritage. *Art Education, 58*(5), 18-24.

A Social Constructivist Study of Adolescent Metaphoric Portrait Drawings and Identity in a Barcelona Secondary School

Mary Stokrocki with Fernando Hernández, Magali Kivatinetz, Eneritz López, and Jordi Macián

Few detailed observations on the emerging links between visual culture and identity within teenage and childhood cultures exist, especially in Spain. When interviewing Spanish teenagers about their preferred television teen series and the way they constructed their adolescent identities outside of school, Corredera (2002), noted that education and social practices developed in school have little relation to art images and visual culture situated outside of school. Trafi (2004) also discovered that preschoolers use images in school originating from popular visual culture, like toys, clothes, and television. Consequently, educators fail to acknowledge such data as school knowledge (Giroux, 1994; Steinberg & Kincheloe, 2000). Scholars need to imagine alternative perspectives for theory and practice, address difficult questions, and encourage multiple views about the psycho-cultural construction of childhood.

Some art teachers incorporate visual culture study into their curriculums using constructivist strategies. Constructivism is "an approach based on the notion that the individual actively builds and adapts experiences into a world view" (Simpson, 1996, p. 53) and emphasizes the learner's experience as central in meaning making and problem solving. Learning goes beyond discovery and becomes interpretive when viewed through new fields of knowledge (Brooks & Brooks, 1993). The constructivist teacher empowers students to connect what they need to learn with their prior knowledge and desire to learn more. "This is a difficult task, in part because all mental activity is constructive and thus, in a sense, all teaching is constructivist ... and constructions can be weak (e.g., arbitrary, rote learning) or strong (connected or transferred)" (von Glazerfeld in Windschitl, 2002, p. 13, n. 6). With this emphasis in mind, we focused on one school, teacher, and art lesson, and asked these questions: What kind of constructivist and visual culture program did the art teacher develop? What images did students use and why? What did they learn? What conceptual, pedagogical, cultural, and political dilemmas emerged?

Method

The dominant research method was micro-ethnography, a systematic process of writing the group's story (Toren, 1996), in this case, a class in one school. We used participant observation, entailing daily note taking, photography, and questionnaires. The study unfolded in several phases. I contacted Professor Fernando Hernández about the possibility of conducting research in one school during my 3-month sabbatical in 2005. He enlisted two graduate students, Magali Kivatinetz and Eneritz López, to interpret daily interactions and documents and give advice in the study's final construction. In exchange, they learned about qualitative methods from me. Although very busy, Fernando offered suggestions and comments, especially in the interpretation of results. One high school student in the observed class, who spoke English, became a key informant. School administrators also expressed interest in the project and allowed us to observe other classes, such as a computer class to understand other disciplines involved. Describing the education system in Barcelona and particularly this school is necessary for readers to understand past and present contextual problems.

Weekly participant observation of ongoing lessons and analyzing students' visual and verbal responses was necessary. While Magali translated verbatim, I took notes, and Eneritz wrote what Jordi and students said. Eneritz translated Jordi's

CHAPTER 29 | A Social Constructivist Study of Adolescent Metaphoric Portrait Drawings and Identity in a Barcelona Secondary School

223

curriculum documents from Catalan into Spanish and English so that we could get an overview of what he taught. Because the unit started in September, no prequestionnaires were distributed. Notes developed into short conversations with students about their images' meanings, and Jordi offered his views on our evolving insights.

Further interpreting and negotiation occurred over the next months as the research team tried to make sense of the data. Artwork also provided evidence as we delved for additional insights on students' identities. Efland, Freedman, and Stuhr (1996) reminded us that such research is complex, eclectic, contradictory, and context-bound.

Context
Art education in Spain was conservative and controlled by the Catholic Church. The nineteenth century brought such reform movements as the Free Teaching Institution that blossomed in Barcelona and spontaneous drawing with little state interference (Hernández, 1998). After the Spanish Civil War (1936-1939), control returned to the Catholic Church and art education resumed practices in mimetic and geometric drawing and handicraft education with division of sexual roles. After the fall of Franco's dictatorial regime, a new economic, educational approach emerged, pursuing expressionism and creativity in schools. Hernández and colleagues at the University of Barcelona championed more socialist and constructivist approaches to art education.

Education today is mandatory and secondary education consists of two (2-year) cycles: for 13-14 year olds and for 15-16year olds. Graduating students can legally enter the labor market, take vocational training courses, or proceed to the upper secondary level. The lower secondary level requires a core program and courses from their chosen specialization, including Art and Technology. The upper level aims to prepare students for professional fields or university entrance. Observed courses are from this upper secondary level.

The observed parochial school, Madres Concepcionistas, located in a middle-class Barcelona neighborhood, is medium-sized (app. 600 students), funded by the Catalan regional government and parents, and consists of preschool, elementary, and secondary levels. The school goals promote personal, cultural and community values and cognitive, affective, and interpersonal skills (Madres Concepcionistas, n.d., Projecte Educatiu de Centre). The art teacher is pleased with his large art room with flourescent overhead lighting. To the several teaching resources on display, students contributed articles, for example, contemporary news about Michelangelo's drawings at the Prado in Madrid.

Participants
Teaching here for 13 years, the observed teacher Jordi Macian graduated from the University of Barcelona with a B. F. A. degree in painting. Hernández chose him because "Jordi is a leader in his school since he is young, kind, and close to the children." The nuns liked his enthusiasm, hard work, and collaborative program. Sister Margarita, Mother Superior, told us, "He is very creative, knows how to relate to students, treats them well, and former students visit him all the time." At the end of the first interview, my research assistants summarized, "He is very energetic, humorous, and makes students think about life." Jordi informed us that students felt excited and important to be asked questions about their work.

Eleven boys and nine girls (14-15 year-olds) participated in the class, which is comparable to high school juniors in the United States. The official language is both Catalan and Spanish, and 20% of the students were immigrants, according to Jordi. Contextual description revealed the difficulties of teaching a liberal contextual pedagogy in a highly conservative educational system. Lack of space forces us to concentrate on one lesson, called Constructing Metaphoric Portraits.

Teaching Philosophy, Program, and Lessons
Constructivist Teaching Philosophy
Jordi's philosophy is based on the belief that education is constructed and knowledge should evolve from students' ideas and continue through dialogue. Lipman (1988) posited that constructivist education "provides opportunities for the child to appropriate culture rather than being indoctrinated by it" (p. 20). Children can make new meanings from other cultural contexts. This means that the teacher leads the student to find educational information and the responsibility shifts from teacher to student. In constructivist teaching, "The creation of self is based on the subject being invested with certain characteristics through symbolic representation, according to Lacan" (Freedman &Hernandez, 1998, p. 191).

Jordi referred to multiple authors who write on adolescent identity: Harter's (1999) identity construct as descriptions of oneself change from using concrete to more abstract terms and from physical descriptions to psychological ones; another's observations of students' changing roles from the primary to secondary school, their diversification of friendships, and the transformation in sexual behavior often associated with the self-image modification; and Castellana's (2003) reconstructive view, which allows for the emergence of students' own interpretations, stories around their daily lives, and the lives of other students. Art offers a way for students to share their successes in domains about which they care and for which they can gain respect and reduce their disappointment in other domains.

Program and Theme

Jordi alluded to the national curriculum, but noted that he designed his own program based on a new theme each year. He planned the years's program with the English and Computer teachers. They chose the theme "Reinvent Yourself" in which students develop knowledge about their own identity, learn how to learn, and gain information about career awareness. The curriculum consisted of *Concepts* that included types of portraits (realistic or abstract and self-portrait). *Procedures* consisted of working on the Internet, pencil portrait measurement canons, ways of constructing gender type, and portraits using a digital camera. He also encouraged dialogue with their family and fellow students about the assignments. *Attitudes* incorporated being sensitive of others feelings when discussing portraits, developing positive work habits, and showing respect for materials.

Visual culture. Jordi proposed that visual culture is interdisciplinary, a convergence of dialogue between many disciplines. Duncum and Bracey (2001) defined visual culture as "a range of all material objects in the environment and has expanded to the performance and virtual images. The aim is to provide students with a set of critical tools for the investigation of human *visuality,* not to transmit a specific body of information or values" (p. 210).

Lesson schedule. The observed class, which started in September and continued all year for three terms, was called Visual and Plastic Education and met once a week. Lessons during this 10-week session included: 1) draw images using the isometric perspective of Escher; 2) write a personal opinion of an advertisement; 3) read about a historical portrait artist [e.g., Rembrandt and major examples of his unfolding work]; 4) make a construction of yourself; 5) produce a profile of a classmate; 6) construct a metaphoric portrait of a classmate with symbols of his/her hobbies; 7) search for an art history portrait that you do not like and explain why; 8) draw a caricature emphasizing exaggeration; 9) create a self-portrait with digital camera; and 10) create a power point document about your family.

Figure 1

Poster motivation for lesson "Reinvent Yourself."

Metaphoric portrait drawing lesson. We concentrated on this lesson that required students to make a metaphoric, nonrealistic portrait[1] of a classmate with symbols of his/her hobbies. For motivation, Jordi used a poster of composite images celebrating Don Quixote *from La Mancha* (El IV Centenario de El Quijote, 2005). See Figure 1. Students discussed the concept of portrait and analyzed different types from art history. They used colored pencils to construct a symbolic portrait of a neighboring student and substituted symbols for head parts. Jordi's constructive teaching style empowered students to elaborate on their ideas.

In summary, constructivist teaching philosophy, involving visual culture, adolescent identity construction, and construction of self, combined with the assignment to make a metaphoric portrait of a classmate will be explored in the following findings about the content of students' metamorphic drawings and what they learned from this assignment.

Findings About Students' Expressive Metaphoric Images

Analysis resulted from research assistants' descriptions and students' informal comments about their collage drawings. This section asked: How do adolescents construct themselves? What images did they use and why? What did they learn?

Sport figures were dominant hero images. Every portrait featured some kind of sport and students

CHAPTER 29 | A Social Constructivist Study of Adolescent Metaphoric Portrait Drawings and Identity in a Barcelona Secondary School

225

Figure 2

Right: Female portrait portrayed from the top-down: a boat sailing on a sea of wavy hair, photos for eyes, cherries—disco logo (*Pacha*) for a nose, keyboard for mouth, and guitar for shoulders.

Figure 3

Below: Another student described media images that included "earphones, Playboy logo for an eye, sport shorts for a mouth, Ram 23, and Homer Simpson.

testified to its importance. They portrayed surfing, tennis, volleyball, tennis, soccer, and racing and sailing images.

For example, a girl featured a sailboat floating on blue waves of hair in her drawing (Figure 2). Another boy incorporated a figure with motorcycle body and soccer balls for eyes. Students also informed us that their favored soccer team "El Barça" again boasted the national championship. Even in the computer class that we observed, students chose sport figures such Victor Valdes for soccer and Valentino Rossi, a famous motorcyclist, and Junior Diaz, hip-hop dancing.

Media celebrity images were rampant. We noticed many music metaphors; such as earphones, CD and disco logos, musical instruments, and techno-rock stars. For example, one portrait portrayed from the top-down: photographs for eyes, cherries for a nose (disco logo *Pacha*), keyboard for the mouth, and a guitar for shoulders (Figure 2). Another student described his media images that included earphones, the Playboy bunny logo for an eye, the Ram 23 logo for a mouth, the punk rock group "blink-182," and an image of Homer Simpson (Figure 3). They chose other media images from the Internet and magazines.

All the portraits featured preferred foods. One female student depicted her favorite cartoon character—Homer Simpson. She interpreted, "I sometimes felt lazy like Homer, and love to eat donuts too" (Figure 3). Another portrait depicted "ice cream eyes, lips that eat it, ice cream nose, margarita flowers for mouth, a necklace of cherries, and pasta for hair with some tomato sauce coloring." Other examples included bananas (smiles) and candy. The class was before lunch, so food was tacitly on their mind.

Opposite sex attraction was noted. Several female students carefully fussed with drawing makeup and hair. One student mentioned, "Looking good to attract attention." Even the boys had strands of hair neatly placed and waved in their drawings.

Students were aware of negative options, such as drugs. For instance, when I questioned one student about what he was drawing, he announced, "[My drawing] has a pot on the head and screws for ears, football eyes, play station for the mouth, and motorcycle shoulders" (Figure 4).

I asked, "What does it mean?" The student replied, "He's a pothead," and expelled from school. Another student told me that his drawing was a portrait of the same "Crazy Guy," who recently left school. The student interpreted the marijuana leaf eyes, the letters IN (insufficient), and a cloud for a bust, as meaning "his head is in the clouds." Because these students were sitting together, they chose this student as subject at the beginning of the project.

Students seemed to enjoy this project, discussed alternative ideas, and helped each other with drawing details. Dominant subjects were sports, media celebrities, picturesque environments, animals, opposite sex attraction, and food. Similar to the Don Quixote model, students constructed a composite portrait of a friend with substitute head and shoulder features. They mostly substituted water for hair and musical instruments, bikes, and mountains for shoulders. They moved beyond the stage of literalism and popular artistic conventions (Duncum & Bracey, 2001). Our key informant summarized, "Everyone here is an individual; each table is another world." We chose examples from students who finished. Since students seemed capable of making metaphoric representations, we turned our attention to what they learned.

Student Learning

We questioned students informally during and formally after their metamorphic drawings about what they learned. Research assistants chose a variety of representative answers from three female and three male responses.

Figure 4

One boy included a figure with motorcycle body and soccer ball eyes and said, "If you loose [lose] screws you go crazy" [screwy].

During the Project

What did you learn about art? Students understood art learning mostly as it relates to drawing ability. Example answers were "I've learnt (sic) that I can take things of life and put them together to create a face"; "I can make a portrait of a person through photos and drawings that represent aspects of a person without the necessity of drawing him like always" [meaning realistic]; and "I can draw somehow." Another student said, "Add more color, use different material, such as paint." A noteworthy comment was "We learned to draw better, more freely. I made my nose more complex by overlapping icecream cones. Here I made an eye into a mountainscape." Another student said that he had transformed his figure (bust) into a motorcycle and hair into weeds (See Figure 4). Some students revealed art learning in a general way, but others could not. Students learned to *juxtapose and substitute forms*.

CHAPTER 29 | A Social Constructivist Study of Adolescent Metaphoric Portrait Drawings and Identity in a Barcelona Secondary School

227

What did you learn about yourself? In regard to themselves, students mentioned: "had imagination"; "discovered parts of myself that I didn't know"; and "concentrate sitting better by myself." Since students were drawing a classmate, they had difficulty relating the project to their own identity.

What did you learn about your classmate [that] you made the portrait of? Most students mentioned hobbies such as sports—soccer, tennis, and basketball. Ellen stated, "[It's a] way of appreciating friends and their hobbies." They revealed "characteristic features" they hadn't seen before but nothing specific.

Post-Project

Which aspects of your personality do you think you have discovered or changed? Three students said "none." Other students referred to boosting their confidance, and still others found the project reaffirmed their views: "I've seen myself inside and I like myself." A revealing answer was "my idols (e.g. Vince Carter) are for me totals." We wondered how much this idol worship affected all students? Students construed the symbolic idea of personality as admiring a media star. Some followup questions are what does this person symbolize and why do you admire him/her?

In which way has this project helped you to look at your classmates differently? One perceptive student revealed, "Each of us has his/her own likes; all of them are strange and different." Other students were critical of classmates: "They are weird and they don't know what they want;" "Some students are taking drugs;" "They are a bit aggressive and curious." Another student confessed that they learned how fellow students really felt. A final student discovered that he changed "the way he judged other students." Perhaps, students' views of classmates changed somewhat because of this assignment, but they need more guidance to go beyond superficial hobbies and sports.

What did you learn about adolescent culture? The most frequent answers were that music, fashion, and friends are important. One insightful student reflected, "In the portrait of my friend, I've discovered that my childhood had influenced [sic] what I've drawn." Another student stated, "I put screws into the head. If you loose [lose] screws you go crazy (screwy)." See Figure 4. The student interpreted adolescence psychologically as a time of turmoil. These findings were noteworthy because we could not directly see these characteristics in any of the students. These were the most meaningful answers in our study.

Why do we need all the material items (CDs, clothes) that we purchase? The dominant answer was "because we like them." Other answers were hedonist—"to have fun or so life is not so boring." A different answer was "because we're in an age when we're capricious and we care a lot about these things." Some students are capable of reflection about the postive/negative outcomes of materialistic thinking and need more opportunities to do so.

In summary, even though Jordi advocates the importance of "a reflective education" we discovered that students had trouble reflecting on their learning. Translators noticed that students were unaccustomed to direct questions and needed time for reflection. Our key informant said, "No one had ever asked them such questions before." Perhaps in the future, we need to interview students and give them alternative "characteristics," such as imagination, art ability, and symbols to consider. Fernando suggested, "Maybe the school is not promoting reflection activities. Perhaps students are only concerned that the teacher wants them to finish their work." Research assistants also complained that students mixed Spanish and Catalan on the questionnaires, making it difficult to understand their answers.

Conclusions and Discussion

Historical, moderate, and radical educational interpretations emerge from this study (Windschitl, 2002). *Historically,* the constructivist stance challenges the traditionally conservative nature of education. Education itself faces an identity crises and Spanish art education suffers from low status. The problem is that schools offer a crowded curriculum that highlights superficial subjects (Dahlgren & Marton, 1978). The conservative government cut time (around 35 hours) for secondary art education classes, reduced the subject name to Plastic Education, with emphasis on manual skills (Hernández, 2003). With this new orientation all the cognitive, visual and cultural learning potentiality of Visual Arts Education may disappear. The obsession with imparting facts (encyclopedia textbook) contrasts the commitment to deep and elaborate understanding of noteworthy essential ideas. Education in the future will need to demand more integrity than it does and a sense of proportion on how it will distribute its energies with respect to a hierarchy of concerns (Lipman, 1988, p. 27). Similar situations exist in other countries.

A *moderate interpretation* of constructivist teaching points to the need for more metaphoric and reflective strategies about what students are learning about themselves and others. The combination of pyschological constructivism with social constructivism—self-knowledge with social ingredients and input from others—can be confusing at times (Cobbs, 1977).

The goals of constructing oneself and attaining a *metaphoric level of knowledge* are complex. Metaphors begin with concrete analogous thinking and proceed with abstract metaphoric combinations of dissimilar things (Lakoff & Johnson, 1980) as in a collage project. Collage as a "process of transforming ephemera by cutting and pasting them in momentarily stable configurations continues to be a particularly effective technique for capturing the chimera of consciousness in action" (Stafford, 1999, p. 146). The brain functions similarly in that it connects ideas by juxtaposing many discrete areas into larger integrated patterns. Marshall (2005) argues for substantive curriculum integration as a way of creating meaning through conceptual collage. Such curriculum attempts take time for teachers to create situational transfer, develop interdisciplinary connections, and for students to process metaphorical understanding.

The metaphoric assignment pushes students away from physical anxieties (over appearances) to shared sociological concerns. In spite of their initial confusion over the metaphoric portrait assignment, students reveal that adolescence is a confusing time and they understand negative alternatives, such as drugs. In spite of trouble reflecting on their artwork and lack of responses, they may construct clever metaphoric collages. Even though they can substitute images of their preferred media heroes, activities, and foods; however, they may not understand metaphorical construction, as their vague answers suggest. This reconstructive view allows for the emergence of students' interpretations and governs their revelations to outsiders, such as myself. Adolescents tend to experiment witht their identity. Recent research claims that a person has multiple identities and identity formation continues throughout life.

A *radical interpretation* reveals the changing nature of adolescence as a materialistic social construction of mixed images, merging codes, and multiple selves (Ruby, 2004), the socially constructed nature of cultural reality, and the tentative nature of cultural understanding. The metaphoric portrait theme allows for exploration of alternative identities and freedom. Students' choices of subject matter, such as (sports, music, foods), disclose the impact of visual culture media on their adolescent identities and their fascination with hero worship, beauty, and the good life (music, fun, and food). Dahlgren and Marton (1978) claim that this type of learning involves memory, skill

reproduction, or superficial knowledge of the other person's identity. Similar to Corredera (2003), we find students' identity—a collage of ideal and fantasy media influences. Teenagehood is a media construction as the prevalence of media images suggest. Construction is not simply a matter of choosing images and arranging them as portraits, but also includes reflecting on these meanings (Freedman, 2003). Students' confusion over assignments and questions about their identity is normal. Gergen (1991) talks about pastiche identity, students as social chameleons. These students share alternative identities with which they're experimenting, until they can consolidate their identity at a later time. The student attracted to Homer Simpson, for example, personifies the indulgent and rebellious adolescent desire in us all. Kellner (1995) similarly finds the series *Beavis and Butthead* as popular with youth's desire to rebel against parent authority and for unlimited freedom. On the other hand, jagodzinski (2004) reports that media immersion offers brief transcendence from these youth's preoccupation with real life problems. Students reveal little about their future selves, perhaps because the assignment didn't stress this aspect. If the theme "re-invent yourself" denotes change, students probably were too preoccupied with their regular studies to notice any change in themselves in a few months.[2]

Teachers and researchers need to understand the deeper issues involved in constructing identity in a global world; in this case—the outside cultural, capitalistic, and political forces. Identity is a complex construction that changes with each context and involves different roles. It [subjectivity] is much deeper than what students understand, may reveal to adults, or even other classmates. Identity, similar to language, is "the interplay and struggle of regional dialects, professional jargons, generic commonplaces" (Clifford, 1988, p. 46) and of insiders' and outsiders' intepretations. Researchers also need to focus more on the different forms of student communication— the languages and visual cues, a tendency called codeswitching (Timm, 1993), a subject for future investigation. Friedman (1999) pointed out that globalism has several dimensions, including political, cultural, financial, technological, and ecological trends. This situation requires that we re-educate ourselves to broaden curriculum in order to produce a new generation of strategists, a complex task in context.

REFERENCES

Brooks, J. G., & Brooks, M. G. (1993). *In search of understanding: The case for constructivist classrooms.* Alexandria, VA: Association for Supervision and Curriculum Development.

Clifford, J. (1988). *The predicament of culture.* Cambridge, MA: Harvard University Press.

Castellana, M. (2003). *La relacio de l'adolescent amb les persones significatives.* Barcelona: P. A. U. Education.

Cobbs, E. (1977). *The ecology of imagination in childhood.* New York: Columbia University Press.

Corredera, L. M. (2003). Exploring visual culture: Television teen series and adolescents identities. In P. Sahasrabudhe (Ed.). *InSEA 31st World Congress Proceedings* (CD-ROM). New York: Center for International Art Education, Inc., Teachers College.

Dahlgren, L., & Marton, F. (1978). Students' conceptions of subject matter: An aspect of learning and teaching in higher education. *Studies in Higher Education, 3,* 25-35.

Duncum, P., & Bracey, T. (Eds.). (2001). *On knowing: Art and visual culture.* Christchurch, New Zealand: Canterbury University Press: University of Canterbury.

Efland, A., Freedman, C., & Stuhr, P. (1996) *Postmodern art education: An approach to curriculum.* Reston, VA: NAEA.

El Quixote IV Centenary. (2005). *IV Centenario de El Quijote.* Retrieved February 7, 2005, from http://www.donquijotedelamancha2005.com

Freedman, K. (2003). *Teaching visual culture: Curriculum, aesthetics, and the social life of art.* Reston, VA: National Art Education Association.

Freedman K., & Hernandez, F. (1998). *Curriculum, culture and art education: Comparative perspectives.* New York: State University of New York Press.

Friedman, T. (1999). *The Lexus and the olive tree: Understanding globalism.* New York: Farrar, Strauss, Giroux.

Gergen, K. (1991). *The saturated self.* New York: Basic.

Giroux, H. (1994). *Disturbing pleasures.* New York: Routledge.

Harter, S. (1999). *The construction of self.* New York: Guilford.

Hernández, F. (1998). Framing the empty space: Two examples of the history of art education in the Spanish political context, In K. Freedman & F. Hernández (Eds.), *Curriculum, culture, and art education: Comparative perspectives* (pp. 59-73). Albany, NY: State University of New York Press.

Hernández, F. (2003). Annual Report on the situation of Visual Arts Education in Spain. USSEA World Council Meeting, The 6th InSEA European Regional Congress in Sweden, August, 2003.

jagodzinski, j. (2004). *Youth fantasies: The perverse landscape of the media.* New York: Palgrave Macmillan.

Kellner, D. (1995) *Media culture.* London and New York: Routledge.

Lakoff, G., & Johnson, M. (1980). *Metaphors we live by.* Chicago, IL: The University of Chicago Press.

Lipman, M. (1988). *Philosophy goes to school.* Philadelphia: Temple University. Press.

Marshall, J. (2005). Connecting art, learning, and creativity: A case for curriculum integration. *Studies in Art Education, 46*(3), 287-241.

Ruby, J. (1996). *Visual anthropology.* In D. Levinson & M. Ember (Eds.), *Encyclopedia of Cultural Anthropology, 4,* 1345-1351. New York: Henry Holt and Company.

Simpson, J. (1996). Constructivism and connection making in art education. *Art Education, 49*(1), 53-59.

Stafford, B. (1999). Recombinancy: Binding the computational 'new mind' to the combinatorial 'old mind'. In B. Stafford. *Visual analogy: Consciousness as the art of connecting* (pp. 138-179). Cambridge, MA: MIT Press.

Steinberg, S., & Kincheloe, J. (Eds.). (2000). *Kinderkulture: The corporate construction of childhood.* Madrid: Ed Morata.

Timm, L. (1993). Bilingual code-switching: An overview of research. In B. Merino, H. Trueba, & Samaniego, F. (Eds.), *Language and culture in learning: Teaching Spanish to native speakers* (pp. 94-112). Washington, DC: Falmer Press.

Toren, C. (1996). Ethnography: Theoretical background. In J. Richardson (Ed.). *Handbook of qualitative research methods for psychology and the social sciences* (pp. 102-112). Leicester, UK: BPS Books.

Trafi, L. (2004). A research on the understanding of visual culture and the production of subjectivity in the context of nursery school. Paper Presented at the InSEA 7th European Regional Congress, July, 2002.

Windschitl, M. (2002, summer). Framing constructivism in practice: An analysis of the conceptual, pedagogical, cultural, and political challenges facing teachers. *Review of Educational Research, 72*(2), 131-175.

ENDNOTES

1   Earlier, students were confused about the nature of a portrait. Several students brought in reproductions of Picasso's *Guernica* and said that they didn't like how it was painted, and Jordi reminded them that they were to repond to a portrayal of someone specific.

2   Thank you Director Josep Ma Domenech Figuera, Sister Margherite, Art Teacher Jordi Macián, Madres Concepcionistas, de la Torre 19, 08006 Barcelona.

The Kids' *Guernica* Peace Mural Project: A Paradigm for Global Art Education

Tom Anderson

In 1995, to commemorate the 50th anniversary of an American plane dropping of an atomic bomb on Hiroshima, Abe Toshifumi of Osaka Women's College asked me to help him develop a children's peace mural exchange between the United States and Japan. The murals were to be modeled after Picasso's *Guernica*, both in size (3.5 meters by 7.8 meters) and in its anti-war intent. In conjunction with Art Japan, a cultural funding agency, we developed this project into a symbolic bridge of peace not just between the United States and Japan but also between countries all over the world.

My first thought, when I was contacted by Professor Abe to do this project, was that it was a wonderful idea. But my second thought was troubling: What can art education possibly contribute to help us better understand the dropping of an atomic bomb? How can children's art be a bridge of peace in the face of such a horrific act of war? To answer these questions it was necessary to build a conceptual foundation for the project.

The Social Nature of Art

As a community muralist (T. Anderson, 1985a) and an aesthetic contextualist (T. Anderson, 1985b, 1989, 1992, 1995), I believe that the purpose of art is communication from one human being to another about things that count (Anderson & Milbrandt, 2005; R. Anderson, 1990; Dissanayake, 1988; Lippard, 1990). Ultimately, significant art is about something beyond itself. This does not mean that we disregard the aesthetic component—the "wonder"—in an artwork. Rather, it implies that the aesthetic is not just for its own sake. The function of the aesthetic, which is usually both prosaic and symbolic, is to serve as a marker that in some way defines the people who make, use, and view artworks or aesthetically framed objects (Anderson & Milbrandt, 2005; R. Anderson, 1990). Art, both as process and as product, is something people do to give them a sense of themselves. Thus art works and the process of making them serve as vehicles for understanding

Figure 1

The first Kids' *Guernica* Peace Mural, executed in Tallahassee, Florida, in 1995.

human nature in particular social contexts. Art is, at its base, a cultural phenomenon (Dewey, 1958/1934). It has been defined as a "principal means of communicating ideas and emotional meanings from one person to another, from one group to another, from one generation to another. When people have experiences, they symbolize the experiences in an art form; they observe their art and then obtain new insights about their experiences" (McFee & Degge, 1980, p. 273).

The meanings conveyed by aesthetic forms—art and visual culture—are inseparable (Dewey, 1958/1934; Geertz, 1983). The formal concerns, composition, lines, colors, and so on, rather than being for their own sake, reflect life concerns of the artist and his or her society. It is the relationship of the thematic content and the means of its expression (style and technique) that makes up the expressive quality of the artwork. If the viewer perceives a unity between what the work seems to be attempting and what is achieved in that viewer's mind and heart, then the result might be called aesthetic.

Simply put, then, art is *visual culture*. That is, art consists of culturally embedded artifacts and performances that objectify a group's concepts of reality (Langer, 1980; McFee & Degge, 1980; Mirzoeff, 1999), making them tangible; making subjective, psychic, and social constructs more concrete, more understandable, more real (Dissanayake, 1988, 1992). Art gives shape to the life of the spirit, the life of the mind, the collective visions of people everywhere, and in that way promotes common understandings and the social cohesion necessary for every group of people's survival (Dissanayake, 1992). That's one of its primary instrumental functions.

Instrumental Ends of Education

Instrumentally speaking, education has some of the same functions as art as described above: namely the identification, preservation, and transmission of behaviors, values, and ideas held in common by the social group (Bruner, 1996; Eisner, 1994a, Dewey, 1938). Formal education, in particular, is a consciously established institution structured specifically for these purposes (Postman, 1995). Through education, children are expected to learn about the values, mores, and ways of doing things that their society holds to be most significant (Anderson & Milbrandt, 2005). As a vehicle for this transmission, they also learn subject matter content such as mathematics and art, but I think that's really secondary to learning society's processes and values (Anderson, 1985c). I would argue, in fact, that disciplines such as art, mathematics, and history are only valued to the extent that they support the primary socialization function of schooling (Anderson, 1992, 1985c).

In formal education, the content areas are assigned a central or peripheral place in the curriculum based on how much they contribute to the socialization process of youth (Anderson, 1992, 1985c). Based on this foundation, art's potential role in education should be obvious. Art, more than most subjects, can serve as an instrument for understanding society and how to live in it. But if this is so, why isn't art at the center of the curriculum?

School Art's Irrelevance to Life

Art has been peripheral in school, in my opinion, because so many art educators have not taught art for *the sake of life* (Anderson & Milbrandt, 2005). They have instead relied on a combination of creative and mental growth (Lowenfeld, 1947) and so called "school art" (Efland, 1976) strategies.

School art (Efland, 1976) traditionally has not been taught like mathematics or other so-called core subjects, to address issues and skills necessary for success in the larger world. Rather, according to Efland, it has served only as a superficially therapeutic outlet within the highly regulated structure of school. Art has been a release, making the culture of school

bearable; beyond that, serving no real function. It is supposed to be fun in an institutionally condoned way, to "vivify school life and break up the deadening routine...minimizing the cost of institutional repression" (Efland, 1976, p. 40). Art, in this schema became a frill: nice maybe, but not necessary.

The second factor is the idea that the point of teaching art is primarily to facilitate creative and mental growth (Lowenfeld, 1947). The creative and mental growth of children was thought to develop through biologically programmed universal stages, which were independent of cultural influences. So the teacher's role was most of all to avoid oppressive adult models that would intimidate the child and stunt his/her "natural" growth. If children are simply provided with nourishment they will unfold according to their own plan like flowers.

The idea of universal development has long been debunked (Dissanayake, 1988, 1992; Feldman, 1980; Gardner, 1991, 1994; Greenspan & Shanker, 2004; Kindler, 2000; Wilson, 1988). The drive to art is biological in the beginning but it begins to be shaped by cultural patterns very early in life, and the culture rapidly becomes the primary pattern-making device shaping how and what we learn. It has become clear that children are biologically programmed to integrate culture: They first emulate, then integrate (Vygotsky, 1962), the patterns presented to them by other people in the world; they are products as much of their culture as their biology.

So it makes more sense for art teachers to present children with patterns they choose, rather than having them pick up whatever patterns from the popular culture. It also makes sense that art educators examine other cultures for patterns in art making and reception, as ways people can understand each other inter and cross-culturally. Wilson (1988) suggested that there are multiple visual languages in the world just as there are multiple verbal languages, and that any one culturally based language "may not carry children as far as they or we need to go" (p.504). Importantly, multi- and cross-culturalism gives insight not only into others, but through comparison, into ourselves, for as Eisner (1994a) said, the culture one is immersed in is often the most difficult to see.

A Locally Specific and Globally Concerned Future for Art Education

If art is taught with the idea that it is meaningful communication between human beings, and that it reflects the values, mores, and ways of doing things of both the individual and the culture, then it will reflect important real-life community values and ways of being, and become centered in general education. I believe that the future of the profession lies in socially grounded (intercultural and cross-cultural), technologically advanced, content and discipline-centered art education. Correspondingly, this strategy will address both locally specific and global concerns.

For the content for art education to be relevant to children, it must be multi and cross-cultural. This is not to say that the dominant European tradition should be abandoned. It's also not to say that Hiroshige should be abandoned as a paradigm in Japan, or that Celadon ware should be ignored in Korea. Core cultures must be respected and understood in common by people in a region or nation if they are to remain unified societies. It is to say, however, that individual children must be respected for who they are, culturally as well as psychologically. And increasingly, children need to be recognized for their diversity and shown paths for success in a diverse world.

Another issue rising from the larger concerns of society is the explosion in computer-generated graphics and information systems technology. The electronic world of computers, iPhones, and the Internet is not a second language or third language to many children, but a first language native mode of communication.

There are difficulties, of course, for the less privileged in this techno-world: technology can divide as well as join us. How will we help kids left out to gain access to the technology resources to make them successful in life? Social justice demands that an answer for this be found, because, in the global culture, multicultural content and electronic proficiency are interdependent and mutually supporting components in art for life.

How to Do Art for Life

Practically speaking, a focus on art for life—that is, on achieving personal and social understanding and competencies through aesthetic means and media competence, including the appropriate use of technologies—demands that art education be centered on *themes* (Anderson & Milbrandt, 2005). The themes should be constructed to address fundamental human concerns such as the sense of self, the sense of place, and the sense of community. Content for these themes should be taken first from contemporary art and culture, because that is what is most accessible to students, then expanded in an organic manner to include a broad cross-section of artifacts and performances from many times and cultures.

Students should be encouraged to immerse themselves in real issues, and to solve real problems that have significance beyond the classroom (Giroux & Simon, 1989), and activities should be developed that foster individual solutions to conceptual and design problems in relation to the issues and problems. Themes and inspiration can be found in works of adult artists but every attempt should be made not to avoid simplistic replication. The idea is to critically engage students meaningfully in the ideas, feelings, and forms of others as stimulus for their own personally significant creative expression. As Bruner (1960) suggested, the process of education must not only transmit culture, but also provide alternative views of the world and strengthen the will to explore them.

Finally, the art activities should include both closed-ended instructional objectives (Eisner, 1994b) designed to teach skills and concepts and open-ended expressive outcomes designed to allow students to express themselves meaningfully. Excellent teaching and learning in an art-for-life curriculum require a natural relationship between skills/concept attainment and creative self-expression. One rises from and feeds the other. Neglect of either a meaningful idea or the skills to carry it off will result in lack of progress. Such a process orientation to learning allows for a more open-ended system that becomes a passage for personal transformation (Arnowitz & Giroux, 1991), an outcome that is highly valued when art is taught for the sake of life.

Kids' *Guernica*: A Locally Specific, Global Example of Art for Life

Since 1995, the Kids' *Guernica* Peace Mural Project has been an excellent example of art for life in a global context. It can be accessed at several websites (www. kids-guernica.org, www.poieinkaiprattein.org, www. productivityofculture.org) and further explored in Anderson and Milbrandt (2005).

Figure 2
Mural executed by high school students in Wollongong, Australia.

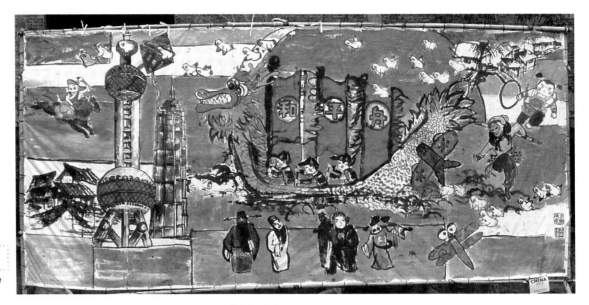

Figure 3

Top: Shanghai peace mural.

Figure 4

Bottom: Children working on a peace mural in Bali.

In the words of international coordinator Kaneda Takuya (2007):

> The main purpose of this project is to foster peace consciousness among children through art activities. The workshops were held in various educational settings such as schools, museums, and community. The participant children vary from kindergarteners to high school students. During these past [13] years of this project, more than 10,000 children from different nationalities, cultures and religions have participated in the Kids' *Guernica* workshops and innumerable people saw the children's wonderful paintings to express their strong wish for peace. (n.p.)

The project celebrated its 5th anniversary with an exhibition and celebration in Nepal in 2000, its 10th in Bali in 2005, and has a 15th-year anniversary celebration projected for Florida in 2010. It also had major exhibitions in Italy in 2002 following 9/11/01, in Greece in 2006, and other locations all over the world. Hundreds of peace workshops have been conducted and more than 150 murals have been executed. Many thousands of children and adults have engaged in the construction of peace murals through this project. Children from Palestine and Israel worked on a mural together. Children in Afghanistan created a mural. Children from Chios, Greece, traveled to Izmir, Turkey, to do a peace mural there. In one case, Iman Nouri returned to Tripoli, Lebanon, from abroad just as fighting broke out between the army and the Palestinians in the refugee camp. Having experienced the Kids' *Guernica* Project in Greece, "she had experienced what it means to be together with others who have a similar vision in mind and who let children touch the canvas with their souls. The painting from Lebanon is...entitled, *Enough. We Want to Live*" (Hatto Fischer, personal communication, 12/22/07).

The roots of this international project are local, in every case: the conditions that give rise to images and ideas as well as the symbolic content for each mural are local. For example, the first mural was done in a parking lot and a non-air-conditioned warehouse gallery in North Florida in the summer on a shoestring budget. The children involved were so called "at risk" kids from the inner city and children who were physically and emotionally challenged. There was very little outside financial sponsorship. I simply believed in the idea, and I engaged others who believed in the idea, and we used local resources to accomplish this first mural. Most of workshops and murals since then also have come together not because of international resources, but because adults and children were dedicated to the idea of the project. Although the 2002 gathering in Kronplatz, Italy, was well funded through EU grants, and sometimes the international organization has the means to offer some financial support for some workshops, frequently local organizers are doing it on their own with no more than moral support from our loose organization. That makes every mural local.

Figure 5

Top: Peace mural
from Spain.

Figure 6

Bottom: Abe
Toshifumi working
with children on a
peace mural in Bali.

The process of making each mural also is as locally specific as the culture it comes from and the problem it tries to solve. In one case, the Palestinian/Israel mural, it was a way to work out differences, to humanize each other through working together to achieve a common goal; in another instance, The American-Japanese exchange, it was a way to help both cultures remember that atrocities were committed in the past and were to be avoided in future; in another, as with the blind boys mural from India, it was way to overcome physical difficulties and garner respect from others; or as with the mural from Papua New Guinea, it's simply a way to say "we exist and here's what we value." Dewey (1957/1934) said the best art is that which manifests in its form the cultural spirit that went into the process of its making. The products/murals resulting from individual local workshops, then, are manifestations that record and reflect each locally expressive process and sharing them is a foundational way we get to know each other. The murals are shown around the world and on the Internet and become artifacts to be received and passed from one group to another for understanding, to humanize us, one to another. In this way we believe that we are helping each other to understand the others' motivations, values, mores, and sensibilities, thus fostering tolerance, and mutual respect: two core ingredients in constructing peace.

The universal aspect to this project begins with the idea that art is global. In spite of its myriad forms, it exists everywhere. So, because we are artists and art educators, we all take art as our primary tool for making peace. Also in spite of the fact that we, participants of the project, are all of different cultures, ages and ways of understanding, we believe that certain

human concerns are universal. One such concern is the right to live in peace. The goals of the project—to foster universal tolerance and respect, as the foundations of peace through aesthetic means—then, are not only local but also global. Through local specificity, we intend to foster global awareness of the possibilities of peace in this world. That's what unifies us.

We are also somewhat unified in process, since there is a pattern we tend to follow in making the murals. Workshops often begin with the exploration of a core concept related to peace, or with brainstorming about what peace means to the participants and how it can be attained. At some point in this process we begin to conceptualize both the content and aesthetic parameters of the mural to be made. Ideally, this is a process of collaboration between adult leaders and the children involved. Kaneda (2007) says, "This project emphasizes the necessity of collaboration to let an imaginative vision become a reality. The collaboration is not only among children but also between children and adults and among different cultures. Kids'

Guernica is not individual artwork. Rather, participant children have to *work together* to complete their huge peace painting" (n.p.)

Another universal aspect to this project is that human beings have difficulties in relationships—even in a peace mural project! As in the usual course of all human interactions, there will probably be disagreements and negotiations, in our case, about what a mural should contain, how it should look and so on. But addressing this is an extremely valuable step in the global effort to construct peace, to realize that even at the local level it's not such an easy task to achieve consensus. This is the crux of peacemaking, when workshop participants have to hang in there with each other, when we have to work to understand that moving forward peacefully can only be attained when we come to understand, tolerate and respect each other's visions and ideas and then take the further step of bending to achieve the larger vision of the group, cooperatively molded and shaped, with everyone's best interests in mind. This, we believe, is a democratic process that fosters purposes of global education articulated by Johns (1989), who said global education should incorporate basic cross-cultural understanding and empathy coupled with an ability to communicate across cultures.

Figure 7

Peace mural executed by junior high school students in Kawasaki, Japan.

So ultimately the power of the project lies in our unity of purpose and our diversity of approaches melded together through the hard work of cooperative personal interaction, using the aesthetic as the means as well as the end. In agreement with Desai (2005) and Tavin and Hausman (2004), we construct themes and solutions that are locally specific to the global problem of constructing peace between the peoples of the world. In this way we think and feel globally and act locally. This process, in conjunction with our loosely organized, non-hierarchical structure, makes the entire project grass roots in nature, and the participants a coalition of equals, with a global vision achieved through local activities. This is a project where no one is in charge, where decisions are made for the good of the group through consensus or at least through negotiation and broad agreement. Frequently the process is messy but in the end it helps to get everyone on board and it keeps us all honest, conceptually, emotionally and aesthetically. "It is important," as international committee member, Hatto Fischer, put it, "to uphold parliamentary democracy or to see how people within Kids' *Guernica* convey that to the children who in turn respond to a world not very convincing when it comes to observing principles of democratic practices" (personal communication 12/22/07).

Finally, while we don't exist in *Second Life*, we do rely heavily on the technology of the Internet for instant communication in planning and sharing ideas, forms, issues, and aesthetic concerns in this project. In our case we are very careful to make our communication processes open and transparent, realizing that, as Duncum (2001) put it, the Internet and other mass communication technologies can become top-down cultural imperialism. We see the Internet as a very valuable tool for democratic communication and social justice. This pertains not just to adult organizers but also to the children involved. Our focus on visual culture as a means of exploring our own visual world and the worlds of others, in other words, not only explores the issue of peace but provides students with the skills necessary to thrive in a world increasingly dominated by the visual image (The New Media Consortium, 2005). As suggested by Davenport (2003), an intercultural approach such as the Kids' *Guernica* Project, facilitated by the Internet, can be a terrific tool for developing a world culture more aware of the issue of peace and more oriented toward peace through art education.

Conclusion

As reflected by the Kids' *Guernica* Peace Mural Project, art education for the sake of all global culture(s) should address art that counts in the personal and social lives of students. It should be about making and critically receiving art that says something of significance that contributes to the human story. Art education should be authentic and theme-based, recognizing works of art as both the windows and mirrors of our lives. Ultimately it should serve as a bridge of respect and understanding between people toward the goal of a global sense of community. This is no easy thing and should not be taken as a simple cliché. It is easy to draw platitudes, across cultures, such as the one that goes, "we are all alike under the skin." But a close examination reveals we aren't. Because we have human culture and that varies, so do we. However, we are all people. And we do have, it appears, some universal impulses, like loyalty to the group and honesty and integrity, a desire to live in peace, and the drive to make art. But these impulses take different forms in different circumstances and in different cultures, and that's the rub. It's the form that counts after all. We take on the ability to engage in (Sarup, 1989; Wilson, 1988) and understand (R. Anderson, 1990) symbolic communication by being embedded in a particular culture. Beyond substance, it is the manner in which something is presented that allows us access to the inner life of the other. Or keeps us out. Making and studying art as meaningful communication in a cultural context can help us understand this. It will require sensitive analysis of social realities and hard work.

These were the premises we used to develop and implement the international Kids' *Guernica* Peace Mural Project. The content and the strategies are real world oriented. They are life based. They are of real interest to, and have a real impact on, the children and adults who participate. The goal is to build a bridge of peace and understanding. The vehicle—not the end, but the vehicle—is art. The overarching goal is to save the world from further devastating warfare. Maybe that's grandiose. Is it too grand to claim that the world can be saved from war through instrumentalist art education? Probably so. But let me reverse the question and ask, if not through art then through *what*? Certainly biology and physics and agriculture and chemistry give us wonderful practical tools to navigate the world, but it is the arts that provide the holistic quality of understanding necessary for social wholeness and cultural health. It is through the arts that we develop the sensibility, the unifying sense, the direction, in short the ability, to use our tools. Let me repeat then, if the world cannot be saved through art then through what?

REFERENCES

Anderson, R. (1990). *Calliope's sisters.* Englewood Cliffs, NJ: Prentice Hall.

Anderson, T. (1997). Toward a postmodern approach to art education, in J. Hutchens and M. Suggs, (Eds.), *Art education: Content and practice in a postmodern era.* Reston, VA: National Art Education Association.

Anderson, T. (1995). Toward a cross-cultural approach to art criticism. *Studies in Art Education 36*(4), 198-209.

Anderson, T. (1992). Premises, promises, and a piece of the pie: A social analysis of art in general education. *The Journal of Social Theory and Art Education, 12,* 34-52.

Anderson, T. (1989). Interpreting works of art as social metaphors. *Visual Arts Research 15*(2), 42-51.

Anderson, T. (1985a). Contemporary American street murals: Their defining qualities and significance for art education. *Journal of Multi-cultural and Cross-cultural Research in Art Education, 2*(1), 14-22.

Anderson, T. (1985b) Thoughts on contextualism and art education. *Bulletin of the Caucus on Social Theory and Art Education, 5,* 51-60.

Anderson, T. (1985c). Hold the pickles, hold the lettuce, special orders do upset us: American art education and the franchise system. *Bulletin of the Caucus on Social Theory and Art Education, 5,* 15-26.

Anderson, T., & Milbrandt, M. (2005). *Art for life: Authentic instruction in art.* New York: McGraw-Hill.

Anderson, T., & Taylor, J. (1995). *A multicultural curriculum framework in the arts for the State of Florida.* Tallahassee, FL: Florida Department of Education (Available from ACE, College of Education, University of Central Florida, Orlando, FL 32816).

Arnowitz, S., & Giroux, H. (1991). *Postmodern education: Politics, culture, and social criticism.* Minneapolis, MN: University of Minnesota.

Barthes, R. (1982b). Lesson in writing. In S. Sontag, (Ed.), *A Barthes reader.* New York: Noonday.

Bruner, J. (1960). *The process of education.* Cambridge, MA: Harvard.

Bruner, J. (1996). *The culture of education.* Cambridge, MA: Harvard University Press.

Davenport, M. (2003). Where do we go from here? Intercultural education for peace. *Journal of cultural research in art education, 21.* 119-125.

Desai, D. (2005). Places to go: Challenges to multicultural art education in a global economy. *Studies in Art Education 46*(4). 293-308.

Dewey, J. (1958/1934). *Art as experience.* New York: Capricorn.

Dewey, J. (1938). *Experience and education.* New York: Simon and Schuster.

Dissanayake, E. (1992). *Homoaestheticus.* New York: Macmillan.

Dissanayake, E. (1988). *What is art for?* Seattle: University of Washington.

Duncum, P. (2001). Theoretical foundations for an art education of global culture and principles for classroom practice. *International Journal of Education & the Arts, 2*(3), Retrieved November 2, 2006 from http://ijea.asu.edu/v2n3/.

Dunn, P. (1996). Interactive technology and art education. *Translations: From theory to practice, 6*(2), 1-6.

Eisner, E. (1994a). *Cognition and curriculum reconsidered.* New York: Teachers College Press.

Eisner, E. (1994b). *The educational imagination: On the design and evaluation of school programs* (3rd. ed.). New York: Macmillan.

Efland, A. (1976). The school art style: A functional analysis. *Studies in Art Education, 17*(2), 37-44.

Feldman, D. (1980). *Beyond universals in cognitive development.* Norwood, NJ: Ablex.

Gardner, H. (1994). *The arts and human development.* New York: Harper Collins.

Gardner. H. (1991). *The unschooled mind: How children think and how schools should teach.* New York: Harper Collins.

Geertz, C. (1983). *Local knowledge: Further essays in interpretive anthropology.* New York: Basic Books.

Giroux, H., & Simon, R. (1989). *Popular culture, schooling, and everyday life.* Westport, CN: Bergin & Garvey.

Greenspan, S., & Shanker, S. (2004). *The first idea: How symbols, language, and intelligence evolved from our primate ancestors to modern humans.* Cambridge, MA: Perseus.

Johns. R. (1986). Help wanted: Art educators for global education. *Art Education, 39*(3), 16-24.

Kaneda, T. (2007). Kids' *Guernica*: International children's peace mural project, personal email communication (originally a report to a local Rotary club in Tokyo.

Kids' *Guernica* websites: www.kids-guernica.org, www. poieinkaiprattein.org, www.productivityofculture.org.

Kindler, A. (2000). From the u-curve to dragons: Culture and understanding of artistic development. *Visual Arts Research, 26*(2), 15-28.

Lippard, L. (1990). *Mixed blessings: New art in a multicultural America.* New York. Pantheon.

Langer, S. (1980). *Philosophy in a new key.* Cambridge, MA: Harvard University.

Lowenfeld, V. (1947). *Creative and mental growth.* New York: Macmillan.

McFee, J., & Degge, R. (1980). *Art, culture and environment* (2nd ed.). Dubuque, A: Kendall Hunt.

Mirzoeff, N. (1999). *An introduction to visual culture.* London: Routledge.

Piaget, J. (1976). *Time and the intellectual development of the child: The child and reality.* New York: Penguin.

Postman, N. (1995). *The end of education: Redefining the value of school.* New York: Knopf.

Sarup. M. (1989). *An introductory guide to poststructuralism and postmodernism.* Athens, GA: University of Georgia.

Tavin, K., & Hausman, J. (2004). Art education and visual culture in the age of globalization. *Art Education, 57*(5), 1-7.

The New Media Consortium. (2005). *The report of the 21st century literacy A global imperative.* www.adobe.com/education/solutions/pdfs/globalimperative.pdf.

Vygotsky, L. (1962/1934). *Thought and language.* Cambridge, MA: Harvard University.

Wilson, B. (1988). The artistic tower of Babel: Inextricable links between culture and graphic development, In G. W. Hardiman & T. Zernich, (Eds.) *Discerning Art: Concepts and issues.* Champaign, IL: Stipes.

Zimmerman, E. (1990). *Teaching art from a global perspective.* http://www.ericdigests.org/ (ERIC Identifier: ED329490). ERIC Clearinghouse for Social Studies/Social Science Education Bloomington IN., Adjunct ERIC Clearinghouse for Art Education Bloomington IN.

AUTHOR'S NOTE

The author welcomes inquiries from anyone who wants to become involved with art for life and art for peace through the Kids' *Guernica* Peace Mural Project: Tom Anderson, The Florida State University, Tallahassee, Florida, USA, tanderson@fsu.edu

CASE STUDIES & PHILOSOPHICAL SPECULATIONS

ABOUT HIGHER EDUCATION: INTERNATIONAL PRACTICES—COLLEGE LEVEL FACULTY AND STUDENTS' TRANSFORMATIONS

Introduction: Section IV

Elizabeth Manley Delacruz

As the many chapters in *Globalization, Art, and Education* demonstrate, themes of glocalization, hybridization, border crossing, interculturalism, and transformation have emerged as important considerations in studies of globalization. Notions of "center/periphery" powers, "dominant/subordinate" cultures and nations, "rivalrous/non-rivalrous" relationships, and "clash/convergence" of civilizations are now being reexamined in recognition of the multiple centers and sites of globalization, as contemporary scholars observe that globalization flows in multiple directions and as they now view individuals and cultures (both young and old) as multifaceted, self-deterministic, interdependent, and dynamic. Globalization's proponents and detractors alike see education as central to the world's state of affairs.

In answer to our call for chapters, the authors in *Globalization, Art, and Education* provide firsthand accounts of the many manifestations of globalization in specific locations with particular people. The chapters throughout this book examine educational challenges and imperatives presented by globalization, considering art and educational theory and practices for early childhood, K-12, higher education, and educational practices with young people and adults in varied non-school settings and online sites. The fourth and final section of this book looks specifically at college level faculty and their students' personal epiphanies and cultural identity transformations resulting from their transnational work as educators, activists, and cultural workers in international contexts.

Readers may recall from earlier chapters both celebratory and cautionary discussions about emerging electronic global communications networks, revitalizations of cultural heritage sites, and the marriage of art, culture, politics, and commerce in the reconstruction of national identities. In the first chapter in this final section of the book, "The Making of *ChinaVine*: Partnering Across Countries," Kristin G. Congdon and Doug Blandy share a compelling and timely case study of the processes, outcomes, goals, and questions emerging from a transcultural, transnational research project involving teams of students and faculty from three different universities—two in the US and one in China—as they created a website to educate English-speaking youth and adults about the material culture of China, starting with a folk art collection in Shandong Province. Their mission was tied into China's late emergence as a new major power on the world stage, its ambitious agenda of rapid modernization, its recognition of the political, cultural, and economic significance of its own cultural heritage, and its recent efforts to foster partnerships in business and education sectors. Also of interest here are Congdon's and Blandy's thoughts about their own processes of engagement in this project, their non-hierarchical and art-based approach, problems of language, concerns about the preservation of fragile cultural heritage sites, and uncertainties about the potential undesirable effects of tourism that could result from their creation of the website.

Jamaican scholar and teacher educator Phyllis T. P. Hill then looks at a growing trend toward "distance education" in her country, an educational delivery system that takes advantage of new technologies, provides educational opportunities to a greater number of people (in this case, off-site teachers), and further accelerates globalization. In "Global Colonization: The Case of Distance Education in Jamaica," Hill examines new technology-dependent distance education models developed for the professional preparation and staff development of teachers in Jamaica. While acknowledging the importance of Jamaican teachers being prepared to teach their learners to effectively and successfully traverse local and global landscapes, at the same time, Hill raises critical questions about equitable practice, cultural relevance, and economic pressures concomitant with distance education, each of which Hill believes undermine Jamaican national sovereignty. Of particular concern to Hill are U.S. corporate influences on Jamaican national policy formation and educational development.

Just as the previous two chapters scrutinize the hopes and problems of new transnational educational collaborations in China and Jamaica, the following chapters provide additional insightful studies of international collaborations in other parts of the world. In "Border-Crossing Dialogues: Critically Preparing Art Educators for Participation in a Global Society" Flávia Bastos describes a partnership involving two art education professors, one in Brazil and one the United States, and their network of art educators, artists, and art education students. Looking in-depth for a deeper understanding of her college students' international experiences, Bastos analyzes program participants' comments, projects, artifacts, and reflections, and describes how these students examined their own cultures, belief systems, and values, and how they developed a more nuanced way of making cultural observations. Bastos demonstrates how transcultural art education experiences both provide opportunities to recognize and transcend familiar boundaries and create new spaces for intercultural dialogue and understanding.

Patty Bode draws from her experience as an a/r/tographer who traveled to a South American community to participate in Secoyan daily life and artmaking. Her chapter, "The Circulatory System of Oil Contamination, Visual Culture, and Amazon Indigenous Life," makes visible the struggles and survival of her hosts by aiming to make Secoyan voices more audible in globalized discourses. Bode's analysis is set against the backdrop of the environmental contamination by global oil production and its influence on the cultural sustenance of one of the indigenous peoples of Ecuador's Amazon region. Bode also reflects on learnings from her own experience with some of her former U.S. high school students, who launched an NGO to address the impact of oil production in the region.

In the following chapter, "Solidarity, Global Scholarship, and the Ethics of Encounter: A Case Study from Guatemala," Rebecca Plummer Rohloff and Peter Rohloff similarly examine both globalization's impact and their own presence and understandings in relation to the environment, language, culture, economies, health, and artistic expressions of a people in their specific locality—in this case, the Kaqchikel Mayan people in the highlands of Guatemala. In their auto-ethnographic study, presented as a dialogue between this traveling international artist-scholar and her partner, a medical worker/medical scholars researcher, Rebecca and Peter document their crises and epiphanies about *the academy* as they worked among Kaqchikel Mayan communities in development of arts-based community programming and medical service provisions. Their dialogue problematizes and then explores notions of voyeurism, tourism, global position, and their own privilege, the mobilization to act and the acquisition of the necessary skills to do so, and finally their recognition of meanings of *solidarity* as a call to radical personal commitment.

Complementing the previous two chapters, Pamela G. Taylor and Christine Ballengee-Morris share an account of the international research experiences of two U.S. art educators and their students with the people and places of Cuba and Brazil, reporting their insights in the form of a five-act play performed as a critically reflective narrative. In "A Cultural Cherishing Drama: Developing International Art Education Relationships through Service-Learning," Taylor and Ballengee-Morris connect this kind of work to service-learning theory and art education pedagogy. Their narrative reveals both their understandings and discomforts with their roles as privileged researchers and tourists, as they converse about Americanization, economic development, poverty, labor rights, environmental safeguards, local art, and educational practices. As do the previous authors in this section of the anthology, their narrative also reveals the personal transformations they underwent with their students as they immersed themselves in and critically reflected on their experiences in these locations.

Enid Zimmerman next provides a case study of a U.S. art educator's teaching experience (hers) in another international context, and discusses her teaching strategies, students' needs, and communication in a second language. Her chapter "'I Could Interpret an Artwork from My Own True Feelings': Intercultural and Empowerment Strategies Used to Teach in an International Setting" attends not only to her own lessons learned as a U.S. faculty member working in Taiwan, but also some of the ways in which her Taiwanese students responded to, engaged, and learned to participate in her Western-styled, constructivist-oriented, and feminist art education offerings which privileged student input and dialogue in the classroom over traditional lecture formats. One of Zimmerman's more provocative educative encounters involved a female artist in one of her classes, who, in venturing forward with her newfound feminist voice by displaying her artworks in public sites, found those artworks immediately vandalized.

As done in the previous chapters, Anniina Suominen Guyas provides a critical self-study of the author's pedagogical practices in "Life and Practice of Transnationalism." Her discussion includes consideration of notions of transnationalism with regard to national culture, institutionalism, communal and individual self-perception, consumerist culture, and corporate stereotypical identity models. Guyas also considers how publicly funded art and how cultural and state institutions endorse models and standards for national identity.

Following, in "Imagining a Faculty of Navigations in the Academy of Radical Generosity as a Future for Art Education," Australian educator Elizabeth M. Grierson describes the author's involvement with emerging digital technologies and new media in a program called the Mobile and Global Art Project. This case study of the project, along with the author's discussion, highlights several themes found to be relevant in previous chapters, as Grierson considers the potential of globalization on new possibilities through art, and examines impacts of shifting demographics, new technologies, and the fast exchange of information, ideas, and capital.

The final chapter in this section provides yet another international vantage point and seems a suitable conclusion to the anthology, *Globalization, Art, and Education*. In "Some Reflections on Globalizing (Visual) Culture" John Steers reflects on art education movements worldwide, highlighting the history and recent trends within The International Society of Education through Art (InSEA), and describes how internationalism, multiculturalism, and interculturalism impact new understandings of visual literacy in the 21st century. Wary of, but not entirely dismissing current leanings in art education academic discourse toward visual culture studies, Steers folds it into his United Kingdom-situated world view that thoughtfully attends to the aims of art education in the global age. Steers concludes that the 21st century requires an *intercultural* visual arts educational approach, one that must be based on the three key tenets of difference, plurality, and promoting independence of mind.

The Making of *ChinaVine*: Partnering Across Countries

Kristin G. Congdon and Doug Blandy

Zhang Yi Gui is in her eighties and lives in Quan Bei Village within Shandong Province, China. Locally, Zhang is known for the shoes that she makes and embroiders for infants. Using multiple colors of thread, Zhang embroiders flower designs on shoes for girls and tiger heads on shoes for boys. The soles are embroidered with evenly placed minute white stitches. Zhang is passing on her craft to her daughter-in-law (personal communication, May 6, 2007).

Within Zhang's lifetime extraordinary political and cultural changes have occurred in China. Born not long after the abdication of the last Qing emperor (1912), China would be ruled by warlords (early 20th century), see the founding of the Communist Party (1921), be occupied by Japan (1931 – 1945), experience a civil war (1946), experience famine killing up to an estimated 30 million (1959), experience a cultural revolution (1966), become a nuclear power (1964), join the United Nations (1971), experience a booming economy (1994), become the world's fourth largest economy (2005), and secure the 2008 Summer Olympic Games.

Zhang, and other folk artists, were brought to our attention by scholars associated with the China Folk Art Research Institute (CFARI) at the Shandong University of Art and Design (SUAD) as part of an aggressive effort on the part of SUAD to partner with other universities outside of China. On September 13, 2006, we traveled to Jinan in Shandong Province to establish a relationship among our three universities: the University of Central Florida (UCF), the University of Oregon (UO), and SUAD. Over a 3-day period Pan Lusheng, President of SUAD and Director of CFARI, Zhao Yi, Vice-Director of the Institute, and the two of us developed a plan for the conceptualization and implementation of a website to educate English-speaking audiences about folk art in Shandong Province. The basis for this website would be the foundational research that Pan, Zhao, and their associates had conducted on the intangible cultural heritage (ICH) of Shandong Province and the extensive folk art collection and archive associated with CFARI. This would be coupled with our own experience in working across cultures for an arts education purpose. Before the September trip, faculty and administrators from UO had already established a partnership with SUAD supporting faculty and student exchanges. A UO and SUAD Memorandum of Understanding (MOU) had been signed formally establishing their partnership. In May 2007, UCF and SUAD formally established their partnership with an MOU signing.

Blandy introduced the idea of a website developed in partnership between UCF, UO, and SUAD to SUAD President Pan Lusheng, when he first saw SUAD's folk art collection in 2005. This extensive collection of traditional folks arts such as papercuts, dough toys, architectural decoration, puppets, kites, jewelry, clothing, paintings, woodblock prints, and numerous

Figure 1

Zhao Jing Lin, printer, Da Zhao Village, Shandong Province, China. Photo credit: *ChinaVine*.

other forms of material culture associated with everyday life in Shandong is based on 20 years of research by Pan and other SUAD faculty and students.

Impressed by the Florida folk art website, *Folkvine* (www.folkvine.org), created by Congdon and other faculty and students at UCF, and wanting to test a community-based research model we developed in 1987 internationally, Blandy believed a three-university partnership would form a strong and promising model from which to work.[1]

Folkvine focuses on ten artists, whose sites can be entered through postcards on the counter of a Florida visitor center. Tour guides and bobble-head scholars help explain humanities' concepts that link the seemingly disparate artists together as they raise questions about identity, creativity, the environment, and community-based practices (Congdon, 2006). Web surfers can also enter a game room that contains two curricular projects for students and teachers. One is for elementary students and is in the form of a board game; the other is a zine for high school students

Project participants from SUAD, UCF, and UO decided that the new website would be called *ChinaVine*, as it grew out of *Folkvine's* approach to non-hierarchical teamwork amongst students and faculty, an arts-based research approach to development and exploration, and a focus on educating participants in an interactive and visual manner. *ChinaVine's* mission is to educate English-speaking children, youth, and adults about the material and intangible culture of China. Our first effort focuses on Shandong Province. The primary means by which the mission is achieved is through an interactive website, created by a diverse disciplinary group of students and faculty associated with UCF, UO, and SUAD. The design, implementation, and hosting of *ChinaVine* is facilitated by UCF and UO.

While *ChinaVine's* first effort was aimed at documenting the folk art of Shandong Province, we anticipate expanding the project to other parts of China. At this writing we are looking at partnerships with other scholars, universities, and provinces in order to have a wider representation of Chinese folk culture represented on the Web.

The focus of this chapter is on the partnership between UCF, UO, and SUAD. The three project goals addressed here are: (1) to concentrate on issues related to communicating effectively, both verbally and visually, for a common purpose; (2) to expand and refine on the partnership research model first developed in 1986-87 and *Folkvine's* model of collaboration by working across three university teams, and two countries and cultures; and (3) to make a successful website for English-speaking audiences that would be easy to use and visually compelling.

Issues of Communication and Context

We did not bring to this project the ability to read or speak any form of Chinese (our Shandong partners speak Mandarin) or with a background as Sinologists. On the other hand, several of our SUAD partners did speak English. At the outset we recognized our limitations. To some extent the research model discussed later in this chapter was designed to address various limitations when working with cultural groups other than our own. We were also familiar with the literature associated with "cultural competence." We recognized that by partnering with SUAD we would be engaging with them in a process that Cross, Bazron, Dennis, and Isaaces (1989) defined as an ongoing pursuit of self-reflection, knowledge acquisition, and skill development, practiced at individual and systems levels, in order to effectively engage a culturally diverse population. The conceptual framework proposed by the National Center on Cultural Competence (NCCCC) (2006) informed our thinking about our own self-assessment, knowing that we would need to consider the differences between our approach to studying material culture and our partners, acquire knowledge in a variety of ways about the context in which we were working, and adapt to the diversity and cultural contexts of the individuals and communities we worked with.

At the beginning of the project we began to immerse ourselves in a variety of readings that would help us understand China. They included scholarly writing (Spence, 1981, 1990; Yang & Yang, 2000), travel writing (Hessler, 2001, 2006), biography (Zhisui, 1994), fiction (Ma, 2001; Tan, 1998, 2001), film and video (Granada/PBS/CPB, 2007), websites (Chinese Village Traditions, 2008), and music (Atkins, 2007). This material addressed the history and culture of China including, but not limited to folk art, vernacular architecture, foodways, folk music, popular culture, Peking Opera, revolutionary politics, and the history of political movements. Of particular assistance was Peter Hessler's book, *Oracle Bones: A Journey Through Time in China* (2006). Hessler's observations on tradition and change in China would become a key topic for discussion and presentation.

Our trips to Jinan have increasingly taught us about the importance of Confucius's teachings in Shandong Province. Confucius' birthplace is in Qufu, which is in east Shandong Province. For example, when eating a formal meal, we quickly learned that there are carefully prescribed places to sit and times to toast. Certain honored guests eat before others, and foods have meanings that teach participants about appropriate roles and behaviors. The Confucius classics that were once banned from the classroom are now being read with great interest and Confucian thought is looked to for answers to current pressing problems (Mooney, 2007). While it instills in its citizenry clarity of purpose, it also prescribes specific roles for people (including faculty and students) that are somewhat less fluid than the practices of U.S. professors and students.

Prior to embarking on our partnership we also learned from Chinese scholars visiting the US that the conceptualization and implementation of *ChinaVine* would be simultaneous with a mammoth ongoing initiative in China to identify, protect, and communicate internationally the nation's intangible cultural heritage (ICH).

Beginning in the mid 1950s the Chinese government began to identify ethnic groups within China; 56 have been identified to date (Yang, 2007). This was a politically contentious process, but a process in which some scholars chose to participate. A primary motivation for their participation over the ensuing decades has been a great concern that some traditions were disappearing because of the lack of political stability in China coupled with rapid industrialization. Questions guiding current scholarship in China include,

whom does folklore belong to? Where is the people's voice? (Yang, 2007).

Informing the desire to maintain traditions in China is the concept "intangible cultural heritage" as proposed in the 2003 United Nations Educational, Scientific and Cultural Organization (UNESCO) *Convention for the Safeguarding of the Intangible Cultural Heritage*. As defined in that document

> The "intangible cultural heritage" means the practices, representations, expressions, knowledge, and skills—as well as the instruments, objects, artifacts and cultural spaces associated therewith—that communities, groups and, in some cases, individuals recognize as part of their cultural heritage. This intangible cultural heritage, transmitted from generation to generation, is constantly recreated by communities and groups in response to their environment, their interaction with nature and their history, and provides them with a sense of identity and continuity, thus promoting respect for cultural diversity and human creativity. For the purposes of this Convention, consideration will be given solely to such intangible cultural heritage as is compatible with existing international human rights instruments, as well as with the requirements of mutual respect among communities, groups and individuals, and of sustainable development. (p. 2)

China is one of the nations participating in these conventions and one of the nations listed as ratifying the 2003 Convention. The US did not ratify this Convention, whereas, in 2004, China did (Feilong, 2005).

Figure 2

Li Yu Cheng, gourd engraver, Li She Village, Shandong Province, China. Photo credit: *ChinaVine*.

Feilong (2005) described China's methods and system for safeguarding ICH. Safeguards are occurring in three ways. First, China is strengthening laws and regulations preserving ICH. Feilong described many such efforts that were first established in the 1990s and continue to the present day across China. Official committees at national, regional, and local levels are producing studies and policy papers associated with these preservation efforts. Scholarly forums and symposia are occurring as well.

Second, preservation programs are being implemented. In 2003 China's Ministry of Culture, the Ministry of Finance, and the National Nationalities Commission, and the Cultural Federation launched a massive effort to preserve ICH—specifically "national and folk culture" (Feilong, 2005, p. 2). The purpose was to identify those forms of ICH in "eminent danger, establish the quite complete protection system of the national and folk culture of China and basically realize the protection of the national and folk culture of China with scientific, standardization and legal system at the end of 2020" (Feilong, 2005, pp. 2-3).

Third, within the provinces of China, prominent organizations, often associated with colleges and universities, have been identified to provide leadership for the preservation program. Within each province these organizations are responsible for collecting and nominating those "masterpieces" needing immediate protection. As such, these institutions are hosting symposia, publishing monographs, and educating professionals around ICH issues (Feilong, 2005).

The Chinese Government, recognizing the enormous attention that would be given China around the 2008 Summer Olympic Games, decided to use the Games as a way to bring attention to China's ICH for the purpose of salvaging, revising, and re-building Chinese folk traditions (Yang, 2007). Scholars within China are examining the numerous exhibits and festivals in which this is occurring (Yang, 2007).

Important also to the context in which we were working was our growing understanding that ICH is of interest to both scholars associated with art schools such as SUAD and the Central Academy of Fine Arts (CAFA) in Beijing and folklorists. Art school curricula in China include courses and degrees related to some of the traditional arts associated with ICH. In addition, one of Pan's goals at SUAD is to inform non-traditional forms of art with ICH forms. For example, students in the digital arts program at SUAD are encouraged to use traditional motifs in their response to design problems. Both SUAD and CAFA have collections of folk art and scholars at both of these institutions have published on this material.

In the early 20th century folklorists began to be involved in collecting and interpreting what is now referred to as ICH (Zhang, 2007). From then until the present day this study would be interrupted periodically by various political upheavals occurring in China. However, enough interest was sustained so that beginning in the 1980s universities began establishing folklore as an area of study. The China Folklore Society (CFS) was founded in 1981 and now has two thousand members (Zhang, 2007).

Through our conversations with scholars associated with art schools and members of the CFS, we have discovered that while there is mutual awareness of the work each are doing, there is no evidence of sustained collaboration. We can only speculate now as to the reasons why collaboration has not taken place, with one possibility having to do with disciplinary orientations. At both SUAD and CAFA the approach to ICH seems to be primarily aesthetic. Within CFS the orientation is folkloric, anthropological, and ethnological.

The Research Model

We brought to *ChinaVine's* research our own long-term commitment to working with communities and cultures. We have been influenced by collaborative research methods within the fields of anthropology and folklore and we believe that such methods as Lassiter's (2004) collaborative ethnography facilitate correct interpretation, representation, or description of a cultural group. In this regard, our method required us to begin working with a new language and to learn to behave appropriately in settings that were totally unfamiliar to us. Congruent with an ethnographic approach was our use of observation, interviews, and field notes.

In 1986 and 1987 we curated an exhibit for the Bowling Green State University School of Art Gallery titled "Boats, Bait, and Fishing Paraphernalia: A Local Folk Aesthetic." Local well-known fishers assisted us in planning the exhibit. This exhibit was on view for the month of February 1987 and included a wooden fishing boat, fishing flies, fishing tackle, clothing worn by fishers, photographs of the Northwest Ohio fishing related landscape, and miscellaneous other objects (Blandy & Congdon, 1988). A significant finding associated with the curation of this exhibit was the development of a method for working in partnership with community members toward the development of cultural programming (Blandy & Congdon, 1993). This model was based on pedagogical guidelines from Freire (1970, 1981) that focus on building nonhierarchical and cooperative relationships among people, methods for critical inquiry, the importance of forging

Figure 3

Lang Xiu Cai, dough
flower maker, Lang
Village, Shandong
Province, China.
Photo credit:
ChinaVine.

a common language, and a conception of culture that is dynamic. The model consists of five overlapping and dynamic phases of activity including orientation, identification of partners, planning, research and implementation, and evaluation.

Following the use of this model, each of us has adapted it to other purposes. In Blandy's case this has included an 1989 anthropological exhibit at UO's Museum of Natural History (Gabai, 1990), an exhibit on tattooing at the Maude Kerns Art Center in Eugene in 1990 (Brookes, 1991), and in 2005 for UO's Knight Library exhibit "Zines and DIY Democracy," and the online exhibit "Zines: Witness this Moment" in 2005 (Blandy & Voelker-Morris, 2005). In Congdon's case examples include *Folkvine*, the 2002 Cultural By-ways Project that placed local history on a free bus system (Congdon, Teicher, & Engell, 2003), and the 1999 research for the exhibition, The Last Harvest, about the closing of the central Florida muck farms (Congdon, 2004). In spite of our many projects, neither of us have had the opportunity to apply our model internationally.

In addition to the collaborative community-based approach we continue to apply to our research projects is the model of arts-based research. In many ways this approach attempts to disrupt academic complacency in its efforts to utilize new technologies and foster democratic approaches while valuing the expertise and critical engagement of students and native communities (Sanders, 2006).

When we first conceptualized and implemented our research model, approval by an Institutional Review Board (IRB) was not required. This is still the case at SUAD. However, both UCF and UO do require a review and *ChinaVine* went through the process. The

IRB application process will be commented on later in this chapter.

The Model Applied
Fieldwork

Associated with our goals was the necessity to do extensive fieldwork in rural Shandong Province. Fieldwork would allow us to become more familiar with the cultural terrain and solidify our teams' relationships as we collect high quality digital images that could be used on the website. Fieldwork was first conducted over a five-day period from May 3-8, 2007. We can only describe our travels within Shandong Province as "spectacular." Our SUAD partner, under the direction of Zhao, facilitated the intensive, exceptionally well-planned fieldwork in the villages of Da Zhao, Li She, Da Yang, Lang, and Quan Bei.

UCF participants included: Kristin Congdon functioning as a project manager and ethnographer, Sarah Long as cinematographer, and Dan Novatnak as technology specialist. UO participants included: Doug Blandy functioning as a project manager and as an ethnographer, Jess Yates as cinematographer, and Rosario Aglialoro, Executive Director of the Northwest China Council in the US and UO alum as translator, photographer, and expert on cultural context. The SUAD team included Professor Zhao Yi, an expert in Chinese folk art, Fu De lei, folk art faculty and ethnographer, Tian Yuan, also folk art faculty who translated the interviews into English, Li Yan, a cinematographer, and Li Ahi Peng a still photographer.

To help solidify our participatory cross-university team approach, we all contributed fieldwork and photographic materials to the ChinaVine archive. We agreed that these materials would be shared equally

Figure 4

Lui Yu Xiang, weaver, Quan Bei Village, Shandong Province, China. Photo credit: *ChinaVine*.

among partners associated with a particular *ChinaVine* project and that contributors would be given credit for their specific project. However, credit will not be listed in relation to particular text and images. Contributors to the *ChinaVine* archive are free to use their materials for purposes outside of *ChinaVine*.

Adapting the Model to the Chinese Context
The Teams

While we looked to *Folkvine*'s nonhierarchal team approach as a way of building *ChinaVine*'s foundational research team, we quickly realized that adaptations would need to be made. The *Folkvine* team was a tight-knit group of faculty and students who worked at each others houses, sent numerous emails on and off the listserve each day, and organized and implemented several public programs with artists and communities each year. *Folkvine* was used to the "feel-good" response that came from working face-to-face. Developing a team of people across three universities and two countries proved to be more difficult, partly because no one person knew everyone.

Since UCF was taking primary responsibility for producing the website, this team was the largest. By January 2008, it was composed of 20 students and 9 faculty from disciplines all over the university, including: Anthropology, Art, Asian Studies, Business, Digital Media, English, Film, History, Humanities, and Philosophy. Even with this many team members, help was needed from the UO team of four individuals on translations, music, and media arts. SUAD provided access to the artists, expertise in fieldwork, translation, and access to their museum collection and archives. For the 4 years that the *Folkvine* team was active, membership was between 12 and 15 members each semester.

Only a few students rotated off each term, and faculty members stayed with the project until it became inactive and efforts shifted to *ChinaVine*.

There are several ways in which our team approach had to be reconsidered with the addition of Chinese partners. First, it appears that it is Chinese custom to know people and trust them before a working partnership is developed. We found this to be true when we traveled to several Chinese universities in September 2006. Repeatedly we heard that U.S. faculty should come and spend time with Chinese faculty, for it is out of relationships that projects develop. Indeed, at SUAD it was emphasized that we had developed a friendship by eating many meals together and sharing a love for folk art. Out of this relationship our project could take place. In the US, we are more apt to develop an idea and then see what kind of expertise is needed and we hope that camaraderie will grow out of a mutual interest in a particular topic. While this beginning step is not always clear-cut, the emphasis on the Chinese friendship before a project starts in opposition to the U.S. way of beginning a research project was noted.

Issues of Formality and Informality

Another difference we noted is that in U.S. universities, when working on a research project with students, informality, rather than formality can often prevail. As students can come to the research table with more expertise in technology or a particular culture than professors, they can be looked to as teachers. This equalizing characteristic was prevalent in the *Folkvine* team, and we expected to build on it in the *ChinaVine* teams. However, in China, faculty is first and foremost an honored and respected individual, and this hierarchy is continuously noted. While Chinese faculty members are friendly and supportive of their students, it remains clear who has the authority in the relationship.

A Chinese folklorist at the American Folklore Society (AFS) in Quebec City in October 2007 told us that there were two ways to do things. One is from the top down, the other is from the bottom up. In China, he informed us, things always work from the top down. This way of working has been characterized by Bhagwati (2007) and Hutton (2007) as one of China's main problems in building its country as an economic stronghold. Without a more democratic way of working, they claim, China hampers free speech and the problem-solving abilities that come with it. Hulbert (2007), focusing more specifically on education, also raises the question on whether China can create an educational system that encourages more openness and flexibility. The Chinese education system has gone though a radical change since Deng Xiaoping reinstated the National College Entrance Exam in 1977, dramatically expanding higher education. As we worked with SUAD over the period of 2 years, an entirely new campus outside of Jinan was built along with numerous other universities. Construction crews worked around the clock and the pressure to move in quickly was apparent.

As has been the case in the US, tests have begun to be the measure for success in schools, raising questions in both countries about student skills in "creativity, flexibility, [and] initiative" (Hulbert, 2007, p. 39). While China may currently see the need to move toward more flexibility, the US seems to be more and more consumed with rote testing.

As we worked on the website, we recognized that formality was continually more evident in China than in U.S. universities. For example, we seldom ask our superiors for permission to travel; we assume that if we can work it into our schedule, we will go. Our SUAD team needed permission from President Pan for travel, and other more everyday events seemed to involve the administration as well. While we recognize that this way of working may have a lot to do with SUAD's student population of about 3,000 compared to UO's 19,000 and UCF's 48,000, we still felt quite certain that U.S. faculty and students have more autonomy.

Freedom of Discourse

U.S. students and scholars generally take for granted the rights and responsibilities associated with discussing regional, national, and international politics. The U.S. team members are aware of reports from rural China about civil unrest and human rights violations. Because our fieldwork took place in rural China we were acutely aware that it was possible that some of these experiences may have impacted the lives of those we interviewed. However, we deferred to our SUAD partners in the degree to which political issues were discussed. In this regard conversations did take place around the rapid industrialization of China and its impact on ICH, environmental issues such as air quality, and U.S. policy in the Middle East. Our SUAD partners did not discuss with us the political situation in rural China. It is impossible to know if this was by choice and/or if they were not well versed in the politics of the rural areas in which we did our fieldwork.

Application of the IRB

Applying what was required of us by the IRB at UCF and UO was very problematic. All members of our teams had to qualify to do the fieldwork as was mandated by our universities. Passing the required test was seen to be time consuming and unnecessary work for those of us who were trained in ethnography and were fully aware of the ethical issues involved in doing fieldwork. But it was the release forms that were most problematic. Congdon insisted that the release forms (in both English and Chinese) be as simple as possible, knowing that even scholars can become confounded by the legal jargon that universities routinely produce. However, even using straightforward release forms presented problems, raising tension and discomfort at several fieldwork sites. Many of our participants couldn't read, write, or sign their names and seemed to have no frame of reference for understanding what was being asked of them. Because dozens of community members came to watch the interviewing process, presenting a written document for participants to sign often placed them in awkward situation. In one case, a granddaughter signed for the artist. In other cases, long discussions had to take place on why such a document was necessary. The fact that we had been invited into the artists' homes showed respect for the process. A legal document they often couldn't read and didn't value raised suspicion. Under the circumstances, we were grateful for Zhao, Yuan, and Aglialoro for their expertise and patience in working with the folk artists to allay their concerns and mitigate embarrassment.

After our fieldwork was done and we were back at SUAD in the folk art museum, a television crew filmed our response to the collection. They later told us that we would need to sign a release form. Falling for the joke, we agreed to do so, and every Chinese person in the room burst out laughing. It was clear from this experience that our mistrust of each other and our need to legalize our actions, which should be based on friendship, disrupted their cultural way of behaving with other. The process caused unnecessary tension that we wished we could have avoided.

The Website
Site Design
The website is designed as a heritage book of Shandong Province. It has drawings, slide shows, and film, and text. Visual and written information reveals information on artists and art forms, as well as folk tales, folk beliefs, foodways, and history. As we progress with the site, it will become more interactive and more complex. We anticipate that other heritage books of other provinces will follow as we explore folk art practices in diverse parts of China.

Licensing
To maximize the usefulness of *ChinaVine* for educational purposes we decided that we would license *ChinaVine* with Creative Commons (CC). Creative Commons "defines the spectrum of possibilities between full copyright — all rights reserved — and the public domain — no rights reserved" (CC, 2008). A CC license permits maintaining copyright while allowing other uses of the work. Visitors to *ChinaVine* are free to share, copy, distribute, and display *ChinaVine* under the following conditions.

- *ChinaVine* must be attributed in the manner specified by the UCF, UO, and SUAD partners.
- *ChinaVine* cannot be used for commercial purposes.
- *ChinaVine* may not be altered, transformed, or built upon.
- Use of *ChinaVine* must make clear that it is licensed for use as described above.

Conclusion: The *ChinaVine* Plan and *ChinaVine* Reality
What is so striking about *ChinaVine* is that it presents a view of China that so many travelers are unable to see. We were most fortunate in May 2007 to have had to opportunity to visit artists in small villages where foreigners are seldom seen. Several of the students and staff from SUAD indicated that even they had previously not been to rural Shandong Province. This fact was often evident to us as people came out of everyday spaces to look at us. Sometimes they giggled as they touched Congdon's and [UCF student Sarah] Long's blonde hair. We were certainly oddities, worth coming to see. This contact, and the ability to film our subjects, is the strength of our project. The opportunities that we have had to capture the images on the website are

Figure 5

Left: Zang Yi Gui, shoe embroiderer, Quan Bei Village, Shandong Province, China. Photo credit: *ChinaVine*.

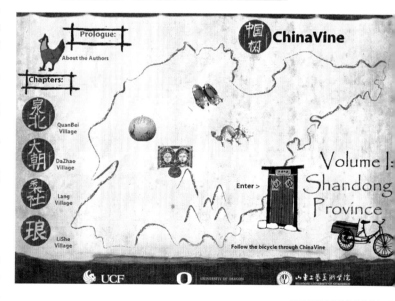

Figure 6

ChinaVine.org, screen capture, work in progress. Photo credit: *ChinaVine*.

clearly due to the years of fieldwork accomplished by the SUAD team.

We will be forever grateful to them for sharing their knowledge and contacts as they have. Many of our colleague and friends have asked to travel with us in order to have the same or similar experiences. Their interest caused us to question what might happen to the small villages we documented if tourists started trekking to their homes. Indeed, the Chinese folklorists we talked to and heard speak at the AFS meeting implied that it was best to document and preserve the villages with as little participation from the government as possible in fear that these heritage places might become like U.S. heritage spaces where tourism is what keeps them alive. We recognize that what is desired in historical preservation is a continuation of living tradition. Because we do not want them to become displays for tourists, we questioned what might happen if *ChinaVine* became popular. We quickly assured ourselves that these villages were so remote and difficult to access that tourism would not be an issue, at least not anytime soon. There were no "comfortable" places for outsiders to eat, sleep, or use the bathroom and it was clear that our access to the village homes was due to the relationship of our SUAD partners.

Many critics claim that today, "China has become the world's hottest contemporary art market" (Vine, Phillips, & Pollack, 2007, p. 49). When this claim is made, the reference to art is not about China's traditional arts. Rather the reference is made to edgy, Art World art that is marketed by powerful museums, galleries, and media conglomerates. In our conversations with SUAD President Pan, he repeatedly told us that he was concerned about Chinese art (associated with art schools) losing its connection the country's heritage. At least some students are concerned about the massive changes that are happening in China as well—and how tradition is being lost and rapidly replaced, not always with something more positive. During fall semester 2007, two UCF film students studied at SUAD to further the work on *ChinaVine*. One SUAD student e-mailed UCF student Sarah Long after she and Mike Diaz interviewed art students about incorporating folk art into their contemporary work. He wrote:

> I had scanned your website, it is so impressive and surprised me. I learned something I had never known before. As a Chinese I think I should say "thanks" to you, because you really did a good job! ... I grow up in [t]he countryside, I like that life style. Now days I always miss those old days I lived there. And the honest people, fresh air, quiet atmosphere are all attracting me a lot. You know all the folk art are come from daily life, so I can experience something truth there. In modern society, the industry and information technical more and more advanced then the handcraft are ignored. (personal communication from Rhys to Sarah Long, November 28, 2007)

We anticipate that *ChinaVine* will continue to grow over the next several years, long after this chapter has gone to print. In the process, we will no doubt answer some questions as we raise others. What will hopefully remain consistent is the power of working in partnership with faculty and students in China.

REFERENCES

Atkins, M. China Dub Soundsystem. (2007). *Made in China* [audio recording]. United States: Bloodshot Records.

Bhagwati, J., Made in China. (2007, February 18). *New York Times Book Review*, 25.

Blandy, D., & Congdon, K. G. (1988). Community based aesthetics as an exhibition catalyst and a foundation for community involvement in art education. *Studies in Art Education*, 29 (4), 243-249.

Blandy, D., & Congdon, K. G. (1993). A theoretical structure for educational partnerships and curatorial practices. *Visual Arts Research*, 19(2), 61-67.

Blandy, D., & Voelker-Morris, R. (2005). Zines and diy democracy: Witness this moment. *CultureWork*, special issue. Retrieved March 1, 2006, from http://aad.uoregon.edu/culturework/zines/index.html

Brookes, K. (1991). *Living art: Tattoo show*. Unpublished Master's Project, University of Oregon, Eugene, OR.

CC. (2008). home. http://creativecommons.org/. Retrieved February 6, 2008.

Congdon, K. G. (2006). Folkvine.org: Arts-based research on the Web. Studies in Art Education, 48(1), 36-51.

Congdon, K. G. (2004). *Community art in action*. Worcester, MA: Davis Publications.

Congdon, K. G., Teicher, S., & Engell, A. M. (2003). Cultural by-ways on the information highway: Contextualizing spaces and places with history and folklore. *Journal of Cultural Research in Art Education*, 21, 27-35.

Chinese Village Traditions (2006). Retrieved January 10, 2008 from http://www.chinalocalculture.net/en.villagetradition.chinalocalculture.net/intro.html

Cross, T. L., Bazron, B. J., Dennis, K. W., & Issacs, M. R. (1989). *Towards a culturally competent system of care*: Vol. I. Washington, DC: National Technical Assistance Center for Children's Mental Health, Georgetown University Child Development Center.

Feilong, C. (2005, December 13-16). *The method and the system for safeguarding intangible culture heritage in China*. Paper presented at the Sub-Regional Experts Meeting in Asia on Intangible Cultural Heritage: Safeguarding and Inventory-Making Methodologies, Bangkok, Thailand.

Freire, P. (1970). *Pedagogy of the oppressed*. New York: Seabury.

Freire, P. (1981). *Education for critical consciousness*. New York: Continuum.

Gabai, C. J. N. (1990). *Ethiopia's braided traditions: Integrating multicultural elements into a natural history museum exhibit*. Unpublished Master's project, University of Oregon, Eugene, OR.

Granada/PBS/CPB. (2007). *China from the inside* [DVD]. PBS.

Hessler, P. (2001). *River town: Two years on the Yangtze*. New York: HarperCollins.

Hessler, P. (2006). *Oracle bones: A journey through time in China*. New York: Harper Collins.

Hulbert, A. (2007, April 1). Re-education. *The New York Times Magazine*, 36-43 & 56.

Hutton, W. (2007). *The writing on the wall: Why we must embrace China as a partner or face it as an enemy*. New York: Free Press.

KQED Public Television and Granada Television, Granada International & BBC, in association with Kostyk Communications (2006). *China: from the inside out*. Arlington, VA: PBS.

Lassiter, L. E. (2004). Collaborative ethnography. *Anthronotes*. 25(1), 1-9.

Ma, J. (2001). Red dust. New York: Pantheon.

Mooney, P. (2007, April 20). Confucius comes back. *The Chronicle of Higher Education*, A46-48.

National Center for Cultural Competence. http://www11.georgetown.edu/research/gucchd/nccc/. Retrieved August 29, 2006.

Rhys (personal communication to Sarah Long, November 28, 2007)

Sanders, J. (2006). Performing arts-based education research: An epic drama of practice, precursors, problems, and possibilities. *Studies in Art Education*, 48(1), 89-107.

Spence, J. (1981). *The gate of heavenly peace: The Chinese and their revolution*. New York: Viking.

Spence, J. (1990). *The search for modern China*. New York: HarperCollins.

Tan, A. (1998). *The hundred secret senses*. London: Vintage.

Tan, A. (2001). *The bonesetter's daughter*. New York: Putnam.

UNESCO. (2003). Convention for the Safeguarding of the Intangible Cultural Heritage. Retrieved January 19, 2008 from http://portal.unesco.org/en/ev.php-URL_ID=17716&URL_DO=DO_TOPIC&URL_SECTION=201.

Vine, R, Phillips, C, and Pollack, B. (2007). Money talks Mandarin. *Art in America*, 3, 49-53.

Yang, L. (2007, February 27). *2008 Olympic Games and the representation and translation of Chinese folk traditions*. Paper presented at the University of Oregon, Eugene, OR.

Yang, X & Yang, Y. (2000). *Chinese folk art*. Beijing: New World Press.

Zhang, J. (2007, October). *An introduction to the China Folklore Society (CFS), and the CFS Delegation to the AFS/FSAC Annual Meeting*. A briefing paper distributed at the 2007 meeting of the American Folklore Society and the Folklore Studies Association of Canada.

Zhisui, L. (1994). *The private life of Chairman Mao* (T. Hung-Chao, Trans.). New York: Random House.

ENDNOTE

1   The Folkvine Team at UCF included many faculty and students who worked from 2003 to 2007 on the Web site. Chantale Fontaine, Folkvine's lead web designer, deserves special recognition for her talent, skill, and vision. The 1987 research model we refer to here is based on the exhibition we coordinated at Bowling Green State University called "Boats, Bait, and Fishing Paraphernalia," a project discussed later in the chapter.

Global Colonization: The Case of Distance Education in Jamaica

Phyllis T. P. Hill

We cannot understand globalization without understanding the structure of the sort of power relations which flourish in the twenty-first century as an economical, cultural and political legacy of Western imperialism.

(ASHCROFT, GRIFFITHS & TIFFIN, 2003, p. 216)

A central issue in the ongoing debate about globalization is that of ideological hegemony, cultural domination and cultural homogenization. In this context the relationship between culture and power becomes critical, especially in post-colonial societies such as Jamaica, where cultural production and the distribution of knowledge have become locations of struggle. This section of my chapter highlights the two major issues—cultural dependency and domination—that occupy the literature on globalization in the Caribbean, paying particular attention to the circumstance of Jamaica. This overview creates a foundation for understanding the economic, political and social challenges with which Jamaica grapples. It also places the issues within a historical context, making it possible to trace the persistent themes of cultural dependency, domination and resistance, within Jamaica's national identity.

Domination and Resistance: The Roots of Jamaica's Economic and Cultural Vulnerability

According to Caribbean writers, Jamaica's vulnerability to cultural, economic and political domination is due to successive cycles of globalization. Like the rest of the Caribbean region, Jamaica has experienced previous rounds of globalization, the first being its violent interaction with Spain, starting in 1494 and resulting in the complete annihilation of its indigenous Amerindian population. Another cycle occurred with the forced relocation of large groups of people from different regions of the world by the Europeans to provide labor on sugar plantations. During each cycle the gains were never equally distributed and the result was an expansion of the economies of Europe, gained through

the exploitation and appropriation of goods and services from Jamaica.

Historically, the Jamaican economy was constructed as an adjunct to the British Empire, and a legacy of reliance on external authorities, suppliers, markets, and global-political agendas continues. The varying waves of colonization created a society with the labor to produce but not the means of production and Jamaica's development continues to falter because of this handicap.

Jamaica gained independence from Britain in 1962, but the influence and control of the Mother Country remained. According to Allahar (2005), Jamaica was granted independence only when

> Britain felt that (1) it had sufficiently cultivated a class of local leaders that was ideologically prepared to take over and run "business as usual", and (2) the direct control of the countries had become both politically anachronistic and economically burdensome. Having made the economies of these countries dependent on those of Britain and other imperialist centers, it was felt that the day-to-day running of the internal affairs politically could be left up to the locals while guaranteeing minimum interference in the flow of economic benefits to the mother country. (Allahar, 2005, p. 122)

Following its independence from Britain, Jamaica looked to the industrialized North as an economic alternative and this, according to Hintzen, created the environment for "anti-colonialism" to become "rapidly transformed into an instrumentality for the penetration of neocolonial forms of global capital" (2003, p. 415). This paved the way for contemporary free trade policies and global financial institutions such as the International Monetary Fund, World Bank, and World Trade Organization to dictate the country's economic policies. The reality is that Jamaica lacks the economic resources to produce and extensively disseminate its own cultural products, and the fear persists that its cultural heritage may be overwhelmed by an imported Western model. Fear of cultural and economic domination is further exacerbated by the increased importance of electronic telecommunications, air travel, dependence on tourism, dependence on overseas remittance, the emerging global culture of mass consumption and free trade agreements. Our local cultural identity is challenged by international cultural products, primarily from the United States of America, such as film, music, cable television, books, magazines, and information technology products.

Decolonizing Education: The Case of Jamaica

Jamaica's system of education continues to be shaped by the processes of globalization. During the colonial period, education was used throughout the Caribbean as a means of control and power, designed to keep the colonized population tied to the plantation economy. Remnants of this ideology persist, leading Ashcroft, Griffiths & Tiffin (2004) to concur that education is the most "insidious and in some way the most cryptic of colonialist survivals" (p. 425) because within systems of education themes of dependence and cultural domination are always present.

As Jamaica continues to reside on the margins of world economic development, education offers a site of resistance to cultural monopolization and of hope for economic prosperity. One impediment to educational advancement in Jamaica, however, is that features of the European models inherited from colonialism remain entrenched within its system of education. The next section seeks to identify (a) the hybridization of ideologies, policies and goals entrenched within the system, and (b) the challenges these pose to the current transformative goals of the system. These two themes will be examined in relation to both general education and art education.

Education: Erasing the Remnants of Colonialism

Throughout the period of slavery the colonial power provided no formal educational opportunities for the slaves and there was no overall plan for mass education until the period immediately before abolition in 1834. The model of education created then had its roots in the belief that the children of freed slaves would follow in the footsteps of their parents as agricultural laborers. The colonial authority advocated a program of learning that it hoped would develop in students

...a willingness to accept the inevitability of their future role as manual workers by providing them with an effective programme of practical, industrial, agricultural or manual training. Such a course of instruction was expected to develop the attitudes, skills and knowledge necessary to increase the student's efficiency in their destined role by inculcating in them the idea that it was their social and moral obligation to work hard. (Bacchus, 1994, p. 121)

Features of this colonial model remain visible in our pedagogical models, schools' organization and management practices, and in the bureaucratic nature of ministerial bodies.

The process of decolonizing education in Jamaica began with an attempt to reform the elitist ideologies, policies and structures which guided the colonial system of education. Norman Manley, the first prime minister of Jamaica, in a 1939 address to Parliament, declared:

We can take everything that English education has to offer, but ultimately we must reject the domination of her influence, because we are not English nor should we ever want to be. (Nettleford, 1971, p. 107)

He also stated emphatically that for education to be culturally relevant in contemporary Jamaica it must be able to prepare each generation to "find the ways and means of liberating itself, whether from the yoke of political domination or the disease of economic insufficiency" (Nettleford, 1971, p. 295). Under his leadership self-government laid the foundation for an educational system focused on social and cultural development. It sought to increase the allocation of funding for education and to develop a national educational policy that would expand the scope of education and redefine educational goals and priorities.

An overarching goal of contemporary education in Jamaica is to create "a people who have a clear national identity and national pride" (Henry-Wilson; 2004, p. 24). Such a citizen, according to Henry-Wilson

knows and is comfortable with him/ herself; who takes responsibility for and is committed to the goals of national and regional development; a citizen who is aware of the history, culture and heritage of Jamaica and the Caribbean and is equipped to participate in the global environment. (p. 24)

So the objective is now to position our learners as global citizens, providing them with the knowledge and skills necessary for them to successfully traverse the global landscape. Thus education's major challenge has become to

...shape the cognitive skills, interpersonal sensibilities and cultural sophistication of children and youth whose lives will be both engaged in local contexts and responsive to larger transnational processes. (Suarez-Orozco & Qin-Hilliard, 2003, p. 3)

This new goal of educational reform is grounded in the premise that we need to foster global awareness while simultaneously maintaining and protecting local knowledge and cultural systems. This approach also underscores the reality that

> Globalization means that the lives of children growing up today will be shaped in no small measure by global processes in economy, society and culture. Educational systems tied to the formation of nation-state citizens and consumers bound to local systems to the neglect of the larger global forces are likely to become obsolete, while those that pro-actively engage in globalization's new challenges are more likely to thrive. (Suarez-Orozco & Qin- Hilliard, 2003, p. 23)

We realize that within this global marketplace our learners need to be informed, engaged, critical citizens if they are to survive in this new millennium. Jamaica's economic and social survival depends on producing citizens who are able to effectively consolidate and navigate both local and global terrains.

Art Education: A Fertile Site of Resistance

The Jamaican art movement evolved as a resistance to the pressures of colonialism and continues as a productive site of decolonization. Our visual arts tradition began with widespread deculturation of the enslaved people. One hundred and fifty years after the abolition of slavery, British art was still held as the standard example and the artistic tradition of the nation. Of the artworks of the Africans who made up more than 90% of the population, David Boxer, art historian, art critic and former director of the Jamaican National Gallery, laments:

> It is one of the tragedies of slavery that so drastic was the decolonization of the Africans, so harsh were the prohibitions against the manufacture of ritual objects, that with the exception of undecorated ceramic vessels not one object exists as evidence of the continuity of African artistic traditions in Jamaica. (1983, p. 4)

Colonization, it seemed had submerged the traditions and value of African art, robbing the Jamaican native of art that reflected his African identity, and in a subtle way had alienated him from his past. Colonization for more than 400 years had forced the descendants of Africa to idealize the history, art and culture of the colonial masters.

The Government of Jamaica has always supported the arts as a tool of national development, recognizing that survival in a global world depends on fostering an environment which will encourage creativity and growth. One long-term goal is their commitment to providing a context for the free practice of the arts, for the nurturing and fostering of individual talent, for the plurality of artistic expression and for the experimental exploration of new ways of cultural expression (National Cultural Policy of Jamaica: M.O.E.Y.C., 2003, p. 6). Currently the arts play a pivotal role in national development, particularly within the field of education where it is nurtured at all levels of the curriculum. Recognizing that there is already overwhelming evidence of an increase in teenage pregnancy, teen prostitution, drug abuse, teens at risk, and poor academic performance in schools, the arts have become a vehicle for the nurturing of individual creativity, and the nucleus of educational curricula at all levels of the system. Educators also recognize that today's youth requires non-traditional, exciting, innovative teaching methodologies, and the arts provide a powerful medium through which to disseminate information and change behaviors. When the arts are used in this way it encourages a continuing dialogue between the formal educational structure and the community.

The Growth of Localism as a Site of Resistance

One important conclusion of the globalization-localization debate is that the global does not exist without the local. Localism grows especially when there is a perceived threat to local identity and culture. Certainly globalization is changing the ways we experience national identities and cultural belonging but, as Yamada Atshshi (2002) argues, the paradox is that localism grows as a resistance to globalization and globalization and localization operate simultaneously—in a process sometimes referred to as 'glocalization.' The idea here is that both processes—globalization and resistance to it on behalf of the local—are evolving together and strengthening each other. This resistance is evident throughout the cultural institutions and systems within Jamaica. In education, British examination models (the British GCE O' and A' levels with the Caribbean Examination Council [CXC]) are being replaced by Caribbean models which we believe have content, methodologies and assessment strategies that are more relevant to our Caribbean students' needs. The curriculum was developed by local educators and stakeholders and allows students to identify, research and evaluate local socio-cultural issues. A major part of this process is that they utilize local knowledge, values, and belief systems to better understand and shape their world. As a response to the "McDonaldization of Jamaica," there is a tremendous increase in the number of local festivals and national competitions aiming to promote traditional heritage, music, dance, cuisine, visual arts, and architecture.

Distance Education: A Center of Power within the Context of Globalization

Distance education is emerging as a centre of power within education and has become Jamaica's most recent challenge, having a direct impact on its system of education. The large influx of distance education programs from North America, Canada and England is not only siphoning funds from its already struggling economy but poses a threat to the values, norms, and ideals that constitute the national character. Distance education programs transcend the barriers of geography, economics and culture, and they bring with them threats of cultural homogenization. Already the local culture is under siege from external cultural products and participation by foreign providers in Jamaica's education system may intensify this.

Education has always determined economic, social, and cultural development and this section examines the ramifications of distance education on the culture and identity of Jamaica. Specifically, it will focus on (a) the policies and trade agreements that influence this growth and the resulting impact on the educational system in Jamaica, (b) the policies in place for governance (control and management) and (c) the current need for the development and integration of distance education programs that are responsive to the country's developmental needs.

Distance Education: Policies & Trade Agreements

Jamaica became a signatory to The World Trade Organization (WTO) General Agreements on Trade in Services (GATS) on April 15, 1994, liberalizing its higher education sector and converting education into a commodity of trade subject to international trade agreements and policies. One central role of the Jamaican education system has always been the exploration, interpretation, and preservation of cultural legacies, and under this trade agreement those legacies are threatened. The liberalization of trade in services seeks to standardize the cultural focus, thoughts, language, and educational themes of individual countries. In essence, the GATS policy attempts to regulate, control or harmonize the movement of knowledge.

GATS is a multilateral, legally enforceable agreement covering international trade in services (as opposed to trade in products). "Services" is defined under this trade agreement as

> ...any service in any sector except services in the exercise of "Governmental Authority". The agreement goes on to further define "a service supplied in the exercise of governmental authority as any service that is supplied neither on a commercial basis nor in competition with one or more service suppliers." (National Council on Education, 2004, p. 3)

Under this trade arrangement, signatory countries commit to incrementally place sectors of their economies under GATS. There are five education sectors covered under GATS (primary, secondary, higher, adult education and other education (testing and certification)) but Jamaica like most other governments have made commitments only for adult education, higher education and other education.

Under GATS, liberalization means that any aspect of "education" in Jamaica is open to foreign competition, inclusive of curriculum development, teacher training, the owning and operating of schools, and the hiring of teachers. Within the terms and conditions of GATS standardization is also institutionalized through international equivalency, and the possibility exists that the uniqueness of local educational institutions will vanish. Liberalization also creates the opportunity for the mass marketing of low quality, generic and culturally irrelevant educational products that are unlikely to have much positive impact on the economies and lives of the purchasers. The end result of this could be the marginalization of national identities.

The Impact of GATS on the Tertiary Level of Education

To succeed and prosper in this new international environment, the Jamaican government recognizes the need for highly educated, knowledgeable and motivated professionals and its manifesto has underscored education as a tool for development. In reaction to the accelerated demand for higher education, the Jamaican government increased "enrollment in all tertiary level institutions through expansion of enrollment on campus, at outreach centers and through distance education" (Mission Statement, Tertiary Unit, MOEYC, 2004, p. 2). Thus the principal use of distance education in Jamaica is for the strengthening and expansion of education, especially at the tertiary level, and it functions as a peripheral rather than central provider. Jamaica's capacity to provide education via distance technologies is severely limited and this has led to a reliance on external providers, primarily from the US, England, and Canada. The significant outcomes of this have been:

- an increase in the number of places at the tertiary level—increased access for more students,
- overseas institutions are setting up educational 'store-fronts' in Jamaica and are now competing with each other and with local institutions in the provision of tertiary level education, and
- increased concerns about quality, accreditation, and national development goals.

The reality is that there is a significant increase in the number of individuals accessing tertiary education but this does not necessarily mean an increase in the quality of education, or that this

> Contributes to national and regional development, meets business and industry demands for productive, well-rounded, skilled workers and serves the country's need for thoughtful, ethical, well-informed and proactive citizens who are lifelong learners. (MOEYC Draft, Strategic Plan Framework Tertiary Education 2006-10, p. 21)

According to Suarez-Orozco and Qin-Hilliard (2003), despite having a well educated population Jamaica has not enjoyed economic success: education by itself does not equate with prosperity.

Policies and Restrictions

Jamaica's reality is that its tertiary level has been growing in an unplanned, unsystematic way, and the current situation demands more strategic planning at the tertiary level, including a national policy that manages the infusion of distance institutions and interventions into the system of education. According to the MOEYC Draft, Strategic Plan Framework Tertiary Education 2006-10:

> At present there is little or no research being conducted to inform and guide the planning of tertiary programming. The absence of valid and useful research data impedes programme planning in the tertiary sector, as it requires several years of planning to develop and implement tertiary programmes. Research skills in Labour Market projection and estimating workforce needs are critically important to build tertiary sector and reduce the exodus of both funds and human resources to apparently more attractive markets. (p. 29)

The absence of a clear national policy on distance education means there is little management of course and program selection; few standards to monitor and ensure levels of teaching, learning and student support; and limited or no research on how distance education meets the defined needs of the society and economy.

Governance of distance education is currently administered by The University Council of Jamaica (UCJ), a statutory body under the portfolio of the MOEYC, whose primary purpose is to establish and maintain a quality assurance system at the tertiary level and that functions essentially as an accreditation and awards body for degrees and other programs. Their primary concern focuses on quality and sustainability and recommends, among others:

- mandatory registration of all off-shore providers of education,
- the registration, certification and licensing of said institutions to be at the discretion of The University Council of Jamaica (UCJ) and The National Council for Technical and Vocational Education and Training (NCTVET),
- compliance with Jamaican law,
- compliance with the Ministry of Education regulations,
- sanctions to be applied in cases of non-compliance, and
- contingency arrangements to guarantee the completion cycle of studies in such cases where the contract is terminated by the service provider.

Compliance, however, is voluntary and is made at the discretion of the provider and/ or collaborating institution.

The Way Forward: Collaborative Distance Education

Without doubt, distance education functions in a market-based educational environment, and as a commodity of trade it may be more interested in profits than in the developmental needs of purchasers. To create a more equitable environment for growth and development, developing nations need to embrace models that foster government to government and institution to institution collaboration. The methodological design of such models would be collaborative and would support an assumption that "everyone must contribute—everyone must gain" (Daniel, 2005). Sir John Daniel, President and Chief Executive Officer of the Commonwealth of Learning, believes that collaboration in the area of distance education "is a means of ensuring that each country can pursue and protect its national interests during the steady internationalization of higher education" (2005, p. 10). Collaboration would also address the issue of brain-drain as it fosters linkages that enrich local research environments and encourages graduates to work in their countries of origin. A collaborative approach would also give developing nations the capacity to create and disseminate their own distance education products.

Within the context of Jamaica it would offer the opportunity for distance education curricula, policies and practices to bolster and validate "local knowledge," local languages, and local culture. In this way participants, prospective students, local policy makers, and educators would be given 'voice,' a space in which to make decisions rather than function as passive subjects. It would also reverse the mistake of transplanting the theories and formulas useful to the US, Canada, and other countries to the Jamaican context.

The *Jamaica Masters Online Project*: A Culturally Responsive Sample

The *Jamaica Masters Online Project* was developed as a response to the need for a culturally responsive distance education model. The Project is a collaborative effort between the Ohio State University Department of Art Education (OSUDAE) and the Edna Manley College of Arts (EMC) in Jamaica. Its purpose is to offer a culturally relevant program of professional development for practicing art teachers in Jamaica and thereby foster the growth of a core of future leaders for art education. Culturally relevant art education in this instance creates, explores and analyzes the relationship between art education, culture and the ways in which art affects the quality of the Jamaican citizen's life. A culturally relevant curriculum would be one in which the social and cultural viewpoint of the Jamaican nation becomes the position against which other values are compared and critiqued. Such a program equips contemporary Jamaican art educators with the requisite knowledge and skill to study, analyze, interpret and, where possible, effect change

in the following areas of cultural relevance;
- National cultural identity and diversity; inclusive of concerns such as empowerment, media influence, technology, youth (youth at risk), cultural heritage, the environment, education, crime and violence, gender, drug abuse and poverty, and
- Cultural industries; inclusive of tourism, reggae and dancehall as avenues for sustainable economic growth and development, and address the negative and positive by-products of these, including prostitution, drug abuse, civic pride, and employment.

This entails utilizing teaching methodologies, content, evaluation strategies and management and administrative policies that complement the peculiarities and cultural context of the Jamaican learners.

Conclusion

This chapter placed Jamaica, a postcolonial, low-income country at the center of the discussion of education and globalization. It outlined the impact of successive waves of globalization on Jamaica's economy and sense of cultural identity using education as the locus for the discussion. Particularly it explored the impact of distance education on the local system of education, highlighting the international trade agreements fueling the growth of distance education and showed the need for national educational policies and gave a relevant example of a culturally relevant distance education model.

REFERENCES

Allahar, A. L. (Ed.). (2005). *Ethnicity, class and nationalism: Caribbean and extra Caribbean dimensions*. New York: Lexington Books.

Ashcroft, B., Griffiths, G., & Tiffin, H. (Eds.). (2004). *The post-colonial studies reader*. London: Routledge.

Ashcroft, B., Griffiths, G., & Tiffin, H. (2003). *The empire writes back*, (2nd ed.). London: Routledge.

Atshshi, Y. (2002). Going local in a global age: Glocalization and techno-nationalism. In R. Oshiba & E. Rhodes & C. Otsuru (Eds.) *"We the people" in the global age: Re-examination of nationalism and citizenship*, (pp. 61-78). Osaka: The Japan Center for Area Studies.

Bacchus, M. K. (1994). *Education as and for legitimacy: Developments in West Indian education between 1846 and 1895*. Canada: Wilfred Laurier University Press.

Boxer, D. (1983). *Jamaican art 1922-1982*. Baltimore: Smithsonian Institute.

Daniel, J. (2005) *Open & Distance Education in the global environment: Collaboration in the time of competition*. Retrieved October 6, 2006 from http://www.col.org/colweb/site/pid/3583

Henry-Wilson, M. (2004). *Sectoral debate*. Ministry Of Education Youth and Culture. Kingston: MOEYC

Hintzen, P. C. (2003). Race, ideology and international relations: Sovereignty and the disciplining of Guyana's working class. In C. Barrow- Giles & D. Marshall (Eds.), *Living at the borderlines: Issues in Caribbean sovereignty and development*, (pp.414-440). Kingston, Jamaica: Ian Randle Publishers.

Ministry Of Education Youth and Culture (2006). *Draft, Strategic plan framework, tertiary education*. Kingston: MOEYC.

Ministry Of Education Youth and Culture (2004). Mission statement, Tertiary Unit. Retrieved February 12, 2005 from http://www.moeyc. gov.jm/divisions/ed/tertiary/index.htm

Ministry of Education Youth and Culture. (2003). *National cultural policy of Jamaica: Towards Jamaica the cultural superstate*. Kingston: Jamaica.

Ministry of Education, Youth and Culture. (2002). *Education: The way upward. A greenpaper for the year 2000*. Kingston: Jamaica.

National Council on Education. (2004). *Guidelines for a policy to govern the establishment of off-shore post-secondary education and training facilities in Jamaica*. Kingston: Jamaica.

Nettleford, R. (Ed.). (1971). *Manley and the new Jamaica: Selected speeches and writings 1938-1968*. Kingston: Longman Caribbean.

Suarez-Orozco, M. M., & Qin-Hilliard, D. B. (2003). *Globalization: Culture and education in the new millennium*. California: University of California Press.

Border-Crossing Dialogues: Critically Preparing Art Educators for Participation in a Global Society

Flávia Bastos

I went into this experience as someone who has never traveled outside the United States. I was looking forward to experiencing a new culture, being engulfed by its people, language, foods, landscape, and arts. [...] I was told São Paulo was a large city, but seeing it from the plane was a sobering reminder of how big the world is and a confirmation of the surprises that were to come my way.

—JENNI MERSCH, GRADUATE STUDENT REFLECTIVE PAPER, SUMMER 2005

According to Friedman (2000), the international economic system of globalization *"is everything and its opposite"* (p. 406, emphasis in the original) and, since it replaced the Cold War system, different countries and communities have seesawed between being attracted to its benefits and repelled by its negatives. A buzzword in today's educational discourse, *globalization* is an all-encompassing concept that alternately entices and frightens teachers from all areas of the curriculum. Whether we like it or not, globalization impacts our lives in ways that are virtually impossible to reverse because they are "driven both by enormously powerful human aspirations for higher standards of living and by enormously powerful technologies which are integrating us more and more every day" (Friedman, 2000, p. 407).

The global education movement initiated after World War II and continuing through the Cold War to present day, followed in parallel tracks the rise of globalization (Davenport, 2000). Including efforts in many disciplines, especially social studies, global education has been defined as the socialization of students into international citizenry, or as a process of acquiring appreciation of human diversity and cultures and of the complexity of the international system (Kirkwood, 2001). Along the same lines, the ubiquitous phrase "preparing students for participation in a global society" conveys the desirability and relevance of understanding globalization. However, if educators are not equipped to engage with our globalized world, they will not be able to carry out this aspect of the educational mission. This chapter examines an international travel program that seeks to expose art educators to the complexities, potential, hindrances, and contradictions of globalization and, at the same time, prompt self-reflection and critical analysis of teaching practices.

Along with several other teacher educators (Arnold, 2005, Charles Jr., 2006, Zimmerman, 1990), I am interested in developing teachers' skills to critically exercise their global citizenship. On the one hand, it is argued that only teachers who have critically examined our globalized condition can adequately prepare students. On the other hand, critical theorists such as McLaren and Fischman (1998) have reminded us that teacher education needs to meet the challenges of the global informational age by not accepting a pervasive notion of globalization that has well surpassed its macroeconomic origins. Therefore, it is imperative that we develop new languages of criticism and interpretation that will fuel a praxis committed to social justice. In my work as a teacher educator, I have developed strategies to prepare art educators to participate in socially engaged praxis that is grounded on an awareness of our new paradigms of living. In my quest, I have been influenced by the ideas of Appiah (2006) who proposes the notion of cosmopolitanism as a guiding principle to assert the importance of difference and a commitment to pluralism in face of the homogenizing potential of globalization. Discussing the ethical imperatives of our current time, Appiah suggests that "in the human community, as in national communities, we need to develop habits of coexistence: conversation in its older meaning of living together, association" (p. xix).

The notion of conversation or dialogue has inspired many of my own cross-cultural initiatives (Bastos, 2006a; Bastos & Ross, 2005), offering guiding principles for inquiry and pedagogy. As a metaphor of equitable exchange that results in new knowledge for all involved, and coupled with the ethical considerations of Appiah's cosmopolitanism, I adopted the notion of conversation as the cornerstone of the international program I developed for my students in Brazil. My graduate students engaged in an international program that promoted an examination of issues of community and its fluid artistic and cultural borders through research and intensive two-week travel in Brazil, involving collaborations with two art education professors, one in Brazil and one the United States, and a network of art educators, artists, and cultural organizations. This chapter (a) describes the goals and structure of this program and, through critical analysis of program participants' comments, projects, artifacts, and reflections, (b) examines its outcomes, and (c) discusses the role of international travel experiences in the preparation and professional development of art educators attuned to the issues of our contemporary global society.

Program's Goals and Structure

I believe that teachers and students should learn to investigate their own cultural traditions, belief systems, and values as well as those of others as a requirement for critical participation in our constantly changing world. In my experience taking students to my home country, I was uniquely equipped to facilitate that *in situ* reflection. My own awareness of the importance of direct experience with other cultures was shaped gradually throughout my experiences as an international graduate student. In the early 1990s, I landed in a professional field that was shaped by multicultural and global education concerns and interests. I was often puzzled by many requests to characterize my culture, artistic experiences, and traditions. As I struggled to understand the slice of United States culture experienced in the Midwest, I realized that requests to speak about Brazilian culture were in fact opportunities to reflect upon a heritage I largely took for granted. These conversations allowed me to create a space of contact between the culture I was bringing with me and the one I was beginning to know. A two-fold process of (a) learning about others and, at the same time (b) reflecting upon one's cultural identity is at the core of making meaning out of the many experiences facilitated by globalization. Coming full circle, through the opportunity of taking my art education students to Brazil I was able to facilitate this process in a guided and intentional manner.

Program Goals

My primary goal was to prepare art educators to learn to inquire about art and culture and investigate the

dialectics of local and global influences within the particular context of Brazil. The 2005 and 2006 trips and related activities were structured to prepare art educators to learn and inquiry about locally produced art, investigating the dialectics of local and global influences. Ultimately, the program encouraged students to examine their own culture, belief systems, and values. I noticed many outcomes from these experiences—an enhanced cultural awareness, a more nuanced way of making cultural observations, and an eagerness to embrace new international experiences. Evidence of these claims include: (a) Caroline Caldwell's lesson about performance art, taught without the help of an interpreter—she spoke a little Portuguese, and her students a little English; (b) Troy Brown's work and the Afro Brasil museum; and (c) Jamie Rahe's decision to return to Brazil after the summer to complete her last academic term of the Master program. My description and interpretation of these cases illustrates the potential impact and relevance of international travel for art educators.

Program Structure

We departed early in June 2005. Our group flew to São Paulo, South America's largest city, and from there to Goiânia, the state capital of Goiás where the university is located. Our itinerary also included Goiás Velho, a colonial town and artists' colony and site of Professor Guimarães research on folk objects (Guimarães, 2001), and Brasília, the nation's capital and modernist architecture landmark. During our 2-week stay we visited museums, galleries and local shops; interacted with Brazilian art education students and local area teachers, visited the University Lab School,[1] traveled between urban and rural areas, enjoyed tourist sites, eat local foods, and took in the different scenery, pacing, and scale.

In 2006 we traveled to Brazil again. Our activities included a 10-day stay in Goiânia and surrounding region and a 3-day stay in São Paulo. A preparation for the trip during the spring term encompassed several evening meetings to discuss selected readings on Brazil's history, culture, contemporary life and tourism. Many students took Portuguese lessons from a native speaker in advance to our trip. We discussed possible gestures of reciprocity and "giving back" that could be adopted as a way to recognize the people who facilitated our many experiences. We arrived in Goiânia in time for the Brazilian team inaugural game in the World Cup. People, places, and things were all clad in green and yellow. This created a context and opportunity to discuss national identity and pride and soccer as a national cohesion force in Brazil.

Figure 1

Goiás Velho, UNESCO World Heritage Site. Photo by Jamie Rahe.

Within a few days of arrival, art education students taught lessons at the University Lab School. These lessons sprang for their own professional/artistic expertise and research interests, including visual demonstrations of studio work, critical analysis of magazine advertisement in Brazilian publications, and a performance art lesson. We visited local museums, galleries, and artists' studios, traveled to historic sites, and partook in a folk celebration involving music, dance, and delicious regional food. In São Paulo we strolled busy streets, went to major museums and galleries, attended music concerts, worked with local community artists, and had a memorable meal, choosing from a Japanese language only menu at the Japanese neighborhood of Liberdade [Freedom]. We had a guided tour of the Museu Afro Brasil [Afro-Brazil Museum] where Troy Brown was to stay on for a two-week internship. All in all, the trip resulted in a collection of meaningful narratives for all involved. Recently, during the 2006 Ohio Art Education

Association Conference, we had the opportunity to interweave our stories during a presentation that in many ways became the impetus for this chapter.

I noticed many outcomes from these experiences—an enhanced cultural awareness, a more nuanced way of making cultural observations, and an eagerness to embrace new international experiences. Another relevant outcome is that my own relationship with the students who participated in the trip became more intimate and it remains that way. Although all these students have graduated, we remain in touch, share their professional accomplishments, and offer and seek guidance. We also occasionally collaborate in projects or research. Recently, when Professor Leda Guimarães, our partner at the Federal University in Goiás (UFG), visited the University in January 24-26, 2008, all past program participants living in the Cincinnati area came to the planned activities and offered to help with logistics and planning. They were definitely motivated to show their appreciation for Professor Guimarães and willing to reciprocate the hospitality and dedication we received from her in Brazil.

Examining Selected Outcomes

The three students featured here participated in the 2006 program. In preparation for the trip they identified research topics of interest. They also devised ways to express their appreciation for the time and attention they received from the people they met. This included gifts from the United States, sharing photographs and sketches created during the trip, keeping in contact with people after the trip through e-mail or even visits.

Moving on the Spur of the Moment: Caroline Caldwell's Performance Art Lesson

Caroline Caldwell is an artist who works primarily in photography and in collaborative projects with a social focus. At the time of the program, she was finishing her first year in the Art Education Master Program and also preparing to become an art teacher. During one of our preservice teaching experiences she taught a lesson about performing art in a public Montessori school in Cincinnati. After some initial anxiety about the unfamiliar experience, her students, ages 6 through 9, became deeply engaged in the process of representing different weather patterns through performance. However, the classroom teacher was concerned that at the end of the lesson, there was no physical evidence of the experience for each individual student to take home. Intrigued about the assumptions relating to art and art education that shaped the teacher's and the students' initial views, Caldwell proposed to teach a similar lesson at the school we were to visit in Brazil.

On the day of her lesson, Caldwell had prepared various visuals with artworks that represented various types of weather—rain, thunderstorms, wind—and a list of the primary words needed in Portuguese for the lesson. Working outside, in the school's front yard, she gathered her fifth grade students in a circle to explain the idea of the lesson, with me as interpreter. "Boa tarde" [good afternoon], she started. "Hello, good afternoon" [Oi, boa tarde], her students replied. As it happens with young people all over the world who listen to pop music in English, surf the Internet, and in some cases also take English lessons, Caldwell's students knew some English and were eager to use it. Because the lesson was primarily experiential and the communication gap was bridged by concerted efforts of students and teacher, my help as translator was not needed. The lesson evolved according to plan, sometimes the process got a little bumpy, but,

in the end, all students participated in creating individual performances that conveyed different types of weather. Caldwell was impressed by the greater comfort of her Brazilian students to express ideas through movement. It also seemed to her that the students she worked with in Brazil were more flexible in their ideas about art and did not have the expectation that an art class should necessarily result in a tangible project. Caldwell was touched by the students' eagerness to communicate with her and speculated whether her own efforts at learning some Portuguese words may have been key.

Today, Caroline Caldwell is a high school art teacher at a rural school. During her time at the University of Cincinnati, she was involved with the Art in the Market Program that caters to urban teens. Caldwell is a competent art educator who enjoys working with students from various backgrounds and is especially interested in urban students. She understands the importance of creating an environment where students feel free to express themselves and is an advocate for exposing students to diverse and unfamiliar experiences.

Re-imagining Race: Troy Brown's Experience at the Museu Afro Brasil

In addition to participating in the planned activities of the trip, Troy Brown participated in an education internship at the newly created Museu Afro Brasil in São Paulo, during the second half of July 2006. As an African American artist and educator, Brow was intrigued by the alignment between the museum's mission and the education department goals of reclaiming the memory of Brazilian Blacks that is so often underrepresented, lacks social prestige and legitimacy, and occupies a peripheral role in discourse about national identity. The museum's project to recognize, understand, and respect the inheritance of Brazilian Blacks is a daring initiative and can be vital in shaping a more inclusive history and memory (Museu Afro Brasil, Education, n.d.).

The change-oriented multicultural mission of the museum highlights the instrumental role art can play in the promotion of social change. However, as can be expected, the implementation of such ideas is not without troubles. During Brown's internship he witnessed some of the challenges educators face. For example, when museum educator Renato Araújo da Silva led a group of elementary students and their teachers through the collection, it was apparent that the teachers had little interest in the artworks. Although their students seemed excited, teachers did not connect with the art or the objects on display. They could not recognize these artifacts as part of their culture, they contended. Silva explained that despite a recent Federal mandate to teach African art as part of school curriculum, not too many teachers have taken an interest in the subject. Brown felt unprepared to deal with the denial and resistance he encountered on the part of the teachers. It seemed to him that Brazilians were quick and proud to accept European influences but hesitant to embrace the nation's significant African heritage. During his first week, Brown and Silva led a group of 20 elementary educators in their fist visit to the museum's collection. Some of the teachers walked away during the educators' presentation, creating their own groups, while others strolled around as if they were walking in a shopping mall. Only a few teachers seemed engrossed by the exhibit and paid close attention to the proposed activities and discussion. After the session, Silva explained that this was behavior he had experienced many times and hypothesized it was due to the teachers' limited knowledge of art history, experiences talking about art, and exposure to museum and gallery visits.

Shadowing another educator, Juliana Ribeiro da Silva, during tours designed for older students, Brown recognized that he was becoming sensitized to Brazil's social hierarchy. He could tell the children who came from private schools and the ones who came from less privileged areas. The private school students were dressed similarly and tended to be of lighter complexion. The poorer schools tended to have kids whose completions were in all shades of brown. Private school children showed more art knowledge and were more comfortable asking questions and making comments during the visit. Frequently, Brown discussed his understanding of racial issues in Brazil with the museum educators. He noticed the deceptive nature of Brazilian racism and its similarities with issues in the United States. For example, the darker you are, the greater the level of discrimination. Also, the overlap between racial and social economic opportunity makes it difficult to pin point and address issues (Richter, 2003).

Brown identified significant differences between the Afro Brasil's and conventional museum education practices in the United States. Specifically, the (a) Large number of educators, 14, working in a modest-sized museum, with a small administrative staff, and limited operating budget indicated the central role of education in the museum's everyday activities; (b) Educators from a variety of disciplines including psychology, religion, sociology, and art history facilitated interactivity and connections, creating an integrated environment for leaning; (c) The central role of education in supporting and furthering the museum's mission is indicated, for example, by the fact that education is the central feature of the museum's website; (d) The most significant difference relates to the potential social change impact of a museum structured around a counter narrative of art inspired by African heritage.

As a result of his Brazil experience Brown has candidly discussed his expanded understanding of racial issues in the United States and beyond. His recent artwork reflects his experiences in Brazil and touches on issues facing people of African heritage that cut across national boundaries. In "Renato" Brown depicts Silva's personal narrative as an Afro-descendant Brazilian who grew up in the favelas [slums] and has overcome tremendous difficulty to become college educated and have access to different social and professional opportunities. Brown describes the work as relating someone's personal struggles with race and status. In appreciation for the hospitality and support from the educators and staff at the Afro Brasil museum, Brown donated an etching he also created upon his return titled "My journey to Brazil." The work has been added to the museum's collection. As it was for Brown, critically understanding the contributions of people of African heritage is meaningful, important, and necessary not only to students but also to the educators who work with them.

Figure 2

Renato, by Troy Brown, acrylic on canvas.

Becoming an International Artist and Educator: Jamie Rahe Returns to Brazil

Jamie Rahe had never traveled abroad or by airplane when she went to Brazil. She was curious and open to learn from the many experiences she was to have. Not speaking any Portuguese, she communicated through the images she created with her digital camera. Many of these compelling images have become the highlight of presentations I give about the program. A ceramics artist, Rahe's primary interest was to learn about Brazilian ceramics. Proving particularly relevant to Rahe's goals, the state of Goiás has a strong tradition of

folk pottery that combines Portuguese and indigenous forms (Guimarães, 2001), and a number of self-taught artists, such as Odon Nogueira, whose studio we visited. As the trip progressed, Rahe became more and more enthusiastic about what she saw.

Returning from the trip visibly energized, Rahe incorporated the artwork of Odon Nogueira into a lesson for high school students she taught during her student teaching. In turn, her students were excited to learn about this artist who their teacher had personally met, whose artwork is highly imaginative and inlaid with personal narratives. At the University, she referred often to the trip and drew from its experiences in her teaching and graduate academic work. However, before the spring term started, Rahe surprised us all with a detailed plan to return to Brazil. Supported by a linkage agreement between the University of Cincinnati and the Federal University of Goiás, and the mentorship of Professor Leda Guimarães in Brazil, Rahe developed a program that included art education and fine arts classes and a time to continue her own artwork. She harbored a desire to have an exhibit in Brazil while there.

Accompanied by her husband, a doctoral student in education who also used the trip as part of his coursework, Rahe accomplished all her goals. She worked with key professors at the university and developed a new body of work in Brazil using plastic resin instead of clay. A week before her return, she had an exhibit at the local art museum that received significant media attention and public acclaim. She has mentioned several times that the trip to Brazil "changed her life." Today, Rahe is an artist with an international exhibition record and a high school ceramics teacher who remains passionate about Brazil and continues to teach what she learned to her students.

Why are International Experiences Important for Art Educators?

Traveling in Brazil with my students during two summers, I witnessed their excitement to understand unfamiliar places, earnest attempts to communicate, and surprising discoveries about Brazilian culture. Earlier in the trip, comments and observations focused on the differences between Brazil and the United States—the smaller proportions of objects and automobiles, the greater density of street life, different materials used in people's homes, the open architecture of schools and university buildings. Gradually, in-depth observations disclosed commonalities between the two countries. Students were surprised to find that in Brazil ethnic lines shaped the social landscape in a parallel fashion to the United States. They learned that these two vast continent-sized countries have comparable historical formation and ethnic diversity. Both countries' official histories start as European colonies. In both countries, colonization led to the occupation of vast territories and the dispossession of indigenous peoples. Afterward, both countries massively imported Africans to form the two largest slave societies of modern times and received waves of immigration from all over the world, ultimately forming large multicultural societies (Bastos, 2006b). As one student put it, "the similarity and humanity of the people's histories was most striking and revealing to me" (Jenni Mersh, reflective journal, summer 2005).

As Elizabeth Bishop said in her poems about her experiences in Brazil, "think of the long trip home. Should we have stayed at home and thought of here?"(1991, p. 93). International travel naturally stimulates reflections about culture. Direct experiences with other places and cultures are complex, involving many rewards and difficulties. Distinct from traditional academic learning, educators and students who embrace new cultural experiences find themselves in a unique space of reflection, not only about the culture they are coming into contact with but also their own. In a concrete way, travel creates a cultural intersession or contact zone between cultures. White and Congdon (1998) suggested that, perhaps more importantly, geographic travel involves a dynamic negotiation of rules and cultural standards. Similar skills are necessary for the conceptual understanding of different artworks, various cultures, and ourselves. Therefore, I advocate in this chapter for art education practices that, while rooted in the different communities in which we participate, we create opportunities to recognize and transcend our familiar boundaries, creating new spaces of dialogue and understanding. This is a required skill to negotiate and interact with a world shaped by homogenizing influences and unprecedented opportunities brought about by globalization.

One of the premises of this chapter is that teachers need to be critically prepared to interact with the unique challenges and possibilities of our times. Drawing from the ethical considerations of Appiah at a time when the world grows smaller and the stakes higher, I come to the conclusion that the ability to carry out conversations that cut across boundaries is a necessary and important skill for educators and citizens alike. Conversations with people from different ways of life are both facilitated and hindered by globalization. For example, on the one hand, various technologies make it easier for us to stay connected, but we tend to choose to do so only with those close and similar to us. On the other hand, because we create tight networks and are linked up, it becomes more difficult to engage in thoroughly new conversations. Each one of the students' stories described here illustrates a different modality of conversation that was not limited by a face-to-face exchange. Relating to collective and individual, material and immaterial, private and public aspects of a culture, sometimes these utterances involved verbal language. Other times, they

required movement or encompassed creative forms. As a teacher educator, I think that programs and activities such as the one described here can create a platform for educators to hone their conversation skills, understanding them as a critical tool to support pluralism. When conversations foster honest inquiry about others and discovery of self, they are a way to establish a meaningful link to other people inhabiting the planet. Furthermore, the notion of conversation, and the engagements it demands, represents a powerful stance to critically reflect on our responsibilities in creating and sustaining relationships. Such an orientation to inquiry and knowledge has the potential to permeate boundaries and establish transformative connections in a world that would otherwise be conceived as full of strangers.

Figure 4

Weavers spinning cotton. Photo by Jamie Rahe.

REFERENCES

Appiah, K. A. (2006). *Cosmopolitanism: Ethics in a world of strangers*. New York: Norton.

Arnold, D. (2005). The many faces of Buddha: A colloquium on religion, culture, and global education. *Independent School, 64*(3), 100-109.

Bastos, F. M. C. (2006a). Border-crossing dialogues: Engaging art education students in cultural research. *Art Education, 59*(4), 20-24.

Bastos, F. M. C. (2006b). Tupy or not Tupy? Examining hybridity in contemporary Brazilian art. *Studies in Art Education, 47*(2), pp.102-117.

Bastos, F. M. C., & Ross, M. (2005). Dialogical perspectives: Subjectivity in Art education inquiry. In: R. Clark M. & M. Stokrocki (Eds.), *Waves, eddies, and currents in art education research*. Seminar for Research in Art Education.

Bishop. E. (1991). *Complete poems*. London: Chatto & Windus.

Charles, A. J. (2006). The global schoolhouse: Developing more globally engaged faculties. *Independent School, 65*(4), 30-34.

Davenport, M. (2000). Culture and education: Polishing the lenses. *Studies in Art Education*, *41*(4), pp.361-375.

Friedman, T. L. (2000). *The Lexus and the olive tree: Understanding globalization*. New York: Anchor Books.

Guimarães, A. (2001). *Objetos populares da cidade de Goiás* [Folk objects from the town of Goiás]. Goiânia, GO: Faculdade de Artes Visuais.

Kirkwood, T. F. (2001). Preparing teachers to teach from a global perspective. *The Delta Kappa Gamma Bulletin, 67*(2), pp.5-12.

McLaren, P., & Fischman, G. (1998). Reclaiming hope: Teacher education and social justice in the age of globalization. *Teacher Education Quarterly, 25*(4), 125-133.

Museu Afro Brasil (n.d.) Educação [Education]. Retrieved March 15, 2008 from http://www.museuafrobrasil.com.br/educacao.asp

Richter, I. (2003). *Interculturalidade e estética do cotidiano no ensino das artes visuais* [Interculturality and everyday aesthics in teaching visual arts]. Campinas, SP: Mercado das Letras.

White, J.H., & Congdon, K. G. (1998). Travel, boundaries, and the movement of culture(s): Explanations for the folk/fine art quandary. *Art Education, 51*(3), pp. 20-24, 41-42.

Zimmerman, E. (1990). Teaching art from a global perspective. *ERIC Art*, December.

ENDNOTE

1   The UFG Laboratory School serves as training grounds for all the licensure programs of the University. Its teachers have University faculty status and engage in classroom research. The school publishes a research journal and other professional publications. As a public school, it is open to all community children who are admitted through a lottery; visit www.cepae.ufg.br for more information.

The Circulatory System of Oil Contamination, Visual Culture, and Amazon Indigenous Life

Patty Bode

Let me be honest. To document the experiences reported in this chapter, I contributed to releasing 3.7 metric tons of carbon dioxide into the atmosphere from the Delta Airline plane on which I sat comfortably aboard, munching peanuts. That is the estimate of C02 emitted from a jet airliner in one round trip flight between Massachusetts and Ecuador. And though I drive a hybrid car to try to placate my carbon guilt, I drive more than "the average American" in my commute to my work as an art educator to a university in Boston, so any offset of my carbon footprint by my Prius is a moot point.[1]

The Circulatory System

Following this arterial awareness of learning, knowledge, and oil consumption emphasizes that my personal carbon responsibilities (and yours) are intertwined with the environmental contamination by global oil production and its effects on the cultural sustenance of the indigenous people of Ecuador's Amazon region, specifically the Secoya people. High school students from a U.S. public school who founded an NGO to take action against global oil contamination also influence my perspectives on oil consumption. This chapter reflects some of what I learned from these two seemingly disparate communities, who both recognize the interdependent influences of late global capitalism in their collective lives. My experiences with the Secoya people and the U.S. high school students intersected in Ecuador's northeast region of the Amazon Rainforest in the summer of 2007 when I was immersed in daily life, art production and cultural questioning with the Secoyas. In what follows, I attempt to make visible the struggles and acts of resistance of the indigenous communities and the students. Taking a sociocultural perspective, I am reflexive about my identities as a teacher, a European-American, a speaker of English, a U.S. citizen, and other traits that I bring from dominating cultures. This reflexive stance brings into focus the role and influence of globalized visual culture in the Amazon rainforest and postcolonial perspectives in U.S. public school classrooms.

What Transported Me to the Amazon?

When I was awarded an Artist International Residency grant from Augusta Savage Gallery at the University of Massachusetts Amherst,[2] I was invited to select a community outside of the United States in which I hoped to reside for 2 weeks in the summer of 2007. I immediately knew I wanted to visit the Secoya community of Ecuador's Amazonian region. I had learned about the Secoyan people and their resistance to oil contamination from students I had taught in my public school art room. My learning stemmed from one student in particular, David Poritz—now a sophomore at Brown University—who had been a student in my art room at Wildwood school in Amherst, Massachusetts in his elementary school years. Later, when I transferred my art teaching to the middle school, I taught David and his peers again, and then again at a summer arts camp where I was the director.

When David was in 6th grade at Wildwood Elementary School, his classroom teacher, Brian McNamara, inspired his study of environmentalism that led to David's heightened interest in the international lawsuit, Maria Aguinda et al. v Texaco (2001), filed by Attorney Cristóbal Bonifaz in efforts to hold Texaco-Chevron responsible for the devastation of indigenous ancestral lands and the ravages on human health that started with oil drilling in the 1960s. When David was in 7th grade, his English teacher, Margarita Bonifaz, was impressed by his persistence and desire to work on the case so she introduced David to her father, Attorney Cristóbal Bonifaz. David worked throughout his middle and high school years to assist Attorney Bonifaz. He also traveled several times a year to the Amazon to engage in humanitarian aid with a social justice lens. As David's research and social action developed through high school, he shared his passion with his peers and teachers. Amherst Regional High School social studies teacher Shari Abbott shared David's dedication and created an after school club. The club worked collaboratively with the NGO that David founded, Esperanza International, Inc.[3] The group of high school students, led by David Poritz and Shari Abbott, traveled to the Amazon every summer, bringing greatly needed goods to the people of the local communities, with an initial focus on providing shoes (to protect their feet from contacting the oil contaminated ground) and then later bringing backpacks filled with school supplies for the children. However, the students realized that humanitarian aid that was devoid of legal action and policy change was limited, and they constantly integrated their efforts to influence international legislation. Each time I spoke to a student who returned from the Amazon, where they witnessed the havoc of oil contamination first hand, they repeated the words that I had heard from David and each student who had gone on the trip the previously: "You just have to see it, Ms. Bode, you just have to see it."

While the story of David and his peers (which continues to unfold as I write this) highlights David's vision, ambition, and determination, it also spotlights the interconnectivity of teachers, students, and mentors through globalization and social action. David's passion was fierce in 6th grade, but without the consistent string of teachers along the way and the mentorship of Attorney Bonifaz, who all recognized his curiosity as purposeful and promising, the story may have been very different. Herein lies the vascular flow of teacher-student curiosity, research, and action entangled with visuality itself, as well as visual culture. The predicament of oil production, oil consumption, and oil contamination was a research topic of high interest, yet before actually seeing the direct results of environmental racism on the indigenous communities in Ecuador, students and teachers reported that it was incomprehensible: "You just have to see it." The story pulses through a circulatory system of student knowledge, teacher leadership, and the astounding impact of visual experience in global social action.

Transfusion of Scholarship and Popular Press

This chapter is much too brief to provide a full-scale review of all that "you just have to see" or to study the history of Ecuador and the indigenous people who have called it home for centuries. However, there is a great deal of literature in both scholarly volumes as well as the popular press (Gerlach, 2003; Roberts, 2005) that provides a context for the histories of

capitalism, opportunism, disease, and migration, as well as resilience and resistance that create the contemporary condition of indigenous lives. For example, the Ecuadorian government's collusion with U.S. oil companies to allow the perpetuation of environmental disasters in Ecuador's pristine rainforest is woven in a collective contaminated web that John Perkins (2006) dubbed the *"corporatocracy"* of the global empire to include corporations, banks, and governments (p. xv). More analysis about the environmental fragility can be found in Darrell A. Posey and Michael J. Balick's volume, *Human Impacts on Amazonia: The Role of Traditional Ecological Knowledge in Conservation and Development* (2006). Nor can this chapter attempt to reveal the countless indigenous lives lost to leukemia and other disease created by a contaminated water supply and environment. An analysis of the public health disaster has been well documented by the nonprofit Amazon Watch[4] at the website of www.chevronToxico.com (that's not a typo; it stems from the word *toxic*). The central event, the globalized 13-year class action lawsuit against Texaco-Chevron that spawned David and his peer's action, is also explained on chevrontoxico.com. Furthermore, the devastation and the subsequent lawsuit has gained mainstream attention outside of the realm of anthropological research and environmental studies through a range of expressions in visual culture and the popular press. A cover story of *Vanity Fair* (Langewiesche, 2007) provided an accessible analysis. Also CNN's 2007 Hero award, in the "Fighting for Justice" category went to Pablo Fajardo, the Ecuadorian attorney on the lawsuit. The recently released documentary film, *Justicia Now!*, MoFilms Productions, provides the opportunity to "just see it" for free online, featuring indigenous activists, the Amazon Defense Front, as well as celebrity Darryl Hannah and aerial artist and activist John Quigley who calls the travesty "time released genocide."[5]

Secoyan Cultural Production

These sources, as well as my students' experiences informed my engagement in the Secoyan community's legacy of artmaking and culture-making that guided my brief visit in 2007. Obviously, the intersection with the industrialized world has changed the Secoya daily life, cultural production and art practices. Despite three decades of oil contamination, loss of life and forced migration, a resilient vibrancy thrives. Because the Secoyan village is in a region of the Amazon rainforest that is accessible only by canoe,[6] it might be surprising to learn that the Secoyan people have developed a tradition of art-making and

Figure 1

A painting by Secoya community artist, Wilfredo Lucitande. Photo by Pablo Yepez.

cultural production that involves painting on canvas. William Vickers (2003), an American anthropologist imported canvases and oil paints just a few decades ago and the Secoyan people transformed the practice of painting on canvas that is typically considered a "Western-world art form" from European and U.S. sources, into a Secoyan tradition. As a result, the Secoyan people developed imagery of the rainforest in self-taught painting methods, that have become increasingly well known in mainstream Ecuadorian society. Many adults in the Secoya community produce compelling canvases of rainforest imagery. But because tubes of paint and canvases are scarce, this practice has not been consistently available to all adults and even less frequently available to children.

At times particular individuals have had more access to supplies than others to focus on painting. In particular, the Secoya painter Ramón Piaguaje's piece won international acclaim in 2000 when he won the first prize of the United Nations Millennium Art Exhibition in aid of UNICEF.[7] Such recognition of Secoya cultural production and artistic achievement brought a great deal of attention to the Secoya's practices, but had little influence on their economic and environmental plights. The modernist-Euro-American view of what counts as art has not necessarily served the broader Secoyan community well. Ramón Piaguaje traveled world-wide after the UN exhibit and has returned to the Secoya community infrequently. Of course, there are other traditional cultural practices that pre-date the painting on canvas by millennia. Pottery making has greatly diminished, to near extinction, as the industrialized world encroaches more on their daily lives. Yet, as communities have moved to escape oil contamination, other practices that are more transportable have thrived, such as the weaving of the Secoya's expertly designed hammocks for which the fibers are derived directly from a palm specific to their rainforest region.

Tensions in the Overlapping Web of Folk Art, Fine Art, and Boundary Crossing

These circumstances highlight the multi-faceted struggles beset by boundary crossing of cultural knowledge as well as the transport of culturally produced objects into the realm of postindustrialized world views of what counts as "art." That which might be a celebration of multicultural awareness and the inclusion of diverse artists in the global artistic discourse also brings tensions. Artists from marginalized groups who are engaged in the making of traditional and ceremonial work face tourist trade consumption and out-of-context exhibition of religious and traditional objects in galleries, museums, and websites (Levin, 1988; Lippard, 2000; Petrovich-Mwaniki, 1997). The modernist narrative which gets applied to these works takes consumers and collectors off the hook from understanding and/or reverencing the context of some of this work. Simultaneously, on another point of the tension of the postmodern Web, many indigenous communities have benefited from the commerce which tourist craft trade has created. The capitalist nature of art commerce has provided many artists in developing communities with more resources to maintain their artistic traditions, as well as substantive support for the broader community. At the same time, these benefits bring questions about the interaction of industrialized communities with others, as the content, traditions and production of art are often influenced by the tourist trade (Staniszewski, 1995). The woven perspectives of daily life of some indigenous communities that may or may not view artmaking as a separate activity from hunting, gathering, and child-rearing points out the tensions between these conceptual incongruities of "fine art" and "folk art" as well as the influence of capitalism on the value of artworks. Continual questions are raised for art teachers about how to best engage their students in the cultural production and works of art of diverse people and the communities who produce the artwork. What might be learned from a position of solidarity with indigenous communities rather than a gaze of consumerism? What might be imaginable in a

social economy that supports the cultural production that is not solely based in capitalism?

Art teachers could study pieces from Secoyan traditional past practices as well as current Secoyan paintings, alongside other contemporary objects that might be found in a U.S. art museum as well as in U.S. guerrilla street art performances and ask many questions, such as: For whom was this object/event created? In what context was it created? To whom was the maker(s) speaking when she or he produced it? Does the product or performance refer to another object, or event? What power structures place these objects in the realm of art or cultural production?

Such questions and the ensuing discussion and artmaking activities (which can be adapted for any classroom from K-12) may reveal a richer understanding of Secoyan histories of tradition, of contemporary indigenous work and of the modernist art world in which "concepts of art" were promulgated. Moreover, these questions may lead students to understand the circulatory system of environmental destruction/responsibility and indigenous culture. As Gude articulates, "The well meaning teacher who uses art from diverse cultures" to illustrate modern concepts "sincerely attempts to infuse multiculturalism into a mono-cultural curriculum structure" (Gude, 2004 p.7). By maintaining a modernist framework on the art from marginalized communities, art teachers inadvertently maintain the marginalization as well.

The postmodern perspective rejects the notion of art being created on neutral ground. Rather it foregrounds the sociopolitical context as woven into the art making process. Art emerges in the postmodern perspective as an expression of individual identity and simultaneously a statement about collective cultural context. A wide body of literature in art education asserts that multicultural art education with a postmodernism perspective asks questions and seeks sociopolitical context of art and art makers (Adejumo, 2003; Anderson, 1997; Armstrong, 1990; Ballengee-Morris & Stuhr, 2001; Barrett, 1997; Cary, 1998; Clark, 1996; Duncum, 2001; Efland, Freedman, & Sthur, 1996; Erickson & Young, 2002; Fehr, 1997; Freedman, 2003, Gude, 2004; Hutchens & Suggs, 1997; jagodzinski, 1997; Marche, 2000; McFee, 1998; Neperud, 1995; Petrovich-Mwaniki, 1997; Stuhr, 1995; Tavin, 2000).

Transporting Questions

Prior to my visit to the Secoya community, I asked if there was anything I could do to be of service during my stay. I was asked to bring art supplies and teach a two-day art workshop. They hoped I would bring paints,

Figure 2

Shaman Delfin
Piaguaje paints
Patty Bode's face to
welcome her into the
community. Photo
by David Poritz.

canvases, and materials from art supply stores. Their
adaptation of painting on canvas has spurred a strong
identification within the community as "Secoyan
Painters," but a lack of those mass-produced materials from industrialized societies made the practice
difficult to sustain.

The evening when I arrived, I met the adults in
the community who were the most practiced painters
and emphasized that I was here to bring supplies and
help facilitate, but that I viewed them as the experts to
teach the children. I discussed the art workshop with
the Shaman and explained my hesitancy to introduce
any imagery that was not already part of the community and received his welcome and his blessing to
proceed.

The morning after I arrived we packed up the
canoe with boxes of art supplies I brought to head
to the community center (Tuike hue), a large open-
air pavilion with a thatched roof. Along the way, we
picked up about 45 passengers, children and adults, in
the two large canoes, and others met us there. There
were about 60 participants on the first day. We collected leaves that had fallen on the rainforest floor
and we made leaf rubbings to learn about how cray-
ons and oil pastels can work. For some children it was
their first experience with those tools. We produced
drawings of leaves and played with the materials. All
the adults painted enthusiastically, completely self-
directed, while I collaborated with some Secoyan

leaders to support the children's exploration in a tri-
angular translation of English, Spanish, and Secoyan
languages.

As we worked, a number of women worked vigorously on preparing the lunch for 60 plus community
members. We stopped for a lunch break of yucca
soup, plantains, and rice with chicken. After lunch
we worked on paintings of rainforest imagery, which
I hesitate to call landscapes because the images seem
to defy categorization. Wilfredo Lucintande, one of
the lead painters, led the children in demonstrations
of how he proceeds with his paintings and the children

Figure 3

At the Tuike
hue Patty Bode
collaborates with
a Secoyan leaders
and David Poritz to
facilitate exploration
of art materials with
children. Photo by
Pablo Yepez.

Figure 4

Right: Secoyan children develop painted imagery that reflects their visual experiences of the river and rainforest. Photo by Patty Bode.

Figure 5

Above: A Secoyan woman works for two full days on her piece depicting rainforest imagery, a Secoyan tradition. Photo by Patty Bode.

of Liberty overlooking a cityscape. On another page, he had drawn a character that looked like a super-hero wrestler. I was dumbfounded. Then I learned that there are some televisions in the community. They recently gained electricity through solar panel installations, and TV quickly followed. Nestor also produced a drawing of a Secoyan man in traditional attire hunting a wild boar with a spear. The juxtaposition of Nestor's imagery emphasizes the intersection and overlap of the (post)industrialized world with the Secoyan world. This raised questions, many questions for me, especially about visual culture.

Nestor's engagement with visual culture from the industrialized world highlighted the intense stream of imagery that is entering the Secoyan world while pointing out that not much of indigenous life or visual culture is influencing outside world, other than a few Secoyan paintings sold in cities. I resist a romanticized view about whether or not TV should be in the Secoya village. The TV is already there, and access to mainstream visual culture will certainly increase. I consider the possibilities of what it might be like to have video cameras in the hands of the Secoya children and adults and laptops from which they could edit and manipulate their visual culture. What would be envisioned in Secoyan production of visual culture through new media? Since they are consuming industrialized world images through mainstream TV, a counter narrative might be for the Secoyas to produce their own images to expand their own cultural production. Would it expand outsiders' understanding of Secoyan life? Might it help sustain the Secoyan community in ways that are yet unimagined? If the outside world is entering through oil company domination and also through televised visual culture, how

eagerly dove into the activity without hesitation. We worked/played until early evening and then got in the canoes to head home before the sun set. The next day we did it all again, with over 80 people participating.

I was struck by the imagery/visual culture of their daily life that the children produced: rainforest imagery, drawings of their friends on the rope swing jumping in the river, canoes filled with families and freshly caught fish. Then, Nestor, a 16-year-old, shared his drawings with me: an image of the Statue

culture and globalization. In what follows I float some vessels to transport understandings and possibilities to the heart of art teaching.

Scholarly research and popular culture could integrate even further to inform and motivate global oil consumers to combat environmental racism. The pulse of indigenous life suffers the embolism of oil contamination, yet the Secoyan community resists domination and adapts for survival. There is a need for in-depth ethnographic studies of the indigenous communities that are thriving despite the detrimental effects of globalization. William Vickers (2003) has provided perspectives into Secoya life and there is a need for updated literature on the status of indigenous communities and the results of the oil production and contamination. The activities of Chevron/Texaco and their so-called clean up are not understood by the general public in the United States. In addition to the MoFilm production of *Justicia Now!* more visual culture production, especially within the realm of democratic media such as cell phone and PDA photos and video, YouTube videos, web media and blogs can ripple through the oil consuming world to create the connective tissue with the worlds from which oil is derived. Art teachers could engage students in analysis and production of visual forms that draw from scholarly research and inspire popular imagination.

Curriculum in U.S. schools is in dire need for education about the specific impact of oil production and consumption on human life, especially in indigenous communities. Students and teachers "just have to see it." While bringing groups of children to the Amazon jungle may be unthinkable for most U.S. public schools, a critical study of visual culture can engage student action, develop critical

Figures 6, 7

Top Left: Sixteen-year-old Nestor Piaguaje's drawing of the Statue of Liberty.
Top Right: Nestor Piaguaje's drawing of a Secoyan man in traditional attire hunting wild boar.

Figure 8

Bottom Left: Nestor Piaguaje paints rainforest imagery. What would be envisioned in Secoyan production of visual culture through new media? Photo by Patty Bode.

might access to production of mass visual culture shift the encounter with the outside world? Is it possible to transfuse the relationship with past practices in contemporary visual culture? The influence of globalized imagery, values, and economies are intertwined with the effects of global oil production.

Vessels of Understandings and Possibilities

There is much to be gained from the Secoya people in art education's expanding questions about visual

Figure 9

The people of the
Secoya community
display their art
production during
the gathering at the
Tuike hue with Patty
Bode. Photo by
Pablo Yepez.

thought and inspire cultural production. The images of the rainforest, the contamination and the indigenous cultural production is available in many forms accessible to classroom teachers. Furthermore, the popular visual culture promulgated by the corporatocracy of the oil industry could enhance student and teacher understanding of their participation in the globalized catastrophe. For example, Chevron recently launched a television commercial campaign, called "Human Energy," stating that "an oil company can practice and espouse conservation." How might an art teacher guide students in a critical comparison of that advertising campaign with the documentary by Martin O'Brien and Robbie Proctor, *Justicia Now!*? There are other curriculum materials such as the unit package offered by Teaching for Change and Rethinking Schools, developed by Bill Bigelow, titled *Oil Companies vs. The Rainforests*. The unit includes interactive activities about indigenous rights and questions about "development," as well as Joe Kane's book *Savages* (1995) and a DVD of *Trinkets and Beads* (Walker, 1996), the documentary film that features the Huaorani Indians defending their culture and the environment in Ecuador's Oriente. These resources might typically be viewed as the territory of a social studies teacher. How might art educators integrate these resources to develop cultural production in U.S. art rooms that connect the arteries and veins of their students to the heart of environmental racism?

Models of economies that are aligned with indigenous knowledge are necessary to sustain indigenous futures. The Secoyan's are becoming much more dependent on the mainstream capitalist world economy in a cash-based system. For capitalism to take over Secoyan lifestyle is to subjugate Secoyan knowledge. Secoyan life is community-centered, not individualistic in nature, and is based on community strength rather than individuals owning goods. To support the Secoyans in developing a robust and sustained manner of thriving, might it be possible to foster "a different economy"?[8] As Julie Graham and her colleagues of the Community Economies Collective (2001) assert: "If we could locate noncapitalist activities here and now, if we could see them as prevalent and sustaining, perhaps we could find more possibilities of participating in their creation" (p.95). The Secoyans are acutely aware that their political struggle against oil company domination is undergirded by their own economic health. What are the possibilities of a fair-trade micro-economy that supports Secoyan painters, weavers, video-producers and yet unimagined cultural production? Julie Graham (2001) emphasizes, the need to "cultivate *a language of economic difference*, within which alternative economic projects can be conceived, and through which alternative economic subjects can be validated and come to self-recognition" (pp. 95-96).

Knowledge among teachers and students needs to be viewed as a circulatory system requiring oxygenation. My relationship with the Secoya people was built on the web of relationships of students whom I first taught when they were in kindergarten. As my students grew and their world expanded, my world enlarged because of them. How can the role of the art teacher and visual culture art education create a crossroads—an intersection—of multicultural education and postmodernism that could bring a tangible, recognizable motivation for change among art education communities? How might art teachers inspire their students—and art students inspire their teachers—to view their global world as more interconnected and ultimately more changeable?

REFERENCES

Adejumo, C. O. (2003). Considering multicultural art education. *Art Education, 55*(2), 33-39.

Aguinda et al. v Texaco. U.S. No. 93 CIV. 7527, 94 CIV. 9266. May 30, (2001).

Amazon Watch. One Hallidie Plaza, Suite 402 San Francisco, CA 94102. Retreived September 5, 2008 from www.amazonwatch.org

Anderson, T. (1997). Toward a postmodern approach to art education. In J. Hutchens & M. Suggs (Eds.), *Art education: Content and practice in a postmodern era* (pp. 62-73). Reston, VA: National Art Education Association.

Armstrong, C. (1990). Teaching art in a multicultural/multiethnic society. In B. Young (Ed.), *Art, culture and ethnicity*. Reston, VA: National Art Education Association.

Augusta Savage Gallery. The University of Massachusetts Amherst. Retrieved September 5, 2008 from http://www.umass.edu/fac/augusta/index.html

Ballengee-Morris, C., & Stuhr, P. L. (2001). Multicultural art and visual culture education in a changing world. *Art Education, 54*(4), 6-13.

Barrett, T. (1997). Modernism and postmodernism: An overview with art examples. In J. Hutchens & M. Suggs (Eds.), *Art education: Content and practice in a postmodern era* (pp. 17-30). Reston, VA: National Art Education Association.

Bigelow, B. (2000). *Oil companies vs. the rainforest*. Washington, DC: Teaching for Change.

Bigleow, B., & Peterson, B. (Eds.). *Rethinking globalization: Teaching for justice in an unjust world*. Milwaukee: Rethinking Schools Press.

Cary, R. (1998). *Critical art pedagogy: Foundations for postmodern art education*. New York: Garland Publishing.

Chevron Corporation. Tapped Energy/Untapped Energy. The Power of Human Energy. Retrieved September 5, 2008 from http://www.chevron.com/about/advertising/?VideoId=UntappedEnergy

Clark, R. (1996). *Art Education: Issues in postmodernist pedagogy*. Reston, VA: National Art Education Association.

Climate Trust, The. CarbonCounter. Org. Retrieved July 1, 2008 from http://www.carboncounter.org/

CNN. Cable News Network. Hero awards. "Fighting for Social Justice". (Dec 7, 2007). Retrieved August, 10, 2008 from http://www.cnn.com/video/#/video/living/2007/12/07/heroes.smits.fajardo.cnn?iref=videosearch

Community Economies Project. Department of Human Geography, Research School of Pacific and Asian Studies, ANU. Retrieved September 5, 2008 from http://www.communityeconomies.org/

Duncum, P. (2001). Visual culture: Developments, definitions, and directions for art education. *Studies in Art Education., 42*(2), 101.

Efland, A., Freedman, K., & Stuhr, P. (1996). *Postmodern art education: An approach to curriculum*. Reston, VA: National Art Education Association.

Erickson, M., & Young, B. (Eds.). (2002). *Multicultural artworlds: Enduring, evolving, and overlapping traditions*. Reston, VA: National Art Education Association.

Esperanza International, Inc. Retrieved August 10, 2008 from www.esperanzainternationalinc.org

Fehr, D. E. (1997). Clutching the lectern, or shouting from the back of the hall: A Comparison of modern and postmodern arts education. *Arts Education Policy Review, 98*(4), 27-31.

Freedman, K. (2003). *Teaching visual culture: Curriculum, aesthetics and the social life of art*. New York: Teachers College Press.

Gerlach, A. (2003). *Indians, oil, and politics: A recent history of ecuador*. Wilmington, DE: Scholarly Resources.

Graham. J., & Members of Community Economies Collective. (2001). Imagining and Enacting Noncapitalist Futures. *Socialist Review, 28*,(3,4) pp. 93-135.

Gude, O. (2004). Postmodern principles: In Search of a 21st century art education. *Art Education, 57*(1).

Hutchens, J., & Suggs, M. (1997). Student complaints and faculty moaning: some antecedents to the essays that follow. In J. Hutchens, & M. Suggs (Eds.), *Art education: Content and practice in a postmodern era* (pp. 7-15). Reston, VA: National Art Education Association.

jagodzinski, j. (1997). *Postmodern dilemmas: Outrageous essays in art & art education*. Mahwah, NJ: Lawrence Erlbaum.

Kane, J. (1995). *Savages*. New York: Random House.

Langewiesche, W. (2007, May). Jungle Law. *Vanity Fair*, 226-236.

Levin, K. (1988). Farewell to modernism. In K. Levin (Ed.), *Essays on art from the 70s and 80s*. New York: Harper and Row.

Lippard, L. R. (2000). *Mixed blessings: New art in a multicultural America*. New York: New Press.

Marche, T. (2000). Toward a community model of art education history. *Studies in Art Education, 42*(1), 51.

McFee, J. K. (1998). *Cultural diversity and the structure and practice of art education*. Reston, VA: National Art Education Association.

Neperud, R. W. (1995). Transitions in Art Education: A Search for Meaning. In R. W.

Neperud (Ed.), *Context, content, and community in art education: Beyond postmodernism*. New York: Teachers College Press.

O'Brien, M., & Proctor, R. (Directors). (2007). *Justicia Now!* [Documentary motion picture]. Available free on line from Mofilms: motion pictures that deal with important issues. Retrieved September 5, 2008 from http://www.mofilms.org/justicianow/index.html

Perkins, J. (2006) *Confessions of an economic hit man*. New York: Penguin/Plume.

Petrovich-Mwaniki, L. (1997). Multicultural concerns in art education. *Translations from Theory to Practice, 7*(1), 1-4.

Posey, D., & Balick, M. (2006) *Human impacts on Amazonia: The role of traditional ecological knowledge in conservation and development*. New York: Columbia.

Roberts, P. (2005). *The end of oil: On the edge of a perilous new world*. Boston: Houghton Mifflin.

Staniszewski, M. A. (1995). *Believing is seeing: Creating the culture of art*. New York: Penguin Books.

Stuhr, P. (1995). Social reconstructionist multicultural art curriculum design: Using the powwow as an example. In R. W. Neperud (Ed.), *Context, content, and community in art education: Beyond postmodernism*. New York: Teachers College Press.

Stuhr, P., Petrovich-Mwaniki, L., & Wasson, R. (1992). Guidelines for the multicultural art classroom. *Art Education, 45*(1), 16-24.

Tavin, K. M. (2000). Teaching in and through visual culture. *Journal of Multicultural and Cross-cultural Research in Art Education, 18*, 37-40.

United Nations. Our World in the year 2000. Retrieved September 5, 2008 from http://www.un.org/events/highlights/world2000.htm

Vickers, W. (2003). The modern political transformation of the Secoya. In N. E. Whitten, Jr. (Ed.), *Millenial Ecuador: Critical essays on cultural transformations and social dynamics* pp 46-74. Iowa City: University of Iowa Press.

Walker, C. (Director & Producer). (1996). *Trinkets and beads*. [Motion picture: documentary]. United States: Icarus films.

ENDNOTES

1 For information on calculating your carbon footprint see http://www.carboncounter.org/

2 For more information about Augusta Savage Gallery please see http://www.umass.edu/fac/augusta/index.html

3 For more information about Esperanza International, Inc. please see their web site at www.esperanzainternationalinc.org

4 Amazon Watch states their mission on the web site www.amazonwatch.org: To work with indigenous and environmental organizations in the Amazon Basin to defend the environment and advance indigenous peoples' rights in the face of large-scale industrial development-oil and gas pipelines, power lines, roads, and other mega-projects.

5 *Justicia Now!* is a documentary by Martin O'Brien and Robbie Proctor about Chevron Texaco's toxic legacy in the Northern Ecuadorian region of the Amazon rainforest and a courageous group of people called Los Afectados (The Affected Ones) who are seeking justice for the ensuing cancer, sickness and death in the largest environmental class action lawsuit in history. See http://www.mofilms.org/justicianow/index.html

6 As this manuscript goes to press, the oil companies are building roads into this region of Secoyan ancestral land, the implications for which have yet to be experienced.

7 For more information about the United Nations art exhibition "Our World in the Year 2000" see http://www.un.org/events/highlights/world2000.htm

8 For more information on J.K. Gibson-Graham's feminist critique of political economy see the Community Economies Collective. Department of Human Geography, Research School of Pacific and Asian Studies, ANU. http://www.communityeconomies.org/

Solidarity, Global Scholarship, and the Ethics of Encounter: A Case Study from Guatemala

Peter Rohloff and Rebecca Plummer Rohloff

Guatemala is a majority indigenous Mesoamerican nation, with a population composed in large part by the descendants and inheritors of the Maya civilization. Marking indigeneity in Guatemala is a complex issue (Metz, 2006); however, several features are perspicuous, including the wearing of traditional clothing, the continued application of subsistence agricultural techniques, and the use of one of more than 20 Mayan languages (Richards, 2003). These practices set the indigenous population apart from the assimilated mestizo (*ladino*) and ruling (*criollo*) classes, who constitute a minority.

The country is one of the most popular destinations in the world for many travelers, including language-learners, artists, missionaries, gallery owners, medical relief workers, and adopting parents. For the majority of these visitors, the reality of indigenous life is carefully and selectively mediated by government and service industries, who promote exotic elements in tourism literature, celebrate the emergence of new democratic processes, and reconstruct a narrative which integrates ancient Maya elements into a single, seamless state history. As a consequence, most remain uninstructed in the ways in which vast disparities in health outcomes (MSPAS, 2003), as well as financial, political, and psychological fallout from a legacy of violence (ODHAG, 2004), continue to be determined primarily by indigeneity.

It is against this background that we take up a consideration of the complexity of transnational life and the role of international academic scholarship in addressing the global burden of disparity. What utility does international scholarship afford disadvantaged populations? How can research programs be responsive to and guided by the self-defined needs of these populations? How do international scholars make the transition from mere critical awareness to a deeper level of engagement?

We began in Guatemala as many do, as a tourist couple ourselves—one a painter and the other involved in medical volunteer work. In our continuing experiences over 5 years among Kaqchikel Maya communities in the highlands of Guatemala, we have moved in and through stages of crisis provoked by a critical analysis of our global position and privilege. In dialogue with each other, the scholarly literature, and friends and colleagues from Guatemala, we have revisited the themes of responsibility and privilege countless times. Here we once again rehearse this dialogue, along the way documenting the "arresting moments" (Katz & Shotter, 1996) that have refined our commitments and led to new opportunities for responsible involvement.

Peter's Journey

I came to Guatemala for the first time in 2003. Before going, I had "read up" on Guatemala, and so I was prepared to observe disparity, the effects of free trade policies, and a residuum of political violence. During the day I studied Spanish and volunteered in a medical clinic. At night I drank beer and talked about human rights with Peace Corps and other volunteers. During these first encounters with Guatemala I saw exactly what I had expected—poverty and an inexorable conformation to global visual and consumer culture.

My first experience with a different side of Guatemala occurred during a trip I made to Nebaj, one of the towns most affected by government-sponsored violence during the civil war. Arriving by public bus, I was surprised to find that my Spanish, just a few months into my learning, was better than most of the people I met on the streets. Walking through the market I heard Ixil being spoken everywhere. Were not Mayan languages dying out? I wondered. So I had been told in my Spanish school and by other international volunteers.

I headed out of the market and into the surrounding agricultural landscape. After a few minutes of walking I heard footsteps at my back. A young farmer moved alongside of me, slowing his pace to match mine. We exchanged a few words, enough to realize that we could not communicate because I spoke no

Ixil and he no Spanish. I accompanied him to his fields, where he reached into his bag and brought out a bunch of bananas. We ate in silence, and then, after shaking my hand, he got up and walked off into the forest. It was at this moment, sitting in a cornfield, that I realized that my Spanish and my politics were of no use here and could neither explain nor engage what I saw before me.

Since that moment, several things have changed. I now speak Kaqchikel Maya and I work with a community-based organization in central Guatemala to develop clinical and community educational resources. Through this work, I am continually challenged to think about difference, friendship, and global solidarity in new ways.

Rebecca's Journey

In the summer of 2004, I boarded a plane to join Peter in Guatemala. Loaded with acrylic painting supplies, I arrived in the historical town of Antigua and endeavored to brush up my perceptive skills by visually documenting my new surroundings. After a month of sitting in quaint parks and on floral-lined street corners, recording the colorful architecture and the occasional interaction with locals and tourists, I proudly returned to the States with 25 paintings. In the fall at a local group exhibit, I heard the comments about these images by onlookers: "Honey, I remember our vacation there, wasn't it just wonderful! We could retire there someday"... and "Hey, that's where I bought this purse; it was so cheap." During these interactions with those who saw my work, I began to realize my own shortsightedness in depicting inaccurate and romantic representations of a mythic Guatemalan reality. With this awareness, I began plans to alter and juxtapose the rest of the prints and paintings in ways that disrupted my own privileged gaze so as to expose the hidden frames of cultural reference. My intent had never been to disparage the other, and yet I know in a profound way I had.

The following year, after engaging in postcolonial studies and regularly communicating with Peter about his new life learning and working among midwives in Kaqchikel communities, I returned to Guatemala with new ideas about what it might mean for myself, as a North American arts educator, to engage in arts service work. During each subsequent trip to various villages, I observed the commercial flows of visual culture and quickly learned that, as occurs in most resource-poor nations, the tourist industry continued to colonize indigenous culture for the sake of its own gain. Given this context I wondered how authentic goods were, and what perceptions villagers had of *gringos*.

Figure 1

Peter facilitating medical training among a Kaqchikel Midwifery Cooperative, San Juan, Comalapa.

During two extensive visits I attended Spanish school, which I found also to be an offshoot of the tourist industry, run by U.S. and European business owners that paid poor wages to teachers who regularly experienced unemployment due to the seasonal flux of students from the global North. Increasingly I recognized my own cultural capital as I sipped $2 lattes in the central plaza each morning: an equivalent of half a day's wage for some mestizos, and surely for many Mayan. Being reminded again of the old axiom, "to whom much is given, much is required," I wondered what *I* could possibly do as an artist-educator to act upon these moments of conscience. I began to envision how to develop an intercultural program where preservice art teachers could learn about and build partnerships with impoverished communities. These initial thoughts took on new complexities as Peter and I began to discuss our individual experiences, which had been shaped and supported by our ongoing reading and research. The following dialogue represents our grapplings with these thoughts, experiences, and aspirations.

Rebecca:

You know it would be a fascinating project for me to go with you to the villages and bring back indigenous knowledge for my research and curricula. I want to open up dialogues with my preservice art teachers about the anthropological (Dissanyake, 1988) and phenomenological functions of arts and aesthetics and expand their views of diversity and global disparity. It seems to me that, in order to train culturally competent teachers (Andrus, 2001), we must engage in a global ethic of human interdependence. Such an approach would challenge students to develop reflexive inquiries and interventions that map both the narrative particularities of identity, experience, and place, and also the dislocations and configurations of relevant social, historical, economic, political, and transnational contexts (Ballengee-Morris & Stuhr, 2001; Congdon, Stewart, & White, 2003; Said, 1993). As a result, students could gain a more global perspective on the functions and potentialities of arts and would be better equipped to assess the nature of their own privileged contexts vis-à-vis the developing world periphery (Keifer-Boyd, Amburgy, & Knight, 2007).

Peter:

I wonder sometimes at the language of the new global pedagogies that we, as educators, employ. For myself, I want to ask "for whom" such education is done, and also "by whom." If we are importing indigenous ways

of knowing into the classroom, does this mean that we are "taught" by this knowledge? In other words, is the indigenous voice the teacher, or is it merely an exemplar embedded in a wider discussion? Do we have an indigenous interlocutor in these situations, or do we mostly hear the voice of the archivist, scholar, or artist?

I think we need to deal honestly with the role that voyeurism plays in our scholarship. Trioullet (2003) discusses the way that anthropological methodologies have constructed the "savage slot." Although, fortunately, scholars no longer call others "savages," the typology that produced this term, which is a typology of a non-Cartesian or other-than-Modern human world, persists, and this remains at the core of our attraction to indigenous contexts. It is striking that in our discussions of the indigenous, we are always very interested in the ways in which it is not "Western"—in other words, we remain at all times deeply concerned with the way in which it throws our own cultural projects into contrast.

When we search for the indigenous, are we not often searching for ourselves? Barrera Nuñez (2005) has documented the ways in which relationships between Maya and foreigners resemble a "transcultural love affair," and he invokes Lacan in this context: "That's what love is. It's one's own ego that one loves in love, one's own ego made real on the imaginary level" (Lacan, as cited by Barrera Nuñez, 2005, p viii). Trioullet (2003) concurs: "It is a stricture of the Savage slot that the native never faces the observer. In the rhetoric of the Savage slot, the Savage is never an interlocutor, but evidence in an argument between two Western interlocutors about the possible futures of humankind" (p 133).

Rebecca:

I recognize that self-interest is a danger as we proceed with the attempt to forge new educational possibilities for our students; however, at the same time, in arts education as a whole there is a desire to transcend the "us and them, the colonizer/colonized" dichotomy. I agree that degrees of self-interest in educational global scholarship is unavoidable; indeed any human project is marked by a certain desire and exploratory interest in "exotic" unknowns because they lead to the expansion of one's own horizons. However, artist-educators generally advocate for building bridges and finding similarities amid the politics of difference. My interests lie not only in recognizing the universals of human experience expressed in symbolic narratives (Campbell, 1949; Jeffers, 1996; Kellman, 1998; Lakoff & Johnson,

of qualitative methodologies, especially the incorporation of autoethnographic components into "field" projects shows (Heike, 1999; Ruiz & Williams, 1999; Staikidis, 2004). However in a quest for universals there is always a dangerous tendency to gloss the ways in which they are conditioned by disparities and discourses of power, and we need to guard against this.

In Guatemala, the best example of this gloss has to do with language. Although there have been a number of arts, visual culture, and education-based research projects in Guatemala among indigenous people in recent years, all with strong autoethnographic components, these have almost without exception been conducted in Spanish, not indigenous languages. I have come across many authors who write intelligently and reflectively about their positioning vis-a-vis their subject at all points except this one; upon arriving at language, one hears that learning an indigenous language is "too difficult," or that there "was not enough time," or that it was not "essential to the research." This is usually the point at which refuge is sought in the "universality" of symbols and artmaking to bridge differences.

How are we able to convince ourselves that research into indigenous artmaking, creativity, symbolism, and identity are not distorted by conducting that research in the colonial language? I think we are able to do so in the end because we believe that the data we collect are the main thing, that the research agenda is valuable enough to justify bypassing the large investment of time required to learn a language or to gain a greater measure of contextual fluency. This view, however, is only justified if we do as Trioullet (2003) alleges that we do, namely work in a way that ensures that the "native never faces the observer"(p. 133). If we, however, envision another way of researching, then we cannot continue to neglect these and similar issues. Among the Kaqchikel Maya, the word used to name their language

1999; Langer, 1953), but also in facilitating voice for those whose stories and sense of being have not been fully recognized and realized (Moustakas, 1995). Such arts-based ethnography is rooted in a social conscience which concerns itself with the human family and with the development of an empathic and critical humanism (Nemiroff, 1992). For example, Staikidis (2006) implements a collaborative model in which Maya arts knowledge is shared through partnering with an indigenous mentor, a process that "transcends certain cultural boundaries" and can "create a kind of 'insidership' that is otherwise not possible to experience" (p. 119). It seems to me that such forms of scholarship attempt to introduce the indigenous mediator by invoking a postcolonial dialogue (Bhabha, 1994; Said, 1993) about the nature of the arts and indigeneity while questioning "Where is the people's voice, and do they make what they want?" (Ballengee-Morris, 2002, p. 241).

Peter:

I agree with you that one of the primary research agenda has to be theorizing these universals of human experience to which you refer. Educators are uniquely positioned to take up these considerations, as the rise is qach'ab'äl—*our language*—*and those who speak it are* qawinäq—*our people. Those who do not are not.*

Rebecca:

So now that you are relatively fluent, are you considered "our people" by the communities you work in? I mean if I came with you and relied upon a translator would this not at least be a beginning toward solidarity? Furthermore, authentic creative expression shared within community is a powerful form of language that forges and unifies relational spaces and cultural boundaries. I am not convinced that such efforts can be negligent. I do think as ethnographers who are also teachers, our time and concern tends to focus upon how new knowledge is of beneficial import for our students, which can easily overlook the reciprocal nature of "living" data, and the life-worlds of the communities we engage with. In fact, teaching broadly of "indigenous culture" as a concept rather than about specific people and individuals'

Figure 3

Magda Mux Sotz describes to Rebecca the historical struggles of her village, depicted in the murals of Comalapa.

experiences, further removes us from the responsibility to relate and participate as global citizens (Clough & Holden, 2002; Young & Commins, 2002). It seems to me that international fieldwork in arts education must adopt a mode of service-learning (Porter & Monard, 2001) that would provide a different lens—one that Ballengee-Morris and Taylor (2004) assert takes on a language of "we" which is attuned to a communally recognized need, requires the ethics of listening, and a committed involvement as a way to "ensure mutually beneficial experiences for everyone involved" (p. 6).

An ethnographic arts model grounded in service relationships could foster self-determined projects in which local Maya community leaders could themselves take "direction of the culture and the manifestation of its forms" (Ballengee-Morris, 2002, p. 241). The role of the arts educator would be to partner with those who uphold the local aesthetic traditions and rituals and to co-facilitate expressive arts projects that offer spaces for lost and silenced stories to be shared and passed on. It also could be a way to share skills of value that could profit the communities not only psychosocially, but also in material and economic ways.

Peter:

In my illustration of how, in Kaqchikel, those who speak "our language" become "our people," I don't really want to advocate for "insidership" (Staikidis 2006), which I think is an attractive but ultimately shortsighted goal. "Insidership" presupposes the ability to delimit the horizon between "inside" and "outside" which is increasingly difficult and theoretically problematic in today's world. Rather, I want to conceive our human experiences as a series of encounters—encounters which can be "arresting" (Katz & Shotter, 1996) to various degrees. Being "arrested" must mean gazing into the face of another human being in a way that engenders and evokes responsible action (Levinas, 2000). I like your use of the concept of service here, because I think this goes a long way in the direction of what that must mean.

Of course we have to guard against a mere "service tourism," which can underestimate the amount of effort and time required to do this sort of thing well. However, if properly conceived, "service" can have the salutary effect of reframing our discussion of "responsible scholarship," which is far too often simply euphemistic for the extraction of data from participants in the most ethically neutral manner possible. As an alternative to mere "responsible scholarship," service connotes an ethic of "responsible action," wherein it is the notion of responsibility, rather than that of the scholarly agenda, which becomes controlling. In other words, when we can leave aside discussions of our data and simply allow ourselves to be arrested by the encounter with another human being, I think we are making progress.

So conceived, scholarship becomes listening and dialogue (Bakhtin, 1982), which leads to what John Shotter (1999) has called "withness writing" as opposed to "aboutness-writing"—with results that evoke the interrelationality of diverse human voices.

> ...rather than extending already existing orders of talk and thought, [our] purpose is to bring previously unnoticed aspects of our lives into dialogical relations with each other...[S]uch writing works to bring them together, not only into a diverse, inter-sensory world, which will, if they can harmoniously inter-relate themselves to each other, be enriched, but also into a diverse world of diverse people, who can be enriched in the same way." (p. 10)

This approach to scholarship has also been called "social poetics" (Katz & Shotter, 1996), which is a fitting name, and most importantly for me, I can see in it a possibility for the emergence of the indigenous interlocutor, for reversing the charge that the "native never faces the observer" (Trioullet, 2003, p. 133).

I should point out parenthetically that, for me, language learning was really just a preamble to learning about this "diverse world of diverse people." Language-learning is not an important accomplishment in and of itself, but what learning an indigenous language does do is allow for the embodiment of one's commitment to encounter, which speaks directly to the second part of your question. It is hard to hitchhike on another's commitment, and translation, as the literature reminds us, dramatically reduces the quality of speech communication, including a virtual loss of all non-discursive, empathetic elements (Aranguri, Davidson, & Ramirez, 2006).

Rebecca:
Well, I guess as scholars we "hitchhike" on the paths that go before us because it feels safe. What I think we are talking about here is the idea that risk is an important element of learning what commitment means, and that if we are not willing to experience significant risk than we will forfeit opportunities to forge relationships with others. The directive of social poetics within global ethnography asks us to live differently, to collapse our professional and private endeavors, and to take stock not only of our own career and life goals, but also of our positioning with regard to global humanity. Rearranging the narrative values that drive our life projects causes us

to reconsider where we place our time, money, and emotional energy. "Narrative itself is the representation of power, and its teleology is associated with the global role of the West" (Said, 1993, p. 273). This challenge to rethink the orthodoxy and authority of the academic center must provoke reflection on how we can, as scholars, place persons—and especially the vulnerable persons whom we study—rather than academic projects at the heart of our lifework.

Such values resonate with Buber's (1970) I-Thou encounters of mutuality and Noddings' (1992) ethics of care, both which have been synthesized into contemporary arts education theory, but often in ways that remain on the academic periphery. As scholars, I wonder how we can engage in global ethics and true solidarity if in our own lives and "homeland" relationships we allow misencounters (Buber, 1970) to dictate and undermine our capacity for moving in empathy. Perhaps what can break through this is a greater vision of what could be possible when we reflectively intervene in our own reactions, uncover their roots in order to respond more creatively—an intention not to hitchhike, or to remain on the margins of the easy and impersonal, but to fully immerse our selves in the hard work and sacrifice it takes to allow real spaces of being for and with others. I think for me this might mean not only clarifying the realities of long-term costs of entering arts-based interactions with the villagers, but also upholding a sense of honor and justice for them, so that I have the vision, endurance, and patience needed in acquiring the skills and experiences which they ask of me. Moustakas (1968) points out that "A potential bridge of meaning always exists between the knower and the known but this reality is elusive and discovering it requires the unique presence of the individual" (p. 5).

I think that within intercultural, global histories and contexts, it is the Indigenous whom deserve our presence. But, I can no longer assume that my own rhetoric of service automatically puts me, or you, or our students, in a position of solidarity. Instead, a true and physical show of solidarity must first emerge from an arrest of self—a process that in facing our own privileged contexts and trading comfort for context, we learn to reserve space in our lives for those men, women, and children whose histories have been silenced (Trioullet, 2003). We are carried by this that is greater than ourselves, and despite Lacan, are moved to face those who we observe with a love that is hybrid and transparent—one capable of being transformed by the reflection of ourselves in the eyes of the Other, and in listening to the Other within ourselves (Bhabha, 1994).

Becoming Arrested by the Other

Through this dialogue we have attempted to document the experiences and paths that have been critical in forming our understanding of the interactions between personal convictions, scholarly work, and "field" involvements. We have found that, for ourselves, this "arrest," which is a "being-arrested" by the Other (Levinas, 2000), opens up an ethics of encounter which can both relativize and revitalize academic scholarship by illuminating concrete paths to radical personal commitment. These commitments must be sustained, and for us we hope they constitute a lifelong journey, as we continue to struggle with questions about the ethics and effectiveness of academic scholarship in Guatemala as well as other developing countries.

REFERENCES

Andrus, L. (2001). The culturally competent art educator. *Art Education, 54*(4), 14-19.

Aranguri, C., Davidson, B., & Ramirez, R. (2006). Patterns of communication through interpreters: A detailed sociolinguistic analysis. *Journal of General Internal Medicine, 21*, 623-629.

Bakhtin, M. M. (1982). *The dialogic imagination: Four essays.* Austin, TX: University of Texas Press.

Ballengee-Morris, C. (2002). Cultures for sale: Perspectives on colonialism and self-determinism and the relationship to authenticity and tourism. *Studies in Art Education, 43*(3), 232-245.

Ballengee-Morris, C., & Stuhr, P. (2001). Multicultural art and visual culture education in a changing world. *Art Education, 54*(4) 6-13.

Ballengee-Morris, C., & Taylor, P. (2004). Service learning: A language of we. *Art Education, 57*(5), 6-12.

Barrera Nuñez, J. O. (2005). *Imaginaries and desires: Transcultural "Love Affairs" in Guatemala.* Dissertation, UMI 3163369.

Bhabha, H. (1994). *The location of culture.* London: Routledge.

Buber, M. (1970). *I and Thou.* (W. Kaufman, Trans.). New York: Charles Scribner's Sons.

Campbell, J. (1949). *The hero with a thousand faces.* Princeton, NJ: Princeton University Press.

Clough, N., & Holden, C. (2002). *Education for citizenship: Ideas into action.* New York: Roultledge Falmer.

Congdon, K., Stewart, M., & White, J. (2003). Identity mapping. In Y. Gaudelius & P. Speirs (2002). *Contemporary issues in art education.* (pp. 198-118). Upper Saddle River, NJ: Prentice Hall.

Dissanayake, E. (1988). *What is art for?* Seattle, WA: University of Washington.

Heike, M. (1999). Mayan education In Guatemala: A pedagogical model and its political context. *International Review of Education, 45*(3-4), 321-337.

Jeffers, C. (1996). Metaphor and meaning. *Art Education, 49*(3), 6-11.

Katz A. M., & Shotter J. (1996). Hearing the patient's voice: Toward a social poetics in diagnostic interviews. *Social Science and Medicine, 43*, 919-931.

Kellman, J. (1998). Telling space and making stories: Art narrative and place, *Art Education, 51*(6), 35-40.

Keifer-Boyd, K, Amburgy, P, Knight, W. (2007). Unpacking privilege: Memory, culture, gender, race and power in visual culture. *Art Education, 60*(3), 19-24.

Lakoff, G., & Johnson, M. (1999). *Philosophy in the flesh.* Chicago: University of Chicago.

Langer, S. (1953). *Feeling and form.* New York: Scribner's.

Levinas, E. (2000). *God, time, death.* (B. Bertino,Trans.) Stanford,CA: Stanford University Press.

Metz, B. (2006). *Ch'orti'-Maya Survival in Eastern Guatemala: Indigeneity in Transition.* Albuquerque: University of New Mexico Press.

Ministerio de Salud Pública y Asistencia Social (MSPAS), Instituto Nacional de Estadística (INE), Universidad del Valle de Guatemala (UVG),CDC, USAID, ASDI, APRESA/UE, PNUD, UNICEF, FNUAP, Proyecto POLICY II, and CARE, Guatemala. (2003). *Guatemala, Encuesta Nacional de Salud Materno Infantil 2003.* Guatemala City, Guatemala: MSPAS.

Moustakas, C. (1995). *Being in, being for, being with.* Northvale, NJ: Aronson.

Moustakas, C. (1968). *Individuality and encounter.* Cambridge, MA: Howard Doyle.

Nemiroff, G. H. (1992). *Reconstructing education: Towards a pedagogy of critical humanism.* New York: Bergin & Garvey.

Noddings, N. (1992). *The challenge to care in schools: An alternative approach to education.* New York: Teachers College Press.

Oficina de Derechos Humanos del Arzobispado de Guatemala (ODHAG). (2004). Guatemala: Nunca más (Versión Resumida). Guatemala City, Guatemala: ODHAG.

Porter, M., & Monard, K. (2001). "Ayni" in the global village: Building relationships of reciprocity through international service-learning. *Michigan Journal of Community Service Learning, 8*(1), 5-17.

Richards, M. (2003). *Atlas Lingüístico de Guatemala.* Guatemala City, Guatemala: Editorial Serviprensa.

Ruiz, J., & Williams, W. (1999). Telling stories-rethreading lives: Community education, women's development, and social change among the Maya Ixil. *International Journal of Leadership in Education, 2*(31), 207-227.

Said, E. (1993). *Culture and imperialism.* New York: Alfred A. Knopf.

Shotter, J. (1999, June). Writing from within "living moments": "withness-writing" rather than "aboutness-writing." Paper presented at the Writing Across the Curriculum Conference: Multiple Intelligences, Cornell University, Ithaca, NY.

Staikidis, K. (2004). *Where lived experience resides in art education: A painting and pedagogical collaboration with Mayan artists.* UMI Dissertation Abstracts 3135382.

Staikidis, K. (2006). Personal and cultural narrative as inspiration: A painting and pedagogical collaboration with Mayan artists. *Studies in Art Education, 47*(2) 118-132.

Trioullet, M. (2003). *Global transformations: Anthropology and the modern world.* New York: Palgrave Macmillan.

Young, M., & Commins, E. (2002). *Global citizenship. The handbook for primary teaching.* Oxford: GB, Oxfam.

A Cultural Cherishing Drama: Developing International Art Education Relationships through Service-Learning

Pamela G. Taylor and Christine Ballengee-Morris

Institutions of higher education increasingly develop international travel study programs to provide opportunities for their students to experience life and learning in different cultures and develop a broader understanding of the world. Linda Chisholm (2003), former president of the International Partnership for Service-Learning, stated, "Service-learning goes beyond mere academic tourism" (p. 259). International service-learning provides students and professors with the opportunity to explore self as a member of the global society. Immersed in a culture, other than one's own, brings a deeper level of discomfort and understandings than study-only or tourist programs. Although similar issues may be present domestically, the possibility to experience cross-fertilization promotes cross-cultural thinkers, stronger leaders and sensitive teachers (Chisholm, 2003).

For these reasons and others, including our value of multiple approaches to both teaching about and making art, we explored international service-learning with our art and education students in Cuba and Brazil. Our experiences were and continue to be both exciting and dramatic stories of negotiation, struggle, acquiescence, and joy. Our goal for this chapter is to critically tell our stories through the form of a five-act dramatic play. Set on a world stage, our play is performed as a critically reflective narrative process that involves negotiating program goals and struggling to establish service-learning programs within an equal, reciprocal, and mutual environment.

Text Play: Arts-Based Research Drama

We chose to report our research and our story within an arts-based methodology for several reasons. Granted, there is always a great deal of drama involved in international travel and study. But, even more than that, we believed that unlike the often distanced-authored characteristics associated (and required) with formal research reporting, an arts-based approach encouraged a more critical form of reflection and introspection of our experiences and emotions. Arts-based research theorists Tom Barone and Elliot Eisner (1997) identified an arts-based approach to inquiry as having "the presence of certain aesthetic qualities or design elements that infuse the inquiry and its writing" (p. 73). As educational researchers, we typically rely on writing and narrative as the primary form in which we share our ideas and findings. Stories, according to Daniel Pink (2005) are the methods by which we as human beings "are freer to seek a deeper understanding of ourselves and our purpose" (p. 113). Transformation and the dialogue that occurs between self with self and self with others demand a dialogic presentation that arts-based methodology provides.

Our dramatic play occurs in three countries, United States, Cuba, and Brazil. The leading actors are Brooke and Rain. Through their personal reflections, they (we) reveal our process of negotiation, communication, and dedication to providing service that responds to the needs identified by the host community. Because the play is relational and dialogic, we gravitated towards a post-structuralist narrative theory of playwriting to construct and deconstruct our experiences through scripted dialogue. French philosopher Jacques Derrida (1997) referred to the binary structures of language as maintaining hierarchies through difference and privileging certain words or terms at the cost of the other (civil/savage, first-world/third-world). Like the ways we often entertain multiple avenues of thought in our own minds, the script of the play featured in this chapter, moves beyond a binary perspective to post-structurally include alternative perspectives, ideas and considerations. Play theorists Sue-Ellen Case, Phillip Brett, and Susan Leigh Foster (1995) advocated post-structuralism as a way of understanding through exploring relationships between language and being. A key to this is the idea of perspective. Our perspective/position (place in the world, identity, and worldview) is in effect, an inter-play. We share our interpretations of specific

CHAPTER 36 | A Cultural Cherishing Drama: Developing International Art Education Relationships through Service-Learning

285

experiences, encouragement, and forces according to their relationship and intersections.

Act One: Privilege, Power, and Is that the Potty?

(Two women, Brooke and Rain, sit on a bed in a hotel room amidst piles of travel memorabilia. Morning light streams through large windows. Sitting cross-legged and dressed in pajamas, the actors drink coffee as they point to and talk about specific items in the piles.)

Brooke: (takes a large drink of coffee and grabs a magazine and newspaper) *Media images and stories like this romanticize anything international. If I didn't know better, from this photograph of Cuba I would think that ALL Cuban people either look like Carmen Miranda or are poor peasants blindly following a dogmatic dictator. And from stories like this* (holds up a National Geographic magazine) *I would associate Egypt with only archaeologists and paleontologists unearthing tombs or long-lost artifacts. And look at these mortifying images of poverty in Ethiopia. It is no wonder that people are shocked by the risks taken in the name of study and research.* (lies back on the bed with a sigh)

Rain: (drops pile of photographs and speaks sarcastically) *But, Brooke, we are Americans! We are from the richest country in the world. We lead the view and goals of a Global Economy and Globalization. We work toward making English a Global language. And although we pride ourselves in visions of the Statue of Liberty* (stands up and lifts her arm to grasp an imaginary torch), *"Give me your tired, your poor, your huddled masses yearning to breathe free. The wretched refuse of your teaming shore. Send these, the homeless, tempest-tossed to me, I lift my lamp beside the golden door..."* (spreading her arms wide, she exclaims) *What is it exactly saying Americanization... taking and reforming those who are different.* (turns and stumbles over a suitcase as she fills her cup with coffee)

Brooke: (softly speaks while sitting up again on the bed) *Globalization has not lived up to its promise of creating universal prosperity, has it?* (holds her empty cup out as Rain slowly fills it with coffee) *It produced a race to the bottom in which companies search the globe for the lowest possible labor costs and weakest environmental safeguards.* (slowly sips her coffee, looking intently at Rain) *Today's global economy actually increases the income gap worldwide, making the rich even wealthier and eroding working families' standard of living.*

Rain: (slowly sets the coffee pot back on the table, walks back to the bed, lies down and covers herself) *It is shocking to some of us and frightening to others that all the people in the world do not see us as we see ourselves.* (shaking her head and gently petting the bed spread) *Or do they see us for who we really are? Why do we feel that if others were like us, this world would be a better place? Honestly, how do you feel? How do you feel when the bathroom is different?* (wrinkles her nose and looks toward the ceiling) *When you can't get ice for your drink? When you can't drink the water...when the salad is warm, when the meat tastes funny....when you can't get that special lotion, ketchup, or candy bar?*

Brooke: (stands up and walks to the window with her back toward Rain) *But, that is a typical traveling syndrome. We feel it even when visiting friends and family.* (whirls around to face Rain with both hands slightly up) *But, what if we take it a step further and imagine visiting people who, on top of the fact they eat and drink differently, value different things. They speak not only a different language but they shout or they whisper...they whine or they silently stare.... They cover their faces, their heads, they walk slowly or quickly, they sit very close, talk with their face inches from yours. Things smell different—all the time.* (wrinkles her nose and whispers) *Things are different—all the time.*

(Stage lights dim to black.)

Act Two: Forbidden Cuba

(Brooke sits in a straight-back chair in the center of blackened stage. Single spot-light.)

Brooke: (speaks toward stage-left) *I was only there for a month over the course of two years.[1] It was not enough. Not enough at all to be talking about it today.* (looks down, pauses and stares at audience) *But, talk I will, because the new issues and regulations governing educational travel make it impossible for me to go there again. I share this experience with you stating up front that mine was only a tiny moment* (making pinching gesture with thumb and forefinger) *and small experience that cannot authentically represent the people and culture of Cuba. Yes, just a tiny moment ... but one that changed my life view forever.*

(The song *Dos Gardenias Para Ti* plays softly. Brooke stands and walks to a battered school desk with a stubby pencil and a piece of crumpled paper. Brooke smoothes the paper.)

Brooke: *The first year, we simply observed in the schools and gave the teachers art supplies. Their didactic, rote memory approach to teaching was a difficult concept for our students to fathom. Although purported as the best education system in the world, we found their approaches archaic and yet, their students were well-behaved and appeared genuinely happy. I cautioned the students in some of our assumptions about the teachers and children. We may not agree. In fact, we may vehemently disagree. But, in our quiet contemplation and gracious gratitude, we may learn something.*

(The music stops and children's voices fill the stage. Brooke smiles, walks to a battered table and sits amidst papers, paints, and brushes.)

Brooke: *The second year, we were permitted to teach in an after-school program. At first, we thought that we should teach a Cuban artist lesson—to show our own value of Cuban art and artists. Upon reflection we realized that no matter how much research we did, we could not speak for a Cuban artist. In fact, we went there to learn about Cuban art and artists. Therefore, we shared a work of art done by a U.S. artist.[2] We tried to ask questions that would provoke thinking and discussion in the class. But, the children remained quiet. We repeated our questions in Spanish and English—still no response. And then our Cuban friends joined in by asking the questions, giving the answers and then having the children parrot their responses in unison. This was not what we had in mind. We were also disappointed with the rather predictable art that the students made in response to our "discussion" and with the way that the Cuban teachers would draw directly on the students' papers. We tried very hard not to reveal our disappointment as we took cues from the other teachers and engaged the young students in simple conversation. In a word, we decided to just interact with these young people in any way that we could. We began to understand that our experiences with the children and the teachers meant more than simply practicing teaching skills. As one young 12-year-old Cuban girl "Elizabeth" said so eloquently, "Invite the children in the US to come here and play with us, make art with us. We want to know you because together we could work toward solidarity between our two countries."*

(Brooke stares directly at the audience and then abruptly jumps from the table and moves back to the straight-back chair that now sits amidst several chairs. Behind the chairs a screen features a video of people talking, moving chairs, tables, works of art, speakers, and microphones amidst crumbling marble columns, walls, and vibrant green plants. Street sounds play loudly and then soften.)

Brooke: *Can you smell that? A mixture of wood and coal smoke, cooking oil, and the distinctive aroma of an old house. You know ... a rich, full bodied fragrance that is foul and fresh at the same time and conjures a memory more than any other human sense. Old Havana has such a scent. It permeates every home, every building, and every park— like a wound. And yet, that wound seems to bind many people together as can be seen in the Casas de la Cultura that are featured in every neighborhood. At these places, art, dance, music and theatre classes are free to the public. They regularly host art exhibitions, performances, and fiestas. We partnered with the Old Havana Casa De La Cultura throughout our experiences. Our partnership included the use of their facilities for classes as well as involving our students in their workshops and weekly critiques. It was at one of these critiques that the teacher from the after school class shared what he had learned from us. He spoke of all the things we talked about and used many of the questions we asked. He had thought about it—really thought about it ... And although we did not see a great deal of discussion even in this audience, we were thrilled that perhaps in addition to learning from this wonderful culture, we may have also shared effectively a little bit of our own. So what did we learn? Understand that although teaching and learning may be approached differently, respect, genuine engagement, and active listening are keys to international study experience.*

(Brooke moves away from the chairs and stands in line with a group of people. Behind her, a screen features the painting *A Path to Follow*[3] by artist Yalili Mora.)

Brooke: *An issue we had throughout our visits was the varying concept of time. We seemed to hurry and wait. Waiting is relentless in Cuba. A book with just such a title documents Cuban art from the nineties. As the book explained, waiting resulted from the "Periodo especial" or Special Period in Cuba when economic and political upheaval at the end of glasnost and the withdrawal of Soviet financial support in 1991 (Power, 1999). Whether people wait for buildings to fall, their water to become safe, stores to open, or a change in leadership, normalcy in Cuba includes and in some cases depends upon waiting.*

(The people in line sit down on the stage and Brooke joins them, sitting cross-legged with elbows on her knees and head propped against her hands. She looks down and then directly at the audience.)

Brooke: *The frustration that we felt about constantly waiting was a steady battle. And in one case, our frustration almost destroyed our program. The waiting game in Cuba involved change. No matter how organized we were, no matter how hard we tried to schedule, plan, and make all of our activities work within our time frame—a museum would close for no apparent reason, the bus would not show up, and/or something would be lost in the translation and someone would be expecting us on a day or time that we had something else scheduled.* (stands up and begins frantically pacing back and forth across the stage) *Without consulting us, our Cuban associates scheduled our visit to the ceramic artist Pellido's studio one morning. But, as most of our students were already on their way to other activities, we told them to cancel the studio visit. In fifteen minutes we found ourselves in the midst of a vehement discussion with people who were suggesting that we may want to leave the country that day!*

(Brooke stops and faces the audience in silence as images of Castro, men in fatigues and machine guns, Guantanamo prisoners, and people in make-shift and sinking boats flash across her face and onto the screen behind her. The stage blackens and only a faint outline of Brooke can be seen.)

Brooke: *What we didn't understand is that "Cuban time" is a multifaceted consequence of daily survival. A bus was late because something broke. The mechanic waited for a part that didn't arrive because the truck had no fuel. The fuel didn't arrive because the driver of the fuel truck couldn't get to work because there were no buses, and so on. When something didn't work, they waited patiently or they changed everything and moved so quickly it was hard to catch up. Sometimes we weren't sure where we were going! But, they did not complain. Not to us anyway. If they did, that is all that they would do. They made the best of each situation and moved along.*

(Light returns to the stage. Brooke moves to a plush overstuffed chair and falls into it.)

Brooke: *We on the other hand, did not understand that. Tired of it all, we wanted to make a decision and our decision was wrong.* (moves to the edge of her seat, looking up and with hands out to her side) *Canceling is not done. Not when it involves such a Cuban treasure as the artist Pellido.* (looks down at her hands) *By canceling, we treated this artist, this country, and all of our Cuban associates with disrespect. They were humiliated and we were clueless!*

(stands and clasps her hand together with arms straight in front of her body) *Fortunately, our ongoing relationship with our Cuban associates and their genuine caring of us encouraged conversation. We quickly rounded up some students and made our way to Pellido's studio. He prepared a feast for us, along with clay vessels ready for our students to glaze. He lectured, shared his home, and worked individually with everyone. It was one of the best and most important experiences of the trip.* (walks back to the single straight-back chair sitting in the middle of a single spot-light) *What did we learn? Flexibility is key to international study. We had to let go of our ideas of structure and embrace alternative opportunities. We learned that although we may not understand or be comfortable with such cultural norms as "Cuban Time," we cannot judge that which we don't know or understand….and therefore we must respect and acknowledge that these people know what they are doing.* (looks down at her hands) *Our Cuban associates held a special fiesta for us on our final day. During the final song, I danced with a young female student saying, "Hold on to this moment. Capture it forever in your mind. It may never happen again." We cried together … for our friends and ourselves as the people had touched our hearts in ways we never knew possible.*

Act Three: So What?

(Brooke and Rain sit at a table amidst a bounty of food.)

Brooke: *While in Cuba I met with the minister of culture of old Havana, a number of policia, the party boss in Florida de Camaguey, and probably (as I discover daily) many more government officials and/or representatives who though watching us carefully rarely impeded our efforts or activities. Those who spoke publicly with us said that programs such as this make a huge difference in not only our perceptions of them but their perceptions of us. As one young woman explained, "I am frightened. We are told that your country is going to invade and destroy our country as you did Iraq and yet, here you are—wanting to learn from us. We just don't understand." Yes, it is much more complicated than just a friendly or not so friendly exchange. Although their socialist ideals preach suffering for the cause, we found our Cuban associates continually frustrated by the exclusionary effects of globalization. They catered to the tourist buses, served huge quantities of food, and escorted tourists to fanciful hotels that they themselves were* *not allowed to enter or have. For me, as we landed in Miami with the thousands of planes, food counters, and unreal air-conditioned spaces, I was again shocked and little embarrassed by the gluttony of capitalism. And yet, I embraced the fact that there was plenty of bathroom tissue, warm water, soap, and paper towels.*

Rain: (places her hand on Brooke's shoulder) *Brooke, we are all contradictions. With all that we experience and all of the inequities that we observe, we battle our own social conditionings and participation. Here we sit with all this food* (her hand waves around the table) *and I have enjoyed it. Would my not enjoying it feed the hungry? You created life-altering experiences for your students and through positive actions and sensitive thoughtfulness, you were change agents in Cuba. I think and hope that our own privilege provides us with possibilities to address inequities.*

Act Four: Rain's Brazil

(Rain walks away from the table and for a moment the spot light searches for her, only to find her standing at the edge of stage-left.)

Rain: *My first trip outside of the US was to Brazil in 1994. It was then that I experienced international travel and immersion that transformed my teaching and research—well—my life. I had no idea what to expect, taste, hear, and feel. I began to know myself, my abilities and weaknesses, and the importance for inner dialogue—that is why journaling is so important on trips.*

(Curtain slowly opens with sounds of howler monkeys, macaws, and running water. Spotlight follows Rain as she turns and walks inside a cement-block 9x10 partially built structure. A small chalkboard leaned on the wall with evidence of math calculations still visible in the dust.)

Rain: *I went to Brazil two more times....(sighs) I was privileged to stay with families in Rio de Janeiro, Recife, Sao Paulo, and unidentified spaces along the Rio Negro River in the Amazonian region.* (runs her hand on the wall, picks up the chalkboard, and pauses) *This school took so much to build—generations of loss of land and lives and yet, it looks like only a cement-block structure. In 2005, colleagues created a pilot exchange program with Brazil. I became involved the next year when our department decided to commit to develop a service-learning model exchange program.*

Through the wisdom of seasoned travelers and the expertise of the Office of International Education, a 10-week course was designed and implemented prior to the travel. (Rain sits on top of one of the tables and Brooke joins her.) *The design of the course was student and needs driven.* (She touches Brooke on the shoulder and smiles.) *Like you said, flexibility was the key. It was important for the students to know there was a Brazil community in Ohio and to hear their stories. This provided a venue for the students to hear multiple Brazilians' perspective and experiences, which also gave our students a chance to reflect within a community space. Although some of the students were seasoned travelers, it was important to review protocols, share travel tips, and discuss the transformation process when immersed in another culture. Travel is a dynamic negotiation of what is known, what is being experienced, cultural and political rules, and understandings. What does it feel like when you can't communicate? How do you handle frustration when difference wears thin? We tried to establish an adventure attitude that was sprinkled with flexibility.*

(Airport sounds, Portuguese language, and automobiles sounds resonate. Curtain closes behind Rain as she walks towards center stage. Spotlight follows.)

Rain: *The preparation quarter flew by and before I knew it we were at the airport ready to embark on our 2-week journey. Had we prepared them enough? Was I prepared to provide leadership? Within only a few hours, the airlines provided us with the first opportunity to practice diplomacy and flexibility. Our first plane was 2 hours late and we were refused entry onto our connecting flight from Chicago to our first stop in Brazil. I am still unsure why they finally allowed us entrance, but in a most confusing way we boarded but our luggage did not—22 pieces—gone for 3 days.* (waves her arms and her voice gets louder) *Flexibility—adventure—flexibility.* (laughs) *We rented a van to retrieve the luggage in Goias. The driver spoke no English and my Portuguese at best is at a two-year old level—just isolated words. I was on the cell phone trying to speak with the airline staff to let them know that we were on our way to pick up the luggage, stating over and over again, "Please don't close, we are almost there* (in both English and broken Portuguese)." *I ran into the airport and went around the counter finding this young tall man with a cart full of luggage. He looked at me and smiled and I just couldn't help it, I hugged him. He seemed to understand and hugged back. We both were talking in our own language, smiling, and walking to the van.*

CHAPTER 36 | A Cultural Cherishing Drama: Developing International Art Education Relationships through Service-Learning

289

(Lights go up, curtain opens and Rain engages with the classroom again. Sitting down at one of the desks.)

Rain: *The 2 weeks were full of opportunities beyond the planned program. The students learned that waiting is embedded and patience is a practiced necessity. The first week was spent on transition to the sounds, smells, and tastes. We experienced a holiday at someone's home with neighbors. We visited local artists' studios—all distinctly different. The students taught at the university lab school and presented workshops and research. Their attempts to speak Portuguese were met with enthusiasm and impromptu language lessons. They quickly learned the importance of communication.*

During the 2 weeks, I found that my epistemological approach to the unknown was a desired state of mind—I loved teachable moments and it was in those student-driven moments that my own learning excelled. My head would buzz with self-reflective questions: how can I direct them to bring this experience to their students—not simply presenting or teaching about—but through recognizing the change of the teacher inside us? Rich and mutual life altering exchanges were many. How can I guide them to replicate this in the confines of a classroom, or can I?

Rain: *Our last 2 days were full of community experiences and traveling. For some, the newness had worn out. They were frustrated and wanted to go home. As one student stated,* (changes her voice to reflect character change) *"I just want to taste normal food. I am tired of getting food that I don't know."* (laughs and shakes her head) *Two weeks was not long enough for them to be able to get past that stage, but it was long enough to recognize that stage and discuss how one might process it and resolve it if they were staying longer.*

(Curtain opens to a bare stage with one table to stage right with a Caipinia drink. Samba music softly plays. Rain dances, twirling and giggling. She picks up the drink and stares at it and slowly savors the taste.)

Rain: *Throughout the 2 weeks, the students compared Brazil to the United States. Such as when they attended a holiday celebration, they remarked how special the food was, how it was full of traditions, and that we did not have anything like that. Through conversations we connected similar holidays and the foods and traditions that are served. It was a "ta-da" moment. It is important to appreciate cultures, but not at the exclusion of one's own* (stops dancing, puts drink down, takes a pen and journal out of her purse,

and begins to write). *But the trip was more than food, drink, and dance. It was about experiencing difference and learning about oneself and one's capabilities when challenged. It was about finding oneself. It was about children and learning to connect to them. One of the assignments was journaling. Specific questions were asked so our students would reflect upon class, race, gender, community action, demographics, education philosophy, types of art and differences and similarities. Their journals revealed that much growth and awareness of their surroundings and self occurred. They recognized similarities and differences and why those differences existed. Their self-reflections revealed a deeper comprehension and/or understanding of privilege, waste, and most importantly, the possibilities they have to give.*

Act Five: Why?

Brooke and Rain

(Brooke enters with 2 chairs and hands one to Rain. They position the chairs facing each other in the spotlighted middle of the blackened stage. With several photos in their hands, they sit down.)

Brooke: *I'm not who I thought I was. Look at these photographs. Can you see the look in my eyes? I was frightened. Genuinely, frightened the whole time I was in Cuba. I'm almost stoic.*

Rain: (leans forward, looks at Brooke's photo, and then holds another photograph up) *Really, you don't look frightened to me. You look brave and actually happy as if you are at a party with friends. Look at this one of me. I look clueless, like an imposter.*

Brooke: *Clueless? I don't see it. You look almost peaceful as you sit amidst your new and very different friends.*

Rain: *Are they our friends? Do we really know that? What did they say when we left? What are they doing now?*

Brooke: *Well, I do receive e-mails several times a year. But, as all communications are closely monitored by the Cuban government, I don't REALLY know what they are actually saying. What did we do, Rain? What did we do?*
Rain: *I don't know if we will ever truly know. But, I do know what it did to me.*

Brooke: *Yes, me, too. I'll never be the same. WE will never be the same. But, is that enough? What does it all mean?*

Rain: *It means, we can't stop going, thinking, learning, hoping ... and indeed cherishing.*

(The lights dim. Natural rain forest sounds resound as again *Do Gardenias Para Ti* softly plays. The sound and music stops abruptly. The stage goes black and a loud voice seemingly spoken through a bull horn, laughs as "s/he" proclaims, *"Viva La Revolucion!"*)

Conclusion

We know the "drama" that seems to play out in both domestic and international travel. No matter how excited we are to go or how much of "home" we take with us, we are never truly comfortable without familiar signs of home. Although, it is doubtful that such personal needs and desires related to international travel will change, we, as Brooke and Rain, recognized and critically reflected upon the ways these desires affected our global relationships as researchers and educators.

When approached through a service-learning methodology that includes critical forms of reflective experience, international study and research experiences may challenge established ways of thinking and acting by encouraging a re-examination of one's own values and practices. This process can build learning communities that support students' and communities' lifelong successes and achievements by creating practices that question social problems, policies and ethical dilemmas.

This inquiry process is important because it creates the potential for critique of one's own national culture at all levels and opens up possibilities for becoming familiar with the national cultures of others. The process is also significant because it facilitates the understanding of the foundations of democracy, its potential, and its risks in achieving our goals of educating responsible, accountable, active members of a global society through arts and visual culture education.

REFERENCES

Ballengee-Morris, C. & Stuhr, P. (2001). Multicultural art education in a changing world. *Art Education, 54*(4), 6-13.

Barone, T., & Eisner, E. (1997). Arts-based educational research. In R. M. Jaeger, T. Barone, & American Educational Research Association (Eds.), *Complementary methods for research in education* (2nd ed., pp. 73-98). Washington, DC: American Educational Research Association.

Case, S., Brett, P., & Foster, S., (Eds.). (1995). *Cruising the performative: Interventions into the representation of ethnicity, nationality, and sexuality.* Bloomington and Indianapolis: Indiana University Press.

Chisholm, L. (2003). *Charting a hero's journey.* New York: IPSL Press.

Derrida. J. (1997). *Of grammatology.* Translated by Gayatri Chakravorty Spivak. Baltimore: John Hopkins University Press.

Pink, D. (2005). *A whole new mind: Moving from the information age to the conceptual age.* New York: Riverhead Books.

Power, K. (Ed.). (1999). *While Cuba waits.* Santa Monica, CA: Smart Art Press.

Taylor, P. G. (Ed.). (2002). *Amazing Grace: The lithographs of Joseph Norman.* Boston: Museum of the National Center for Afro-American Artists.

ENDNOTES

1   One author facilitated a study-abroad experience in Cuba with University of Georgia Professor Joseph Norman in 2003 and 2004.

2   The art education students taught the Cuban children about *Target Practice: Take this Take that!* by artist Joseph Norman (Taylor, 2002).

3   In *A Path to Follow* Cuban artist Yalili Mora realistically painted the legs and torsos of people waiting in line. In sepia and grayed tones, the personality, gender, and plight of each represented figure is symbolically represented with bandages, tattered shoes, frayed hemlines, and gestures or stances that appear characteristically submissive or surrendered to a plight of suffering. See http://www.havanagallery.co.nz/artists_flash.html

"I Could Interpret an Artwork from My Own True Feelings": Intercultural and Empowerment Strategies Used to Teach in an International Setting

Enid Zimmerman

Teaching in Taiwan

Teaching in global contexts has potential to provide rich and expansive experiences for both teachers and students. In fall 2005, I spent a semester teaching two classes in Taiwan, where I faced many language and communication challenges. One class was an undergraduate art appreciation class and the other was a graduate class in gender issues in art and education. I co-taught the art appreciation class with Gilbert Clark and was the sole instructor of the graduate class. The classes were taught in a rural town in Taiwan with 1,000 students on a branch campus of National Chiayi University (NCYU). The main NCYU campus is in Chiayi City in central Taiwan, a half an hour's drive from the branch campus. I was invited to teach by Jin-Shiow Chen, a professor at NCYU and former Indiana University doctoral student, who also suggested the main themes for the classes Clark and I taught. In both classes, emphasis was on crucial roles art teachers can play in promoting tolerance and understanding diversity of peoples in a global context. Data for this study were derived from observations of in-class student responses, student assignments and interviews, digital photographs, and videos recordings of class activities. Content-comparative analyses were conducted to provide topics for interpretation of the data (Stokrocki, 1997).

Intercultural Approaches to Art Education

In the art appreciation class, intercultural approaches to art teaching were emphasized, with a focus on diversity of peoples and their beliefs and values in a global context. Understanding commonalties shared by all peoples and appreciating differences between and within various cultures provided a rich context for teaching art appreciation in an increasingly interconnected world (Davenport, 2000; Davenport & Zimmerman, 2001; Zimmerman, 2003). The students were encouraged to gain tolerance of points of view that differed from their own and at the same time to develop abilities to read images based on personal meanings (Chalmers, 1996; McFee, 1996; Stuhr, Petrovich-Mwaniki, & Wasson, 1992; Wasson, Stuhr, & Petrovich-Mwaniki, 1990; Zimmerman, Clark, & Chien, 2007). Teaching from an intercultural perspective empowered the students to examine their own cultural identities and to engage in dialogues with other students by expressing reactions to artworks connected to their own experience (Ladson-Billings, 1995). The students also used technology that provided opportunities to overcome geographical, language, and cultural boundaries. As Clark and I discovered, it was a challenge to conquer obstacles of verbal communication and cultural differences and to teach a course in Taiwan that emphasized an intercultural approach in which students observed artworks[1] and engaged in writing and talking knowledgably about them (Wilson & Clark, 2000).

The Art Appreciation Class

There were 28 students (16 women and 12 men) in the art appreciation class, most in their last year of undergraduate studies and majoring in fine arts. The class met twice a week for one and a half hours. Most of the students had studied English in elementary and/or secondary schools, but the majority was not able to read or write English with any fluency. Clark and I were the first professors to teach in English in the art program at this campus. We do not read or speak Chinese and no translators were assigned to the class, so we used a variety of teaching strategies to bridge the language gap.

Teaching Strategies

In the first half of the semester, students participated in teacher-initiated dialogues that called attention to critical features and meanings of works of art and helped them develop an appropriate vocabulary. In the second half of the semester, students engaged in a variety of experiences with artworks and shared their findings with one another. They were required to complete all assignments, read required materials, participate in class discussions, and prepare projects for in-class presentations (Zimmerman, Clark, & Chien, 2007).

The students viewed images from cultures around the world, created at various times from past to present, focusing on traditional Asian and Western art, as well as contemporary arts and popular visual culture. Rather than employing a lecture approach typical in Taiwan, Clark and I emphasized informal discussions with questions about images and objects shown in class. Class content was based on image-related themes rather than a more familiar historical approach. We purposefully chose images that connected to the students' lives and had meanings for them; we also offered them opportunities to make selections for discussion from an array of images. NCYU students usually listen to lectures and take notes, and these new teaching approaches meant they had to assume responsibility for interpreting and discussing artworks with their peers.

To communicate with the students, Clark and I drew images on chalkboards, used many non-verbal acting techniques, and were helped by those students who had some English skills. One means for developing student confidence in speaking and writing in English was to have almost all responses to assignments negotiated through group discussions. A student who had some facility with English was placed in each group and other students were randomly assigned as group members. First, they expressed their ideas through large group discussions. Next, they engaged in smaller discussion groups that led to individual presentations about their interpretations of art works.

Use of technology also helped students translate from Chinese to English and research information about particular images or artists. To make the students comfortable and reduce their anxiety about using English, Jerry Chien, a professor at NCYU who helped facilitate technology for the class, brought laptop computers for researching information on a variety of websites and using Microsoft Word to check English spelling or grammar mistakes. They also used their mobile phones, pocket translators, or computer software (such as Dr. Eye) to assist in translating Chinese into English. In addition, the art education department had two computer classrooms and students were encouraged use them to access English websites.

Class Assignments

There were seven class assignments, besides the outside readings–principally examples of art analyses and criticism that Clark and I rewrote to simplify the language. The first half of the semester was devoted to oral discussions and increasing students' comfort levels and their willingness to use English. A considerable amount of time was spent on translation and negotiating meaning, and it took three times longer to cover material than in a similar art appreciation class in the United States. For the first assignment, students, in groups of six, were asked to contrast and compare pairs of images on postcards. For the second assignment the students, still in groups of six, selected an image from an array of postcards and answered questions in English about it. For the third assignment, the groups chose a pair of images and worked outside of class, responding to more complex questions about how the artworks made them feel and what meanings were conveyed to them. For the fourth assignment, students met in groups of four outside of the class, chose any artist working in any medium, and answered the same questions as in the previous assignment. Influenced by their art history backgrounds and information in English found on the Internet, a majority chose well-known Western artists from the 19th and 20th centuries.

Clark and I noticed that most groups chose well-known, Western male painters. For assignment five, therefore, they were asked to contrast and compare works by two women artists from the East or West. For the sixth assignment, we brought many, small, three-dimensional art objects to class, mostly from Eastern cultures. The students responded to general questions about the objects, such as where the object was from, its use, and materials from which it was made. For the final assignment, students were asked to chose an artwork that had particular meaning for them, do some research about it, and make connections between the artwork and their own lives. They all chose to do an oral presentation in class; 17 chose Asian artists' artworks, including some craft objects, and 11 students chose artworks by Western artists.

Students who chose to interpret Asian artworks said that they felt comfortable expressing their own opinions about works that had personal meanings for them and sharing their thoughts and feelings about images from their own cultural backgrounds. Comments from two students, given below, were particularly meaningful to Clark and me.

> This artwork (an ink painting of a house created in 1986 by Guan Zhong Wu) displays the oriental culture...I think of my past...when I was a child there were many

people in my family and we all lived together. We did not care about petty things...good time does not last long because everyone grows up...in this picture there are few people and there is no warmth.

Vincent's painting ("Portrait of the Artist with a Bandaged Ear" created in 1889 by Vincent Van Gogh) affects me. I often meet predicaments of life and I'm not happy... with worried matters... My father suffers from melancholia and I realize this feeling and could melt into this situation.

Assessment of the Art Appreciation Class

After we had assigned students' final grades, we developed, along with Chien, a questionnaire to evaluate the students' responses to the class. Chien interviewed 17 students for half an hour, using the questionnaire as a protocol. He asked five questions in Chinese and translated students' answers into English. We then used content analysis to place these responses into categories (Stokrocki, 1997). Here are the questions, followed by categorized student responses, and a few representative quotes.

What did you learn about looking and talking about art in this class? Eighty eight percent of the students mentioned that open discussions with other students and instructors helped them organize their ideas and appreciation of works of art. Understanding that there are multiple points of view to think about art was cited by 52%, and expressing personal feelings about works of art was a learning experience for 18%. Student comments such as the two given here seemed to reflect the thoughts of the group.

Artworks from other cultures broadened my vision and increased my ability to think about art.

We didn't just need to use textbooks; I also could interpret an artwork from my own true feelings.

What teaching methods did you learn to look and talk about art? Teaching methods that were new included guiding students to appreciate artworks step-by-step (82%); having students express their own feelings and ideas (76%); creating opportunities for dialogues between students and their teachers (41%); using many different strategies to talk about art (35%); and spending time observing and discussing one artwork rather than many (24%). Their insights about teaching are reflected in these student comments.

A teacher should guide students to different aspects of thinking and not one narrow dimension.

Focus first on the work and students can bravely express their feelings about it; then you can think about who did the artwork and when they did it.

What do you think about the group activities? Positive reactions to the group activities included

finding inspiration from other students (88%), being in a setting where everyone could express his or her opinions (29%), and collaborating to find answers to questions posed by the instructors (24%). Some challenges were that consensus couldn't always be reached (29%), not everyone contributed to discussions (23%), and that it was hard to communicate conclusions in English (29%). These students understood the benefits of classroom dialogue and inquiry, as indicated in two comments offered here:

It made me rethink my original plan and sometimes I would change my thoughts after hearing someone else's opinion.

Sometimes we couldn't come to a common opinion about an artwork and it was frustrating.

What were differences were there between the art appreciation class and art history classes you had taken previously? Differences mentioned focused on student input rather than 'correct' answers as in art history classes (59%). The main method in art history classes was usually lecture and not the dialogue method (53%). Students appreciated the classroom dynamics of discussion, as reflected below.

Taiwanese teachers tend to cram lectures into students; it is hard to have students think in a critical and active way.

More emphasis on hearing different opinions of everyone rather than a correct response gave us more opportunities to respond.

Did using computers help you with assignments and discussions? Most students thought computers were convenient for retrieving information (65%) and that they saved time and helped with English writing and learning about artists (79%). There were questions about the reliability of information found on the computer and time taken from group discussions to use computers (41%). Both positive and negative aspects of computer-facilitated learning were noted by students:

It helped with homework and offered abundant information about artists from different places and backgrounds.

Spending too much time on computers may lead to reduction of discussion and thinking.

Was the class helpful in developing your English skills? How? The majority of students said that they developed English reading, writing, listening, and speaking skills (76%) and gained confidence in speaking English (76%). A quarter of the students felt learning about art appreciation with new methods was more important than learning English language skills.

Gender Issues in Art Education

As a feminist art educator, I have been involved for three decades, with Frances Thurber, in encouraging women in the United States to take leadership positions in a variety of educational contexts (Zimmerman, 1997a, 1997b). My focus is on empowering art teachers to find their own personal voices and develop collaborative voices with others in order to eventually form public voices (Thurber & Zimmerman 1996, 1997, 2002).

When teaching the gender issues class in Taiwan, I wanted to provide my students with support and at the same time be critical. I tried to put into practice a teacher/student relationship, described by Pence (1995), where there is trust, mutual respect, and a commitment of the teacher to assist students in sharing ideas, thoughts, failures, and success with each other. An ambiance of cooperation, collaboration, equality, and support can be constructed by recognizing that no pedagogy is value-free and that gender issues may operate differently in different contexts, especially in international settings.

Of primary importance was to create dialogues with my students and to have them dialogue with each other. Reinforcing positive images of women, I encouraged them to speak freely without fear in a caring community where students work together collaboratively and personal reactions to diverse issues are validated (Hegelsen, 1990; hooks, 2000; Irwin, 1995; McCall, 1995; Noddings, 1992). Ultimately, they could expand their self-concepts and their relationships to local and broader worlds that surrounded them.

Gender Issues in the Art and Education Course in Taiwan

The purpose of this course was to promote awareness, understanding and inquiry into gender issues, particularly women's concerns, in art and education. This was done by exploring the nature and extent of women's contributions to art and education in a global context, discussing women's issues in art education, and relating this information to strategies and resources for art education practice. The class began with an historical overview of women's art in the East and West and discussion of contemporary concerns about women's art and education.

There were seven women in the class, all teachers or prospective teachers at various stages in their master's degrees. The class met once a week for two and a half hours. Most of the students had some modest degree of English reading and speaking skills; I was their first English-speaking professor. To stimulate the students to be active class participants, I used many of the strategies used in the art appreciation class, including feminist teaching strategies. As in the undergraduate class, students used their mobile phones, pocket translators, or computer software to assist in translating Chinese into English.

Class Assignments

The first class assignment was to read, in Chinese or English, a biography or autobiography about a woman artist from the East or West, make an oral presentation in class about the artist, distribute a one-page outline to classmates, including some gender issues discussed in class and reflections about how to teach about this artist and her works. The final project was to create an artwork about a gender issue in art and/or education that had an impact on their personal lives. The students also read and discussed selected articles in English related them to topics discussed in class.

The artists that the students chose were mostly contemporary, including Saito Chino, a Japanese *manga* artist; Pan Yuling, a Chinese calligrapher; Yayoi Kasama, a Japanese sculptor, designer, and painter; Ava Hseuh, a Taiwanese a creator of fabricated objects; Georgia O'Keeffe and Mary Cassatt, American painters; and Cindy Sherman, an American performance artist and photographer. Their interpretations were generally historically oriented and did not include much emphasis on gender issues. Often, comments were "In Taiwan, we cannot do feminist kinds of things, women's roles are very traditional," "We are supposed to get married, have children, and serve our husbands," or "It is easier for women in the US to be independent." These were typical comments before they read assigned articles in English about the women's movement in the 1970s and 1980s in the United States, contemporary readings about Asian and Western women artists' lives and their works, explanations about traditional women and their artworks, and articles about feminist pedagogy. An article I wrote in 2005 contained areas of concern that resonated with these students. Asian doctoral students, in the article, spoke about studying in United States and experiencing feeling they had to have right answers, and speaking and challenging others' ideas in public arenas. Trust and a willingness to share ideas, failures, and successes with each other and with their teachers were new concepts for the NCYU students. In another article the students read, Chao (2003) explained that art educators in Taiwan needed to take responsibility for "eliminating unjust conditions in society and establishing gender balanced art education practices" (p. 153).

Jin-Shiow Chen, who attended a number of class sessions, discussed with the students an incident that happened to her artwork when it was on public display (Figure 1).

> [In Taiwan several generations ago,] daughters and mothers used to bury their beautiful days in needlework. They sewed one stitch after another carefully and delicately onto stretched fabric to create works overflowing their stories, passions, tenderness, and dreams ... My project was done in a similar way, using wooden hoops to stretch pieces of silk and stitching flower motifs from old fabrics onto the stretched silk... I intended to make my artwork related to the past needlework ... women had made in the past. (Chen, 2007, personal correspondence)

Figure 1

Top: Chen's exhibit in a train station.

Figure 2

Right: *Devil's Ivy*—oil painting.

Jin-Shiow Chen explained further that she was invited to participate in a group exhibition in the 2005 Art Festival organized by the Art Site of the Chiayi Railway Warehouse. The artwork she created for this art exhibition was entitled *Women's Needlework.*

Women's Stories. Chen decided to display her work on a railway platform near the warehouse. The next day, when Clark and I, along with Chen, attended the opening of the art exhibition, we were stunned to see that many pieces were slashed with knifes or poked with sticks, and some were spit upon with betel-nut juice. Chen said:

> I was irritated seeing my artwork attacked. I had a feeling that I was ... punished for speaking up for women and their art ... The sad thing is that no one really cared about gender issues underlying the violent behavior after I reported the incidence to the art exhibition organizers. (Chen, 2007, personal correspondence)

The class members' reactions to this issue galvanized them as a support group. This unfortunate incident brought home concerns they had been engaged with in class. The destruction of Chen's artwork deeply influenced their final art projects, as a model for expressing their own meanings, through their artworks, about women in Taiwanese society.

Final Projects

All seven students in the class submitted final art projects with short explanations in English. Themes included male domination, recognizing gender inequities in Taiwanese society, and gaining confidence to speak in public. As examples, I will present four abbreviated final projects that represent a variety of responses. The first, an oil painting titled *Devil's Ivy* (Figure 2), was explained this way:

> Women in the past were bound by codes of society and standards of their family and husbands. Most women would obey those rules even though they are unreasonable. My painting shows that women are strong enough to challenge men and the world. Devil's Ivy is green and its leaves are leathery ... There are not many limits to its living environment ... that is why it is called Devil's Ivy. As long as water is provided it will grow. The upper leaves grow larger than the lower ones. Just like women who suffer many challenges, when they become mature women they can grow.... I may meet many resistances ...but I will learn the spirit of the Devil's Ivy to oppose conditions that are not fair or biased.

Another student described her black ink and watercolor painting, *No Girl Speak Aloud*[2] (Figure 3):

> In a traditional patriarchal society, girls are educated to keep silent and take care of housekeeping and families. At the university, even though the number of girls outweighs boys, boys are more dynamic and inquisitive than girls. .... Girls who desire to have romance and good relations with others have no choice but to 'shut up'... In my painting, the girl ... doesn't have a mouth and simply opens her big eyes. The lines stand for striving and confused thoughts and the red cloth stands for passion. I will build confidence gradually and dare to speak out loudly any time anywhere. Silence is an unwise action that is yielded to the pressure of power.

A third student justified the content of her collage, *Taiwanese Betel-nut Girls* (Figure 4):

> We often see young girls standing by the road and calling attention to their bodies and dressing to stimulate

men's desire to buy betel-nuts... The center figure represents a betel-nut girl whose body is bound by ropes. The ropes represent masculine domination, market exploitation, and wrong values... Women's bodies are objects to meet men's desires. Betel-nut businessmen utilize females' bodies to make money. The women's almost naked bodies become the main target to draw customers .... They do not know this situation will send them to an invisible jail.

Modern Women in Taiwan (Figure 5) is the title of a ceramic plaque made by a fourth student. She wrote:

Taiwan women are still limited in some customs and the gender bias of traditional Chinese masculine-dominated viewpoints. My work shows the situation in modern Taiwan and reminds women to stand up for themselves. The nipple ... is a symbol for women's responsibility to care for babies and work at the same .... Taiwanese women are like the bird in a cage that wants to escape ... The pipe symbol is for masculine domination, but it also is a high heel for women to wear and be watched by men. The lines and spots represent water. Water is a symbol for women, because Taiwan females look soft as water on the surface, but they are strong as water that can run through hard stones and have power to generate enormous power for electricity.... Women in Taiwan do not have to build their confidence on men's recognition.

Assessment of the Gender Issues Class

At National Chiayi University, graduate students are required to anonymously evaluate their classes. Jin-

Figure 3

Top Left: *No Girl Speak Aloud*—watercolor.

Figure 4

Top Right: *Betel-nut Girls*—collage.

Figure 5

Left: *Modern Women in Taiwan*—ceramics.

Shiow Chen translated the students' responses and in general, most wrote about receiving positive images of women and being able to speak freely in class. I used content analysis to place these responses into categories for discussion (Stokrocki, 1997).

All seven students wrote they became reflective practitioners. Two mentioned positive effects of participating in a community of teachers and developing collaborative voices with others. Four said that their abilities to understand and express themselves in English improved because they were in a kinship with other art teachers. Four wrote that I helped them to find their own personal voices:

> Our instructor brings us to think deeply and make us concerned how women stand in society.

> We were encouraged to talk about gender issues from our own personal experiences and perspectives.

Four students mentioned trust, mutual respect, sharing ideas, and having dialogues with each other as successful aspects of the class:

> The friendly and kind manner of the class made me feel encouraged to speak up and work with others.

The class was taught in an approachable manner with skillful methods to make complicated concepts clear and easy to understand. Two students observed that the form and content of gender issues should operate differently in global contexts:

> I recognized ways American people's values sometimes are different from Taiwanese [values].

> We were introduced to multiple perspectives about gender issues and works of art created by women.

This class was a beginning for most of the students and resulted in their feeling empowered to make modifications in their own lives and begin forming communities of teachers with collaborative voices. In the future, perhaps some will become change agents who transform the place of women in their local communities or beyond.

Conclusions and Recommendations

This chapter describes my insights gained as, and reflections about, a U.S. art educator teaching two different courses in Taiwan. Students in both of my classes gained understandings of other peoples and their beliefs and values in a global context and became tolerant of viewpoints that differed from their own. Group discussions in the art appreciation class inspired students to express their own opinions and collaborate to read images meaningfully and from a vantage point that was not at first familiar to them. Through discussions students were empowered to express their reactions to artworks and connect them to their own experiences.

In the gender class, students were able to study women's contributions to art and education in a global context, explore problems related to women's issues in art education, and be reflective practitioners who could talk and write about these issues. They also were empowered to find their own personal voices, develop collaborative voices with others, and eventually form public voices. In both classes, the students became risk takers in a teaching/learning community where they could trust their classmates and instructor when they shared their ideas.

Computer technology helped students in both classes search for information and introduced them to many artists and concepts of which they had no previous knowledge. Technology also played an important role in facilitating communication between the NCYU students, Clark, and myself. In both classes, students gained confidence in expressing their thoughts and feelings in English. Communication by non-verbal means, such as facial and body expression, drawing visual representations, or by collaborating and cooperating both in groups and individually, helped them negotiate meaning about art and its place in their lives. As an instructor in both classes, I valued the student engagement with course content and approaches to teaching that were new and challenging for them. I too learned that to teach effectively and productively in a global context it was necessary to leave my own comfort zone and participate in both classes as both a learner and a teacher.

REFERENCES

Chalmers, F. G. (1996). *Celebrating pluralism: Art, education, and cultural diversity*. Los Angles, CA: The Getty Education Institute for the Arts.

Chao, H.-L. (2003). External and internal approaches for empowering Taiwanese women art educators. In K. Grauer, R. L. Irwin, & E. Zimmerman, *Women art educators V: Remembering, revisioning, reconsidering* (pp. 153-161). Kingston, Ontario: CSEA and Reston, VA: National Art Education Association.

Davenport, M. (2000). Culture and education: Polishing the lenses. *Art Education, 41*(4), 361 -375.

Davenport, M., & Zimmerman, E. (2001). Teaching art from multicultural, community- based, global, and intercultural perspectives. *For your information: New York Foundation for the Arts, 10*(2), 13.

Hegelsen, S. (1990). *The female advantage: Women's ways of leading*. New York: Doubleday.

hooks, b. (2000). *Feminist theory: From margin to center* (2nd ed.). Cambridge, MA: South End Press.

Irwin, R. L. (1995). *A circle of empowerment: Women, education and leadership*. Albany, NY: State University of New York.

Ladson-Billings, G. (1995). But that's just good teaching! The case for culturally relevant pedagogy. *Theory into Practice, 32*(3), 159-165.

McFee, J. (1996). Interdisciplinary and international trends in multicultural education. *Journal of Multicultural and Cross-cultural Research in Art Education, 14*(1), 6-18.

McCall, A. L. (1995). The bureaucratic restraints to caring schools. In D. M. Dunlap & P. A. Schmuck (Eds.), *Women leading in education* (pp. 180-198). Albany, NY: State University of New York.

Noddings, N. (1992). *The challenge to care in schools*. New York: Teachers College Press.

Pence, L. J. (1995). Learning leadership through mentorships. In D. M. Dunlap & P. A.

Schmuck (Eds.), *Women leading in education* (pp. 125-144). Albany, NY: State University of New York.

Stokrocki, M. (1997). Qualitative forms of research methods. In S. D. LaPierre & E. Zimmerman (Eds.), *Research methods and methodologies for art education* (pp. 33-55). Reston, VA: National Art Education Association.

Stuhr, P., Petrovich-Mwaniki, L., & Wasson, R. (1992). Curriculum guidelines for the multicultural art classroom. *Studies in Art Education, 45*(1), 16-24.

Thurber, F., & Zimmerman, E. (1996). Empower not in power: Gender and leadership issues in art education. In G. Collins & R. Sandell (Eds.), *Gender issues in art education* (pp.144-153). Reston, VA: National Art Education Association.

Thurber, F., & Zimmerman, E. (1997). Voice to voice: Developing in-service teachers' personal, collaborative, and public voices. *Educational Horizons, 75*(4), 180-186.

Thurber, F., & Zimmerman, E. (2002). An evolving feminist leadership model for art education. *Studies in Art Education, 44*(1), 5-27.

Wasson, R., Stuhr, P., & Petrovich-Mwaniki, L. (1990). Teaching art in the multicultural classroom: Six position statements. *Studies in Art Education, 34*(4), 234-246.

Wilson, T., & Clark. G. (2000). Looking at and talking about art: Strategies of an experienced art teacher. *Visual Arts Research, 26*(2), 40-50.

Zimmerman, E. (2005). Art education experiences of three Asian women formally doctoral students in the United States. *Research in Arts Education,10*, 1-23.

Zimmerman, E. (1997a). Building leadership roles for teachers in art education. *The Journal of Art and Design Education, 6*(3), 281-284.

Zimmerman, E. (1997b). I don't want to sit in the corner cutting out valentines: Leadership roles for teachers of talented art students. *Gifted Child Quarterly, 21*(1), 33-41.

Zimmerman, E. (1999). ' No girls aloud': Empowering art teachers to become leaders. *Australian Art Education, 22*(2), 2-8.

Zimmerman, E. (2003). Intercultural art education offers a means to promote tolerance and understanding. *Journal of Cultural Research in Art Education, 19 & 20*, 68- 80.

Zimmerman, E. (2005). Art education experiences of three Asian women formally doctoral students in the United States. *Research in Arts Education, 10*, 1-23.

Zimmerman, E., Clark, G., & Chien, J. (2007). Negotiating meaning in an art appreciation class taught in English to Taiwanese college students. *Journal of Research in Art & Education: Korean Society for Education through Art, 8*(6), 127-160.

ENDNOTES

1   *Artworks* here refer to objects created by artists from many different cultures and include 'fine art' as well as artifacts created by traditional peoples to images and constructions from popular culture.

2   The title comes from an article I wrote in 1999, "No Girls Aloud:" Empowering Art Teachers to Become Leaders, that the students read in class.

Life and Practice of Transnationalism

Anniina Suominen Guyas

This chapter articulates an epistemology that emphasizes diversity education and the development of critical equity, while repositioning the learners' active and relational selves at the center of all learning. Although the focus is to discuss the concept of transnationalism and examples of a pedagogical practice sensitive to issues of equity and diversity, my interest is also personal: I have struggled to find a 'home' within the various practices of diversity education that have dominated writing in the field of art education for the past two decades. My personal transmigrant experiences and my interactions with others in similar voluntary or professional relocation situations, as well as through my studies and conversations with people who have gone through forced migrations and who, as a consequence, have invested great efforts into redefining their cultural, communal, and personal identities, have proven that the modernist concepts of migration, citizenship, and cultural identities tied to one or two localities and/or states are no longer sufficient concepts and need to be re-examined (Glick Schiller, Basch & Blanc-Szanton 1995; Grewal, 2005; Wimmer & Glick Schiller, 2002). People no longer travel across continents and oceans to resettle permanently in new geographic locations, thus allowing for simple definitions of place, identity, language, and belonging defined through 'what was then' versus 'what is now.' People now experience more complex, fluid, and rhizomic identifications of self and subjectivity within various physical and imagined contexts. Despite the contemporary globalization trends and transnational nature of everyday life and experience, more states are being formed to unite nations, and nationalism continues to be "a powerful signifier" used for "different purposes and political implications" (Wimmer & Glick Schiller, 2002, pp. 326-327). In the following sections, I inquire the role and impact of *collective memory* and the *institutionally reinforced national identity* on education and one's self-perceived subjectivity (Alasuutari, 2001; Gould & Pasquino, 2001; Kristeva, 1993; Orchard,

2002; Paasi, 1997). Moreover, I suggest that ontological, epistemological, and methodological questions in relationship to the life and practice of transnationalism be brought to the center of diversity education and the role of nationness and use of national symbols in the creation of communal unity be studied. Finally, I make suggestions for pedagogical practice and relate the concept of transnationalism to the pedagogical discussion about self, other, place, community, and diversity education through two current research projects.

Nation-states, Nationalism, National Symbols, and State Funding for the Arts

The concept of a nation is indeed complex since one has the urge and inbuilt need to belong and be alike, while simultaneously claiming difference and uniqueness, and actively choosing to unbelong. In *The Changing Face of European Identity* Robyn (2005) argued that "Two-thirds of the conflicts in the world today could be of the 'identity-based' type that characterizes nationalist motivations (p. 2, citing Regehr, 1993). Supported by research in various fields (Geisler, 2005; Robyn, 2005; Paasi, 2005; Spickard, 2005; Gould & Pasquino, 2001) as well as based on my observations and analysis of people's everyday behavior, attitudes, and beliefs, and the continuous media representation, *nationalism*, *nation*, and *national identities* are deeply rooted concepts of self and society. What I find problematic about much diversity education (multiculturalism, interculturalism, crossculturalism, pluralism) is its focus on the *cultural*, assuming a difference between culture and politics. A level of innocence is assigned to the study of the cultural practices by dismissing the often-problematic political issues surrounding the history and practice of specific cultural traditions of cultural groups within and across nations. To study the arts and culture, one needs to acknowledge the direct and problematic relationship between culture and politics bound to and associated with specific ethnic groups located within geographic boundaries. Orchard (2002) asserted that in the discourse of nationalism and nation "'cultural difference' becomes 'cultural identity' and functions as the basis for recognition: from the outside as a basis for entitlement, and to demarcate a particular object of study, and from the inside, as the basis for solidarity and 'belonging'" (p. 420). Following this line of thought, if *self* is understood to be defined and formed within and as a reflection of larger *collective narratives and memory*, and within the context of a location (Geisler, 2005; Kuhn, 1995; Paasi, 2005), national epics promoted through visual and verbal narration in private and public contexts play an important role in constructing this awareness of self. Considering the insufficiency of the concept of *a nation specific to a state* to respond to the multilayered complexity of one's cultural identity, I find it increasingly alarming to observe the strong promotion of the state-nation union in diversity education.

To further analyze nations and national identities, two traits identify the nation-state union: First, "*fusing a nation to a state*" (Geisler, 2005, p. xv, emphasis added) (e.g., the strong nationalist movement that dominated the political and cultural environment in Finland before and after it gained its independence from Russia), and second, using a constructed collective memory with a strong promotion of *national symbols* and narratives *to create a nation specific to a state* (e.g., the United States). Besides symbolizing the collective memory assumed to unite the nation, these symbols also "represent the power of the state to define a nation" (p. xvi). Functioning through "direct textual reference," "connotation," or "education" (p. xvi), these national symbols promote a "shared mythic past" and a communal future to which one's personal narrative becomes intertwined and inseparable. Daily encounters in commercial, educational, leisure, and personal contexts with these symbols "generate the feeling of 'large scale solidarity,' which keeps us from opting out of the nation either physically or ideologically" (p. xvi). According to Alasuutari (2001) "art has served as a symbol of the state-centered and expert dominated society and at the same time provided legitimacy for that society" (p. 179). State substitutions are often granted to what is considered *culturally valuable* art projects to preserve vanishing cultural traditions or to support noncommercial 'high' culture. The basic assumption behind the state substitutions for culture is that citizens of the state need *education in culture,* and while consumers are readily engaged in the forms of commercial or entertainment culture, these state substitution systems protect and promote the forms of culture that do not lend themselves to

such competitive commercial venues and functions. Simply put, specialist groups of cultural experts orchestrate the maintenance of valuable forms of culture that individuals are too ignorant or misguided to engage in or support.

In my concern about state-regulated funding for the arts, I rely on my personal experiences in Finland and in the Midwest United States. Through these experiences I propose that the institutionalized support for arts and culture suggest that profound acceptance of complex diversity is yet to be achieved and remains superficial and decorative. Norms and standards are based on the idealized notions of what is Finnish or 'American,' mainly defined or explained through stereotypes. Yet these reductionist notions about nations dominate the funding of education and cultural studies, as seen in standardized testing or the continued use of the terms/concepts of ethnicity and race as the main identifiers of a person's culture and/or as measures of diversity within geographic borders, and/or differences and similarities between or within groups (Spickard, 2005). Racial thinking, whether called *racial* or *ethnic*, dominates the research, policy, and cultural funding in most, if not all, areas of the Western world. Deeply embedded in these ideologies and language of human diversity are the complex practices of domination often bound to geographically bordered states and nations (Spickard, 2005).

Border Talk and Nation-states

The major problem with the highly institutionalized (and publicly funded) practices of nation-state systems and nationalism is that they still operate under the concepts of communities that are localized and function within the boundaries of a specific context (Mirón, Darder, & Inda, 2005). What then is the meaning of place and state in the context of globalization? Imprinted in our spatial and cultural understanding is a globe with its distinct and separate areas marked by *borders* (Paasi, 2005). Here we come to an area of research that has received much interdisciplinary scholarly interest. To further question the nationalistic notions, I follow Paasi's (2005) definition of borders as boundaries that are to be

> understood not merely as static lines but as sets of practices and discourses which 'spread' into the whole society and are not restricted to the border areas. The production and reproduction of boundaries is part of the institutionalization of territories--the process in which their territorial, symbolic and institutional 'shape' is determined. Therefore boundaries manifest themselves in numerous social (economic, cultural, administrative and political) practices and discourses that may be simultaneous and overlapping. (pp. 119-120)

With globalization, discussions about *borders* have established their central place in everyday as well as in theoretical conversations. Vanishing borders, border protection, immigrant rights versus border patrol, increased number of humanitarian projects targeted to empower individuals through seemingly effortless and minor contributions are some of the topics that seem to unite the *global human nation*, yet complicate public and private negotiations of entitlement and belonging. The sense of belonging to nation-states versus a borderless world is additionally problematic, as Europeans now commonly identify with two governing institutions: a nation/state and the EU. This duality between supposedly open and fluid borders of a state opposed to the individual nations' strong sense of national identity could be disputed to have caused the increasing fear of the foreign and the need to identify 'us versus them,' arguably causing the support for nationalist parties and other less structured nationalistic movements in Europe (Robyn, 2005). The increasing support for the openly conservative Christian attitudes and policy in the United States evidences a similar trend (Robyn, 2005). Some of the reasons for these increasingly conservative attitudes are easy to identify: We are constantly reminded to fear the unknown and cautioned for the need to protect ourselves from the 'evil' that is ever-ready to penetrate the cozy, highly idealized reality of the white middle class. Besides the threat of direct physical and mental violence, the global economy further complicates these matters and introduces other imaginary and real threats. The rise of nationalist and conservative patriotic attitudes conflict with the move toward assuming a more inclusive notion of diversity associated with the marketed borderless global society.

Transnationalism

Having hopefully provoked rethinking the concept of nation and the association of nation-states with diversity education, it should be noted that I do not consider all things relating to *nation* harmful and intentionally conservative patriotism; however, when notions deriving from cultural domination and a limited sense of *us* influence a child's education and upbringing at all institutional levels, these concepts are in need of further inquiry. To begin to think about cultural belonging and citizenship through a polyglot, Mirón, Darder, and Inda (2005) suggest the "notion of citizenship that goes beyond legalistic definitions to encompass the more informal aspects of how people are integrated into their cultural milieus, in this case milieus that are not confined to just one national

space" (p. 293). This polyglot perspective on viewing an individual's discursive and contextual identity suggests multiple subjectivities, fluidity, flexibility, and inherent relationality. The term *transnationalism* especially appeals to me in the context of immigration studies because attention is directed to the individual's relational experiences within multiple real and imagined contexts without overemphasizing and tracing back the meaning of an individual's life narrative to the location of suggested origin. The definition of transnationalism used in this chapter relies heavily on the discussion of the concept by Mirón, Darder, and Inda (2005) and Glick Schiller, Basch & Blanc Szanton (1995). But to begin addressing transnationalism requires redefining the migrants as people

not uprooted themselves, leaving behind their homeland and facing the often painful process of incorporating into a new national culture; instead, in part because the facilitation of two-way traffic, both physical and metaphorical, made possible by modern technologies of transport and communication...they have been able to forge multistranded ties that link together their society of settlement and origin. (Mirón, Darder, & Inda, 2005, p. 290)

Transmigrants are immigrants whose daily lives depend on multiple and constant interconnections across international borders and whose public identities are configured in relationship to more than one nation-state. (Glick Schiller, Basch, & Blanc Szanton, 1995, p. 48)

I emphasize that in addition to public identities, private identities are formed in complex interactivities bound to more than one or two contexts and nation-states or smaller scale localities, as well as within the hybridity of philosophical structures that define one's sense of self and belonging. I propose that citizenship, contextual identities, and belonging "must be [re]thought in terms of the strategies migrants use to navigate transnational spaces" (Mirón, Darder, & Inda, 2005, p. 290). This suggestion is not meant to be associated only with large-scale, or profoundly life-altering, migration narratives but considered relevant to all levels of mental or physical migration. When considering transnationalism in the context of globalization, I also propose viewing the individual through multiple active subjectivities that create and act within complex discourses and in relation to and aware of the globalization of economics, politics, environmentalism, ontological understandings, and communication. By underlining the importance of the *active role of the cultural citizen* who simultaneously belongs to multiple social structures at different geographical locations, I acknowledge the uneven ability of individuals to participate in the above listed aspects of actively creating their subjectivity in the global sense as their transnational subjectivities are not bound to access to information. Instead it is formed most significantly in reactions/relation to their living situation, context, and everyday experiences. While my life is privileged in its access to technology, information, and possession of some cultural and educational power and authority, my sense of self is no more or less transnational than someone's whose life is lived through the cultural hybrid of everyday without analyzing it using theoretical concepts and arguments. However, I certainly promote developing an increasing critical awareness, which is also where I see the educational potential of this approach. While the research on social studies might have been restricted by "methodological nationalism" (Wimmer & Glick Schiller, 2002) and social and cultural policy has been narrowly defined through the assumed and natural social order of nation-states, the same limitations apply to education.

Transnational Civil Society, Transnational Citizenship, Nationalism, Nationness

Central to my pedagogical understanding and practice are the relational individual experiences and the firm belief that to develop an educated and personally committed understanding of diversity, the learner has to be located at the center of all learning. Although self-reflection and critical study of self is at the heart of learning, inquiry about humanity can be extended to wider social contexts and concepts. Since the inaccuracy and insufficiency of the nation-states has been established, considering a society through the concept of transnational civil society could be useful. As Appadurai (2006) explains it:

> The term 'transnational civil society' suggests something already formed, fixed, and institutionalized, a sociological noun of some kind. But in fact, it is several other things: it is a project, a process, and a space, all in search of an unresolved sociological form. (p. xi)

Within this framework, I see transnationalist identities and cultural actions performed within the interstices of established and institutionalized, in between something that one has overgrown, such as pre-given categories of identity (race, gender, etc.). Practices and identifications are formed based on the established and learned but reach for something more hybrid and fluid that better fits the constantly changing collaborative, communal, cultural, political, spiritual, artistic, sexual, private, and public self and us. According to Mirón, Darder, and Inda (2005), "Rather than displace the meaning of place, the processes of globalization and transnationalism propel local actors through their vast social networks to fully

engage in the politics of place making" (p. 289). The strength of many of the transnational effort derives from the individual "struggl[e] to make democratic claims that can no longer be made within an older model, in which civil society was—roughly speaking —the social space between the family and the State" (Appadurai, 2006, p. xi). Herein lies the potential for diversity education that promotes cultural empowerment and responsibility.

Pedagogy and Epistemology: Inquiry into the Author's Practice

For those invested in promoting social awareness as a component of a meaningful, authentic, and contextual art curriculum the question that remains to be answered is how to teach sociocultural equity in politically changing and sensitive environments. How one defines one's subjectivities in relation to the imagined, ideological, and physical contexts and how these varied and complex contextual identities influence a person's professional and private experiences is the focus of the following section. Through brief explanations of two research projects I demonstrate my attempt to respond to the institutionalized hidden curricula that promote cultural domination and superficial acceptance of diversity and rely on embedded stereotypical notions of self within the localities. First, a self-study of the author's teaching of preservice art educators in a largely Caucasian Midwestern college in the United States is used in reference to the author's developing pedagogical understanding. Second, a research and pedagogical project focused on immigrant experiences and studied through photographic representations is used to elaborate on the pedagogical potential I associate with the transnational notion of identity.

In my pedagogical thinking I rely heavily on concepts derived from critical pedagogy. Especially useful is the focus on understanding education within wider sociopolitical contexts. However, I find the strong binary thinking inherent in the practice of critical pedagogy limiting. Based on my educational background in the Finnish art education tradition, I suggest that emphasis on one's deep and complex relationships with nature and environment, if studied through critical reflexivity and relationality, naturally promotes social and cultural responsibility, empowerment, and agency. I find some support from Gude's (2007) "principles of possibility" that draw attention to "attentive living," "forming self," "investigating community themes," "encountering difference," "empowered experiencing and making" (pp. 8-12). Social reconstructivist multiculturalism, and interculturalism, while conveying important messages of (critical) acceptance and study of differences, similarities, and variety, are ideologically based on ethnic and "racial thinking and signifying," which are also the "means to naturalize [the] oppressions and resistances" (Spickard, 2005, p. 22). I see the role of art and art education, as well as research in art and education, as a means of forming complex understandings of identity beyond predetermined models, such as gender, ethnicity, age, and abilities, of subjectivity. I understand *self* to be performed and relational, and constructed in a constantly changing complex relationship with perceived familiarity, 'otherness' and 'strangeness within.' Self and one's multiple subjectivities and the continuous process of forming one's life narratives are formed in the intersections of continuity and incoherence, lifestory and temporality, the multilayeredness of the performed, and singular and multiple identities. It is important to recognize the tensions between past, present, and future as these influence one another in the active construction of self. Learners are understood to be active in creating contextual subjectivities when forming critical understandings of wider social and cultural issues, and it is thus important that the learners are engaged in reflecting on the continuous interplay between smaller and larger scale contextual understandings, such as one's family identity versus communal or national identity. Interplay and critical reflections need to also occur between a single subjectivity versus the complex web of one's multiple subjectivities. For example, in the preservice art education courses a learner might initially reflect on one aspect of identity, such as professional identity, but is then led to engage in other reflexive exercises (visual, written, instructional) about how this aspect of one's self-perception is developed in relation to the other subjectivities one assigns to them. Besides, and perhaps despite, the cultural context of learning, meaningful and advanced critical understandings and agency of cultural pedagogy can be formed when social issues, self, art, and culture are studied in tandem.

Implied in my approach to curricular development is a critical self-study and continuous evaluation of the purposefulness of my practice. Research, educational practice, art creation, and one's private life are seen as inseparable components, each contributing to theory and practice. This assumption creates a structure for curricula that interweaves art creation, pedagogical idea development, and theoretical reading, as well as builds on the continuous interplay between private life-experiences and public discourses. Deeply affected by my personal immigration and assimilation/dissimilation experiences, I have come to modify my pedagogical practices and

to develop theoretical understandings that are sensitive to the everyday issues of equity and diversity. I have faced the issues of belonging to and ownership of culture and society through professional and private experiences. It continues to astound me that families are not automatically united through citizenship. Love neither unites people, nor does it "buy" a membership of a community, but money does, as there is a monetary price for a citizenship. Still, possessing a formal citizenship or legal residential status does not grant one an access to cultural and social ownership: one is still measured against a norm, majority, and dominant social behavior. Further, a full membership can only be acquired through assimilation, which, if one agrees with Spickard's (2005) statement about how "*Race is about power, and it is written on the body*" (p. 2, author's emphasis), is denied to those who do not or cannot, physically or ideologically, modify their subjectivities to fit the norm. For these reasons (e.g., promotion of state-nation union, cultural domination through legislation and funding, and the persistent reliance on the concepts of nation, race and ethnicity) I argue for the need to further explore the concepts of sociocultural self and identity, and develop a pedagogy that empowers learners and equips them with practices and knowledge of meaningful art creation. However, a reflexive approach towards life-experiences alone does not help one to gain insights about education, society, and art. Social issues, relationality, and one's subjectivities need to be studied through a combination of theoretical development, engagement in and with art, and a practice of these developing ideologies. Aligned with Peña (2005), I am still working toward developing pedagogical practices sensitive of plural theories, a "spiritual yet a non-religious kind...integration, inclusiveness, inter-and intra-dependence, environment, equity, ecology, transcendence, love and finally race as a place" (p. 23).

The guiding principles of my practice when designing learning components for undergraduate and graduate courses are very simple. They are designed to interweave components of art, visual culture, and/or material culture analysis, artistic creation, written reflection, and concept development. Assignments emphasize open-ended objectives that allow students to engage in the inquiry process at their level of comfort and theoretical/pedagogical maturity. During and after every assignment, students reflect on three aspects of learning: What did I learn about myself, about/from my peers, and about the topic/issue studied. Also, rather than studying groups of people, I direct attention and inquiry to the study of an individual's relational experience. If, for example an artist or craftsperson is interviewed about their philosophy of art and perceived role in the community, students engage in creating meaningful, personal art inspired by the interviewed person. Also, reflections on the process are guided to combine the perspectives of multiple persons (students, peers, interviewed artists) and the contributions of each person's positionalities. The projects my students engage in could be seen to combine some of the ideas introduced by Gradle's (2007) notion about learning dispositions through practice and through curricular development that mimics engagement in/with art, and Walker's (2004) notion of "big ideas" that guide art creation.

Visual Anthropology Project

The study discussed in this final section is an ongoing collaboration with Paula Toiviainen, a Finnish art educator, and her students at the Helsinki City College of Social and Health Care. All participants are refugees or recent immigrants pursuing 2-year preparatory degrees in health and social sciences. The program introduces students to various areas of social and health care while also teaching language and social skills. In the study, students' cultural (transmigrant) identities and experiences are explored through analyzing photographic representations and verbal narrations. Participants perform visual inventories to explore various signifiers of identity located in private living spaces and public places of comfort. Although the study is in its early stages, a few observations pertain to the continuous negotiation of complex cultural identities through everyday interactions that do not readily lend themselves to dualistic categories of Finnishness or 'other' but require a much more complex understanding of self. Students study the concepts of locality, nationalism, globalization, transnationalism, as well as group and individual identities through critical visual anthropology/ethnography (Grimshaw & Ravetz, 2005; Pink, 2001; Rogoff, 2000; Rose, 2001; Wiles, 2008). The first group of students was asked to photograph several important objects in their homes, then a place of comfort and safety both at home and outside their home environments. Students then narrate these photographs. Analysis of these photographs is a weighty responsibility because they are concrete and honest representations of the participants' lives. While it is too early to draw any specific patterns between participants or discuss individual contributions in great detail, the early examples from

this study have helped me to revisit the terminology and theories I relied on when designing the conducted pedagogical practices. Performing these visual inventories, these representations of self, that include pictures of families, classmates, churches, grocery stores and bus stops among other concrete topics, indicate the precarious balance between belonging-unbelonging, social empowerment, and mobility that increase with learning the sociocultural roles of location. Through continued conversations with the participants I am hoping to understand more of the visual complexity presented to me.

With the next group of students, an initial photographic and visual autobiography will be performed through sharing several photographs or other visual and/or verbal documents. While the submitted visual material is of high interest to the researcher/educators, hopefully this activity will concretize the power of representation and intentional construction of narrative.

The participants' willingness to share their stories is a touching gesture of an honest desire to be understood. Looking at the images of their family members—for example, a baby smiling at the camera—I am reminded of the value and significance of individual stories, and the urgency to work toward understanding the complexity of everyday transnationalism.

Many texts in visual and material culture studies and semiotics successfully promote the deconstruction of symbolism associated with cultural icons and inquire the corporate power of creating reality. I urge further studies that explore the everyday use of *material, visual, and linguistic symbolism in relation to one's personal or communal ideologies*, as well as discourse studies about how educational institutions, such as museums, schools, universities, and public funding for arts and culture promote and reinforce a limited sense of 'us, as a nation.' This can lead to further explorations of educational practice and its effects on one's sense of self as an active agent partaking in the process of renegotiating and recreating 'us' specific to and beyond geographic localities. As Geisler (2005) argues, national symbols and the sense of nation is in the constant remaking, therefore I believe it should be of prevalence to educate students in ways that help them become active participants in this process of reformation and reinvention of the collective narratives and past beyond geographic locations or socially constructed groupings of people.

REFERENCES

Alasuutari, P. (2001). Art, entertainment, culture, and nation. *Cultural Studies—Critical Methodologies, 1*(2), 157-184.

Appadurai, A. (2006). Foreword. In S. Batliwala, & D. Brown (Eds.), *Transnational civil society: An introduction*. Bloomfield, CT: Kumarian Press.

Geisler, M. E. (2005). Introduction: What are national symbols—and what do they do to us? In M. E. Geisler (Eds.), *National symbols, fractured identities: Contesting the national narrative* (pp. xii-xlii). Lebanon, NH: Middlebury College Press.

Glick Schiller, N., Basch, L., & Blanc-Szanton, C. (1995). From immigrant to transmigrant: Theorizing transnational migration. *Anthropological Quarterly, 68*(1), 48-63.

Gould, C. C., & Pasquino, P. (Eds.) (2001). *Cultural identity and the nation-state*. New York: Rowman & Littlefield Publishers.

Gradle, S. (2007). Random weave: Developing dispositions to teach art. *Art Education, 60*(4), 6-11.

Grimshaw, A., & Ravetz, A. (Eds.) (2005). *Visualizing anthropology*. Bristol, UK: Intellect.

Gude, O. (2007). Principles of possibility: Considerations for a 21st-century art & culture curriculum. *Art Education, 60*(1), 6-17.

Grewal, I. (2005). *Transnational America*. Durham, NC: Duke University Press.

Kristeva, J. (1993). *Nations without nationalism* (translated by L. Roudiez). New York: Columbia University Press.

Kuhn, A. (1995). *Family secrets: Acts of memory and imagination*. London: Verso.

Mirón, L., Darder, A., & Inda, J. X. (2005). Transnationalism, transcitizenship, and the implications for the "New World Order." In C. McCarthy, W. Crichlow, G. Dimitriadis, & N. Dolby (Eds.), *Race, identity and representation in education, 2nd ed.* New York: Routledge.

Orchard, V. (2002). Culture as opposed to what? Cultural belonging in the context of national and European identity. *European Journal of Social Theory, 5*(4), 419-433.

Paasi, A. (1997). Geographical perspectives on Finnish national identity. *Geo Journal, 43*, 41-50.

Paasi, A. (2005). Boundaries as social practice and discourse: The Finish-Russian border. In P. Gangster, & D. E. Lorey (Eds.), *Borders and border politics in a globalizing world* (pp. 117-136). New York: SR Books.

Pink, S. (2001). *Doing visual ethnography*. London: Sage.

Peña, R. A. (2005). Water is clear like me: A story about race, identity, teaching, and social justice. In R. A. Peña (Ed.), *Community and difference: Teaching, pluralism, and social justice* (pp. 1-24). New York: Peter Lang.

Robyn, R. (2005). Introduction: National versus supranational identity in Europe. In R. Robyn (Ed.), *The changing face of European identity,* (pp. 1-16). New York: Routledge.

Rogoff, I. (2000). *Terra infirma: Geography's visual culture. New York: Routledge.*

Rose, G. (2001). *Visual methodologies*. New York: Sage.

Spickard, P. (2005). Race and nation, identity and power: Thinking comparatively about ethnic systems. In P. Spickard (Eds.), *Race and nation: Ethnic systems in the modern world,* (pp. 1-29). New York: Routledge.

Walker, S. (2004). Big Ideas: Understanding the art making practice—reflective practice. *Art Education, 57*(3), 6-12.

Wiles, J. (2008). Sense of home in a transnational social space: New Zealanders in London. *Global Networks, 8*(1), 116-137.

Wimmer, A., & Glick Schiller, N. (2002). Methodological nationalism and beyond: nation-state building, migration and the social sciences. *Global Networks, 2*(4), 301-334.

Imagining a Faculty of Navigations in the Academy of Radical Generosity as a Future for Art Education

Elizabeth M. Grierson

MOBILITY, FLUIDITY, INTERACTIVITY are words that sum up the global world of today. As students, artists, educators we are part of this new condition of practice whereby we move easily from place to place, idea to idea, product to product, language to language, work to work.

—GRIERSON, 2007A, P. 3-4

Imagine a new Faculty of Knowledge for the future of the art academy.

—DELISS, 2006

How may we envision the future for the art academy? How may we name new faculties of knowledge to meet the needs of a globally mobile world with its unlikely juxtapositions of people, practices, and places? How may we encapsulate a newly defined ethic as a way of working globally and responsively to each other and our environment? These were the challenges as we set out to imagine art education futures not constrained by institutional boundaries and political protocols. This story of interlocking mobile art projects has its beginnings in Melbourne 2005 and 2006, then moves to Tokyo in 2006, Germany in 2007, and back to Melbourne, 2008. Through introducing the players and places, the challenges and outcomes, I will show new possibilities for our educational futures. Ending this particular narrative in Melbourne 2008 does not imply closure. Rather it reveals an opening, a clearing for the occurrence of new pedagogical models of art education.

The setting is the university art academy but the implications from the project go beyond one level of education. The project works on a networked, cross-cultural, inter-cultural model of global mobility with art production and knowledge transfer as the centrifugal force.

The Beginnings

Without seeking origins I will attempt to map the genesis of this project. It was May 2005. Balanced precariously on the upper-deck front-seat of a Hong Kong double-decker bus, wending its way from Wan Chai to Stanley Markets, Irene Barberis turned to me with a

proposal for a new sort of research hub. This was to be an internationally mobile site for international pathways through which the instigation of collaborative, networked, globally linked art projects could occur for artists, educators and students. Funding would be sourced externally, and art methodologies would enable the quick transfer of knowledge unencumbered by institutional blocks and boundaries. This hub was envisioned as something that could exist both inside and outside the academy at one and the same time. It would be attached to the academy and serve its strategic aims but it would have a limbic flexibility and vascular system of its own. Mobility was its key and innovation its mantra. From this starting point the international research hub *Metasenta*[1] was born. Back in Melbourne I had the task of validating *Metasenta* through the institutional system (where there was an embargo on the construction of new research centers at the time—hence the name 'senta' as a semiotic slight of hand) while Irene was busy with the organisation of *Metasenta's* first guest, Dr Clémentine Deliss from Edinburgh. This was the starting point of a journey of international linking, networking, mapping, exchanging and transferring ideas and practices in the name of art education.

At the time I was considering how art could work effectively as a site of knowledge to re-imagine and map our global living spaces. I was establishing a research cluster called *Art, Knowledge and Globalization* in the School of Art to bring together researchers with a common interest in the mobility of art practices as forms of knowledge transfer with pedagogical potentials of cross-border mobility and imperma-nence. When art starts to lose its purchase in the face of media saturation and digital hyper-connectivity, then it is time to rethink its potential and possibilities in the non-territorial realm. If we see art as a social semiotic, then we may need to engage more robustly through the practices of art to reveal the weave and texture of a global world. Art's position in a global domain morphs with shifting demographics, new tech-nologies, and fast exchange of information, ideas, and capital. Art puts these issues of space, place, site, tech-nologies, identity, and identifications on the academic agenda—and it is art educators who can mobilize the social syntax of art to explore, reflect, and interrogate the physical, cultural, and political territories that make up the social fabric of our knowledge spaces.

As knowledge is bought, sold, and transferred with the speed of a mouse click, the boundaries of our worlds are fast changing, the institutional corridors of power are crumbling, and with them the bastions of hierarchical structures bend as hollow reeds in the wind. Yet here we are today, positioning our institu-tional lineages, marketing our brands, competing for funding and students while we speak of partnerships and collaborations. How may art educational worlds function when we move beyond the borders of national and partisan interests, institutional and financial pro-tections? How may we hold the creative potentials of our subject and envision our global footprint beyond the confines of institutional tick-box mentality?

Melbourne 2005 and 2006

An outcome of much of this thinking and question-ing appeared in the book, *Metronome 11 What is to be Done? Tokyo* (Deliss, 2007), and continues today through the *Metasenta* projects. As is so often the way with creative projects, they have a peculiarly trusting reciprocity at their heart and circuitous route to their manifestations. That is the way of creative arts meth-odologies. Our mapping takes us to the School of Art at Royal Melbourne Institute of Technology, RMIT University, Melbourne. It is 2005, and then 2006, and the School of Art is hosting visits from Dr Clémetine Deliss, the editor and founder of *Metronome Press* and *Future Academy*, to work with postgraduate students and present her work in a public forum.

Metronome, founded in Dakar by Dr Clémentine Deliss in 1996, is an alternative publication organ "modeled closely on the seminal magazine 'Docu-ments' edited in 1929 by Georges Bataille in Paris" and produced each year in a different location—Da-kar, Berlin, Basel, Frankfurt, Vienna, Stockholm, Oslo, Copenhagen, London, Paris, and most recently Tokyo.

Deliss sought a means "to short-circuit the mass of information available on art within an increasingly global context, and thereby animate a specific pro-fessional interest between artists who operate from different parts of the world" (RMIT School of Art website).

In 2006 RMIT School of Art invited Deliss to return to further the *Metronome* and *Future Acad-emy* projects in the art academy environment of Melbourne. The project was activated through joint funding from diverse institutional sites from RMIT Foundation, RMIT School of Art, and Victoria College of the Arts Melbourne, with *Metasenta* providing the organizational and academic impetus, thus enhancing the collaborative nature of globalized work. Without the necessary funding many creative projects simply do not arrive at their destination of possibility, no matter how well intentioned, and we see their seeds dissipate in the winds of economic necessity. But somehow this one took flight.

The Project in a Framework of Globalization

The project trajectory at this stage was threefold: the future of the art academy; an alternative model of art publication arising from the future academy; and, through *Metasenta,* a future for enhanced mobility and flexibility within and beyond the academy. Involved are artists, art educators, curators, and arts coordina-tors crossing borders to exchange ideas on the future of art education at an international Think Tank in Tokyo. This involves art academics from academies in Edinburgh, Paris, London, Tokyo, China, Singapore, Melbourne and Sydney, and artists and cultural work-ers from outside the institutional environment.

The need to review the state of art education and the academy is situated within the cultural-political context of globalization. In the market-driven cul-tures of education, art too easily becomes one more commodity, one more service, one more instrument of rationalized time, space, and technology. For a subject requiring time for reflection, critique and processual working through materiality—with all its attendant technical requirements and challenges—this makes for a very restricted set of conditions for creative pro-cesses to germinate and find form. This situation is now well recognized by art educators as they juggle the realities of reduced time to accomplish more tasks, increasing demands from management, exter-nally imposed requirements, and reducing budgets to meet primary necessities for art production—let alone allowing for expansion of opportunities beyond the borders of classroom or studio. What I have described here is the production model of industry translated to a consumption model with fast input-output transfers in market consumer economies of globalization with which we are now quite familiar.

How can we imagine the ethos and practicality of art education as an ambition beyond mere input-output, beyond the demands for codification and reductive explanation? Is it possible to see an art education based on the mobility of exchange where art as *tacit* knowledge, rather than primarily codified knowledge, can exercise its potential for transmission of ideas and understandings beyond the borders of the already thought? Such a model might go some way to bring otherness into closer proximity of ethical relations across personal, social, cultural and political borders—something that is urgently needed in this globalized world we are constructing and inheriting.

Taking this idea further, one wonders if it is possible to introduce a completely different model into art education when so much is proscribed and so much expected of teachers and students by way of fitting the glass slipper of policy and practice. It is arguably easier to take the risks needed for global mobility through art practices in higher or tertiary education where a greater degree of flexibility may exist for the interventions of new practices in teaching and learning models. However, tertiary art educators are also facing severe restrictions of time and budgets along with increasing demands for strategic positioning, international marketing, and capacity building to meet teaching profiles and research output targets and demands.

There are increased efficiencies of knowledge production, accumulation, and transfer in the global reconfigurations of education, yet we must look beyond to seek creative solutions in spite of external pressures. Is it possible to find solutions through art? I would argue that art is a knowledge-subject that can expose porous borders of potentiality that are much needed in the fault lines of 21st-century knowledge economies. You could say of art today, "Here lies our strength and our salvation," to put it in apocalyptic language; and perhaps this is the message we need to broadcast right now in a globalized world marked by swarming violence, terror, and mistranslations.

As Hélène Cixous says, "When an event arrives which evicts us from ourselves, we do not know how to 'live'. But we must… we are launched into a space-time whose coordinates are all different from those we have always been accustomed to" (cited in Merewether, 2006, p. 045). In context of these new configurations the fundamental questions I am posing here are: Can art be returned, projected to, and sustained as a cross-border, mobile site of tacit knowledge? Furthermore, how might we conceive of mobility and impermanence

in the structures of our future institutions? Or in the words of *documenta 12*, "What is to be done?"

Project Challenges: International Think-Tank, Tokyo 2006

Prior to the Tokyo Think-Tank participants were invited to propose a new *Faculty of Knowledge* for an imagined *Future Academy*. The responses were many and various. The challenge was to look to the future by devising new faculties for the art academy in an age of globalization. As participating researchers, Irene Barberis and I decided to work together on our new faculties of knowledge, drawing from our own artistic and life experiences. Mine was the *Faculty of Navigations*; Irene's, the *Faculty of Breathing Space*. Suggesting we position these faculties in a context of respect and reciprocity to provide an ethical dimension, I devised the *Academy of Radical Generosity* from Emmanuel Lévinas and his philosophical writings on ethics. The aim was to consider the ways art moves across borders via mobile practices of reciprocity and exchange, and the way art might address implicitly the ethics of respect in the radical forms of coexistence that comprise global public space.

The forum in Melbourne 2005, and then again in 2006, culminated in three intensive days of discussions, performances, and exchanges at an international Think-Tank on the future of the art academy at Academy Hills, Mori Art Centre, Tokyo, in September 2006. The event was organized by Arts Initiative Tokyo and *Metronome Press*, and widely supported by a range of partner institutions.[2] It comprised 125 international participants including 5 from Australia.[3] The Think-Tank was set to explore some key issues to be raised further by *documenta 12* and *documenta magazines*. It was addressing the global complexity of cultural difference, asking how art education and academic publishing could be reconfigured within the broader contexts of the academy. It was concerned with the mediations of research in art and discursive modes of art publishing including artist commentary, interviews, photo reportage, and creative writing and the value ascribed to these within the notion of research in the academy.

With the aim of productive exchange, *documenta 12* posed three key themes or *leitmotifs* that would be reflected in the *documenta* publications. These themes were informing the Tokyo Think-Tank: *Is modernity our antiquity? What is bare life? What is to be done?* Taking these questions further:

> Is humanity able to recognize a common horizon beyond all differences? Is art the medium for this knowledge? What is to be done, what do we have to learn in order to

cope intellectually and spiritually with globalization? Is that a question of aesthetic education and cultivation? What constitutes life when everything is subtracted which does not belong essentially to life? Does art help us out to get through to what is essential? (See Endnote 3. http://www.documenta12.de)

Celebrating Difference

In context of the work we were doing in the *Art, Knowledge and Globalization* research cluster and *Metasenta* at RMIT in Melbourne, I considered that it would be reasonable to problematize the first question. Why would we want to go "beyond all differences" when contemporary art is founded in discursivity and difference? It is those juxtapositions of difference that make art so fluid and fascinating, activating the capacity to create and reveal elements of collective meanings in a culture without seeking a common order of those meanings or assuming a "common horizon."

There are different ways of considering difference and working through its inevitable manifestations in social, cultural and intellectual landscapes. Difference may imply contradiction or even contra-distinction, which may describe two conditions in opposition to each other. The dialectical model of reasoning from the 18th-century German philosopher, G.W.F. Hegel, seeks a resolve of this contradiction of difference through synthesis of the thesis (idea) and the antithesis (contradictory idea). Dialectic argument and critique may be the methodology to work through this process.

Then there is another way to consider the juxtaposition of difference, a way that does not follow the urge to tidy up difference, to beat opponents, synthesise or overcome their different viewpoint. The 20th-century French philosopher Jacques Derrida shows the logic of difference not as contradiction that requires resolving, not an antagonism or argument but as a productive site of deferral, a place where difference can coexist as we recognize the traces of difference in self. This is a way of reasoning that allows for difference to remain as difference, with all its specificities in tact. Derrida shows how meaning is always in flux when ideas, forms, images, objects, actions, people or words appear in juxtaposition then each defers to another in the search for meaning. Thus meaning is in play and not fixed in one text or form or artwork or person; it is made up of a series of traces of the other. Derrida calls his method deconstruction as a way of noting the overturning of the position that regards "an artwork or art object as a privileged container of meaning, that it has meaning *in* it, through its very *presence*, or by its representational values it is representing meaning which must by definition be situated somewhere in the world..." (Grierson, 2000, p. 154).

In his book *Positions* (1981) Derrida is suggesting that difference cannot and need not be resolved; difference need not be tidied up into another order. Thus in the juxtaposition of differences in the global world of people, places, products, languages, ideas, images, objects, artworks, and events, we see a field of texts, signs, images, or forms suggesting meanings in deferral as they open our minds to new possibilities. Seen this way the juxtaposition of difference is a productive state in the processes of exchange and interchange with potential for understanding the needs of otherness in pedagogy and social life.

Navigating to *Documenta 12*, Kassel, Germany 2007

With those thoughts to the fore, the methodology of the Think-Tank followed the discursive practices of difference, with artists, writers, academics, and curators addressing questions of art, globalization, and knowledge through informal and formal discussions, performances, panels, and debates. Working my *Faculty of Navigations in the Academy of Radical Generosity* alongside artist and art educator Irene Barberis' *Faculty of Breathing Space* was a way to bring the otherness of practices together in a creative instrument of address. Images sourced from New Zealand photographer, Nicholas Gresson's *Birds of Navigation* series, and Irene Barberis' mobile, inflatable drawings in space, accompanied the presentation at the Think-Tank and found form in the publication, *Metronome 11 What is to be done? Tokyo* (2007), included in *documenta 12* at Kassel, Germany (June to September, 2007).

There, at this far-reaching contemporary art event in 2007, the focus was on art and art education with similar questions informing art exhibitions and associated publications. Held every five years and claimed today as a "seismograph of contemporary art" (documenta website), *documenta's* genesis was in Kassel in 1955, initiated by the artist and art educator, Arnold Bode. The aim was one of reconciliation in a post-Nazi world, to bring together German public life in a confrontation with its past and possible future. "Since then Documenta has occurred every five years with a new director and new exhibition direction. Every year visitor numbers increase, with more than 650 thousand visitors attending Documenta 11 (2002)." (http://www.documenta12.de)

What was unique about this *documenta* was a full acknowledgment of the importance of education through art. In the words of Curator Roger M. Buergel (2006), "Education will appear as art's advocate and the audience's counterpart. It will dedicate itself to the task of engaging with the visitors in coming to terms with things that we do not understand." Buergel adds, "*Bildung*, the German term for education, also means 'generation' or 'constitution,' as when one speaks of generating or constituting a public sphere." (http://www.documenta12.de)

Within this context of generation *documenta 12* and *documenta 12 magazines* opened significant sites of critical engagement and contemplation. *Metronome 11 What is to be done? Tokyo*, arising from the Tokyo Think-Tank was one of over eighty invited print and on-line periodicals from across the world to consider *documenta 12*'s three *leitmotifs*—Is modernity our antiquity? What is bare life? What is to be done?

Artists as Navigators

My starting point for the *Faculty of Navigations in the Academy of Radical Generosity* as published in *Metronome 11 What is to be done? Tokyo* (2007) was situated in my own act of navigating between Aotearoa New Zealand and Australia in 2005 to embark on a new academic position in a new land, a new institution. "It was my act of practice, the evidence of my mobility and impermanence..." (Grierson, 2007, p. 190). These comments need to be seen in the perspective of navigating the condition of absence having recently faced the *aporia* of death where impermanence and radicality had become the conditional fabric of the everyday and where "blank spaces ... take on importance" (Derrida, 1981, p. 3). I was facing bare life. Art and the academy in the proposition of *The Academy of Radical Generosity* (Grierson, 2007) had its tenuous links in the irreconcilability of death in life. I was no stranger to conditionality and the global need for an ethic of practice in the everyday realm of human existence.

"From this point as *tautai*—or academic navigator—my Faculty of Navigations is born. *Tautai* is the Samoan word for 'navigator'—an expert in all things related to the sea" (Grierson, 2007, pp. 190-191). There is a particular knowledge about navigations when you are a Pacific person; the sea becomes a way of knowing and locating:

> The Pacific navigators steered by the stars of the Southern Cross or Matariki. They kept their eyes on the stars as we keep our eyes on the political weather. ... The Faculty of Navigations is an essential condition for the Academy of Radical Generosity: it reminds us to keep our eyes open in the act of steering our way, the way of knowledge, the way of generously going out to the Other and inviting the Other into our midst (other idea, other practice, other person, other field of interest and understanding). (Grierson, 2007, p. 191)

Such an academy, *The Academy of Radical Generosity* is a globalized place where ideas and practices can be itinerant, mobile, cosmopolitan, while engaging with and respecting local tradition and practice; it may have its constitutional base in one country adhering to national regulations of governance, but it finds a way of going beyond juridical boundaries. Borders become porous in the way a virus can mutate from one form to another, one host to another, one site to another. This is the scope of art and artists; they have the capacity for this kind of risk and flow. As imagined, *Academy of Radical Generosity* can mark a way of being and radicalizing the ethics of practice as a sustainable condition of knowledge exchange.

Navigating Public Art Interchanges

Beyond the academy walls, we might meet in unlikely places, work together in communal spaces in a mode of reflexive engagement and reciprocity with otherness. Here are some examples of the *Faculty of Navigations* in action. In 2006, a group of public art students and academics from RMIT School of Art worked with Turkish fisherman on a community art project painting a sea wall in Sile, Turkey.[4] They went out to listen, meet, talk, share, and exchange in Sile before any art was produced. But what was this art? Where lay the art of it? Some geometric colors on a wall in Sile might be deemed aesthetically to be non-art, graffiti almost. But according to Adorno, "Nothing concerning art is self-evident any more" (1997, p. 1); we can no longer be sure of art's practice, aesthetics, or relationship to the life-world. The value of the Sile project lies, it would seem, in its way of engaging with others in that act of reciprocity. There is no closure of arts' meaning, no finite assumption of Western arts' aesthetic value, no global expansionism or imperialist epistemologies in this act. The group of Turkish and Australian artists, fishermen, and educators worked together in Sile with the radical generosity of accepting that something new or previously unthought may happen there.

Another example is the field-trip undertaken frequently by RMIT students of public art to Xian Yang Province in China, where Australian students work alongside Chinese students in a response to the local environment. As they work together, their visual projects reveal different kinds of 'building'—of communities, scaffolds, stone carvings, paintings, and bridges across languages and cultural differences.

What is the role of academic managers in these events? It takes an act of trust on the part of academic governance to enable these encounters to take place as managers must see beyond the borders of economic rationalism to the potentiality of art as a medium for cross-border knowledge, a way of promoting awareness of and respect for global difference. Of these

RMIT global art projects in Melbourne, Turkey, and China, Lucy Lippard writes:

> Collaboration is difficult enough on common ground. Collaboration across cultures, west to east, south to north, is a true challenge, especially for artists, who in the west, at least, are pointed toward rugged individualism and self expression rather than ego-suppression. ... The artists and their colleagues, the builders, gardeners, bureaucrats who support and share their achievements—contribute to building partnerships and important works of public art. Their practice, as much as their products, provides a model for those all over the world who know that art really does build bridges and bears witness to its time. (Lippard, 2003, p. 3)

As artists and art educators our role is not just about creating for the economic machine, or about creating as a panacea for humankind. It is about bearing witness to our time and creating the conditions of practice for radical generosity as an ethic in action. Radical generosity is an ethical practice where one defers to another as one differs from the other. There we may witness the *Faculty of Navigations* (Grierson, 2007a) and the *Faculty of Breathing Space* (Barberis, 2007) going beyond the borders of the already thought, beyond the primary commodification of education, to give shape to an *Academy of Radical Generosity*. I would argue that only through exercising an operational politics of difference, without reducing everything to the same, can global mobility of our practices be sustainable beyond a dominating attitude of consumption and economic privilege.

Reflecting On What Is To Be Done

The questions posed by *documenta 12* and threading through these interlacing projects and positions, are offering some crucial challenges for artists and art educators as we face the mounting pressures of a globalized economic ordering of knowledge. The story of my navigations over 4 years with *Metasenta, Metronome, Future Academy*, Tokyo Think-Tank, *documenta 12*, and RMIT Public Art shows that the art educator's role is to displace the naturalized assumptions about "common horizons" with its appeal to sameness. When we engage with the social, cultural, historical, personal, and political conditions of difference in ourselves and in others, then we can recognise and celebrate the contingent world of knowledge that is shaping our futures. Looking to a future economy of exchange in our educational *habitus* (a term used by French sociologist, Pierre Bourdieu, referring to a set of social and cultural dispositions that generate cultural production), we might ask why education is so intent on predicting outcomes. We need to face the question of trust and ask: How can an artist and art educator trust *to not* knowing what might be the outcome?

The projects discussed here go further toward exercising this trust. Our time with *Metronome* and *Future Academy* has passed and *documenta* is over for another 5 years. However, the impetus and energy of *Metasenta* and the public art projects continues, with the public art students working in Italy, collaborating with communities of practice in Tuscany. *Metasenta* has established *The Drawing Space Melbourne* as a mobile site for *Activating Dormant Spaces* enabling students of drawing to work with international artists by proxy or proximity in dormant architectural spaces of the academy, university or city.

My navigations through these projects give evidence of how artists and art educators can work together as globally networked collectives activating an art academy beyond our present conditions. This is my way of shaping our educational futures. Testing the limits of the border on joint projects, meeting in unlikely places, moving as global cosmopolitans, navigating a way from site to site, idea to idea, aesthetic to aesthetic, economy to economy, might bring us closer to understanding the different knowledge frameworks of a global world; and there we come face-to-face with difference as a condition of practice. Ultimately, in asking the question of *documenta 12*, "What is to be done?" we may find the courage to live with the irreconcilability of difference and to contemplate truly, in the words of Roger Buergel (2005), "That part of our existence from which no measure of security will ever protect us," that is to face bare life in others as in ourselves.

REFERENCES

Adorno, T. (1997). *Aesthetic theory*. (Robert Hullot-Kentor, Trans.). London: Athlone Press.

Barberis, I. (2007). Faculty of Breathing Space in the Academy of Radical Generosity. In C. Deliss (Ed.) *Metronome 11 What is to be done? Tokyo*, in collaboration with Documenta 12 Magazines (pp. 196-198). Tokyo & Paris: Metronome Press (English and Japanese).

Buergel, R. M. (2005). *Documenta Kassel 16/06 – 23/09 2007: Lietmotifs*. Retrieved April 26, 2008, from: http://www.documenta12.de/leitmotive.html?&L=1

Buergel, R. M. (2006). *Documenta 12*. Retrieved February 21, 2007, from: http://www.documenta12.de

Deliss, C. (2006). E-mailed conversation with author.

Deliss, C. (Ed.). (2007). *Metronome No. 11 What is to be done? Tokyo*. Special edition for Documenta 12 Magazines. Tokyo: Metronome Press.

Derrida, J. (1981). *Positions*. Alan Bass trans. Chicago: the University of Chicago Press. Originally published 1972 by Les Editions de Minuit.

Grierson, E. M. (2000). *The politics of knowledge: A poststructuralist approach to visual arts education in tertiary sites*. Doctor of Philosophy thesis, The University of Auckland, New Zealand.

Grierson, E. M. (2007a). Faculty of Navigations in the Academy of Radical Generosity. In C. Deliss (Ed.) *Metronome 11 What is to be done? Tokyo*, in collaboration with Documenta 12 Magazines (pp. 190-195). Tokyo & Paris: Metronome Press.

Grierson, E. M. (2007b). Foreword. In *Mastermind 2007*, Catalogue, Pao Galleries of Hong Kong Arts Centre (pp. 3-4.). Hong Kong: RMIT University and Hong Kong Arts Centre.

Lippard, L. (2003). Foreword. In *Outer site: Cross cultural public art from RMIT and its predecessors* (p. 3). RMIT University, Melbourne.

Merewether, C. (2006). Taking place: Acts of survival for a time to come. *2006 Biennale of Sydney: zones of contact* (pp. 045–060). Sydney: Biennale of Sydney.

Metronome 10, Metronome Press. Retrieved April 28, 2007, from: http://www.metronomepress.com/issues/metro10.html Metronome http://www.metronomepress.com/

RMIT School of Art (2007). *Clementine Deliss, Melbourne 10th-15th August 2005*. Retrieved April 28, 2007, from: http://www.rmit.edu.au/browse/Our%20Organisation%2FDesign%20and%20Social%20Context%2FSchools%2FArt%2FNews%2FClementine%20Deliss/

ENDNOTES

1   *Metasenta* is the registered business name of Irene Barberis and operates within RMIT University. The name *Metasenta* may not be used for any other entity.

2   Partner institutions included Academy Hills, Tokyo; Edinburgh College of Art, The University of Edinburgh; University of Dundee School of Fine Art; Scottish Arts Council; RMIT School of Art, and Global Art *Metasenta* at RMIT, Melbourne; Cultures France; and Sun Chlorella.

3   Participants of the Think-Tank from Australia were Dr Irene Barberis, Director of *Metasenta*, Nigel Brown, postgraduate student, and Professor Elizabeth Grierson, Head of the School of Art, RMIT Melbourne; Michelle Mantsio, postgraduate student, Victorian College of the Arts; Professor Richard Dunn, Sydney College of the Arts. Others included Dr David Elliott, Director of Mori Gallery, Tokyo; Fumio Nanjo, Deputy Director of Mori Gallery, Curator of the Singapore Biennale; Ruth Noack, Curator of *documenta 12;* George Schöllhammer, *documenta 12 magazines*; Professor Ian Howard, Professor Karen Forbes Visser, Edinburgh College of the Arts; Tracy Mackenna, University of Dundee; Thomas Boutoux, Metronome Press, Paris; Hu Fang, Vitamin Creative Space, Vienna/Guangzhou; Yuko Hasegawa, Museum of Contemporary Art Tokyo; Roger Mcdonald, Art Initiative Tokyo, Deputy Curator Singapore Biennale; Tony Trehy, Poet-Curator, Manchester.

4   Coordinator of Public Art programs at RMIT University is Geoff Hogg who was awarded the title of Honorary Professor for his work in Xian Yang Province, China in 2006.

Some Reflections on Globalizing (Visual) Culture

John Steers

Much has been written about art education's contributions to and reliance on globalization. Most recently coming from visual culture advocates, an argument appears to be that by consciously engaging with 'global culture', art education can contribute to the directions globalization takes, or, alternatively, the 'globalization of culture' (Duncum, 2000). The adoption of such ideas needs to be approached with caution by art and design educators. The implications are complex and contradictory, and it may be prudent to look carefully before we leap. In this chapter, I examine some recent discourse about art education in relation to issues of globalization, consider claims and assumptions from varied and competing points of view, and pose an alternative vision of our goals and practices from an international perspective. These considerations do not necessarily negate a visual culture orientation in art education; rather they problematize it, build from it, and expand our thinking to address what I believe to be larger and more important issues.

Advocates of visual culture education often assert that the domain of art education must expand to embrace all forms of visual culture, and as it occurs or is expressed in a globalized world. This implies a global perspective on culture. But the globalization of culture is as yet a limited phenomenon, perhaps merely the chimera of a privileged minority; and it should be remembered that unrestricted access to global information, production, commerce, and communication is still a very long way from being universal for a variety of practical, social, economic and political reasons. We live in a world full of gross inequalities where more than half the population is yet to make a telephone call, let alone log on to the Internet. As Bauman argues, "What appears as globalization for some means localization for others; signalling a new freedom for some, upon many others it descends as an uninvited and cruel fate" (1998, p. 2).

There is a utopian vision, perhaps misguided, of ending divisive and often destructive cultural differences through globalization and globalized education. In reality being local in a globalized world is often a condition of social deprivation and degradation. Moreover, does globalization actually divide as much—or more—than it unites? Will increased cultural hybridity and homogeneity encourage intercultural tolerance or give rise to intensified localized inequities, resistance, and violence? Also to the point is the question of whether art education really contributes to the globalization of culture. And if so, are we at all sure that this is what we want? What other choices do we have? As many anthropologists and social scientists have observed, in cultural terms the local identity of the individual is often at least as powerful and significant as the global; and perhaps maintaining cultural diversity and individual identity should be a primary concern of art education for much the same reasons we wish to preserve bio-diversity. There are some who now wonder if globalization is but colonization by another name and thus might question the lead on visual culture education coming from the United States for reasons evident here:

> ...it is in the economic and political interests of the United States to ensure that if the world is moving toward a common language, it be English; that if the world is moving toward common telecommunications, safety, and quality standards, they be American; that if the world is becoming linked by television, radio, and music, the programming be American; and that if common values are being developed, they be values with which Americans are comfortable. These are not simply idle aspirations. English is linking the world. American information technologies and services are at the cutting edge of those that are enabling globalization. (Rothkop, 1997)

Tentative Definitions and Speculations

Recent and not so recent discourse in art education relies heavily on conceptualizations about culture, literacy, and globalization. Significantly, missing in some of that more recent discourse is much about art and design. Culture, globalization, and literacy, nevertheless, are important notions for educators to understand.

Clifford Geertz (1973) views culture as an organised collection of socially established signs and symbols on which people's cultural behaviour patterns are shaped and meaning is given to their experiences in order to sustain their social life. He suggests, '...man [sic] is an animal suspended in webs of significance he himself has spun, I take culture to be those webs' (p. 5).

My dictionaries define *globalization* as the action or an act of globalizing ("Globalization," 1998) or the process enabling financial and investment markets to operate internationally, largely as a result of deregulation and improved communications ("Globalization," 2004). Globalization is generally seen as a process leading inexorably to greater interdependence and mutual awareness of economic, political and social issues. It is often suggested that globalization entails a compression of space and time, a shrinking of the world, brought about increasing information flows, driven by digital technologies and the imperatives of international trade and macro-economic politics. However, Bauman suggests that rather than homogenizing the human condition: "...the technological annulment of temporal/spatial distances tends to polarize it" (1998, p. 18). And, although there is freedom for some, "...for others it portends the impossibility of appropriating and domesticating the locality from which they have little chance of cutting themselves free..." 1998, p.18). Economists, sociologists, geographers, politicians, environmentalists, anti-capitalists, and a myriad of other protest and single issue groups all have their own slant on what globalization is and what its effects might be. The crux of the matter seems to be that most of the outcomes of globalization are neither anticipated nor intended: "'Globalization' is not about what we all, or at least the most resourceful among us, wish or hope *to do*. It is about *what is happening to us all*" (Bauman, 1988, p. 60). The worldwide financial crisis of 2008 is a case in point.

The terms *art education*, and *visual culture* or *visual literacy* are not synonymous although they may share a lot in common. The term *visual literacy* has found favor in England despite being a problematic notion, seen generally as the semiotic reading of signs and symbols associated with the kind of analysis commonly associated with literary texts. In recent discourse, it is concerned with broader readings of visual images, recognising that gender, ethnicity and class can lead to widely different and many layered interpretations. In its postmodern permutations, visual literacy provides a valuable tool for visual education offering a means of interrogating prevalent assumptions—by questioning who makes the rules and how those rules are legitimated.

Similar to visual literacy discourse, Freedman (2003) offers a definition of *visual culture* that is concerned with critical analysis of multiple forms of visual communication:

> The forms of visual culture include all of the visual arts and design, historical and contemporary: the fine arts, advertising, popular film and video, folk art, television and other performance, the built environment, computer graphics and other forms of visual production and communication. Teaching visual culture is not just teaching about popular culture, nor is it a process of uncritical acceptance. It is a reasonable response to contemporary realities in which the visual arts from past and present, and from multiple cultures, are infinitely recycled, juxtaposed, co-mingled, and reproduced. Today, art education must have less to do with information distribution and more to do with ideas, analysis, and appraisal. Teaching visual culture is about students making and viewing the visual arts to understand their meanings, purposes, relationships, and influences. (p. 11)

To my mind, the core aim of courses in visual literacy or visual culture alike, is to provide a set of critical tools for the *investigating* the visual world. As Freedman points out, it is not merely about the transference of specific knowledge or values.

Some Caveats and Considerations

I am not opposed *per se* to many of the ideas embedded in visual culture education discourse, but I do want to raise some issues for careful consideration. I think that promoting any single vision of the curriculum is dangerous; more diversity is needed. I also believe that enthusiasm for visual culture education must always be tempered with more sensitivity to diverse cultural traditions, artforms, values, developments, and needs worldwide. I am also hesitant because in the United Kingdom the idea of visual culture/visual literacy education does not seem so radically new. A very similar concept has been current for over a quarter of a century. The English national curriculum sets out a broad spectrum of art, craft and design activity and associated critical and contextual studies. The range and content of the subject is extensive (QCA, 2007). Of course, I recognize that here in the United Kingdom as elsewhere there is quite a gap between theory and practice (Steers, 2003; 2004). The content and range of school art practice is often more restricted and locked into unquestioned orthodoxy than it might be (Downing & Watson, 2004).

I am also torn between utopian and dystopian visions where increasing impacts of globalization, including *globalized visual culture education*, might be leading. On the one hand, there is the hope that a globalized visual culture approach might promote the urgent educational objective of increasing intercultural, interethnic, interfaith understanding, and tolerance. It may help address the uncertain futures our students seem destined to face in a very unpredictable world of cultural crossovers, hybridity, and fusion brought about by mass movement of people and globalization. But pessimistic views of the effects of globalization are more common. Barber, for example, asserts that, "We have globalized our economic vices crime, drugs, terror, hate, pornography, and financial speculation but not our civic virtues" with the consequence that there is "...a growing tension between the beneficiaries of globalization and just about everyone else" (1992, p. 1). I would hope that a contemporary visual cultural approach might not only explicitly interrogate such tensions as it currently does, but also at the same time further inquiry into the continuing importance of teaching about those culturally valued forms of artistic expression embedded in diverse localized cultural contexts around the world.

In support of a utopian vision of globalization, it is worth recalling how, in the aftermath of the 1939-1945 World War there was a spirit of optimistic internationalism, fuelled by a post-war economic boom. There was a conviction that such a disaster must never be allowed to happen again that contrasts vividly with current pessimistic acceptance in the West of the protracted inevitability of the so-called 'War on Terror.' It was the era in which the United Nations and UNESCO were founded, organizations designed to resolve conflict through diplomacy and to extend the benefits of educational, cultural and scientific exchange. In the early 1950s, the founders of the International Society for Education through Art (InSEA), itself a UNESCO non-governmental organization, echoed similar optimistic beliefs that are still reflected in its constitution. Specifically, they argued that, because creative activity is a basic need common to all people, it should act as a unifying force, and that as a consequence international co-operation and better understanding between peoples can be fostered through art education. Toward the end of his life Sir Herbert Read, who was instrumental in founding InSEA, issued a challenge that still has great resonance suggesting that potentially art education "...is packed with enough dynamite to shatter the existing educational system, and to bring about a revolution in the whole structure of our Society" (Read, 1965, p. 1). A stirring sentiment but is it believable or achievable? Can international co-operation and better understanding between peoples be furthered through art education or visual culture education? Do we have much choice but to try?

Chalmers (1996), an admitted cultural relativist, cites Pankratz (1993) who writes of the need to accept and respect the "co-equality of fundamentally different frames of thought and action characteristic of diverse cultures" rejecting, apparently as does Duncum (1996), any hierarchical ordering of cultures or arts. Clearly such idealistic pluralism is threatened in a world dominated by major stereotypes, where cultural exchanges are often one-way, and where the ability to exploit or overwhelm a culture is a consequence of the strength of power and money. Cultural interaction is too often an occasion for looting and cultural oppression rather than co-equality. If some cultures seem immune to subjugation, it is often at the expense of the disempowerment of all those less vigorous within a particular cultural group, those more local and underclass subcultures that have been damaged or destroyed in the process of economic development, colonisation and globalization. In such cultures, rather than celebrating hybridity, the crucial issues are those concerned with survival, territory, security and local identity. It is a justified fear of globalization that often drives demands for political devolution and increased recognition of distinct cultural, religious and ethnic identities in many parts of the world.

Clearly, as cultural studies scholars and many others have observed for many years, globalization is seen to have negative impacts on local cultures worldwide. Brand names such as Nike, Coca-Cola, Disney, Microsoft, Ford, McDonalds, and Marlboro are ubiquitous and instantly recognizable world-wide. They are often seen as evidence of invasive cultural domination. In France, for example, anti-American feeling is usually expressed by burning down the local McDonalds outlet. The homogeneity implicit in globalization is not culturally neutral but rather it is principally a product of cultural domination, often cemented by the impact of advertising, film, music, and television industries. Hutton cites the example of the control of film distribution in Britain and in Europe by Hollywood studios and the Motion Picture Association—noting, for example, that 70% of films shown in French cinemas are from Hollywood. He provides examples of how the cultural impact of film is founded on the priorities of another culture, often with disregard for historical truth, and he gives examples such as *Saving Private Ryan, Enigma,* and *The Patriot* where "British audiences collude in their own character assassination to serve the cultural and political agenda of another country" (Hutton, 2002, p. 40). A trivial complaint perhaps, but it is indicative of a much more widespread commercial commodification and plundering of cultural identity and cultural self-esteem that leads to resentment.

Often citing the proliferation of globalized media and new communication networks as critical components of globalization, art educators are keen to recognize the increased need for art education to engage these forms. Given the inventiveness, rapid expansion, and pervasiveness of published, transmitted, and digital media and the scope for investigating visual culture this affords, many educators both within and preceding visual culture camps have long argued for a greater emphasis on information and communication technologies (ICT) in the art and design curriculum. No doubt the interpretation of visual data in one form or another is an essential skill in just about every discipline and the new media and technologies will continue to bring a rush of profound changes to the way we perceive the world. We recognize the profound shift from text-based to global information technologies that are increasingly image-driven, and the unresolved educational challenges presented by this revolution.

But in reality, do increasingly globalized (Western) media serve as a window on diversity? Or do the media barons channel worldwide essentially the same hollow dross that is often insensitive to local cultural impact? Egyptian scholar Sid-Ahmed (1998) has argued that the technological tools now available to bring cultures closer together, such as the Internet and satellite broadcasting, also impoverish culture. He stressed the familiar, inherent paradox of globalization that it is as likely to lead to marginalization as to integration. Similarly, Bauman considers that the much-vaunted interactivity of new media is greatly exaggerated and the reality is a one-way medium where the many observe the few:

> Contrary to what academics, themselves members of the new global elite, tend to believe, the Internet and the Web are not for anyone and unlikely ever to become open for universal use. Even those who get access are allowed to make their choices within the frame set by the suppliers... (1998, p. 53)

Giddens points out that globalization "...looks uncomfortably like Westerni[z]ation–or, perhaps, Americani[z]ation, since the US is now the sole superpower, with a dominant economic, cultural and military position in the global order" (1999). Paradoxically, the oft-lauded U.S. notion of a multi-cultural but unified society is seen by some as yet another form of Americanized cultural hegemony. In the West, multiculturalism has generally been seen as a self-evidently 'good thing' but there are many societies that wish to remain mono-cultural.

The InSEA inspired book *Beyond Multicultural Art Education: International Perspectives* (Boughton & Mason, 1999) is an honorable exception to the rule concerning Western dominance of this subject. For example, Barbosa from Brazil writes about the tendency in the developing world to copy from the developed metropolis and how what goes on in the USA, Japan or France legitimates visual arts practice in her country. She warns that "...pre-packaged solutions and dependency on others for validation of a phenomenon's merit or worth implies a surrender of social consciousness" (Barbosa, 1999, p. 187). Barbosa raises a further issue: that of the class prejudice that she claims is the great enemy of multiculturalism in the Third World whereby "Everything made by the poor is labelled 'craft' or 'folklore,' not 'art'" (1999, p. 196) and how everything that does not correspond to the First World's aesthetic values is rejected by the colonized elite. She suggests that this is a concept that originated with the English upper classes to distinguish forms of cultural production that did not correspond to their own cultural code.

In a review of regional, national and global trends in multicultural art education, Mason suggests that its variations include an emphasis on *cultural pluralism* in North America, while a *cross-cultural* communication model that emphasises *intercultural* artistic exchange is dominant in Western Europe (Boughton & Mason, 1999). In nation states in the modern third world that are recovering from cultural aggression in one form or another, *cultural identity* and *cultural resistance* are central concerns. No longer dominated by the Soviet Union, Eastern Europe can again accept the dynamic of *cultural diversity* that is its heritage. *Cultural survival* is a prime concern of ethnic or national groups that experience migration, occupation, population dispersal and loss of territory. Mason concludes that although the commitment to pluralism is shared, cultural identity is the core construct in global multicultural art education reform. She writes:

> ...concern with this reverse side of pluralism means that arts and crafts serving to convey unique cultural identities are the focus of attention together with teaching art heritage.... While the wide variety of regional and national emphases indicates the complexity of multicultural art education it is likely there will be more diversity, not less, in a world society that is becoming decentralised. Objections to the trend are that cultural and political identity are not one and the same thing and that art educators must not neglect global culture. (Boughton & Mason, 1999 p. 15)

More recently, Phillips (2007) has argued that the increasingly maligned concept of multiculturalism is still worth supporting; however, she emphasizes, only if we reject unified and homogenized conceptions of culture and begin to understand that the individual should not be taken as representative of a cultural group as a whole. She suggests that the problem derives from often misguided and misleading representations of culture. She claims cultures have been represented, by supporters and critics of multiculturalism alike:

> ...as more distinct from one another and less marked by internal contestation than is ever the case. This misunderstanding of culture has damaged our perceptions and, to a lesser extent, practices of multiculturalism. My own view is that we need a multiculturalism 'without culture': a multiculturalism that can acknowledge and respect difference without falling into the determinism and simplification of culture. (Phillips, 2007. p. 29)

Phillips warns that the way boundaries are drawn around a culture's supposedly defining practices and beliefs tends to reflect either the need of outsiders to categorise and make sense, or an internal power struggle. She argues for multiculturalism grounded in the rights of individuals rather than the rights of groups:

> I do not see cultures as having rights to respect or funding or survival; only individuals do. I do not see cultures as all inclusive ways of life that can be categorised according to core beliefs or traditions. I do not see multiculturalism as a way of distributing power and resources between different cultural groups. In particular, I would be wary of any policies that accede authority to groups over their so-called members, which give them the power to regulate the lives and activities of members in particular ways. Such policies reflect what I regard as dangerously unified and homogenised conceptions of culture and cultural group. (Phillips, 2007. p. 31)

Ending Divisions?

Is globalization the key to the utopian prospect of ending divisive cultural and ethnic differences? Would increasing cultural homogeneity also increase intercultural tolerance? Not necessarily, according to Gray (2007), who argues that utopianism is always a futile attempt to achieve an impossible state of affairs. In today's world the secular project of utopianism, evident in the foreign policy of the US and its few allies, is a version of the European apocalyptic millenarianism of the Middle Ages. He wryly notes, "Although mass violence and mass killing is ubiquitous, mass killing with the aim of perfecting humanity and creating a perfect world is distinctively Western, deriving from its religious traditions" (Gray, 2007, p. 29).

In *The Clash of Civilizations?*, Huntington famously hypothesised that in the future culture would constitute the crucial agent of division among human beings:

> ...the fundamental source of conflict in this new world will not be primarily ideological or primarily economic. The great divisions among humankind and the dominating source of conflict will be cultural. Nation states will remain the most powerful actors in world affairs, but the principal conflicts of global politics will occur between nations and groups of different civilisations. The clash of civilisations will dominate global politics. (Huntington, 1993. p. 1)

Perhaps the primary significance of Huntington's theory is his recognition that culture can act as a powerful source of conflict as it represents a crucial factor in shaping identities and affiliation in contemporary societies. The evidence can be seen in the rise of separatist movements, religious fundamentalism and ethnic intolerance around the globe. Yet maybe it is more the case that "Culture becomes a tactic, a tool, not a fundamental cause of conflict itself, and the necessary policy responses are to address, not culture on its own terms, but the socio-economic circumstances that bring culture to the fore" (Mazarr, 1996).

Barber (1995) explores two opposing tendencies of globalization in his book *Jihad versus McWorld*, while raising the question of the future of democracy and civil society in a world dominated by free trade. He argues that whilst the fragmenting tendency he names *Jihad* aims at recreating sub-national borders based on culture and ethnicity, *McWorld,* driven by international markets, operates as a strong homogenising force and aims at promoting uniformity. He suggests these forces "operate with equal strength in opposite directions, the one driven by parochial hatred, the other by universalising markets. ...They have one thing in common: neither offers much hope to citizens looking for practical ways to govern themselves democratically" (Barber, 1995, p.53). So it is possible to argue that "We are all emerging from out of the security of our tribes, traditions, religions and worldviews into a global civilization that is dazzlingly, overwhelmingly pluralistic" (Rorty, 1989). Or, to take a contrasting view: "New tribal and fundamentalist tendencies... are as much legitimate offspring of globalization as the widely acclaimed hybridization of top culture" (Bauman, 1998, p. 3).

Further concerns relevant to these issues, as cultural scholars and political scientists are quick to note, include the growth of private supra-national corporations, effectively absentee landlords, many of which have economies bigger than the majority of individual states. These organizations weaken the sovereignty of nation states and their growth has seen no commensurate development of effective, global, political and civil institutions or regulation. In a world where financial, commercial, cultural and technological flows are faster and more awesome in scale than ever, notions of global citizenship and global civil society are yet to be entrenched in permanent and accountable institutions. We can only hope that international treaties on climate control, weapons of mass destruction, sustainable development and the formation of an International Criminal Court will no longer be spurned by the most powerful on grounds that fail to mask callous self interest. Hutton (2002) warns that the world needs a more subtle and sophisticated order:

> Security, prosperity and justice are global goods. They cannot and should not be provided as any one country dictates, or as a by-product of what it considers its interests; rather, their provision needs to be international and predicated upon an acknowledgement of interdependence. (p. 11)

Toward an Intercultural Curriculum

This chapter has explored complementary and contradictory explanations of globalization, with consideration of some of the claims and recommendations promulgated by visual culture, multicultural education scholars, and others. From my vantage point, it seems that we are in greatest need of an intercultural approach in art education, informed by but not limited to views expressed by advocates in varied scholarly camps (or tribes?). Intercultural education seeks an understanding of multi-cultures, and the dynamic shifts that occur in an increasingly globalized world. In such a framework, one would engage issues such as how local cultural traditions and changes are expressed artistically and convey cultural identities, values, and aspirations. In such a framework, one would then consider the interface of such traditions, changes, and value systems with notions of global citizenship; sustainable development; conflict resolution; values and perceptions; diversity issues; human rights; social justice and interdependence and understanding the way individuals and communities affect and are affected by others. The creation and study of the arts, insofar as they express, embody, or lead to such considerations, are central to such a framework. In my own country, the United Kingdom, the Development Education Association (DEA) suggests that the global dimension of the arts:

> ...helps pupils to understand and respect how diverse cultures and experiences lead to many different artistic expressions and to explore the global nature of the arts. It enables them to use the arts as a means of studying different global contexts and issues and to explore how the arts reflect and interpret the world rather than looking at different artistic forms in isolation from the community and circumstances in which they came about. It enables pupils to expand and develop their understanding of the arts, as they see it through the lens of diverse cultures, communities and broader society. The global dimension to the arts also allows pupils to explore their own identity and to see how the arts can be a tool for positive social change (DEA, 2007. p. 3)

Such goals are difficult to attain. The election of New Labour, a center-left party, in 1997 in the UK saw a commitment by government to modernise and to reaffirm "...a sense of national identity while at the same time embracing diversity and valuing cultural mix"—a difficult balancing act (Back, Keith, Solomos, & Shukra, 2002, p. 23). Ten years on, the celebration of multiculturalism in British multi-faith, multi-ethnic society seems less certain. Most analyses point to underlying socio-economic causes related to a lack of social cohesion and an environment where there is little real contact between majority and minority communities (perhaps a microcosm of what happens on a global scale). The policy emphasis now seems to be shifting from multicultural to assimilation strategies that, it is hoped, will integrate diverse ethnic, cultural and religious identities in a common set of values. Consequently, "There is an urgent need for a serious debate about the boundaries and limits of a multicultural democracy, the role of competing rights and obligations, the impact of racism and racial inequality and conditions that can allow us to thrive in a culturally diverse society" (Back, et al., 2002, p. 23). This is a debate that is also needed on an international scale.

In November 2001, shortly after the destruction of the World Trade Center, UNESCO adopted a Universal Declaration on Cultural Diversity. Member states reaffirmed their conviction that intercultural dialogue is the best guarantee of peace. Article 7 of the UNESCO Declaration optimistically identified cultural heritage as the wellspring of creativity:

> Creation draws on the roots of cultural tradition, but flourishes in contact with other cultures. For this reason, heritage in all its forms must be preserved, enhanced and handed on to future generations as a record of human experience and aspirations, so as to foster creativity in all its diversity and to inspire genuine dialogue among cultures. (UNESCO, 2001)

Conclusion

In *A Manifesto for Art in Schools* we argued for a view of art, craft, and design in education predicated on three fundamental principles: celebrating *difference*; exploring *plurality;* and developing *independence of mind* (Swift and Steers, 1999). We also set forth the view that curricula should be planned to raise consciousness of crucial personal, social, international, and global issues and their representation in past and present art, craft, and design forms and images. Nine years later, a new English secondary curriculum is being phased in, commencing in 2008 (QCA, 2007) and most of the issues raised in the *Manifesto* have been addressed. The vision is to offer increased opportunities to develop wider skills for life and learning, as well as making links to the major ideas and challenges that face society and individuals. It is recognized that some subjects share key concepts and processes; curriculum opportunities highlight the potential for links between subjects; and dimensions such as enterprise, creativity, cultural understanding, and diversity can be used to cut across the curriculum. The school curriculum is seen as the entire planned learning experience—not just 'lessons,' but also the events, routines, visits, and activities that take place out of the classroom, beyond the school. Cross-curricula dimensions include identity and diversity; healthy lifestyles; community participation; enterprise and entrepreneurship; the global dimension and sustainable development; technology and the media; creativity and critical thinking. In art and design the key concepts are creativity, competence, cultural understanding, and critical understanding. Schools are encouraged to develop their curriculum to meet the specific needs of their particular students and a great measure of teacher autonomy has been restored.

The lesson that I think has been learned by my own government is that 'global' solutions to the curriculum do not work. The curriculum has to be innovative to meet the profound changes taking place in society and, above all, [must be] localized. Not national, let alone global, but *local*. This will require a radical shift in teachers' education if they are to become skilled intercultural guides and interpreters capable of sensitively addressing profound issues of race, ethnicity, faith, class, gender, and identity. Perhaps achieving this goal might provide the real dynamite in an education through art or visual culture which Read (1965) envisioned? These are issues not only for those who seek to address the tensions of the multi-ethnic and multi-faith societies in which they live: They are just as crucial in societies with a steadfast commitment to maintaining a monoculture. The 21st century requires a locally relevant but intercultural visual arts curriculum designed to sympathetically and critically explore a labyrinth of cultural diversity issues as a source of creativity and cultural understanding, whilst acknowledging both the grave threats and possible opportunities presented by globalization.

In the 21st century, in many part(s) of the world, culture is not necessarily limited by tradition, by what is bequeathed locally by family, class, religious community, tribe, or nation. We have access to vastly greater sources of information and inspiration and also the responsibility to scrutinize what we have, what we value and what we want to preserve both locally and worldwide. Education is perhaps the principal arena in which to carry out that scrutiny and the sharing of knowledge and ideas. A well-considered intercultural art and visual education clearly can make a crucial contribution to such a project.

REFERENCES

Back, L., Keith, M., Solomos, J., & Shukra, K. (2002, June 14). Challenge of unrest brings out Labour's true colours. *The Times Higher Education Supplement*, pp. 22-23.

Barber, B. (1992, March). Jihad versus McWorld. *Atlantic Monthly*, pp. 53-56. Retrieved November 16, 2007, from http://www.theatlantic.com/doc/199203/barber

Barber, B. (1995) *Jihad versus McWorld*. New York: Random House Times Books.

Bauman, Z. (1998). *Globalization: The human consequences.* Cambridge: Polity Press.

Barbosa, A. M. (1999). Cultural identity in a dependent country: the case of Brazil. In D. Boughton, & R. Mason (Eds.), *Beyond multicultural art education: International perspectives*. Munster, Munich, Berlin and New York: Waxmann, pp. 185-198).

Boughton, D., & Mason, R. (Eds.). (1999). *Beyond multicultural art education: International perspectives*. Munster, Munich, Berlin and New York: Waxmann.

Chalmers, G. (1996). *Celebrating pluralism: Art, education and cultural diversity*. Los Angeles: Getty Education Institute for the Arts.

Development Education Association (DEA). (2007). *The arts: the global dimension*. London: Author.

Downing, D., & Watson, R. (2004). *School art: what's in it?* Slough, UK: National Foundation for Education Research.

Duncum, P. (1996). From Seurat to Snapshots: What the visual arts could contribute to education. *Australian Art Education, 19*(2), pp. 36-45.

Duncum, P. (2000). How art education can contribute to the globalization of culture. *Journal of Art and Design Education, 19*(2), pp. 170-180.

Freedman, K. (2003). Recent shifts in US art education. In N. Addison & L. Burgess (Eds.), *Issues in Art and Design Teaching* (p. 11). London: Routledge Falmer.

Geertz, C. (1973). *The interpretation of cultures: selected essays*. New York: Basic Books.

Giddens, A. (1999, April 11). *Runaway world*. [Radio broadcast]. London: BBC Radio 4. Retrieved April 15, 1999 from http://news.bbc.co.uk/hi/english/static/events/reith_99/default.htm

Globalization. (1998). In *Oxford talking dictionary* [CD-Rom]. Oxford: The Learning Company.

Globalization. (2004). In *Collins Internet-linked dictionary* [CD-Rom]. London & Glasgow: HarperCollins.

Gray, J. (2007, October). Rivers of blood, in the name of a perfect world. *RSA Journal*. p. 49.

Gundera, J., & Fyfe, C. (1999). Intercultural visual literacy and art history. In D. Boughton & R. Mason (Eds.*), Beyond multicultural art education: International perspective* (pp. 87-102). Munster, Munich, Berlin and New York: Waxman.

Huntington, S. quoted in non-attributed article 'Culture, Citizenship and Identity in the Global Age', *Interchanges* 27, p.1. (Newsletter of the Centre for Creative Communities). See also Huntington, S. (1996) 'The Clash of Civilizations and the Remaking of World Order', New York, Simon & Schuster.

Hutton, W. (2002). *The world we're in*. London: Little Brown.

Mazarr, M. (1996, Spring). Culture in international relations. *Washington Quarterly.*

Pankratz, D. (1993). *Multiculturalism and public arts policy.* Westport, CT: Bergin & Garvey.

Phillips, A. (2007, October) Divided on culture. *RSA Journal*. pp. 28-33.

QCA (2007) *National Curriculum.* Retrieved November 15, 2007, from http://curriculum.qca.org.uk/index.aspx

Read, H. (1943). *Education through art*. London: Faber & Faber.

Read, H. (1965). *Education through art: A revolutionary policy*. A lecture given by Sir Herbert Read at an Open Meeting at University, College London, January 3, 1965 (Pamphlet published by Society for Education through Art, United Kingdom.)

Richard, C. (2002). Body, time and craft in contemporary South African art. Programme notes for the Arts Council of England conference from *Material things: Art and artefact in the 21st century.* Held at the British Museum on February 22/23, 2002.

Rothkop, D. 'In praise of cultural imperialism? Effects of globalization on culture', *Foreign Policy. 107*(1997): 38.

Rorty, R. (1989*). Contingency, irony and solidarity*. New York: Cambridge University Press.

Sid-Ahmed, M. (1998, August 6-12). Globalizing culture: a non-starter? *Al Ahram Weekly*. Issue 384.

Steers, J. (2003). Art and design in the UK: The theory gap. In N. Addison & L, Burgess (Eds.), *Issues in art and design teaching* (pp. 19-30). London: RoutledgeFalmer.

Steers, J. (2004). Art and design. In White, J. (Ed.), *Rethinking the school curriculum: Values, aims and purposes* (pp. 30-44). London: RoutledgeFalmer.

Swift, J., & Steers, J. (1999). A manifesto for art in schools. *Journal of Art & Design Education 18*(1), 7-14.

UNESCO (2001). *Universal Declaration on Cultural Diversity*. Retrieved November 26, 2007, from http://unesdoc.unesco.org/images/0012/001271/127160m.pdf

Utrecht School of the Arts website. www.hku.nl/cvo/forum/ accessed 23 June 2002.

About the Editors

Alice Arnold is Associate Professor of Art Education at East Carolina University in Greenville, North Carolina. She taught art in the public schools for several years prior to coming to East Carolina University, and has since published and presented her work in numerous scholarly and educational venues. Alice's interests have included community engagement and outreach, contemporary artistic practices, interdisciplinary arts, ecology, and international programming. She is a frequently invited speaker and consultant to school districts, museums, and community organizations throughout the Eastern United States, and at regional and national art education conferences. She serves on the editorial board of *Visual Arts Research: Educational, Historical, Philosophical, and Psychological Perspectives, The International Journal of Arts Education,* and the *International Journal of Education through the Arts.* Alice has been an active member of the United States Society for Education through Art, serving in many capacities and offices, including President of the organization from 2005-2007, and Executive Secretary, her current position.

Elizabeth Manley Delacruz is Associate Professor, Editor of *Visual Arts Research*, Research Fellow at the Center on Democracy in a Multiracial Society, and former Chair of Art Education at the University of Illinois, Urbana-Champaign. She taught K-12 art, graphic design, and language arts for many years prior to her appointment at UIUC. She earned an EdS from University of Florida and her PhD from Florida State University. Elizabeth's research is published in numerous scholarly journals and anthologies, and she authored the book *Instructional Theory, Research, and Practice in Art Education: Design for Inquiry.* Elizabeth is a recipient of significant awards, including the UI Vice Chancellor's Teaching Scholars Award, a National Endowment for the Arts grant, the 2009 NAEA Women's Caucus June King McFee Award, and the 2009 NAEA Higher Education Division Art Educator of the Year Award. Her work fuses scholarship and teaching with public engagement, and considers the nature and value of culturally diverse artistic expressions, from folk art to new digital media, and the role of visual arts education in promoting global civil society.

Ann Kuo is a Professor in the Graduate Institute of Fine Art at National Taiwan Normal University in Taipei, Taiwan. An experienced teacher, University art educator, administrator and artist, Ann is the founder and president of both Taiwan Art Education Association (TAEA) and Global Chinese Society Education in the Arts (GCSEA), and President of InSEA (International Society Education through Art) 2006-2008. She has published widely, been a keynote speaker and presenter at numerous international and national conferences and workshops, and exhibited her work in many individual and group exhibits. Ann's contributions to international art education have been recognized through numerous international and national awards, including 2002 El Bassiouny Award from InSEA in recognition for her outstanding contributions to InSEA, the 1997 Edwin Ziegfeld Award from United States Society for Education through Art in honoring her for distinguished international leadership in art education, the 1999 Outstanding Contribution and Achievement Award in the domain of art education from Ministry of Education in Taiwan, the 1998 Cultural Education Award for her distinguished Achievement in the development of International Art Education from the Ministry of Education in Taiwan, and the 1997 Special Achievement Award for her leadership and achievement in the field of Art Education from the National Art Association in Taiwan.

Michael Parsons was born and educated in England, and earned a PhD in Philosophy and Education at the University of Illinois. He taught philosophy of education at the University of Utah and art education at The Ohio State University for many years, with shorter appointments at Penn State University, the University of British Columbia, National Changhua University of Education (Taiwan), and the Hong Kong Institute of Education. He has served as department chairperson and associate dean. Michael has published on the development of children's understanding and response to art, teaching aesthetics to children, issues of interpretation in a postmodern society, contemporary directions in art education, integrated school curriculum, alternative methods of assessment, and various approaches to cognition in art. He has worked with schools in Ohio on art education and issues of school and reform, has promoted programs of e-learning for art teachers, and has become interested in post-colonial thought and movements in art education around the world. In 2006 he retired from the Ohio State University as an Emeritus Professor, and is now a Research Professor at the University of Illinois.

About the Contributors

Tom Anderson is the Jessie Lovano-Kerr Professor of Art Education at Florida State University. He is the former editor of *The Journal of Cultural Research in Art Education* and *The Journal of Social Theory and Art Education* and the former publications editor for *Studies in Art Education*. He is the 1998 Manuel Barkan Award recipient (with Sally McRorie), the 2004 InSEA Edwin Zeigfeld Award recipient, and 2006 National Higher Education Art Educator of the Year, and he is a founding member of the Kids' *Guernica* Peace Mural Project. Tom's publications include two commercially published books including *Art for Life* (with Melody Milbrandt), two additional books produced by public institutions, and about a hundred paper-length publications, which appear as journal articles and book chapters. A new book is forthcoming—edited by Tom Anderson, David Gussak, Kara Hallmark, and Allison Paul—to be published by NAEA, and titled *Art Education for Social Justice*.

Michelle S. Bae is a visiting assistant professor in the the Art Education Program in the department of Art and Design at University of Illinois, Urbana-Champaign. She has been teaching and supervising undergraduate art education majors and student teachers in digital media technology and visual culture at UIUC. Her research has revolved around youth identity and culture, issues of media education and technology and implements of postmodern pedagogy to secondary education. Particularly, her current study lies in minority teenage girls' lived experiences and gender identities in web cultures and cultural productions, including image-making, video-making, and website development. Her scholarly experiences have been shaped within multidisciplinary studies crossing Art Education, Women's Studies, Media Studies, and Asian-American Studies, and she has presented her work at NAEA, QI, InSEA, SLSA, and UIUC feminist scholarship series in Gender and Women's studies.

Flávia M. C. Bastos is Associate Professor at the University of Cincinnati, where she also directs the Graduate Program in Art Education. Her research and teaching focus on the encompassing and mutually complementary dimensions of community-based and international art education. In Cincinnati, she has directed the Art in the Market Program for 7 years. This unique service-learning initiative connects urban youth and art students to revitalize an underprivileged, historic neighborhood and their residents through art. In partnership with a Brazilian university and a museum, she spearheaded an international program supporting exchange and collaboration, and faculty and student exchange for the last 3 years. Inspired by the ideas of fellow Brazilian educator Paulo Freire, she engages in teaching and research that embrace real-time life experiences and can be a referent for change. She is the current editor of *Art Education*.

Christine Ballengee-Morris is Associate Professor of Art Education and American Indian Studies at The Ohio State University, Founding Director of the Ohio State University Multicultural Center, past president of the United States Society for Teaching through Art, and the 2006 J. Eugene Grigsby, Jr. Award Winner for her commitment to diversity. She is co-author of *Interdisciplinary Approaches to Art Education in High School*, published by the National Art Education Association. Her research examines social justice, social reconstructivism, and Post-colonialism as it relates to arts policy, curricula development, integrated curriculum, pedagogy, and identity development. Christine's teaching experiences include 14 years in the public school system, artist-in-residencies, undergraduate and graduate level college courses, and international teaching in Chile, Brazil, Australia, and Ireland.

Doug Blandy is Professor and Associate Dean for Academic Affairs in the School of Architecture and Allied Arts at the University of Oregon. He directs the Arts and Administration Program and the Center for Community Arts and Cultural Policy. He is the past Editor for *Studies in Art Education*. Douglas' research and teaching attend to the relationships between art, education, community, and place. His research has been published in *Studies in Art Education*, *Art Education*, *the Journal of Multicultural and Cross-Cultural Research in Art Education*, and *Visual Arts Research* among other journals. He has been associated with the editorship of five books. Douglas received the Mary J. Rouse Award, NAEA Manuel Barkan Research Award, and a faculty excellence award at the University of Oregon.

Patty Bode is the Director of Art Education for Tufts University in affiliation with the School of the Museum of Fine Arts, Boston. Her research interests include how multicultural education informs art education, especially urban education, and the role of visual culture in student knowledge and political action. Her recent work focuses on self-determined indigenous knowledge in globalized art education contexts. Years of experience as an activist public school teacher and teacher educator inform her art-making, research and teaching as an a/r/tographer. She was named the 2005 *Multicultural Educator of the Year Award* from the National Association for Multicultural Education. She has presented lectures within a range of educational communities including keynote addresses at Massachusetts Art Education Association (2006) and National Association for Multicultural Education (2007). She is co-author with Sonia Nieto on the 5th edition of *Affirming Diversity: The Sociopolitical Context of Multicultural Education* (2008).

B. Stephen Carpenter, II is Associate Professor of Art Education and Visual Culture in the Department of Teaching, Learning and Culture at Texas A&M University. He teaches courses in curriculum development, curriculum theory, cultural foundations of education, visual culture, and arts education research. His research on art education, ceramics criticism, curriculum theory, and hypertext curriculum theory and practice has been published in book chapters and journal articles. He is co-author of *Interdisciplinary Approaches to Teaching Art in High School* (2006), published by the National Art Education Association. In 2010 he will assume the role of co-editor of the *Journal of Curriculum and Pedagogy*, with Stephanie Springgay.

Sheng Kuan Chung is Associate Professor and Graduate Program Director of Art Education at the University of Houston, Texas. He holds a BEd from National Hsinchu Teachers College in Taiwan, an MA from New York University, and a doctorate from the University of Illinois, Urbana-Champaign. Sheng has authored over 30 papers published in the UK, the US, and Taiwan. His research interests include: social reconstructionist art education, multiculturalism, visual/media culture, social issues, and Asian aesthetics. Sheng is editor of the NAEA anthology, *Teaching Asian Art: Content, Context, and Pedagogy.* He has served as an art judge for the

National Scholastic Art Competition and a grant reviewer for the Texas Commission on the Arts. His artworks have been shown in over 20 juried exhibitions. He is currently on the editorial board for *Art Education*, the Journal of the National Art Education Association.

Kristin G. Congdon has taught art in public schools, correctional settings, treatment facilities, museums, and universities. She is Professor of Philosophy and Humanities at the University of Central Florida and Director of the Cultural Heritage Alliance. She has published extensively on folk art, community arts, and feminism in an effort to celebrate artists and who have had little visibility in the art world. Her most recent books include *Artists from Latin American Cultures* and *20th Century United States Photographers* (with Kara Hallmark), *Just Above the Water: Florida Folk Art* (with Tina Bucuvalas), *Community Art in Action*, and *Uncle Monday and Other Florida Tales*. Kristin has been president of the Florida Folklore Society and a member of the Florida Folklife Council. She has also been a World Congress Member for the International Society for Education through Art, and past president of the National Art Education Association's Women's Caucus. She is the current editor of *Studies in Art Education*.

Karen Frostig is Associate Professor and Coordinator of Partnership Initiatives at Lesley University, and Visiting Scholar at the Women's Studies Research Center at Brandeis University. She exhibits her work extensively in the US and Europe; her latest project "Erinnerung aus dem Exil/Exiled Memories" is permanently installed at the University of Vienna's Institute for the Philosophy of Law. She lectures internationally, is a recipient of numerous fellowships and awards, and has published several essays in professional journals related to art education. Book publications include co-editor of *Blaze: Discourse on Art, Women and Feminism* (2007) and co-author of *Expressive Arts Therapies in Schools* (1998), translated into Korean by Sigma Press (2007). She is currently a member of the national board for the Women's Caucus for Art and regional coordinator for The Feminist Art Project. Holding dual citizenship with Austria, her current research encompasses ideas about diasporic identity, traumatic memory, and feminist theory supporting transnational activism.

Charles R. Garoian is Director, School of Visual Arts and Professor of Art Education at The Pennsylvania State University. He is the author of numerous scholarly articles, book chapters, and books including *Spectacle Pedagogy: Art, Politics, and Visual Culture* (2008) with Yvonne Gaudelius, and *Performing Pedagogy: Toward an Art of Politics* (1999). Charles has performed and lectured in colleges and universities, galleries and museums nationally and internationally, and received significant awards for his research and creative accomplishments. He has served on the Editorial Review boards of the *International Journal of Education and Art (IJEA), Studies in Art Education, Qualitative Inquiry* journal, and the *Journal of Social Research in Art Education.*

Yvonne M. Gaudelius is Professor of Art Education and Women's Studies at The Pennsylvania State University and in 2007 was appointed Assistant Vice President and Associate Dean for Undergraduate Education. Prior to her current appointment, she was an Associate Dean in the College of Arts and Architecture and served as interim dean of the college. Gaudelius has been a Penn State faculty member since 1993, after receiving a doctorate in art education from Penn State. Yvonne is author of numerous articles, chapters, and books relating to art education theory and practice, including the books *Contemporary Issues in Art Education* with Peg Speirs, and *Spectacle Pedagogy: Art, Politics, and Visual Culture* with Charles Garoian. She received the 2001 Mary J. Rouse Award from the Women's Caucus of the National Art Education Association.

Elizabeth M. Grierson is Professor of Art and Philosophy, and Head of the School of Art, Royal Melbourne Institute of Technology (RMIT) University Melbourne; Adjunct Professor at AUT New Zealand; and Fellow of the Royal Society of Arts, UK. She is World Councilor of InSEA, executive member of Art Education Australia (AEA), Deputy Chair of Australia Council of University Art and Design Schools (ACUADS), and past president of Aotearoa New Zealand Association of Art Educators (ANZAAE) (2001-2005). At RMIT she is executive leader of Design Research Institute, Intervention through Art program, and leader of Art and Urbanism projects in Global Cities Research Institute. She is executive editor of *ACCESS: Critical Perspectives on Communication, Cultural & Policy Studies,* consulting editor of *Educational Philosophy and Theory* and board member of *International Journal of Education through Art* and *Australian Art Education.* She speaks and publishes widely in the history, theory, and philosophy of art, education, and globalization.

Anniina Suominen Guyas is an Assistant Professor at the Florida State University. Her research interests include interdisciplinary research, critical theory, feminist theory, arts-based educational research and a/r/tography, visual, silent and embodied knowledge, narrative as educational research/teaching/learning method, diversity education, and relational and contextual identities. She received her PhD from The Ohio State University in the US and her combined master's and bachelor's degree from the University of Art and Design in Helsinki, Finland. Prior to working at FSU she was an Assistant Professor at the Kent State University.

Fernando Hernández is Professor in the Unit of Psychology of Art and Visual Culture Education at the Fine Arts Faculty of the University of Barcelona, and Coordinator of an Experimental Program on Initial Teacher Education for Art Education in Secondary Schools. He also coordinates the Inter-universities Doctoral program on "Visual Arts and Education: A Constructionist Approach," where several researcher projects are conducted on how primary and secondary students and teachers understand art education issues and notions. He is Director of a master program on "Studies and Projects on Visual Culture." His latest book is *Espigadores de la Cultura Visual. Otra narrativa para la educación de las artes visuals.* Barcelona: Octaedro (2007).

Phyllis T. P. Hill is an Associate Professor at Northern Caribbean University, Department of Teacher Education, Jamaica. She received her master's degree and PhD from The Ohio State University, Department of Art Education. Her experience in the field of education is extensive and includes working in the area of educational reform throughout the Caribbean. Her research concerns issues of cultural identity, homogenization, and Western hegemony in an age of globalization, and focuses primarily on Distance Education as an emerging site of power. Within the Caribbean, she is actively involved in educational policy development, curriculum development and implementation, the development of educational resources for all levels of the education sector, e-learning and teacher training.

Magali Kivatinetz and Eneritz López are doctoral students in the "Visual Arts and Education: A Constructionist Approach" Program at the University of Barcelona. Magali is studying identity formation of museum educators, and Eneritz is searching for underlying conceptions at museum education activities. Jordi Macián graduated from Visual Arts at the University of Barcelona. He develops interdisciplinary and visual culture units with fellow teachers at a secondary school in Barcelona.

Herman Jiesamfoek is Assistant Professor at the School of Education, Brooklyn College, City University, New York. He studied dance at the Rotterdam Dance Academy, art history at the State University of Leiden, and visual art at the Royal Academy of Fine Arts in Antwerp and the Academy of Fine Arts and Architecture in Rotterdam. During his studies of Art Education at Teachers College, Columbia University, he carried out fieldwork among the Bush Negro people of Suriname, which led to his Doctor of Education degree and the publication of his first article on the Surinamese Bush Negro People in the *Journal of Intercultural Studies*. From 2003 to 2007, he was Adjunct Assistant Professor at Teachers College, Columbia University, and from 2004 to 2007, Education Officer at the New York City Department of Education. His research continues to center on the artistic practices and traditions of the Bush Negro people of Suriname.

Rachel Bailey Jones is Assistant Professor of Education in the Social and Psychological Foundations of Education at Nazareth College in Rochester, New York. She taught art at the elementary level in North Carolina before receiving her PhD in Curriculum and Teaching with a Specialization in Cultural Studies from the University of North Carolina at Greensboro in 2007. Her main research interests include colonial and postcolonial forms of education, gender, and sexuality in education, and the relationship between art and education. She has a special fascination with colonialism and its role in shaping and educating us about normal and appropriate racial, gender, and sexual roles.

Koon Hwee Kan is Associate Professor in the Art Education division at the Kent State University School of Art. Her doctoral research, entitled "A Story Told Visually: The Singapore Secondary School Art Style," was co-winner of the 2006 Dissertation Award from the American Educational Researcher Association, Arts and Learning Special Interest Group; and she also received the Marilyn Zurmuehlen Award for Distinguished Research in Art Education from the National Art Education Association in 2007. She has made more than 23 solo and 12 group scholarly presentations locally at Kent, regionally, nationally, and internationally, and has published in *Art Education, Arts and Learning Journal, Journal of Cultural Research in Art Education,* and *Visual Arts Research*. Her research interests include adolescent artistic learning, art teacher education, and qualitative methodology, especially visual narrative inquiry.

Karen Keifer-Boyd, Professor of Art Education and Affiliate Professor of Women's Studies at The Pennsylvania State University, co-authored *Engaging Visual Culture* (Davis, 2007) and *InCITE, InSIGHT, InSITE* (NAEA, 2008), co-edited *Real-World Readings in Art Education: Things Your Professors Never Told You* (Falmer, 2000), and served as editor of the *Journal of Social Theory in Art Education* and guest editor for *Visual Arts Research*. She is co-editor of *Visual Culture & Gender*. Her research on feminist pedagogy, virtual museums, inclusion, and cyberactivism is published in more than 40 peer-reviewed research publications and translated into several languages. She has been honored with several teaching, arts administration, and research awards, including a Fulbright (2006).

Hyungsook Kim is Assistant Professor of Art Education at Seoul National University. She studied Art Theory (MA) at Seoul National University in Korea and studied Art History (MA) and Art Education (PhD) at The Ohio State University in Columbus, Ohio, US. Her research interests lie in the areas of museum education, art history and criticism in art education, and curriculum development, policy, and administration of art education. She has contributed to developing the long-term plan of cultural art education and the national art curriculum of Korea. She is the chairperson of the Committee of Curriculum Review and vice president of the Editorial Advisory Board of the Korea Art Education Association and the Korean Association of Arts Education. As the chair of the General Congress, she has organized the 2007 InSEA Asian Regional Congress in Seoul.

Anna M. Kindler is Professor in the Faculty of Education and Vice Provost and Associate Vice President of Academic Affairs at the University of British Columbia, Vancouver, Canada. She is a graduate of the Academy of Fine Arts in Warsaw, Poland and the University of Illinois at Urbana-Champaign. Her cross-cultural research in artistic development and social cognition of art has been complemented by her creative work in photography resulting in over 100 publications and exhibitions. Former Vice-President of the Canadian Society for Education through Art, and former Dean of the School of Creative Arts, Sciences and Technology at the Hong Kong Institute of Education, Anna is a recipient of the British Columbia Art Educator of the Year Award, the NAEA Lowenfeld Award for Outstanding Achievement and Exemplary Service, and the Sam Black Award for Excellence in Education and Development in the Visual and Performing Arts.

Wanda B. Knight, PhD, is Associate Professor of Art Education at The Pennsylvania State University, where she serves as Coordinator of Graduate Programs in Art Education. Besides university level teaching, she has taught art at all grade levels and has served as public school principal, museum registrar, and assistant museum curator. Focusing on pedagogies of difference (i.e., race, class, gender, and ability), Wanda serves as editor of the *Journal of Social Theory in Art Education*. Further, she has presented in local, state, national, and international venues and has published widely in leading journals in the field. Moreover, having served as chair of NAEA's Committee on Multi-ethnic Concerns, Wanda's leadership and extensive work in the field have been recognized through various honors and teaching awards including Teacher of the Year, *Who's Who in American Education*, and the J. Eugene Grigsby Jr. Award for outstanding contribution to the field of art education.

Chien-hua Kuo is an Assistant Professor at the Graduate Institute of Children's Literature, National Taitung University in Taiwan and a member of the Children's Literature Association, US. She earned a PhD degree in Art Education at The Ohio State University, US. Before entering the field of higher education, she worked for two non-profit education foundations and a private public relation company. Her university teaching has focused on

children's picture book studies, images of childhood in media, introduction to children's literature, children's literature and extension education, and qualitative research methodology. Her primary research interests are related to issues of cultural representation and identity through visual cultural forms, intertextuality in relationship to author—text—reader, and the application of children's literature to museum activities and policy.

Jae-young Lee earned his BA in Elementary School Education, a MA in Art Education from the Daegu National University of Education in South Korea, and his PhD in Art Education at University of Illinois at Urbana-Champaign. Following 6 years of full-time public school teaching at elementary schools, he taught undergraduate practical pedagogical models for teachers of art for a year. His research has been published and presented regionally and nationally in South Korea. He is currently interested in inquiry-based approaches in art education and qualitative research in art curriculum. His current research describes what ways and to what degree elementary school students engage concepts and principles informed by a visual culture approach to art education; that includes critical analysis of the impact of images in contemporary society and in a globalized society.

Ching-Chiu Lin received her PhD in Art Education at the University of Illinois at Urbana-Champaign. Currently she is a faculty advisor supervising student teaching in visual arts at the University of British Columbia, Canada. She has a BEd in Art Education from National Pingtung Teachers College, Taiwan and a MEd in Art and Art Education from National Taipei Teachers College, Taiwan. While at the University of Illinois, she served as an instructor teaching Art in the Elementary Grades, a supervisor for preservice art education student teachers, and a research assistant developing learning modules for community-based multicultural youth organizations. Ching-Chiu's research interests lie in issues of technology and community in art education, and in maintaining scholarly collaborative partnerships in cross-disciplinary environments. Her doctoral dissertation received honorable mention for the 2009 NAEA Seminar for Research in Art Education Elliot Eisner Doctoral Research Award.

Marjorie Cohee Manifold is Associate Professor of Art Education, School of Education, Indiana University, and an Affiliate Faculty of the Center for the Study of Global Change, Indiana University. Her responsibilities include teaching methods courses in the art teacher certification program, and instructing graduate seminars in art education. She is President of the United States Society for Education through Art (USSEA) and is a North American World Councilor to the International Society for Education through Art (InSEA). Her scholarship of research looks at the aesthetic sensibilities and artistic practices of artists within real and online communities. She explores how interactions of these individuals and groups may foster appreciation of local and cosmopolitan perspectives and encourage respectful, responsible participation in global citizenship. Marjorie's findings have been reported in papers given at national and international conferences, and published in numerous articles and book chapters.

Julia Marshall is Professor and Head of Art Education at San Francisco State University. She holds an MFA in sculpture and an EdD in education. Before coming to SFSU she taught elementary and middle school art as a teaching artist. She maintains her practice as a visual artist and has recently completed a commissioned public artwork in China. Her interest in globalization and culture stems from her extensive travels in Asia and Europe and her service-learning work in El Salvador. Her other scholarship and interests lie in arts integration, the intersection between imagination, creativity, and learning, and the uses of contemporary art and visual culture in art education. Julia has published articles in *Studies in Art Education, Art Education* and numerous chapters in art education anthologies. She has also presented papers on her work locally, nationally, and internationally.

David Ogega Nyaberi received a Bachelor of Education degree in Fine Art from Kenyatta University in Nairobi, Kenya and started his career as a high school art teacher in Kisii, Kenya. He later became an art instructor at Kericho Teachers' College in Kericho, Kenya. Nyaberi joined Purdue University in 2002 and in December 2003 graduated with a Master's of Arts degree in Art Education. He attended the University of Illinois at Urbana-Champaign in August 2004, and completed the requirements for a PhD in Art Education from the University of Illinois in 2008. David's research interests are in the influence of colonial education in Kenya's postcolonial curricular policies and practice, and how art education curricular practices in Kenya are informed by and contribute to the notions of intercultural and national unity. He is currently Assistant Professor of Art Education at Lane College in Jackson, Tennessee.

Nancy S. Parks is an Assistant Professor of Art Education at Indiana University-Purdue University, Indianapolis, Indiana, where she directs the graduate program in art education. Nancy has taught art in the public schools, worked with teaching-artists in the Western New York's aesthetic education program, and taught undergraduate and graduate level courses. Dr. Parks has presented her research at state, national, and international conferences. She has examined representation of non-Western art and culture in the classroom by Western art teachers, race and representation issues in visual culture, and new media as social reconstructionist sites in her research. She is the author of "Is it Hutu or Tutsi or Tutsi or Hutu: Memory and Social Reconstructionist Art Education" (2007) in the *International Journal of the Arts in Society;* other published articles have appeared in *Studies in Art Education, Journal of Cultural Research*, and *Art Education.*

Martina Riedler completed her PhD in Art Education at the University of Illinois, Urbana-Champaign, where she ws also a Fulbright Scholar. Her research focuses on the role of national museums and identity formation, questions on critical pedagogy in art museums, and issues of contemporary museum studies. She has worked with the adult interpretive education programs at the Solomon Guggenheim Museum New York, the education programs at ZKM/ Center for Art and New Media Karlsruhe, Germany and has been a lecturer at the cultural studies department at the Carl-von-Ossietzky University of Oldenburg, Germany. Martina earned her MA in Art Education at the Academy of Fine Arts Vienna in Austria. She is an editorial board member of the *International Journal of Progressive Education* and advisory board member of the *International Journal of Education and the Arts.*

Rebecca Plummer Rohloff received her PhD (2008) from the University of Illinois. She is currently a visiting Assistant Professor of Art Education at the Pennsylvania State University. Her research interests reflect interdisciplinary, arts-based inquiries as they apply to preservice art education curricula, and community service such as the expressive arts within medicine and healthcare settings. She envisions eventually pioneering a service-based relationship between art educators and the indigenous Guatemalan communities affiliated with Peter's NGO, Wuqu' Kawoq. A gallery of her portfolio and student work can be seen at http://rprgallery.com.

Peter Rohloff received a PhD (2003) and MD (2007) from the University of Illinois. He currently serves as executive director of Wuqu' Kawoq, a nongovernmental organization that works in Guatemala at the intersection of medical care delivery and Mayan language revitalization. His research interests include language revitalization, Mesoamerican linguistics, tropical medicine, resource-poor health care delivery systems, and ethnobotany-ethnomedicine. Information on his work in Guatemala can be found at http://www.wuqukawoq.org

Ryan Shin is Assistant Professor in the School of Art at the University of Arizona. Prior to joining the Art and Visual Culture Education Division at UA, he taught art education and directed the art education program at the University of Wisconsin at La Crosse between 2002 and 2007. He earned his doctorate in art education from the Florida State University, and his MA from the Seoul National University in South Korea. His current research focuses on Asian folk and performance arts from a cross-cultural perspective. He is also interested in Asian visual and material culture studies in North America, and emerging online ethnic communities and their culture. His articles have appeared in *Visual Arts Research* and *Journal of Cultural Research in Art Education*. He also has published several book chapters, and actively presents at state, national, and international conferences.

Michelle Simms is a PhD student in the Department of Teaching, Learning, and Culture at Texas A&M University, where her research focus draws upon her experience as a National Science Foundation Graduate K-12 Teaching Fellow, her diverse background and experience in the sciences, and her love for creative expression. She is exploring the effects of virtual globes and mass media on cognitive development and developing techniques for formal and informal learning experiences using these tools. She has a special interest in utilizing cinematic story structure as the engine for developing curriculum and meaningful learning experiences with new media such as virtual globes. She holds a Bachelors of Science degree in Geography, a Masters of Agriculture in Natural Resources Development, and a Masters of Science in Geography specializing in Geographic Education. These experiences have resulted in specialized skills in spatial thinking skill development and geospatial technologies such as geographic information systems and Google Earth.

Borim Song is Assistant Professor of Art Education at the School of Art and Design of East Carolina University, Greenville, North Carolina. She holds her EdD and EdM from Teachers College, Columbia University. Her scholarly interests include digital art instruction, preservice teacher education, incorporation of contemporary art into K-12 curriculum, cross-cultural and intercultural movements in art education, and particularly a pedagogical use of cultural identities as creative and critical constructs. Borim has given presentations nationwide, including Boston, Honolulu, New York, and University Park, Pennsylvania. Her writings on art, art education, and cultural studies appear in publications in both the US and Korea.

John Steers has been General Secretary of the National Society for Education in Art and Design since 1981. He has been a member of the editorial board of the *International Journal of Art and Design Education* for 27 years since its inception. He was the 1993-96 President of the International Society for Education through Art and served on its executive committee in several capacities between 1983 and 2005. He has served on many national committees for and as a consultant to government agencies, and has published widely on curriculum, assessment, and policy issues. He is a trustee of the Higher Education in Art and Design Trust and Chair of the Trustees of the National Arts Education Archive, Bretton Hall. He was a visiting Senior Research Fellow at Roehampton University, London from 1997-2007 and is currently joint national subject leader (art & design) for the introduction of the new secondary curriculum in England.

Mary Stokrocki is Professor of Art, Arizona State University and former Vice-President and currently World Counselor for The International Society for Education through Art. She also is past president of USSEA. She is the recipient of the 2007 College of Arts & Architecture Alumni Award, Pennsylvania State University; 2007 Women's Caucus June King McFee Award; 2005 Lowenfeld Award; 2002 USSEA Ziegfeld Award; 2002 NAEA Distinguished Fellow; and 1995 NAEA Manuel Barkan Award. She edited *Interdisciplinary Art Education: Building Bridges to Connect Disciplines and Cultures* (2005), published by NAEA. Her ethnographic and visual culture studies have involved teaching in the inner-city Cleveland; Rotterdam, Holland; Ankara, Turkey; Sao Paulo, Brazil; Warsaw, Poland; Barcelona, Spain; Evora, Portugal; and the Yaqui, Pima/Maricopa, Ak-Chin, Apache, and Navajo Reservations in Arizona. She spent 2 years as a curriculum consultant in Turkey for their National Higher Education Development Project, sponsored by the World Bank.

Pamela G. Taylor is Chair and Associate Professor, Department of Art Education, School of the Arts, Virginia Commonwealth University in Richmond, Virginia. She earned her PhD from Penn State in 1999, receiving a J. Paul Getty Doctoral Dissertation Fellowship for her study "Hypertext-based Art Education: Implications for Liberatory Learning in High School." Her research is published in *Art Education, Studies in Art Education, Journal of Cultural Research, Innovate, International Education Journal, International Journal of Education & the Arts, Computers in Schools, Journal of Educational Multimedia and Hypermedia*, and *FATE in Review*. Her books include *Amazing Grace: The Lithographs of Joseph Norman* and *Interdisciplinary Approaches to Teaching Art in High School*. From 2006-2008, Pamela served as Editor of *Art Education*, the Journal of the National Art Education Association. She presents papers at regional, national, international, and online conferences and conventions on such topics as service-learning, interactive digital technology, emerging media, visual culture, curriculum, and criticism.

Christine Marmé Thompson is a Professor of Art Education in the School of Visual Arts at The Pennsylvania State University. Christine earned her PhD in Art Education at The University of Iowa, and taught at the University of Illinois at Urbana-Champaign from 1985-2001. Her research focuses on issues of children's culture and art learning, with particular attention to the social contexts of early childhood art, peer influence and dialogue. She is co-editor, with Liora Bresler, of *The Arts in Children's Lives: Context, Culture, and Curriculum* (2002), editor of *The Visual Arts and Early Childhood Learning* (1997), and a section editor and contributor to *The International Handbook of Research in Arts Education* (2007). Her writings have appeared in national and international journals in art and early childhood education, and in numerous edited collections, including Jonathon Fineberg's *When We Were Young: New Perspectives on the Art of the Child* (2006).

Frank Vigneron received a PhD in Chinese Art History from the Paris VII University, a Doctorate of Fine Arts from the Royal Melbourne Institute of Technology, and a PhD in Comparative Literature from the Sorbonne University. His research focuses on the history of Chinese painting from the 18th century onwards and on different aspects of contemporary Chinese art seen in a global context. He teaches courses on the history of Western Art, contemporary Chinese art, Hong Kong art, and Chinese and Western comparative aesthetics. Frank has been living in Hong Kong since 1990; he is now Associate Professor in the Fine Arts Department of the Chinese University of Hong Kong.

Yuehchen Wang was born in Taiwan, and is currently a doctoral candidate in Art Education at the University of Iowa. She received her Master of Arts in Studio Art from Indiana University of Pennsylvania and a Bachelor of Education in Fine Arts and Crafts Education with an Art Teacher Certification from National Hsinchu University of Education in Taiwan. She has presented numerous research papers related to visual art and art education to many international and regional conferences and has exhibited in many international juried art exhibitions. She is currently a member of the National Art Education Association, College Art Association, and Art Educators of Iowa Association. Yuehchen has been actively involved with art advocacy and promotion on the local and regional level by contributing student artwork to exhibitions throughout the community and creating an after school art club for grade 3-12 students during her teaching in Taiwan.

Li-Yan Wang is Associate Professor of the Department of Art and the Graduate Institute of Art Education at National Changhua University of Education in Taiwan. She received her PhD degree from The Ohio State University in 2000. Her research has focused on issues related to computer-mediated art instruction and cross-cultural understanding and dialogue attained through the study of art. She has published research articles in numerous academic journals and participated in over 30 national and international conferences in Taiwan, Hong Kong, the US, Portugal, and Germany. In addition, she is currently an editorial board member of *Research in Art Education* and *International Journal of Education through Art*. Since 2005, her research has focused on the historical development of art education in Taiwan.

Courtney Lee Weida is Assistant Professor of Art Education at the Ruth S. Ammon School of Education, Adelphi University, Garden City, New York. She earned her EdM in Arts in Education from the Harvard University Graduate School of Education and her Doctorate in Art and Art Education from Columbia University Teachers College. Courtney's creative, research, and teaching interests engage the layering of studio craft, gender theory, cultural studies, contemporary practices of artists and their shifting roles in cultural/communal contexts, arts museum education, and art education research methodologies. She has presented both her art and her research at regional and national conferences, and her art has been recently exhibited in Sumei Multidisciplinary Arts Center, Newark, New Jersey, and the International Fiber Collective Interdependence Project, Huntsville, Alabama. Courtney's work has been recently published in *Teaching Artist Journal*, *Spaces: Arts and Humanities Journal*, and *Terra Cotta Journal*.

Enid Zimmerman, Professor Emerita at Indiana University, has authored or co-authored over 130 articles, 20 book chapters, and 25 books and monographs in areas of art talent development, art teacher education, feminist art education, leadership and mentoring in art education, intercultural and global art education, and curriculum and policy issues in art education. Her most recent book is *Teaching Talented Art Students* (with Gilbert Clark); she was editor of the Teaching and Teacher Education section for the *Handbook for Research and Policy in Art Education*. In respect to international art education, she has taught or conducted workshops in art education in over 25 countries, was senior editor of the *Journal of Cultural Research in Art Education*, served as an International Society for Art Education World Councilor, and was recipient of a USSEA Ziegfeld Award. She recently has consulted on projects with the Hong Kong and Korean Departments of Education.